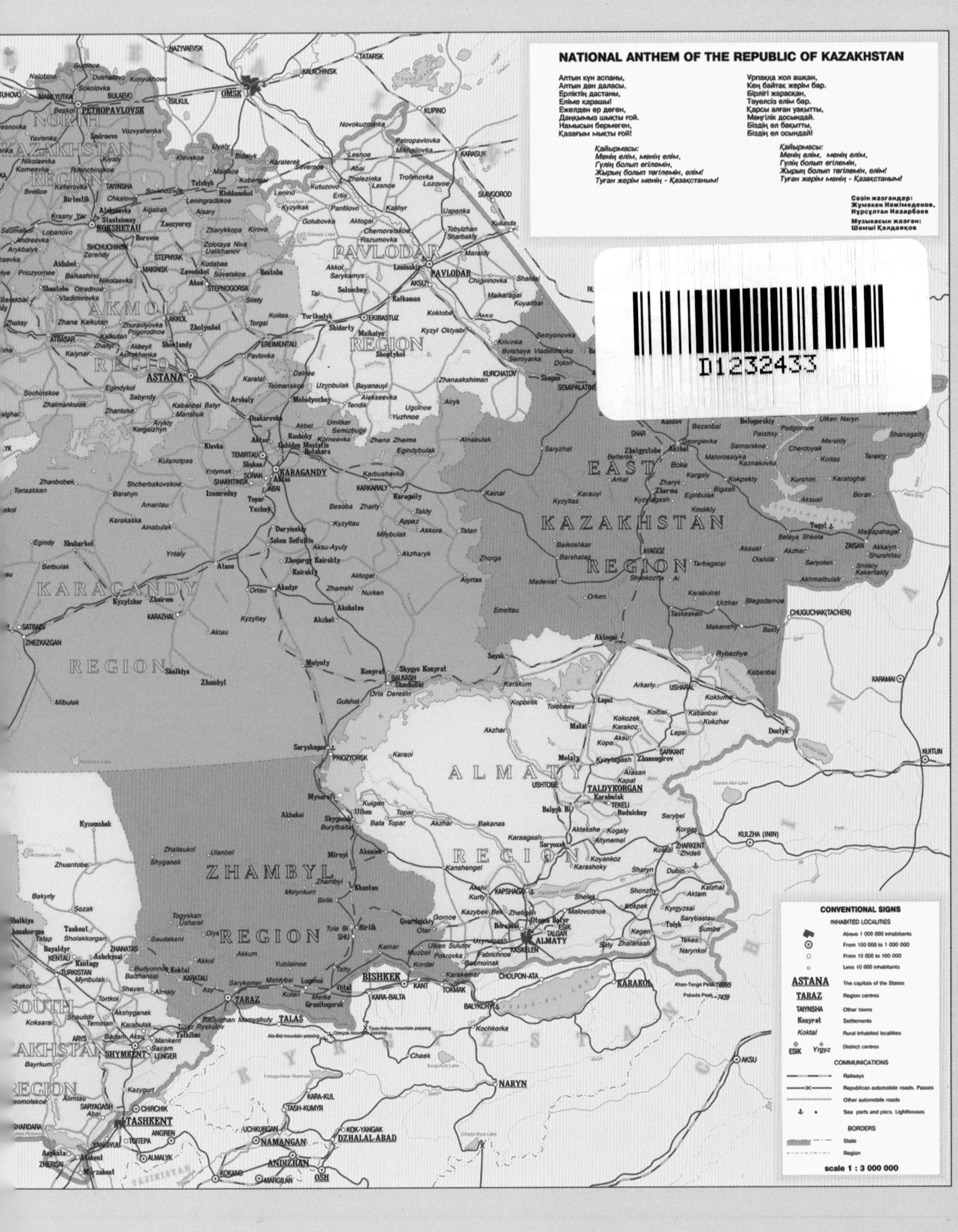
NATIONAL ANTHEM OF THE REPUBLIC OF KAZAKHSTAN
Алтын күн аспаны,
Алтын дән даласы,
Ерліктің дастаны,
Еліме қарашы!
Ежелден ер деген,
Даңқымыз шықты ғой.
Намысын бермеген,
Қазағым мықты ғой!
Қайырмасы:
Менің елім, менің елім,
Гүлің болып егілемін,
Жырың болып төгілемін, елім!
Туған жерім менің - Қазақстаным!
Ұрпаққа жол ашқан,
Кең байтақ жерім бар.
Бірлігі жарасқан,
Тәуелсіз елім бар.
Қарсы алған уақытты,
Мәңгілік досындай.
Біздің ел бақытты,
Біздің ел осындай!
Қайырмасы:
Менің елім, менің елім,
Гүлің болып егілемін,
Жырың болып төгілемін, елім!
Туған жерім менің - Қазақстаным!
Сөзін жазғандар:
Жұмекен Нәжімеденов,
Нұрсұлтан Назарбаев
Музыкасын жазған:
Шәмші Қалдаяқов
D1232433
NORTH KAZAKHSTAN REGION
PETROPAVLOVSK
OMSK
KOKSHETAU
PAVLODAR REGION
PAVLODAR
AKMOLA REGION
ASTANA
KARAGANDY
KARAGANDY REGION
EAST KAZAKHSTAN REGION
SEMIPALATINSK
ALMATY REGION
TALDYKORGAN
ALMATY
ZHAMBYL REGION
TARAZ
SOUTH KAZAKHSTAN REGION
SHYMKENT
TASHKENT
BISHKEK
KARAKOL
NARYN
NAMANGAN
ANDIZHAN
DZHALAL-ABAD
OSH
CONVENTIONAL SIGNS
INHABITED LOCALITIES
Above 1 000 000 inhabitants
From 100 000 to 1 000 000
From 10 000 to 100 000
Less 10 000 inhabitants
ASTANA The capitals of the States
TARAZ Region centres
TAIYNSHA Other towns
Konyrat Settlements
Koktal Rural inhabited localities
ESIK Yrgyz District centres
COMMUNICATIONS
Railways
Republican automobile roads. Passes
Other automobile roads
Sea ports and piers. Lighthouses
BORDERS
State
Region
scale 1 : 3 000 000

Recent Reviews of other Odyssey Guides...

"Thorough and beautifully illustrated, this book is a comprehensive—and fun—
window into Afghan history, culture, and traditions. A must have for travel
readers and a gripping read for anyone with even a passing interest in Afghanistan."
—Khaled Hosseini, author of *The Kite Runner*—

"...for coverage of Chongqing and the Gorges, and of the more placid and
historically notable sites below Yichang and downriver to Shanghai, it is unrivalled..."
—Simon Winchester—

"It is one of those rare travel guides that is a joy
to read whether or not you are planning a trip..."
—The New York Times—

"...Essential traveling equipment for anyone planning a journey of this kind..."
—Asian Wall Street Journal—

"If travel books came with warnings, the one for *AFGHANISTAN: A COMPANION AND GUIDE* would read, 'Caution: may inspire actual voyage.' But then, this lavishly
produced guide couldn't help do otherwise—especially if you're partial to adventure."
—*TIME*, August 22nd 2005—

"Above all, it is authoritative and as well-informed as only extensive
travels inside the country can make it. It is strong on the history.
In particular the synopsis at the beginning is a masterly piece of compression."
—*The Spectator* (UK)—

"A gem of a book"
—*The Literary Review* (UK)—

"...Quite excellent. No one should visit Samarkand,
Bukhara or Khiva without this meticulously researched guide..."
—Peter Hopkirk, author of The Great Game—

"The Yangzi guide is terrific"
—Longitude Books—

"...The bible of Bhutan guidebooks..."
—Travel & Leisure—

"...It's a superb book, superbly produced, that makes me long to go back to China..."
—John Julius Norwich—

"...Odyssey fans tend to be adventurous travelers with a literary bent.
If you're lucky enough to find an Odyssey Guide to where you're going, grab it..."
—National Geographic Traveler—

BUCKINGHAM PALACE

FOREWORD

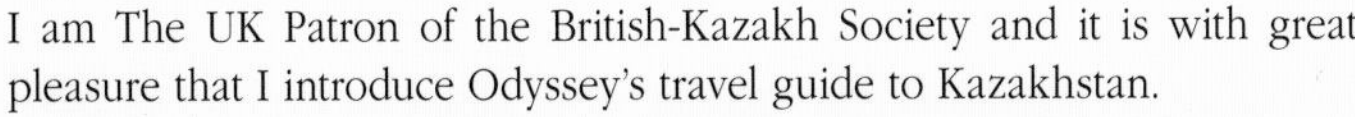

I am The UK Patron of the British-Kazakh Society and it is with great pleasure that I introduce Odyssey's travel guide to Kazakhstan.

Having 12% of its land area in Europe and the rest in Asia, Kazakhstan is unique in covering a vast expanse of northern and central Eurasia, from the Caspian Sea in the west to the Tien Shan and Altai mountain ranges in the east; from the deserts of Turkmenistan and Uzbekistan in the south to the Russian Siberian steppe in the north. The territory of the Republic of Kazakhstan is equivalent in size to Western Europe. For millennia it has been a crucible for human civilisation, a crossroad of cultures and a confluence for conquering armies.

Five thousand years of human history have enriched this region; from the Neolithic pastoralist communities of the Altai and Tien Shan mountains to the classical nomadic culture of the Sak; from the golden era of the Silk Road, the Huns and Kypchaks to Genghis Khan's Mongol horde and the armies of Tamerlane; from the Greater, Middle and Lesser Hordes who united as the "Kazakh" nation in the 16th Century, until the inexorable advance of the Russian empire in the 19th Century. As part of the Soviet Union Kazakhstan saw new waves of emigrants flood into the steppe, including thousands exiled from other parts of the Soviet Union.

This potted history is intrinsic to understanding Kazakhstan and the people of modern Kazakhstan today. With well over 100 ethnic nationalities the country is a true "melting pot" of cultures.

Since independence in 1991 Kazakhstan has made significant progress toward developing a market economy. Kazakhstan is not only one of the world's largest repositories of natural resources in oil and natural gas, but has one of the widest varieties of mineral deposits in the world, and has become an increasingly important economic partner in this strategically significant region.

Kazakhstan now features increasingly on business people's travel itineraries; but the riches and beauty of its vast and varied geography have yet to be discovered by more than a relatively small number of intrepid travellers. I have been fortunate enough to have seen at first hand some of Kazakhstan's imposing mountain scenery, the beauty of the steppe and the majesty of its desert, rivers and gem-like lakes. The country truly offers travellers a unique combination of adventure, history, culture and legendary hospitality—all set against a backdrop of pristine landscapes.

I very much hope that Odyssey's ***Kazakhstan*** guidebook will give you more of an insight into and a greater understanding of this vibrant country. It might, perhaps, inspire you to plan your own visit to discover for yourself all that Kazakhstan has to offer.

HRH The Duke of York

Domestic and International Route Network

Moscow
Amsterdam
London
Hanover
Oral
Aktobe
Atyrau
Frankfurt
Aktau
Istanbul
Antalya
Dubai

About Air Astana in Brief

- One of the fastest growing airlines in the world
- Operates to 20 international and 27 domestic destinations from its capital Astana and main operational hub in Almaty
- Fleet of western aircraft – Boeing 767, 757, Airbus A320, A321 and Fokker 50
- Carries over 5000 passengers per day
- Operates under European EASA/JAR-145 safety standards

Air Astana Call Centres

Domestic

Алматы / Almaty
+7 7272 506850

Астана / Astana
+7 7172 210764; 210765

Ақтау / Aktau
+7 7292 300400; 300401

Ақтөбе / Aktobe
+7 7132 550588; 548501

Атырау / Atyrau
+7 7122 355340; 355345

Жезқазған / Zhezkazgan
+7 7102 722311; 724616

Қарағанды / Karaganda
+7 7212 566991; 567522

Қостанай / Kostanay
+7 7142 546875

Қызылорда / Kzylorda
+7 7242 270392

Орал / Oral
+7 7112 515151; 515044

Өскемен / Oskemen
+7 7232 576675; 576676

Павлодар / Pavlodar
+7 7182 320091; 534594

Петропавл / Petropavlovsk
+7 7152 490187

Семей / Semey
+7 7222 560818; 560262

Тараз / Taraz
+7 7262 456656

Шымкент / Shymkent
+7 7252 549861; 549863

International

China (CN)

Air Astana BEIJING
Tel: +86 10 64651030, 64665067
E-mail: beijing@airastana.com

Cargo Service: Beijing DODA International Cargo Transportation Co., LTD
Tel: +86 10 85631471
Fax: +86 10 85610796
E-mail: genmake@x263.net

France (FR)

Air Astana Discover The World Marketing, PARIS, Tel: + 33 1 70 64 46 77
Fax: +33 1 58 22 20 10
E-mail: PAR.sales@airastana.com; PAR.reservations@airastana.com

Germany (DE)

Air Astana FRANKFURT
AVIAREPS Airline Management Group AG
Tel: +49 (0) 6105 206022, 6105 206028
E-mail: fra.reservations@airastana.com

Frankfurt International Airport:
Aviation Handling Services Ticket Desk,
Tel: +49 (0) 6969 061465

Cargo Service: ATC AVIATION SERVICES LTD., Tel: +49 (0) 6969 80 53 64
Fax: +49 (0) 6969 80 53 20
E-mail: vonkalckstein@atc-aviation.com; otto@atc-aviation.com

Air Astana HANOVER
Tel: +49 (0) 6105 206022
E-mail: fra.reservation@airastana.com

Hanover International Airport ticketing:
Aviation Handling Services Ticket Desk
Tel: +49 (0) 5119774166

Holland (NL)

Air Astana AMSTERDAM
Menzies Ticket Desk, Hall 3
Schiphol Airport, Tel: +31(0) 20 446 6354
E-mail: ph_ticketdesk@menziesaviation.nl

Cargo Service: Eurosky Cargo
Tel : +31(0) 20 795 2900
Fax : +31(0) 20 795 2909,
E-mail: matthijs@euroskycargo.com; Colette@euroskycargo.com

India (IN)

Air Astana DELHI
Deepika Travels
Tel: +9111 51521425, 23711225, 23711226
E-mail: del.sales@airastana.com; del.reservations@airastana.com

Cargo Service: Deepika Travels
Tel: +91 11 2371 1225 / 26
Fax: +91 11 2371 3869
e-mail: cargo@deepikatravels.com; airastana@deepikatravels.com

Indonesia (ID)

Air Astana c/o PT AVS, JAKARTA
Tel: +62 21 3929949
Fax: +62 21 2300253
E-mail: avs@aviationindonesia.com; erhan-alhabshy@aviationindonesia.com; djatmiko-hp@aviationindonesia.com

Italy (IT)

Air Astana AVIAREPS AG, MILAN
Tel: +39 02 4345 8391, + 39 335 7785911, Fax: +39 02 4345 8373
E-mail: Mil.reservations@airastana.com; Mil.sales@airastana.com

Malaysia (MY)

Air Astana Cargo Service
c/o ABDA Aviation Sdn Bhd., SELANGOR

From the heart of Eurasia

www.airastana.com

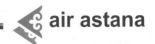

Kazakhstan

Nomadic Routes from Caspian to Altai

Dagmar Schreiber

with
additional material by

Jeremy Tredinnick

Odyssey Books & Guides is a division of Airphoto International Ltd.
903, Seaview Commercial Building, 21–24 Connaught Road West, Sheung Wan, Hong Kong
Tel: (852) 2856 3896; Fax: (852) 2565 8004
E-mail: sales@odysseypublications.com; www.odysseypublications.com

Distribution in the USA by
W.W. Norton & Company, Inc., 500 Fifth Avenue, New York, NY 10110, USA
Tel: 800-233-4830; Fax: 800-458-6515; www.wwnorton.com

Distribution in the UK and Europe by
Cordee Books and Maps, 3a De Montfort St., Leicester, UK, LE1 7HD, UK
Tel: 0116-254-3579; Fax: 0116-247-1176; www.cordee.co.uk

Kazakhstan: Nomadic Routes from Caspian to Altai
ISBN: 978-962-217-789-5
Library of Congress Catalog Card Number has been requested.

Grateful acknowledgement is made to the following authors and publishers; all materials remain the property of their respective copyright owners as indicated: The Ilyas Yesenberlin Foundation for *The Nomads* by Ilyas Yesenberlin © 2000; John Murray Publishers for *Diplomatic Baggage: The Adventures of a Trailing Spouse* by Brigid Keenan © 2005 by Brigid Keenan; Alma B. Kunanbaeva for "*Nomads*" © 2002 by Alma B. Kunanbaeva; The Long Riders' Guild Press for *A Ride to Khiva: Mounted adventures in Central Asia*, 1876, by Colonel Frederick Burnaby.

Managing Editor: Jeremy Tredinnick
Design: Au Yeung Chui Kwai
Maps: Mark Stroud (Back end paper map), On The Road Cartography
Production by Twin Age Ltd, Hong Kong
E-mail: twinage@netvigator.com
Printed in China

Front cover: A hunting eagle spreads its wings on the winter steppe (Vladimir Tugalev, top); monumental landscape on the Ustyurt Plateau (Dagmar Schreiber, bottom)
Front end paper map courtesy of the Agency on Land Resources Management of the Republic of Kazakhstan

Pages 4–5: The first Kolsay Lake in the Tien Shan range (Jeremy Tredinnick)
Page 6: The Mausoleum of Khoja Ahmed Yasawi in Turkistan (Jeremy Tredinnick)
Pages 8–9: Sharyn Canyon in the Zhetisu region (Christopher Herwig)
Left: The KazMunaiGaz building in Astana (Christopher Herwig)

Acknowledgements & Thanks

A book of this size and scope involves the work of many people. The publisher and editor would like to gratefully acknowledge the following individuals and organizations for donating their time and resources, thereby making a valuable contribution to this book:

Ambassador Erlan A. Idrissov, Oral Abubakir and Zhanbolat Ussenov at the Embassy of the Republic of Kazakhstan to the United Kingdom (**Note:** Ambassador Idrissov is now Ambassador to the United States of America)

Consul General Usen A. Suleimenov and Faizrakhman Kassenov at the Consulate of the Republic of Kazakhstan in Hong Kong

The Ministry of Tourism and Sport for the Republic of Kazakhstan

Rashida Shaikenova and Shakira Adilbekova at the Kazakhstan Tourist Association

The Agency on Land Resources Management of the Republic of Kazakhstan

The Akim of the East Kazakhstan Region

Gauhar Bramley-Fenton of the British-Kazakh Society

Baitursyn Umorbekov and Amir Jadaibayev at the Kasteyev State Museum of Art

The Central State Museum, Almaty

Dagmar Schreiber (for tireless assistance far beyond the call of duty)

Jack Hemsley (for much-appreciated editorial, translation and research work)

Folke von Knobloch and the Central Asia Tourism Corporation

Charles van der Leeuw at Caspian Publishing House

Richard Allcorn at Fauna & Flora International

E.J. Milner-Gulland of the Saiga Conservation Alliance

CuChullaine O'Reilly of The Long Riders' Guild

Brigid Keenan

Alma Kunanbaeva

Elena Romanova of the Foundation for International Arts and Education (www.fiae.org)

Lucy Kelaart and Summer Coish of *Steppe* magazine

In addition, the editor would like to express his thanks to the following individuals for assistance and friendship openly given during research in Kazakhstan for this book: Anara Zhenisovna, Gulzhan Kirgizbayeva, Ernur Baekeev, Zarina Tokumtayeva, Renato Sala, Jean-Marc Deom, Maksat and Rahima Nurgaliev, Kseniya and Aydan, Yevgeniy Yurchenkov, Nurlan and Aldiyar Toktarov, and Edda Schlager.

Rakhmet!

Right: The Holy Ascension Cathedral, Panfilov Park, Almaty (Jeremy Tredinnick)
Following pages: A Kazakh hunter rides out on the steppe with his trusted eagle and tazy *hound (Christopher Herwig)*

EDITOR'S NOTE

Producing a guidebook to a country like Kazakhstan presented us with considerable problems. A relatively young independent state, largely unknown and geographically vast, it is developing at a rapid pace, emerging on the global stage as an economic and political power within Central Asia (an increasingly important region), and now finds itself very much in the spotlight thanks to "Borat", where only a few years ago it was a blank in most people's minds. Clearly an English language guide to the country was needed as soon as possible, but the task of finding an individual able to accurately, informatively and enthusiastically describe the entire country, its culture and people, appeared Herculean given the short time frame involved.

In a stroke of good fortune, however, Odyssey Books & Guides became aware of just such an individual in Dagmar Schreiber, whose knowledge and love of Kazakhstan had resulted in the German guidebook *Kasachstan entdecken* (published by Trescher Verlag, www.trescherverlag.de). A translation had already been made for Kazakhstan-based Caspian Publishing House, and it is a version of that text that Odyssey has used as the foundation for the book you hold in your hand. It is hoped that despite the difficulties of translating German into flowing and entertaining English text, something of Dagmar's vivacious personal style has remained.

The English spelling of both place and people's names in Kazakhstan is a minefield of troublesome transliteration, for example in the mixed use of "i" and "y" (Katon-Karagay or Katon-Karagai, Abai or Abay, Pobediy or Pobedy, Aiteke Bi or Ayteke Bi, Kostanay or Kostanai, Altai or Altay, etc); "zh" and "j" or "dj" (Zhungar, Jungar or Djungar); "sh" and "ch" (Shymkent or Chimkent, Shu or Chu, Sharyn Canyon or Charyn Canyon)... and so on. As much as possible spelling has been made consistent, but in many instances "common usage" can refer equally to at least two spelling variations, while the existence of a disparate state language (Kazakh) and lingua franca (Russian) only adds to the confusion, with official Kazakh spellings replacing historical Russian ones, often resulting in both being used at the same time (see the list of new and old spellings in the Language section on page 547).

Inevitably there will be inconsistencies within this book, but for this we do not apologize. Rather, you should look at it as a valuable lesson in preparing for the many different spellings you will come across either during further literary exploration, or on the road during a sojourn in this remarkable and rewarding country.

Jeremy Tredinnick, 2007

Opposite page: Kazakhstan's highest mountain, 7,010-metre Khan Tengri, the "Lord of Heaven" (KanTengri Mountain Service)

CONTENTS

Previous pages: The majestic eagle is an icon of Kazakh culture and symbol of freedom (Vladimir Tugalev)

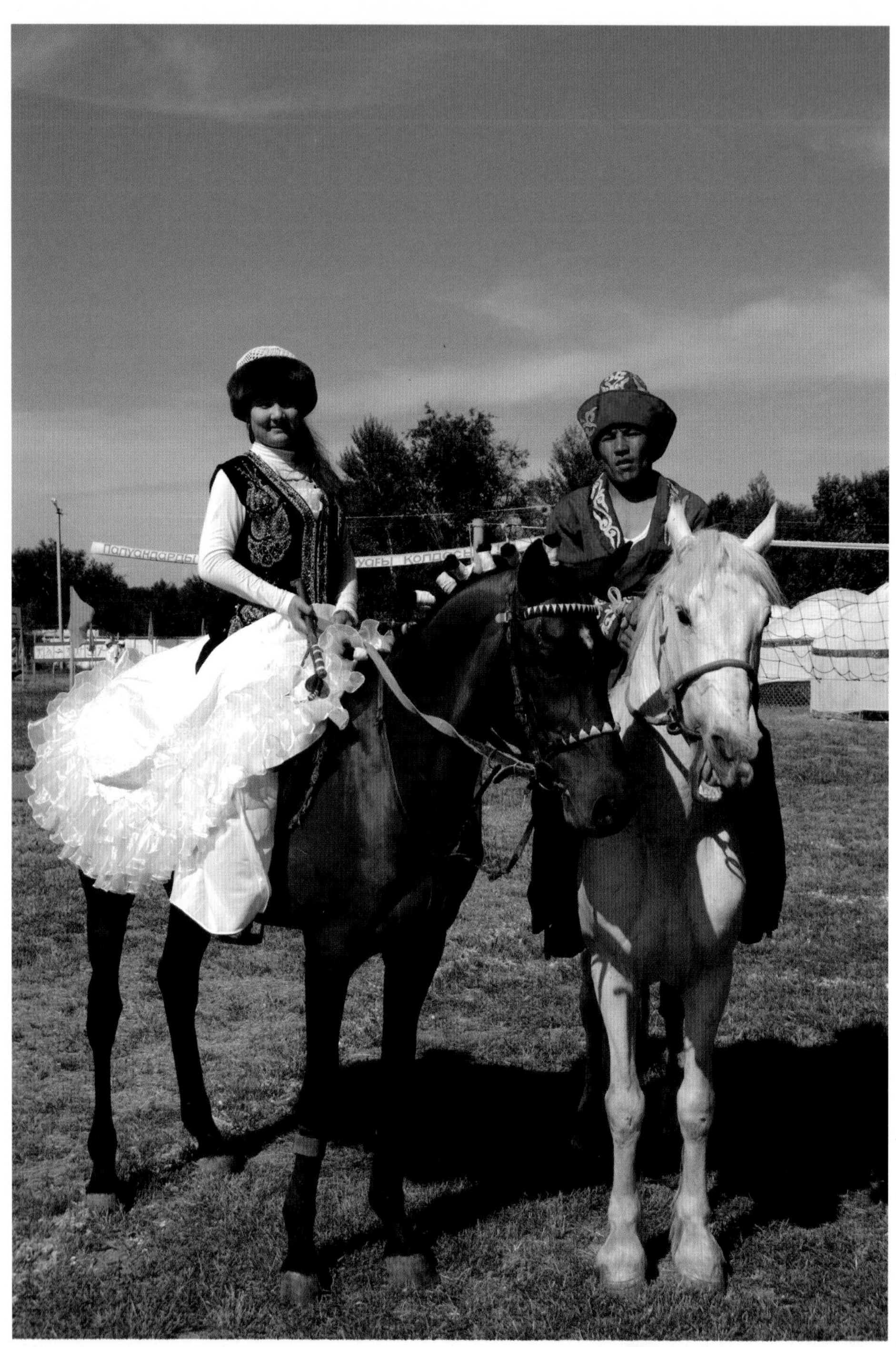

Above: Richly attired in traditional festival clothing, a young couple sit proudly on their steeds at an event in Ordabasy, South Kazakhstan. Right: Verdant hill steppe rises towards the Tien Shan (Jeremy Tredinnick x2)

THE LAND AND ITS PEOPLE

Whoever takes an interest in Kazakh culture, one of the most original and richest cultures in Eurasia, pays tribute to a nation which even during the hardest years offered refuge to many people.

Nursultan Nazarbayev

GEOGRAPHY

Kazakhstan is the world's ninth largest country, boasting 2.7 million square kilometres of land, an area larger than all the other former Soviet Central Asian member states put together, and four times the size of Texas. Put another way, with an east-west range of 2,800 kilometres and spanning more than 1,600 kilometres from north to south, the territory would be large enough to encompass Spain, Portugal, France, the Benelux states, Italy, Austria, Switzerland, Germany, Sweden, Denmark and the United Kingdom within its territorial boundaries. The most central of Central Asian countries, Kazakhstan has extensive land borders with Russia (6,467km), Uzbekistan (2,300km), China (1,460km), Kyrgyzstan (980km) and Turkmenistan (380km). Add to this its maritime border on the Caspian shelf, which stretches over 600 kilometres, and Kazakhstan's total border length reaches around 12,187 kilometres.

The perennially snow-covered peaks of the Tien Shan mountains dominate Kazakhstan's border with Kyrgyzstan (Dagmar Schreiber)

Topography and Mineral Resources

From the lowlands and plains in the west and north, to the high mountains in the southeast and south, Kazakhstan's territory has an altitude range of more than 7,000 metres. The country features an exceptional variety of landscapes, the most visually impressive being the high mountain ranges. The Tien Shan, a northern branch of which—the Zailiyskiy Alatau—separates Kazakhstan from Kyrgyzstan over a distance of 300 kilometres, is a folded massif which was formed during the Neo-Palaeozoic and Tertiary eras and later rose again as an anticline fault line ridge.

This mighty mountain chain stretches 2,500 kilometres from Kazakhstan across Kyrgyzstan into China. The Chinese called it the Mountains of Heaven, and at a height of 7,010 metres on Khan Tengri, Kazakhstan's highest summit, one gets close to Heaven indeed—and each year, due to the high seismic activity of the mountain range, up to five millimetres closer. The northern Tien Shan distinguishes itself by its ruggedness: within

Right: The country's wealth in mineral resources also results in some spectacularly colourful landscapes (Gunter Kapelle)

the relatively short period of time since the mountain range's formation, the strong erosive forces of ice and water have formed steep, deep valleys and filled them with rock debris, but failed to round off the peaks and ridges. Towards the north, the Tien Shan massif extends to the Zhungar (Dzhungar) Alatau, which occupies a vast area along the border with China, and reaches heights of up to 4,622 metres. Further to the north rises the wild, rocky Tarbagatay mountain chain, the highest peak of which reaches 2,992 metres.

The second major mountain range of Kazakhstan, the Altai, is also young in geological terms. The Altai's main chain consists of schist rock, which was folded and pushed up from the surrounding steppe and large plateaus until the Quaternary Era. The last Ice Age froze the Altai hard, and the snowline lay about 1,000 metres below its present-day level; as a result, today a rich variety of glacial formations are found: broad, bath-shaped valleys, coarse gravel fields and numerous lakes. The Altai is rich in polymetallic resources, particularly on its western, Kazakh slopes.

Characteristic of Kazakhstan's landscape are the Kazakh Uplands (*Melkosopochnik*) that occupy the entire eastern territory of Kazakhstan from the foot of the high mountains to the Syr Darya plains and the Torgay Depression, and the Kazakh plains that stretch westwards over 1,500 kilometres to the Turan Lowland.

The Talgar Peak is not far from Almaty; surrounded by glaciers it presents an awe-inspiring sight to trekkers unused to having such tremendous panoramas so easily accessible from a major city (Vladimir Tugalev)

In the west of the country lies the Caspian Depression, which has its lowest point, 132 metres below sea level, near Aktau. Here one finds the bare steppe and the vast, rich oil deposits of the Caspian Shelf. In the northwest, the southern spurs of the Urals mountain range stretch into Kazakhstan. This region is best known for its rich deposits of ore.

Erosion has played and continues to play a key role in forming Kazakhstan's landscape. The annual snowmelt shapes the many branches of the dry valleys in the steppe. Mountain rivers such as the Sharyn and the Aksu have dug grandiose valleys and canyons, while the trough-like valleys in the high mountains reflect the slow, inexorable work of glaciers through millennia. In the deserts and semi-deserts, dunes demonstrate the power of the wind. Only in very few countries in the world can one admire such a variety of impressive forms of erosion.

Its rich geological past has blessed Kazakhstan with a variety of mineral resources. Almost all existing chemical elements are hidden under Kazakhstan's surface, most of them in sufficient quantities to make their exploitation commercially viable. Oil, natural gas and hard coal, iron and chrome, manganese, wolfram, nickel, cobalt, molybdenum, copper, aluminium and bauxite, lead and zinc, tin, gold, silver, uranium and beryllium as well as a multitude of earths, stones and salt are mined. However, this wealth has been a double-edged sword for the country: unprecedented overexploitation of natural resources has occurred in many places with no genuine attempt to restore the land to its original health.

Climate

Kazakhstan is farther from any of the world's oceans than any other country on the planet. As a result its climate has a pronounced Continental character: extreme fluctuations in seasonal temperatures and poor precipitation. Hot, dry summers almost skip autumn to become cold, mostly dry winters with little snow, followed once more, almost overnight, by fast-rising temperatures.

In the north, the average summer temperature is 18°C, and winter averages -20°C. These values, however, say nothing about the extremes. In the northeast and the central steppe and desert areas especially, winter temperatures of -40°C are not exceptional. Summer temperatures in these regions also reach record highs, 40°C being far from rare. In the south, in the shelter of the Tien Shan, the climate is somewhat milder with less contrast.

In the regions bordering Uzbekistan, winters are relatively mild, with January temperatures averaging -1°C, spring comes early and summers are hot, with temperatures in July averaging 30°C. As a result, vegetable and fruit cultivation yields several harvests per year.

Total annual sunshine in some areas reaches 3,000 hours. Average precipitation reaches 1,500 millimetres in the Altai, 580mm in Almaty, while in the central steppe to the east of Lake Aral it is only 100–200mm. By comparison, the average annual precipitation in Germany is 800mm.

The low level of humidity makes the extremes in temperature more bearable for travellers. Even at temperatures in the order of 40°C, a stay in the steppe can be pleasant due to refreshing breezes and use of shade. Also, it's worth noting that a dry atmosphere with a temperature of -20°C often feels much better than a humid one at 3°C, provided the air is still. However, when the Buran—the long-lasting northeasterly wind that sweeps across northern Central Asia—rages, comparative studies of fresh air are simply unviable.

The high mountains often have their own microclimates. Mountain hikers and alpinists should therefore not rely on general weather patterns. Even in the low-risk season for mountain visitors, from June till mid-September, it can become very hot during the day and bitterly cold at night. Sudden changes in the weather, with heavy rains and snow on higher levels, are far from rare especially in June and July. Only when most of the snow on the glaciers has cleared can one expect stable weather in the high mountains.

Changes in the global climate are also being felt in Kazakhstan, where they result in ever hotter summers and the accelerated dwindling of the Tien Shan's large glaciers.

Above: A horse waits patiently at his post near the first Kolsay Lake, a stunning region for trekking even when the sun is hidden by layers of atmospheric mist (Dagmar Schreiber). Right: A waterfall gushes between slabs of rock on its descent to Rachmanov Lake in the Altai Mountains (Jeremy Tredinnick)

WATER

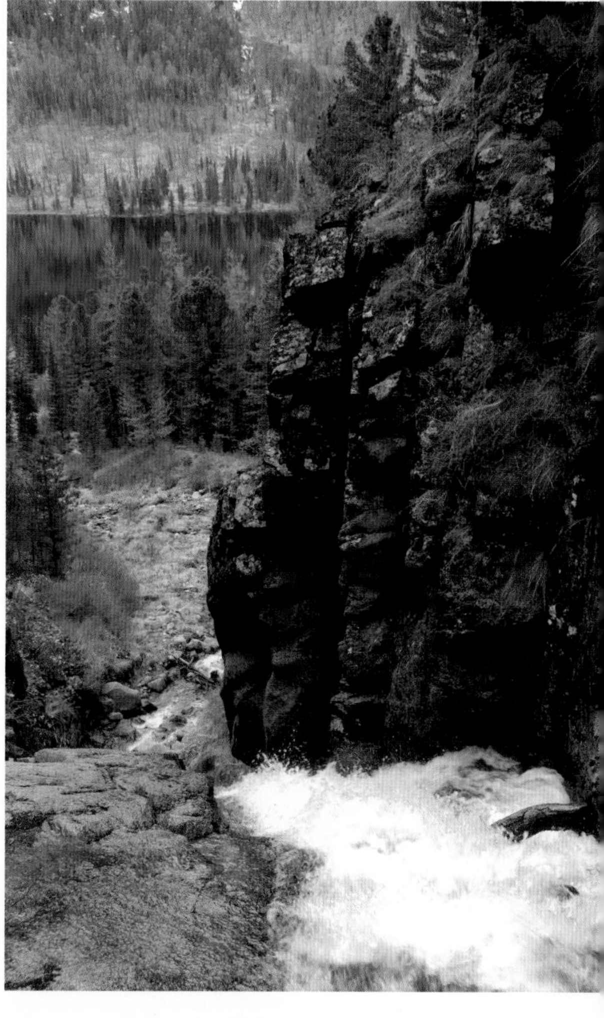

Water is life—and in continental and precipitation-strapped Kazakhstan this saying has profound meaning. The country has a wide variety of water resources. To the west, Kazakhstan borders the Caspian Sea—or Caspian Lake, as it should actually be called, since with a surface varying between 374,000 and 438,000 square kilometres it is the largest inland water basin on Earth. Having no outlet, and supplied by several rivers, the mightiest of which are the Volga and the Ural, evaporation is the main factor determining its water level. Situated in the Caspian Depression, its deepest point is 980 metres. In its northern sector, off the coast of Kazakhstan, however, the waters are extremely shallow. This zone's salty water is particularly appreciated by sturgeon species such as the osetra and sevruga, as well as Caspian seals.

Scientists are mystified by the sharp fluctuation in the level of this vast lake. In the 1970s and 80s, explanations blamed large reservoirs along the Volga. Other scientists claimed that water was "disappearing" into subterranean fissures in the Kara Bogas Gol (Bay of Kara Bogas) in Turkmenistan. Tectonic movement in this relatively active seismic zone has also been cited as the reason for the water level's fluctuation. Of late, the Caspian Sea is on the rise again. Some suspect that a thin layer of oil, originating from the numerous test and production drilling operations in the northern and western parts of the shelf, prevents evaporation. Other theories are based on uplifts in the floor of the sea. Whatever the cause, what is undisputed is that the Caspian needs greater protection because of its role in moderating the region's climate, its unique flora and fauna, and for the survival of its coastal inhabitants.

The tragedy concerning Lake Aral, once the fourth-largest inland water basin in the world, which Kazakhstanis reverently call *Aralskoye Morye*, the Aral Sea, has been widely reported throughout the world. The people who lived on its shores were once proud of the beauty of its turquoise surface, its wealth of fish resources, its wildlife in the river deltas of the Amu Darya and Syr Darya, and its picturesque isles—the Kazakh word "*aral*" means island. Its 65,000-square-kilometre surface area once almost equalled that of Ireland.

Tragically, the gigantic Soviet irrigation projects of the 1950s, called the Virgin Lands reclamation programme, have cost the lake its life. Driven by the ambition to turn the Soviet

A dust storm sweeps over the depleted Aral Sea—the small expanse of water in the north is now called the "Lesser Aral" (Satellite image courtesy of the Modis Rapid Response Project at NASA/GSFC)

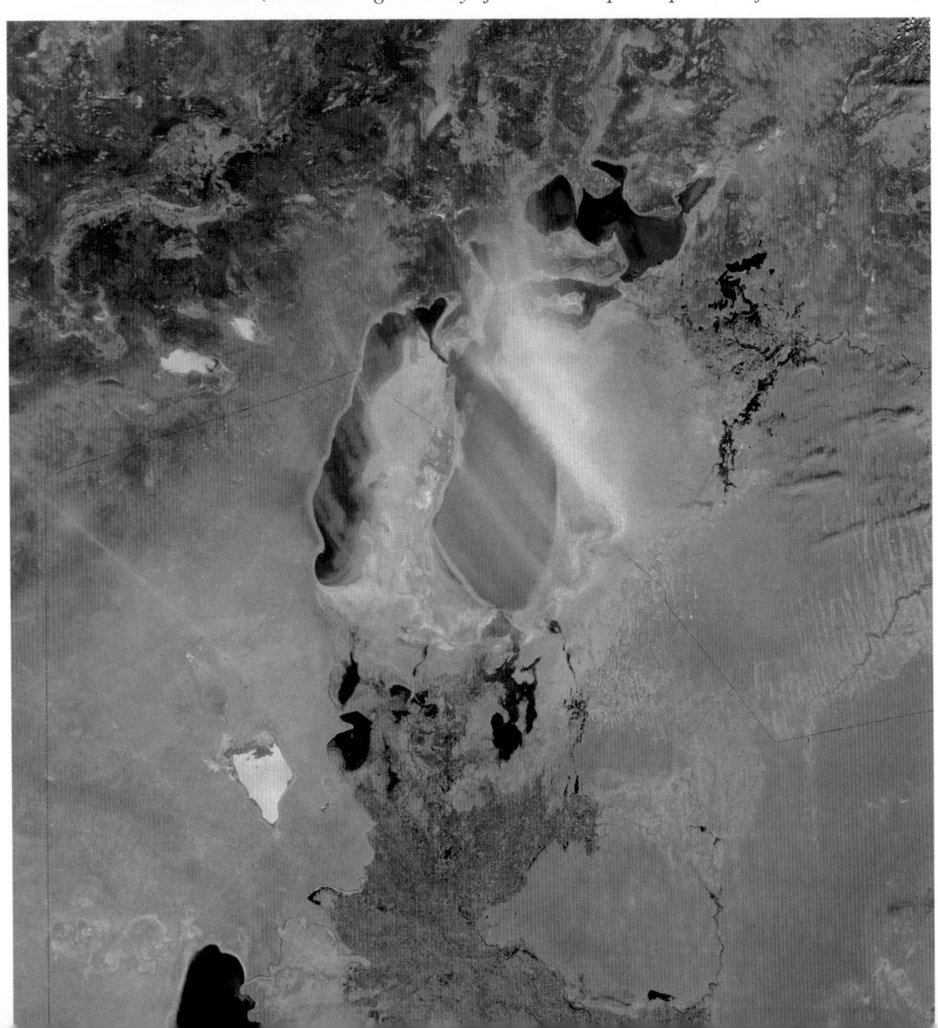

Union into an important exporter of cotton, planners pushed their luck too far. Their open canals, dug through the hot desert sands over distances of hundreds of kilometres, allowed more water to evaporate than eventually reached the crops. Nowadays the once mighty rivers of Amu Darya (2,540km) and Syr Darya (2,800km), end up as pitiful rivulets where the Aral's coast used to be. The shores of the Aral Sea have retreated dozens of kilometres, leaving behind thick salt marshes. Where once tigers roamed through the deltas' reed thickets, forbidding emptiness now prevails. By 1992, the lake had shrunk to half of its original area and to as little as one-third of its volume (see pages 324 and 328).

Whether or not this remnant can be saved depends on political decisions regarding the future of cotton. One thing is certain, however: the Aral Sea plays a vital role in Central Asia's climate. The water's salinity has risen sharply, not to mention its contamination from disproportionate use of fertilizers, herbicides and insecticides. The entire region has turned into an emergency zone, with people living under unbearable climatic, epidemiological and social conditions.

Glaciers within the mountain ranges of the Tien Shan, Zailiyskiy and Zhungar Alatau and Altai feed numerous rivers. Thus, in the south the Land of Seven Rivers ("*Semirechye*" in Russian, "*Zhetisu*" in Kazakh), a fertile piece of land the size of Hungary and Greece combined, is crossed by a large number of rivers that have their origin in the Zailiyskiy Alatau. The largest among them, the Ili, which has been dammed to the northeast of Almaty by the large reservoir of Kapshagay, is the main water supply of Lake Balkhash further downstream. This lake, with a surface of 18,200 square kilometres, has become Kazakhstan's biggest inland water basin as the Aral Sea dries up. In the southwest, where the Ili flows in, the water is fresh, whereas beyond the Uzynaral Peninsula in the east it becomes salty. Almost all steppe lakes are shallow and salty; with no outlet, the minerals and salt that flow into them accumulate fast. The best known among these is Lake Tengiz, to the southwest of Astana. In the east, near the Zhungar Gate, is the relatively shallow and fish-rich Alakol, also a salt lake, with a surface area of 2,100 square kilometres.

The Ertis (also Yertis, or Irtysh in Russian) has its source in the Altai. This mighty river, however, is losing more and more of its strength, because on the Chinese side of the mountains the steadily growing population increasingly taps its upstream resources. The Ili is also threatened with a similar fate, unless politicians in both countries can come to an understanding and effect a mutually agreeable and lasting solution.

With a total length of 4,250 kilometres, the Ertis makes its way through eastern and northern Kazakhstan for 1,700 kilometres. It flows into Lake Zaysan's eastern end, and out of it again 100 kilometres away from its northwestern tip. After another 340 kilometres, it flows into the Bukhtarminsk Reservoir, after which, already on Russian territory, it joins the

Esil (also Yesil, or Ishim in Russian) that comes from the Kazakh steppe. Finally, it joins the Ob, one of the largest rivers in the world.

From the Ural Mountains originates the river of the same name (in modern Kazakh *Oral*, in ancient Kazakh *Zhayik*), which makes its way through northwestern Kazakhstan until it flows into the Caspian Sea south of Atyrau. With its broad meandering, it is a good example of a river that has remained largely unharmed and left in its original state. It winds across Kazakhstan for just over half of its 2,534-kilometre length.

Many of Kazakhstan's rivers are characterized by strong changes in water volume; after snowmelt in the highlands and rare rainfall they can flow in full spate, but at other times they can only be recognized by their dried-up beds. Dry riverbeds, the longest of which are the Shu (Chuy in Kyrgyz, Chu in Russian), the Torgay and the Surysu, are shown as dotted blue lines on maps.

Above: A saksaul *bush survives the harsh environment of Altyn Emel National Park (Jeremy Tredinnick)*

SOIL AND VEGETATION

Kazakhstan is very clearly divided in its soil and vegetation zones. In the north, beyond Latitude 52, a strip of black earth occupies nine percent of the country's total land area. This soil is relatively thin, half being unsuitable for agriculture without irrigation. This is also the case with the belt of dark chestnut-brown soil to its south. This was the soil on which the Virgin Lands reclamation programme was concentrated.

In many ways, much of Kazakhstan is nature's poor cousin in terms of soil conditions. Gravel, sands and loam dominate the overall picture, and deserts, semi-deserts and steppe occupy 84 percent of the country. However, vegetation has adapted itself wonderfully to the rough conditions. The *saksaul* (haloxylon), a bush or tree with moisture-absorbing needle-shaped leaves and long, far-reaching roots, prospers in the desert; it grows slowly and produces an extremely hard and resistant wood. If it becomes too dry, it sheds its leaves. Unfortunately, this wood is being systematically plundered for its good meat-grilling qualities, and if the state does not intervene, it will soon be found only in nature reserves.

The *karagach*, an elm species, is equally hardy with 20-metre-long roots like piles, and is therefore planted as a windbreak in areas sensitive to erosion. Tamarisks produce pretty flowers which belie how tough these drought-proof bushes are, while ephedra and sand-thorn bushes also survive on meagre soils, their charming berries adorning the yellow-brown landscape.

Bulbous plants survive the harsh winter underground in the steppe and come to life in April and May when the meltwater penetrates the soil. During this brief period, apart from the small steppe tulips (among which botanists distinguish various subdivisions), you can see wondrous cistanche, graceful lilies, crocuses and anemones; even garlic has attractive flowers. Many of our cultivated garden plants have their ancestry here in the steppe and sheltered mountain valleys of Kazakhstan.

Late in May, swathes of common poppy cover the immensely vast steppe like a purple carpet. Only a month later, when everything has shrivelled, comes the time for humble plants. Many unassuming kinds of drought-resistant and hardy grass, sedge and shrubbery give the steppe its typical character.

Right: The rare Kaufmann's tulip (L. Bjelousowa)

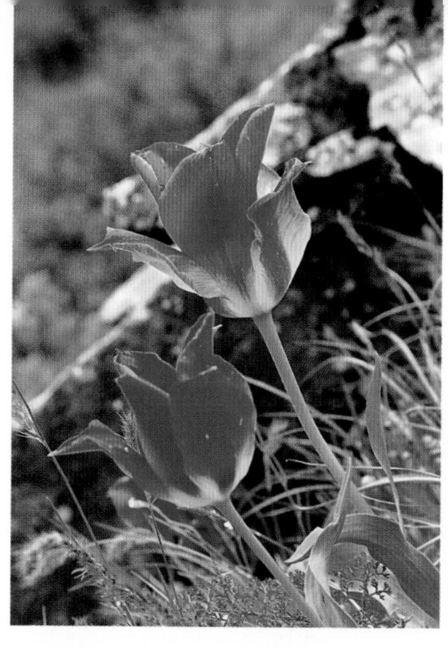

Short- and long-grass steppes, the latter looking delightful with their long, silver-gleaming clumps of feather or heron grass, are blessed with more precipitation and fertility.

In the foothills of the mountains, the grass steppe gives way to wormwood meadows. The meat of sheep that are grazed here is known for its exceptionally aromatic taste, and these herbaceous areas are popular with many other herbivorous animals as well. On the numerous slopes of the high mountains the elegant Tien Shan spruce grows straight as an arrow, while valleys are covered with juniper woods. Wild apple, pear, cherry and apricot trees that grow in the lower mountains are the forerunners of our garden fruits. In the alpine meadows below the glaciers marigold, primrose, edelweiss and gentian grow profusely. The Tien Shan's alpine zone contains more than double the number of plant species than that of the Alps.

A wide variety of plants prosper in the fertile wetlands of the lower river valleys. Torgay woods, as they are called, with Turanga poplar, ash, tamarisk and reed border the rivers as they flow through the semi-deserts and steppe. In some places, primeval forests dating back millennia have been preserved. The most sensational is situated downstream on the Sharyn, where a mixed willow and ash wood from before the last Ice Age has been preserved. The high-lying pine-tree forests on the Ertis are also worth seeing.

Kazakhstan's vegetation consists of 5,700 plant species, of which 700 are endemic. Some travel agents offer special botanical excursions—the best time for these is in May and June.

WILDLIFE

In 1867, the German zoologist Alfred Brehm, while exploring southern Siberia and Central Asia, found a true paradise in the area now known as Kazakhstan. Excited, he wrote in a report titled "On the tracks of the arkhar": "From the rocks, where Finsch's wheatear, Godlewski's bunting and red-fronted rosefinch carry on, the faint song of the stone thrush resounds, jackdaws swarm around the upper peaks, and above them circles the golden eagle by day, and soundlessly glides the Eurasian eagle-owl by night—both keen on catching the abundant rock partridge or a careless marmot. The most interesting of all is the arkhar… the argali in the words of the explorer, one of the giant mountain sheep of Central Asia, as tall

Above: Tulipa greigii is one of the largest of Kazakhstan's many tulip species (L. Bjelousowa). Left: Coniferous forest blankets the northern slopes of the Tien Shan (Jeremy Tredinnick)

as European red deer... They climb effortlessly up and down almost vertical slopes, jump wide crevasses and come down from on high, as though they could fly."

Unfortunately its nimbleness has not saved the argali from having been all but wiped out. These days, they are included in the red list of animal species under threat of extinction. They share this fate with many other animals: the ram-snouted saiga antelope, the elegant *dzheyran* or goitred gazelle, the *kulan* (wild ass) and numerous birds of prey. There was little that Brehm could know then about the dangers threatening the snow leopard, the brown bear and even the wolf.

The causes of the decimation of so much of Kazakhstan's wildlife are manifold. First was the conversion of 25.5 million hectares of steppe—a surface equal to that of Great Britain—into agricultural territory in the 1950s and 1960s. This large-scale destruction of natural land, known as the Virgin Lands programme, irreversibly deprived many animals of their habitat. The grasslands of the kulan, saiga, dzheyran, fox, wolf, songbirds and birds of prey disappeared to make way for dubious monoculture. What had taken centuries to grow in the harsh climate of Central Asia was ploughed out within a decade. Even now that large-scale agriculture with chemical agents has ended, it will take decades before the original steppe vegetation, able to support large herds of antelope, gazelle, wild donkey and birds, can be restored.

Another cause for the virtual disappearance of many steppe animals is hunting, which once was—and still is, illegally—celebrated in true orgies of killing. The Kazakh and Russian passion for hunting has always been proverbial. But it was social need that drove many inhabitants of Kazakhstan to systematically slaughter the saiga antelope, wild sheep, *maral* and wild boar, as well as to over-fish the sturgeon population in the Caspian Sea. Pelt hunters still hunt snow leopard and bear, while poachers plunder falcon and eagle nests and sell eggs and fledglings to rich sheikhs and other falcon hunt lovers. In the famine-stricken steppe of Betpak Dala, where the herds of saiga used to be counted in tens of thousands, now only around 1,000 animals survive, whereas in other areas small numbers are thought to linger on. Only in 2001 was the antelope species, under threat of extinction, put under total protection. Some kulan survive in the protected zone of the Barsakelmes Peninsula on the Aral Sea and in Altyn Emel National Park, and thanks to strict protection the animals are multiplying once more.

Back in 1867, Brehm, who was an avid ornithologist, was impressed by the rich bird life in the steppe. Even though this can only be observed today in a handful of remote steppe regions, it still makes for a very worthwhile trip. Tours in these areas support the efforts of national and international nature conservation organizations to open people's eyes to the beauty of these animals and to sharpen their awareness of the need for preservation of all Kazakhstan's wildlife.

Birds & Beasts of Mountain and Steppe

By *Richard Allcorn*

Kazakhstan is a country blessed with an exceptional natural heritage set amidst vast, stunning landscapes that stretch from the high skylines of the celestial Tien Shan Mountains to the far horizons of the immeasurable steppe. It has extraordinary wildlife, a rich culture and a generous and hospitable people whose traditions are founded on their coexistence with and deep respect for their land and nature.

Kazakhstan harbours a richly diverse biogeography and attendant biological diversity. The northernmost region is covered with the taiga, mixed forest and forest-steppe of the Siberian lowland. Further south, the arboreal influence disappears and extensive steppe and desert ecosystems dominate. The Central Asian deserts are the richest desert complexes in Eurasia. There are more than 34,000 lakes, including the saline Caspian and Aral Seas, and large freshwater bodies such as lakes Balkhash and Tengiz, as well as associated and extensive reed beds and marshes. The majority of the rivers, the

Above: The dzheyran *or goitred gazelle, once a common sight on the Kazakh steppe (Vladislav Yakushkin).*
Inset: The fierce and coveted saker falcon (Vladimir Tugalev)

Volga and Ural, Syr Darya and Ili feed into these large lakes. Only the Irtysh, Ishim and Tobol rivers flow north across Siberia to the Arctic Ocean. The Tien Shan and Altai mountains form natural boundaries around the Kazakh Basin and contain different types of forest, alpine meadows, tundra, permanent snow belts and glaciers.

Although a land-locked country, Kazakhstan's western border is formed in part by the inland Caspian Sea—home to the smallest species of seal, the Caspian Seal. The fisheries of the Caspian are very important both in terms of biodiversity and the economy of the Caspian countries. Within its expansive waters live six species of sturgeon, including the beluga, shovelnose and starlet (90% of the global sturgeon population), as well as herring, zander (sander), sazan and the Caspian roach.

The fauna of Kazakhstan is as exciting and diverse as the landscape it inhabits, with wildlife spectacles to rival anything on Earth. Over 489 bird species have been recorded, 178 mammal species, 49 reptile species, 12 amphibians and 104 species of fish. Some of these are familiar species, but many are wonderful or rare, from the enigmatic snow leopard and bizarre-looking saiga antelope to the huge-horned argali sheep, desert dormouse, swan goose, relict gull, Siberian crane and sociable lapwing. The meadow viper and Central Asian salamander are two of the more exotic reptiles and amphibians. There are also exceptional numbers of invertebrates, with more than 100,000 species described so far and tens of new species being added each year, such is the country's geographic size and diversity.

Many of these species have cultural value, forming part of the spirit and identity of Kazakhstan. The national flag features the majestic golden eagle, one of 35 species of bird of prey found in Kazakhstan. The beautiful and

Przewalski's horse once ranged across large areas of the steppe (Vladimir Tugalev)

elusive snow leopard is considered a national icon, often depicted supporting the equally iconic golden warrior of Almaty. The charismatic saiga, an antelope of the harsh desert, is emblematic of the region; esteemed in local culture and folklore, it reflects the traditional nomadic lifestyle of the people of the steppe.

The saiga is the keystone species of the steppe and deserts that cover almost two-thirds of Kazakhstan. It is perfectly adapted to the harsh and unpredictable conditions of the region, with a distinctive oversized and flexible nose that warms the air in winter and filters out the dust in summer. Historically, saiga occurred in vast herds 100,000 strong. Their migration across these dusty arid plains was a spectacle to rival the mass ungulate migrations of East Africa. Until the middle of the last century these herds were accompanied by predators including wolf and wild dog, Asiatic cheetah and Caspian tiger. Sadly, only the wolf can now be seen in Kazakhstan, and tragically the last Caspian tiger was hunted to extinction in the 1950s. Recent changes in land management and high levels of illegal poaching decimated the saiga herds—from more than a million individuals just two decades ago, perhaps fewer than 40,000 now remain, although intervention by the government has now halted the population collapse (see the special topic "Saiga saga" on page 370).

Kazakhstan is a grazer's paradise, originally home to a wealth of herbivores, including Asiatic wild ass (kulan or koulan), Bactrian camel and Przewalski's horse. Domesticated camels are now common, and are a key component of the rural economy. Przewalski's horse is locally extinct and the wild ass very rare, but conservation efforts are being initiated to help them both recover in the region. Rodents are abundant in all the habitats of Kazakhstan. In the steppe and semi-desert ecosystems they play an important role, their ground disturbance recycling nutrients and activating seeds. Marmots, sousliks, hamsters, gerbils and jerboas are common, and several rodent species are only found here, such as the desert dormouse and comb-toed jerboa.

The great eagle owl is a top predator (Jeremy Tredinnick)

Corsac fox, honey badger, sand caracal and Pallas's cat are typical semi-arid carnivores found in the region, although many of these are sadly in decline. The steppe (its grasslands and water bodies) is also home to many exciting bird species, from raptors such as the saker falcon to sociable plover, black-winged pratincole, demoiselle crane, black lark, the rare saxaul jay and the desert sparrow. Reptile diversity is also very high, including many species of snake, gecko and toad agama—some only found here, such as the grey monitor specific to the Kyzylkum Desert.

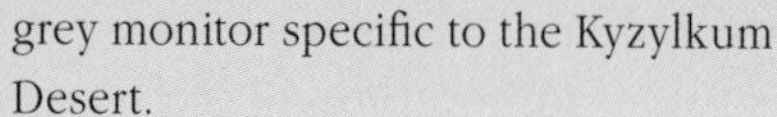

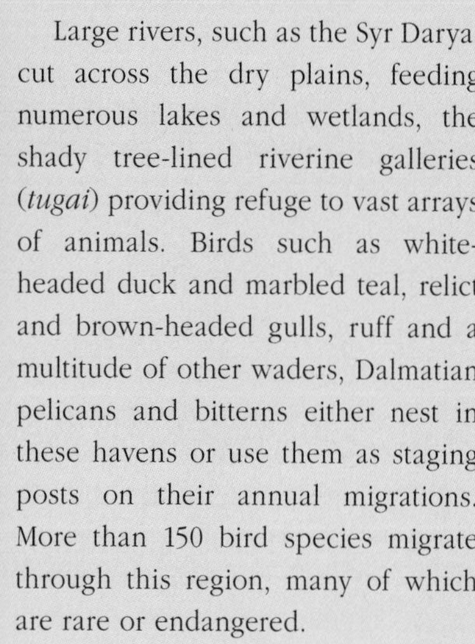

Large rivers, such as the Syr Darya, cut across the dry plains, feeding numerous lakes and wetlands, the shady tree-lined riverine galleries (*tugai*) providing refuge to vast arrays of animals. Birds such as white-headed duck and marbled teal, relict and brown-headed gulls, ruff and a multitude of other waders, Dalmatian pelicans and bitterns either nest in these havens or use them as staging posts on their annual migrations. More than 150 bird species migrate through this region, many of which are rare or endangered.

Bats are plentiful, as are rodents such as flattooth rat and tamarix gerbil. Wild boar, Bukhara deer and goitred gazelle use the tugai for shelter from the steppe; hyena, jungle cat and jackal hunt in the forest glades. Amphibians are common with grey, green and Central Asian toads and Anatolian, lake, grass, Siberian and black-spotted frogs all present. Reptiles are well represented too, with geckos, skinks and snakes either resident or wintering in river cliffs or wooded areas away from the harsher open landscapes.

The rivers are fed by the snows and glaciers of the two magnificent mountain ranges that border Kazakhstan, the Tien Shan in the south and southeast and the Altai Mountains in the northeast. Both isolated regions are

The Asian paradise flycatcher inhabits woods and mountain forests (Rolf Behlert)

home to many rare and special species. The most charismatic species of the higher altitudes is the snow leopard. Solitary, shy and well camouflaged, this exquisite creature is very rarely seen. It is well adapted to the cold, harsh landscape, protected from the snow and the cold by thick, smoky-grey fur. Sure-footed and silent, snow leopards are capable of leaping 10 metres and taking prey three times their own bodyweight. Although not aggressive to humans, they continue to suffer by our hand, so that now no more than 100 survive in Kazakhstan.

A mixed suite of other predators can be found, from Altai ferret, wolverines and jungle cat to wolf and lynx. The red bear, an increasingly rare subspecies of brown bear, can still be found in the Tien Shan. Arkhar sheep and maral deer graze the middle elevations, whilst on the higher rocky slopes ibex and argali can be found. On the northern slopes of the Altai, reindeer herds from Siberia graze across the tundra slopes. Rodents are again plentiful in number and diversity, with birch mouse, voles and shrews abundant in the foothills and arctic ground squirrels and Siberian chipmunk in the alpine environments.

The lammergeyer, the bone-breaker vulture, rules over these peaks, sharing the skies with Eurasian and Himalayan griffon vultures, golden and steppe eagles, buzzards, eagle owls and peregrine falcons. Alpine choughs tumble above the rock faces. Finches, buntings and redstarts fill the woody valleys with their varied calls whilst the forests are home to game birds like the rare snowcock and hazel grouse. A rare resident of the relic mountain coniferous forests is the Central Asian salamander, found only in the headwaters of small mountain streams in the alpine forest-meadows.

Richard Allcorn is Eurasia Projects Manager for Fauna & Flora International, the world's longest established conservation society, which works to conserve threatened species worldwide, choosing solutions that are sustainable, based on sound science and taking account of human needs. For more information visit www.fauna-flora.org

An agama lizard scurries across the scrub desert floor (Manuela Offenzeller)

ENVIRONMENTAL PROTECTION

Environmental awareness and activity in Kazakhstan focuses on sustaining biodiversity, and the restoration of its large number of damaged areas: a quarter of the country's land has been heavily affected. Among these regions are the former nuclear arms zone near Semey (Semipalatinsk), the test zones of Saryshagan, Azgir and Taysoygan, the shrinking Aral Sea, Lake Balkhash (which is also retreating), the rising and warming of the Caspian Sea, and the areas surrounding major conurbations. High salt concentration in the soil is a problem, as is the retreat of the country's glaciers, as well as overuse of drinking-water resources. But the biggest problem for environmental initiatives is the poverty of the population in many of the worst areas. People live with no infrastructure to speak of, and where, apart from livestock breeding, there are hardly any sources of income. Poverty leads to illegal logging, overfishing, poaching and overuse of pastureland. Given this situation, the benefits of ecotourism are potentially valuable, creating new prospects for local people.

Much is being done through the country's scientific research institutes and also by international organizations to analyse the problems and improve the situation step by step. Unfortunately, so far Kazakhstan has not been able to provide the necessary financial resources to preserve the impressive multitude of plants and animals within its borders. In a few areas plans are under way to create UNESCO biosphere reservations and global natural heritage protection zones, and to pursue programmes for the protection of biodiversity. The best results of these efforts have been in the Altai, in the lake district of Tengiz-Korgalzhin and in the dry steppe of Naurzum.

A good example is the work of the German Naturschutzbund (NABU) to expand the natural reserve of the vast wetlands around Lake Tengiz (which was established as early as the 1950s), to upgrade it to a UNESCO biosphere reserve, and to protect it against uncontrolled and improper agricultural exploitation. A group led by the German biology professor Michael Succow has been engaged in Tengiz on this pilot project for years. His work includes research and lobbying, public relations, equipping of wardens, support for a local nature protection initiative, and the participation of the local population in the development and adaptation of management schemes for the area, which should lead to exemplary sustainable land use. Also included are practical protection measures such as the replacement of high-tension cables, lethal for many large birds, by decentralized solar power generation equipment. Ecotourism here is particularly desirable (see Chapter 5, Sary Arka: the Great Steppe).

RESERVES AND NATIONAL PARKS

Kazakhstan has nine natural reserves and four national parks, all of which charge entry fees and are partly open to tourism. Nature reserves (*zapovedniki*) are large protected areas, mainly designated as closed reserves that can only be entered with permission and are under constant scientific observation.

Kazakhstan's nature reserves are:

• **Naurzum**: Dry wormwood-, salt- and pasture steppe with scattered, ancient fir-tree vegetation in the north of the Torgay Depression, with numerous fresh- and saltwater lakes.

• **Korgalzhin Lakes and Tengiz**: A salt steppe landscape to the southwest of Astana, with large salt lakes and dense reed vegetation, a rich variety of waterfowl, birds of prey, wading birds and salt steppe plants.

• **West Altai**: A forest-covered, medium-high mountain range on the Russian border with a dark and black coniferous forest taiga.

• **Barsakelmes**: A partially reed-covered peninsula, formerly an island, in the Aral Sea with typical salt desert vegetation and a population of kulan, saiga and dzheyran.

• **Ustyurt**: A vast, untouched desert plateau east of the Caspian Sea, stretching into the Turan Lowland. Special protection is granted to the endemic Ustyurt moufflon, as well as saiga, dzheyran and reportedly some cheetah.

• **Aksu-Zhabagly**: High mountain landscape with juniper forests between Shymkent and Taraz, together with the adjacent Karatau mountain range; one of the areas with the largest biodiversity.

• **Almaty Reserve**: Varied landscapes of low steppe foothills reaching to the high mountain slopes of Zailiyskiy Alatau; significant biodiversity.

• **Markakol**: An almost untouched, large mountain lake situated in the far eastern tip of Kazakhstan, surrounded by fir, spruce and larch forests; great wealth in plant, bird and mammal life.

• **Alakol**: A chain of lakes not far from the Chinese border, consisting of two large salt lakes and a giant reed-covered moist biotope in the Tentek delta on the freshwater lake Sasykkol.

Kazakhstan's state national parks are:

• **Kokshetau**: Forest-covered, medium-high mountain "island" with many lakes in the middle of the steppe between Astana and Kokshetau, best known for its health resort of Burabay (Borovoye).

• **Bayanaul**: An area between Pavlodar and Karaganda; as with Kokshetau Park, it is an azonal (not divided into zones) region of fir and birch forests on the granite massif in the dry steppe, requiring careful preservation.

• **Altyn Emel**: Steppe and semi-desert area with rich wildlife, wandering dunes, Scythian barrows/tumuli and rock carvings, located on the north bank of the Kapshagay Reservoir and bordered to the north by the Altyn Emel highlands. Established for the protection of kulan, dzheyran and arkhar.

• **Ili-Alatau**: The most northerly chain of the Tien Shan, between the southern outskirts of Almaty and the border with Kyrgyzstan. In this region more than any other, the compatibility between enjoyment of nature through leisure activities and careful protection of the environment has to be proven. Here, as in the Altyn Emel National Park, limited, strictly controlled hunting is permitted.

History

Present-day Kazakhstan is the result of centuries-long emerging and fading of tribes and states in the vast steppe between the Altai and the Volga. The development of separate statehood was long delayed, due both to the nomadic lifestyle of the tribes living on the territory and to frequent incursions from outside, ethnic migration movements and, last but not least, due to everlasting inner struggles for power among Kazakh tribal associations.

Early History

The fertile areas north of the Tien Shan and the hillsides and green valleys of the Alatau Ranges were inhabited long before the beginning of our era. Encampments belonging to primitive humans have been found in sheltered and forested locations rich in water and wildlife in many places in present-day Kazakhstan. The richest finds have been made in the valleys of the Karatau Mountains in southern Kazakhstan. Perhaps contrary to expectations, Kazakhstan's earliest history lies in settled agricultural communities rather than in nomadism. Artefacts dating from the end of the Neolithic Age demonstrate that as early as 5,000 years ago farming, and particularly the domestication of livestock, was practised on the northern outskirts of the Tien Shan.

At the beginning of the Bronze Age, archaeologists have been able to detect a coherent culture—the Andronovo Culture—reaching from the Ob and Yenisei Rivers in Siberia, down through the foothills of the Altai into Kazakhstan. In general, the people of this age (c. 2000–1500 BC) lived a sedentary life in simple dwellings, with plank beds, hearths, and pits sunk into the ground to keep their provisions. These small houses were often gathered into settlements, clustered around ploughed fields or cattle enclosures. Their principal industry, aside from breeding livestock and making garments from their wool—fragments

Petroglyphs have been a part of the region's many developing cultures through millennia (Vladimir Tugalev)

of pounded-woollen caps from this time have even been found in their graves—was that of metallurgy. Copper ore primarily was mined in shallow pits and surface deposits in the Altai and Kalbin ranges, and craftsmen used clay or composite stone moulds to forge spearheads, daggers and blades.

The observable remains of the religion of these people, including offerings in tombs of agricultural produce, milk and vegetables, bears testament to the nature of the society, ultimately concerned with cultivation. However, it is in this time that the first foundations of nomadism were laid down. The horse, which was an animal originally hunted, was domesticated, and it is perhaps during this period—although some scholars disagree—that the people of the steppe began to learn how to ride. It is also to this time that many date the invention of the wheeled chariot, the use of which perhaps preceded horseback riding.

The Andronovo Culture was succeeded by the Karasuk Culture (c. 1500-800 BC), a change signified by different burial customs, and tombs of unworked rectangular stone slabs within circular enclosures. Despite this difference, the technologies possessed by the people continued to evolve, and it can be said beyond doubt that full-scale pastoral nomadism had come into being by this time. The improving skill in metalworking not only allowed for the creation of highly wrought artefacts—daggers and ornaments with the heads of horses, rams, goats and even tiny bells—but also for the invention of the bronze bit, allowing for the wider and more long-distance use of the horse. This combined with further inventions—the felt tent, the hooded cart, products from milk including *kumis* and cheese—allowed for the evolution of a nomadic stratum of society that was, for its everyday requirements, self-sufficient.

Nonetheless, the sedentary and agricultural element was still very much present, and we can envisage the nomadic and the sedentary populations living in symbiosis. Each would exchange their native produce with the other, and the nomads would also be responsible for the appearance of long-distance trade and contacts between established centres. The nomads also contributed to the world of ideas, creating a rich mythology of religion based on a dualistic struggle between the heavenly gods of light, and the evil gods of the underworld.

A pair of winged horses with ibex horns, part of the "Golden Man's" headdress (Courtesy of the Museum of Gold and Precious Metals, Astana, and the Foundation for International Arts and Education, www.fiae.org)

The Sak

The lands of Kazakhstan, after the eighth century BC, gradually came under the control of a wave of Indo-European speaking immigrants, the Sak (also known as the Saka or Sacae). These are thought to have been one of the tribes or branches of the Scythians, a people who are thought ultimately to have migrated from the inner Asian regions north of China, and settled from the coasts of the Black Sea to as far as southern Siberia.

Little can be said for certain of their political history. What literary evidence we have of them is generally found in ancient Persian and Greek sources, and often this is vague and contradictory. Even with respect to such writers as the historian Herodotus, it is difficult to pin down geographical locations, or see through the haze of myth and rumour. (Sak horsemen were reputed to have been the first to shoot with bows and arrows from a galloping horse and to have mastered the art of iron forging before any other nation did. Excavations have revealed that the Sak penetrated deep into mountain ranges on their hunting expeditions—an arrow tip of Sak design was found at 2,000 metres.)

However, descriptions are given of their nomadic behaviour and customs, and of them Herodotus writes in book IV of his *Histories* that "all carry their houses with them and are mounted archers, living not by the plough but by cattle, [and some] whose dwellings are upon cars, these assuredly are invincible and impossible to approach."

His elaborate descriptions of divination and interment rites are also to a certain extent confirmed by the recent excavation of Sak burials throughout Kazakhstan and further afield.

The most famous of their tombs, or *kurgans*, is the Issyk Kurgan, discovered in 1969. It contained the skeleton of a Sak warrior (the "Golden Man") clad in ornamental golden mail finely wrought with a variety of animals, including horses and griffins, snakes and leopards. An inscription on a silver goblet points to an indigenous and as yet undeciphered alphabet, and the rest of the artefacts suggest a high level of culture and development. However, the title "Golden Man" may be a misnomer, since it is unknown whether this specific skeleton is that of a man or a woman. Yet, in a great number of instances, skeletons which are clearly female have been found dressed as warriors, and it gives some credence to the theory that these regions are also to be associated with the legendary female warrior tribe, the Amazonians.

The Silk Road

The history of the region at this time is both obscure and somewhat confusing, being mostly found in fragmentary accounts and evidence of tribal movements of which we can say little for certain. However, the haziness of the period is thrown into relief by the evolution of the Silk Road, and the growth of international trade. In 138 BC, the Chinese Emperor Han Wu-di, threatened by the nomadic powers of Inner Asia to the north of his kingdom, sent a diplomatic mission under a courtier, Zhang Qian, to see if there were any powers in the far west with whom the Chinese could ally. Zhang Qian's journey took him from the ancient Chinese capital Xi'an into the depths of Central Asia and Afghanistan, and although he

The "Golden Man", one of Kazakhstan's greatest archaeological finds (Renato Sala and Jean-Marc Deom)

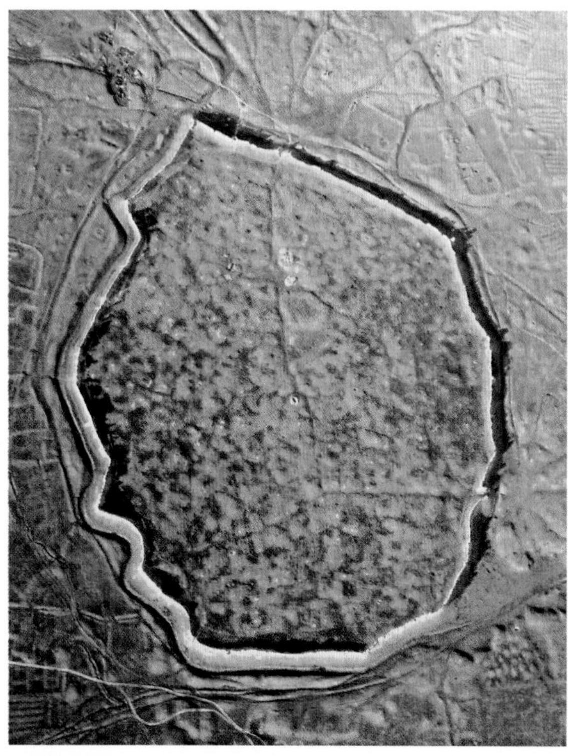

was unable to set up any alliance with the Central Asian Kingdoms, he brought back to Xi'an a wealth of information about these previously unknown areas. This, over the following years, allowed for the development of contacts and eventually regular trade between the great empires of the ancient world. By the beginning of the first century BC, embassies had been exchanged between China and Persia, and by the end of it, Chinese silk was well known in Rome.

The Silk Road, a wide, multi-branched network of caravan and trade routes, branches of which crossed modern-day Kazakh territory, began to evolve. Not only luxury merchandise of all varieties, but also religions, cultures and customs were exchanged along this network; for example, Greek art and religious motifs were taken up and echoed in nomadic artefacts of the steppe. The nomads themselves played a significant part in the trade, conducting caravans of merchandise between major centres, as well as trading their own produce from the steppe in urban mercantile centres such as Tashkent. In this way, despite the appearance of these more formalized routes of international trade, the pattern of life and coexistence between nomads and the settled population, had in essence not changed since the earliest period.

THE GREAT MIGRATIONS

As the Silk Road evolved, the movements of tribes and peoples across the Steppe continued. Around 300–200 BC, the Sak were gradually overrun from the east by another eastern people, the Usun. These were a confederation of Turkic-speaking pastoral nomads, perhaps of Mongol descent. According to Chinese sources, by the first century they numbered over 600,000, and had divided into two sections: the former composed primarily of sedentary

Above: A bird's-eye view of the ruins of Sauran, a Silk Road city and later a military stronghold for the White Horde and Tamerlane (Renato Sala and Jean-Marc Deom)

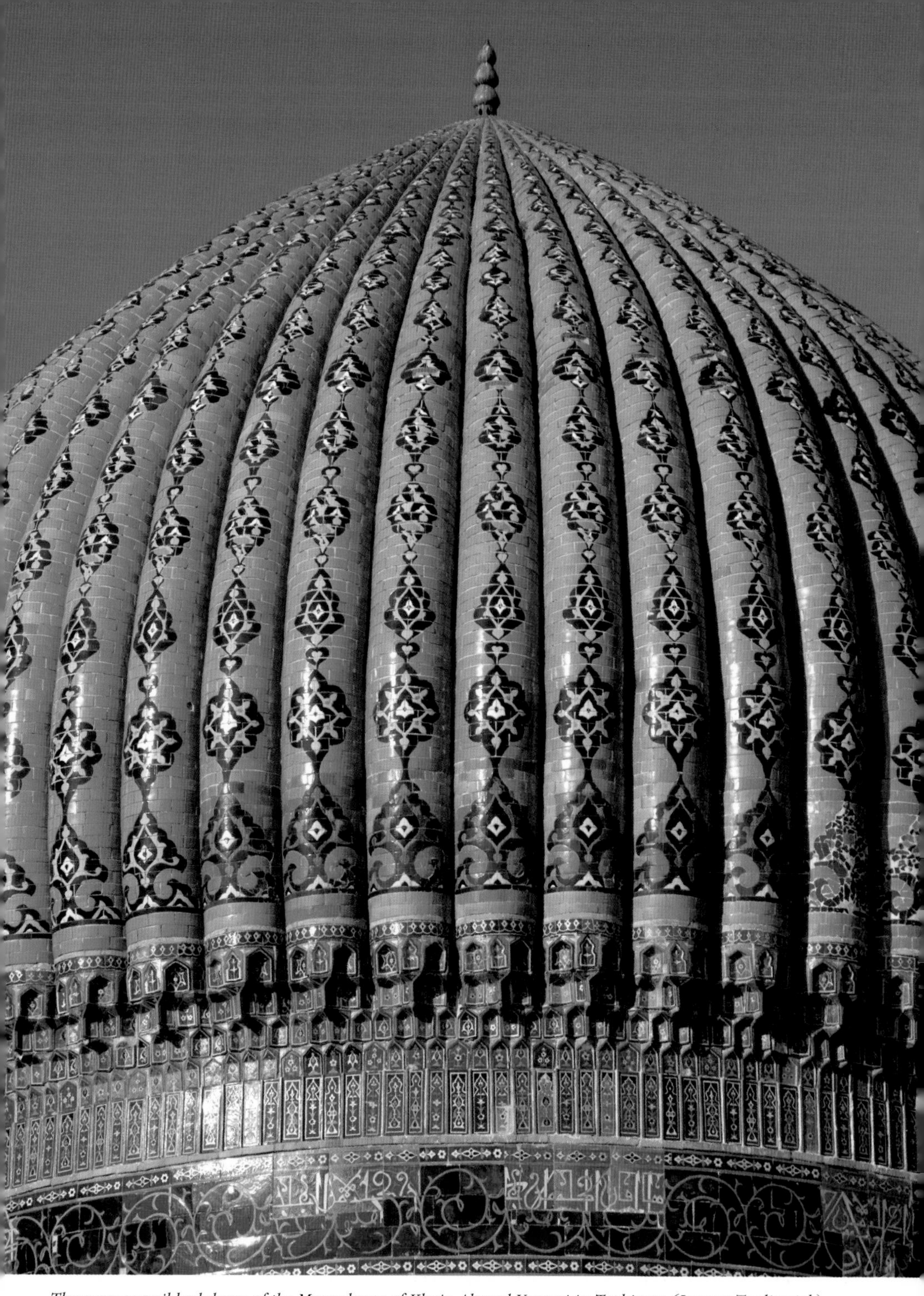

The gorgeous ribbed dome of the Mausoleum of Khoja Ahmed Yasawi in Turkistan (Jeremy Tredinnick)

farmers, who settled in the Karatau region and also along the middle stretches of the Syr Darya; the latter made up principally of nomads, who migrated across the regions north of the Caspian and Aral Sea. Recent excavations at Aktobe near the Ilek River have uncovered archaeological remnants of this time, including two-storey dwellings with courtyards for use by tribal leaders as winter residences.

The power of the Usun Empire began to collapse around the fifth century AD under the pressure of further waves of Turkic immigration and invasions from the Altai. Its place was taken by the Western Turkish Khaganate (Empire), and later, in the 7th–8th centuries, by the Turgesh Khaganate. One scholar says of these empires that they were "complex and stratified societies consisting of aristocrats, urban traders, oasis farmers, pastoral nomads, and a professional warrior class..." Of the former Khaganate, we have various glimpses in both Western and Chinese literature. The Byzantine Empire exchanged embassies with the Western Turkish Khaganate in the second half of the sixth century, hoping to engage their military support against their enemies, the Sasanian Persians. The Western Turks, for their part, wished to find a way of selling silk and iron to the Byzantines without using the Persians as intermediaries.

On one occasion, members of a Byzantine delegation were compelled, for the sake of diplomacy, to join in a mourning ceremony for one of the noblemen, slashing their faces and participating in human sacrifice. Later, in 630, a Chinese Buddhist monk, Xuanzang, visited the Khagan (ruler) at the capital Tokmak (now in modern-day Kyrgyzstan), and describes discussions with him about his religion, and mentions that he slept in a bed made of iron. At this time, the empire was at its height, stretching from the Hindu Kush to the Zhungar Mountains, and from the upper Yenisei to the Crimea. However, despite its strength, and that of its successor, the region was unable to withstand attacks from the Arabs, newly united under the banner of Islam. The Arabs managed to attack the Turgesh across the Syr Darya in 739, and as a result of the weakness caused by this assault, the Khaganate disintegrated within 30 years.

In spite of this collapse, a new Khaganate was established in 766 under the leadership of the Turkish Karluk tribe. It seems that the cities of the steppe, such as Taraz and Otrar, were greatly extended under their leadership. The Karakhanid tribe, which took control of the Khaganate in 940, continued this period of stability and economic growth. The system of irrigation on the steppe was developed so that fruit and vegetables, as well as cereals, could be freely cultivated in the region. The number of sedentary farmers increased rapidly, and the capital, Taraz, grew to boast over 10,000 inhabitants. It is also notable that in 960, the Karakhanid ruler accepted Islam, though there was no wholesale conversion of the general population during that time.

During the 12th century, the Khaganate became vulnerable on account of changes in balance of power throughout Central Asia, and the Karakhanids fell to a rapid series of invasions from the east by various peoples, including the Karakitae—a Mongol people —and the Naimans and Terei, who were different Turkic tribes. As a result the region was weakened, and at the beginning of the 13th century, was less able to maintain the security and stability that had been built up over the previous centuries.

The Greater Mongol Empire

In 1207, Temuchin, crowned "Unbending Lord" or Genghis Khan, started the build-up of an empire that was to stretch from Peking to the Danube. Starting in 1218, he attacked and conquered Semirechye (Zhetisu, the "Land of Seven Rivers" between the Tien Shan and Lake Balkhash), and in 1220 moved on to desolate Otrar, and the rest of the cities of Central Asia. Genghis Khan incorporated the area into his strictly organized world empire. From there on, the name "Golden Horde" gained currency, probably after the Khan's golden tent. After the Great Khan's death in 1227, the Golden Horde's rule became institutionalised by Batu Khan, one of Genghis Khan's grandsons, who ruled over the western part of the Greater Mongol Empire. His domain stretched from the Irtysh in the east to Khorezm in the southwest and to the Lower Volga in the west. Residing in Saray, present-day Russian Saratov, he reigned over the Kypchak, as they were called, until his death in 1255.

Although the agriculture and the infrastructure of sedentary society in the region of Kazakhstan had been devastated by Genghis's invasion, with the establishment of *Pax mongolica*, the trade routes across the continent were restored, and caravans could once more travel through without being bothered by tribal feuds and attacks. From the notes of travellers such as Marco Polo and others who ventured into the region at the time, it can be concluded that tolerance prevailed. Thus, the Great Khan was in frequent communication with Christendom, and Christian belief spread among Asian courts. The Mongol world empire at this stage was a true amalgam of cultures.

Disintegration and Subsequent Reunification under Tamerlane

While still alive, Genghis Khan divided his entire territory among his sons. The territory of Kazakhstan was split into three parts: The major slice, the immensely vast steppe between the Irtysh, the northern boundary of Semirechye and the lower Volga, was allocated to his eldest son Juchi, after whose premature death the region was to be governed by his son Batu, whose expansive campaigns extending to the Crimea have been amply recorded. Chaghadai obtained the south and southeast of Kazakhstan as well as eastern Turkestan. Ogedei, the youngest of the sons, inherited the northeastern part of Semirechye, western Mongolia and the upstream Irtysh basin. Infighting and divisions, raids and conquests among their heirs, however, were soon to be the order of the day.

This period came to an end under the dominion of Tamerlane from 1360. A warlord and military genius of Turkic-Mongol descent who married into Genghis Khan's family, from his fief in Turkestan and on the debris of the Mongol Empire Tamerlane built up a second Mongolian Empire with Samarkand as its capital. In swift military campaigns he conquered Central Asia, Persia, India down to the mouth of the Ganges, the southern Caucasus and Russia to the outskirts of Moscow. His death in the city of Otrar in 1405 thwarted the already-prepared conquest of China.

The Kazakh Khanate

The Kazakh nation as such, with a statehood of its own, did not take shape until the 15th and 16th centuries. At first there emerged three major tribal confederations (hordes or *zhuzy*, and clans, *ordy*). Some historians link their origins to the presence of three major landscape forms, whereas others trace them back to political factors such as the division of the territory under the heirs of Genghis Khan.

The Senior Horde, which united the tribes of the Alban, Uysun, Daoulat, Zhalayr, Kang-Li, Su-An, Sgrely, Oshakht, Ysty and Shahprashty, and their 32 clans, occupied the area between the Syr Darya and Semirechye. The Middle Horde inhabited central and northern Kazakhstan and included the major tribes of Argyn, Kerei, Kongrat, Kypchak, Nayman and Ouak with their 40 clans. The Junior Horde was settled downstream along the Syr Darya, on the banks of the Aral Sea and in the Caspian Depression. To it belonged the tribes of the Alimulek, Bayuly and Zhetiru with 25 clans.

From the middle of the 15th Century these three hordes became known as "Kazakhs", a Turkic word designating them as "free" or "independent" people. This term's background possibly reveals the events that preceded the establishment of the Kazakh Khanate: in 1450 two scions of Genghis Khan, Zhanibek Abusayid and Kerei (also spelt Girei), and their adherents disassociated themselves from the Khanate of Abulkhair, centred in present-day Uzbekistan, after having refused him allegiance. In neighbouring Mongolistan they were well received by Yesen Buga Khan, and were granted fertile places to dwell in the Chuy plains. In 1465-67, following Yesen Buga Khan's death, they proclaimed the Kazakh Khanate, and thereby, according to tradition, laid the foundation for the first formation of a Kazakh state. Numerous followers of the Uzbek *ulus* (tribe) adhered to their new state, which resulted in the Khanate's expansion towards the north with the inclusion of the Kypchak, Nayman, Kang-Li and Kerei tribes.

A little later, under Burunduk Khan, fighting broke out over the cities in the south, with Suzak, Sygnak and Sauran being taken from the Sheybanids (descendants of Batu) and incorporated into the Kazakh Khanate.

In the first half of the 16th Century, the Khanate expanded even further under Kasym Khan, and ended up stretching from the Urals down to the Syr Darya and from the Mangyshlak Peninsula to Semirechye in the east. Shortly afterwards, however, the struggle for power within the Khanate took off. Under Tahir Khan, separatist trends started crystallising with several tribes splitting off. The Khans Hak-Nazar, Shigay and Taukel were able to stop the process during their reigns and by the end of the 16th Century the Khanate was once again more or less stable. For a brief period of time, the Kazakh realm included Samarkand, Bukhara and Fergana. In 1598, under Yesim Khan, a peace treaty was signed with Bukhara in which Tashkent and the cities on the Syr Darya were included in the Kazakh Khanate.

Power Struggles

Wherever there is prosperity, envy tends to follow—and therefore, during the 100 years that followed the peace accord, it was inevitable that the sultans' claims to power were to increase within the Khanate. The struggle for influence within the hordes also increased. The power of the tribal aristocracy (*beys*) and warlords (*batyrs*) became stronger and stronger.

The statue of the "three sages" next to the High Court of Justice in Astana (Gunter Kapelle)

A typical Russian house, steep-roofed and blue-shuttered (Dagmar Schreiber)

The adherents to the supreme power in the Kazakh Khanate viewed themselves as successors of Genghis Khan. They dubbed themselves Ak-Ayek ("White Bones"). People at the other end of the social scale, the Kara-Shalyk ("Black Backwards"), had to submit to certain regulations. These regulations were recorded in the Zheti Zhargy ("Seven Rules"). These feudal regulations were developed under the rule of Tauke Khan in the beginning of the 18th Century by the "three sages" Ayteke Bi, Tole Bi and Kazybek Bi, to settle the internal conflicts within the tribes and to reinforce the state.

Nevertheless, further fragmentation, continuing struggles over supreme power in the Khanate, combined with a strong social polarisation, led to the weakening of the state. The Zhungars, a Lamaist-Buddhist tribe in western China, took advantage of this weakness and attacked in the early 18th Century. The Khanate was forced to seek protection from Russia, its powerful neighbour to the north, and in 1717 Tauke Khan appealed for help. At that time no actual intervention was necessary, but when Tauke Khan died in 1718, his successor did not consider himself committed to his word.

Part of the Russian Empire

The "Years of Great Distress", as these times of continuing and increasing Zhungar raids are remembered, resulted in a temporary consolidation of forces, most of all within the middle and lower levels of the population. Abulkhair Khan of the Junior Horde and Ablai Khan of the Middle Horde succeeded in uniting the Kazakh tribes for a short period. All-Kazakh gatherings (*kurultay*) took place on a regular basis, and a popular defence force was formed.

However, in 1731, for lack of confidence in their own defence forces, the tribal elders of the Junior Horde under Abulkhair Khan concluded an assistance pact with Russia and placed themselves under Russian sovereignty. In the course of the following 150 years the entire Kazakh territory became part of the Russian Empire. An initially peaceful process of colonisation subsequently took place.

Cultural transformation took place gradually in comparison to other countries, but also irreversibly. On a political level, this culminated in the replacement of khans as representatives of power by Russian governors in 1822. Protests arose against this weakening of the traditional patriarchal order. By 1837, unrest had spread over the entire territory and taken on the dimension of a powerful uprising under the leadership of Kenesary Kasymov.

More than 300 uprisings in the course of the colonisation process by Russia illustrate that the much-professed voluntary character of integration with Russia had its detractors. The elders, in part due to sincere confidence in an improvement of the situation, in part with Russian "encouragement" through *bakshish* and force, had forfeited their territory to Russia.

With its victory over the Khan of Kokand in 1868, Russia conquered all of present-day Kazakhstan's territory. In the process, numerous Russian farmers were settled in the borderlands. Nomads' pasturelands were confiscated, and a harsh tax system was introduced. In this manner, livestock-breeding Kazakhs were gradually deprived of their livelihoods. Masses of people were hit by incredible poverty. An imperial decree on the conscription of the Kazakhs into war-imposed labour forces in June 1916 appeared to be the last straw. Under the banner of Islam, the "Great Revolt", initially a united front of nomads, farmers, officials and traders in Central Asia, broke out. It was harshly suppressed, but with the October Revolution of 1917 erupted once more.

Soviet Power and Autonomy

The downfall of Tsarism deprived the liberation movement of its adversary, but revived nationalist thinking. Hopes for an independent development of a democratic society took shape, for instance, in the Alash Party, which demanded a democratic constitution and the introduction of the function of president. In October 1917, at the first All-Kazakh congress, which took place in Orenburg, in present-day Russia, the first provisional autonomous people's council of Kazakhs was appointed. Orenburg (spelt Orynbor in Kazakh) became the first capital of the Kazakhs. Following the turmoil of the Civil War, which in Central Asia took place most of all in the form of bloody battles between *basmachi* rebels and Bolsheviks, an autonomous republic within the Russian Federation comprising Kazakhs and Kyrgyz was proclaimed in 1920. It was split up only in 1936, when Stalin pursued his nationalities policy and through arbitrarily designed borderlines put the gunpowder in place for later decades.

The reorganization of Central Asia, a markedly multinational region, which had not known any fixed borderlines for centuries, was carried out through several administrative reforms. In 1936, with the professed goal of national delimitation, but in the end based on political and economic calculation, the union's republics of Uzbekistan, Turkmenistan, Kyrgyzstan, Tajikistan and Kazakhstan were created.

Forced Collectivisation

As in the case of all nomadic nations within the Soviet realm, the Stalin period inflicted incurable wounds on the Kazakhs. Under the pretence of liberation from the yoke of backwardness, Kazakhs were prohibited from following a unique culture and way of life adapted to the conditions. As it did in all other Soviet republics, the dispossession of the *kulaks*, as large-scale farmers were called, annihilated the rural upper and middle levels. Not just the rich beys and *beaks*, but also many of the elder and respected persons in *auls*, themselves in the possession of smaller herds, were dispossessed and deported. The "Kazakhstan Tragedy", as the dramatic events of the 1920s and 1930s are called, culminated in the nomadic population's collectivisation.

Livestock-tending families, who could not survive without moving their herds from one place to another on the scanty steppe soils, were forced to settle down with the remainders of their livestock in designated sedentary zones. Wandering and migrating were punishable. This lunatic policy led to the death by starvation of almost two million people, with another million moving out of the country. Today, most of the latter live in western China, but also in Mongolia, Iran, Afghanistan and Turkey. The Kazakh diaspora of more than five million people now lives in more than 40 countries.

Exile in the Steppe

In the process of forced collectivisation, the Kazakhs had lost half of their population. Deported people, convicts and settlers were now placed in the abandoned territories in random fashion.

During the years preceding the Second World War and during the war, entire peoples were deported to the vast lands of the Kazakh steppe. Volga Germans, Koreans, Chechens, Crimean Tatars, Kalmyks, Greeks, Balkarians, Ingush and other ethnic groups suspected by Stalin of collaboration with the enemy were sent there. Many people died of starvation or froze to death, and it is only thanks to the generosity of the Kazakhs that tens of thousands survived—in the Kazakhs' yurts and clay huts, and in the earth huts and refugee camps that were built with their help.

In continuation of the Russian tradition of banishment, prison camps were established in inhospitable areas of Kazakhstan. Entire economic sectors rested on the shoulders of the people detained in them. During the war, many important enterprises were evacuated from the European part of the Soviet Union to the far side of the Urals and into Kazakhstan. All of a sudden, the Central Asian republics played a vital role in the supply of the front and in maintaining civil life in the Soviet republics.

THE VIRGIN LANDS PROGRAMME

In 1954, now with Nikita Khruschev at the helm, the cultivation of the "virgin lands" was introduced and therewith an influx—this time predominantly voluntary—of young people and adventurers from the other republics began. On the territory of present-day Kazakhstan alone, 255,000 square kilometres of steppe land came under the plough and was made fit for the cultivation of cereals. Today, it is known that the Virgin Lands Programme, with its short-lived economic effect, inflicted irretrievable damage both to the steppe's vulnerable ecosystem and to traditional extensive livestock breeding. However, the massive human migration also led to organizational, social and cultural problems, the dimensions of which have only just begun to be recognized.

ATOMIC TESTS IN THE STEPPE

In 1949 an area of steppe near Semipalatinsk in the country's northeast was chosen as a testing ground for atomic bombs. A series of huge test explosions were detonated above ground until 1963, and continued underground thereafter. This was a perfect example of Stalinist ideology and its contempt for human life; in the name of Soviet wellbeing, individuals, groups hostile to the system and entire communities were sacrificed. This appalling situation was compounded by the arms race that developed during the period of the Cold War. However, by the late 1980s staunch campaigns by the human rights movement Nevada-Semipalatinsk protested against and lobbied for the cessation of nuclear testing, and finally ensured the closure of the testing ground in 1991.

BALANCE

While considering the huge cost of all these tragedies, crackdowns and deplorable decisions, one should nevertheless understand that Kazakhstan as a Soviet republic did make some incredible achievements, among them the transfer of large parts of the Soviet Union's heavy industry, as well as cultural and scientific institutions, from the European USSR to Central Asia; the conversion of enterprises into equipment manufacturing; and the absorption of around two million refugees—the human achievement of the Kazakh population should not be underestimated.

Consider also the reconstruction following World War II, the struggle to survive the gigantic and megalomaniacal development projects of the 1960s, and the stagnation of the

1970s and 1980s, followed by the change in course of the late 1980s—put into context, the achievements of a people who became multinational in the process, who despite many strategic mistakes by politicians managed to meld together to become the Kazakhstan nation, should not be taken lightly.

Perestroika, Openness, Sovereignty

In a development mirrored by other republics of the Soviet Union, with the coming of perestroika Kazakhstan witnessed a political shift that had been preceded by almost 20 years of economic crisis. Although this period of instability developed in a less turbulent manner than in Russia's cities, social movements and informal organizations did emerge. In December 1986, thousands of students in Almaty rebelled against the fossilized governmental structures in favour of more national independence. As they demonstrated in Almaty's main square they were shot at; the number of dead has never been officially declared, although it is estimated that more than 200 people died, and hundreds were arrested. Since that infamous day, 16 December has been celebrated as a national memorial day.

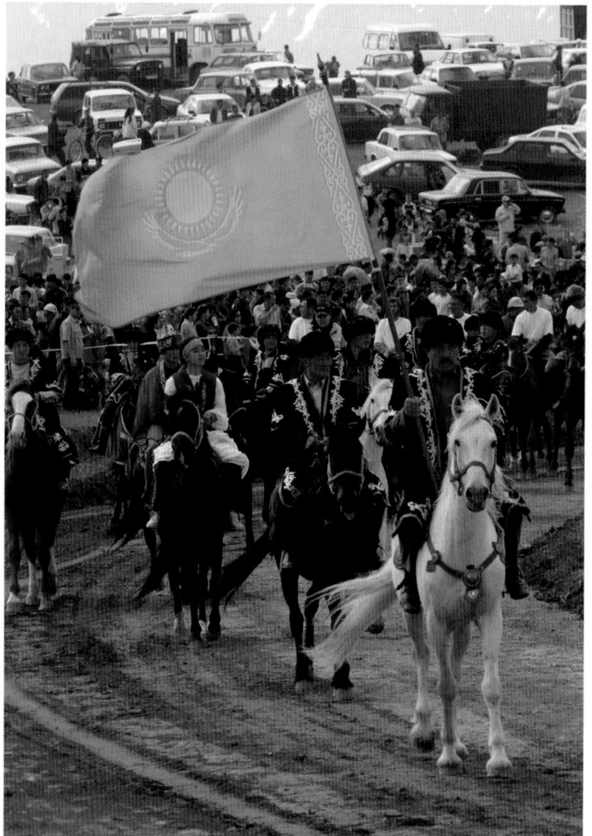

Kazakhstan's national flag is a symbol of great pride for the people of this relatively young nation (Gunter Kapelle)

On 25 October 1990, the Supreme Soviet of the Republic of Kazakhstan passed the "Declaration on the state sovereignty of the Socialist Soviet Republic of Kazakhstan". Well over a year later, following the break-up of the USSR, political independence was proclaimed. President Nazarbayev intentionally chose 16 December 1991 as the day for the Law on Independence to be adopted. Kazakhstan was the last member state to leave the USSR—taking into account its close economic relationship with the Russian Federation, this was by no means an easy step.

Yet, despite its initial difficulties, Kazakhstan has been able to prosper since independence. In spite of some friction with a separatist movement among portions of the ethnic Russian population, it has been generally free of the communal tensions that have troubled other former Soviet Republics. Benefiting from this stability, it has attracted a great deal of foreign investment, on account of which it has been able to exploit its vast reserves of minerals and natural wealth. Most notably, a number of oil pipelines have been constructed, linking Kazakhstan to markets it was not previously able to reach. Prominent among these are the lines connecting the Tengiz oilfield in the west of the country across the Caspian to the Russian Black Sea port of Novorossiysk, and the more recent line to Alashankou and western China, opened in 2005. It is estimated that its current oil exports are one million barrels per day, and the government hopes that within 10 years, Kazakhstan will be one of the world's largest producers of oil.

Nonetheless, Kazakhstan still faces many challenges. It has a legacy of pollution from the Soviet period, and one of its leading concerns is the drying-up of the Aral Sea. In the economic field, with the newfound income from oil and mineral exports, there are now also anxieties over the disparity in wealth among the population. However, there is already a full consciousness that the wealth to be derived from oil extraction is only to be relied on until the supplies are spent, and that it is necessary to diversify well before that time. In that Kazakhstan is now attempting to move into areas such as light industry and banking, and develop itself as a regional financial and trading centre, it may be said that Kazakhstan is returning to its ancient Silk Road roots, making use of its position between East and West to establish itself as a centre of international commerce.

The Economy

Kazakhstan boasts significant riches in raw materials: it has giant deposits of oil and gas, coal and minerals, semi-precious stones and construction materials. It ranks first in the world in terms of zinc, wolfram and barite reserves, second in uranium, silver, lead and chrome ore, third in copper and fluorites, fourth in molybdenum, and sixth in gold reserves.

In 2006, the country had proven oil reserves of more than 39.6 billion barrels, with estimated possible reserves of between 60 and 100 billion barrels; by the year 2015 it is set to be among the 10 largest oil-producing countries in the world. In order to make the country less sensitive to oil price fluctuations, a national oil fund was established in 1999, into which every tenth petrodollar is paid and which as of June 2004 already contained US$3.7 billion. Infrastructure projects will be financed from this fund.

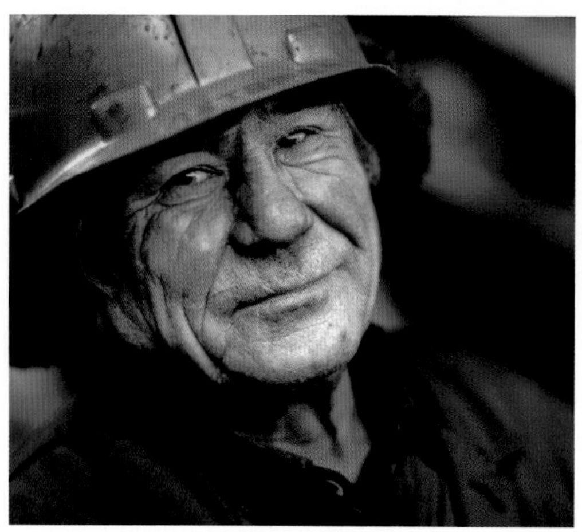

Following its political independence and the collapse of the USSR's state-controlled employment system, Kazakhstan needed to build a functioning economy within a relatively short period of time. Taking the giant step from being a socialist economy to becoming a free market economy is known simply as a "transition economy". The first, enormous task demanded the liberalisation of the economic system. The abandonment of price controls in January 1992 with its subsequent effect on purchasing power led to enormous inflation. External trade came to a virtual standstill, because Kazakhstan had no structures for import and export industries. The privatization of most state enterprises resulted in the bankruptcy and subsequent closure of many of them, which could simply not survive in a market situation. For the first time, unemployment occurred. The introduction of a national currency, the tenge, in November 1993, brought the value of citizens' rouble-denominated accounts down to next to nothing.

The result was severe deprivation among the population. In 1994 and 1995, Kazakhstan found itself at rock bottom. Most badly hit had been the agricultural sector; as a consequence of the social needs of the population, livestock holdings had been drastically reduced, harvests could no longer be fully gathered due to derelict technology, and a dramatic exodus from the countryside began.

However, from 1996 onwards, the currency started to work as a lever, triggering a gradual pick-up in conditions. Trade and services began to flourish, employees awoke from their apathy, and a spirit of entrepreneurship started to develop. The government's economic policy started to bear fruit. The Asian financial crisis and the depreciation of the rouble were a setback, since the tenge also had to be devaluated, but after a short period of shock, this actually brought about the stimulus by which the economy was brought back to health. It became economical once more to process commodities within the country, and agriculture, food processing and light industries profited from this. Today, the shelves are again full of domestically produced food and beverages, and the export of meat is now back on the agenda. The country is self-supporting in food, and a decisive step on the road to economic independence has been made.

Portrait of a coal miner—though a life of hardship is etched on his face, so is a wry smile (Christopher Herwig)

Since 2002, Kazakhstan, with an annual growth in gross domestic product of 8–10 percent, has left the other post-Soviet countries behind. Gradually, the overall economic benefit is reaching those who in the early years of consolidation had to make the biggest sacrifices. The population's savings deposits are on the rise once more—full restoration of losses inflicted back in 1993 have even been reported—and confidence in stable economic development is growing. In order to secure this stabilisation and to obtain economic independence, the government increasingly focuses on the processing of raw materials within the country's boundaries.

Major efforts to create a strong middle class are being made. Ninety percent of all enterprises have now been privatized, and a strong domestic entrepreneurial class has developed. Investment facilities for domestic and foreign entrepreneurs are being created; many domestic enterprises, though, still lack capital. However, the stabilisation of the banking sector and increasingly reliable economic development have slowly led to the relaxation of one-time rigid credit allocation practices.

In 2000, Kazakhstan was recognized by the European Union as a market economy, and in 2002 the USA endorsed this recognition. This is a major step in the direction of Kazakhstan's membership of the World Trade Organization, to which the country aspires.

A monstrous machine eats up the landscape at one of the world's largest open pit coal mines in Ekibastuz (Christopher Herwig)

Falcon in one hand, bow in the other, a Scythian warrior stands on a winged snow leopard atop a huge column in Almaty's Republic Square (Jeremy Tredinnick)

POLITICS AND GOVERNMENT

NATIONAL IDENTITY AND NATIONAL SYMBOLS

Following the establishment of the state in 1991, the language and culture of Kazakhstan, until then confined to rural areas, underwent a wide resurgence. The Kazakh nation has re-found, rather than recovered, its national identity—a process that is ongoing today.

There is a tale much recounted in Central Asia of *mankurts*—people without thought. These date back to the time of the Zhuan-Zhuan, a tribe with gruesome customs who more than once invaded the Kazakh steppe from the east. They were said to cover the heads of men who refused to be subdued with animal skin, letting it shrink under the heat of the steppe. The infernal pain to which the tortured victims were exposed, the unbearable thirst and fear, left those who survived the ordeal in a state of oblivion of their past. During the years of colonisation, oppression and dispossession of the Kazakhs, this fear of collective forgetfulness was ever present. And not without grounds: in 1960, only a handful of schools in Almaty provided education in the Kazakh language.

Kazakhs have a clear definition of their historic background and that of their land, along with the values that connected them. Discount the period of colonisation by Russia and the suffering of the Stalinist period, and the history of the Kazakhs is that of free and independent nomadic and semi-nomadic tribes within an all but limitless steppe landscape. Symbols of this way of life are the yurt, the horse, the wide turquoise sky, the sun and the steppe eagle. Therefore, one finds on the gleaming turquoise national flag the golden sun, and under it the eagle with its wings spread. These symbols stand for peace and unity, honesty, loyalty and hope, wealth and generosity, vigilance and the free flow of thought. The symbolic markings on the left edge of the flag show the ever-recurring motif of animal horns intertwined with plant tendrils.

The national heraldry of Kazakhstan shows the profiles of two winged unicorn steeds. Between them is the roof opening of a yurt (the *shangyrak*), symbol of homely peace and hospitality. The winged unicorns stand for immortality, development and spiritual riches of the peoples who in Kazakhstan live together under a single shangyrak. Connecting the unicorns and the shangyrak are a multitude of sunbeams. An equally popular symbol on display is the very rare snow leopard, known as *irbis* in Kazakh or *bars* in Russian. It stands for independence, wisdom, persistence and the power to leap forward. Sculptures of the irbis are found everywhere, most frequently in Astana. The most well-known snow leopard statue sits atop a high column on Republic Square in Almaty. In particular the irbis symbolises the jump into the future that is supposed to occur by the year 2030. The strategic programme "Kazakhstan 2030" was developed at the instigation of President Nazarbayev in the 1990s, at a time when there was a communal lack of vision.

continued on page 76

KAZAKHSTAN'S ENERGY OVERLOAD

By *John Roberts*

Kazakhstan's mineral wealth abounds. The oil boom pays for the astonishing architecture in Astana and accounts for the new business centres in Almaty, Atyrau and Aktau. Without the oil—and in future the gas and uranium—Kazakhstan would be a vast land of great strategic interest but with far fewer ways of making a splash in the world.

The resources are massive, capable of turning Kazakhstan into one of the world's great oil exporters and making it quite possible that, in time, it will fulfil its goal of becoming the world's foremost producer of uranium. Over the next seven or eight years it expects to double its output from around 1.3 million barrels of oil a day (mb/d) in 2006 to 2.5 mb/d in 2015. Eventually the country could well produce as much as four mb/d, with exports exceeding three mb/d, thus accounting for around four percent of global world output —and perhaps as much as seven or eight percent of the world's cross-border oil trade.

What's more, although much has already been discovered, there's a feeling that much more remains to be found.

What we know already is that Kazakhstan possesses some 39.6 billion barrels of oil and some 3 trillion cubic metres of gas in proven reserves—reserves that can actually be developed and turned into actual production. That's about 3.3 percent of the world's oil reserves and 1.7 percent of its gas reserves. In the energy business, those are very big numbers indeed. It's particularly important because Kazakhstan, unlike most of the OPEC countries, is prepared to allow international energy companies—whether from the US, Europe, Russia, China, India or elsewhere—a role in developing its resources on a profit-sharing basis. In other words, if these internationals find a major new oil or gas field, they can make a huge amount of money, whereas in much of the Middle East—where two-thirds of the world's oil is located—they can only secure fees for their services.

Kazakhstan is very much the energy world's new frontier. The US Chevron signed a contract in 1992 to develop Tengiz, a giant onshore field at the edge of the Caspian Sea that had previously defeated the best efforts of Soviet oilmen. British Gas and Italy's Eni teamed up the same year to develop the giant gas—and gas condensate—field at Karachaganak on the border with Russia, signing a production-sharing agreement for the field in 1995. Away from the Caspian, a group of Canadians turned a cluster of lesser fields in the centre of the country into the major PetroKazakhstan operation before selling out to the China National Petroleum Corporation in 2005. And, alongside these, a cluster of smaller companies began developing new fields or helping revive or prolong Soviet-era operations.

One field alone can be used to sum up the Kazakh experience: Kashagan, discovered in July 2000 after years of survey work and test drilling—and the world's biggest offshore oil discovery for a generation. To begin with its ownership structure is important, with Kazakhstan waging a three-year campaign from 2003 onwards—fought in defiance of Kashagan's major shareholders, ExxonMobil, Total, Shell and Italy's Eni, the field's operator— to secure a stake in the venture for its own KazMunaiGaz.

Then there is the reserves issue. Initial test wells disclosed the presence of some 38 billion barrels of "reserves-in-place". Using the traditionally cautious formula that for every five barrels of oil in place you might reasonably be able to extract one barrel of oil, that produced an initial assertion of seven billion barrels of proven reserves. But as the technicians at Kashagan got to grips with the field, they revised their estimates upwards. Now they estimate they can extract 13 or even 15 billion barrels. That's about as much as the current proven reserves of the entire North Sea. It also means that for every man, woman and child in Kazakhstan, Kashagan alone possesses perhaps 1,000 barrels of oil worth around US$60,000 at current prices and available for production over the next 30 years or so. That's a useful foundation for developing not just an economy, but a whole new social structure.

But if Kashagan shows how Kazakhstan's oil reserves can grow as further data becomes available—and there are also plenty more prospects that might yield fresh major discoveries in the Caspian Sea close to Kashagan—it also illustrates the problems of developing large fields.

Kashagan is, geologically, highly complex. The oil is under very high pressure and it is also highly sulphurous (and thus dangerous to handle). The field, ice-bound in winter, is also located in very shallow water of no more than a few metres' depth. This latter point might seem to make it easier to develop, but in fact it is one of the main reasons why environmental considerations have to be taken so seriously. An oil spill in an ocean is, if not quite a drop in the ocean, at least a problem that nature can in time resolve. But a spill in a couple of metres of water is an ecological catastrophe for a highly delicate marine environment such as exists in the Caspian Sea.

The original plan was for Kashagan to produce its first commercial oil in 2005. However, the target date was subsequently deferred to 2008, and now the expectation is that Kashagan will start producing commercial volumes in 2010 or 2011. It's a long wait, albeit one made easier to bear by the increase in oil prices in recent years, which has ensured that Kazakhstan's finances have boomed despite export constraints resulting in slower-than-expected oil production increases.

Kashagan also demonstrates another key Kazakh energy dilemma: how to get its oil and gas to market. When the country declared its independence in 1991, its energy links with the outside worlds were those inherited from the Soviet Union. All were directed at, or through, Russia. Indeed, oil and gas produced in the energy-rich Caspian regions in the northwest of the country were routinely exported north to Russia, whilst the industrialised southeast of the country actually received its oil and gas imported southwards from Russia.

Now Kazakhstan has new horizons. A new oil line linking eastern Kazakhstan with western China entered service in July 2006, and will almost certainly prove the precursor of a full-scale system to carry oil from western Kazakhstan all the way across Kazakhstan itself to join the existing China line. A gas export pipeline covering much the same ground was also under serious discussion in 2007. Both the oil and gas lines could be operational as early as late 2009.

But most of Kazakhstan's oil will continue to head west, either through the Russian pipeline system or through a new pipeline, built with extensive private sector participation, which links the Kazakh oil centre of Atyrau with the Russian Black Sea port of Novorossiysk, or by means of the Baku-Tbilisi-

Ceyhan (BTC) pipeline, which opened in June 2006. For Kazakhstan to gain access to BTC—and BTC was firmly built with the idea it would eventually carry quite a lot of Kashagan's output—the oil will first have to cross the Caspian. With Russia opposed to trans-Caspian pipelines, Kazakhstan and Azerbaijan have agreed that they will set up a new tanker service to link their respective terminals.

However, if Kazakhstan is to export any of its gas westwards, it will either have to strike deals with Russia or find a way of developing a pipeline or alternative gas transit system across the Caspian that does not offend Russia... and this could prove a difficult task.

Meanwhile, Kazakhstan is starting to learn how to use its wealth. The government is taking seriously the issue of Dutch disease—an economic concept explaining the problem that an influx of oil wealth routinely results in a contraction of local industry, with the government increasingly furnishing subsidies to more and more of its citizens. To counter this, President Nazarbayev is pushing for his country to become one of the world's 50 most competitive economies.

The oil companies are playing their part, too. They are sponsoring a massive expansion of technical education and this, together with the development of a relatively youthful technocracy, is already having a major impact on Kazakh society. It is still not clear, however, that Kazakhstan will be able to overcome the "oil curse"—all one can say at present is that it is well aware of the problem.

Oil and gas aside, Kazakhstan possesses a wealth of minerals, from iron to fuel the steelworks to gold and, with an eye on the very near future, uranium. By 2010, Kazakhstan intends to become the world's leading producer of uranium, producing 17,000 tonnes compared to 4,365 tonnes in 2005. That's an impressive rate of growth at a time when the industrialised world is taking a fresh look at nuclear power because of concerns about relative lack of investment by leading OPEC producers in oil and gas.

It's quite possible that Kazakhstan is not only the last great new frontier of the oil age, but that it may also become the first new frontier for a reborn nuclear age.

THE CASE FOR ALTERNATIVE ENERGY

Consider Kazakhstan's geography: the majority of its land is vast, open steppe, sparsely populated and scoured for long periods each year by powerful winds that sweep down from Siberia; in its southwestern regions, sunshine reigns for all but a few weeks a year; while from the mighty peaks of the Tien Shan and Altai ranges that comprise the country's southeastern and northeastern borders flow myriad rivers down steep, narrow valleys. Kazakhstan is, in fact, brimming with potential for development of "clean" energy sources such as wind, solar and hydroelectric power.

The fact that little has so far been done in these sectors is due in the main to Kazakhstan's huge wealth in the more mainstream energy resources of oil, coal and natural gas, which mean energy costs are low and will provide ample supplies for decades. The presence of massive reserves of uranium, making nuclear fusion a viable future energy alternative for the nation, only serves to make the case for "green" energy production more difficult to argue.

But nevertheless, the government is aware of the possibilities—and positive long-term benefits—of these alternative resources, and in 2006, with help from the United Nations Development Programme (UNDP) and the Canadian International Development Agency, it launched its first solar energy project, located in the southeastern Almaty region and predicted to provide electricity for 1,500 residents of the former capital. Solar power could prove to be particularly useful in remote and hard-to-access parts of the country, once cost-efficiency increases.

In 2007 the UNDP and the Kazakh government launched a three-year programme to develop a wind-based energy industry—the country's wind potential is estimated at 1.82 trillion kilowatts per hour, the world's largest potential of wind power resources per capita, according to the Kazakh research and development institute Kazselenergoproekt. The institute also reports that Kazakhstan has a unique geographical location in the wind belt of the Northern Hemisphere. It has identified 15 promising sites to construct large wind power stations, with experts noting that "the intensity of wind potential in a number of locations in the country is as high as 10 megawatts per square kilometre—such wind potential is unique".

The Zhungar Gate (near the Chinese border) and the Chilik Corridor (closer to Almaty) in particular show great promise, with average wind speeds varying between 5 and 9 m/s; as a result, the government is now in the process of building a five-megawatt wind power station—to be completed by 2010—in the Zhungar Gate, the first major project in the programme. Funding has come from the Washington-based organization Global Environmental Facility (GEF), which is providing US$2.5 million, US$4 million allotted by the government, and private sector investment. The plan is to build 500 megawatts of installed wind power capacity by 2030.

Hydroelectric power is far more advanced in the country—73 percent of Kazakhstan's water resources being concentrated in the most populated eastern and southern regions, on the Irtysh, Ili and Syr Darya rivers. However, only 13–14 percent of feasible potential is being used, and an increase in the number of hydroelectric power stations is planned, with new facilities scheduled for Mainak (300 megawatts), Semey (78 megawatts) and Kerbulak (50 megawatts).

Smaller hydroelectric power stations, with a capacity of less than 10 megawatts, are also part of the strategy. According to some estimates, Kazakhstan has more than 450 abandoned small hydroelectric power stations with a potential capacity of 1,370 megawatts and an annual electricity production potential of six billion kW per hour.

Put all these plans together, and the government's renewable energy development programme looks very promising—it would certainly contribute to a sizeable reduction of greenhouse gas emissions, held primarily responsible for global warming. However, the fact remains that today about 90 percent of Kazakhstan's electricity is still generated from coal and gas. Most of the remaining 10 percent comes from hydroelectric power—the current share of renewable power resources like solar and wind energy remains marginal, as little as 0.2 percent of total electricity production.

But the positive steps taken so far illustrate Kazakhstan's efforts to develop alternative energy resources—in the process alleviating its dependence on oil and gas. If wind, solar, hydropower and even biomass energy production is promoted actively, the future for the country's energy use could be as green as the steppe in springtime.

Text created using source material from the Government of Kazakhstan.

Democracy Kazakh Style

By *Gerald Frost*

With the sudden and dramatic collapse of the Soviet Union in 1991, Kazakhstan became an independent state—but by default rather than design. There had been signs of growing national consciousness during the 1980s, but this had not developed into anything resembling a liberation movement. As Shirin Akiner put it in *The Formation of Kazakh Identity: From Time to Nation-State* (The Royal Institute of International Affairs, London 1995): "...there was no freedom struggle: the Kazakhs were bereft both of the organizational experience of such a period of preparation, and of the ideological bonding of the fight for a common national goal; hence there was no legacy of audacious national deeds to celebrate, no emotive slogans and symbols, no heroes, no national myths."

National independence was declared on 16 December 1991. At a hastily arranged summit in Almaty a few days later, a further announcement proclaimed that Kazakhstan, along with seven other former Soviet republics, would join an enlarged Commonwealth of Independent States (CIS).

Seventy years of Soviet rule and 150 years of Tsarist autocracy do not provide the ideal background for those building a system of parliamentary democracy. But while Kazakhstan's political system clearly remains in its infancy, it has withstood the strains resulting from rapid political and economic change and proved more stable than those of its Central Asian neighbours. The system is defined in the Constitution of 1991—amended three years later to strengthen presidential powers—as "a democratic, secular state whose highest values are the individual, his life and freedoms."

Compared to the political systems of Britain and America, Kazakhstan's political institutions are highly centralised. The most obvious comparison is with the French Fifth Republic. A powerful presidency has the responsibility for the broad outlines of domestic and foreign policy, for representing the country at home and abroad, and for appointing and dismissing Prime Ministers and cabinets. The appointment of the Prime Minister, but not cabinet members, is subject to parliamentary approval. The President is also responsible for appointing judges and *akims* (regional governors), and has control of the security and armed forces.

Nursultan Nazarbayev, the son of a nomadic shepherd, has steered the infant state of Kazakhstan since its independence, having become President of the Supreme

Soviet of Kazakhstan during the last stages of Communist rule. He was elected as President of the newly independent Republic of Kazakhstan in an unopposed contest in December 1991 (his most likely rival had failed to get the 100,000 signatures necessary to be a candidate). After extending his period of office by means of a referendum, Nazarbayev stood for re-election in December 1999, when he received 79.9 percent of the popular vote compared to the 11.7 percent achieved by his rival, the Communist Party leader Abdil'din Serikbolsyn.

Six years later when Nazarbayev stood for a further term some Western reporters, encouraged by figures in the opposition, predicted that Kazakhstan was on the brink of a "coloured revolution" similar to those that had occurred in Georgia and the Ukraine. In fact, the election passed off without violence of any kind and Nazarbayev, by far the most popular politician that Kazakhstan has known, increased his share of the vote to 91 percent; turnout at the election, which was monitored by more than 1,200 foreign observers, was 77 percent. The size of Nazarbayev's majority is not difficult to explain: record levels of inward investment in the country's booming energy sector, plus shrewd economic management, had produced growth rates of around 10 percent per annum over the previous five years; in turn these had led to rising living standards and a reduction in those living below the poverty line. Political upheavals elsewhere in Central Asia, some involving bloodshed, had clearly served to reinforce the widespread desire for stability and continuity.

Parliament, the supreme representative and legislative body of the Republic, consists of two chambers: the Senate (39 seats) and the *Majilis* or lower house (77 seats, of which 67 are filled by majority voting and 10 on the basis of party lists). Election to the lower is conducted by direct secret ballot; the upper house consists of two representatives elected by 14 *oblast* and city assemblies with the remaining seven senators appointed by the President from among the ranks of prominent public figures.

Parliament has the power of approval over the government programme, the budget, and a number of appointments on the basis of presidential recommendation.

The Organisation for Security and Cooperation in Europe (OSCE) has criticized Kazakhstan's record on elections on the grounds that these have fallen short of the highest international standards, even though it has acknowledged progress in particular areas. However, a close analysis of the OSCE findings and those of other independent observers shows that each of the elections to have occurred in the country's brief history as an independent state marked a significant advance on the previous election. There is no doubt that the most recent elections—those for the Majilis in September 2004 and the 2005 Presidential election—were genuinely competitive and that the latter was the freest and fairest in the country's history. Among those monitoring the election was a team of British observers under the chairmanship of Lord Parkinson, the former Conservative Party chairman, which concluded: "At this election, Kazakhstan has taken a major step forward in becoming a full democracy."

The President's own attitude to democratic change appears to be that a gradual process of organic political reform against a background of economic growth provides the best guarantor of sustainable democracy. In his view it is unreasonable for foreign observers to expect his country to complete overnight processes that in the West took hundreds of years. He takes care to stress that his country's democracy remains in its infancy, might easily be damaged by hasty or ill-considered decisions and should not be regarded as the finished political article.

In March 2006 a state commission was charged with the responsibility of recommending further steps in the democratic reform process. At its sixth meeting in February 2007 it announced that future reforms would concentrate on strengthening parliament, the reform of local government, steps to improve judicial and law enforcement agencies and measures to assist the development of political parties. The commission also backed a proposal to give a proportion of parliamentary seats to the People's Assembly of Kazakhstan, a consultative body that directly represents more than 100 ethnic groups living in the country.

In May 2007, during a speech to the Joint Session of the Chambers of the Kazakh Parliament, the President reviewed the lessons that he said had been learned by his government since 1991 and reiterated the basic philosophy that has underpinned the development of the country's fledgling democracy, namely "first economy and then politics". He promised that the next stage of democratization and reform would include reforms to enhance the effectiveness, transparency and accountability of the executive branch, anti-corruption measures as well as steps to decentralize state administration and develop local government. The President also committed himself to strengthening the powers of the Kazakh parliament and to ensuring the independence of the judiciary.

These reforms have been well received by the US, which sees them on balance as a positive move, even given that the Kazakh president is now allowed to remain in office for life. "It's a step—ultimately, when you look at the balance of these things—in the right direction," said US State Department spokesman Sean McCormack, commenting on the reforms, which include raising the number of parliamentary deputies and letting parliament play a bigger role in choosing the prime minister.

The record to date suggests that future reform will be gradual, measured and designed to meet the specific characteristics of Kazakhstan.

Hard political and economic realities place severe constraints on policy-making. As in the past, political reform will need to reflect the cultural aspirations of the Kazakhs, the country's titular people, while also respecting the political rights and religious freedoms of the country's ethnic minorities. As Kazakh society becomes more diverse, power must be devolved if a way is to be found to mediate differences of interest and satisfy the aspirations of a new generation of political leaders, many educated in the West; however, this must be accomplished without disturbing the present social equilibrium.

In the economic sphere the process of liberalisation will need to continue if Kazakhstan is to join the WTO and achieve the President's ambition of making the country one of the top 50 enterprise economies in the world, but ministers will not wish to surrender control over key economic assets. In managing foreign policy Kazakhstan will wish to build on its good relations with the US, the country's biggest source of inward investment. But it will also wish to maintain close ties with Russia, with whom it shares the world's longest land border, and with China, the other nuclear power on its doorstep as well as an increasingly important customer for its oil. In balancing these conflicting interests and pressures, Nazarbayev's eventual successor will consequently need to display the same skill as the country's highly pragmatic Founding Father.

Few countries have found themselves faced with the task of building an independent nation, a market economy *and* democracy all at the same time; thus far Kazakhstan has succeeded against the odds. Its success to date and its emergence as the Central Asian pacesetter gives grounds for cautious optimism for the region as a whole.

GOVERNMENTAL STRUCTURE AND THE CONSTITUTION

Kazakhstan's political system is most easily described as a presidential democracy. President Nursultan Nazarbayev, re-elected in 1999 following an amendment to the Constitution in October 1998, has been granted far-reaching rights and authority. He is simultaneously the supreme head of state and the most senior state servant; he appoints the government, the prime minister—with the agreement of Parliament—and has influence on the composition of the Senate. In case of a vote of no confidence against the government by the legislative power, he can dissolve Parliament. He appoints the head of the state auditor's office. The President has the right to present bills and decrees and decides whether or not to hold referendums. In addition, he is also the commander in chief of the armed forces, has the right to appoint and dismiss their leadership, and can proclaim a state of emergency in the country. Recently, on the initiative of President Nazarbayev, various changes in the Constitution grant him an all-powerful position within the state that will last until the end of his life.

Nonetheless, the principles of the state under the rule of law and the separation of powers are defined within the Constitution. Parliament is responsible for legislation. Kazakhstan has a two-chamber Parliament, consisting of the Senate (Upper House) and the *Majilis* (Lower House, House of Representatives). Of the senators, who keep their posts for six years, 32 are elected by assemblies of local representatives, and seven are appointed by the President. Of the Majilis' 77 deputies, whose period in office lasts five years, 67 are directly elected to single-mandate constituencies in a secret vote, and 10 proportionally through nationwide party lists. The government, headed by the prime minister, exercises executive powers, whereas jurisdiction lies with the Supreme Court.

Administrative divisions

Kazakhstan is divided into 14 administrative Regions (*oblysy* or *oblasts*):

Area	**Area capital**
Akmola (Akmola oblysy)	Astana
Aktobe (Aktobe oblysy)	Aktobe
Almaty (Almaty oblysy)	Taldykorgan
Atyrau (Atyra oblysy)	Atyrau
West Kazakhstan (Batys Kazakhstan oblysy)	Oral
Karaganda (Karaganda oblysy)	Karaganda
Kostanay (Kostanay oblysy)	Kostanay
Kyzylorda (Kyzylorda oblysy)	Kyzylorda

Mangystau (Mangystau oblysy)	Mangystau
South Kazakhstan (Ongtustik Kazakhstan oblysy)	Shymkent
Pavlodar (Pavlodar oblysy)	Pavlodar
North Kazakhstan (Soltustik Kazakhstan oblysy)	Petropavlov
East Kazakhstan (Shyghys Kazakhstan oblysy)	Oskemen
Zhambyl (Zhambyl oblysy)	Taraz

The cities of Astana and Almaty have their own administrative status and do not belong to any oblast. Each area is headed by a governor (*akim*), who together with his local government (*akimat*) rules with a high level of autonomy. The President appoints the governor. Each administrative area, as well as the two autonomous cities, is subdivided into 167 districts (*rayons*). Each rayon in turn has its own akim and corresponding akimat. The district akims are also appointed. So far, only the heads of municipalities (*auls*) are elected.

Domestic Politics

The Constitution adopted in 1995 defines Kazakhstan as a democratic, secular, constitutional and social state and guarantees the upholding of human rights. The Constitution also guarantees the right to freedom of opinion and the freedom of the press. Consistent implementation of these rights, however, has initially met with difficulties—not unusual in the first years of any state's independence. Thus, even though interference by the state in the affairs of political parties and social organizations is banned by the Constitution, attempts to influence parties have intermittently occurred—for instance through semi-legal financing of parties loyal to the President such as the Otan (Fatherland).

Political parties in Kazakhstan are still a long way from filling the role their counterparts in Europe enjoy. Most citizens don't expect them to be true representatives of their interests, and vote for individual personalities rather than political party programmes. In Kazakhstan, 10 political parties have been registered, compared to around 4,500 nongovernmental organizations. As expected, the Otan Party, loyal to President Nazarbayev, won a clear majority in parliamentary elections in autumn of 2004. Four parties managed to get more than seven percent of the vote to obtain seats in the Majilis: AIST (the agrarian-industrial coalition) and Asar, the relatively young party of the President's daughter Dariga Nazarbayeva, both of which support the President's policies, and the opposition parties Ak-Zhol (Bright Way) and the Democratic Party of Kazakhstan. Eighteen independent candidates also managed to win a seat in Parliament. Parties working outside Parliament can be roughly divided into opposition parties and neutral ones where the governing party is concerned.

Worth mentioning is the fact that President Nazarbayev holds regular meetings with party representatives—including those of the opposition, thereby creating a dialogue on important issues concerning internal political life. Regular conferences on further democratisation, established in autumn of 2002, also involve nongovernmental organizations.

More than 2,000 printed media, internet periodicals, television and radio stations compete for the attention of Kazakhstan's citizens. Despite the fact that leading media such as the television broadcasting system Khabar are in the hands of the presidential family, the sheer number of media sources can by and large be considered an indicator of democracy and freedom of expression. In newspapers especially, open and controversial discussion can and does often take place.

Nevertheless, cases of intimidation of journalists have been reported, and pressure on newspapers' editorial boards, including their closure, is not unknown. Inventive editors and journalists, however, time and again manage to continue publishing under a different name. Some newspapers get support from the state through advertising assignments and financing —this is true in particular of publications dedicated to ethnic minorities, which could not survive in a competitive market without such support.

Foreign Politics

After independence in 1991, Kazakhstan entered the international arena as an autonomous state for the first time. Because of its geographical location on the Eurasian continent and its wealth in raw materials, the country finds itself in the midst of a region full of tension. It therefore wisely maintains a position of political and military neutrality and non-interference with regards to foreign policies.

The US is among many major "players" attempting to gain influence in this region. Russia, of course, being the largest former Soviet republic, expects a fair share in the proceeds of Kazakhstan's wealth in raw materials; its influence remains strong—there is still a large ethnic Russian population in the country. The European Union, meanwhile, concentrates its presence through aid and training programmes, and this unobtrusive and benevolent attitude results in a high level of respect in Kazakhstan for the EU.

Big neighbour China is playing an increasingly important role in Central Asia. The most striking example is the ongoing migration of more than 40 million Chinese into the province of Xinjiang, the region bordering Kazakhstan to the east. The Chinese government is accused of attempting to neutralize the "threat" of Muslim Uygur and exiled Kazakhs in this region. Many Kazakhs watch this population increase with discomfort. Within a short time, a mass of people—three times Kazakhstan's entire population—will live on the other side of the border. Potential conflicts abound, the issue of water usage being one of the most volatile—consider the effects of the draining of the Ili and Ertis rivers on Kazakhstan's environment and river communities.

Other Asian and Eurasian countries such as Turkey, Iran, India and South Korea are active in Kazakhstan on the political-economic level, with investments from those countries increasing by the year.

Within the framework of the Commonwealth of Independent States (CIS), the founding document of which was signed in Almaty on 21 December 1991, the country actively contributes to the integration of the former USSR member states. Within the CIS there are a number of smaller economic, social, military and ecological associations, of which Kazakhstan is a member, for instance the Eurasian Economic Community, originating from the common Customs Union between Russia, Belarus, Kazakhstan, Kyrgyzstan and Tajikistan.

Kazakhstan is an active member of the United Nations. At the UN General Assembly in October 1992, President Nazarbayev took the initiative for a conference for cooperation and confidence-building in Asia. Many states followed the call, and are at present members of the conference, the declared goal of which is the prevention of conflicts in Asia.

As a member of the Shanghai Cooperation Organization (SCO), which was founded in 1996 as a result of border negotiations with China, Kazakhstan, together with the major powers Russia and China as well as with neighbours Kyrgyzstan, Tajikistan and Uzbekistan, is engaged in security and cooperation in the region for an effective platform in the struggle against international terrorism as well as the determination of conflict-free borders. The latter, awkward issue can be traced back to the Soviet policy of drawing frontier demarcations based on economic considerations in Central Asia. Today, as the one-time administrative borders between Soviet republics have become state borders and interests such as access to subsoil water resources determine international politics, much sensitivity is required in the process of defining terms of agreement on border demarcations. Since 2002, the border demarcations between Kazakhstan and Kyrgyzstan and Uzbekistan respectively have been settled, and since 2004 that between Kazakhstan and Russia has been mutually recognized.

Education and Science

A standard compulsory education of at least nine years exists in Kazakhstan, while high-school pupils attend classes for 12 years. Everyone is entitled to free education, but good schools generally charge extra. Teachers, parents and pupils have a very serious attitude towards learning—this Soviet legacy has fortunately been preserved and freed from its ideological constraints. However, targets set for the country—a modern, personality-oriented upbringing, technical, musical and moral education, and computerization in all schools—have met with a major obstacle: insufficient material provision for many schools, along with an extremely low pay rate for teachers.

In many schools, classes take place in two or three shifts for the simple reason that there are not enough classrooms. All the more amazing is to see with what inventive improvisation the best is made of what is available, and with how much enthusiasm the children learn. Also impressive is parents' readiness to make all the sacrifices they can possibly afford so that their children receive good schooling.

The consequence of this idealisation of education is an incredible run on universities. In September each year, a mass movement of tens of thousands of well-dressed, excited 17- and 18-year-olds gather in front of the gates of the universities of Almaty, Astana and other cities in order to obtain the results of their entry tests. Enthusiasm is at its strongest at the tradition-rich Al-Farabi Almaty State University in Almaty, and the Gumilyov Eurasian University, established in Astana in 1996.

The Academy of Arts and the Kurmangazy Conservatory, both in Almaty, enjoy a particularly good reputation, as does the recently opened musical academy in Astana. But the Medical University, the Technical University and the Agrarian University in Almaty also attract crowds. These establishments use the title "national"—meaning that they belong to the top-ranking universities. Those who cannot make it here, however, can still choose between several hundred state and private institutes with the status of academy and vocational school. Most of these, however, would never meet European criteria for a university, even though strolling through Almaty you can find buildings displaying signs reading "university" on virtually every street corner.

Those who can afford it attend universities abroad, while the best graduates compete for stipends from the state. In all, more than half a million students are enrolled at Kazakhstan's universities on a yearly basis. Many universities have research facilities attached. The National Academy of Science, founded in 1946, has 30 research institutes, of which the institutes of astronomy, mathematics, protein synthesis and phytochemistry are well renowned, as are those of astrophysics, geological and seismology. These days, much value is placed on sectors such as petrochemicals, metallurgy, physiology, fuel technology, machine building and electronics, as this provides impetus for the national economy.

The Presidential Palace occupies a prime position in the new city area of Astana, the nation's capital (Jeremy Tredinnick)

The People

More than 100 ethnic groups live in Kazakhstan—precisely 126 according to some written sources. To explain this, look to the migratory movements and campaigns of conquest in which the history of Central Asia is so rich, as well as the wheeling and dealing along the Silk Road which led to a situation, even before the establishment of Soviet power, in which the Kazakh territory was already home to a kaleidoscopic range of peoples: Kazakh, Uzbek, Turkmen, Kyrgyz, Persian, Chinese, Uygur, Dungan, Russian, Ukrainian, Tatar and many others already dwelt here long before Stalin started his deportation campaign. Forced migration following the outbreak of World War II resulted in an influx of over a million Koreans, Germans, Chechens, Ingush, Poles, Crimean Tatars, Turks, Greeks and other nationalities. For a long time after the war's end, these people were prohibited from returning to their places of origin. Their final rehabilitation had to wait until perestroika.

In addition, during the Virgin Lands campaign representatives of many nationalities from all over the Soviet Union came to Kazakhstan and settled there. As had happened during the land confiscation by the Russians 200 years previously, the country once more attracted many to its "land without owners".

A newspaper stand in Almaty Station shows the breadth of media available to Kazakhstan's population (Gunter Kapelle)

Kazakhstan today, therefore, genuinely represents a true melting pot of peoples. In a political sense, its citizens are correctly known as Kazakhstanis, whereas only the members of its titular ethnic group are called Kazakh. Thus, for instance, it does make a difference if one speaks about Kazakhstani or Kazakh cuisine, and Kazakh wedding customs differ from those of Uygurs—even though the latter (who live in the country) are no less Kazakhstani. In common practice, however, people often refer to something as "Kazakh" when the longer form would be technically correct.

Significantly, the number of Kazakhstanis has decreased over the last 10 years, whereas Kazakhs show a clear increase in population. In 1990 nearly 17 million people lived in Kazakhstan, but according to a census in 1999 the population was a little over 15 million. As of January 2007 it was still only 15.4 million, 53.4 percent of whom are Kazakh, 30 percent Russian, 3.7 percent Ukrainian, 2.5 percent Tatars, 2.5 percent Uzbek, 2.4 percent German, and the remaining 5.5 percent other nationalities.

Outside the cities, small-town life follows more traditional rhythms (Vladimir Tugalev)

Kazakhstan's ethnic mix can be seen in the faces of these young women (Gunter Kapelle)

Such a dramatic decline—of almost 10 percent of the population—within a 10-year period has more than one cause. After the opening up of the state borders and a new course in the direction of national sovereignty, many non-Kazakh subjects chose to return to the lands of their forefathers, since they feared nationalist unrest or discrimination. More than three million Russians, Ukrainians, Poles and Germans emigrated (the number of Germans in Kazakhstan dwindled from 831,000 to 272,000 between 1992 and 2002). These *Fehlende* (literally "those who failed") now try to gain footholds as returnees in their "historic homeland".

Another cause for the decline in population was a lowering of life expectancy after independence. The Soviet period, for all its terrible faults, never knew the levels of poverty and sickness of the 1990s. Only in recent years has money been invested once more in the obsolete health sector to rectify the problem.

Meanwhile, ethnic Kazakhs have increased in number by 1.4 million, and today they represent the majority of Kazakhstanis. This increase is due partly to the traditionally higher birth rate in Kazakh families, but also because an integral part of state policy has been to bring Kazakh emigrants back to their land of origin. These *Oralmany*, as they are called, come mainly from China, Mongolia, Iran and Afghanistan.

continued on page 97

The Yurt

The yurt is the traditional dwelling of Central Asia's nomadic nations. In Kazakh, it is called the *kiyiz üy*, or felt house. The yurt's invention was fundamental to the Turkic nations' mobility and consequently their expansion into Eastern and Central Europe. Without yurts, there might have been no "exodus of nations" under Attila or Mongol world conquest under Genghis Khan.

Today, for Kazakhs, Mongols and Kyrgyz the yurt is once again more than just a symbol. For decades the Communist state had inflicted a regime of forced collectivisation and brutal measures aimed at imposing a sedentary life on livestock breeders; as a result, in Kazakhstan the yurt fell towards oblivion, considered a remnant of a backward past, to be seen in museums at best. Thankfully it is that cruel regime that has faded, and the yurt is regaining its reputation as an extremely practical dwelling: warm in winter, cool in summer, variable in size and furnishing. It is the ideal shelter for

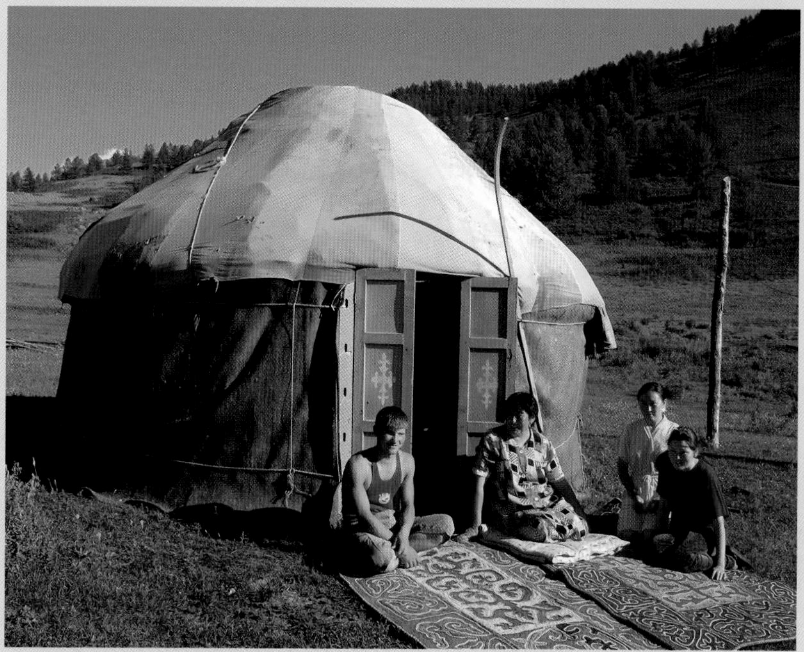

Felt rugs provide a comfortable sitting-out area in front of a typical yurt in summer pasture land (Hermann Schulz)

The interior of a yurt is made as rich and comfortable as a family's means allow; these furnishings represent significant wealth (A. Kruse)

semi-nomads who in early summer move with their herds into the steppe or into the green mountain valleys. It allows people to move to their next location with minimal trouble when the grass is finished or the pastures are dried up.

The yurt's skeleton is a framework (*suyektery*), consisting of a circular wooden concertina frame (*kerege*), curved roof bars (*uyk*), a wooden roof opening (*shangyrak*) and a double wooden door. The kerege is made of willow, birch or poplar and has a maximum height of two metres. Leather strips are pulled through holes drilled in the bars where they cross each other, and allow the structure to be folded up. According to the size of the yurt, from four to 12 bars are generally used, although khans' yurts have been known to use up to 30 bars. An opening is kept free for the entrance. After

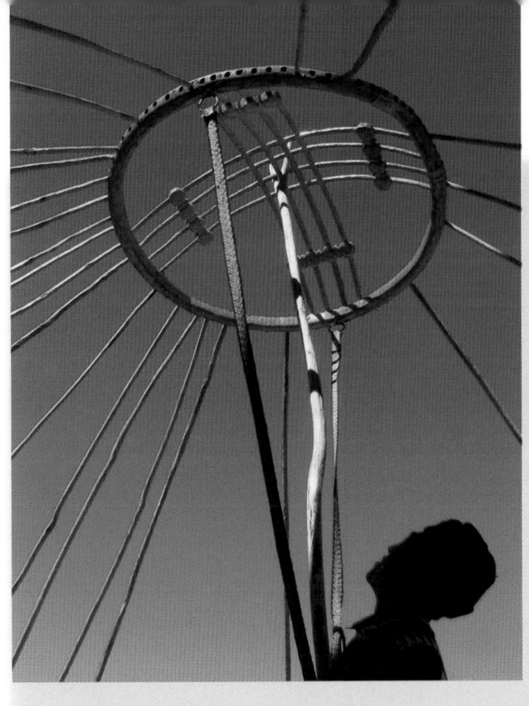

the frame has been raised, the edge structure of the shangyrak is lifted on a fork-shaped tool (*bakan*) and attached to the upper crossings of the kerege with roof bars.

Although putting up the yurt is the women's job, the raising of the shangyrak is a privilege reserved for the head of the family. The shangyrak is more than just an outlet for smoke—for Kazakhs, it is a symbol of home and family and represents an opening up to the world. Anyone who has spent the night in a yurt and peered through the shangyrak to watch the starlit sky before drifting off to sleep, will understand this meaning. All other components of a yurt can be replaced, but the shangyrak stays, and is passed down from father to youngest son. The most resistant wood is used for its construction and treated with special care. A solid ring, with holes drilled for the roof bars, is held together by several transverse bars. These bars are in turn attached with lasts, the latter often decorated with carvings or metal ornaments.

The curved roof bars are pulled down from the shangyrak and attached to the forked upper edge of the kerege, held in place by thick strips of wool. Then the doorframe and the wooden door are put in place in the door opening. Traditionally, the door is supposed to creak in order to indicate people entering—hence its nickname *sykyrlauyk*—"creaking". In poorer yurts, the entrance is simply covered with a thick felt.

A circular mat, made of reed stems or thin willow twigs, often painted or covered with coloured needlework, surrounds the kerege, and this mat is then covered with felt. A long piece of felt encloses the entire frame and the lower part of the roof structure, to which it is attached with canvas. After that, pieces of felt are pushed up to cover the roof, thrust over the roof structure and also attached. The shangyrak is covered with a special piece of felt, with

The raising of a yurt's central roof opening, or shangyrak, *is a symbolic affair reserved for the head of the family (Edda Schlager)*

a rope attached to it that allows it to be opened and closed. A piece of felt, rolled up above the door opening, can also be let down in bad weather or at night.

The yurt must now be stabilised: multicoloured strips attach the shangyrak to the frame, while pieces of strong canvas connect the yurt to pegs driven into the earth. In this way, a nomad's dwelling can resist even violent storms. The entire process of erecting a medium-size yurt takes no more than 45 minutes.

The yurt's interior is split in two—the right half for the women and the left for the men. Household equipment is stored on the right side, with tools for hunting and livestock maintenance on the left. The interior is furbished with multicoloured strips of cloth, tassels and carpets—the finest rug is always attached to the canvas behind the wooden bed (in poorer yurts, the nomads sleep on mats). During the day, everything is placed in boxes and closets, or hung on the wooden bars of the frame. The space inside the yurt is then used to prepare and consume meals—eating on seats or benches around a tablecloth —and to work.

Six to 10 people live in a standard-sized yurt (with a diameter of four metres). During cold nights young calves and lambs often also find shelter within the warmth of the dwelling. Wealthy families possess more than one yurt, divided according to function: a yurt to cook in, one to dine in, another to sleep in, and a yurt for guests.

The Central State Museum in Almaty, the Presidential Cultural Centre in Astana and the Abai Museum in Semey each display a number of exceptionally fine yurts. In Tausamaly (Kamenka), a suburb of Almaty, an enterprise manufactures quality yurts; it can be contacted through the museum shop at the National Museum.

Strong braids of wool tie the uyk *roof bars to the top of the* kerege, *the yurt's concertina-style wooden wall frame (Gunter Kapelle)*

Are there Still Nomads?

In June 1995, I prepared questionnaires together with a project team for the World Bank in order to research living standards in Kazakhstan. Our partners at the State Statistics Committee were of the opinion that we could skip the question "Do you possess a yurt?" since there were no more yurts in Kazakhstan.

Ten days later, while driving from Almaty to Kapshagay, we spotted an enormous cloud of dust on the side of the road. First a camel broke out of the cloud, loaded sky-high with various sticks and packs. The centre of the cloud, however, was moving at the side of the road—hundreds of sheep hooves were kicking up the desert sand. The sheep were accompanied by a donkey and by some people on horseback, young men and women, who readily stopped and proudly answered our questions. Each year at this time they drove their herds to the mountain pastures, where they stayed until September or October, before returning to their winter quarters. And yes, of course they had a yurt —as though we had not already spotted their camel.

This nomad's yurt on the Assy Plateau combines the old—a traditional bread-making oven in the foreground—with a modern solar panel on its outer wall (Vladimir Tugalev)

Our colleagues from the Statistics Committee declared to us the next day that this had been an exception. These people had been forced to turn to nomadic-style livestock breeding once more in order to escape the poverty in the villages. So a way of life, which had been prohibited and punished for more than 60 years, was just reappearing? Highly improbable.

In reality, this way of life never really died out. The Kazakhs and their ancestors have maintained nomadic traditions on the open steppe for 3,000 years—this culture is the only sophisticated way to survive within the steppe's dry vegetation, its scarce water resources, its summer heat and its winter cold. Since the end of the Soviet period, the nomadic way of life has demonstrated its ability to support life at a time of material penury and difficult self-rediscovery for the Kazakhs. The yurt, in some places preserved with much care, has regained its place of honour. Knowledge about the behaviour of the weather, the characteristics of plants, water and animals is once more being applied.

Meanwhile, nomadic migrations such as the one we observed are no longer exceptional, and in summer you can find mobile nomad settlements in many steppe valleys and on mountain pastures. Smoke rises from the yurts or army tents, and children play around them. In the evening, shortly before dark, mounted herdsmen with dogs arrive, driving herds of goats, sheep, cows or horses in front of them. The animals have spent the day in the pastures of nearby valleys or on the higher grassland plateaus, but are driven to the compound for the night. From the yurts, humming and laughing is heard throughout the evening hours. Anyone who joins the company will be offered a bowl of kumis or tea, along with round flat bread. These encampments are

Above: Father and son sit in a nomadic encampment in the Kayindy Valley (Dagmar Schreiber)
Right: Nomads on the move (Gunter Kapelle)

called *zhaylau*, and the very sound of this word can provoke a smile on the face of proud Kazakhs throughout the country.

In winter camps, called *kystau*, things have changed slightly from a century ago, with the herdsmen now living in huts or houses, in most cases supplied with electricity. However, even in winter the animals are still driven out to graze—only in bad weather are they kept in the stables and fed hay. These communities of herdsmen, who during the warm season follow the food and water with their herds, but in winter occupy fixed dwelling places, are called semi-nomads.

Meat is the main food of Kazakhs. When winter comes, a horse is chosen for slaughter, as its meat is considered the best energy provider during the cold season. A young bull's meat is considered the best dish for spring, and mutton is available year round. Mutton tastes particularly good in summer, when the sheep are grazed in herb meadows.

Semi-nomadic livestock breeding has a bright future in Kazakhstan. It is recovering well, with families gradually gaining a position of modest prosperity—to the extent that the travellers who are invited in for a bowl of kumis inside the yurt, may find to their surprise that a refrigerator and TV set have been added to the room's many colourful decorations.

NOMADIC CULTURE—A NATURAL RHYTHM

By *Alma B. Kunanbaeva*

Excerpted from a paper titled *"Nomads"*, prepared by the author as part of an event named *The Silk Road: Connecting Cultures, Creating Trust*, at the 36th Annual Smithsonian Folklife Festival On The National Mall, Washington, D.C.:

Nomads and nomadism have been intimately linked to Silk Road trade and culture since ancient times ("nomad" derives from the Greek nomos, *meaning "pasture"), and at the debut of the 21st century, still constitute a vital, if all too often endangered economic and social force in large parts of central Eurasia. From Siberian reindeer herders and Kazakh horse breeders to Turkmen shepherds and Tibetan yak drivers, modern-day pastoralists preserve a way of life that embodies some of the Silk Road region's most time-tested and ingenious traditions.*

Marking the frontiers of the great civilizations of China, Iran, India and Greece, the historical borders of the nomadic world have been indefinite and diffuse. Nomads and settled peoples have long existed in a complementary relationship, and in the history of trans-Eurasian trade and cultural exchange, nomads have been like blood vessels that circulated the oxygen of ideas and distributed new technologies and products along the Silk Road. Nomads can be proud of their historical achievements, which include movable dwellings, clothing suitable for riding horseback, felt and leather utensils, and the equine harness. They invented kumis *(fermented mare's milk), the art of hunting with birds of prey, and bowed stringed instruments that are the ancestors of the cello and violin...*

...Nomad civilization has its own laws governing the organization of time and space, and nomads follow very sensitively the cycles of nature. In the words of one song, they are in continual pursuit of eternal spring. The primacy of movement serves as the basis of the nomads' entire worldview. For them, everything that is alive is in movement, and everything that moves is alive: the sun and moon, water and wind, birds and animals.

The low fertility of the soil does not allow nomads and their herds to stay in a single area for a long time. Overgrazing can have dire results—at the extreme, removing a pasturage from economic use for a period of years. In order to maximize the yield of a pasturage, nomads have to be able to judge on which exact day to drive their herds from one pasture to the next, leaving the abandoned area to rejuvenate over the course of a year. Migration with livestock is an unavoidable fact of survival, and during the process of natural and forced selection, sheep, goats, cattle, camels and horses have been selected for their suitability for lengthy migrations. Indeed, the symbol of nomadism is the horse, whose praise is sung in songs, epic tales, and stories. The winged flying horse, called by various names—Tulpar, Jonon Khar, like Pegasus of the ancient Greeks—is a beloved character of legends and a source of poetic inspiration.

At the earliest signs of spring, nomads drive their cattle to spring pastures where the animals give birth to their young, sheep have their spring dip, and are shorn. Spring is a time of hope and the beginning of the new cycle of life marked by the observance of the New Year, called Nawruz *("New Day" in Persian) among the Turkic nomads. Without lingering long, nomads drive their animals on to summer pastures, where the happiest time of the nomadic year begins. Summer is a time of fattening for the animals characterized by an abundance of food, games and holidays for the young, and meetings with relatives as different migratory paths cross. At the same time there are preparations for the hard winter ahead: sewing clothes, weaving rugs, beating felt. With the onset of the first cool days, nomads undertake their migration to fall [autumn] pastures where they carry out the fall shearing of sheep and camels, the preparation of milk and meat for the winter, and the return to winter quarters.*

This nomadic cycle, renewed from year to year, is not exactly the same each year, for the seasons themselves are not the same from one year to the next. Yet what remains constant for the nomad is the sensation of a natural rhythm of movement, stable forms of social organization, and abiding relationships among people. Success in nomadic life depends on mastery of a vast body of collective knowledge amassed over centuries. This knowledge, passed on from father to son and mother to daughter, embraces an entire complex of tradecraft, domestic know-how and moral norms...

...The yurt is the universal dwelling of nomads in central Eurasia, and represents a unique achievement of human genius. As the name of a kind of

dwelling, "yurt" entered general usage from Russian. In Central Asia itself "yurt" is a polysemous word that can mean "community", "family", "relatives", "people", "land" or "countryside". Turkic-speaking nomads call their dwellings kiyiz üy *or "felt home"—Mongolian speakers use the term* ger.

For nomads, the yurt is rich in symbolism that represents both the macrocosmic and microcosmic world. Under the endless hemisphere of the sky, called Tengri, which is also the name of God among nomadic animists, the yurt duplicates this hemisphere with the round opening of the smoke hole symbolizing the sun... quite simply, the yurt is at the heart of the traditional nomadic worldview. It provides a model and symbol of humanity and the universe, and is the key to understanding nomadic civilization.

> Only one who, after a long journey on a windy, grey winter evening has stepped into a warm, bright, spacious, radiantly coloured yurt
>
> Only one who, melting from the smouldering intensity of noon heat in summer when everything is silent and even time seems to stand still, enters the dry semi-darkness of a yurt
>
> Only one who, after quickly washing up, falls onto the cool surface of a yurt's silken comforters and buries her head in an aromatic bowl of astringent, frothy cold kumis
>
> Only one who has awakened in the early morning from the joyous sensation of warm sunlight on her face and, shivering from the morning chill, emerges into the blooming steppe to meet the sun
>
> Only such a person can appreciate the yurt in its full range and depth.

Putting together a yurt is a magical act that for nomads represents the original creation: the transformation of Chaos into the Cosmos, Disorder into Order. Conversely, dismantling the yurt creates a reverse transformation. Each step in erecting a yurt has a symbolic meaning of which participants in the process are keenly aware. Moreover, the yurt has been anthropomorphized so that its parts are described by the same words used to name parts of the human body. For example, the centre of the yurt where the hearth is located is known as the "navel"; walls are "thighs"; the interior of the lattice frame is the "womb"; the roof is called the "shoulders;" the opening in the smoke hole is an "eye"; the wooden frame is called the "bones" or "skeleton," and the felt covering is "clothing." Herders say that each yurt has its own spirit, which is why guests bow their head and pronounce greetings when entering a yurt, even if no one is home.

The inside of a yurt has a sacred character and is also imbued with its own symbolism. The spot opposite the entrance is the place of honour and is reserved for people who are closer to the Upper World by virtue of their social status, age or artistic gifts. At the same time, this seat provides a vantage point from which the occupant can view the entire yurt, with men conventionally seated on the right side, and women on the left.

In their traditional daily lives, nomads do not know an unadorned space. All of their surroundings, beginning with the internal appointments of the yurt, are adorned or ornamented by their own skilled hands. To "ornament" is to domesticate, to turn an object into a part of one's own cultural universe. Thus everything that is locally produced, from simple household necessities like drinking vessels and blankets to specially crafted items like horse harnesses and jewellery, represents an inviolable link between art and life. Moreover, ornaments serve not simply as decoration, but comprise a special language that is essential knowledge for an understanding of nomadic arts...

...The nomadic diet is high in protein, and consists mostly of meat and milk products. Such food provides the energy people need to engage in hard physical labour and symbolizes not only physical but spiritual survival. The daily meal, with its symphony of tastes, customs and rituals played and replayed in the life of every nomad since childhood, serves as a cornerstone of self-identity, and the shared meal is in its turn at the very epicentre of traditional nomadic culture. The ritual of seating guests around the yurt neatly sums up the social and familial relations of people in any given group, demonstrating hierarchy and priorities.

Nomadic hospitality rituals are strongly regulated and provide an opportunity to exchange news and for guests—at the behest of their host—to talk about themselves, their travels and events in the place where they live. Genealogical ties between hosts and guests are thoroughly discussed, and elders recount historical legends and stories. Among the means of communication particular to life on the steppe is a unique form of transmitting information known as the "long ear": whatever is discussed around the dastarkhan *(tablecloth) can already be known the next day for hundreds of miles around. How, and by what means? Who knows!*

Nomadic life is marked by eternal circles—the circle of the sun, the open steppe, the circumference of the yurt, the horned circular scroll of ornaments, the life cycle of the müshels *or "12-year animal cycle." The completion of one circle leads to the beginning of the next, and each moment of transition is consciously and carefully marked by the appropriate customs, rituals and holidays. One of the turning points is Nawruz, the beginning of the calendar year that occurs on the vernal equinox, 21–22 March.*

Preparations for Nawruz begin early: homes are cleaned, new clothes are sewn. On the eve of Nawruz, nomads light bonfires and jump over them, young people wander about with lighted torches, women gather to cook large pots of a soup called sumelak *or* Nawruz kozhe *made of seven ingredients—water, salt, meat, wheat, millet, rice and milk. Stirring the soup, they sing special songs and pronounce blessings. With the sunrise, they sit down to the first meal of the new year, and as they eat, wish one another a long life. Then they call upon relatives, who await them in their yurts with spreads of delicious food. The holiday continues with horse competitions. At meals, elders are offered a boiled sheep's head, there are songs, and bards engage in verbal duelling competitions. Meanwhile, young people play games like "White Bone", which consists of looking for a sheep's tibia bone that has been thrown into the open steppe—into a magical night full of laughter and freedom under a spring sky filled with stars.*

The holiday has provided a short but joyous respite on the path of life, and as it recedes into memory, a new morning arises in the endless steppe, signifying yet another beginning, another rebirth. It is a rebirth in which nomads believe wholeheartedly, a rebirth that carries them through snowstorms and intense heat, losses and disappointments, betrayals and challenges, and all the tests of fate that lead to the future.

Alma Kunanbaeva specializes in ethnomusicology, cultural anthropology and linguistics. She is the author of more than 40 articles and two books, has taught at universities in the United States, Russia and Kazakhstan, and is currently a Visiting Professor at Stanford University's Cultural and Social Anthropology Department.

The Social Condition

Having lived through hardship, this matriarch is cautious of what the future holds (Gunter Kapelle)

According to the World Bank's Human Development Report, Kazakhstan was set to advance on the world list of social welfare conditions from 83rd place in 2000 to 78th in 2004. Life expectancy stands at 65, but there are major contrasts between the cities and countryside.

Over the past century, and in particular during the last 16 years, Kazakhstan has lost a significant percentage of its rural population to the cities. At present, 57 percent of the population lives in cities, mainly due to the labour market. In rural areas, predominantly in southern Kazakhstan, many families exist on low cash incomes, with monthly income per capita in the order of 14,000 tenge (around US$100 dollars); the average income per inhabitant in the oil centre of Atyrau is four times as much.

Reports show that 30 percent of Kazakhstan's population lives below the poverty line. Among these are a majority of pensioners (in 2003 the average pension amounted to 7,100 tenge), the unemployed (if they can receive social security money, it is only for a period of three months and in negligible amounts), students, single mothers and numerous inhabitants of rural regions.

City life in Kazakhstan is as multifaceted as in European and Asian cities: there is a mix of many nationalities, living in both large and small family units, with married and unmarried couples as well as single people living alone. In order to stem the influx from the countryside, the government declared the years 2003–2005 "Years of the Aul" and carried out various programmes in rural areas. These included the improvement of drinking water (over a million people get their drinking water from springs and sometimes dubious-quality wells), better medical treatment, and better allocation of micro-credit for small and medium-size farms.

Yet in spite of radical changes and strong urbanisation in Kazakhstan, its society is still characterized by strong solidarity between the old and young. This can be attributed in large part to the importance of learning the art of survival under the tough conditions of nomadic life. Traditionally, the knowledge necessary for the maintenance of an extensive pastoral agriculture was acquired through decades-long observation of the weather, vegetation growth and animal behaviour. Thus young people developed a huge respect for the elderly and experienced, which remains noticeable in Kazakhstan to this very day. Particularly in the countryside, an *aksakal*—"white-beard"—is a venerated person given honour by all. Important decisions are only made after asking the aksakal for advice, and at family parties he is addressed in a most respectful manner, gets the place of honour and the best piece of meat.

Swings are a popular traditional game in rural areas (Jeremy Tredinnick)

In a Kazakh family, adult children never abandon their parents. Either the youngest son or a daughter stays in the parents' house and lives there with their family. They, and a daughter-in-law in particular, are required to be obedient towards the family elders. It still remains the custom, though no longer obligatory, that grandparents bring up the first grandson. The young parents hand over their son as soon he has been weaned. This tradition relieves the young parents, who often have their first child very early, from the multiple burdens of education, work and the child. Moreover, it allows the grandparents' rich experience in life to be passed on to their grandchild and later on the grandparents can rely on the support of the child when it grows up.

Another factor explains the closeness between young and old generations. The social structure of a family—again particularly in rural areas—does not allow it to live scattered in small units. A large family is an economic community; several generations live together under a single roof, take care of the livestock, cultivate a piece of land and keep the family's cash inflow for their joint disposal.

Officially, women have always enjoyed great freedom in Kazakhstan. They have never been forced to wear veils or robes down to their ankles. Traditionally they took part in many mounted sports and could freely put their strength to the test. A particularly fine example is the *kyz syny* contest during the New Year festivities, when girls and young women compete against each other with poems, songs, proverbs and epigrams, but also in their knowledge of the national cuisine.

However, in spite of this, there are sometimes major distinctions in equality between men and women. The great writer Abai Kunabayev noted that poverty often put women in a position of dependence and injustice. The days when a wealthy bey could abuse a poor

An honoured aksakal, *or "white beard", on the steppe (Gunter Kapelle)*

orphan girl and get away with it are long gone, but poverty is still particularly severe on women. The nightlife in major cities gives ample evidence of this, with prostitution as evident as in developing—and developed—cities the world over.

In the north of Kazakhstan, as well as the metropolises of Astana, Almaty and other cities, women are equal in terms of civil rights, showing no real difference with nearby Russia. Women here are well-educated, qualified employees and many of them hold responsible positions.

By contrast, in the south and in Kazakh-dominated rural regions, women are still often confined to the role of mother and spouse. The influence of Islam is noticeably stronger here, and the cultural conditioning of women's lives accordingly more rigid. Though prohibited by law, the traditions of bride kidnapping and polygamy still occur. It is true that often the ritual of kidnapping takes place with the bride's consent and is motivated by the need to save on a costly dowry and the no less costly traditional wedding party. But this aside, cases of violent kidnapping of women still occasionally take place. The causes of polygamy vary from social aspects such as "taking over" a deceased relative's wife in order to take care of her and her family, to womanising out of hedonism or for prestige.

The official minimum age of marriage in Kazakhstan is 16. Marriage between elderly men and very young women is relatively common. Men tend to explain this trend with the succinct observation that women in Kazakhstan tend to age rapidly. In the countryside especially, this explanation turns into a self-fulfilling prophecy due to frequent childbirth and hard physical labour.

As elsewhere in Central Asia, women in Kazakhstan find themselves caught between their traditional role and the broader possibilities of emancipation, with the latter either officially propagated as a legacy of Soviet times, or imposed by economic necessity and the prospects of a market economy. The fact that a significantly greater percentage of university students is female gives an indication of the fairer sex's willingness and motivation to succeed in every level of society. One thing also cannot fail to catch the visitor's attention: women in Kazakhstan are beautiful, self-assured and extremely feminine.

A picnic dastarkhan, *or dinner table, is blessed by the head of the family, wearing a* kalpak *felt hat (Alexander Kolokolnikov)*

Customs and Traditions

Hospitality

Hospitality is the supreme commandment of the steppe. Every traveller can be certain that wherever he sets foot he will be given shelter at all times. In such a vast territory of climatic and geographic extremes, this cultural imperative means survival.

"*Kuday konakpin!*" says a guest upon entering a dwelling. This means "I am God sent"—and the guest is treated accordingly. A ram used to be—and often still is—slaughtered in honour of the guest, and cooked in a large cauldron. Often neighbours are invited to take part in the feast. The guest is served the best piece of the meat on a plate, cuts it into mouthfuls and divides it among those present according to age and status: first to the host, then the lady of the house, and then the others according to rank.

After this substantial and lengthy welcome, and before he leaves, the guest is bound to be offered a *sarkhyt*—or food for the road—since the journey to the next yurt could be as much as a day's ride. The host will often take the opportunity to accompany his guest along the road for some distance.

Such feasts in honour of one or more guests occur more infrequently these days. However, one should be aware of this type of hospitality in order to react appropriately. Certainly as a visitor to Kazakhstan you will be treated with great hospitality wherever you go, and you should be prepared to spend many hours around a dining table, giving and receiving toasts over bottles of vodka or cognac. Indeed, the Russian love of strong liquor has been embraced by the majority of Kazakhstanis, so be firm if you do not wish to drink tumbler after tumbler of vodka, or be prepared to be drunk under the table and suffer the following day, when it will begin all over again!

Weddings

A wedding starts with the wooing of the bride (*kuda tussu*). The wooer, the groom and the latter's relatives appear in front of the bride's parents, offer them the richest gifts they can afford and ask their permission for the marriage. This having been granted, the dowry (*kalym*) is settled and the date of the wedding determined. Sometimes, the bride has the last word; a blunt refusal is considered impolite—setting an impossible task is more courteous.

Wedding couples pass in and out of a Karaganda mosque, melding modern dress with traditional ceremony (Christopher Herwig)

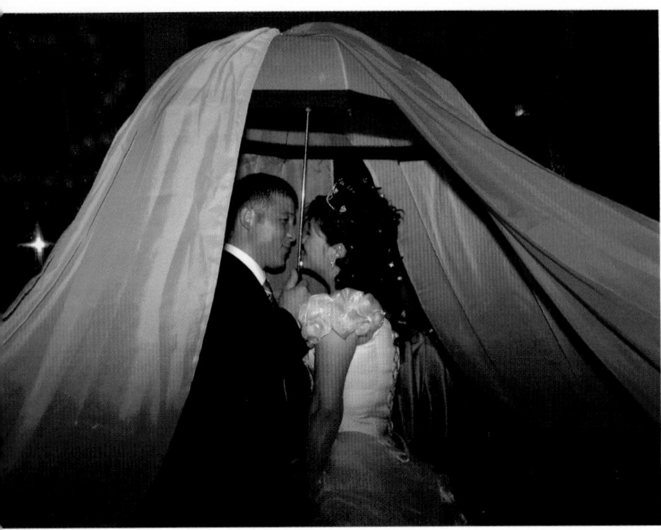

If all is agreed, however, the preparation for the event starts. This can take time, since it is the custom to invite all relatives and acquaintances—and they can amount to hundreds. The wedding party proper is a long and complicated process, the culmination of which is the *batashar,* or the uncovering of the bride's face by one of the groom's relatives—usually a young boy. In times of old, this ritual had more significance than it has today, since in those days the groom hardly got the change to see his future wife's face beforehand.

The batashar is accompanied by the performance of a special, very long litany, sung by a *zhyrau* (bard). In the litany, the names of all the invited guests are recited in order, each of whom steps forward on hearing his/her name to offer the young married couple gifts—usually household items. On receiving each gift, the bride bows, and the boy briefly lifts her veil from her face. At the end of the ceremony, the cloth is removed.

The batashar is preceded by a very intimate procedure among the women. The mother-in-law takes the bride into her home or yurt, takes a little animal fat into her hands, warms it briefly and then touches the bride's face with her greased hands. This means that the bride is welcome and that things will go well for her in her new family.

In order to save on dowries, many less prosperous couples revert to the old variant of kidnapping. A kidnapped wife must be married as swiftly as possible, in order to save the family from disgrace. In these cases, the wedding is not as lavish. In earlier times a woman's dress code would change after marriage. While young women were free to cover their hair with a hood or silk shawl or not, a married woman was not allowed to show her hair in public. They would wear a *kimeshek*, a cylinder-shaped turban wrapped in a cloth that left an opening for the face. These days, such rules are still observed in the south of Kazakhstan and in remote areas, if less strictly.

Above: Though many Kazakh weddings are modern affairs these days, traditional themes are often woven into the event as reminders of their cultural roots—here an umbrella and bolts of silk symbolize a yurt, under which the happy couple embrace (Jeremy Tredinnick)

Contests and Games

Physical contests are massively popular in Kazakhstan; from wrestling in a ring to wrestling on horseback, from archery to various forms of horsemanship, all are popular at festivities. Horseracing and other competitions on horseback are without doubt the top-ranking national sports—unsurprising given the crucial role of the horse in Kazakh society. (The significance of the horse is also reflected in the Kazakh language, which has some 50 different words indicating the colour and shading of horses.)

A straightforward race, often involving young boys, is known as the *bayga*. Often without using saddles, the participants set off at breakneck speed on a course either 20km *(tok bayga)* or 30km (*alaman bayga*) long.

Top: An international wrestling competition in Ordabasy (Jeremy Tredinnick). Above: A bayga *in full swing at a large event in the mountains (Gunter Kapelle)*

The sport of kokpar *is a rough and often dangerous pastime, requiring great horsemanship, courage and boldness (Vladimir Tugalev). Inset: The very same skills apply to horse wrestling (Gunter Kapelle)*

A very popular sport throughout Central Asia is *kokpar* (known further south as *buzkashi*), a sort of horseback rugby where two teams of horsemen compete to grab and win possession of a headless goat carcass, then carry it and throw it across the opposition's goalline. It is played in a ferocious manner, and often the participants wear a padded helmet for protection against blows from both men and horses.

The *kyz-kuu* ("catch the girl") is a horserace in which women participate. Young men (*dzhigits*) pursue a young girl on horseback, who sets off with a small advantage. The winner is the first one to catch up with the girl and kiss her whilst still at a gallop. This game can also be one-on-one, but if the unlucky dzhigit does not manage to catch and kiss his target before the finishing line, the girl has the right to beat him with her whip all the way back to the starting line—much to the amusement of onlookers.

Hunting

Hunting is one of the Kazakhs' great passions. One shoots ducks with his shotgun, another stalks bigger game on horseback. Most hunters these days respect the hunting seasons, but unfortunately poaching still occurs—not only for food, but also out of sheer hunting fever. Tourists with enough money, as well as high-ranking state guests, can arrange to go hunting with birds or dogs. In winter, when the wild animals' fur is thick and valuable, Kazakhs set out into the steppe or mountains on horseback with a golden eagle (*berkut*) on their arm. This kind of hunting, mostly for steppe foxes and wolves, used to be a rich man's pleasure.

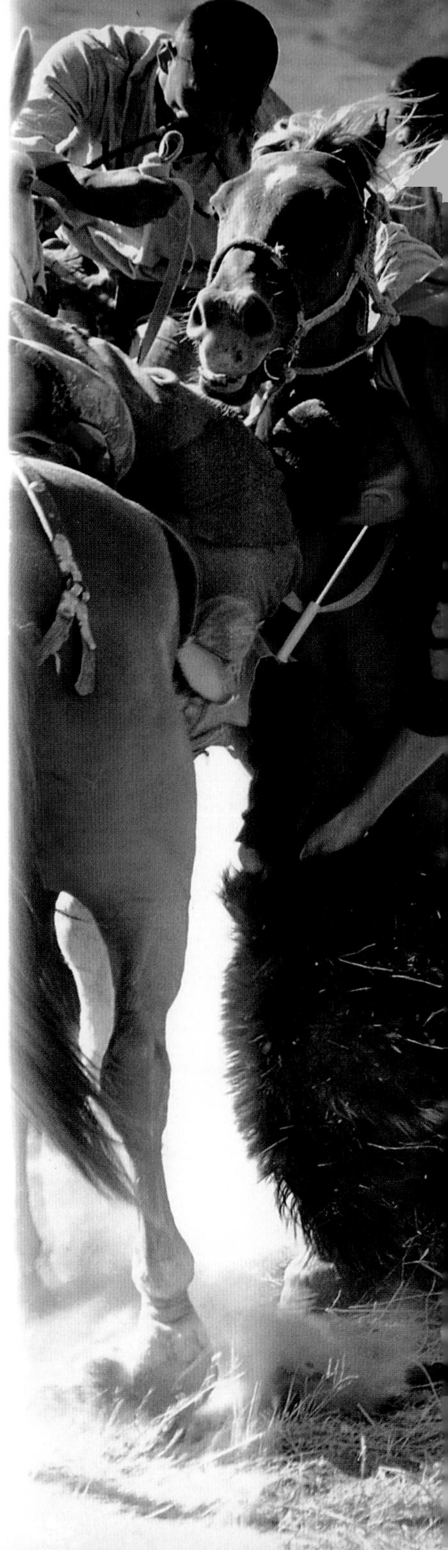

Only they could afford golden eagles, imperial eagles or saker falcons for hunting: the price of a trained golden eagle could be as much as five or six camels.

These days, there are only a few people who still practise the art of training hunting birds. A *berkutshe* must have great physical strength, knowledge, patience and absolute authority in order to tame and train a heavy eagle or fierce falcon. This man is held in great esteem, his profession surrounded by myth. People used to be convinced that an infertile woman could be cured if she spent the night with a berkutshe. Her husband would personally take her to this "therapy"...

Eight different kinds of eagles, falcons and hawks were used for hunting, and noble dogs often accompanied the royal birds. The borzoi—or *tazy*—is considered the epitome of greyhound breeding in Kazakhstan. These dogs have excellent eyesight, develop phenomenal speed, and are enduring and very courageous. Even snow leopards were hunted with these dogs. They were so highly valued that one borzoi could replace 47 horses as a dowry. Another similar breed, the saluki, is also used.

Battling over a headless goat carcass during a game of kokpar, *this young man risks being unseated and trampled in the melée (J. Bjelousov)*

Intrigue at the Hunt

From times past royal hunts in the steppe were arranged as major feasts. During those festivals beks and sultans could show off their riches in a grand way, boast of their magnificent steeds, their precious harness and weapons. At the same time the hunt was meant to be a kind of military parade where each man showed his courage, gallantry, resourcefulness and marksmanship. Quite a few braggarts were known to take leave of their senses in fear when a deadly scared hare suddenly jumped out right from under their feet; the more so when one heard the growling of a tiger or a fierce leopard. Some ran away in terror, dropping their arms and sometimes even famed marksmen, who at a contest could shoot down from a tree branch a purse stuffed with money at a distance of one hundred steps, were not able to hit a huge beast three steps away from them.

Besides, during the hunt the courage of young warriors who appeared amongst the grown men for the first time was tested and confirmed. Indeed, when there is no war going on where is one supposed to show his worth? The one who would not falter seeing a huge boar with atrocious half-metre teeth running right into him and send his three-edged arrow three fingers deep into its forehead would do the same to an iron-clad foe on the battlefield. It was not for nothing that in the steppe hunting was called the fair of courage.

Ultimately, after taking counsel with Kerei, Sultan Janybek decided to accept the invitation of the khan, considering the fact that there was no apparent reason for declining it. "What is to be, will be," thought he. "It is not for nothing that they say one cannot hide away from death even in a gold coffer. While if you are destined to stay alive not one of the thousand arrows aimed at you will hit you!"

"Yes, we must join the hunt and pretend we suspect nothing," agreed Kerei. "But we will have to take along the most reliable warriors who will stick close to us all the time. If we don't go now that wolf Abulkhair will realise that we know what he is up to and will surely find a way to get rid of us. After all, they say the one who got undressed will surely jump into the water..."

Janybek prepared for hunting very thoroughly. Like all steppe people he liked best the light-footed argamak horses and hunting birds. One of the most famous kushbegi, the trainers of hunting eagles and hawks in all the steppe of Desht-Kipchak, was a young sultan. Alongside his white yurta there were small black tents and in each one of them there lived a domesticated hawk, eagle, hen-harrier or kestrel. Real hunting birds cannot be kept in the same room...

In spite of tradition, the sultan was chasing birds of prey not with the help of fledglings but with strong full-fledged fighters. Although it was far more difficult to tame such birds it was immensely more useful. An eagle that was grown free is stronger and more ruthless than the one fed by hand.

So, Sultan Janybek did not trust anybody to raise his eagles. Normally the birds would not give in to training but he would stubbornly and patiently keep on repeating everything from scratch. They would put a leather hood, tomagu, on the head of a proud bird and settle it on a swing for it to get accustomed to riding on horseback. Then they would gradually feed it right off one's hand with meat drained of blood in water. Hunger made the eagle submit and gradually it got used to taking meat only from the hands of its master. Tomagu or no tomagu, it recognised the master from afar.

It was only much later that they took the cloth off the eagle's head and the master began feeding it on red meat. Seeing the meat the eagle screamed with impatience but it only took it from its master's hand. After that a race in the steppe began. Janybek let the eagle free and soon called it back, each time giving food to it. That way he would ultimately tame it, making it a hunting bird.

No matter how long you might tame an eagle, still when it sees a flaming-red fox it falls on it like a rock sinking its claws into its victim and flies up into the sky. That very moment it hears its master's call, flies towards him and gets a double or triple reward. Having registered it in its memory it can't but wait for another hunt.

Janybek had several such hawks. During the summer they had a good rest and were eager for hunting. For his hunt the sultan took his famed hawk Sombolak that had been glorified in the songs of his songsters. And beneath his hunting gown Janybek was wearing thin iron-chained armour, a sharp-edged sword and newly feathered arrows...

An orderly team of buglers came out on a hill and the steppe resounded with their brass calls summoning the hunters. Sultans, beks and emirs decorated with feathers and shining with rich armour began coming together from all sides.

Suddenly clouds of dust swirled on the road from the khan's headquarters. A large group of horsemen raced towards the hill and in front of them the khan himself was riding an extraordinarily beautiful bay steed with a white spot on its forehead and its mane and tail tied in knots. The accompanying riders' horses had their manes and tails tied up. The spirited beasts were biting their steel bits prancing with impatience. The whole retinue were clad in light hunting armour, their heads crowned with finely patterned, shining silver helmets. Immediately after the khan and his retinue followed his guardsmen, all of them his most faithful warriors and bodyguards, or nukers...

There were three or four women in this brilliant crowd. One of them, who was dressed better than the rest and sitting astride a golden gulsary-akhaltekin horse whose name Ortek, meaning "The Dancing Ibex", was known all over the steppe, was attracting the attention of everyone. Her beauty had a blinding effect on all men around and each one wanted to meet her eye.

She was the fourth wife of Abulkhair and the daughter of the great scholar Ulugbek, grandson of Timur. They called her Rabia-Sultan-Begim and said there was no woman on Earth as beautiful as she. Her clothes, her saddle, bridle, spurs and shabrack were decorated with wrought gold. The contrary wind was swaying the plume on her pointed cap lined with otter, an expensive necklace was glittering in the sun shining with all the colours of the rainbow, but especially beautiful was her white clean-featured face with fine arched eyebrows and a black cascade of numberless braids...

When the khan and his majestic retinue approached the hill another group of horsemen came in sight galloping towards them from the open steppe. In front of them Sultans Janybek and Kerei were riding dark-grey argamaks, with a hawk on the shoulder of each one.

Janybek and Kerei were wearing light hunting caftans trimmed with sable, Kazakh caps on their heads. Among those following them there were women too. Zhakhan, Janybek's second wife and the mother of young Sultan Kasym, was the most beautiful of them. Being the daughter of a warrior from the nomadic Kerei clan she looked regal astride a milky-white mount nick-named Kibikayak which means "Deer's Legs". Unlike those of the beautiful Rabia-Sultan-Begim her saddle, shabrack and the rest of the harness were only adorned with chased silver, which especially suited her steppe beauty and physique.

Besides, there was something else which made the beautiful Zhakan so different from the wife of Abulkhair. Her right hand was gripping firmly a thin pointed spear. Her proud and slender figure of a horsewoman breathed courage. The people milling around greeted her with an enthusiastic uproar. Abulkhair himself could not help taking a look at her and her beauty astounded him. "That's alright, if God is willing tomorrow she will be mine!" the khan thought to himself and put spurs to his horse. It was not the first time that he had seen her, and he had long decided she was worthy of his yurta...

A berkutshe *prepares to loose his eagle on the winter steppe (Vladimir Tugalev)*

However, Sultan Janybek was on the alert and watched the khan closely. He had noticed the changing expressions on Abulkhair's face and was now certain that the khan was up to something evil. Janybek glanced over the bright-coloured crowd furtively, trying to determine the one who was to kill him. Suddenly he spotted three horsemen whose clothes were not as rich as those of the rest. They stayed away from the crowd and the sultan sensed the stare of the one a little ahead of the other two. "These commoners have never before taken part in the khan's chases," he thought. "Besides, they can hardly be from the khan's retinue. So it is them that I have to beware of..."

Ilyas Yesenberlin, The Charmed Sword, Part 1 of The Nomads, translated into English by the Ilyas Yesenberlin Foundation, 2000

Birth and Infancy

During the first 40 days following childbirth, a mother and her child may only be visited by their closest relatives. During this period, the child remains nameless. The reason for this originally pagan habit can be traced to the high rate of child mortality in nomads' yurts in days gone by. It was thought that newborn children were envoys from the underworld and that this world constantly called them to. After 40 days, one could be more or less certain that the child's attachment to the underworld was weakening, and so the child was given its name at the morning prayer on the 40th day.

Namegiving is performed either by the mullah or by the eldest person in the family. He reads loudly from the Koran and speaks the child's name into its ear three times. Thereupon the child is washed in a bowl with 40 spoonfuls of water, coins and silver jewellery. Among Kazakhs, silver has a magical, purifying significance. For the first time, the child's hair and nails are cut. After the cleansing, the silver is divided among the women in the company. Sweets are wrapped up in the infant's shirt, which is hung around the neck of a dog, which is then driven away. A merry chase ensues: the sweets are for the children who catch the dog. A woman who wishes to bear a child takes the shirt. This custom is called *iy kopek*—dog's shirt.

When a child takes its first steps, another beautiful old ritual is celebrated: cutting the bonds (*tunas kisser*). Two intertwined tapes, one black and one white, are tied in a figure of eight around the child's ankles. A guest especially invited by the family for the occasion then cuts the child's bonds from its ankles. This ritual is believed to strengthen the child's good fortune in life.

Some Kazakhs celebrate their anniversaries not simply each year, but in cycles of 12 years according to the Eastern calendar. This birthday is called *mussel has* and is celebrated with great pomp; after all, it has to count for another 12 years.

Death, Mourning and Remembrance

In 1867 Alfred Brehm wrote of Kazakh funerals: "Every family is ready to make the greatest sacrifices to celebrate a splendid party in the honour and memory of a deceased family member; everyone, including the poorest, seeks to adorn the tomb of his dead loved ones to the best of his ability, and everyone would consider it contemptible not to give the greatest honour to the dead."

All friends and relatives are invited after the death of a family member. Only men take part in the funeral; women perform the lamentation of the dead and prepare the funeral meal, which takes place seven days after the deceased's death. The funeral takes place at a *befit*, a cemetery far from the deceased's dwelling place. After having been washed, the body is wrapped in a shroud that he bought himself during his life. Thus covered, he is brought to the grave on a camel, a horse—or these days, in a car. He is laid in a grave, which is no more than chest-deep, in a vault facing Mecca. The tomb is not closed, but simply covered with planks or stones. The body dries out within a few weeks in this remarkably hygienic manner of burial.

The women lament the deceased for a whole year. After exactly a year, the friends and relatives meet again for a grand memorial feast, which marks the end of the mourning period when "normal" life resumes. Mourning clothes are exchanged for normal dress. In days of old, the dead man's horse used to be slaughtered for the occasion and its meat divided among the poor.

Remembrance of the dead is held more sacred among Kazakhs than anything else. A Kazakh sees the place where his ancestors are buried as his home forever. It is an unwritten law that each Kazakh knows his ancestors' names back at least seven generations.

National Dress

The *kalpak* or felt hat with its upright edge is still often seen in the countryside. It provides ideal protection against both sun and rain. The *tyubeteyka*, a round cap, is also widely worn. Unfortunately, other elements of national dress have become relatively rare. In fact, Kazakhs' traditional costumes used to have a rich variety according to dwelling place,

A row of aksakals *attend an event decked out in beautifully embroidered* shapans *and* kalpaks *(Yevgeni Bjelousov)*

Resplendent in national costume showing emblematic motifs, a family of Kazakhs stand proudly with their coveted eagles and tazy *hunting dogs (Vladimir Tugalev)*

tribe, membership of lower or upper levels of the population, as well as the occasion. What they had in common was their colourfulness and their rich adornment with fur trimming and ornaments, embroidered or appliquéd with felt and leather. Men's costumes mainly displayed animal motifs, whereas on those of women plant tendrils or blossom themes prevailed. Kazakhs were once able to recognize to which tribe another man belonged by his garment's ornaments, but with the abandonment of national clothing, this feature has disappeared as well.

On festive occasions many elderly, but also some younger Kazakhs, dress up in national costume. The men's costumes include the *shapan*, a long coat made of heavy velvet, and the kalpak or tyubeteyka as headwear, which in winter are replaced by the *boric*, a round fur cap, or the *tymak*, a beautiful fox pelt hat with ear and neck protection. During the cold season, a heavy sheepskin coat replaces the shapan.

According to their status, girls and women wear a long gown with a lavish flounce or patterned border or a skirt, a white or multicoloured silk shirt and over it a hip-length waistcoat, or *kamsol*. The men's waistcoat is called a *kaftan*. The coat-like cover worn over it is called a *khalat*. Particularly beautiful furs are made for women. Both men and women wear trousers (*shalbar*) under the shapan, gown or skirt respectively. Trousers as we know them today were in fact invented by the Central Asian nomads, who introduced this practical garment for riding. Leather boots could also be an invention of the steppe, with or without felt stuffing according to the season. They are often richly adorned, those for women being high-heeled.

A proper Kazakh bride wears a *saukele* on her head. This is a tall hat, with or without a plume. Its position high up in the air symbolises the bride's purity. Making clothes for the family is a woman's obligation and demands a lot of skill. To understand just how intricate and beautiful Kazakh traditional clothing can be, simply visit the Central State Museum in Almaty, the Presidential Cultural Centre in Astana or one of the many local history museums.

Religion

Even though Kazakhs are traditionally Sunni Muslims, Kazakhstan is not an Islamic state. President Nazarbayev firmly stresses to the outside world, and increasingly at home since the terrorist attack of 9/11, the value of a secular state policy and equal rights for all religious beliefs. There are three main religions in Kazakhstan: Islam, and Orthodox and Evangelical Christianity. As well as these, there exist a wide variety of independent communities of

The Maschur Zhusup Mosque in Pavlodar is a huge and impressive building (Dagmar Schreiber)

believers. It is quite natural that Kazakhstan, with its multitude of different peoples, should harbour a diverse collection of religious creeds.

Polytheistic and shamanistic beliefs were initially predominant among the nomad peoples living in the territory of Kazakhstan, elements of which melded with Islam and other religions as they grew in power and influence. Islamic islands existed in the south of Kazakhstan's present-day territory, usually among sedentary communities, and Islam obtained a strong foothold here in the 8th and 9th centuries following the Arabian conquest.

During the 18th and 19th centuries the Russians brought the Orthodox faith with them as they conquered the land; the Volga Germans introduced the Evangelical faith, and at a more modest level Catholicism.

Today, the construction of mosques can be seen everywhere. But along with this, although with less fanfare, synagogues and Christian places of worship are also being opened. Both Islam and other beliefs fit well into efforts to counter post-Soviet ideological doctrine, and national self-awareness and Islam are being linked together. A religion stressing esteem and hospitality, tolerance and respect for the elderly, resonates with Kazakh traditions. Islam is

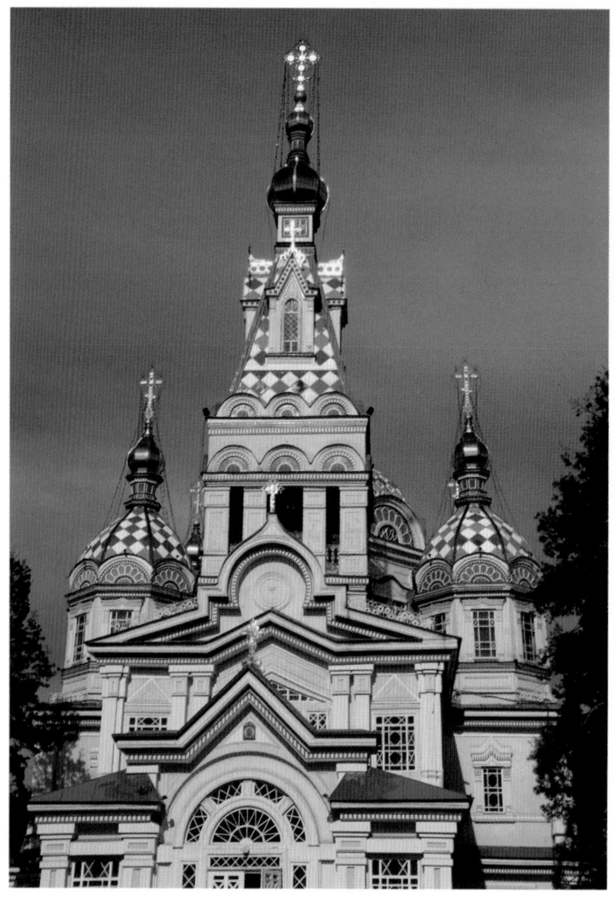

of great cultural significance here, but is rarely put into practice in an overtly religious manner. There also remain many ancient and traditional elements within the culture that mingle with Islam.

Many factors will determine the answer to the oft-posed question of whether Kazakhstan will become more Islamic in the future. Of these, the country's social development and level of education are the most important. Of course fluctuations in domestic and foreign politics are bound to play a role in the process as well. An attempt to reinforce pan-Islamism is inevitably taking place, since on the Islamic world's northern flank all sorts of interests are at stake—not least Kazakhstan's economic wealth. At present, however, neither the President's moderate religious policy nor the attitude of the country's believers give any reason for concern. According to data provided by the Institute for Socio-Economic Information and Strategic Studies, only 15–20 percent of the 42 percent of the population who consider themselves Muslims, are profoundly religious.

In September 2001, Pope John-Paul II paid a visit to Kazakhstan. President Nazarbayev received the head of the Catholic Church as a state guest, and hundreds of thousands turned up in order to be blessed by him, including many "officials". In his address, the Pope praised the spirit of openness and good neighbourliness that facilitate the peaceful coexistence of so many peoples within the borders of a single country. It seems President Nazarbayev's concept of allowing religious freedom is working very well.

The crosses of the Holy Ascension Cathedral in Almaty's Panfilov Park shine in the late-afternoon sunlight (Jeremy Tredinnick)

THE ARTS

The Kazakh homeland and the hard but free way of life on its vast steppe have always been the fundamental subject for all forms of Kazakh art. For many centuriest the art of steppe nomads and sedentary farmers and craftsmen was by and large functional in some way. It consisted of adornment, symbols of tribal adherence on implements such as clothing, carpets, yurts, horse bridles, furniture and tools, a constant accompaniment to daily life and popular festivities, serving to pass on knowledge and experience.

The separation of art and life's daily routine took place relatively recently, in the middle of the 19th Century. At this point, written Kazakh literature took shape, followed by Kazakh theatre, and soon schools of fine art and musical academies began to appear (music and story-telling through the spoken word had become embedded in nomadic culture centuries earlier). In all these artistic sectors, Kazakhstan has produced masters of the first rank within a relatively short period of time.

APPLIED ARTS

Hardly a single visitor leaves Kazakhstan without a felt, woven or sewn carpet, a saddle bottle, a horsewhip or a piece of white silver jewellery embellished with semiprecious stones. Many a tourist has already taken a dombra or a beautifully carved box home, while the number of travellers who have received a shapan (coat), kamsol or kalpak from a generous host must number in the thousands.

Traditionally, any object of utility is always adorned and decorated. Even if today this custom is practised mostly for the sake of tourism, and national clothing is only seen at festivals, the applied arts are still passed on to future generations. A good example of the will to maintain this cultural connection with the past is the "arts village" of Sheber Aul near Almaty, where fine-arts masters publicly display their workmanship as artisans, and teach apprentices eager to carry on the tradition. Walk round Almaty's galleries and you will find plenty of—mostly—tasteful crafts.

MUSIC

Music has played a dominant role in Kazakhs' lives for centuries. During the golden era of the Kazakh nation and its nomadic culture in the 16th Century, a person was literally accompanied from the cradle to the grave by music. Every life event had its own special customs, accompanied by songs and instrumental pieces (*kyu*). A young girl had absolutely no moral claim on marriage if she could not add a self-composed song to the dowry. A young man could only declare his love for a girl in the form of a song. Complex musical compositions were played during wedding parties. A person's death brought about a new song as well. And if an ageing man could not discover a gifted songwriter among his

acquaintances, he would compose the mourning lament himself and leave it behind for the occasion.

Music and poetry are the very thought of the Kazakh nation. Through them religious and cosmic allegories could be expressed, and knowledge of nature, man and historic events could be passed on. In centuries past, music and song were vitally important because they compensated for the overall absence of a written language. This led to the formation of a remarkable unity between singers, called *akyn*, and the people who listened avidly to their music. By improvisation and in dialogue with his audience, the akyn created both a work of art and a testimony to his life and times. The audience decided in a "democratic" manner whether or not the piece of art was to survive: it was accepted or else sank into oblivion.

This direct and democratic evaluation of music and poetry remains alive in the tradition of the *aytis*. An aytis is a public contest for akyns, each of whom picks up a special theme to create a song, or *kyui*. This particular Kazakh form of art reached its apogee by the turn of the 19th and 20th centuries. At that time, society had become engaged in many arguments, which were expressed in a poetical and musical form of debate. Representatives of different genres took turns during the aytis in rivalling one another: *zhyrau* (poets and performers of epic verse), *zhyrshy* (storytellers of great epics), akyn, *seri* and *saly* (improvising poets) and *kyuishi* (composers and instrumental virtuosos) all competed. Music and speech always formed an inseparable unity in the process (the kyuishi presented their kyui with an explanation of their content prior to their performance). This form of aytis dwindled during the second half of the 20th Century and has only been rejuvenated in the last decade (winners now receive valuable prizes). It is also interesting to observe how the Kazakh art

Above: Beautiful examples of classic dombras can be seen in the Museum of Folk Musical Instruments in Almaty (Jeremy Tredinnick). Left: For Kazakhs, music is an intrinsic part of their cultural and artistic roots (Gunter Kapelle)

Kazakh Gold

By *Renato Sala and Jean-Marc Deom*

During the first millennium BC, the Eurasian steppes from Hungary to Manchuria were blessed with a cool, moist climate that proved a fertile home for nomadic groups famed for three cultural elements: horses, weapons and gold. Greek and Roman historians such as Herodotus, Eforus, Diodorus, Posidonius, Strabo, Pliny the Younger, Ptolemy, Dio Cassius and Marcellinus all referred to the presence of these nations, as did inscriptions on Achaemenid Persian monuments. They were tribes of mounted and armed shepherds, prospering on a diet of milk and meat, patriarchal but very respectful towards women, organized around military leaders of aristocratic lineage and often uniting in large confederations to plunder distant bounty. When their chiefs died, they were buried with weapons and harnessed horses in huge funerary mounds (*kurgans*) aligned majestically with the undulations of the steppe, together with a staggering amount of golden jewellery, appliqués and horse trappings, shaped and adorned with animal motives in Scythian-Siberian animalistic style.

Today, the treasures of the early nomads displayed in Kazakhstan and at the Hermitage museum in St Petersburg represent only the remnant of tons of golden objects dug from tombs and smelted during the 17th and 18th centuries, and indeed during millennia prior to that.

Why precious metals?

Huge treasure troves of precious metals hidden as hoards appeared among settled peoples in the Middle East and Europe during the Early Bronze Age, and by the second millennium BC were being converted into accumulative commercial capital through trade. However, among the pastoralist peoples of the steppes, wealth was mainly represented by herds of animals. These also had an accumulative potential: they grew quickly when wider ecological niches were exploited through mobility, but were highly perishable when immobile or badly managed. Additionally, they were very sensitive to environmental and political changes, determining quick changes in fortune.

As a result, when in the hands of mounted nomads free to move in open spaces by social alliances or military superiority, herds played the role of "pastoralist capital"—wherever they were at any given time was the centre of power. Given this geographical shifting, the function of funerary monuments broadened to become a vital element in land claims, used as signs of genealogical association and tribal identification. With this socioeconomic background, the nomads came to view precious metals not as treasure or a means of exchange, but more indirectly as a status symbol, a seal of alliance and confederation. This explains their extraordinary abundance in funerary monuments in the form of items endowed with canonical traits.

Silver and gold are ideal for metalwork due to their high malleability. In the steppe region they were abundant and could be worked to a high standard using techniques already well developed in the Middle East since the third millennium BC. These included the production of sheet metal and wires; relief work by hammering out a traced leaf of 0.1–0.3mm from the reverse side on a negative mould (embossing), or by beating down its right side to the ground of a positive mould (chasing, eventually by double positive-negative mould); engraving a design on leaves of 0.8–1.2mm by removing material with a sharp tool (chiselling); one-sided casting by pouring hot metal into an open mould, or two-sided casting through a double-mould and lost-

An aerial view of the Issyk Kurgan—where the "Golden Man" was discovered—gives an idea of the sheer size of these important sites (Renato Sala and Jean-Marc Deom)

wax process; welding together different metal pieces; enamelling of holes in the metal with vitreous substances; and the setting of precious stones (lapis lazuli, turquoise, emerald, garnet, carnelian, sardonic, chalcedony, quartz and agate) with a cabochon cut. All these techniques have been found among Kazakhstan's ancient metal relics.

What was their purpose?

The golden artefacts of the early nomads were of a functional, ritual or strictly decorative nature, but were all expressly produced to be elements of the funerary assemblage. They consisted of body ornaments (diadems, hairpins and combs, earrings, necklaces and pendants, armlets, bracelets, rings), articles of clothing (plaques and beads, fibulae, breastplates, belts and masks), trappings for horses, cups, weapons (arrowheads, spearheads), hilts and sheaths of daggers and swords, handles of mirrors and whetstones, and appliqués for wooden objects (ritual vessels and ceremonial goat-horns).

All of these had an equivalent for daily use in poorer materials (ornaments, cups, weapons, mirrors, whetstones) but, when created in or adorned with silver or gold and buried with the dead, their symbolic meaning was emphasized, connected with the culture's world-views and heraldic functions. Metal has in itself an alchemic significance due to its ability to be fashioned into specific forms from its hot liquid state, while gold also exhibits incorruptibility. Body ornaments and necklaces were endowed with symbolic power through clenched, protective forms; weapons provided defence, with whetstones to sharpen them; and mirrors and masks duplicated reality.

Style and form

Many artefacts were shaped and engraved with forms of animals typical to the steppe environment. Figures of lions, deer and reindeer were characteristic of the ancient steppe north of the Black Sea; wolves, bears and stags in the Urals; leopards, horses, camels, mountain goats and bighorn sheep in the Kazakhstan steppe; and tigers and elk in the southern Siberian regions. Also represented were wild boars and hedgehogs, eagles and griffon vultures, wild geese, ducks and swans. As well as animals, fantastic chimerical creatures such as griffins (a combination of a bird, a land predator and a hoofed animal), horned horses and camels with jaws, as well as some human images have been found.

A close-up inspection of the Kargaly diadem (a crown-band) shows the high level of skill attained by the ancient craftsmen who worked gold and semiprecious stones into stunning pieces of jewellery (Renato Sala and Jean-Marc Deom)

Geometric and floral forms and simple metonymic elements like horns were used to decorate small plaques or peripheral edges. Generally speaking, during the 7th–4th centuries BC in the western steppes, decorations using single animals were abundant; during the following classic era (4th century BC–2nd century AD) and always in the southern Siberian regions, complex compositions depicting predators attacking and overthrowing hoofed animals were more commonly found. Different animals were chosen for different metal objects: predator-prey scenes decorated breastplates and belts; heads of ovicaprids decorated the top of hilts and handles; predators decorated the edges of incense burners or coiled up around a ring.

The predator-prey composition and the so-called "animalistic" style of its artistic realization were the main aesthetic features of the artistic tradition of the early nomads. This is manifest in both the rock art and metalwork of the region, but it is within the latter, in adapting to the limited space of the metal objects, that it reached its highest expression. There are three main stylistic features: the dynamic, tense, realistic but hyperbolic forms of animal bodies; their realization through an assemblage of fixed stylized iconographic elements valid for different species; and their dramatic contortion and complex composition in order to fill the whole surface of an object. The

European steppes and the southern Siberian regions represent two radiating poles of the so-called "Scythian-Siberian animalistic style": the former offers more classic features inspired by the Greco-Hellenistic world, while the latter presents the most original and exaggerated variants, with the introduction of metaphoric forms and sometimes bizarre constructions.

Meaning

As a whole, the subjects and styles of Kazakhstan's ancient gold artefacts reflected the world-views of the military elite of the early nomadic mounted warriors. Power and swiftness were essential qualities of life, underlined by a reverence for very aggressive or highly dynamic animal species. Conflict was an immutable law of nature; sacrificial animals such as stags or bighorns with bent legs reflected the positive presence of death within the circle of life. A triadic partition of the world (quite evident in the decorations of the hat of the Golden Man of Issyk) was represented by different species: birds for the sky; ungulates for the Earth's surface; predators, hedgehogs and mysterious carnivorous animals for the underworld.

A beautifully wrought snow leopard leaps up from mountain peaks (Courtesy of the Museum of Gold and Precious Metals, Astana, and the Foundation for International Arts and Education, www.fiae.org)

Some animals constituted a bridge between these three spheres. For example, the link between earth and sky was provided by some ungulates playing the role of sacrificial animals endowed with psychic powers: stags, because of their tree-like antlers; bighorn sheep and mountain goats, with annually growing horns, measuring the yearly cycle of the sun; horses as the speediest carriers. So we also find metaphorical stags with beaked muzzles and horses with wings and stag or ibex horns. Predators were menacing underground forces, but in some cases could become protectors: dogs, being the toughest fighters, plunderers, killers and, together with vultures, eaters of corpses, were symbols of military groups. The link between the forces of the underworld and the earth's surface was provided by the wild boar, half carnivore and half-hoofed, sometimes curled and sometimes elongated, and by the camel, ungulate but potentially furious and malicious.

Key sites

In Kazakhstan, significant golden objects of the Scythian-Siberian tradition have been discovered in dozens of sites. Four of them have provided the most impressive finds: the "Golden Man" of the Issyk kurgan in Semirechye (early Iron Saka period, 5th–3rd centuries BC); the appliqués on horse outfits of the Berel barrows in the Altai region of East Kazakhstan, attributed to Saka tribes of the 5th–3rd centuries BC; the Kargaly diadem in Semirechye (a detail of a man riding a griffin, early Iron Wusun period, 1st–2nd centuries AD); and the Aral-tobe "golden warrior", attributed to the Sarmatian tribes of the 1st–2nd centuries AD. They have all provided heraldic emblems for the newborn Republic of Kazakhstan, and are now displayed in the Museum of Gold and Precious Metals in Astana.

Archaeologists Renato Sala and Jean-Marc Deom have lived and worked in Kazakhstan for more than 10 years. They are members of the Laboratory of Geoarchaeology, part of the Institute of Geologo-Geographical Research, Ministry of Education and Science of Kazakhstan. For more information on their important work visit www.lgakz.org

A golden hoop earring with horse detail (Courtesy of the A. Margulan Museum of Archaeology, Almaty, and the Foundation for International Arts and Education, www.fiae.org)

of musical improvisation links up with a similar form of art from the other side of the globe: jazz. Kazakh ethno-jazz is a burgeoning form that is well worth checking out if you are a jazz lover.

Visitors to Kazakhstan are often astounded by how many songs—with so many stanzas—their host knows, and is willing to perform at the drop of a hat. Many Kazakh men and women can accompany themselves on a musical instrument. This is usually a *dombrya* or *dombra*, a double-stringed plucked instrument with a rich timbre. Listen to an experienced dombra player drawing lofty and passionate tones and rhythmic patterns from his instrument and the association with the vast steppe and the clip-clop of horses' hooves is obvious. In general, Kazakhstan's natural world is an extremely rich source of musical inspiration. One of the earliest and most important collectors and explorers of Kazakh popular music, Alexandr Viktoryevich Zatayevich, called the Kazakh steppe a "sea of music".

This is not only reflected in the music of the dombra but also in that of the legendary *kobyz* (a two-stringed bow instrument), with a far-reaching, magical timbre, the faint melodies of the *zhetig* (a seven-stringed plucked instrument) and the lofty melodies of the *sybyzgy* (flute).

Folk orchestras such as Sazgen, Otrar Sazy and Sybyzgy Sazy and most of all the folk ensemble Shalkyma of the National Eurasian University have revived ancient musical instruments such as the *kyl-kobyz* and *astayak*, and percussion instruments such as the *dabyl*, the *dauylpas* and the *shandauyl*, which were outlawed in Soviet times for being "shamanistic tools". For the majority of audiences, including Kazakhs, such sounds are still thought of as exotic. These orchestras play Kazakh classics: famous dombra works by Kurmangazy Sagyrbayev and Dina Nurpeysova, Dauletkerey, Tattinbet, Kazangap and others, sybyzgy pieces by Sarmalay, kobyz music by Khorkhyt and Yshylas, but also by modern composers such as Adil Bestybayev, Serik Abdinurov and Beybut Aldenbayev.

Kamerata Kazakhstana, a chamber orchestra founded in 1998 by Gaukhar Mirzabekova, has become renowned for the great talent of its exclusively young musicians. Violin virtuosos Marat Bisengaliyev and Ayman Musakhodzhayeva, pianists Zhanya Aubakirova and Vyacheslav Uzbekov, kobyz player Raushan Orazbayeva, vocalists Bibigul Tulegenova and Nurzhamal Uzenbayeva, the instrumental ensemble Ulytau, the rock group Roksonaki—all of these are world-class representatives of a highly musical nation.

If at all possible you should try to experience the richness of the Kazakh musical sound at a concert, but if this is not possible make a visit to the Museum of Folk Musical Instruments in Almaty, which offers a modest overview and a chance to hear the instruments.

The Meeting, *a 1927 painting by Salihitidin Aitbayev, hangs in the Kasteyev State Museum of Art (Jeremy Tredinnick)*

VISUAL ARTS

Visual art has existed in the territory of Kazakhstan in the form of rock drawings, or petroglyphs since the Neolithic Age (see Special Topic on page 224), but the modern form of artistic painting is relatively young in Kazakhstan. The Kasteyev State Museum of Art in Almaty offers a comprehensive and very impressive overview of works by Kazakh painters (as well as sculptors) from the 19th Century to today.

The realistic works of the master Ablaikhan Kasteyev (1904–1973) show a country full of contradictions. They include early pieces such as the light and whimsical portrait of folk minstrel Zhambyl, and the image of a crowd at the natural ice-skating rink of Medeu, to a panorama showing the construction of the Turksib railway through the steppe, and the construction of a dam on the Ili River at Kapshagay—more serious works undertaken to illustrate the progress of Russian "civilization" of the Kazakh homeland. What Kasteyev's works all have in common is a high level of drawing precision. For 40 years, Kasteyev accompanied the development of Kazakhstan with his paintings.

Many paintings from the 1940s and early 1950s can be described as "socialist euphoria". Painters like Bortnikov were forced to glorify Soviet power. The national themes persisted, but euphoria disappeared as the 1950s wore on. After the ideological reckoning of Stalinism had been settled, the arts were also engaged in efforts to find an identity of their own. Works of people like Telzhanov, Shayakhmetov and Ismailova show a cautious trend away from uniform ideological positions.

The 1960s and 70s generated a huge variety of both critical and less critical social-realist paintings. A wonderful example is the painting *Prazdnichiy dyen* (Festivity Day) by Aralbayev, which hangs in the Kasteyev State Museum of Art. During the 1980s, realism went over the top, and paintings could be described as "satirical realism" (the paintings of Aliyev should be mentioned in this context). In addition, two Kazakh sculptors, whose expressive works catch the attention, have boosted the appeal of this form in the country. The first is Rakhmanov, whose work is also exhibited in the Kasteyev Museum, and the second is Shokan Tolesh who creates small, emotional bronze and stone sculptures.

A wide variety of artistic schools and trends coexist in independent Kazakhstan. From picturesque landscapes and political portraits to mysticized historic and national themes,

Below right: Ablaikhan Kasteyev's Portrait of Khan Kenesary, *a 19th Century Kazakh hero*
Below left: Contemporary paintings such as this beautiful work are exhibited and sold in the Kasteyev State Museum of Art's second-floor gallery (Jeremy Tredinnick x2)

A vibrant 1940 painting by Leonid Leontiev named Marketplace in Kolhoz *(Jeremy Tredinnick)*

often shrouded in veils of oil and chalk, from surrealistic representations of a changing world to still lifes—anything can be found. A good place to look into modern visual arts is the Tengri-Umay gallery in Almaty. In 2002 the highly motivated staff of this gallery organized the Kazakh artistic biennale of the same name. What strikes one in the paintings of most Kazakh artists is their colourfulness: the magic of their strong, warm, earthy colours is enchanting.

Architecture

In comparison with Europe, Kazakhstan has very little to offer in terms of ancient architectural treasures. That said, a must-see building is the magnificent Mausoleum of Khoja Ahmed Yasawi in Turkistan, dating from the time of the Timurids and now recognized by UNESCO as a World Heritage site. Its classic Islamic style was used as the template for many of Samarkand and Bukhara's later architectural masterpieces. More or less identifiable remnants of the cities of a northern branch of the Silk Road have been preserved in many places in the south of Kazakhstan.

This aerial shot of the impressive Mausoleum of Khoja Ahmed Yasawi shows the ruins of the ancient town to the west (Renato Sala and Jean-Marc Deom)

Throughout the country, graveyards (*mazary*) and mausoleums can be spotted, some of which have been skilfully sculpted in stone, while others consist of either raw or burnt clay tablets. On the Mangyshlak Peninsula dozens of important necropolis sites unexpectedly pop up in the middle of the desert, scattered with sandstone mausoleums, ornamented tombstones and stelae.

In the cities, buildings more than 100 years old have already been classified as historic. Most of the current cities were built in the 19th Century in the wake of the Russian conquest; not much is left of the early citadels and the plain wooden houses surrounding them—and unfortunately what is left of them tends to disappear under the tracks of the bulldozers which clear the site for the villas of the nouveaux riches. Prestigious 19th Century Russian buildings can still be seen in Semey (Semipalatinsk), Petropavlovsk, Oral (Uralsk) and some other cities—including a few Russian Orthodox churches. A few simple mosques have also been preserved.

Almaty contains many fine examples of buildings constructed during the earliest phase of socialist development, but you can also find them in rather unlikely places such as Kyzylorda. Many universities, theatres and government administration buildings were built in the impressive Soviet classical style. However, visitors cannot fail to note how all Kazakh cities contain an excess of gigantic block-like socialist buildings. One can explain this gruesome homogeneity of many cities by the pressure to urbanize following the establishment of major industries. However, this hardly makes their image any more aesthetically appealing.

Classic Timurid tile and window detail on the Yasawi mausoleum's walls (Jeremy Tredinnick)

The only city being completed and modernised according to an overall master plan is Astana. The new capital is the perfect example for those who want to study modern Kazakh architecture. Government buildings feature much glass, exotic curvature and elements in the omnipresent Kazakh sky-blue. Often, domes such as those on the Presidential Cultural Centre, the Congress Hall and the Palace for State Receptions imitate the roof of a yurt. There has also been a revival of the Emperor Style from the 1950s, of which the new building of KazMunaiGaz is an example. A carefree mix of styles can be seen in residential buildings—a short distance towards the river from the KazMunaiGaz building stands a brand-new development that could have been transplanted from New York City. On the river's right bank, The Palace of Peace and Concord, a huge pyramidal structure created by UK architect Norman Foster, has been so well received that Foster's company has been employed to work on another mammoth project named Khan Shatyry, the world's largest "tent", that for its walls uses a plastic compound which absorbs the sun's heat, meaning temperatures inside will be high enough to sunbathe while it is -30°C outside during winter. Astana will soon stand alongside the likes of Dubai, Shanghai and Hong Kong in avant-garde architectural style.

Literature

Kazakh literature is rich in folkloristic poetry: sagas of Kazakh knights (*batyrs*), love tragedies, heroic epics like *Alpamys* and fairy tales, in which witty rascals rip off rich and ignorant beys. A striking assessment of this traditional art comes from Yuri Rytcheu, an author from the Chuchi people: "No other human craft breathes such optimism, such belief in the victory of good over evil, such refined humour and such sensitive understanding for social harmony and justice, as we find it in the oral tradition of popular poetry." The amazing thing is that countless verses, songs and tales of truly epic length have passed from generation to generation for centuries with great accuracy, both in terms of meaning and wording, to the extent that historic events can be accurately reconstructed with the help of other sources.

A statue of Abai Kunanbayev stands at the eastern end of Abai Avenue in Almaty (Jeremy Tredinnick)

In the second half of the 19th Century, scholars such as Abai (Ibrahim) Kunanbayev started writing down their compatriots' legends. Other important Kazakh writers came to the fore, like Ibray Altynsarin, who demanded that literature should not only narrate but also provide food for deep thought, and Chokan Valikhanov.

Tragically, the 1930s witnessed the annihilation of an entire generation of humanist writers: Saken Seyfullin (1894–1938), Akhmet Baytursinuly (1873–1938), Mirzakhyp Dulatov (1885-1931), Magzhan Zhumabayev (1893-1938) and Beimbet Maylin (1898-1937), among many others. Those few who did not end up in Stalin's death camps only succeeded in doing so by renouncing their convictions on the advice of their colleagues. A prominent example is Mukhtar Auezov (1897–1961); during the 1930s Auezov came under attack for allegedly propagating a feudal Kazakhstan in his life's work, the four-volume *Abai's Way*, which is a crucial contribution to Kazakhstan's self-awareness. Ultimately, Auezov was granted the Order of Lenin for his four-volume book after Stalin's death, recognizing that it offers an encyclopaedic view of the Kazakh way of life during the 19th and early 20th centuries.

Many good writers dedicated their work to historical topics. The most important are Anwar Alimzhanov (1930–1994) and Ilyas Yesinberlin (1915–1983), whose trilogy *The Nomads* is a thriller-like description of Kazakh history from the 15th–16th centuries, and to this day is among the best-read books in Kazakhstan. In his books and dramas Takhaoui Akhtanov (1923–1994) depicts everyday life in the countryside during the 1950s and 1960s. His book *Confession in the Steppe* has also been published in German.

A gradual transformation from enthusiastic believer in Soviet progress to disappointed sceptic can be seen in the books of Kyrgyz-Kazakh writer, publicist and politician Chingis

Aitmatov (born 1928). His books, *The Day Lasts More Than a Hundred Years* and *The Place of Execution*, are set in Kazakhstan. His other works, set in the Kyrgyz mountains and the valley of the Chuy, display the comparative life of the neighbouring countries.

Olzhas Suleymenov (born 1936) is also known both as a politician and a writer. His personal development from the writer of early poems like *Earth, Bow before Man!* into a vehement critic of the atomic tests near Semipalatinsk, is noteworthy. Suleymenov was one of the initiators of the protest movement Nevada-Semipalatinsk and after its legalisation he became its chairman. In 1975 he published his nonetheless controversial work *As y ya*—"I" (in Kazakh) followed by "and I" (in Russian)", pronounced "Asia" when spoken together. In this work, Suleymenov tries to demonstrate that Kazakhs are a nation born to rule the world. This should perhaps be understood in context—at that time the self-confidence of Kazakhs was very low—but the book can certainly lead to misunderstandings.

Abish Kekibaliyev (born 1939), like Aitmatov and Suleymenov, is not only known for his historical, epic and poetical work and for his numerous translations, but also for his civic engagement.

Mukhtar Shakhanov (born 1942) went from tractor driver to writer and politician and became one of the most respected authors in Central Asia. The work of this lyricist, essayist, playwright and prose writer has been translated into 30 languages. In the 1970s he became engaged in civil rights and ecological movements. His work *Four Mothers* gives his impressions of Kazakhstan's rebellious youth movement in 1986. *The Wandering Path of Civilisation* is a grim poem on progress and loss of values. *The Weeping of the Hunter Over the Abyss* and *Night of Thoughts on Socrates*, both of which he wrote with Chingis Aitmatov, are works of great wisdom, the relevance of which stretch far beyond Central Asia.

Dukenbay Doszhan (born 1942), though sharing his literary contemporaries' historical pessimism, ostentatiously stays aloof from public life. He published his selected works in 13 volumes in 2002. *Silk Road* brings the Shah of Khorezm and Genghis Khan back to life. In 1983, his work *Wind-lions' Manes* was translated into Russian by Anatoly Kim and into German by Herold Belger. Doszhan broke away from the Soviet-style polarising of heroism at an early stage. He adds a human dimension to his historical heroes, after the tradition of Dostoyevsky, recognizing that no man is only good or evil. His biography of Auezov, *Mukhtar's Way*, is among the best-read Auezov biographies in Kazakhstan.

Abdishamil Nurpeysov (born 1924) is the chairman of the PEN Club in Kazakhstan. His best-known work is *Blood and Sweat*. The one-time fisherman also won fame with his book *The Dying Sea*, a stirring, admonishing work on the fate of a fishermen's village beside the Aral Sea as the great lake shrank drastically.

ALDAR KÖSE'S MAGIC FUR COAT

Aldar Köse is one of the great characters of Kazakh folklore—similar to the Uzbek Hodzha Nasreddin or his Flemish-German counterpart Tijl Uilenspiegel/Till Eulenspiegel. The anti-hero of numerous stories repeated through the centuries around yurt fires across the steppe, the scoundrel Aldar Köse always has a sharp nose when it comes to tricking rich but ignorant contemporaries, or engaging in adventures with demons, giants and monsters.

In a society where a long beard and the possession of large herds of livestock were a precondition for membership of the upper class, tales of the wandering, quick-witted "beardless deceiver"—the literal translation from Kazakh—served as a lightning conductor for the frustrations of the lower classes. The oral tradition of satirical tales about Aldar Köse has endured, with the sympathies—naturally—always lying with the waggish champion of the poor and repressed. Below is a typical tale of Aldar's cunning and mischievous humour:

One can only survive a cold winter like this in a fox fur coat! But Aldar Köse froze day after day in his short, threadbare coat, full of holes. One day, he was riding over the steppe, his hands and feet already completely stiff and his nose blue from the frost. If only he could find a warm yurt at last! The wind was howling and all but tore the rascal's ears off. And nowhere in the wide steppe was the smoke of an aul to be seen…

He whipped his mount, but it failed to make the old bag of bones run any faster. It merely shook its mane and trotted on.

"When the horse is bad, the road is long," the horseman said to himself and shook his head. He would have to ride on for a long, long time, no sound of dogs barking, not a single yurt to be seen in the steppe. Who knew what could happen with such a frost.

All of a sudden, the horseman spotted another rider coming up from the opposite direction. The powerful trot of the horse made it easy for Aldar to guess: there comes a bey. Immediately, an idea struck the rascal. He flung his coat wide open, sat upright in the saddle and started to sing a cheerful tune. When the travellers met, they halted their horses and greeted one another according to etiquette. The bey in his fox fur coat was shivering with cold. Aldar Köse, however, had pulled back his cap and fanned himself with his hand, as though he were sitting under the mercilessly hot rays of the sun.

"Are you not cold?" the bey asked the scoundrel.

"Why, it may well be cold under your coat, but I am sweating under mine," Aldar Köse replied.

"How can you sweat under such a coat?" the bey asked in disbelief.

"So, do you not see it yourself?"

"Frankly speaking, what I see is that crows must have picked your coat to pieces. It has more holes than fur!"

"But the good thing about it is that it has so many holes. The wind blows in through one hole, and whoosh!—it blows out again through the other. And I remain warm."

"I have got to get that magic coat from him," thought the bey to himself.

"Oh how warm I would be if only I could put on the bey's fur coat," secretly rejoiced the scoundrel.

"Sell your coat to me!" said the bey in a commanding voice.

"Not for anything in the world, without my coat I would certainly freeze!"

"You will not freeze! Take my coat," proposed the bey. "It is also warm enough."

Aldar Köse turned away and pretended to be unwilling to listen. But with one eye he peered at the fox fur, while he squinted at the rich man's well-fed horse with the other.

"I shall give you my fur coat and money as well," the bey tempted him.

"Money I need naught. But if you give me the horse with the coat, I might think about it."

The bey was delighted and agreed. Immediately, he took off his fur coat and leapt from his horse. Aldar Köse put on the fox fur coat, jumped on the bey's swift horse, gave it the spurs and he was off, faster than the wind.

Now Aldar Köse had a good ride, and in his warm fox fur he wandered from aul to aul on his smart-looking horse. And wherever he came, in each yurt he was asked: "Tell us, Aldar—where did you get that fine fur and that swift horse?"

"I obtained them in exchange for a magic fur, with 70 holes and 90 patches besides!"

And Aldar cheered up the people by telling his tale of how the bey had hurled himself upon his coat full of holes and had given him his fox fur coat instead. The people laughed their heads off and thanked the comical storyteller generously with kumis and fresh flat round bread. And always when the laughter had died down, Aldar Köse added: "Only he who has covered the road can tell whether it is long or short. And only he who eats can distinguish the sweet food from the bitter."

Kyzylorda's Kazakh drama theatre was built in 1926 at a time when the town was the Russian capital in Kazakh territory (Dagmar Schreiber)

Theatre

Kazakh theatre has its roots in traditional festivities and song contests. The art of improvised declamation of poems, verses and songs was widespread both among the common people and the upper classes, and was continually cultivated and refined. The artists who entertained the people at festivals, family parties and markets with their witty performances were called *ku* or *shanshar*.

Theatre came to Kazakhstan as an independent art form along with the Russians. Drama theatres were started up in Orenburg, Omsk and Uralsk, followed later by Tatar travelling theatres. Societies of theatre lovers were established within the Kazakh intelligentsia from 1910 on, celebrating ethnographic musical evenings with performances including short satirical pieces. Today, the birth of Kazakh theatre is considered to have been the first performance of Mukhtar Auezov's *Enlik-Kebek* in 1917. Auezov had scrupulously prepared the performance as a wedding gift for one of his relatives. The performance took place in two yurts, joined together and fitted out as a theatre.

From there on, the development of Kazakh theatre moved ahead swiftly, since the Revolution, the civil war and socialist reform positively craved the accompaniment of inflammatory propaganda performances. In 1926, the first Kazakh drama theatre was founded in Kyzylorda, which was the capital at the time. In 1929, the company moved to the new capital Almaty. In the 1930s, the first actors graduated from the newly established theatre school in Almaty, which had attracted graduates from Moscow and Leningrad as teachers. The actors performed Shakespeare and Gogol, and works by a growing number of Kazakh playwrights as well. Auezov played a leading role in this.

Almost all Kazakh writers also wrote, and still write, for the theatre. All major cities in Kazakhstan have at least one theatre, in which usually one Kazakh and one Russian company perform. The best known among them are the Auezov Kazakh Drama Theatre in Almaty, in which pieces are also translated into Russian, the Lermontov Theatre in Almaty, and the Kazakh Musical Drama Theatre in Astana.

There are two grand opera houses in Kazakhstan—one in Almaty and one in Astana. Here, in addition to European opera classics, Kazakh opera and ballet are also performed. One should try to attend at least one performance of Abai, Kyz Zhibek, Birzhan y Sara, Aysulu, Yer Targyn or Alpamys.

FILM

Kazakh cinema was born in 1929 with the establishment of the first film studio Vostokkino. Most of the films made here were documentaries about Soviet development. The first feature film with a Kazakh theme and Kazakh actors, *Amangeldy*, was shot at Lenfilm in Leningrad. Based on the life of the hero Amangeldy Imanov, the film depicts life and suffering in pre-revolutionary Kazakhstan and the Kazakh liberation movement.

In 1942, during wartime, the renowned Mosfilm studios were evacuated to Almaty and stayed there until 1944, when it was safe to return to Moscow. Most of Sergey Eisenstein's well-known film *Ivan the Terrible* was shot around Almaty. Numerous war films were also made here.

With the experience gained from Mosfilm, Almaty was now able to produce its own films. The first achievement by Kazakh filmmakers was the film version of Mukhtar Auezov's *Abai's Way*. Since then, more than 100 feature films and numerous documentaries have been shot in Almaty. Both in terms of content and of form, most of them reflected the social development and political conditions of their time. Films like *Zhambyl, His Time Will Come* (about Chokan Valikhanov), *Kyz Zhibek, Sultan Beybar* and the award-winning *Land of the Forefathers* (after a novel by Olzhas Suleymenov) were about the search for Kazakh identity. A combination of literature, musical creation and cinematic art has resulted in some high-quality filmmaking.

Since the mid-1980s Kazakh film has become more self-critical, experimental and cosmopolitan. Works such as *New Worlds, Signs, Killer* and *Zhol* are the product of young film directors who display the contradictions of our times. Since 1990, more than two dozen new private film studios have been established. The fruits of this free market competition have also found important recognition on an international level. The enormous creative potential of Kazakhstan's filmmakers, however, stands in sharp contrast to the difficult working conditions.

The multi-award-winning film by Sarybaldy Narimbetov, *The Young Harmonica Player's Song*, is a perfect example of the new generation in Kazakh cinematography, in which its themes intertwine history and the modern day in an extremely impressive and sensitive manner. More recently, the epic movie *Nomad*, filmed in Kazakhstan but produced by the US-based Weinstein Company, and starring US actors in the main roles, has shown the growing interest from the West in Central Asian filmmaking potential.

As in all post-Soviet countries, a vital artistic scene has emerged which, with curiosity and a talent for improvisation, explores its own identity and possibilities—from time to time using its new liberties to an excessive degree.

Famous Kazakhs

Al-Farabi (870–950)

The real name of the man who was called the second Aristotle because of his universal knowledge was Abu-Nasr ibn-Mohammed Tarkhan ibn-Uzlag Al-Farabi. He came from the renowned city of Farab, later renamed Otrar. His studies in Baghdad and Aleppo acquainted him with the teachings of the Greek philosophers. In 160 treatises, Al-Farabi, with his creative use of the works of Plato, Aristotle, Pythagoras and Ptolemy, built up a world of ideas aimed at the reconciliation of science, philosophy and the philosophical concept of faith. There is hardly a scientific area on which he did not publish his views: philosophy and religion, ethics and aesthetics, political theory, logic and rhetoric, music, mathematics, physics, astronomy, medicine and scientific theory. Al-Farabi spent the last years of his life in Cairo, Aleppo and Damascus, where he died. The country's biggest scientific institute, the Al-Farabi Almaty State University, bears his name.

Ablai Khan (1711–1781)

Abdulmansur Ablai was a sultan until he was proclaimed Khan of the Middle Horde in 1771. He played a major role in the unification of the three Kazakh Hordes. Ablai Khan maintained an austere and thoroughly organized hierarchy of power and a strong army. At the same time, he developed a network of diplomatic and commercial connections with Russia, China and the Khanates of Zhungaria, Bukhara and Khiva. In 1740, he swore allegiance to Russia and requested integration. This saved him from imprisonment by the Zhungars: in 1740 he was released thanks to the intervention of a Russian embassy. In 1772, he reconfirmed his vow of loyalty to Russia. The Russians amply demonstrated their gratitude for the service rendered to them by Ablai Khan. The peaceful submission of a major part of the Kazakh steppe was rewarded with annual transfers of money and other forms of support. The Khan's head was displayed on the 100 tenge banknote (now replaced by a coin).

A statue of Al-Farabi looks towards the Khoja Ahmed Yasawi mausoleum in Turkistan (Jeremy Tredinnick)

THE BORAT PHENOMENON

By *Lucy Kelaart*

After the film *Borat: Cultural Learnings of America for Make Benefit Glorious Nation of Kazakhstan* debuted in cinemas throughout Europe and the United States in the autumn of 2006, Borat Sagdiyev, the pseudo Kazakh TV presenter, became Kazakhstan's best-known personality, eclipsing even President Nazarbayev on an official visit to the US by holding a mock press conference outside the White House whilst the two leaders met within.

Love him or hate him, Borat has put Kazakhstan on the map. Gone are the days when a person's first reaction to the country was "Where's that?". If you agree that there is no such thing as bad PR, then this film and Borat's associated antics have increased interest in Kazakhstan to previously unimagined heights. Within months of the film's release, the UK currency firm, Travelex, had received thousands of expressions of interest in the Kazakh tenge; one travel website rated Kazakhstan at the top of its tourist destination polls, beating both Spain and Turkey; and Kazakhstan became a media star, her pros and cons discussed on talk shows, in national newspapers, and in lifestyle magazines to a degree that would be the envy of any media-hungry celebrity.

Opinion was, of course, divided. There were those who loved the film, people who found Borat's naïve, clumsy and crude approach to life amusing and his extreme humour compelling; and those who found the film rude, offensive, and—in the case of Jewish lobbies in the United States—anti-Semitic. In an interview with *Rolling Stone* magazine, Sacha Baron Cohen (who created and played Borat) explained Borat's racist acts by stating that those parts of the film are a "dramatic demonstration of how racism feeds on dumb conformity as much as rabid bigotry". According to the film's executive producer, Dan Mazer, "Borat holds a mirror up to people; if they're horrible they'll appear that way when they're with him, and vice versa." Some of Borat's more innocent victims disagree, however, and a series of lawsuits have been filed against production company Twentieth Century Fox by individuals who felt duped by the Kazakh journalist with the innocent smile, from a pair of American college students in South Carolina to a whole gypsy village in rural Romania.

But it cannot be denied that the Kazakhs have weathered the greatest impact. It is not now possible to be a Kazakh abroad without enduring at least some mention of Borat. In Kazakhstan, on the other hand, Borat has only permeated the consciousness of the young and the urban (and state) elite. When Borat first surfaced on UK and US TV screens as part of *Da Ali G Show*, the official government response was limited to concern about Borat's moustache rather than his portrayal of their country: "He looks more like some Turk or Arab," they said. But as Borat's stature grew, so too did the Kazakh defence. By the time the film was released, Kazakh officials were eager to distance themselves from Mr Sagdiyev, instead attempting to portray the "real Kazakhstan"—a racially tolerant, secular, modern and prosperous country (a response which, according to Borat, was merely defamatory Uzbek propaganda).

As media interest continued unabated, the Kazakhs revised their strategy and began to appreciate the importance of getting the joke. Soon President Nazarbayev himself relaxed, and in a move entirely unprecedented for the leader of a post-Soviet country which still has anti-presidential defamation laws, he said: "This film was created by a comedian—so let's laugh at it —that's my attitude." While the presidential seal of approval has permeated some layers of Kazakh society (there is even a spoof website called www.stopborat.com where you can buy "Kazakhstanis Against Borat" Y-fronts, and sales of the DVD have soared to the top of Amazon.co.uk's exports to Kazakhstan), there are also those who still find Borat hard to swallow.

But as Mazer points out, Borat was never intended to be a joke on Kazakhstan. The producers chose Kazakhstan because it was a country that existed, but one people knew relatively little about. When the team was researching *Borat*, they found that the only books available were post-Soviet studies or geopolitical tracts which tended to concentrate on Kazakhstan's rich natural resources—not, as Mazer puts it, rich pickings for jokes. As a result, Borat was able to tell people anything and they were prepared to believe it—for example, that there are only seven swimming pools in the entire country, that women travel on the outside of buses, that until recently homosexuals had to wear blue hats, and that the national sport is *shurik* or dog shooting. Write it like that and it's hard to believe that anybody could believe him, but believe him they do. The people he interviews see him as an "innocent" bigot, which helps draw out their own prejudices both towards him and the kind of society they think he comes from. In this sense, Mazer says Kazakhstan is "a Trojan Horse that we've used to bring out people's prejudices". The joke is on Borat's victims rather than on Kazakhstan. "Kazakhs," he says, "should pat themselves on the back for taking Borat with such good grace."

Indeed, such is the turnaround in general opinion of the ambivalence of Borat's influence, at a performance in the heavenly surroundings of London's St James Church in May 2007, Kazakh virtuoso violinist Marat Bisengaliev led his Turan Alem Philharmonic Orchestra in the premiere of *Zere*, a work in the Kazakh idiom composed by none other than Erran Baron Cohen, Sacha's older brother. In fact, Bisengaliev invited Erran to write *Zere* after hearing his rollicking score for the Borat movie. Whether *Zere* represents an olive branch of reconciliation or a fig leaf to hide embarrassment, it certainly gave rise to rapturous applause from Kazakh and Brit alike in the audience. Nor could one mistake the affection shown to the young composer at the reception afterwards, with the Kazakh Ambassador to the UK praising Erran for "capturing the authentic spirit of the Kazakh steppe", and jokingly offering to make him an honorary Kazakh citizen.

Kenesary Kasymov (1802–1847)

It took decades before the real effects of the 18th Century khans' submission to Russia became obvious. In part due to patriotic considerations, but certainly also due to personal gain, they had sold the Kazakh steppe to the Russians. Kenesary Kasymov, a grandson of Ablai Khan, did not share these principles. At a time when the khans had been stripped of their authority by the Russian occupiers, while reinforcement of the Russian military presence in the steppe meant that the Kazakhs were being pushed away from their fertile pasturelands, he fought for his country's independence, the reinstating of the Khanate, and the re-engagement of the beys. Between 1837 and 1846 he commanded a movement—at times counting 20,000 armed men—and put vast stretches of land under its control.

Against the officially declared prohibition of the Russian authorities, Kenesary was elected Khan in 1841, in the rebel-controlled Torgay steppe. He initiated economic reforms and attempted to settle relations with the Russians in a peaceful manner. This failed completely, and an army was prepared to march against him. In his attempts to mobilise the entire Kazakh population against this army, he resorted to punitive action against auls that were unwilling to submit themselves to his vision. This lost him his social base and he was forced to withdraw onto a peninsula in the Ili delta, which was hard to capture. Following the unconditional surrender by the Middle Horde to Russian authority, he tried to continue his struggle from the Kyrgyz mountain range. Eventually, together with 32 of his sultans, he was taken prisoner and executed.

Chokan Valikhanov (1835–1865)

The life of this man, who died of tuberculosis before he reached the age of 30, reflects the way in which the Kazakh people were torn apart at the height of Russian colonisation. Valikhanov was a great-grandson of the renowned Ablai Khan. Being a sultan's son with the rank of officer, he received an excellent education at the Russian cadet school in Omsk. He spent much time reading and visiting Russian intellectuals who had been sent into exile in Siberia. He became a Russian army officer at 18, and served as an adjutant to the Russian governor-general Gasfort. Later, he was promoted to the rank of captain. He used his right of access to the Omsk archives to enrich his knowledge of history, geography and ethnography. As his superior was also

Chokan Valikhanov

responsible for the Kazakh steppe areas, Valikhanov also had to accompany him on his journeys through those lands as an interpreter and negotiator. This strengthened the young Kazakh's interest in the fate of his people. During one of these journeys in 1855, he got to know Fyodor Dostoyevsky in Semipalatinsk. The latter was enthralled by the young Kazakh nobleman's historical expertise and state of mind. A profound friendship developed between the two.

Valikhanov spent the next couple of years as a member of a diplomatic and fact-finding mission in Semirechye on numerous trips, which took him as far as Issyk Kul, Kuldzha and Kashgar. He collected valuable information, wrote, commented and drew. On one of his travels, he met the famous Russian explorer Semyonov, later known as Semyonov Tienshansky. Thanks to the latter's influence, Valikhanov's work came to the attention of people in Moscow and St Petersburg. Valikhanov was given recognition, became an ordinary member of the Russian Geographical Society, and was allowed to present the voluminous results of his research in St Petersburg. He was awarded the Order of Saint Vladimir for his scientific work. He stayed in St Petersburg for more than a year, dedicating himself exclusively to scientific activity and cooperating in the design of a map of Central Asia and Eastern Turkestan.

In 1884, Valikhanov was offered a place on an armed expedition with the aim of incorporating southern Kazakhstan into the Russian Empire. Horrified by the gruesome character of such a mission, he requested his premature dismissal on grounds of his tuberculosis. He retired to a remote corner of Semirechye. Here in the last year of his life, he cherished the thought of setting up a Turkestan liberation movement, but was unable to make this scheme materialise. Valikhanov was the first Kazakh to receive a first-class European education. He is seen as a leading example for the Kazakh young generation.

Abai Kunanbayev

Abai Kunanbayev (1845–1904)

Ibrahim Kunanbayev, the son of a rich and powerful Kazakh provincial prince, gave himself the pen-name Abai the Righteous.

His father sent him to the Koran school in Semipalatinsk, where he spent many years studying and got to know exiled Russian intellectuals. The library that the young Russians had established, their seminars and discussions, made an impression on Abai that was to influence his entire life. Once back in his aul, he was confronted with the conflict between learning and rural custom. He was married against his will and had to bow to all his father's whims. Henceforth, he vowed to dedicate all his work to the effort to liberate his nomadic people from ignorance. He took topics from his immediate environment, transformed them into poetry and put them into literary shape. By translating them into Kazakh, Abai made important works from Russian and European literature accessible to his compatriots. He concentrated on Kazakhs' national self-consciousness. As the best prerequisites for this he recommended education and moral integrity. His literary and philosophical masterpiece, the *Book of Words*, is dedicated to this theme. His writings provided a powerful impulse to Kazakh literature; today, Abai is honoured as the founder of Kazakh literature.

MUKHTAR AUEZOV (1897–1961)

Born in Abai's hometown and directly surrounded by his descendants, Auezov grew up with admiration for the great poet. During the 1920s and 30s, Abai's work and his literary heirs were attacked by Stalinist slander. The label "backward-looking, aiming at the restoration of feudal order" was used to pursue dozens of great names in Kazakh literature, who were put in camps and even executed. Auezov was given advice by his colleagues, themselves already detained, to glorify Soviet power in order to be able to complete *Abai's Way*, on which he was already working. The four volumes of this work, which depicts Kazakh life during the 19th and early 20th centuries in a grandiose portrayal, were published between 1942 and 1956. Mukhtar Auezov was awarded a USSR state prize for the first two volumes. Kazakhs honour him for the fact that with his biography he essentially saved Abai from oblivion. He also built a true and lasting monument to Kazakh culture through his encyclopaedic portraits of nomadic life.

Mukhtar Auezov

Auezov's histories make their way through a series of changes in social conditions and conflicts, and many of his works were made suitable for drama. The Auezov National Kazakh Drama Theatre in Almaty is named after him.

AKHMET BAYTURSINULY (1872–1937)

The story of Akhmet Baytursinuly stands as an example of the entire group of patriotic-minded Kazakhs who were systematically annihilated during the 1930s. Baytursinuly started his career as a teacher after finishing his studies at an Islamic School. He dedicated his life to the education of his compatriots. Baytursinuly translated the Russian poet Ivan Krylov into Kazakh, wrote his own poetry and distinguished himself as a turkologist and ethnologist. Between 1913 and 1918, he published the newspaper *Kazakh* at a time when his people were still called Kyrgyz. Baytursinuly knew better; he had undertaken a thorough study into the Kazakh language and the family tree of Turkic languages.

A member of the Alash Orda Party, he was accused of trying to restore the feudal order of the beys. Baytursinuly proved the contrary and put his talent at the disposal of Soviet development. He was first minister for education and a member of the Kyrgyz Revolutionary Council, an expression which at the time still referred to both the Kyrgyz and Kazakh peoples. It was in this position that in 1920 he wrote an impressively analytical and courageous letter to Lenin. He complained that the Revolutionary Council's work had contributed nothing since it had no clear goals. The Council's members were close to concluding that the communists were newly elected oppressors. There were only two roads that could be taken in the direction of further development: the easy way which consisted of the continuation of oppression, or the difficult way of laboriously convincing the Kyrgyz that the New Order really would bring about liberation. To choose the second option, one would have to mobilise the national intelligentsia. Baytursinuly proposed to have two-thirds of the revolutionary committees occupied by "Kyrgyz intellectuals" and recruit the remaining members among "genuine" communists. It is not known whether he ever got a direct answer to his letter. But it is likely it was a decisive reason for his later persecution.

In 1928, Baytursinuly became professor in the Kazakh language at the Kazakh National University, but was not given much time to exercise this appointment. He and his family were sent into exile from 1929 to 1933. It was only thanks to the intervention of Maxim Gorky's wife that he was temporarily set free. After a short period, he disappeared into the Stalinist camps, where, after terrible abuses and with his health destroyed, he was shot as an enemy of the people in 1937. It was only in 1988 that his reputation was rehabilitated "for lack of evidence". His wife's rehabilitation followed in the same year, and that of their daughter in 1990. At least the daughter lived to receive compensation. She built a museum in honour of her father in Almaty, a visit to which is recommended.

Zhambyl Zhabayev (1846–1945)

This Kazakh bard became a Soviet celebrity in 1927 after he performed his work, *The Course of Time*, in front of a large audience of Kazakhs. The epic verse, entirely in Kazakh tradition, expressed the theme of the new Soviet era for the first time. Born in a village at the foot of the Zailiyskiy Alatau and growing up a celebrated aytis from childhood, Zhambyl at the age of 81, using all his moral authority, put himself at the vanguard of Kazakhstan's Sovietisation. His emotional poems *Home Nation*, *The Big Construction Site*, *My Life* and *To Youth*, however, found their way more easily into Kazakh hearts than into the decisions of party councils. In 1938 he was elected to the Supreme Soviet of the Kazakhstan Soviet Republic. Zhambyl appeared on the parliamentary rostrum as a musician and singer. When nearly 100 years old, he dedicated various works to the resistance of his Soviet homeland against the fascist intruders. Radio listeners in Leningrad during the blockade could hear his appeal *People of Leningrad, My Children* time and again. His last song, *From a Hundred-year-old Heart*, can be seen as the continuation of an ancient Kazakh tradition according to which one writes his own funeral song if one cannot find somebody worthy of doing so for him. Even though the context in which Zhambyl wrote his works is now viewed differently, recognition of this Methuselah's passion and talent among his present-day compatriots has not diminished. The district and town where he was born bear his name to this day.

Dinmukhamed Kunayev (1912–1993)

The longest-serving First Secretary of the Communist Party of Kazakhstan, originally a miner, was extremely popular among the Kazakh population, because in spite of his rapid rise in politics he always stuck to a simple lifestyle. Many a street remains named after him. Nowadays, this statesman's name is always evoked when the bright side of Kazakhstan's survival as a Soviet republic comes to mind. Kunayev did a lot for his Union Republic. Of course, he enjoyed some freedom of decision since the Soviet Union was relatively prosperous during his tenure. Even in the "years of stagnation", what is now called "Kunayev's Kazakhstan" was noted for a lot of building and stable social welfare. The charismatic politician had a better grip on his power base than many of his peers, and he succeeded in tapping funds for his republic's budget. After 26 years in office as head of the Kazakh Soviet Republic, Kunayev was replaced by a Russian named Koblin in December 1986 by a decree of the Central Committee. His dismissal led to a popular uprising in Almaty, at the cost of many dead and injured. The event contributed more than a little to the Kunayev legend and is viewed as the beginning of a process that in the end led to Kazakhstan's independence.

Nursultan Nazarbayev (Born 1940)

Nursultan Nazarbayev, Kazakhstan's president and architect of its successful development (Gunter Kapelle)

The only President of the Republic of Kazakhstan so far was born into an ordinary family in Almaty oblast. He started work as a metal factory labourer. Following his training as an engineer, he obtained an additional post-academic degree in economic science. His political career started in 1969 in the Soviet youth organization Komsomol. Ten years later he became a Secretary of the Communist Party of Kazakhstan, and after another 10 years he reached the post of First Secretary. Five years earlier, he had already found himself at the head of the Council of Ministers. In 1990, he became President of the Soviet Socialist Republic of Kazakhstan, and when his country was cut loose from the Soviet Union, he was elected President of the Republic of Kazakhstan. Since he first attained this position in December 1991, he has consolidated his control through astute political manoeuvring. He combines all crucial powers in the country, including the right to presidency for life. Members of his family occupy influential posts: his wife Sara is engaged in charity, education and health; his eldest daughter Dariga, a doctor of political science, is in charge of the state television company Khabar, and in 2003 founded the political party Asar, a broad movement to support her father's policies and to include ordinary citizens in the social process.

With his consistent policy of state neutrality and international understanding, Nazarbayev has gained great respect as a statesman. He volunteers as mediator in regional conflicts and shows strong engagement in keeping the many nationalities within Kazakhstan's borders working together and thinking as a single nation. Nazarbayev is an enthusiastic sportsman (downhill skiing, tennis, horseriding, swimming and volleyball) and huntsman. His penchant for historical, philosophical and economic literature is reflected in his own numerous political essays and books.

Language

The Kazakh language belongs to the group of Turkic languages. The first Kazakh linguist, Akhmet Baytursinuly, designed a language family tree almost 100 years ago, showing the origins and branching of the Turkic nations' tongues. Apart from the Turks, the Kyrgyz, Turkmen, Uzbek, Azeri, Tatar, Uygur, Bashkir and many other peoples belong to this group, and their various languages are strongly interrelated. A distinction of the Turkic languages that clearly sets them apart from the Indo-European language family is their grammar. All words are formed according to a specific system that consists of a mainly unchanging root to which large numbers of prefixes and suffixes are added.

It is hard to tell how many of the 10 million or so Kazakhs worldwide are masters of their mother tongue. Due to their Soviet past many Kazakhs, especially in the cities, speak Russian rather than Kazakh. Though Kazakh is the official state language, Russian is recognized as the lingua franca. Many Kazakh words have been borrowed from Russian, eg *tramvay* (tram) and *svetofor* (traffic light), and words from other languages have also been appropriated. *Taxi*, *teatr*, *telefon*, *politika*, *kompas*—many terms introduced in the 19th and 20th centuries have entered the Kazakh lexicon.

Kazakhstan still uses the Cyrillic alphabet even since the end of the Soviet era. Arabic script had been in use well into the 20th Century, but after linguistic reforms in the Soviet Union in 1924 it was replaced by a Latin script until 1940, when it was in turn replaced by Cyrillic. There are, however, some additions to the Russian alphabet in Kazakh Cyrillic, since there are vowels and consonants that exist in Kazakh but not in Russian—this expands the Kazakh alphabet to 42 letters.

The Kazakh tongue sounds strange to Western ears. Many consonants sound

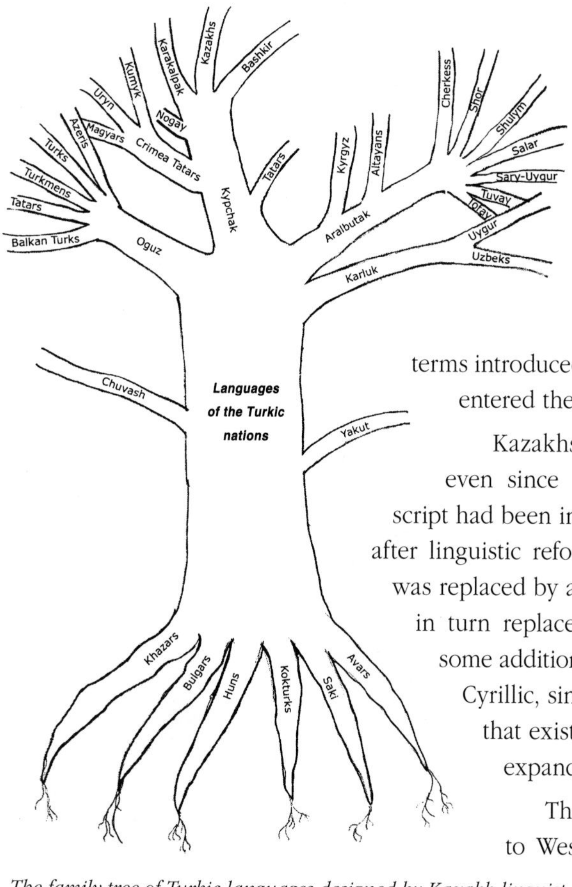

The family tree of Turkic languages designed by Kazakh linguist Akhmet Baytursinuly

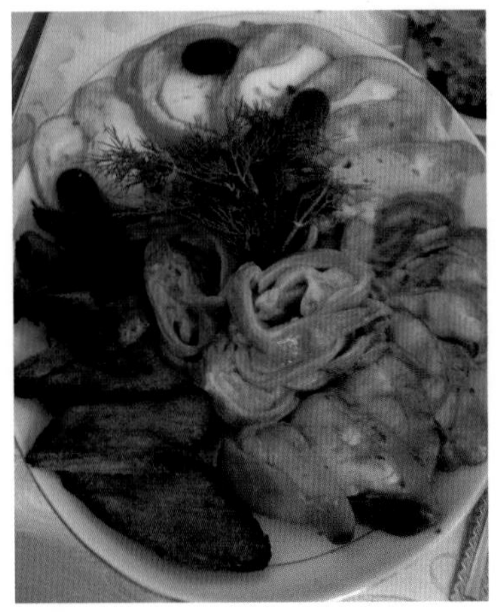

mute and guttural. This is due to the deep-throated pronunciation of consonants and a number of very short vowels. Most Western Europeans have trouble with pronunciation. However, you should practise a few expressions and have them ready as an icebreaker, since the joy and surprise of Kazakhs, whenever they hear their own language from the mouth of a foreign guest, is wonderful to see.

CUISINE

Kazakhstan's cuisine is hard to distinguish from that of its neighbours, and it is difficult to identify dishes the Kazakhs can really claim as their own. Mostly these are meals prepared from cooked mutton, and camel and horsemeat. The milk of these animals, served in tea or fermented in the form of kumis (mare's milk) or *shubat* (camel's milk), is the apéritif for every classic Kazakh meal, served along with *baursaki* (fried dough), raisins, *irimshik* (sour cow's cheese) or *kurt* (salted cheese balls).

Most guests feel full after only the first course, but a feast in a yurt always lasts a long time, and many more sumptuous meat dishes follow. These dishes are usually served with *shorpa*, a strong broth in which the meat has been cooked. Thinly rolled pieces of dough cooked into large noodles provide the carbohydrate portion of the meal. Another round of kumis, followed by tea, concludes the meal.

Many dishes of Arabian, Tatar, Uzbek, Uygur, Korean and Russian origin have been added to the Kazakh culinary lexicon, and they also grace the *dastarkhan*, a richly filled dinner table, named after the Persian word that means a tablecloth spread on the floor. If you are lucky enough to be invited to a dastarkhan you should join it with an empty stomach but not empty-handed. A small souvenir from your own country would be especially appreciated by your hosts. Otherwise, a bottle of good wine or cognac or a cake is welcome.

If you are a non-drinker you will need a very good excuse, or else the *tamada*, the toast-master—generally a highly esteemed person at

Above: A platter of cold horsemeat is a common starter (Jeremy Tredinnick). Right: A streetside shashlyk seller cooks up a storm (Gunter Kapelle)

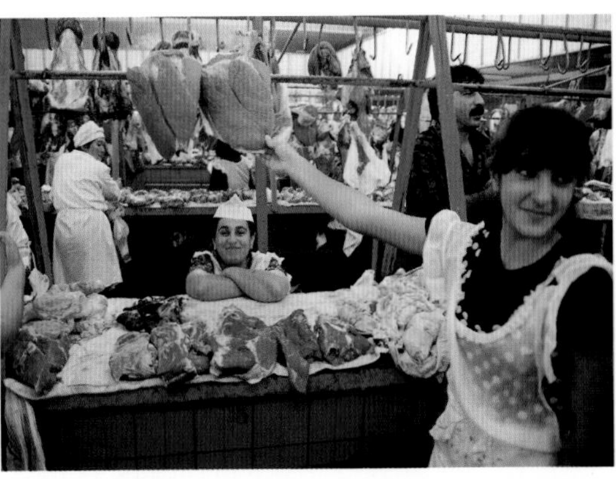

the table who is responsible for the proper order of toasts—will be successful in his friendly but persistent attempts to ensure you drain more than one tumbler of either vodka or cognac, both of which are ever present at Kazakh meal times.

These days, meals start with a variety of salads, most of which originate from Russian cuisine. First courses also include mutton or horsemeat, and smoked fish. By helping yourself moderately to these delights, you can still enjoy the next round of meat dishes without embarrassing yourself with your pitiful appetite. It is sometimes hard to hide your amazement at the sight of the heaped plates of meat that arrive on the table, but the Kazakh ability to eat is legendary. Meat dishes are still the core of any dastarkhan, and the splendour of these feasts is measured by the sheer size of those dishes. Fortunately, there are many guests, the evening is long, and the vodka is in abundance. When the feast is finally coming to an end, the hostess will serve up cake or pastries along with large dishes of dried fruits and sweets. Tea is the courteous sign for an imminent conclusion to the night's revelry. The last, obligatory toast by the guests is to the host and hostess. Before leaving, you should drain your glass and say, *"Zhol ayakh!"*—meaning "May we return home safely". A dastarkhan is an unforgettable experience; the great variety of dishes and drinks, the witty toasts, the heaviness in the stomach, will for long be a subject of conversation.

Food and Drink

Kazakhs have developed a number of techniques to preserve and prepare their main commodities, meat and milk. These methods are still in use today: salting, drying, smoking, pickling or even a combination of these. In the past, one rather piquant process of salting and tenderizing was to place a flat piece of meat under your saddle until it was "ridden to tenderness", the horse's sweat serving to salt the meat. Travellers may find comfort in the thought that this kind of preservation is no longer practised.

The following glossary of food and drink should make it easier to read menus and provide visitors to a dastarkhan with some background information. The most popular Kazakh dishes and a number of commonly eaten Korean, Uygur, Uzbek and Arabian dishes are included.

Above: The meat section at Almaty's Green Market is large and always well stocked (Gunter Kapelle)

Drinks and Dishes Based on Milk

Kumis/kumys: Mare's milk fermented in a smoke-cured leather bag—a surprisingly refreshing, thirst-quenching drink.

Ayran: *Kefir* or a type of salt lassi made from skimmed or full-fat cow's, sheep's, goat's or mare's milk.

Katyk: Sour milk heated in the oven.

Shubat: Camel's milk with a high fat content, fermented in a leather bag. Shubat is used to treat tuberculosis and intestinal pain.

Irkit: A well-shaken mix consisting of freshly boiled, cooled and soured milk.

Koyirtpak: A cocktail, rich in calories, of fresh milk, ayran, katyk, kumis and shubat.

Ashygan Kozhe: Boiled and soured groats from wheat, millet or rice, mixed with wheat flour and usually with milk, ayran or sour cream.

Chay po-kazakhskiy: "Kazakh tea"—black tea prepared in a special way. Heated milk is poured into a *kese* (tea bowl) and tea is added to it. People take special care not to fill up the bowl to its edge to prevent guests from burning their fingers. It is served with dried fruits, sweets and baursaki.

Kurt: Small dried balls from soured cow, sheep or goat's milk.

Balkaymak: Honey cream, made from boiled cream, mixed with sugar, honey and flour and added to tea.

Irimshik: Dried raw milk quark (low-fat soft cheese).

Saryssu: Dried small flans made from boiled and cooled whey.

Suzbe: Strained and salted quark made from ayran.

Dishes from Cereals

Zhent: Also called Kazakh chocolate. Millet and irimshik are mixed in a mortar with sugar, butter and raisins. The mixture is stiffened by cooling and cut into small slices.

Zhanyshpa: Soft dessert from ground millet, sugar, butter and sour cream.

Millet with kurt: Millet poured into pounded kurt, softened in hot water.

Talkan: Roasted millet, wheat and maize pounded in a mortar, with butter, sour cream, stock or raw eggs then added.

Sut Kozhe and *Kurniyas*: Millet soup with milk, sometimes thickened with flour.

Cold First Courses

Kazy: Usually lean horse rib, well seasoned, and dried in horse intestines, then hot-smoked and cooked. It is cut into slices and served on large plates as a starter.

Shuzhuk: Like *kazy*, with the same ingredients, but with half fat and half lean horsemeat.

Zhaya: Salted, dried and subsequently smoked and cooked meat from a horse's hip, served in slices.

Zhal: The long strip of fat under a horse's mane is cut off with a thin layer of flesh and prepared in the same way as zhaya.

Sur-Yet: Tender horsemeat with tendons and gristle removed is first salted and dried, and then served cooked.

Fish platter "Assorti": Noble fish (sturgeon, salmon, carp) served on a large platter with caviar and bread. Take care in restaurants, where this "assorti" can turn out to be particularly expensive.

Bottles of vodka and cognac are ever present at the dinner table (Jeremy Tredinnick)

Shalgam salad: Spicy salad from finely sliced radish and paprika.

Korean salad, carrots Korean-style: Spicy salad from finely sliced carrots.

HOT FIRST COURSES

Shorpa: A nourishing meat broth with mutton, sometimes with rice, sometimes with baursaki. *Shorpa Kozhe* is thickened with cooked millet.

Kespe: Another meat broth with mutton, less often with poultry, with thin pasta noodles.

Salma: Meat broth with mutton or beef, with large square noodles.

SECOND COURSES

Myaso po-kazakhskiy (meat Kazakh-style): The classic Kazakh dish—a sumptuous meat repast of mutton, beef or horsemeat, with onions, herbs, large square noodles and in some cases potatoes, cooked into a stew and served on a platter. It is also called *besparmak* or *beshparmak*—meaning Five Fingers. This is because traditionally it is eaten with your hands: pick up a noodle, wrap a piece of meat in it and put it into your mouth, smacking your lips loudly to express your appreciation.

Ryba po-kazakhskiy (fish Kazakh-style): A rich fish dish, prepared in a similar way to meat beshparmak.

Kuyrdak: Also an original Kazakh dish, with internal organs such as liver, kidneys and heart, fried in mutton fat, seasoned with salt, onions and pepper, and served with bread.

Meat Kuyrdak: Mutton, beef, horsemeat or game fried in fat and then braised and covered with sour cream, served with potatoes and vegetables. Can also be prepared with rabbit or chicken.

Basturma: Marinated sausages of mutton, tomato and onion pieces, grilled, and served with fresh vegetables.

Tostik: Breast of mutton grilled on skewers, cut into pieces and served with sauerkraut and tomatoes.

Beydene: Fried back of mutton sliced and served with rice, tomatoes, cucumbers and vegetables.

Zhambas: Leg of mutton, larded with mutton fat, braised with carrots, and served with potatoes, pickled cucumbers and tomatoes.

Stuffed zhauryn baglana: Roasted shoulder of mutton stuffed with vegetables (carrots, radish, pumpkin, onions) and minced meat.

A typical dinner table, boasting plates of meat, salad, fried bread and bowls of kumis (Jeremy Tredinnick)

Manty: Large, steamed pieces of pasta filled with soft, coarsely minced beef or mutton, onions and thinly sliced pumpkin.

Shashlyk: Skewers of juicy mutton, sometimes supplemented with liver, barbecued over *saksaul* wood or coal.

Pelmeni: A dish of Siberian or Chinese origin, but also very popular in Kazakhstan. Small pieces of pasta are filled with mutton or beef with onions, boiled in salted water, and served with sour cream or brown butter. Fish, mushroom or potato can also be used for the filling.

Orama: Steamed rolls of pasta filled with coarsely minced mutton and onions.

Zhuta: Large, boiled rolls of pasta filled with thinly cut carrot or pumpkin, butter and a little sugar.

Lagman: A delicious Uygur dish consisting of boiled noodles which can be very long indeed, over which a sauce of thin pieces of fried meat and vegetables (garlic, potato, tomato, carrot, radish and cabbage) is poured.

Kazakh plov: Pieces of mutton fried with onion rings and slices of carrot, then topped with rice and broth and simmered. There is a rich variety of plov, with all kinds of things added: boiled eggs, peas, raisins, diced dried fruit or pomegranate seeds. The richest variety is called *festival plov*. There is also a vegetarian *sweet plov* with dried fruits and almonds.

BREAD AND PASTA

Taba nan (wheat bread): A round flat loaf made from yeast sourdough and baked in a closed pan on glowing coals.

Damdy nan, tandyr nan: A flat loaf from yeast sourdough baked in a stove pipe or in a special oven (*tandyr*).

Kazanzhappay: Thin bread from yeast sourdough baked in a pot (*kazan*).

Salma nan: Pieces of pasta in a kind of noodle dough, cooked in boiling water or broth.

Baursaki: Dough rolls from a heavy yeast dough baked in sizzling fat. There is also a variety called *ay baursaki*, in which yeast is replaced by soda dough and a larger number of eggs are added. *Domalak baursaki* uses quark as the raising agent. When they are prepared with sheep's tail fat and made into rings, they are called *jespe baursaki*.

Zhelpek: Rectangular pieces of yeast sourdough based on ayran and/or kefir, fried in boiling fat.

Kuymak: Pancakes of runny dough with or without yeast, fried in a pan.

Samsa: Half-moon shaped plain flour dough packets fried in fat and filled with minced mutton or beef and cooked rice. Sometimes the filling consists of lung, heart and liver.

Belyashi: A yeast sourdough roll fried in fat and filled with minced mutton or beef.

Chebureki: A plain flour dough roll baked in fat and filled with minced mutton.

Pirogiy with meat or fish: A large round and tasty pastry made from yeast dough, filled with meat or fish and rice, and baked in a pan in the oven.

DESSERTS

Orekhi s sakharom (nuts with sugar): Caramelized sugar with a variety of nuts.

Chak-chak: A roll from very heavy dough baked in melted butter and then drenched in honey.

Khvorost: A pastry made from curved strips of dough, fried in vegetable oil.

Sourdough pirogiy: Small yeast rolls filled with meat, cabbage, potato or egg and baked in the oven.

Honey cakes: A biscuit sprinkled with poppy seed and made of spicy, heavy honey dough.

Kauynkak: Dried melon.

Khalva: A sweet dish made of sugar with vanilla, dissolved in melted butter, and saturated with roasted flour.

ALMATY: THE CITY AND ITS ENVIRONS

Gardens, water canals, the delightful city.
Singing vastness above one's head, wind, birds, sunshine.
And on the horizon the white-crowned mountains.
Alma-Ata! In the face of your beauty my words are powerless.

Tahir Zharokov

ALMATY

For most foreigners, their introduction to **Almaty**, formerly **Alma-Ata**, starts in the dead of night, when most international flights land. This is regrettable, since at night, although Almaty is a big city very much alive during the evening and early hours, everything that contributes to its charm remains hidden in the dark.

By contrast it's an unforgettable impression, when, on a domestic flight in summer, one sees the first sunrays of dawn burst out and shine over the majestic backdrop of the northern **Tien Shan** mountain chain. Glacier-covered peaks stand in solitary splendour more than 4,000 metres high under the azure-blue sky, the green slopes march vividly forward in the morning light, and everything looks as though one can grasp it. Embedded in a green sea of oak, poplar and birch, the million-plus city of Almaty lies below, with its clearly distinguishable landmark, the television tower on Koktobe hill.

The Alatau range to the south and the steppe and desert outskirts to the north determine the city's climate and colourfulness. Mountain streams and canals provide the city with water all year round, and everything is green and blooming. The city is built almost entirely on a slope, rising into the foothills of the mountains. This makes it easy for newcomers to find their way around: north is downhill, south is uphill. Only the metropolis's northern outskirts penetrate into the steppe's flatland. The strict north-south street pattern has been designed to allow the mountain breeze to blow through the streets as effectively as possible in summer, when the heat becomes unbearable. The city's lavish greenery also contributes to making life bearable here during the hot season, although Almaty does not have the extreme temperatures that the steppe is known for. Here, on the edge of the mountains, even the notorious *buran*, the harsh, cutting wind that sweeps south across the steppe from Siberia, developing infernal power over distances of thousands of kilometres, calms down.

In this—for Kazakhstan—comparatively mild climate, a rich variety of fruits, vegetables and flowers prosper. The sheltered valleys in the lower mountains are home to wild fruits, which have grown there since primeval times. Apples, especially, have a great history here, reflected in several place-names. The legendary giant apple, *Aport,* which brought the city fame under the Tsars and later in Soviet times, is cultivated on the slopes overlooking Almaty. In fact, Alma-Ata translates as "The Father of Apples".

The green city of Almaty lies right at the foot of the Tien Shan mountains, whose 4,000-metre peaks form a superb backdrop to the cityscape (Jeremy Tredinnick)

History

The fortress of Verniy, or **Fort Verniy** (the faithful fort), was founded in 1854 on territory in the mountain foothills where once the settlement of Almatau (Apple Mountain) or Almata (rich in apples) had stood, before **Tamerlane** destroyed it back in the 14th Century. The city of Alma-Ata developed around the new fort over the course of time.

Fort Verniy was built on the assumption that the Russian troops, brought in by the Kazakh Khan in order to help defend the country against marauding tribes from the east and southwest, could best accomplish their mission with the construction of a string of forts in the Land of Seven Rivers—the name given to the region between Lake Balkhash and the Tien Shan, and which is still in use today: it translates as **Zhetisu** in Kazakh, and **Semirechye** in Russian.

Verniy was one of those fortresses, and within a year of its construction the first settlers arrived: Cossacks and farmers from Siberia and Russian officials. They created the Greater and Lesser Almaty Cossack settlements (*stanitsa*). Soon, a Tatar settlement sprang up next to them, where Tatars from the areas around Semipalatinsk, Tyumen, Omsk and other cities made a new home. According to tradition, the newcomers swiftly integrated with the inhabitants of the nearby Kazakh *auls* (villages), to whom they offered expertise in agriculture, horticulture and craftsmanship. In 1857, the first water mill was built next to the wooden houses of the inhabitants of this strip of land. The following year, the first brewery

was put into operation, and in 1860 the first post office and hospital were opened. At the time, around 5,000 people lived here in 677 houses, of which only one was built of stone.

Verniy's first baptism of fire in its original function as an outpost against warring neighbours came in 1860, when a large host of the Khan of Kokand poured into the Land of Seven Rivers. The 700 soldiers who occupied Fort Verniy marched forward to meet the enemy, and defeated the khan's 21,000-strong army. A monument commemorating the battle can still be seen in the present-day village of Uzynaghash.

After that, the outpost's development continued in a peaceful manner. In 1865, Igor Redko, a settler from the governorate of Voronezh, brought a sapling of the *Aport* apple with him and thereby laid the foundation of the city's subsequent fame. On 11 April 1867, Fort Verniy was granted city rights. It became the centre of the Semirechye *voyevodstvo* (province) and the area's entire governorate moved to it.

Of course, uncontrolled growth of the city now had to come to an end. A committee for urban development was established to draft a settlement plan. Within the year, it was decided to extend the city's construction sites towards the south and the west of the Greater Stanitsa. The streets were to be almost 35 metres wide and supplemented with squares and parks. At first 11 of these squares were designed, five of which were designated as marketplaces: a vegetable market, a hay market, a wood market, a horse market and a row of inns. In December 1874, 33 lampposts with stearin (beeswax) candles were erected on the squares.

By 1879 the number of Verniy's inhabitants had grown to more than 18,000 and the lack of organisation became noticeable, so it was decided to give names to the first 43 streets. The names indicated their function, such as Barracks Street, Court House Street, (river) Bank Street, etc.

At this stage, the city's architecture consisted of so-called *razryadiy*, or "grades". The first grade consisted of the most splendid buildings such as the military governor's house with its gallery of columns, the farm and home of the Bishop of Turkestan, the officers' mess, the boys' and girls' gymnasiums (schools), the cathedral, the regional printing house and others. These buildings were in the area between Court House Street (now Kaldayakova Street), Commerce Street (Zhybek Zholy or Silk Road Street), Serigopolskaya Street (Tulebayeva Street) and Commander Street (Bogenbay Batyr Street). The second grade, bordered on the east by the Lesser Almatinka River and on the west by Barracks Street (now Panfilova Street), consisted of less impressive houses belonging to officials, officers and traders. The third grade covered the rest of the city. Here, in mud huts and holes in the earth, poverty reigned.

Left: A winter cladding only adds to the picturesque beauty of the Holy Ascension Cathedral in Panfilov Park (Vladimir Tugalev)

The Abai Opera and Ballet Theatre, with the Television Tower on Koktobe on the far left and snowy peaks behind (Gunter Kapelle)

In 1887, the young city was hit by a devastating catastrophe, when a strong earthquake razed 1,798 of its buildings to the ground. Only one building remained standing, and it can still be visited today: it is found at 51 Gogol Street, on the corner of Pushkin Street. Unfortunately, because of the earthquake only archive documents now show how Fort Verniy looked during its founding phase. The remnants of the fortress rampart stretching to the Lesser Almatinka and a barracks built of fir tree trunks can now be seen only on Zhetisu Street. Both are rather hidden, surrounded by sheds.

A larger number of architectural monuments dating from the early 20th Century have, however, been preserved. Many wonderful-looking wooden buildings by master builder Zenkov from St Petersburg still stand, owing their relatively long lifespan to their earthquake-proof construction. Even the 56-metre-high **Holy Ascension Cathedral**, made entirely from wood without a single metal nail being used, survived the strong earthquake of 1911, and can now, beautifully renovated, be admired in the bucolic surroundings of Panfilov Park. Two other very fine examples of Zenkov's architecture can be seen on Zenkova Street, to the east of the cathedral: still in the park is the old officers' mess, built in 1908—today it harbours the **Museum of Folk Musical Instruments**; and not far from the Green Bazaar on Zhybek Zholy Street is the attractive **Dom Tkanyey**, the textile market. Zenkov was also responsible for the expansion of the broad north-south main streets.

Right from its foundation Verniy took special care with its greenery, which was meticulously planned from the start. After the first year, two large boulevards were constructed—these can be recognised today by the old, dense lines of trees that still flank them. The first one is the Sophia Allee, now called Pushkin Street, and the second, the road to Tashkent, is now Raimbeka Avenue. Planting in the main city garden started in the same year. Today called Central Park, the garden offers shelter to thousands of Almaty's inhabitants looking for cool shade in summer. In the 1870s, a church park was laid out, today's **Panfilov Park**. In 1892, master forester Eduard Baum took the initiative for the planting of a large forest-park. Today, the place is named after its creator: Roscha Bauma—Little Baum Forest. General Kolpakovsky, the governor of Verniy at the time of master builder Zenkov's period, ordered that each inhabitant who planted a tree should be paid one *gryvennik*, but also that illegal logging should be punished with a public flogging. One is still inclined to thank the governor for that during hot summer days.

Given the high risk of earthquakes, a meteorological and seismic station was opened in Verniy in the early 20th Century. A department of the Geographical Society was founded, which started exploring and mapping the area. By 1913, the population had grown to 40,000. Some of the cottages and houses built in the Russian style during this period can still be seen in the area between Bogenbay Batyr Street, Kabanbay Batyr Street and Kasteyev Street, as well as in the eastern part of the city to the south of the Cultural Park, though as modernisation speeds up these are disappearing fast.

Panfilov Park is a favourite spot for relaxing and enjoying the shade on a hot sunny day (Jeremy Tredinnick)

The October Revolution of 1917 reached Verniy in March the following year. In the night of 2-3 March 1918, an armed uprising resulted in the proclamation of victory for Soviet power. On 14 March 1921, the city was renamed Alma-Ata by decree of the Central Executive Committee of Turkestan. Eight years later, the capital of Kazakhstan was moved from Kyzylorda to Alma-Ata. The main reason for the increased importance of Alma-Ata was due its location on the **Turksib**, a railway line that linked Central Asia with Siberia, and which in 1930 became connected to the Trans Siberian Railway. The Turksib ran through Alma-Ata and gave the city's development a strong boost. From then on, there was no way to stem population growth. From 1926 to 1939, Alma-Ata increased from 45,000 inhabitants to 222,000. During this period, the city's infrastructure was enlarged, with 30 new industrial complexes and bus and tramway lines. Alma-Ata expanded vigorously towards the north and west. In the centre of the city, splendid stone buildings with two to four stories replaced old wooden houses. The main post office, railway station Almaty-2, numerous government buildings, scientific institutes and various theatres are examples of construction dating from the period of Soviet development in the late 1920s and 1930s. The beautiful, recently restored building of the **Opera and Ballet Theatre** was completed in 1941, during the early months of World War II.

During the war years, many large Soviet enterprises as well as cultural and scientific institutes were moved to Almaty, among other places, in an evacuation from European sections of the Soviet Union designed to place them out of reach of the invading German army. Tens of thousands of workers followed the enterprises and in spite of the war Alma-Ata witnessed significant growth. Almost the entire Alma-Ata 1 district, with its rings of terraced houses surrounding industrial sites, originates from this period. For many years following the war, Alma-Ata continued to grow. Former Volga Germans found their new home here, as well as Koreans who had been evacuated due to the Korean War, and Uygurs from western China. These, and the many Kazakhs who migrated from the countryside gave Alma-Ata the official status of a million-plus city in 1982. The city's uncontrolled growth after the war is reflected in the mix in architecture, with two- to four-storey residential buildings from the 1950s and 1960s in some places and the typical high residential complexes, the so-called *mikrorayons*, from the 1970s and 1980s. The latter have often been decorated with oriental ornamentation to liven up their façades, while many of the former have been urgently razed.

In addition to the construction of functional residential areas, there was also a drive, led by Dinmukhamed Kunayev, Communist Party First Secretary for many years, to give the city its own grand identity. Examples of this are the earthquake-proof **Hotel Kazakhstan**, the **Circus** building in the form of a giant yurt, the Palace of Pupils, the television tower on

Koktobe Hill, the central *banya* (sauna) of Arasan and the campus of the State University between Al-Farabi Avenue and Timuryazova Street. Some of the buildings constructed in the 1980s, for example the monumental government buildings around **Republic Square** and the **Auezov Theatre** opposite the Circus, were designed to inspire respect and awe among visitors.

In 1993, as the capital of the now independent Republic of Kazakhstan, the city's name was changed to Almaty. From there on, many new buildings appeared, enriching the city's image: Western-style hotels, department stores, office and residential buildings. Fortunately, investors have also been found who are willing to engage in the restoration of older buildings. In this way, many buildings dating from the Soviet Classical period have been allowed to shine once more. Cinemas and other cultural buildings, which had become dilapidated in the course of post-Soviet stagnation, have been given a new life. The present-day image of Almaty is an incredible mix of monumental facades, grand statues, utilitarian housing estates, splendid single-family mansions in all sorts of building styles, glass and steel office blocks, giant marketplaces—both modern malls and old bazaars—and the occasional surviving wooden house.

Even the loss of its function as capital—since the government moved to the steppe town of Akmola and renamed it **Astana**—has hardly affected the role of Almaty as a metropolis. It remains the country's centre of commerce, science and culture, and therefore the city, often called the "southern capital", continues to be the most popular destination for visitors.

Almaty has the most vibrant cultural life in Kazakhstan, and in this respect it is still very much the capital. It owes its cultural riches to its history, not least because of the numerous cultural institutions the Soviet Union removed here during World War II, but also because many artists remained in the southern sun after the war—this is why the city boasts such a large number of universities, academies and music schools. A plethora of theatres, the opera, concert halls, galleries, libraries, numerous revamped cinemas and a developing alternative scene all combine to create a city with something for every taste.

Almaty presents itself to visitors as the most cosmopolitan and modern metropolis in Central Asia, a rare location in the centre of Eurasia where you can use your credit card without any problem, find hotels in every price category, enjoy a shimmering night life, watch new skyscraper skylines compete with the inspirational mountainscape—even get stuck in a traffic jam at any hour of the day. The negative side of this development, meaning the widening gap between haves and have-nots, is visible only to those who go looking for it.

continued on page 176

An Architectural Tale of Two Cities: Almaty and Astana

By *Lucy Kelaart and Summer Coish*

The generally observed history of Kazakhs is of steppe nomads who left no architectural legacy. However, political independence has had a significant impact on Kazakhstan's heritage of construction. Buildings reflecting the foreign rule that dominated Kazakhstan for nearly two centuries under the Tsarists and the Soviets are now juxtaposed, and at times make way for, visions of architectural modernity and progress swathed in glass and steel. Nowhere is this architectural contrast better demonstrated than in the edifices of Kazakhstan's two capital cities. Almaty, the former political capital and now cultural and financial centre, began as a nomadic settlement that evolved into a Russian outpost and later a major Soviet capital. These cultural influences are reflected in the variety of architectural styles that tell the city's history. Meanwhile, Astana, the political capital, is an entirely new city—a monumental project designed to demonstrate Kazakhstan's growing role as a key player in the global sphere of influence; its natural resource wealth reflected in the city's many mirrored skyscrapers.

The recent redesign of Kazakhstan's currency is, perhaps, an apposite reflection of architecture's new place in the country's identity; one side of the new 5,000 tenge note shows Almaty's late-1970s Soviet-built Hotel Kazakhstan, while the flip side shows one of the first construction projects in Astana—the

The Hotel Kazakhstan, built in the 1970s, is still Almaty's highest building (Jeremy Tredinnick)

imposing 97-metre-high Baiterek (Tree of Life) tower, which has become the unequivocal symbol of the new Kazakhstan.

While both structures tower above their neighbours, the view from the top of each is radically different. From Hotel Kazakhstan's top floor Cosmos restaurant in central Almaty, the Tien Shan Mountains dominate the southern skyline and present an immutable barrier to the city's expansion. Thousands of years ago, trade and nomadic herding routes skirted these mountains and led to the establishment of an ancient settlement in the area. In 1854, the Russians, advancing on Central Asia, built a fort at Verniy (present-day Almaty), and as the Russian intent in Central Asia changed from protection to colonisation, a small town was established. Buildings in this period were constructed of wood (easily available from nearby forests and the most durable material for construction in an active seismic zone). Siberian-style Russian log cottages were built in residential areas, while larger, more elaborate buildings such as Zenkov Cathedral, today's Museum of Folk Musical Instruments and Zhibek Zholy's "Trade Building", were built in the central area in and around modern-day Panfilov Park.

Almaty's transformation from a small sleepy town into a major Soviet capital began with the arrival of the TurkSib railway in 1929. As Almaty (then known as Alma-Ata) expanded its role as a trading centre, officials established a town plan radiating southwards from the Tsarist centre. As with all Central Asian capitals, parks, public gardens and tree-lined boulevards were drawn into the plan to give a sense of the open countryside within the town, a feeling which still dominates today.

During the late 1920s and early 1930s, bold architectural practices gave rise to buildings such as the Post Office (Kirova and Ablai Khan), both constructivist in style and exemplary for its day. In 1931, Moisei Ginzburg, founder of Moscow's "Organization of Contemporary Architects" and most

The crown of Astana's landmark Baiterek tower, the "golden egg" from which Kazakhstan's city of the future can be seen in all its glory (Jeremy Tredinnick)

famous for his Gosstrakh Apartments and Narkomfim Building in Moscow, designed a constructivist-style government building in Alma-Ata (now the University of Almaty). A walk around Almaty's central streets unveils further buildings from this period.

The late 1930s–1950s saw a halt in such radical architectural and artistic ideas with their "external" influences, and construction began to follow the narrow Stalinist "Empire" style—a mix of neoclassical form and local ornament, manifested most dramatically in Alma-Ata in the Opera and Ballet Theatre (1941), the Union of Writers (1956) and the Academy of Sciences (1957).

Some of Alma-Ata's most monumental buildings emerged, however, under the leadership of Dinmukhamed Kunayev, first secretary of Kazakhstan's Communist Party from 1959–1986. A close friend of Brezhnev, Kunayev was the only Central Asian representative in the Soviet Politburo, the select committee of super-elites who controlled the workings of the USSR. With such high connections, Kunayev was able to obtain a generous budget for the city, which allowed him to carry out his dream of monumentalising Alma-Ata.

Under Kunayev's rule, the Palace of Culture (1970), the Circus (1972), the House of Friendship (1972), the Wedding Palace (1971), Medeu Sports Complex (1972), the Kasteyev Art Museum (1975), Hotel Kazakhstan (1978), the Republican Palace of Schoolchildren and Pioneers (1983), Kazakhfilm Studios (1983) and the Arasan Banya (1983), amongst others, were built. These late Soviet buildings displayed a high level of interior and exterior design, whose style is finding followers among architectural students today.

Almaty's most recent transformation, to a city laced with glass-and-steel skyscrapers, began in the early 2000s as it transitioned from being the administrative capital to becoming the country's financial capital. Spurred by tremendous natural resource wealth, a stable emerging market and increased foreign investment, construction has become one of Kazakhstan's fastest growing sectors. Modern office buildings and apartment blocks emerge in record time, whilst quality control and adherence to building codes go largely unchecked. The rapid development and consequential increase in real-estate values have resulted in the demolition of many of the historic wooden structures that once defined central Almaty. As the city continues its high-density expansion, it would be well served to recognise the importance of protecting and preserving its architectural heritage.

In contrast to Kunayev's impressive Soviet capital, Astana presents an entirely different perspective on the new Kazakhstan. A golden imprint of President's Nazarbayev's palm inside the spherical glass and metal observation tower at the top of Baiterek (symbolising the egg of Samruk, a Kazakh legend in which the mythical bird of happiness lays a golden egg in a poplar tree) makes clear whose city this is. Seen from this observation tower, Astana spreads out before the eye in all directions, placed, it seems, unceremoniously in the middle of nowhere.

Built, like Almaty, on the site of a Tsarist fortress called Akmola, the two cities differ in almost every other respect. Nazarbayev's government relocated here in 1997, and some $15 billion later, Astana has become one of the world's largest building projects—its surreal skyline dotted with skyscrapers in stark contrast to the vast emptiness of the surrounding steppe. The official move to Astana offered a more central location from which to govern a country five times the size of France and is a direct result of a campaign to create a new vision for Kazakhstan. Its rapid development has resulted in the doubling of its population in the last ten years, and approximately US$2 billion dollars is spent on Astana's construction every year, despite the reluctance of many officials to move there. Those who have made the move, claim to notice weekly changes to the city's skyline, although observers remark that Astana's rapid growth has not yet allowed the city to establish its own identity.

The new city (on the left bank of the River Ishim) is laid out along a central axis with Baiterek dominating the main square and the Avenue of the Republic—a well-manicured city boulevard and the city's main axis (reminiscent of the National Mall in Washington, DC) flanked by modern government buildings and ministries. The placement of buildings along this axis hints at their official significance, with the President's Palace and the KazMunaiGaz headquarters (the state oil company and one of the first buildings to be constructed in Astana) at opposite ends of the boulevard, representing the most prominent players in Kazakhstan today. Between these two landmarks lie shiny government buildings including the Senate and Parliament, the Supreme Court, the Ministries of Defence and Foreign Affairs, the National Archive and the National Library.

Although Astana's master plan was designed by visionary Japanese architect Kisho Kurokawa, Nazarbayev himself is the city's unofficial chief architect.

Grandeur is never lost in the city's new architecture where some buildings have elaborate designs that hint at their function: the Ministry of Finance is shaped like a US dollar sign, the National Academy of Music resembles a giant white grand piano and the Ministry of Transport is built, somewhat more enigmatically, in the shape of a giant cigarette lighter. Among Nazarbayev's other designs is the Palace of Peace and Reconciliation (also called the Palace of Peace and Concord), a pyramid built behind the Presidential Palace. Completed in 2006, it is a permanent venue for the Congress of Leaders of World and Traditional Religions, a triennial event promoting religious tolerance. British architect Norman Foster (known for monumental projects like Beijing's airport, the world's largest and most advanced) completed the 62-metre-high pyramid in just 21 months.

Nazarbayev was so pleased with his pyramid that he offered Foster another commission: Khan Shatyr, the world's largest tent. Containing an indoor city, the transparent tent will have a 150-metre-high dome and will be clad in material that absorbs sunlight, creating a summer-like temperature

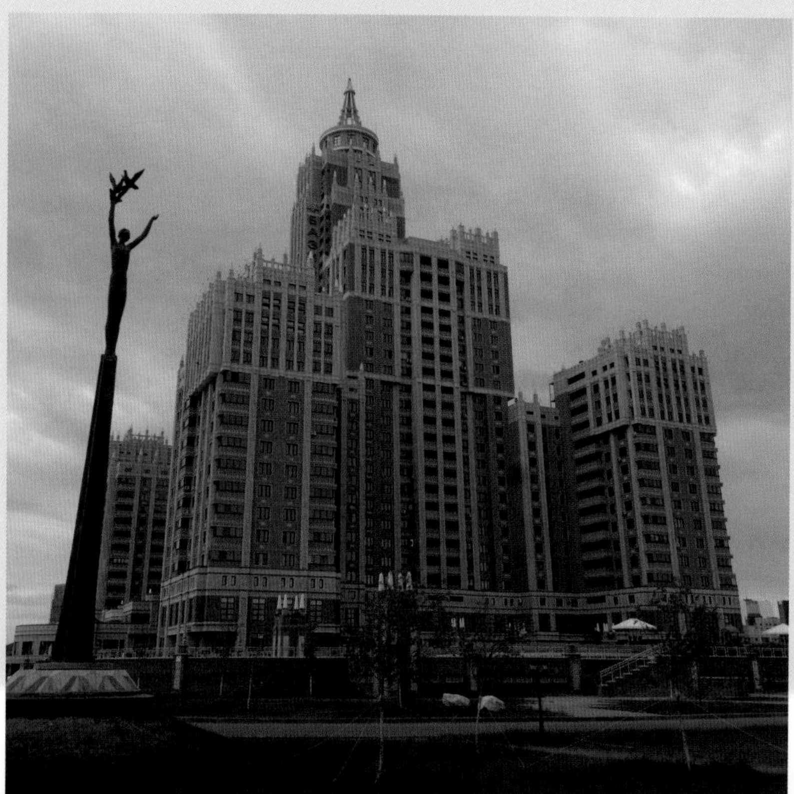

year round. Covering an area larger than ten football stadiums, it will be a city with cobbled streets and squares, an urban-scale park, shopping and entertainment venues, a golf course, cafés, restaurants and an indoor beach resort. From late 2007, Astana residents will be able to enjoy this year-round summer paradise—even when it is -30°C on the snow-covered steppe outside.

The old and new architecture found in Kazakhstan's two capital cities displays an eclectic mixture of forms and styles, a perfect illustration of the split state of the country's society with the flashy new Kazakh vying for attention among those of a more traditional, often Soviet mindset. The architecture of Almaty and Astana encompasses these trends and tells part of the story of a nation slowly, but surely, stepping into global focus.

Lucy Kelaart and Summer Coish are the editors of Steppe *magazine—Central Asia's first glossy cultural magazine. For more information, visit its website at www.steppemagazine.com*

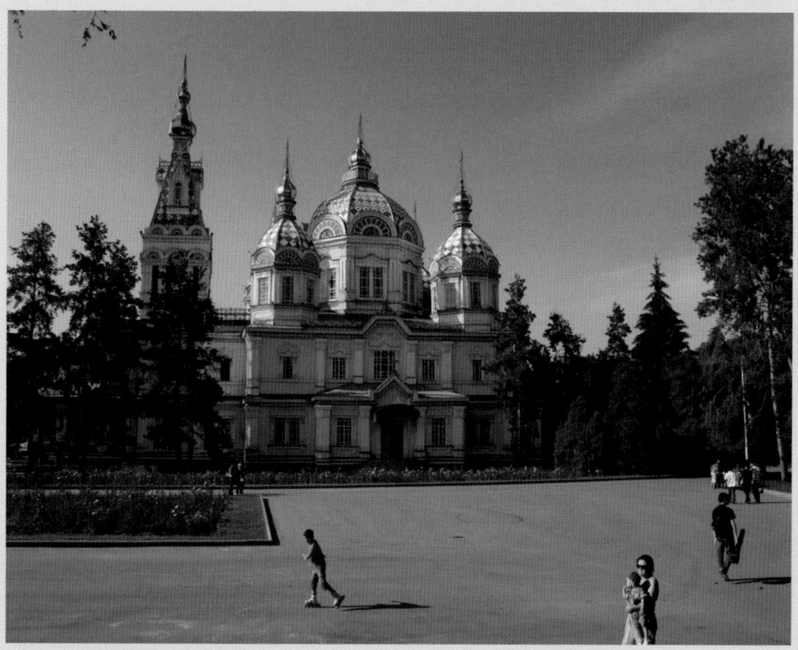

Above: The Imperial Russian splendour of Almaty's Holy Ascension Cathedral. Left: A huge new residential building in Astana is reminiscent of New York's early 20th Century building boom (Jeremy Tredinnick x2)

BAZAARS AND BUILDINGS

I feel very much aware of being in the middle of an enormous empty landmass thousands of miles from the sea. It's surreal.

Decided to waste no more time moping about and to get Yuri to drive Nina and me to the Zelioni Market (that means Green Market) to do some shopping. I love markets and this turns out to be a really good one: Long trestle tables stretch down a huge covered hall selling all sorts of stuff. Babushkas wearing headscarves like those Russian dolls that fit inside each other stand behind these trestles selling mare's milk (fermented and unfermented; the fermented tastes better—or should I say, less awful—than the unfermented), camel's milk (not bad), cream, home-made cheeses, smoked chicken and fish, caviar in big plastic tubs, honey of all sorts, veg, fresh chicken, etc. I said "quack quack?" to Nina and she took me to the duck counter, where we bought one for supper.

A couple of metres of trestle table are devoted to all sorts of extraordinary mushrooms and fungi that you'd pay a fortune for in England, and there are certain things—some strange dried berries for example—that I have never seen before. The counters selling raw meat have pictures of cows, pigs, sheep and horses so you know what you are buying. I am sorry to say that the horsemeat stand is the biggest—one of the delicacies of Kaz is the horsemeat sausage, the fattier the better. Towards the front of the market are jolly, gold-toothed Tajiks selling dried fruits (including the dried apple that Barrie Juniper talked about) and nuts from Uzbekistan, Turkey and Iran. If you buy anything from them you get lots of perks—I was given handfuls of dried apricots and sesame-sugar-coated peanuts.

On the way home we drove past a huge stone blockhouse with oriental domes which turns out to be the vanya *or bathhouse. One of the more attractive Soviet-style buildings in town, it was put up in the early eighties by an extremely popular Kazakh Communist First Party Secretary called Kunaev. Apparently you can have a Finnish, Turkish or Russian bath there. I wonder what the difference is, and I would also like to know if you can get your legs waxed there. Must investigate, but don't know who to ask...*

...Yesterday In the lunch hour AW and I went into town and bought a TV set and video, and this morning I set of with Yuri to buy a TV table to put them on.

In the course of this search I had a good look at Almaty. It has some really pretty architecture: there are hundreds of charming wooden cottages with carved window frames and shutters all painted in different colours—these, I am told, were built by the Russian Pioneers who, in last century, came east to this empty land in search of a new life. They remind me of a children's book our daughters loved called The Little House on the Prairie, *about an American family who went west to seek there fortune; the Central Asian version of the story would have to be called The Little House on the Steppe. I suppose most of these will ultimately disappear as the town is developed. I'll ask Yuri to take me round so I can photograph some of them.*

Then there are the Old Russian civic buildings of Almaty—long and low, with columned facades painted in shades of yellow or blue. Yuri pointed out the house where Brezhnev lived when he was First Part Secretary here; it is ravishing, painted blue with white stucco work. I wondered in sign language where Trotsky and his wife lived when they were exiled here by Stalin, but Yuri didn't know.

In between all these pretty things are huge apartment blocks which look semi-derelict, the president's new white marble palace like a gigantic sugar cube (very similar to the president of Syria's—perhaps they come in colossal kits), and huge Soviet-style edifices such as the Palace of Youth and Culture, which has a tower so phallic it would be better placed on an institute of Human Anatomy. Some of the Soviet buildings—such as the bathhouse, and the neoclassical Opera House, and the enormous National Museum, which looks like a mosque with a blue dome—are rather wonderful.

I wish I could have been in charge of Almaty in the 1970s and '80s and encourage the Old Russian style—especially the attractive Russian/Oriental combinations they have here (basically classical but with little Oriental touches such as pointy Moorish windows). Almaty could have become one of the prettiest places in the world.

Brigid Keenan, Diplomatic Baggage: The Adventures of a Trailing Spouse, *2006*

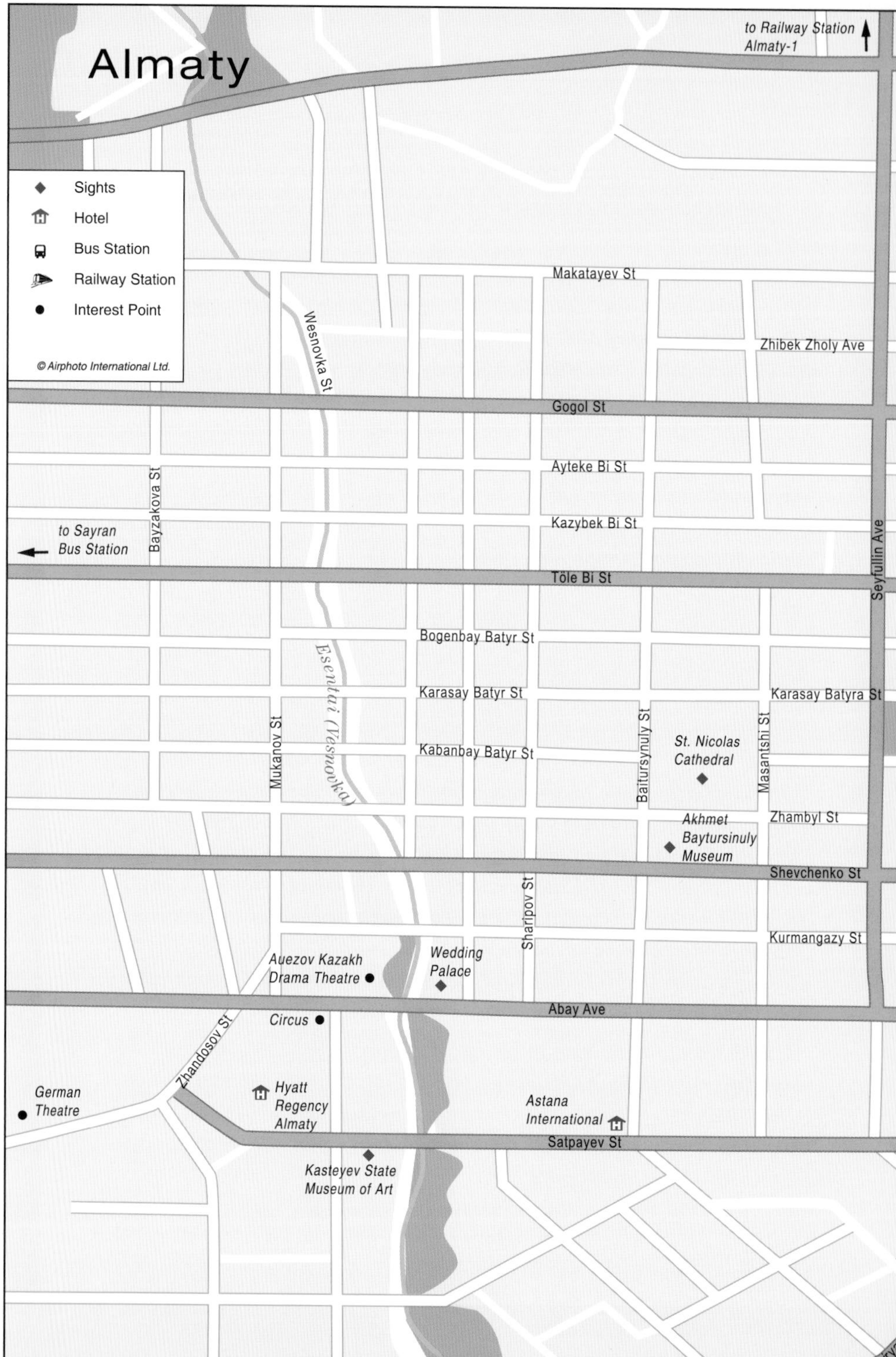
Almaty
to Railway Station Almaty-1
Sights
Hotel
Bus Station
Railway Station
Interest Point
© Airphoto International Ltd.
Makatayev St
Wesnovka St
Zhibek Zholy Ave
Gogol St
Ayteke Bi St
Kazybek Bi St
Bayzakova St
to Sayran Bus Station
Töle Bi St
Seyfullin Ave
Bogenbay Batyr St
Esentai (Vesnovka)
Karasay Batyr St
Karasay Batyra St
Mukanov St
Kabanbay Batyr St
Baitursynuly St
St. Nicolas Cathedral
Masantshi St
Akhmet Baytursinuly Museum
Zhambyl St
Shevchenko St
Sharipov St
Kurmangazy St
Auezov Kazakh Drama Theatre
Wedding Palace
Abay Ave
Circus
Zhandosov St
German Theatre
Hyatt Regency Almaty
Astana International
Satpayev St
Kasteyev State Museum of Art

Hippodrome
Sayakhat
Bus Station
mbeka Ave
Railway Station
Almaty-2
Central
Mosque
Pushkin St
Tulebayev St
Makatayev Ave
Zhetysu
Tsum
Department Store
(Pedestrianized Area)
Green
Market
Zhibek Zholy Ave
Otrar
to Central
Park
Gogol St
Gogol St
Arasan
Baths
Holy
Ascension
Cathedral
Panfilov Park
Museum of Folk
Musical Instruments
Furmanov St
Kazybek Bi St
Kasteyev St
Töle Bi St
Töle Bi St
Astana
Square
Zheltoksan St
Ablay Khan Ave
Panfilova St
Bogenbay Batyr St
Dostyk Ave
Zenkov St
Kaldayakov St
Post Office
Mukanov/Musrepov
Museum of Literature
Book Museum
Almaty
Kabanbay Batyr St
Abai Opera and
Ballet Theatre
Zhambyl St
Archaeological
Museum
Nature
Museum
Furmanov St
Tulebayev St
Kunayev St
Pushkin St
Shevchenko St
Dostyk
Kazakhstan
British,French,German
Consulates
Mukhtar Auezov
Museum
Geological
Museum
Cable Car
Abay Ave
to Koktobe
and TV Tower
Zheltoksan St
Independence
Monument
atpayev St
Republic Square
InterContinental
Almaty
Former
Presidential
Palace
Central
State Museum
Mal. Almatinka

GETTING AROUND

Almaty's urban transportation system is dense, with two tramway lines, nine trolleybus lines and over 100 bus and *marshrutka* (minibus) lines, which render the use of a car virtually unnecessary. As of 2007, local transport costs on average 40 tenge. If you want to get to a city destination quickly, taxis are cheap: just stand on the pavement (sidewalk), hold out your arm, finger down, and you won't have to wait long before a car pulls over. Don't be put off by the lack of any "Taxi" signage on most of these vehicles—many are private cars whose owners are simply looking for spare cash; they will accept or reject you depending on whether they are going in your general direction or not.

For 200–300 tenge (foreigners with an accent are asked double that amount or more) you can get anywhere in the city centre. For 500–1,000 tenge one gets to the outskirts of the city, for 1,500–2,000 to the airport, and for 2,000 to the mountains. At night, prices go up slightly. (As of summer 2007, US$1 = approx 120 tenge.)

Almaty desperately needs an **underground railway**. Motor traffic is literally suffocating, air pollution levels rise every year, and 75 percent of all emissions into the atmosphere come from cars. There are traffic jams everywhere and in the rush hour it is best to go on foot (take this seriously into consideration when heading for business meetings, and always allow plenty of time to get to an appointment, although your host will most likely be understanding of the situation). In the 1980s, construction of an underground line more or less under the course of Abai Avenue was started, but then halted in the confusion of the collapse of the Soviet Union. With the help of local and foreign investors, work has begun again and is continuing, but the date of completion is not definite. The future underground's logo has been painted on the fences of station construction sites.

NB: It is important to understand that the lingua franca in Kazakhstan is Russian, and hardly any English is spoken in normal day-to-day situations. If your Russian is poor or nonexistent, you will need the help of a translator, be it a friend or paid guide, to do anything more than the most basic sightseeing walking tours and supermarket shopping. President Nazarbayev has stated his desire for the entire population to become fluent in Kazakh, Russian and English within the coming years, but it will certainly take time and the development of education institutions to allow this to happen.

Many streets in Almaty were renamed following independence. This makes direction finding difficult if you travel by taxi The older generation of taxi drivers, especially, often know only the old names—city maps even show streets with both their old and new names. maps in this book show only the new names for the sake of clarity, but below is a list of old names for some of Almaty's most popularly used thoroughfares:

New name	Old name
Ablai Khan Avenue	pr. Kommunistiychkiy (pr. means Avenue)
Ayteke Bi Street	ul. Oktyabrskaya (ul. means Street)
Altynsarina Ave	pr. Pravdy
Baytursynuli St (Baytursinova)	ul. Kosmonavtov
Bogenbay Batyr(a) St	ul. Kirova
Valikhanova St	ul. Krasina
Dostyk Ave	ul. Lenina
Zheltoksan St	ul. Mira
Zhybek Zholy St	ul. Gorkova
Zenkova St	ul. Proletarskaya
Kazybek Bi St	ul. Sovetskaya
Kaldayakova St	8 (Vosmovo) Marta
Karasay Batyr(a) St	ul. Vinogradova
Kunayeva St	ul. Karla Marksa
Makatayeva St	ul. Pastera
Manasa St	ul. Chapayeva
Nauryzbay Batyr(a) St	ul. Dzerzhinskogo
Raimbeka St	ul. Tashkentskaya
Suyunbaya Ave	Krasnogvardeyskiy Trakt
Tole Bi St	ul. Komsomolskaya
Turgut Ozala St	ul. Baumana
Utegen Batyr(a) St	ul. Mate-Zalki

There is no need to starve as you wander through Almaty, however poor you are. Over the last couple of years, cafés, bars and restaurants have mushroomed not only in the city centre but also in the suburbs. The numerous cafés offer the opportunity to eat fast, affordably and well for those in a hurry or short of cash. Kazakh cuisine, in most cases combined with traditional Russian dishes, is available everywhere, and on the street there is *shashlyk* of variable quality. As the city's overseas population has grown, new restaurants offering "exotic" cuisine such as Egyptian, Thai and Chinese food have sprouted up.

SIGHTS

A stay in Almaty should begin with a familiarization walk for a couple of hours. Don't stick only to the broad main streets, wander up and down the half-hidden secondary streets as well, from time to time peeping around corners into the many courtyards and squares. Sit down in any of the many small parks and look around, and you'll soon realize that the city's most interesting aspect is all around you: the people. A melting pot of nations, Almaty

Republic Square with the Independence Monument centrestage, flanked by two large office blocks and surrounded by statues and a relief showing Kazakh history (Jeremy Tredinnick)

has a Babylonian mix of faces, dress codes and languages. The liveliness of the streets and courtyards is striking. Children play till late in the evening, young adults frequent the cafés and disco bars till deep into the night, conversations take place on every corner. One often receives a giggle or a curious look. The pretty girls draw particular attention—Almaty has a demographic bias in favour of women, and being a university town there always seem to be many groups of stylishly and/or provocatively dressed young women about.

Of course, Almaty also has "genuine" places of interest to offer, but these would only be half as interesting without the surrounding mélange of Almaty's 1.5 million residents. An example of this is **Koktobe**. Close to the towering Hotel Kazakhstan and set back from the junction of Dostyk and Abai (Abay) avenues, a cable car whisks you up to the 1,070-metre-high summit of the "Green Hill" for 200 tenge. There, at the foot of the television tower, you can look out over the city and mountains, a magnificent panorama that draws hundreds of people at a time in the evenings and at the weekend. Most are city inhabitants, romantic couples and families appreciating what a beautiful place they live in. Sunset is a particularly popular time, enjoyed with a portion of shashlyk, wine and music—at times a little too loud.

Panfilov Park was named after General Ivan Panfilov's regiment, which, during the battle of the Volokolamsk Shosse near Moscow destroyed 50 German tanks—the 28 brave guardsmen lost their lives in the process, but a massive and evocative statue of the general and his men remembers their courage, and an eternal flame in front of it is often flanked by bouquets of flowers. The large park, with its old trees and peaceful ambience, is frequented by countless people every day. Some seek spiritual help or a blessing in the *Svyatno-Vosnesenskiy Sobor* (**Holy Ascension Cathedral**), Zenkov's wooden creation that is an architectural joy; others simply come to bear witness to Almaty's past, to relax, to take a coach or horse ride, eat an ice cream or sit down on one of the many benches for a game of chess. Bridal couples surrounded by their numerous guests and relatives visit the park and lay a garland on the monument to the guardsmen, before proceeding to the Wedding Palace for the ceremony, then perhaps on to Medeu to celebrate their wedding day in great revelry.

At the **Wedding Palace** (*Dvorets Brakosochetaniya*), 101A Abai Ave, a distinctive round, white building modelled on a yurt, couples are married at the weekend in a procedure that lasts just a quarter of an hour. Take care: if you show your camera too openly you can easily be engaged on the spot as a wedding photographer, and possibly end up part of the wedding party, only to wake up the next day with a terrible headache in an unknown home! When the Wedding Palace proved insufficient for Almaty's population growth, a new wedding palace was built on the corner of Timuryazova Street and Bayzakova Street, where, in addition to the state wedding ceremony, Muslim and Christian wedding celebrations are also held.

Top: The statue dedicated to General Panfilov and his 28 brave guards is an impressive monument. Above: Sidewalk cafés are all the rage in Almaty (Jeremy Tredinnick x2)

Another spot where one is sure to meet many people is *Ploshchad Respubliki*—**Republic Square**, where the impressive **Independence Monument** looks across to the old Presidential Palace. Situated between Furmanova Street and Zheltoksan Street, the square is normally nothing more than a meeting of the broadest streets in the city—trying to cross it is a lesson in courage and fast reflexes. On holidays, however, the square is turned into a place of festivity with stages, market stalls and crowds of fun-seekers. Fireworks shoot into the sky, music blasts out from the stage and through loudspeakers, and people eat, drink and dance.

The Independence Monument's statue of the Scythian warrior standing on a winged snow leopard has been added to the collection of Kazakhstan's national symbols. At its foot, next to a print of the President's hand, the history of Kazakhstan, starting with the Scythian migration through to the uprising of December 1986, is depicted in a series of reliefs. It is here that the uprising reached its tragic climax. To the south of the square are the splendid buildings of white marble where, before the capital moved to Astana, the President and the government were located. As for the Parliament, it used to gather on **Old Square** (*Staraya Ploshchad*), between Ablai Khan and Furmanov on Tole Bi Street. This square features lavish parks and lawns, with attractive water fountains surrounding the main colonnaded building. Here, in the heart of the city, numerous offices, shops and restaurants create an atmospheric buzz.

The **Central Mosque** (*Tsentralnaya Mechet*) on the corner of Raimbeka and Pushkina, with its large blue domes can be spotted from some distance. It is relatively new, built in 1999, and can accommodate 3,000 worshippers. The building was jointly financed by a large number of Islamic states. Its outer walls are made of white marble, while the inside is an attractive blend of modern Islamic architecture. At first, Kazakhs were hesitant of how to make use of such an impressive building, but today it is full of life, especially on Friday, the Day of Prayer. The Hall of Prayer and its adjacent rooms quickly fill with praying men, and many now also carry out their prayers in the courtyard. On holidays, and most of all on the occasion of weddings, many less religious Kazakhs come here in order to secure the support of Allah. Non-Muslims can enter freely, except on Fridays. Women must keep their head, neck and arms covered, and miniskirts are taboo.

The dress code is less severe at the **Nicholas Cathedral** (*Nikolskiy Sobor*), a charming, newly restored Russian Orthodox cathedral that can be reached by leaving the **Nikolskiy Bazaar** on the corner of Baytursynuly and Kabanbay Batyr to one's left. The proximity of the bazaar to the church is practical in every sense. In the rare instance that the House of God is closed, you can instead enjoy the colourful mix of vegetables, household items, souvenirs and flea market bric-a-brac. Those who beg for alms around the church often spend the tenge received from generous passers-by in the market place.

A leisure park surrounds the architecturally interesting **Circus**, built in the shape of a yurt, on Abai Avenue. This park is popular among the citizens of Almaty, in particular at the weekend and in the evening during the warm summer season. There are carousels, karaoke, a chamber of horrors and numerous fast-food stands, and the sound of pop and rock music resounds around this area of the city.

The **Central Culture and Leisure Park**, or simply **Central Park**, at the eastern end of Gogol Street is somewhere for those looking for relaxation and shade, and features a collection of ancient trees and a beautiful range of flowers. There is the zoo at the far side with more than 4,000 species of animal, but it is in a sad state, with an obvious lack of funding to house the animals properly. Though you can see rare indigenous animals such as the snow leopard, Tien Shan bear and Kazakh steppe wolf, the condition of the animals in their narrow cages can be depressing.

The vast **Botanic Garden** (*Botanicheskiy Sad*) behind the trade exhibition centre (entrance: 48 Timuryazova Street) has also seen better days. Founded in 1932, it used to be not only a popular leisure spot for city folk, but also a national research centre. The large estate of 108 hectares has been badly neglected since the 1990s and is now closed. A sign hangs at the entrance with constantly changing instructions about whom to report to for a visit to the garden, but for the moment it seems it is only open to group tours. It is possible to creep in through the dilapidated fence on the Al-Farabi University side, but you risk a US$50 fine if you are caught. Real Kazakh games can be witnessed at the **Hippodrome** (*ipodrom*) on Akhan Sere Street. During national holidays and on certain weekends, you can watch Kazakh horseriding contests here.

The **Arasan Banya** (Baths) on Ayteke Bi Street is a must-visit destination to get a feel for local life. Housed in a huge white slab of a building opposite the western edge of Panfilov Park, with a fascinating interior of coloured glass and Art Deco angles, you can easily spend an entire day here—preferably in the company of friends—for a very affordable price. There is a choice of Russian (humid), Finnish (dry) or Turkish (mild) saunas, almost all kinds of massage can be arranged, and the circular pool is a great place to relax. Small groups have the option of hiring a luxury private room in the basement for 1,500 tenge an hour.

MUSEUMS

The **Central State Museum of the Republic of Kazakhstan** (*Tsentralniy Gosudarstvenniy Muzey*), a giant building with sky-blue domes constructed in 1985, is a landmark that can easily be spotted from Koktobe Hill. In spite of the fact that many of its best items have been moved to Astana, it still has a lot to offer. (Copies have been made of important exhibits so that the inhabitants of Almaty are not left without them.) An example is *Altyn Adam*—the Golden Man. His costume, a leather kaftan clad with almost 3,000 golden plates found in Issyk, not far from Almaty, is the ceremonial costume of a Scythian warrior dating from the 4th Century BC. Exhibits in the museum illustrate the amazingly well-developed culture that had developed in the territory of present-day Kazakhstan as early as the 8th Century BC. One department is dedicated to the Silk Road. Paintings, allegories and models of mosques and fortresses take the visitor back to the times of Genghis Khan, the Golden Horde and Tamerlane. Especially impressive are the numerous objects from the daily lives of the Kazakhs and their ancestors: finely wrought miniatures in gold and silver, tools and household equipment made of wood and leather, beautiful robes and mantles, weapons showing the strength of those who used to carry them, skilfully wrought woven, knotted and felt rugs, strange-looking folk instruments and a fully equipped yurt. Carpets, pictures, felt objects and books are on sale in various souvenir shops in the museum lobby.

The **Museum of Folk Musical Instruments** (*Muzey narodnykh musikalnykh instrumentov*), situated on the east side of Panfilov Park, is neglected by many tourists but should not be missed. If you are lucky enough to be guided personally by the Kazakh

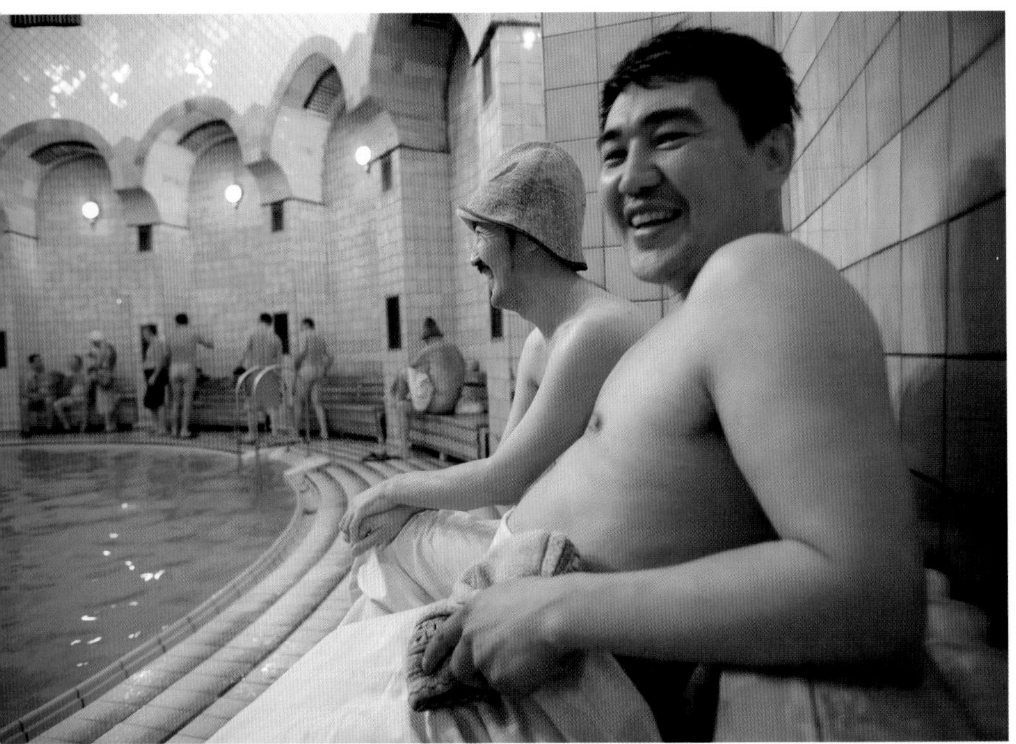

The main pool inside the Arasan Baths; a few hours of sauna, swimming and relaxation with Kazakh friends is a great way to unwind after a long day of sightseeing (Christopher Herwig)

Clockwise from top right: Statue of a graceful dancer in front of the Circus (Gunter Kapelle); this monument to Taras Shevchenko stands at the eastern end of the street that bears his name; a statue of Zhambyl is located in the same fashion; the Museum of Folk Musical Instruments (Jeremy Tredinnick x3)

Summer in the City

Summer has brought out some odd sights. Panfilov Park is suddenly full of brides in white dresses and veils flitting through the trees. It's like some kind of surrealist French film. The reason is the strong tradition in this society for honouring the dead: brides are photographed in front of war memorials, and since Panfilov Park is the home of the most powerful memorial in Almaty—commemorating the Kazakhs of the Panfilov division who died defending Moscow—this is their first choice. It's one of my favourite places too: the memorial is so dramatic it gives you gooseflesh. A colossal bronze map of Russia is the background, and poking out of it, impossibly grim, are the helmeted heads of the Kazakh defenders with their high cheekbones and oriental eyes. In front of them all stands the figure of Panfilov, their Russian officer, with his arms flung wide, biceps bulging, thighs like tree trunks, protecting the homeland behind him.

Not far away, outside the Green Market, babushkas are selling flowers and fruits from their gardens, as well as bunches of wild flowers gathered in the steppe, and old gypsy fortune-tellers have set up their stalls on upturned boxes with cards, cowries shells, and other odd bits and bobs. Their customers—usually young men or women with desperately earnest faces—crouch beside old ladies listening intently. I long to hear their stories.

This week I saw babushka sitting behind a table with just one enormous root on it. When I questioned her it turned out to be asafoetida: people were buying chunks of it for medicinal purposes. She gave me a little piece and told me to mash it with honey and use it as a facemask. So I did—and gave some to Nina and Ira. It certainly made my skin soft, but I couldn't get rid of its horrible pungent smell.

Brigid Keenan, Diplomatic Baggage: The Adventures of a Trailing Spouse, *2006*

composer and singer, Abylai Tugelbayev, you'll learn a lot about the history and culture of Kazakhstan, get demonstrations of all popular instruments and finally have the privilege to listen to a 15-minute concert performed by Tugelbayev, accompanying himself on the dombra. He has a phenomenally powerful voice for his years.

The excellent **Kasteyev State Museum of Art** (*Gosudarstvenniy Muzey Kasteyeva*) houses works of lesser-known European painters from the 16th Century, Russian paintings from the 18th and 19th centuries, and a superb collection of about 1,500 paintings and sculptures by Kazakh artists, including a room dedicated to the works of the museum's namesake Abil Khan Kasteyev, considered the first professional Kazakh painter A large room features applied arts, with woven and felt rugs, woven strips for the decoration of yurts, jewellery, ceramics, instruments and household equipment of leather and wood. Contemporary and abstract art by talented young artists is also displayed upstairs. Guided tours in English and German are available.

A **Book Museum** (*Muzey Knig*) is located on 94 Kabanbay Batyr. Original copies of rare books and manuscripts explain the origin and development of the written Kazakh language. The **Mukhtar Auezov Museum** is dedicated to the great Kazakh writer, who spent the last 10 years of his life here. Visitors interested in literature can find the **Mukanov Musrepov Literature Memorial Museum** nearby.

Two museums are recommended to lovers of antiquity. The **Archaeological Museum of the Institute of Archaeology**, 44 Dostyk Ave on the corner of Zhambyl Street, behind the Zhambyl statue, displays an exhibition of the culture of the Scythians/Sak in Kazakhstan and an interesting map showing all the excavation sites in the country. The **Museum of Geology** on the corner of Dostyk and Abai, through the side entrance of the Kazakh Business Centre, provides a valuable exhibition on rocks and mineral subsoil resources in Kazakhstan. It is open from Tuesday to Saturday between 10am and 4pm. Even laymen get enthusiastic about the variety and beauty of the treasures hidden under Kazakhstan's soil.

The **Natural History Museum** (*Muzey Prirody*) of the Academy of Sciences, situated in the east wing of the academy, 28 Shevchenko Street on the corner of Pushkin Street, is an interesting place to see Kazakhstan's nature and its prehistoric fauna and flora.

On the corner of Baytursynuly and Shevchenko there is the small private museum in memory of **Ahmet Baytursynuly**. The chances are you will leave this place impressed by the fate of the great Kazakh linguist, pedagogue and politician, who was shot in 1937, as well as the fate of his numerous contemporaries who did not survive the Stalinist repression. It is open on weekdays between 1pm and 6pm.

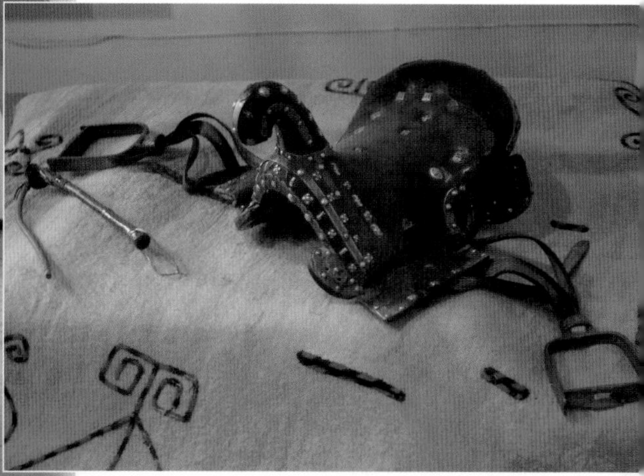

The Kasteyev State Museum of Art displays a variety of treasures. Clockwise from above: A classic Kazakh saddle rests on a felt blanket; Sabur Mambeyev's 1961 At the Yurta*; a painting by the German artist Breuhmer, who documented Kazakhstan's development in the early 20th Century; an 1891 work by self-taught artist Nikolai Khludov named* In the Yurta*; a 1986 metal sculpture by Erkin Merganov called* Meeting*, a reference to the cultural blending of Kazakh tradition with the modern world (Jeremy Tredinnick x5)*

MARKETS

The **Green Market** (*Kok Bazaar* in Kazakh, *Zelyoniy Rynok* in Russian) is situated in the rectangle bordered by Zhibek Zholy, Pushkin St, Makatayev St and Kaldayakov St. It is one of the city's classic Central Asian landmarks, and is an essential destination for visitors—those who do not go can barely claim to know Almaty. Hundreds of stands offer everything you can imagine. In the main hall, dried and fresh fruits and vegetables are displayed in a picturesque manner; massive heaps of meat and offal from a variety of animals are sold in huge amounts; and roots and herbs, honey and flowers spread seductive odours reminiscent of *A Thousand and One Nights*. Korean salads, fish and caviar compete with turtles and confetti. The market cries of the colourfully dressed women selling fruit and the butchers in their bloodstained overalls are remarkable. Outside, you can find drinks and ice cream, felt socks and CDs, bread and tools, workshops where anything can be repaired, key cutting services and money changers, babushkas selling old personal items, and beggars. It's perfectly normal to leave the Green Market heavily laden and considerably lighter in tenge. The market is closed on Mondays.

Every citizen of Almaty knows the **Barakholka**, a kilometre-long stretch on Kuderina Street, parallel to Ryskulova Prospekt. This market offers Asiatic flair, abundant merchandise and sensationally modest prices. Traders both inside and outside offer any and everything: food and beverages, clothing, furs, household equipment, building materials, technical equipment, junk and branded goods at wholesale prices or even less. Branded jeans can be bought here for 10 euros, good mountain boots for 12 euros and coats made of karakul fleece for four times that price. It is quite an experience even if you aren't intending to buy anything. One should, however, keep a tight grip on one's wallet and passport.

Other markets are found in the outskirts of the city. Most of them specialize in something, for example the market on the corner of Tole Bi St and Mikrorayon Aksay-1 offers, apart from fruit, vegetables and other food and beverages, live animals, in particular the popular Central Asian and Caucasian sheepdogs. Closer to the city centre, in the marketplace on the corner of Tole Bi St and Brusilovskovo St, you can find a broad range of furniture and craftwork tools.

PRACTICAL INFORMATION

The dialling code for Almaty is +727. When dialling within the Almaty city area this prefix is not necessary; however, the figure 2 (from the old city code) now has to be prefixed to all six-figure city numbers. Most people use mobile phones; local SIM cards are available at the airport and at many locations around the city—these prove far more economical than submitting to hotel phone rates.

The main post and telegraph office is located at the junction of Ablai Khan/Bogenbay Batyr St. The entrance is at the back across the parking lot. Open Mon–Fri 8am–7pm, Sat/Sun 9am–6pm. The main building of KazakhTelecom is at 100 Zhybek Zholy St, open daily 8am–10pm.

Money exchange booths can be found on almost every street corner in the city, and the rate they offer is generally better than that offered by banks. Favourable US$/euro/tenge rates can be obtained around the Green Market, on the corner of Seyfullin and Shevchenko St, on the corner of Seyfullin/Kurmangazy St and on Gogol St.

Internet cafés have sprung up everywhere, unsurprisingly. Their rates are far lower than hotel rates (the Hyatt for instance charges US$1 per minute), usually around 500 tenge per hour. Following are some of the most convenient:

Internet Café, Dostyk Ave, behind Dovrets Respublika, 2/F (equivalent to UK system's 1/F), open 10am–1am

Computer store in Ramstore, 226 Furmanov St, open 10am–10pm

Net@Café, 87 Gogol St, 11am–12 midnight

Net-Klub Internet, 167 Auezov St, open around the clock

Stalker Internet, 20 Tole Bi St, open 6pm till midnight

Internet access is also available at the main office of KazakhTelecom and the National Library (free of charge). A very useful English language website is the Almaty Expat Site **http://expat.nursat.kz**, which provides a huge amount of useful and updated information on what to do in the city.

TRANSPORTATION

Almaty is the major international entry point for Kazakhstan. Its airport is situated 18 kilometres northeast of the city (1 Maylina St, for information tel: 2 540 555, ticket reservations: 2 795 821/2 795 597, website: **www.almatyairport.com**) and can be reached by bus/marshrutka (minibus) lines 38 (Timuryazov-Baytursinov-Seyfullin), 79 (Timuryazov-Baytursinov-Panfilov Park-Sayakhat bus station), 446 (from Sayran bus station), 492 (Abai-Zheltoksan), 501 (railway station Almaty-2), 540 (Dostyk-Kazybek Bi) or 572 (Green Market).

Air Astana is the national carrier (www.airastana.com). It operates flights to Moscow and St Petersburg in Russia, London, Amsterdam, Frankfurt and Hanover in Europe, Istanbul and Antalya (seasonal) in Turkey, and Dubai, Tashkent, New Delhi, Bangkok, Beijing and Seoul in Asia. Domestic routes include several flights a day to Astana, daily flights to and from Karaganda, Kyzylorda, Shymkent and Pavlodar, while Aktau, Atyrau, Oral, Aktobe and Oskemen are served several times a week. Many other airlines also operate into

TUMAR
White metal. Total length- 40cm; size of the plates: 11x9cm;
CSM RK KP 26795/1

KUDAGI ZHUZIK Western Kazakhstan Silver, gilding. 7,5x6 cm
CSM RK KP 16486

1906
Quiver with arrows. Zoomorphic ornaments. Leather, wood, feather, stamping. XVIII c.

24457
Ishik - woman's fur coat. XIXc. Western Kazakhstan.
Sheepskin, ivy, threads, beads, metal.

A selection of exhibits to be found in Almaty's Central State Museum, from a saukele-crowned mannequin to ancient gold and silver (Courtesy of the Central State Museum, Almaty)

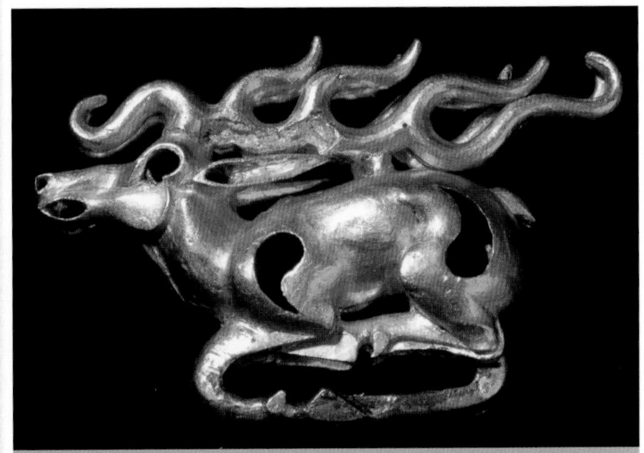

22030/9
Sculpture of a deer. V-III cc. B.C. Zhalauly village. Almaty region.

10337
Duliga- helmet. XVII- XVIII cc. Metal, gilt, notch, weaving, casting.

Almaty, primarily from Russian and other CIS cities in the region. China Southern Airlines connects Almaty to Urumqi in Xinjiang Province. To check updated flight schedules, consult Central Asia Tourism's (CAT) website at www.centralasiatourism.kz. Information can also be obtained at the airport bus station ("Aerovakzal"), 111 Zhibek Zholy/Zheltoksan St, from where shuttle buses leave for certain flights.

Railway station Almaty-1 is a terminal located at the northern end of Seyfullin St (information tel: 2 963 392). Trains from China and the Central Asian republics to the south stop here, and link up with connections to the Russian Federation.

Railway station Almaty-2 is located at the northern end of Ablai Khan St. From here, trains to various destinations in the country depart, including a special night train that leaves for Astana in the evening five days per week. This is the brand-new Spanish "Talgo" train, with air-conditioning, bar, restaurant, and compartments for six, four and two persons. Tickets can be booked at several travel agencies around town.

Booking offices of the national railway company are located at the following addresses:

Zheltoksan/Zhibek Zholy, tel: 2 396 939
50 Timuryazov/Zharokov, tel: 2 604 637
249 Tole Bi/Brusilovskovo, tel: 2 408 949
126 Zheltoksan/Bogenbay Batyr, tel: 2 692 253
59 Dostyk/Zhambyl, tel: 2 914 982

The Sayran Long Distance Bus Station is at 294 Tole Bi St, next to Lake Sayran (information tel: 2 762 676/2 262 677). The Provincial Bus Station is at 1 Suyunbaya/Raimbeka, north of the square in front of the Central Mosque (information tel: 2 302 529/2 302 829).

Accommodation

Almaty's hotel offerings cover the full gamut from cheap and cheerful hostels to international-brand luxury establishments, although rooms in mid- to top-end hotels are by no means cheap, and purported four- or five-star service and standards may not always meet expectations. In many mid-range hotels the Soviet legacy still holds sway, which can be frustrating but also an interesting and not unpleasant experience.

InterContinental Almaty (formerly the Regent Almaty)

181 Zheltoksan Street, tel: (7 727) 2 505 000, fax: (7 727) 2 582 100, e-mail: info@interconti-almaty.kz, website: www.intercontinental.com

A five-star international-brand hotel close to Republic Square and the burgeoning business district to the south. Offers all the luxury facilities you would expect from this hotel group, including the Ankara Spa.

Hyatt Regency Almaty (formerly the Hyatt Rakhat Palace Hotel)

29/6 Akademik Satpayev Avenue, tel: (7 727) 2 501 234, fax: (7 727) 2 508 888, e-mail: almaty.regency@hyattintl.com, website: http://almaty.regency.hyatt.com

The first five-star hotel in Almaty, this luxury property has an enormous lobby atrium complete with a lounge bar area in the shape of a giant yurt. Nearly all its 258 rooms and suites boast panoramic views.

Astana International Hotel

113 Baitursynuly Street, tel: (7 727) 2 507 050, fax: (7 727) 2 501 060, e-mail: info@astana-hotel.com, website: www.astana-hotel.com

A solid four-star hotel located within minutes of both the downtown and new business districts. Features Wi-fi internet connection, good restaurants and small but comfortable rooms.

Hotel Alma-Ata (Almaty Hotel)

85 Kabanbay Batyr Street, tel: (7 727) 2 270 047/052/070, fax: (7 727) 2 720 080, e-mail: info@hotel-alma-ata.com, website: www.hotel-alma-ata.com

Situated in a pleasant and convenient area next to the Old Square parks, many of the Almaty Hotel's rooms have superb views over the Opera and Ballet Theatre to the mountain ridges of the Zailiyskiy Alatau.

Hotel Kazakhstan

52 Dostyk Avenue, tel: (7 727) 2 919 101, fax: (7 727) 2 919 600, e-mail: info@khotel.kz, website: www.hotel-kazakhstan.kz/en

The tallest building in Almaty and a landmark in its own right, this four-star, 26-storey business hotel has recently renovated its rooms, lobby and restaurants. The city views are splendid, and the panorama from the top-floor restaurant is magnificent.

Hotel Otrar

73 Gogol Street, tel: (7 727) 2 506 830/840/848, fax: (7 727) 2 506 809, e-mail: otrar@group.kz, website: www.group.kz

This popular four-star hotel has possibly the best location in the city, facing south over Panfilov Park towards the Tien Shan mountains.

KazZhol Hotel

127/1 Gogol Street, tel: (7 727) 2 508 944, fax: (7 727) 2 508 927, e-mail: hotel-kazzhol@arna.kz, website: www.kazju.kz

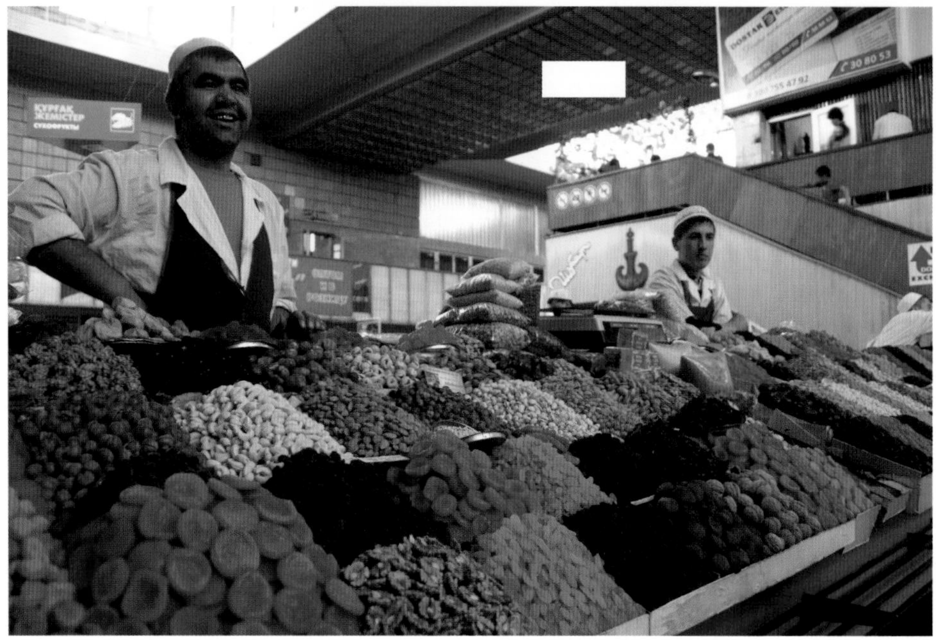

A three-star hotel only a 10-minute walk along the main shopping street from Panfilov Park with a good restaurant.

Grand Hotel TS Tien Shan

115 Bogenbay Street, tel: (7 727) 2 449 600, fax: (7 727) 2 444 007, e-mail: mailbox@ts-hotels.kz, website: www.ts.hotels.kz.

A pleasant four-star hotel in a reconstructed 1930s-period house in the old centre of town, with good service and facilities, restaurants and a spa.

Hotel Zhetysu

55, Ablai Khan Avenue, tel: (7 727) 2 500 400/407/444, fax: (7 727) 2 500 416, e-mail: info@jibekjoly.kz, website: www.zhetysuhotel.kz

A small three-star hotel, located a short walk from the Zhibek Zholy pedestrianized area, with a helpful travel agency based in the hotel.

Food and Drink

Given its multiethnic population and the recent influx of money and expatriates, it comes as no surprise that Almaty presents a feast of dining options. Cafés, bars and restaurants open and close, become fashionable then make way for the latest trends, so it's best to ask local friends or business associates where is best to eat. However, following are just a tiny sampling of currently respected and popular places to drink and dine.

Above: Dried-fruit vendors at the Green Market. Right: Babushkas relax in the shade of Panfilov Park (Jeremy Tredinnick x2). Top right: Almaty's young generation are an effervescent and energetic lot (Gunter Kapelle)

CAFÉS & BARS

For snacks and coffee, try any of the **Kafeinya** chain of coffee shops around the city, as well as **Coffeedelia**, 50 metres east along Kabanbay Batyr from the Furmanov St junction, where the smart moneyed set gather, paying Western prices to indulge in coffee and cakes while seeing and being seen. Good coffee and other drinks, as well as light lunch dishes including toasted sandwiches, salads and sushi snacks are served at **Moka Loka** on the pedestrian zone next to the Tsum department store (Zhibek Zholy, nicknamed "Arbat" after its counterpart in central Moscow). Another popular place with an outdoor terrace during the warm season is Bombolo, also on "Arbat" near Tsum.

The young crowd, students in particular, meet at the **Vogue Bar** (Satpayev/Furmanov) or the **Di Wang Bar** (75 Zhambyl/Tchaikovskaya). In summer, the **Rock Café** on Ablai Khan St between Gogol and Zhibek Zholy has an outdoor terrace. If you fancy comrades Lenin, Trotsky, Che Guevara and other communist heroes looking over your shoulder from

the walls try the **RVS** bar (Furmanov/Ayteke Bi). A nice place for lunch in the colder seasons is the new café **Le Jardin**, 10 Satpayev St, opposite the Gros supermarket.

Western-style food of varying quality is also served in bars where the majority of customers are expatriates from Europe and the US. The most popular are the **Dublin Bar** (off Bayseitov St between Abai Ave and Republic Square), **Mad Murphy's** (just east of Tole Bi/Zenkov), the **Guinness Bar** (71 Dostyk Ave) and **Soho** (65 Kazybek Bi/Furmanov).

Central Asian Cuisine

For a taste of good-quality Kazakh food the restaurants of the major hotels are usually up to scratch; the **Yurt Hall** at the Otrar hotel and **Sulu** at the Astana International Hotel are recommended. But private restaurants often provide a more traditional atmosphere, and are generally cheaper.

Zherulyk restaurant, 500 Seyfullin St, near Karasay Batyr St—in the evening and on holidays people dance to the sound of the dombra here.

Kishlak restaurant, 540a Seyfullin St/Abai Ave—Kazakh and Uzbek dishes in a folky atmosphere and at friendly prices (reservations recommended; tel: 2 615 601).

Alasha restaurant, 20 Marata Ospanova St—good food in a great atmosphere (tel: 2 715 670).

Dastarkhan (75 Shevchenko St/Nauryzbay Batyr St) and **Tomiris** (48 Dostyk Ave)—good Turkish and Kazakh cuisine is offered at rather high prices by both these restaurants.

Yubileyniy (Ablai Khan/Gogol)—part of the popular Dastarkhan restaurant chain, well-priced dishes from traditional to pizza (tel: 2 598 901).

A trip out of town to **Kazakh Aul**, a yurt village behind the Medeu Hotel next to the skating stadium of the same name, allows you to enjoy the country's traditional music as well as great Kazakh cuisine—reading the bill is a pleasant surprise too.

Along the road to Medeu are the open-air restaurants **Aynabu** (also dubbed AB, located at Dostyk/Tattimbeta) and **Sabanty** (Gornay/Marata Ospanov—on the left side). People sit in separate pavilions on the bank or on the bridge over the Malaya Almatinka stream. The menus have a wide range of Central Asian and international dishes.

International Cuisine

Top-quality international food is served in the restaurants within the more luxurious hotels, but as usual the prices will empty your wallet unless you have a generous expense budget. Elsewhere in the city and its environs, the choice seems endless.

Fort Verniy (179a Tole Bi/Auezov)—Russian, Kazakh and European dishes are served in a rustic atmosphere reminiscent of a hunter's cabin, with more than 50 salads, a wide variety of meat dishes and two-dozen brands of beer on the menu. Prices are moderate and the music almost allows normal conversation.

U-Afanasicha (123-8 Dostyk Ave, opposite the end of Chaikina St)—a Russian café with a terrace behind an artificial rampart; ideal for hot summer days.

Zhili Bili (43 Kurmangazy/Furmanov)—another combination of a good atmosphere and excellent Russian cuisine.

Zvezda Davida (42 Furmanov St)—Jewish, Indian and European food at relatively high prices.

Aztek restaurant (66 Kazybek Bi St)—a very popular place with Mexican and Italian cuisine and a lively Latin atmosphere.

Sumo San (163 Baytursynuly St)—excellent Chinese, Thai, Japanese and other Oriental dishes, including an excellent sushi bar at moderate prices.

Three Oranges (*Tri Apelsiyniy*) (Satpayev St, on the left side 100 metres before the junction with Dostyk Ave)—a fine selection of Korean, Thai, Uygur, Chinese, Italian and local dishes are served at good prices and with friendly service. Frequented by students and teachers of the international school of economics (KIMEP).

Brno (64 Zhibek Zholy/Valikhanov)—a tasty and affordable Czech restaurant.

Staraya Angliya (134 Bogenbay Batyr St)—a British restaurant with relatively high prices.

Prussia, (95 Rozabakiyev/Satpayev)—a popular German restaurant.

"**Schwäbisches Haus**" (121 Ablai Khan/Kabanbay Batyr)—another German eatery that advertises itself as "open 25 hours a day".

Rumynskiy Dvor (courtyard of 135 Ablai Khan St)—a rustic atmosphere, friendly service and a fine selection of Balkan dishes.

Stetson (128 Furmanov/Kabanbay Batyr)—sophisticated cuisine with good wines and a large beer menu.

Senator bar and restaurant (corner of Shevchenko/Shagabutdinov)—a cheerful mood thanks to the many students from the nearby Institute of Foreign Languages.

Open-air restaurants can be found at the Tau-Dastar "restaurant township" in the valley of the Greater Almatinka River, on the road that leads to two of the most popular leisure resorts, Bolshoye Almatinskoye Ozero and Alma Arasan. Cuisines on the various restaurants' menus include Georgian, Bavarian, Tibetan and others. The smaller restaurants and grills next to them are also worth trying. Prices in general are relatively high, as this road is part of the regular tourist trail.

NIGHTLIFE

Almaty has a vibrant but ever-changing nightlife scene. The internet is the best source of up-to-date information on where to go for your own particular brand of entertainment. The Russian website www.spravka.kz has links to individual clubs' websites, most of which have English pages as well, or try http://expat.nursat.kz. However, be careful to check out the clubs before you visit them, and avoid entering clubs at random, since many feature hustlers and in some physical violence—due to the amount of strong alcoholic drink that is routinely consumed—is fairly common. Another thing to be on the lookout for is drug abuse—Kazakhstan has tough laws and follows strict policies on this. At time of writing, the following discos and clubs are known to have a good reputation:

Jazz Café Bourbon Street (Adi Sharipov/Kurmangazy).

Members' Bar (Hyatt Regency Hotel)—good live jazz music every day.

Stars Club (171a Zheltoksan St).

Petroleum (100 Shevchenko/Seyfullin)—a more mature crowd.

Ankara, in the hotel of the same name (181 Zheltoksan St).

Grand (52 Gogol St).

Metro (2b Zhandosov/Bayzakov)—a mixed crowd.

Pyramid (152 Karasay Batyr/Nurmakov)—Popular with the younger generation.

Dafreak (Pushkin/Gogol)—a young crowd, mainly students.

For something a little different try the **Real Club** (corner of Masanchi/Raimbekova), which began life as a gay club, but these days is about a 50/50 mixed crowd. Transvestite shows with all the usual humour, glamour and glitter are on Friday and Saturday nights, starting at 2am and lasting till dawn. "Face control" at the entrance keeps the crowd civilized.

SHOPPING

At shopping centres such as **City Centre** (136 Tole Bi/Bayzakova), **Promenade** (44a Abai Ave) and **Ramstore** (226 Furmanova St), everything from food to tools is available, and Visa and Eurocard are accepted. Nowadays, all the Western luxury brands from Boss to Givenchy and Gucci can be found downtown on and around **Gogol Street**. For a shopping experience more akin to Soviet times, head for the somewhat chaotic department store **Zangar** (formerly Tsentralniy Universalniy Magazin, or **Tsum**) on the corner of Zhybek Zholy St and Ablai Khan St. Mobile phones and accessories, food and beverages are on the ground floor; souvenirs on the top floor. Well-stocked souvenir shops can also be found in all major hotels. Beautiful silver jewellery by the artist Serzhan Bashirov, as well as felt

Kazakhstan embraces the modern world, but many of its citizens remain parochial (Gunter Kapelle)

and leather goods can be bought at the studio business of Gulmira Bashirova (gulmirabash@mail.ru, tel: 2 371 273).

The Central State Museum shop offers a selection of fine carpets. Mostly factory-made rugs can be found at **Almaty Kilem** (187 Tole Bi/Zharkova, www.almaty-kilem). A visit to the carpet weavers on Kabanbay Batyr St between Panfilov St and Furmanov St is an experience. Here, at the firm At Atkul Carpets, you can watch carpets being designed and made—buying one is of course an option.

Beautiful felt rugs can be bought on the top floor of the Tsum. Nearby, a bit farther up "Arbat" towards the Silk Way Shopping Mall, oil paintings by Kazakh artists are displayed on the street and in shops. Most of the work is junk offered by the painters at knockdown prices, but it is possible to find the occasional piece with genuine artistic merit. For real quality, one should turn to the galleries around town.

Bookshops (often also selling maps) can be found on almost every street corner, although what is available on any one day is something of a lottery. The chains Rarity and Economix offer the best collections and the best service. Another useful place is Akademknia (Shop 2, 139 Furmanov/Kabanbay Batyr, tel: 2 727 981). Caspian Publishing House sells its English language collection at the postcard shop Koza, on Panfilov St near the corner of "Arbat", and at its office beside the CAT office at 20½ Kazybek Bi St. The Ramstore supermarket on Furmanov St and the Hyatt and InterContinental hotels have English bookstores with a relatively varied stock.

For trekking equipment the best quality is located at the Korgan-Centre Robinson, 60 Ablai Khan St, near the Tsum (tel: 2 327 640).

Museums, Galleries & Theatres

Central State Museum, Mikrorayon Samal-1, building 44, tel: 2 642 200. Open daily 10am–6pm.

Museum of Folk Musical Instruments, 24 Zenkova St on Panfilov Park, in front of the (new) Officers' House, tel: 2 916 316/326. Open Tue–Sun, 10am–5:30pm.

Kasteyev State Art Museum, 30a Satpayev St/Musrepov St, tel: 2 922 343/2 478 356. Open Tue–Sun, 10am–6pm.

Book Museum, 94 Kabanbay Batyr St/Kunayev St, tel: 2 623 821. Open Mon–Fr, 9am–5pm.

Mukhtar Auezov Museum, 185 Tulibayev St/Abai Ave, tel: 2 637 467/2 629 274. Open Tue-Sat.

Mukanov/Musrepov Literature Memorial Museum, 185 Tulibayev St/Karasay Batyr St, tel: 2 635 912/2 638 286. Open Tue–Sat.

Archaeological Museum, 44 Dostyk Ave/Zhambyl St, tel: 2 918 585/2 918 632. Open daily.

Geological Museum, 85 Dostyk Ave/Abai Ave, side entrance of the Kazakh Business Centre, tel: 2 635 283. Open Tue–Sat, 10am–4pm.

Nature Museum, 28 Shevchenko St/Pushkin St. Open daily, 10am–4pm.

Akhmet Baytursinuly Museum, Baytursinuly St/Shevchenko St. Open Mon–Fri, 1pm–6pm.

Tengri Umay Gallery of Modern Art, 43 Abai Ave/Ablai Khan St (in the foyer of the Lermontov Theatre), tel: 2 620 309, e-mail: filat@itte.kz—a new exhibition each month of fine arts from Kazakhstan and the rest of Central Asia, as well as applied arts, good-quality jewellery and gadgets on sale. Open Mon–Sat, 10am–6pm.

Ular Gallery for Modern Art, 29 Kurmangazy St, to the east of Kunayev St, Room 304 in the House of Scientists, tel: 2 914 773—high-level fine arts exhibitions and photo exhibitions. Open daily, 10am–6pm.

Tribuna Gallery, 14a Republic Square, on the tribune's ground floor, opposite the Golden Man statue—modern Kazakh art, often by young artists. Open daily 11am–6pm.

Central Exhibition Hall, also dubbed the Museum for National Applied Arts, 137 Zheltoksan St/Zhambyl St, tel: 2 692 090/086—changing exhibitions of paintings, artefacts and rugs. Open Mon–Fri 11am–6pm, Sat 11am–2pm.

Bakhyt Centre for Decorative Art, 56a Abai Ave, to the east of Manas St, tel: 2 425 777/2 426 400—artefacts and works of art by young, talented artists and artisans. Open Mon–Sat, 10am–6pm.

Art Salon, 53/1 Ayteke Bi St/Panfilov St. Open Mon–Fri, 10am–5pm.

Gallery Antique-M, Apt 45, 131 Ablai Khan St/Shevchenko St (entrance in the courtyard), tel: 2 699 173—good, high-priced works of art, jewellery, woven artefacts on sale. Open Mon–Sat 11am–8pm.

Asia Craft Salon, 85 Kazybek Bi, Apt. 26 (between Tchaikovskovo and Navruzbey Batyr St), tel: 2 320 528. Open Mon–Sat, 11am–7pm.

Gallery Oner, Shevchenko/Furmanov St, tel: 2 625 951—paintings, souvenirs and artefacts.

Modern art gallery Orkhon, 62 Ablai Khan St/Zhibek Zholy St (3/F of the Tsum department store), tel: 2 332 914/2 330 329.

Abai Opera and Ballet Theatre, 110 Kabanbay Batyr St/Panfilov St (opposite the Almaty Hotel), tel: 2 722 934/042—the full classical repertoire.

Auezov Kazakh Drama Theatre, 103 Abai Ave/Zhandosov St (opposite the Circus), tel: 2 926 378—plays are performed in Kazakh with Russian translation in the two auditoria of this large, well-equipped theatre.

Novaya Stsena ("New Stage"), 103 Panfilov St/Zhibek Zholy St, tel: 2 335 766/2 323 849—classical Russian plays and avant-garde. Open daily, 6pm.

Republican Palace, Dostyk Ave (behind Hotel Kazakhstan), tel: 2 915 523—beautifully decorated auditorium for 3,000 people, all kinds of concerts and other performances.

Children's and Youth Theatre, 38 Ablai Khan St/Mametov St, tel: 2 714 237.

Uygur Musical Comedy Theatre, Nauryzov Batyr St/Karasay Batyr St, tel: 2 691 817—wide variety of Uygur, Kazakh, Russian and European plays with a resonance that reaches beyond Almaty.

Korean Musical Comedy Theatre, 70/71 Papanina St, tel: 2 469 713.

Kazakh State Puppet Theatre, 63 Pushkin St/Gogol St, tel: 2 335 656.

Central Concert Hall/State Philharmonia, 35 Kaldayakov St/Tole Bi St, tel: 2 722 934/042—mostly classical music.

KazKonsert Concert Hall, 63 Ablai Khan St, to the south of Ayteke Bi St, tel: 2 616 364/2 610 712.

Kurmangazy Conservatory, 90 Ablai Khan St, between Bogenbay Batyr and Karasay Batyr St—high-quality students' concerts beginning at 6pm.

Circus, 50 Abai Ave/Vesnovka, tel: 2 927 923.

Hippodrome, 10a Akhan Sere St (formerly Omarov St)/Zhansugurov St (road to Kapshagay), tel: 2 939 433/2 948 600—horse races at weekends and on public holidays. To get there, take bus lines 30 and 34, and trolleybus line 7, or use a taxi.

Chekhov City Central Library, 109 Gogol St/Zheltoksan St. Open Mon–Fri, 9am–6pm.

National Library, Abai Ave/Ablai Khan St, tel: 2 629 590. Open daily, 10am-8pm.

Arasan Baths, Ayteke Bi St/Kunayev St. Open Tue–Sun, 10am–10pm.

Within easy reach of the city, Big Almaty Lake is a popular camping and hiking destination, its clear turquoise water surrounded by high forested ridges and peaks (Vladimir Tugalev)

The Almaty Environs

Not surprisingly, the Tien Shan mountains are the most impressive of Almaty's surrounding attractions. In 1996, the **Ili-Alatau National Park** was founded. It descends almost into Almaty from the mountain heights, stretches over 120 kilometres from east to west between the rivers Turgen and Shamalghan (Chemolgan), and south to the border with Kyrgyzstan. The park contains 1,400 plant species and 240 kinds of vertebrate, many of which are endemic and rare.

You can make numerous day trips from Almaty into the nearby mountain areas either by city bus or taxi. For multi-day guided treks or package bus trips simply go to one of Almaty's numerous travel agencies—the Almaty environs is the best-developed region for tourism in all of Kazakhstan. A list of recommended travel agencies can be found at the end of Chapter 3, Zhetisu: the Land of Seven Rivers.

Medeu, Shymbulak and the Tuyuksu Glacier

City bus 6 (204 at weekends), or a 30-minute taxi ride, will bring you to **Medeu** and its legendary ice stadium at a height of 1,609 metres, 15 kilometres to the south of the city. Early birds can also take the only bus to Shymbulak, which departs from the corner of Satpayev and Baitursynuly at 8am every day.

When Almaty citizens praise "their" Medeu, they will tell you that more than 120 world skating records have been set here. The site was under reconstruction for a long time and was reopened in 2002. The skating arena is used only occasionally for competitions, and people can go skating almost throughout the year.

From the stadium you can carry on into the mountains either on foot or by taxi. A large, 150-metre-high dam overlooking Medeu was built in 1966–67 to protect the city against mud slides. The two explosions carried out in the dam's construction caused subterranean tremors that registered 7 on the Richter scale. Its protective wall of reinforced concrete stood the test in 1973, when a strong heatwave and increased melting of the glacier created a powerful landslip of mud and boulders—the giant mudflow wiped out a major part of the village of Talgar in the neighbouring valley.

On foot, you must climb 830 steps to reach the upper edge of the dam. From there, you turn south, past the meteorological station to the forester's house. You now have the choice of two directions. Either you turn sharp right across a nettle field to reach a path

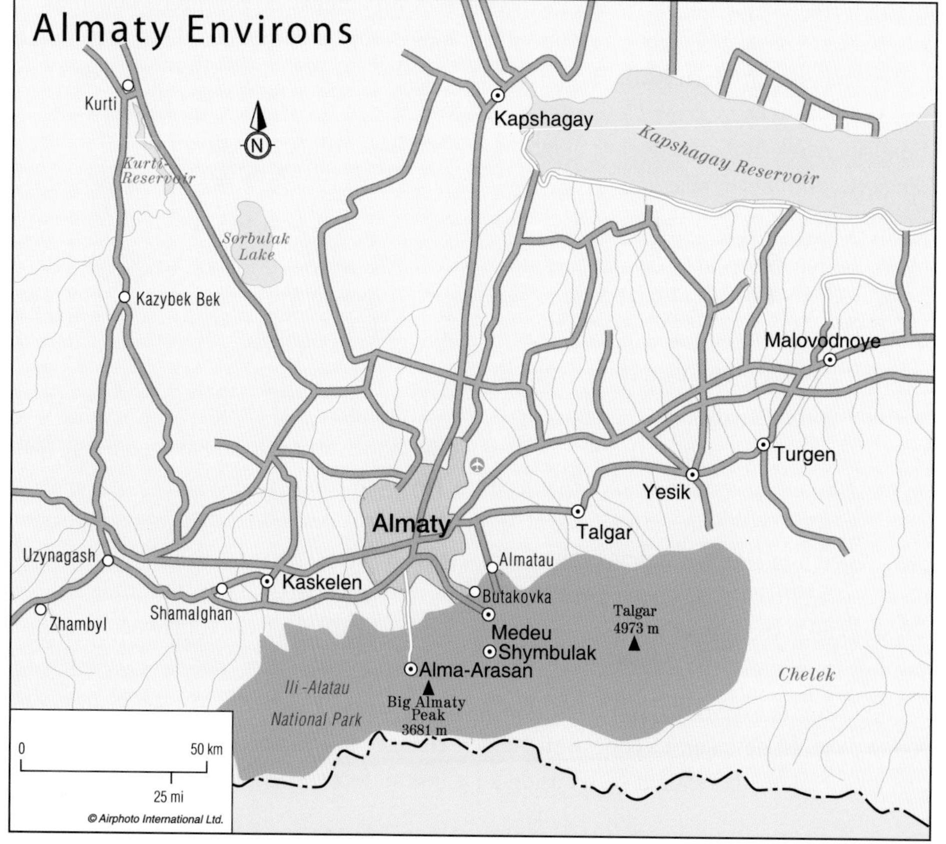

that leads to the right through a fir forest, past picturesque rock formations and another meteorological station on the upper reaches of the Gorelnik stream to a waterfall, where, after a break, it's time to think about returning. Or, alternatively, at the forester's house turn only half-right and follow the road to a bridge that crosses the Gorelnik. Warm sulphur springs beyond the bridge feed the river. A swim alleviates fatigue and is recommended before taking the road back. Along the right bank of the river you can walk up to the former Gorelnik Inn, which was destroyed during an avalanche in 1973.

It takes about three hours to walk from Medeu to **Shymbulak**, and the view of the slopes with their towering Tien Shan spruces—which grow between 1,500m and 2,800m altitude, reach 50 metres in height and can be centuries old—cannot fail to impress. Of course if you are reluctant to walk there is a road, very busy at weekends, and a parking place for 1,000 cars.

Shymbulak is a popular ski resort—even the president is spotted here from time to time—with hotels and seven cable and chairlifts; there is 60-80cm of snow on average near the resort base, while higher up 1–2 metres of snow is common. The chairlifts take people to the Talgar Pass at a height of around 3,000 metres. In clear weather, the pass offers a view of magnificent Talgar Peak. Here, you can sunbathe on any of the 330 sunny days each year, ski or snowboard from November till May on one of the pistes with varying degrees of difficulty, trek in the summer or climb. Skiing schools, including some for children, offer their services in Shymbulak.

Shymbulak will host the 2011 Asian Winter Games, and with this in mind work has already begun on a cable car connecting Medeu to Shymbulak with a capacity of 2,000 people per hour. A new hotel is also planned, and already there are two dozen large wooden chalets on the road up to the resort. These cater to groups of 10 or more, and can be booked at major tour agencies in the city.

Hotel Vorota Tuyuksu is recommended as a starting point for alpine tours. It is named after the rock formation directly behind the building, which stands in solitary splendour like a gate to the entrance of the valley that leads to **Tuyuksu Glacier**. This large valley glacier at a height of 3,500 metres at the foot of Mount Lokomotiv can be reached in two to three hours. There is a research station of the Glaciological Institute of the Academy of Sciences at the top—the Tuyuksu has been scientifically observed since 1902. (Sadly, the studies show that since 1923 the glacier has receded nearly one kilometre, a situation blamed on global warming by scientists worldwide.)

Jeeps can manage the gravel track, which comes pretty close to the glacier. Appropriate clothing should be taken to cope with sudden changes in the weather. To remain on the safe side, a whole day should be set aside for a trip on foot.

PRACTICAL INFORMATION

ACCOMMODATION

Hotel Premier Medeu, 582a Gornaya Street, tel: (7 727) 2 716 254, fax: (7 727) 2 716 255/256/257, e-mail: amsmax@nursat.kz,—from US$125 in winter, with discounts in summer. At a height of 1,600 metres near the Medeu ice stadium, on the left side of the large parking place. Renovated rooms, a bit chilly in winter. Nice view, good starting point for many alpine tours.

Hotel Shymbulak, tel: (7 727) 2 738 624, fax: (7 727) 2 733 329, e-mail chimbulak@ nursat.kz, website: www.chimbulak.kz—family rooms and suites from US$102, without breakfast. Full board for US$10–15 extra. At a height of 2,200 metres, this sports hotel is 100 metres from the ski lifts, has an equipment rental shop, ski school, sauna, bowling and billiards. Crowded in winter, quiet and affordable in summer.

Hotel Vorota Tuyuksu, tel: (7 727) 2 508 585, fax: (7 727) 2 640 448, e-mail: alp21@ mail.ru—a nice-looking Swiss-style wooden chalet, with 26 cosy double rooms from US$40; cottages from US$50–80. Situated at a height of 2,500 metres in the valley of the Malaya Almatinka, two kilometres beyond Shymbulak, right by the gravel track that leads to the glacier; a picturesque location, with winter sports equipment for rent.

BUTAKOVKA

It costs 40 tenge on city bus 429, departing from the corner of Dostyk Ave and Gornaya St, to get to the village of **Butakovka**. This is a village full of contradictions; wealthy citizens have built huge mansions and surrounded them with walls and tall iron railings for protection on the best spots on the slope, with a fantastic view of the mountains of Shymbulak—but the poor neighbours in their dilapidated *dachas* (wooden cottages) seem little disturbed by it. A handful of Kazakh families, one of which even lives in a yurt, breed horses. You can see the half-wild animals in the evening as they come to drink from the brook in the shadow of the majestic mountain peaks. The many pensioners appear to survive on the clear water of the Butakovka mountain stream and the apples that grow on the slopes. Repairs to their once charming homes will have to wait until solvent buyers respond to the signs reading *prodam dom*—"For sale".

On sunny autumn days, one can hardly get enough of watching the yellow-red leaves of the apple trees with the red apples glowing as if in competition. The 3,000m+ peaks behind them are already clad in their first winter snow; the sky is clear blue. It is warm enough to climb the trees in shorts to shake down the apples. Very brave souls might follow the example of cold-water therapy enthusiasts, who gather here every day to undergo shock treatment under the waterfall of the Butakovka stream. Ever since Sara Nazarbayeva,

Above and below right: The Medeu ice skating rink has seen its fair share of records set in competition, but it is more often used by Almaty residents for recreation. It is open virtually all year round, as popular in summer (above) as in winter (below right) (Ernst Ischovits x2)

the president's wife, announced that the therapy of the Russian health expert Ivanov is extremely healthy and demonstrated it by submitting her own body to this treatment, there has been no end to the influx of eager participants.

You reach the waterfall by following the tarmac road eastwards, passing the military-style fenced villas of the nouveaux riches, to the new sports hotel. Here, you must leave your vehicle, since the land beyond is private property. You can, however, continue on foot following the brook along the track. Where the gorge gets narrower, you leave the main path that leads to the Butakovka Pass, take the side valley to the left, and reach the waterfall in 10 minutes.

The 20-metre-high waterfall is also very beautiful in winter, when the frozen cascade looks like the castle of an ice princess. Fit hikers can continue across the fairly easy Kimasarovskiy Pass to Medeu. Locals say that the walk is easier from Medeu to Butakovka—it is almost entirely downhill. In Butovka you can enjoy Central Asian and Russian cuisine outside the friendly and affordable Cafe Bike, situated on the left side of the road that leads to the waterfall.

The last bus from Butovka to the city leaves at 5:10pm, but if you miss it you can always find someone to drive you to the city for 300–500 tenge. The travel agency Indra Tours offers a longer, guided trek of several days from here to the village of Talgar.

ALMA ARASAN AND THE PROKHODNAYA VALLEY

Alma Arasan is a former health resort situated at a height of 1,850 metres. It can be reached on bus 93 from the roundabout that joins Al-Farabi Ave with Novoi St, or by taxi for 1,000 tenge. There is an inviting walk along the Prokhodnaya mountain stream, and a warm sulphur spring (37°C/99°F) next to a tea pavilion, unfortunately wrecked, is popular among local people for bathing, but is not currently recommended for hygiene fanatics. There are 16 such hot springs here, to which the place owes its name, Arasan (sweat bath). The **Prokhodnaya Valley** is good for a couple of hours of easy hiking, and a swim afterwards is refreshing. Good trekkers will make it to the foot of Mount Saw, named for its shape. You should plan your route in such a way that you can catch the last bus back to the city from Alma Arasan, which leaves at 6:30pm. Alternatively, you can spend the night in the Alma Arasan sanatorium, an aged building with a sauna, pool and beautiful view of the mountains from the balcony. One night costs as little as US$10.

Prokhodnaya Valley is a popular starting point for walks to **Issyk Kul** in Kyrgyzstan. Those who choose the easiest track still have to cross two mountain passes. The trek takes two to five days, depending on fitness and load.

The Sunkar Sanctuary for Birds of Prey

Taking the marshrutka 560 minibus from Almaty-2 Railway Station or bus 93 from the roundabout at Al-Farabi/Navoi, you'll head towards Alma Arasan but get off after about seven kilometres behind the massive avalanche protection wall at the entrance to the national park. The **Sunkar bird sanctuary** is situated right behind the ecological observation post to the right on the slope.

Here, injured hunting birds are lovingly cared for, eggs abandoned by birds of prey incubated, and the fledglings raised under conditions as natural as possible. You can admire falcons, eagles, owls—among them some protected species—at close quarters. Staff will teach you a lot about these animals, and about traditional hunting with dogs—primarily the ***tazy***, a type of borzoi—and hunting birds. Some Kazakh tazys are kept at the facility, together with Central Asian shepherd dogs. A falconry show takes place daily in the warm season, where you'll see saker falcons, eagle owls, golden eagles and even a griffon vulture all being flown and put through their paces. Entry is 1,000 tenge per person.

If you want to stretch your legs you can walk and climb pretty far into the valley behind the sanctuary. The **Valley of Stone Flowers** (*Kamenniy Tsvetok*) is a picturesque karst valley which forks more than once and over a distance of about five kilometres, leading to summer pastures. Trips up here on horseback are also possible from the sanctuary.

A two-storey wooden house with seven double rooms is available for those who want to overnight here—one night costs US$10. Call Ashot Ansarov, head of the sanctuary (tel: 7 701 799 2028), Galina Osipova (office administrator, tel: 2 524 122) or Falconer Peter Pfander (tel: 7 701 166 5409) for information on schedules and options.

Kok Zhaylau Alpine Pasture

Two major mountain valleys emerge on Almaty's doorstep: the **Lesser (Small) Almatinka**, in which the famous ice stadium of Medeu is situated, and the **Greater (Big) Almatinka** (*Bolshoye almatinskoye ushchel'ye*) with the lake of the same name. The walk from one valley to the other across the ridge and **Kok Zhaylau**, the meadows in the valley of the Kazatshka brook, is demanding but rewards hikers with wonderful panoramas.

Take city bus 24 or 6 from Dostyk Ave in the direction of Medeu, and jump off at the Prosveshchenets Inn. Here, you turn right towards the southeast at first, climbing steadily up along a mountain path through a beautiful birch forest and thence towards the west, flanked by firs and wild plum trees. After having climbed some 1,100 metres in altitude, you're rewarded with a break at the pass and a wonderful view over the city—if it is visible in the haze, of course. A path leads east from the pass's lowest point to a waterfall. Experienced walkers can include a two-hour climb of the **Kumbel Peak** (3,618 metres) in

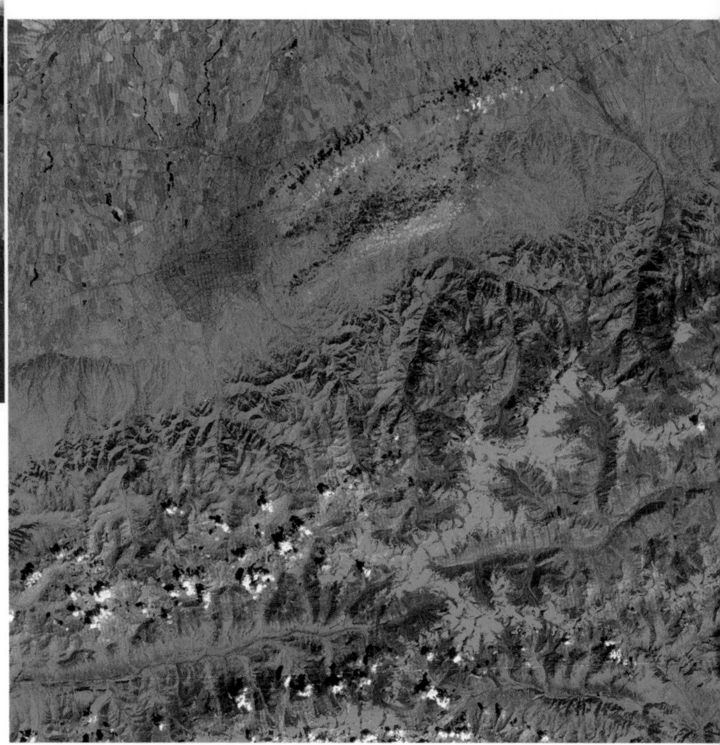

Above: The Space Observation Station on the slopes of Big Almaty Peak (Jeremy Tredinnick). Right: A satellite image shows Almaty's proximity to the mountains (NASA Landsat image courtesy of USGS and Global Land Cover Facility, www.landcover.org). Below: Big Almaty Lake gets a covering of ice in winter (Vladimir Tugalev)

this trek. It starts on the southern side of the pass, and towards the top you get a panoramic view of the mountain peaks that surround the valley of the Lesser Almatinka, the highest of which is the **Ordzhonikidze Peak**.

Back on the pass, you head off down the 14-kilometre-long track across the green Kok Zhaylau meadows, rich in medicinal herbs. Kok Zhaylau means green summer pasture, and the area used to be heavily used by herdsmen. Even now you can encounter herds of sheep and cattle during the spring and summer seasons. In winter, this long and gently sloping track is popular for skiing and tobogganing. Even in summer skiing is still possible in some of the side valleys of Kok Zhaylau, since the snow lasts there until the beginning of June.

Having arrived in the Greater Almatinka Valley, you head back to Almaty on city bus 28 or 93. The whole excursion will take 8–10 hours, a solid day's hiking requiring preparation, food and plenty of water.

Big Almaty Lake and Big Almaty Peak

A tarmac road from Novoi St leads from the city to the hydroelectric power station GES-II. Bus lines 28 and 93 get there and a bit beyond. At the checkpoint you have to pay for entry into the national park—people on foot pay 100 tenge, a car or a minibus costs more. But a walk to the lake is not only preferable because of the difference in price; from the last bus stop to the lake is an easy 16 kilometres, but the road becomes worse with each kilometre.

The 38-metre-deep **Big Almaty Lake**, as it is most commonly known, is the nearest lake in the **Zailiyskiy Alatau** region, set like a beautiful azure jewel in the surrounding mountain scenery. It is situated at a height of 2,511 metres in the valley of the Greater Almatinka River, to which it owes its name. The water temperature does not rise above 8°C even in summer. You can camp here—a warm sleeping bag is strongly advised—or spend the night in an inn for the modest sum of between 500–1,000 tenge. The lake is at its most beautiful in June–July after the snow has melted, or in September when the glacier has released its highest level of water during the summer.

From the lake, a climb to the **Space Observation Station** on the slopes of **Big Almaty Peak**, also called BAP, is possible. The station is at 3,681 metres, but no special equipment is required for the climb, only stout, well-fitting shoes and warm clothes, since an icy wind blows on the top. You can spend the night in a sturdy house next to the observatory—it's worth it just for the sunrise. Camping is also possible if you have the right equipment.

The road splits in two on the dam that crosses the lake. To the right is the starting point for the popular multi-day walk to Issyk Kul across the **Ordzhonikidze Pass** at the head of the valley. To the left (east) the road leads to the Tourist Pass into the valley of the Left Talgar.

PRACTICAL INFORMATION

Hotel at the Observatory—a simple inn that houses 34 people, with rooms for one to three persons, dilapidated communal toilets and showers, a kitchen, dining room and sauna, US$40 including all meals. Bungalows are also available with rooms for one to two persons. Reservations through Aidar Kuratov, e-mail: aidarskiy@mail.ru, tel: 7 777 247 5537.

"Student bungalow" for 18 persons, rooms for three to four undemanding trekkers, facilities "across the yard". Reservations through Slava Plyetnyev, tel: 2 759 385 (work) or 2 977 560 (home).

Alpiyskaya Roza—a small, 12-room hotel in the valley of the Greater Almatinka Valley at a height of 2,235 metres, tel: 2 552 356, fax: 2 640 448, e-mail: alpina@citiserv.net, alp21@ mail.ru; double rooms in cottages from US$50, single occupation negotiable. Winter sports equipment can be rented.

THE ARTISTS' VILLAGE OF SHEBER AUL

On the road to Big Almaty Lake is the village of **Kokshoky**, some nine kilometres beyond the Al-Farabi/Novoi roundabout and 25 metres down the left fork for Alma Arasan/Big Almaty Lake. Craftsmen of the Trade Corporation of Kazakhstan have been engaged for years in turning the dilapidated buildings into a handicraft village (***sheber aul***) where one can see craftspeople at work and buy traditional items such as felt rugs and toys, silver jewellery, and goods made of wood, leather and fur. Unfortunately, little progress can be seen due to lack of funding. During the warm seasons, however, it is worth the excursion. After all, each visitor contributes a little to the local economy.

There is accommodation here, the **Hotel Kumbel**, tel: 2 507 527, fax: 2 507 526, e-mail: kumbel@asdc.kz, a quiet place with 13 rooms from US$110 and a separate comfortable wooden house, restaurant, sauna, swimming pool and sports facility.

LAKE SORBULAK

This vast lake on the right side of the main Almaty-Astana road, some 50 kilometres to the northwest of Almaty, has for years attracted large numbers of pelicans, who breed here. Any visit to **Lake Sorbulak** must be made in the full understanding that protection of the colony of large birds on the lake is paramount. Discretion is required so as not to upset the environment of this large collection of majestic waterbirds.

ZHETISU: LAND OF SEVEN RIVERS

High over the yurts, high like roaming cranes, floated tender, grey-blue clouds; flocks of sheep poured in a quiet, wide stream over the hill; a waterfall crashed from the rock and blinded the eyes with its white wisps of foam.

Chingis Aitmatov

Seven main rivers flow down off the steep slopes of the **Tien Shan** and the **Zhungar Alatau** to the northeast; they gave their name to the fertile hills and plains that they created: **Zhetisu** (**Semirechye** in Russian), the "**Land of Seven Rivers**". These rivers include the **Ili**, which flows in from China, and the Shelek, Tentek, Lepsy, Aksu, Koksu and Karatal; along their banks numerous settlements have turned the land southeast of **Lake Balkhash** into the most densely inhabited area in Kazakhstan. Today, the term Zhetisu refers to the entire Almaty Region, the capital of which has been **Taldykorgan** since 2001. With a land area of 224,000 square kilometres, the Land of Seven Rivers is larger than the US state of Utah, and almost as big as Great Britain.

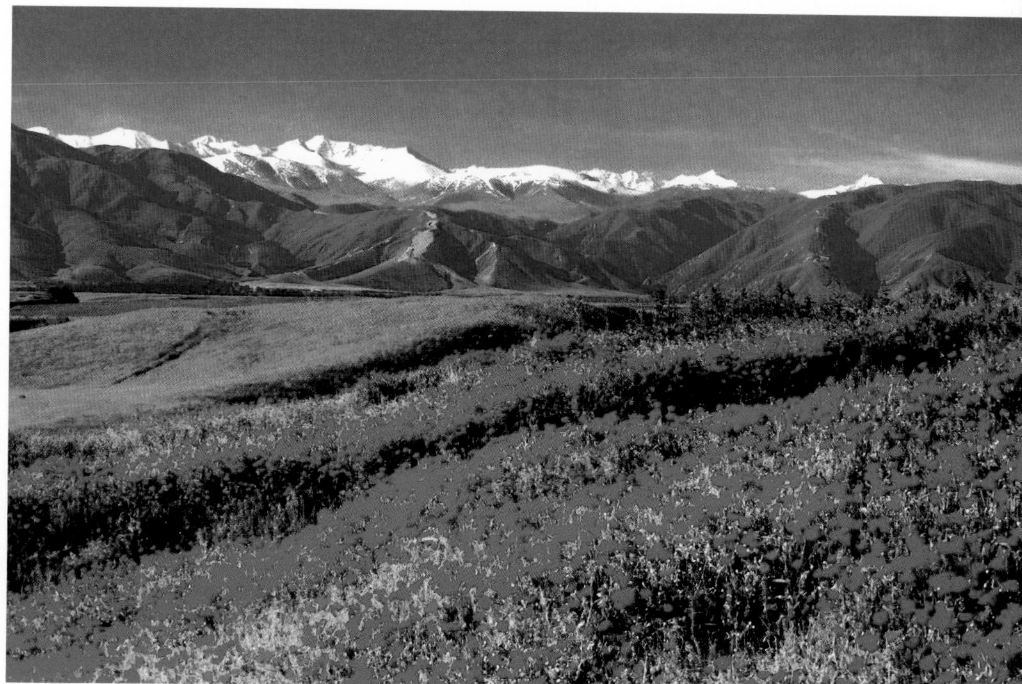

Above: Nature paints an Impressionistic picture in Zhetisu during the spring bloom (Vladislav Yakushkin). Left: The rich pastures of Kok Zhaylau have been used by nomads for centuries (Vladimir Tugalev)

It is frequently boasted that in a matter of few hours you can drive or even walk across six different climatic and vegetational zones in Zhetisu—from desert and semi-desert through scattered deciduous and mixed forests, the conifer forest taiga, the treeless alpine meadow or tundra zone, to the eternal ice of the glaciers, the arctic climatic zone. The region is relatively well developed for visitors; for some time tourism as a source of income has been seen as increasingly important, and the development of infrastructure is in progress accordingly. A tourism department has been established in the regional capital, Taldykorgan, which provides information on request through tkoblakimat@global.kz.

Zhetisu can be roughly divided into the mountainous areas of the Tien Shan in the south, the Zhungar Alatau in the east and the core area of the Land of Seven Rivers, characterized by steppe, desert and river valleys, which stretches to Lake Balkhash and the lakes of **Alakol** and **Sasykkol**, marking the boundary of the area to the northeast.

Guided tours to all parts of Zhetisu are possible, using many different forms of transport: on foot, camel- or horseback, by mountain bike or with a jeep, on river boats or canoes, by bus or even in a hot-air balloon or helicopter. A large number of travel agencies offer their services (a selection are listed at the end of this chapter), and anyone deciding to go on an extended trip, whether as part of a group or alone, should always use a guide—the deserts and steppe are vast and broken, and the mountains are treacherous, especially at heights above 2,500 metres.

The Mountain Ridges of the Tien Shan

Tien Shan is a Chinese name meaning Mountains of Heaven. The highest peaks of this 12-million-year-old—and therefore geologically young—mountain range reach over 7,000 metres in hight, and Kazakhstan is proud to number one of them within its own territory. Until recently, **Khan Tengri** was officially recorded at 6,996 metres, just failing to reach that magic number. However, after new, more accurate measurements it has now been established that in fact Kazakhstan's highest peak measures 7,010 metres in height.

Comprising the mountain ranges of **Zailiyskiy Alatau**, the **Kungey Alatau** and the **Khan Tengri massif**, the Tien Shan forms the southeastern border of Kazakhstan with Kyrgyzstan. One season is not enough for those who want to explore all its main valleys and perhaps climb some of its easier peaks. Trekking time starts in the middle of May and ends in September, with even less time available for climbing higher peaks. This does not mean that there are no good days for trekking outside that season, but ambitious trips between October and May are not recommended.

Two-Country Tour to Issyk Kul

A trek across the mountains to the legendary **Issyk Kul** in Kyrgyzstan is high on the must-do list for many visitors to Kazakhstan—and this is relatively easy to arrange. Issyk Kul is the largest lake in the Tien Shan, 182 kilometres long, up to 58 kilometres wide, up to 700 metres deep, and only 50 kilometres from Almaty as the crow flies. A visa is required to cross the "green" border, but it is easily obtained at Kyrgyzstan embassies abroad or in Almaty. Rules for an entry visa are the same as for Kazakhstan. However, don't forget that if you want to return to Kazakhstan after the trip, a **double-entry visa** for Kazakhstan is required.

The physical effort to cross the mountain barrier is an entirely different matter. Depending on your time, purse and physical condition, you can choose to cross the two mountain ridges of the Zailiyskiy Alatau and Kungey Alatau from Almaty by coach, car or jeep, mountain bike or on foot. The 500-kilometre trip by coach from the central bus station takes about 12 hours. You can book the various trips, including accommodation in hotels or guesthouses, at almost every travel agency in town.

During the summer, there is a shortcut from Almaty to Issyk Kul which you can take using a jeep or a mountain bike. This path—it hardly deserves the name road—leads from the left (southeastern) shore of **Big Almaty Lake** to the **Kyzylsay Plateau**, from there to the Ozzhyorniy Pass and down into the Chong-Kemin Valley. There is a bridge across the river, from where it is not very far to a road in the true sense of the word. This subsequently leads over the Kokayryk Pass to Issyk Kul in Kyrgyzstan. It would be in the interest of this protected area if further tarmacking were discontinued to prevent a much-frequented road from further degrading the habitat of animals threatened with extinction.

Another road that runs east from the Sharyn, through Kegen, Karkara and over the Samakh Pass is in better condition, though still not particularly good. The routine visa and customs formalities take place four kilometres before the actual border.

There is a well-developed tourist infrastructure around **Cholpon Ata**, on the north shore of Issyk Kul. For a dollar or two, almost all private homes have beds on offer in rooms, redecorated stables, summer huts and alcoves. The place is very much alive, with watersport and leisure facilities, though it's easy to move away from this and find yurt camps, belonging to natural protection projects, where you can stay in large, comfortable yurts and experience the simple life of a Kyrgyz family—a glimpse of mountain nomad life.

If you want to trek from Kazakhstan to Issyk Kul on foot, you should join a small group with good guides and possibly porters or horses. The simplest route takes you from Alma Arasan across the Almaty or **Prokhodnoye Pass** (3,599 metres), which even in high

The art of eagle hunting is still very much alive in Kazakhstan—man, horse and eagle are perfectly at home in the vast steppe (Christopher Herwig)

summer is often snow-covered, and leads to the valley of the Chong-Kemin River. On this trail you often meet shepherds minding their flocks, and they may ask you to join one of their meals. In exchange for a small contribution—cigarettes, tea or a bottle of vodka—you can drink kumis and ayran, and eat shashlyk. Strengthened by this, you're ready for the next mountain ridge, the Kungey Alatau. You follow the Ortokoysu watercourse downstream, then cross the snow-covered **Kokayryk Pass** (3,889 metres) to the village of **Chon Sary Oy**. This trek takes five days.

Yet another route goes from Big Almaty Lake across the **Ozzhyorniy Pass**, reached along a somewhat longer trail from Medeu through Shymbulak and across the **Greater Talgar Pass**. It meets the first route at Ozzhyorniy, and from there ascends the Kungey Alatau and crosses the **Ak-Su Pass** to the north. This tour takes 9–10 days and is described in detail in the useful pocket book *The Road is the Goal: Trans-Alatau, from Alma-Ata to Issyk Kul.*

A timeless scene on the rolling green steppe (Alexander Kolokolnikov)

A third route, more remote but very beautiful, takes you through the valley of the three **Kolsay lakes** and the across **Sarybulak Pass** to the eastern shore of Issyk Kul, providing breathtaking views along the way. This trek is much in vogue because of the beauty of the lakes and their surrounding scenery, and the fact that the track leads across only a single 3,274-metre mountain pass, which is hardly ever snowbound in summer, meaning mountaineering equipment is not required at all.

Of course there are many variations of treks in this area, some covered in the following Turgen Valley and Left Talgar Nature Reserve sections. Trekkers with proper training and in good health can safely undertake these trips from June till September, provided they have the equipment to endure sudden changes in the weather and cold nights in the mountains.

THE ZAILIYSKIY ALATAU MASSIF

"Multi-coloured mountains beyond the Ili" is the translation of the Russian-Kazakh name of this, the northernmost spur of the Tien Shan. The unusually rich colours of the wild fruit tree woods and mixed forests in autumn could be the origin of the Kazakh name, Alatau. The nomads have certainly valued the sheltered and fertile valleys of this mountain spur for centuries. The range is situated south of the Ili River, which makes its way westwards from China through the centre of the Land of Seven Rivers, accumulating water from myriad mountain streams rushing out of the Alatau, before flowing into the giant reservoir of Kapshagay, then on for a further 300 kilometres across Zhetisu to empty finally into **Lake Balkhash**. The name "Zailiyskiy" was added by Pyotr Syemyonov "Tienshansky", the Russian scholar who in the second half of the 19th Century explored and mapped large areas of Kazakhstan, in particular the Tien Shan, on the orders of the Russian tsars.

Large areas of the Zailiyskiy Alatau between the valleys of the rivers Shamalghan and Turgen belong to the 2,023-square-kilometre **Ili-Alatau National Park**, which was established in 1996. This protected area is the home of many endangered species, including **snow leopard**, ibex, arkhar, brown bear, red wolf, lynx, wild boar and many rare birds. The variety of plants in the park is impressive, with 1,200 different species recorded. Trekkers can observe the mighty Tien Shan spruce, juniper trees, wild apple and apricot trees, berberis, primeval forms of many well-known garden flowers, edelweiss and other rare plants. Thanks to its range in altitude and climatic zones, the national park has everything to offer from semi-desert and steppe vegetation to alpine meadow flora.

THE KASKELEN VALLEY

In the west of the Ili-Alatau National Park we find the valley of the **Kaskelen River**, which flows through the town of the same name. **Kaskelen** was among the first places in Zhetisu, together with Issyk (now Yesik) and Talgar, where Russian customs posts were established. President Nazarbayev was born in the district of Kaskelen, in the village of Shamalghan, which could be why the surrounding areas are so well taken care of. The valley's main attraction is the Uyi-Tas, the Yurt Stone—a giant piece of rock consisting of grey granite in the form of a yurt five metres high and six metres in diameter, which has stupefied geologists because there is not one crevice in it, nor any other rocks nearby. The stone yurt stands alone on the top of a ridge that flanks the valley. How did this bizarre 500-tonne rock get here? No one has the answer as yet.

The river valley is 30 kilometres long and covered with relatively dense woods in its upper reaches. Logging has created some rough tracks and you can climb a long way up by jeep. The valley has a fork where the "Left" and "Right" Kaskelen flow together shortly before the tree line. Both valleys are good for trekking, especially as there are no crowds. The **Left Kaskelen** has its origin at the West Kaskelen Pass on the border with Kyrgyzstan. On reaching it you can also carry on to Issyk Kul—a distance of 60 kilometres. The trail follows the Chong-Kemin River valley—there is even a bridge across the river—and crosses the relatively easy West Dyure Pass (3,734 metres). The way down to Issyk Kul is long and smooth, passing the small village of Chyrptykty after just over 30 kilometres.

Up the valley of the **Right Kaskelen** you reach the Northern and Upper Bassa Dzhaya passes, situated close to one another at heights of 3,770 and 3,830 metres respectively. You can also walk down from them to the Chong-Kemin and from there on to Issyk Kul.

TAMGALY (TANBALY)

Kazakhstan boasts more than 1,500 known sites with rock drawings and carvings, called **petroglyphs**. They are almost always found in places that must have been good campsites for nomadic tribes: in valleys, by springs, in caves. Most of the drawings represent scenes from the lives of a hunting, nomadic community: deer and ibex, sheep, cattle, horses, riders. The carvings give their name to the sites; many of them are dubbed *Tamgaly* or *Tamgaly Tas* which means "a rock illustrated with the symbol of a tribe".

There is no lack of such sites in the Land of Seven Rivers, the most important of which is **Tamgaly** in Zhambyl Region, some 170 kilometres to the northwest of Almaty. Officially "discovered" by archaeologists in 1957, Tamgaly now claims UNESCO status as a **World Cultural Heritage** site.

Zhetisu in spring is a land of vast blue sky, dark-green forest and colourful wildflowers (Vladimir Tugalev)

The drawings on the almost vertical rock walls are estimated to be about 3,000 years old; however, not all artwork dates from the same period. It is assumed that the valley's "artistic creations" continued well into the first millennium of our era. The drawings testify both to the daily lives and to the spiritual world of the people who used to live here: hunting and herding scenes, divine beings or shamans with sun-shaped heads, rituals, dances, female forms, falconry, ornaments and tribal symbols. In all, the rock walls contain some 4,000 remarkably clear images. The indigenous communities also call the site the Sun Temple. If you visit on a sunny day you will understand this: voices echo strangely between the canyon walls, and looking up, one gets the impression of being under a turquoise orb. Under the hot sun, the senses get blurred and you can imagine yourself flying back in time 3,000 years, when the first humans began their rock art carving.

Sadly, unmistakable signs bring the visitor back to the present: some of the stone images are damaged. It is hard to tolerate the stupidity of our fellow man, some of whom feel they have to leave their own mark as initials on the stone walls. Also, certain cracks in the walls are not the result of major shifts in temperature or other natural phenomena, but recall that this was used as a tank training area in Soviet times!

To reach Tamgaly, turn right off the road to Bishkek some 80 kilometres from Almaty, after driving through the village of Targap. The crossroad is called Degeneres and can be recognized by its picnic site with yurts. Take the road signed "Kopa" and having passed the

Left: A lone horseman follows the contours of the steppe towards the mighty Tien Shan (Christopher Herwig)

village of the same name, drive for two more hours (minding the holes in the road) to Mount Anrakay, at the foot of which is the hamlet of Karabastau. Four kilometres farther up the road, a blue sign indicates a path to the left, which after approximately one kilometre ends up at the entrance of a narrow rock canyon, in which numerous very clear rock drawings are visible. Grave mounds and sparse remainders of a settlement not far from the gorge also testify to the fact that this area was inhabited from the 15th to 11th centuries BC.

On the way to Tamgaly you can visit the monument to a famous battle against the Zhungars, which is on top of a hill next to Km Stone 38. It is composed of one high block of red granite, and a lower, partly split one of grey granite, which symbolize both nations respectively—the victorious Kazakhs and the Zhungars, finally subdued. A circle of stones with images of the oriental Zodiac surrounds the blocks.

In the village of **Zhambyl** at the foot of Mount Kastek, on the western fringe of the Zailiyskiy Alatau, there is a museum dedicated to the great *akyn* (poet-minstrel) **Zhambyl Zhabayev**. An exhibition of his musical work is in the house where the aged bard lived during the last years of his life, and the mortal remains of the poet are there as well. The great Kazakh composer, Nurgisa Tlendiyev, is also buried here. You can reach the village by turning left off the road to Bishkek after Uzynaghash.

THE AKSAY VALLEY

A tiny, but still active, monastery with a few monks still exists in the valley of **Aksay** on the far heights of Mount Kyzylzhar. The monastery can only be reached on foot, but a visit is worthwhile, if only for the beautiful view. To get there, drive west from Almaty to the village of Tausamaly (Kamenka), which has all but become part of Almaty as expansion steams ahead. Keep going west to the valley of the Aksay River, then turn south. The fence of the national park lies beyond a toll post, across a once well-settled area, now full of neglected and abandoned dachas on a serpentine road, the condition of which deteriorates quickly. Here, you have to leave the car. Walking upstream along a clearly visible path, you pass through pastures and half-wild apple orchards. In late summer, you should try the shrunken but delicious apples. Now you have to cross the river before venturing upward on a steep path, then steps and even ladders. The last barrier before your destination is a fir wood. Having crossed it, you enter a meadow and suddenly you find yourself overlooking a marvellous panorama of Almaty.

The monastery consists of a charming new wooden church and a community house. The monks themselves live all year in earth caves. Monastic solitude obviously suffers from the crowds of curious visitors who arrive weekend after weekend in spite of the laborious climb. Don't be surprised if the monks, who made their dwelling up here in the 1920s in an attempt to escape persecution by Red Guard zealots, look for even better hideouts in years to come. To respect the brothers' constant prayers for peace and wellbeing in the land, one should behave quietly, unpretentiously, and not smoke. However, sometimes the monks themselves come out to talk to visitors.

The Aksay Valley is relatively broad and in its middle reaches it consists of dense woodland. Above the tree line it splits in two. Both subsequent valleys wind up between high peaks covered with year-round snow and cross into Kyrgyzstan. With the exception of Mount Akbulak (3,690 metres), all of them are covered with glaciers and are over 4,000 metres high—all in all, no place for mere day-trippers. Up here, you still have a good chance of seeing ibex jumping from crag to crag and golden eagles soaring in the blue sky.

THE LEFT TALGAR NATURE RESERVE

The green town of **Talgar** is no more than 20 kilometres from Almaty, on the outskirts of a forked mountain ridge, the highest peak of which is **Mount Talgar**. With a height of 4,973 metres, the tooth-shaped mountain is higher than Mont Blanc. It is hard to climb, and an ascent takes three to four days. The valley of the Kotyrbulak brook, which runs between Almaty and Talgar, as well as the valleys of the Left, Middle and Right Talgar are all excellent for hiking. In summer, you can pick the wild fruits from raspberry and currant bushes as you go.

To reach the national park, leave the main road in the centre of Talgar behind the streetlamp next to a small mosque, and from there drive to the right (south) crossing Abai Street and passing by the fairground, till you come to the office of the national park and the museum—which is worth a visit. After four more kilometres along the Talgar River, you reach the entrance to the national park. After a while along the relatively well-maintained southbound road, you come to a fork: the **Left (*Lyeviy*) Talgar** comes from the right side and the **Right (*Praviy*) Talgar** from the left.

The valley of the noisy, foaming Left Talgar stretches up to over 4,000 metres on the border with Kyrgyzstan, where the river originates from a giant glacier massif. This area has a special protection status within the Ili-Alatau National Park due to its natural beauty and its rich variety of animal species. An identity card is needed at the checkpoint and an entry ticket can cost up to 800 tenge.

Many beautiful walking routes link the valley of the Left Talgar with those of Butatovka, Medeu and Shymbulak, and the valley of Big Almaty Lake. The landscape along the way includes Komsomola Peak (4,376 metres, recently renamed Nursultana in honour of the president), Ordzhonikidze Peak (4,409 metres) on its western flank, and the peaks Koptau (4,152 metres) and Bogatyr (4,580 metres) to its east. By crossing the latter's glacier, experienced mountaineers and climbers can reach the wonderful glacier-lake of **Shokalskovo**, which flashes up from the valley like a sky-blue eye. The stream is already

continued on page 230

ROCKS OF AGES: KAZAKHSTAN'S PETROGLYPHS

By *Renato Sala and Jean-Marc Deom*

The rock art of Kazakhstan pertains to the *Centrasian* (Central Asian) tradition, and its traits are found across a huge territory, from the Indus Valley up along the piedmonts of the Pamir, Tien Shan and Altai mountain ranges to the basin of the Yenisei River in southern Siberia. Among the various monuments used in the culturalization of the Kazakh landscape (including pictograms, petroglyphs, cupmarks, stelae and geoglyphs), petroglyphs (engravings on rock) are by far the most abundant.

They are executed on open-air stone surfaces, mainly along a 200km piedmont corridor endowed with excellent metamorphic rock material, weathered smooth and patinated by sunlight, and offering the most favourable surfaces for the preservation of precise incisions over thousands of years. They have slowly accumulated through millennia, forming sites of different dimensions having anything from a few to more than 1,000 engraved surfaces. The largest and most significant sites are those of Arpauzen in the Karatau

Above: An early Saka period deerstone petroglyph at Eshkiolmes. Above right: A Kuljabasy hunting scene dating to the mid-Bronze Age (Renato Sala and Jean-Marc Deom x2)

range, Kuljabasy and Tamgaly in the Chu-Ili mountains, and Eshkiolmes and Bajanzhurek in the Zhungarian range. These engravings were created over a period of more than 4,000 years, from Neolithic times (circa 3000 BC) to the Turkic period (1200 AD), and reach a quantitative and qualitative peak during the period spanning the Bronze Age (2000–800 BC) and Early Iron Sak period (800–250 BC). The aesthetic taste for landscape background, techniques, styles and subjects vary from period to period.

In general, Kazakhstan's petroglyphs can be categorized into seven periods: Archaic; Early-Mid Bronze; Late Bronze; Early Iron Sak; Early Iron Hunnic-Wusun; Medieval Turkic; and Late Medieval Ethnographic. The earliest engravings are represented by rare figures of wild bulls (*bos primigenius*, extinct from around 1000 BC) chipped by stone tools onto a single horizontal surface set in an astonishing landscape scenario. The bulls are two-dimensional figures, often of huge size (up to 2m x 1m). This Archaic period can be considered a primordial act of landscape culturalization, the figures' creators being hunters and gatherers of the Kelteminar Neolithic culture.

With the Early-Mid Bronze period (2000–1200 BC) came the first aesthetic revolution in the development of the Centrasian tradition, and the blossoming of the rock art of Kazakhstan. The importance of the landscape diminished in favour of the figures themselves, evidenced by the use of clusters of proximate surfaces that created a visual chorus of images. Figures during this period were hammered with metal tools as medium-sized silhouettes, and a natural style was achieved through the use of images in perspective for three-dimensional effect. The repertory of subject matter grew richer, with more than 40 different subjects and, more importantly, compositions consisting of certain images found in recurrent scenes.

All the main species of large wild mammals were represented: wild bull, bighorn sheep, mountain goat, deer, horse, camel, bear, wolf, jackal and fox. Human figures were also used: men with an erect penis, depicted with a tail and wolf-mask; men raising their hands, holding weapons (bows, hand-axes and clubs) or crosiers, shaking hands and fighting; sex scenes can be found between men and women, as well as between men and goats; and there are scenes of hunting, dancing, caravans and chariots. In addition to humanoid figures were geometrical and abstract signs such as solar circles, wheels and square grids. The artists of these increasingly complex petroglyphs were communities of settled shepherds and metallurgists of the Andronovo culture.

The Late Bronze period (1200–800 BC) saw a diminution not so much in the quantity but certainly in the quality of the engravings. Their location indicates a preference for the presence of previous figures, which were then filled by smaller images with a diachronic purpose. The style of this period lost three-dimensional effects, the images tended to become linear, several wild animals were not depicted while some domesticated species were introduced, such as horses and herds of sheep and goats, together with scenes of domestication and horse riding. This period corresponds to the full colonization of the steppe expanses, the growth of metallurgical activity, the rise of patriarchal aristocratic clans, and, from an aesthetic point of view, represents an important transitional phase.

The Early Iron Sak period (800–250 BC) represents the second and last revolution in the development of the Centrasian tradition, which saw a change in all aesthetic factors. Locations were chosen avoiding former surfaces and rock groups, preferring horizontal surfaces in untouched areas. Together with hammering techniques, scratching and polishing techniques were introduced. New styles now appeared (the Scythian-Siberian animal style), showing the influence of patterns developed in the southern Siberian region and paying witness to the intrusion of northeastern tribes: the figures of this era are realistic and two-dimensional, shaped by plastic contours and internal spiral decorations that emphasized volume. Iconographic elements ceased to be exclusively used for individual species and were instead used as generic parts of any ungulate body, underlining their lightness, dynamism and tension.

At the same time, the repertory of subject species was drastically reduced to only a few: wild goats, bighorn sheep, deer, wild boar, archers and riders. Rhetoric forms become more abstract, connotative of qualities, carrying symbolic, emblematic and heraldic meanings. On the whole the petroglyph expression from this period consisted of the same patterns found on golden artefacts buried in funerary mounds. It comes as no surprise that at this time powerful aristocratic tribes of mounted warriors were controlling the steppe: funerary complexes of aligned kurgans had become the main form of landscape culturalization, satisfying a need for genealogical records and reducing the petroglyph sites to a complementary heraldic function.

The Early Iron Hunnic-Wusun period (250 BC–500 AD) followed the fall of Sak rule with the immigration of military confederations and mixed-farming shepherds from eastern territories. Petroglyph art now saw its first clear phase of decay, becoming quite poor and insignificant in value. Engravings of small figures (10cm x 10cm) spread wider in the territory, but the surrounding landscape and rock material were less important, with rock outcrops near settlements being favoured. The style in this period was strictly linear, with subjects being reduced to domesticated ovicaprids in a grazing position, hunters and riders.

The Turkic period (500–1220 AD) saw to the domination of the steppe by successive powerful Turkic military confederations, and seems to represent the last renaissance of the Centrasian petroglyph tradition. The Turkic tribes reintroduced from south Siberia the importance of monumental petroglyph sites and a taste for beautiful engravings. This period saw the revisiting, with less originality and in an eclectic way, of the stylistic patterns and subjects of the Sak animalistic style, together with the introduction of some new subjects of military-political character which represented the best contribution of the period: riders with banners and detailed depictions of clothing and paraphernalia, for which techniques of scratching and polishing were preferred. At this time, highly centralized urban centres dominated the whole steppe territory, introducing religions, writing, drawings and frescoes and, at the end of the period, paper. This new urbanization undermined the importance of the petroglyph sites and, as a whole, the old communication system based on stone faded, overwhelmed by a new one based on paper.

Under Mongol domination (1220–1450 AD) petroglyph work decreased everywhere to almost nothing. It recovered slightly during the Ethnographic Kazakh period (1450–1900 AD) when, in scattered sites, figures of goats, sheep, hunters and riders were created in a simple linear style on poor rock surfaces surrounding shepherd camps. An extraordinary exception is presented by the petroglyphs of the Mangyshlak Peninsula, elegantly scratched on the walls of mosques and mausoleums with forms and subjects typical of Sufi cosmology.

The petroglyph sites of Kazakhstan were initiated with the intention of decorating the landscape, and developed with the artistic aim of continuing the growth of these ancestral art galleries. The artists did not so much describe the world in which they lived, but rather looked to the world of their forefathers, conscious of lost ways of life: archers appeared when hunting was already a pastime, and pastoral scenes when society started to be ruled by aristocratic clans. In this sense the meaning of the images, expressed by denotations, metaphors or symbols, doesn't pertain to the phenomenological world but rather to that of collective and subconscious memories. Petroglyph sites are, in fact, the archives of ancestral dreams.

Above: One of the earliest petroglyphs at the Kuljabasy site, from the Archaic period (Renato Sala and Jean-Marc Deom). Right: Rocky landscapes throughout Kazakhstan's territory have served as natural canvases for rock art through the ages (Vladimir Tugalev)

beyond the watershed and carries its water into the Shelek on the far side of the Zailiyskiy Alatau ridge. Two routes are particularly popular to get to Issyk Kul through the valley of the Left Talgar. One leads across the Turistov Pass, a 3,920-metre shortcut over the glacier, followed by the ice-free Ozzhyorniy Pass, while the other, more difficult one, leads across the Razvyedochniy Pass (4,170 metres), and includes crossing a glacier. Both routes meet in the valley of Chong-Kemin. From there on, one still has to cross the Boztery Pass, which, at 4,110 metres, is also difficult.

The valley of the Right Talgar can be travelled by car for approximately four kilometres. From there, it is about a four-kilometre walk to the point where the Middle Talgar flows into the Right Talgar. Following the Middle Talgar upstream, you come to the foot of the peak where the river has its origin—at this point you are at 2,520 metres. Even if you don't want to climb to the summit you can get close to the beautiful glacier by following the path that winds upwards for about five kilometres. From here, at a height of 3,000 metres, a marvellous panorama reveals itself.

The valley of the Right Talgar has a less spectacular view, but here one can also follow a four-kilometre track into the mountains. Sure-footed trekkers can reach the Yesik Valley from here in a day's march across the 3,475-metre Birkaragay Pass.

Practical Information

Tourist guesthouse Tau Turan, in the Belbulak Valley, tel: (7 727) 2 939 540, fax: (7 727) 2 650 394, e-mail: turpost@nursat.kz.

Mountaineers' guesthouse Sunglade, in the Koturbulak Valley, tel: (7 727) 2 692 649—has a ski piste and sauna.

Ak Bulak Sanatorium, in the village of Shymbulak, tel: 27446 179/299—medical treatment on request, pool, sauna.

Ak-Kain Sanatorium, in the village of Kamenskoye Plato, tel: (7 727) 2 548 392/118—from US$30 per night, including full board, separate bungalows outside the sanatorium, medical treatment on request, pool, sauna.

Almatau, on the slope of Kotyrbulak, tel: (7 727) 2 730 076—nice ski and mountaineering resort from US$25. At a height of 1,860 metres between the Left Talgar Valley and Malaya Almatinka, 25 kilometres to the southeast of Almaty.

Yesik, the Blue Lake

In the village of **Yesik** (formerly Issyk), some 50 kilometres to the southeast of Almaty in the direction of Narynkol, a broad, tarmacked road that starts after the bridge across the Yesik River leads southward into the mountains. Following it, one reaches the picturesque woodlands of the Yesik River valley and the lake of the same name. *Yesik* means "hot", and here there are subterranean springs, which not only slightly warm the lake but also give it its particular milky-blue colour. The Yesik lake was once called the "Pearl of the Tien Shan", until fate took a hand in 1963, when a terrifying mud avalanche thundered down into the valley. What is left of the lake today is being restored—and it seems that the attempt is likely to be successful.

Unfortunately, the site's numerous visitors leave lots of rubbish behind; nevertheless the lake's southern shore is relatively clean. Climbing the slopes on either shore is only recommended for experienced mountaineers. The valley here is covered with dense woods, and leads all the way to the lakes Akkol and Muzkol, with the Talgar Peak, surrounded by the largest collection of glaciers in the Zailiyskiy Alatau, a bit further to the west.

On the way back to town, stop to taste the local wines of the **Issyk Wine Company**. The red and white grapes have seen so much sun that even the dry blends have a slight taste of dessert wine to them.

Yesik is also known for its **kurgans**, Scythian grave mounds dating from the 4th Century BC. In 1969 a sensational find took place in one of the numerous kurgans on the outskirts of Yesik. In a side-room of the tomb, next to the huge, six-metre-high and 60-metre-wide main hall (unfortunately already plundered), the complete ceremonial costume of a warrior (a female warrior according to the latest assessments by some anthropologists) was found, skilfully adorned with pieces of gold. This unique artefact used to be displayed in the Central State Museum in Almaty, and can now be admired in the Presidential Cultural Centre in Astana. The costume consists of a high, pointed headdress with 150 golden ornaments, the most remarkable of which are in the form of winged horses, and a leather kaftan with 3,000 golden ornaments sewn on, those on the edges in the form of a tiger's head. Leg-shields and a golden dagger complete the find. In addition, numerous wooden, clay and silver bowls and dishes were excavated from the site.

Practical Information

You can stay at the **Tau Samal Sanatorium** or the **Issyk Tourist Inn**, right on the shore of Yesik Lake at the end of the tarmac road. Reservations can be made for wine tasting at the Issyk Wine Company through the Otrar Group; e-mail: otrar@group.kz.

Following pages: The grand scenery of the Akkol Valley in the Khan Tengri massif is just reward for these horse trekkers (Vladislav Yakushkin)

TURGEN VALLEY

One of the most picturesque valleys of the Zailiyskiy Alatau is that of the **Turgen River**, which starts on the high **Tassy Plateau** and is 44 kilometres long. Wild mountain streams and rich flora accompany trekkers; the trail leads through dense mixed and fir woods, and over subalpine and alpine pastures, with plenty of opportunity for gatherers of herbs and berries. On the Tassy Plateau in summer, you are sure to meet nomads with their yurts and flocks. This vast, high flatland has been a favourite summer meadow for centuries, as many rock carvings with fine images of animals testify.

The Turgen Valley is known for its waterfalls; at the **Bears' Cascade**, the Turgen drops more than 30 metres, while the **Boguz Cascade** has bored a tunnel through the rock. A trip here from Almaty leads east through Talgar and Yesik to the charming, quiet village of Turgen, awash with green and situated at the foot of the mountains. Shortly after entering the district you take the first tarmac road to the right, marked by a sign that reads "*Tsentr aktivnovo otdykha*" (active leisure centre). From here the valley can be ascended by car for about 20 kilometres.

The area is relatively well developed to the left and right of the road for weekenders, campers and more demanding travellers. For a 100-tenge entry fee visit the ethnographic visitor's centre located right behind the checkpoint to the right. A bit further on there is a trout farm where you can catch your own fish. A number of cafés in yurts and buildings offer shashlyk and other local dishes, there are picnic sites and a campsite (with toilets, which is rare) on the bank of the Turgen. This is a good starting point for walks in the beautiful side valleys. For more comfortable accommodation you can choose between inns, artists' cottages and a brand-new, very comfortable ranch named Stetson Rancho (www.stetson.kz) situated in the lower 10 kilometres of the valley.

Further up, the valley gradually narrows to a gorge. Here, the water foams and roars between the rocks, and small bridges with crooked railings barely take the weight of the buses that cross carefully. The original stopping place, **Batan**, has now developed into a small settlement consisting of shashlyk bars, yurts, a restaurant and a hotel. A branch of the valley leads from here to the charming mountain lake, **Zhasylkol**. A contest in hunting with birds and hounds takes place in Batan every year.

At the end of the road, behind the parking place for coaches and cars, the valley splits into three branches. Three streams come together here: the Turgen, the Shenturgen from the west and the Kishturgen from the east. From here, you must walk to the waterfalls, or even further to the glaciers from which the streams originate. Up high near the spring of the Shenturgen is a curious botanical sight: the *Chinturgenskiye Yelniki*—a moss fir wood that extends right to the edge of a massive expanse of glacial ice.

The Turgen and the Kishiturgen valleys can also serve as a starting point for a number of treks to Issyk Kul that take several days and vary in length and degree of difficulty. A particularly good but considerably longer route than the others is to go via the Kolsay lakes and from there on over the relatively easy Sarybulak Pass (3,250 metres) to Issyk Kul.

THE KUNGEY ALATAU MASSIF

The Tien Shan mountain spur known as the Kungey Alatau is actually situated "behind" the Zailiyskiy Alatau, to its south, with a large part in Kyrgyz territory. The Kungey Alatau comes into its own in the Uzunbulak/Zhalanash area, where the Zailiyskiy Alatau gets lower and ends in rolling foothills and plains. The road to this mountain region leads through the valleys of the Sharyn and the Shelek rivers.

SHARYN CANYON

The road east from Almaty in the direction of Narynkol follows a northern branch of the Silk Road of old. The southern side of the road offers fantastic views of the mountains, while the northern side overlooks fertile river valleys, the Kapshagay Reservoir on the horizon and further on, the mountain steppe of Shodak and Altyn Emel. Along the road you often see herds of horses, cattle and sheep. In September, dried tobacco hangs in the front gardens, and everything the gardens yield is neatly displayed along the roadside. Near Km Stone 52 is a **botanical park**, planted about 50 years ago with some 1,500 different species of trees and bushes from all over the world—everything seems to grow willingly in the fertile ground.

Around 195 kilometres from Almaty, the **Sharyn River** has cleft a rough gorge, 154 kilometres long and up to 350 metres deep in places, into the red sandstone; local people like to compare it with the Grand Canyon, and although this is a little ambitious, it is still impressive and does have a particular charm of its own.

The road to Sharyn Canyon winds over the mountain ridge of **Sogety**, passing a side road shortly before the village of **Kokpek** that leads to the reservoir of **Bartogay**, which is worth a separate visit. The main road leads through Kokpek to Sharyn Canyon and the Sogety heights looming behind it. This large, seemingly barren area is a favourite place for hunting with birds; it is said that many an Arab sheikh has enjoyed his favourite hobby here, attended by high-ranking local politicians. Ground squirrels are nonetheless present in abundance—the plain is full of their holes.

Shortly before reaching the end of the plain a checkpoint appears, where you must pay a fee of 300 tenge per car and 100 tenge per person to enter the national park. The last 11 kilometres through the canyon lead along a natural track over the barren highlands. One can drive directly into the canyon with a 4WD or robust car, though hikers tend to find this particularly annoying.

Above: The first Kolsay Lake is fed by clear mountain streams and surrounded by a wealth of biodiversity (Vladimir Tugalev). Left: The Sharyn River cuts deep through red sandstone landscape to form the impressive Sharyn Canyon (Jeremy Tredinnick)

The road down into the canyon is not too difficult, but strong shoes are recommended: the crumbling sandstone has caused many a hiker to fall. Side branches of the canyon bear evocative names like Fortress Valley and Witches' Valley. The fairy-tale sandstone formations along the road through the canyon have also been given names, some slightly embarrassing, like Notre Dame, Penguin, Duck or Winnie the Pooh. In summer, visitors are accompanied by the deafening sound of cicadas and the sight of unusual vegetation, including saksaul, ephedra, thorny bushes and a mass of small succulents. Avoid turning over stones—you don't want to disturb scorpions and poisonous spiders. But rest assured, they never attack passers-by who treat them with respect.

Through the centre of the canyon flows the Sharyn River, brown and foaming. It flows fast, so take care when swimming there. There are a few shallow places where you can swim near the bank without much risk. From down in the canyon, you are free to explore, climb up the peaks and ridges—with varying degrees of difficulty—and enjoy the breathtaking view, which changes with every twist and bend in the canyon. There are no fences or warning signs, so it is up to you to take account of the danger. The best time to visit the canyon is from April till October, although in the middle of summer it can become very hot inside the gorge.

Upstream, the Sharyn Valley has more places of interest to offer. You need either a strong rubber raft with a knowledgeable guide or a few days in hand and a good map for hikers to visit the **Valley of Snakes** and the **Temerlik Valley**. In its lower reaches, the river offers one more thing worth seeing. These are the ash-trees—a forest of so-called relic trees, which have been there since before the last Ice Age and survive only here. The ecosystem of this 48-square-kilometre primeval forest, which consists of Sogdanian ash and Turanga poplar, is more than 10,000 years old. Some of the trees are so thick that five people joining hands cannot get their arms around them.

The **Scythian grave mounds** that lie scattered on the edges of the wood suggest that this forest had a profound significance for the ancient horse-riding nation. Further east, shortly before Chundzha, there are the remains of a prehistoric settlement called Aktobe.

To get to the "**Relic Forest**", follow the road some 10 kilometres southeast of Kokpek that bends in the direction of Chundzha/Zharkent.

In Chundzha there is a small hotel, and 20 kilometres south there is another in Kyrgyzsay. If you decide to stay here for a couple of days, you'll have the opportunity to trek up to the mountain ridge of **Ketmen** (*Khrebet Ketmen*). Numerous roads lead from the main road towards Kolzhat and the Chinese border to the south, through lovely forest-covered valleys. Here, nomads still live in significant numbers, and life is simple and easy. A permit is required to enter the border zone beyond Chundzha.

If you are looking for a quiet, atmospheric visit to the Sharyn Valley, try to go during the week. But if you enjoy the whirlwind of crowded markets, visit at the weekend when they take place in all the towns and villages. Particularly recommended is the horse market in Malovodnoye, some 80 kilometres to the east of Almaty. Take care, though: the last petrol station before the canyon is in Shelek.

PRACTICAL INFORMATION

Yasinyevaya Dacha Tourist Inn in the village of Sartogay, tel: (7 727) 7 821 443—a wooden house for 20 people, with communal toilets, from US$8.

There are private boarding facilities in **Nira**, the village of the eagle-trainers, 140 kilometres to the east of Almaty, information and reservations tel: (7 727) 2 420 675, e-mail: akoval@nursat.kz (for the attention of Andrey Kovalenko).

There is a guesthouse in **Baiseit**, for 17 people in 8 rooms, from US$15, without breakfast, fax: (7 727) 2 500 416.

THE KOLSAY LAKES

Many of those who trek to Issyk Kul choose to start in the valley of the interconnected **Kolsay lakes**, partly because of its great natural beauty, but also because it leads over the relatively easy **Sarybulak Pass**. However, whether you are heading over the pass or simply visiting the lakes before returning to Almaty, several days should be set aside to fully appreciate what the lakes have to offer.

Situated in the northern branches of the Kungey Alatau range, this valley in the upper reaches of the River Shelek can be easily reached on foot from the village of **Saty**. A bus from Almaty to Saty runs once a day, taking six hours to complete the journey. You can also drive—if your vehicle is up to it—to the trailhead starting point, some 320 kilometres from Almaty via first the road to Narynkol, then right to Alargas/Zhalanash, and finally up a gravel track through Karabulak to reach Saty in the Shelek Valley. Five kilometres to the west of Saty the Kolsay stream flows into the Shelek. Turn left here, where you pay 100 tenge per person and between 300 and 800 tenge per vehicle at the entrance checkpoint of the ecological reserve. This procedure repeats itself further up at the entrance of the national park.

You can make it by car up to the **first Kolsay Lake**, situated some 15 kilometres from Saty; for this reason it's not surprising to find some basic but decent infrastructure by the lake's shore. As well as a campsite, small wooden cottages have been built on a hill overlooking the lake, which is a gorgeous blue, and mirrors the forest lining its shore and snow-capped mountains in the distance. Having recently been given its own special status within the national park, local officials are attempting to develop tourist accommodation but in an environmentally friendly way—essentially meaning low numbers, basic comforts to minimise energy needs, and an attempt to educate visitors to take their rubbish away with them.

More adventurous souls will want to move farther into the mountains, though: hike a couple of kilometres beyond the lake and you'll quickly find yourself virtually alone with nature, and a plentiful choice of prime camping grounds next to sweet, babbling brooks. About 10 kilometres and 450 metres in altitude brings you to the equally beautiful **second Kolsay Lake**—the track along the stream to get there is renowned among mushroom gatherers and trout fishermen. In a side branch of the valley are some stables where you can get a snack of kefir and kumis.

It's another 400 metres of climbing over a distance of about eight kilometres to reach the **third Kolsay Lake**, the ice-cold water of which hints at the proximity of the nearby glaciers. If you want to camp here, make sure you are prepared for night temperatures below zero.

It is not recommended to stay here off-season, from September to June. The third Kolsay Lake is situated at 2,670 metres, but in spite of that, there is still lavish vegetation. The tree line is at 2,800 metres, beyond which you enter wonderful meadows filled with gentian, edelweiss, yellow poppy and calendula, willowherb and lady's mantel.

One to three days' walking is needed for those who decide to march on from here to Issyk Kul. Unhurried trekkers should choose a sheltered spot in a valley below Sarybulak Pass as their next campsite. The following day involves a difference in altitude of 1,800 metres, first climbing 200 metres up to the 3,274 metre pass, and from there down to the lake in Kyrgyzstan. From the pass, the view of Lake Issyk Kul and the 5,000-metre plus mountains on the far side of it is inspirational, while the descent through a steep, picturesque valley also has much to offer. In the village of **Balbay** you come to a tarmac road where you can either continue by bus—which is "scheduled" to stop here every couple of hours—or simply by hitchhiking. A good alternative to foot power is to make the trip on horseback—there are horses for rent in Saty. There is also a good information point here for all manner of trips in the surrounding area.

Practical Information

Cosy cottages with a sauna and fantastic view belonging to the travel agency Zhibek Zholy are available from US$30, without breakfast—use of the kitchen carries an extra charge. They can be reserved through Almaty, tel: (7 727) 2 500 400, fax: 2 500 416, e-mail: joly@kazmail.asdc.kz or joly@arna.kz.

Wooden huts managed by Kolsay Nature Park, tel: (7 727) 77 27638.

Sergey and Marina Volkov's guesthouse in Saty; rustic wooden house with clean toilets and sauna in the yard, good food, many excursions on foot or horseback on offer. From US$70 with full board, tel: (7 727) 77 27645 or in Almaty at (7 727) 2 203 778; booking also possible through alextravel4x4@mail.ru (Alexander Kucheryavko).

Lake Kayindy

A little known treasure hides not far from the Kolsay lakes. The geologically very young **Lake Kayindy** was only formed in 1887, the result of an avalanche after a tremendous earthquake. The valley was blocked and the Kayindy River gradually swelled into a lake. The pressure of so much water broke part of the natural barrier 50 years later, and today the lake is somewhat smaller. What sets this lake apart from the many other picturesque bodies of water in this region are the drowned fir trees of the original valley floor, whose tops stick out of the water like the masts of a fleet of ancient shipwrecks.

Top: The enigmatic, and recently formed, Lake Kayindy (Vladimir Tugalev).
Above right: A local official at the Kolsay lakes (Jeremy Tredinnick).
Above left: A mirror-like calm on the first Kolsay Lake (Alexander Kucheryavko)

Lake Kayindy is situated in a valley east of the first Kolsay Lake. It can be reached from the road to Kolsay Lake by turning left about one kilometre before Saty, next to the cemetery, and from there along a track which leads to the picturesque river valley for around nine kilometres before the nature reserve's checkpoint appears, requiring the usual 100-300 tenge fee; you then continue for another four kilometres down to the lake—a 4WD is preferable for this track if you're not hiking, but walking is by far the nicest way to get here; the track is not difficult; the distance from Saty is only 15 kilometres and the difference in altitude only 600 metres.

Kayindy means "place of birches", and the lake is known for a large wood of these attractive trees that you must pass through shortly before reaching the lake, and which is unexpected at this altitude.

THE KHAN TENGRI MASSIF

Most locals' knowledge of this region extends only to the road sign that reads Narynkol. They know simply that beyond this town, up the river of the same name, is the border with China—but few have any idea how beautiful this remote area is. Because of its status as a border district, you can only visit the **Khan Tengri massif** by buying a permit through one of the larger travel agencies in Almaty.

Travelling from Almaty to the Khan Tengri region takes a whole day. (There is a bus service to the area—starting from the Sayakhat bus station in Almaty—for patient travellers with great patience and endurance.) Driving time for the 350 kilometres in private transport is at least six hours, and it is hard to resist the temptation to stop and enjoy the beautiful views from 200 kilometres onwards. Fifteen kilometres after the hamlet of Kegen, after having passed many tomb mounds, most of which date from the 5th to the 3rd centuries BC, the road crosses the 2,000-metre **Sholadyr Pass**. The enormous, multi-forked high-level valleys of the rivers Kegen, Shalkodysu and Tekes, each with their own tributaries and flanked by the mountain chains of **Terskey Alatau** to the south and **Ketmen** to the north, has so much to offer in terms of natural beauty that you could easily stay for a couple of weeks there to explore the salt lake of Tuzkol on the right side of the road from Karasaz to Sarybastau, the river valleys of the Tekes, the Orta-Kokpak, the Ulken-Kokpak, and Bayankol and Narynkol. To the south, the Terskey Alatau rises mightily towards the Khan Tengri massif—especially from the Tekes Valley, it offers views that will live long in your memory. You can drive a considerable distance into the mountains by car along the rivers Tekes, Orta-Kokpak and Ulken-Kokpak, up to the slopes of Kaynar, Kokpak and Karatogay, but for this region 4WDs are a must.

The two most beautiful valleys are the **Karkaratal**, on the border with Kyrgyzstan, and the **Bayankol Valley** with its side branch of **Akkol**, reached through the towns of Zhambyl and Karatogay. The valley splits after the checkpoint where the border zone starts. To the left, the idyllic main valley of the Bayankol River leads directly to the Saryzhus mountain ridge, behind which stretches the northern **Inylchek Glacier**. There is even a rough track that leads to the gold mine of Zharkulak. To the right, the Akkol Valley begins; following the shore of Lake Akkol on foot or horseback will bring you very close to the mighty mountain that is held in such esteem by the Kazakh people. In this closed region, riding a staunch, obedient Kazakh horse is surely the best, fastest, most comfortable and ecologically sound way to travel. But remember: given the vastness of the territory, a mountain guide is strongly recommended, if not essential.

This is an ideal area for camping, and particularly beautiful is the Akkol campsite. It is situated at 2,600 metres on the middle reaches of the Bayankol River where the Akkol flows into it, and near the mountain lake of the same name. As a base camp for mountaineering groups attempting to conquer Khan Tengri, it even has a helicopter landing site. You can use the main building's kitchen and dining room on condition that you bring your own food. Electricity is generated at a small hydroelectric plant, and there is a sauna with a dipping pool and wooden toilet cabins. There are even rather spartan huts to sleep in for US$10–20 per night.

The base camp of **Karkara** is also wonderfully situated and well equipped; it can be reached by turning right in Kegen and driving through Karkara towards the Kyrgyz border. Be sure to keep to the left, since the border with Kyrgyzstan is immediately at the Karakara Valley's entrance. There is accommodation at the Khan Tengri Tourist Inn in Narynkol and at the sanatoriums Kayshi and Shogansay in Zhambyl, should you want to base yourself there and make multiple excursions into the mountains.

KHAN TENGRI

"Lord of Heaven", and also "Lord of Spirits" is what the name of Kazakhstan's highest peak means. The oldest reference to it, in Chinese chronicles, goes back 1,200 years. This impressive peak is sacred to the nomadic nations throughout Central Asia, since it is the place where their most powerful god, Tengri, who rules over all celestial beings, dwells.

The first European scientist to enter this forbidding area was the Russian, Semyonov, who in 1856 penetrated into the very heart of the Tien Shan. The German explorer, Dr Gottfried Merzbacher, reached the snow basins of the northern and southern Inylchek glaciers in 1902–3 (the lake on the northern glacier near the point where they come together was named Lake Merzbacher in his honour). In 1931, a Ukrainian expedition lead by Mikhail Pogrebetsky reached the summit across the southern Inylchek Glacier and the western ridge, and in 1933, Yevgeniy Kolokol, a mountaineer from Almaty, followed in his footsteps.

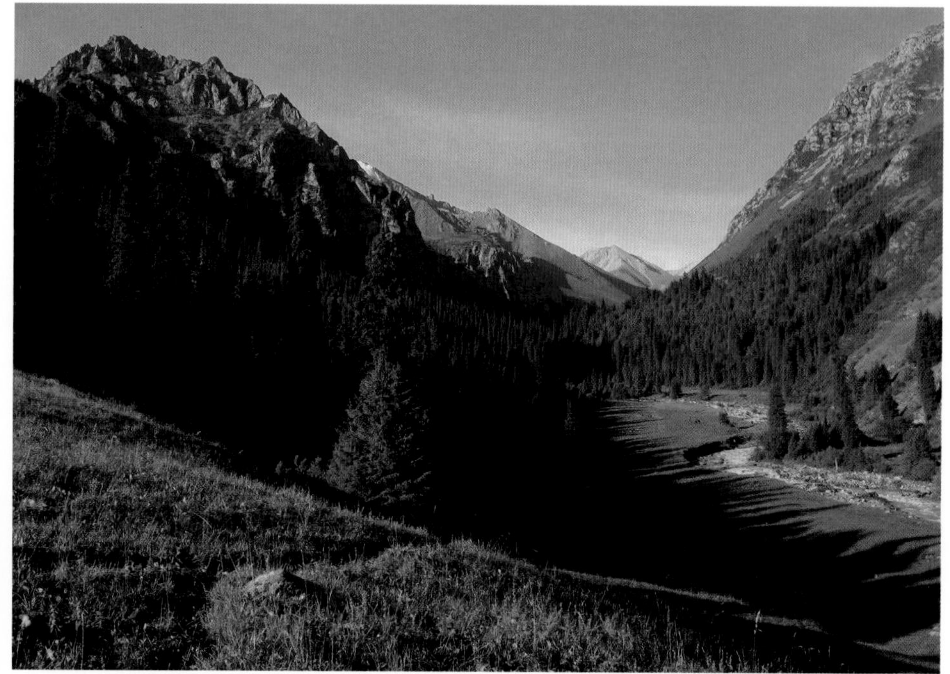

Connoisseurs view the 7,010-metre-high **Khan Tengri** as one of the world's most beautiful mountain summits. Its majestic, symmetrical marble pyramid can be seen from far away; fascinating scenes at sunset are common, when the lower mountains become shrouded in darkness but the Lord of Heaven still radiates light like a gigantic pink tulip amidst the ice and snow. This colour display has given it the nickname of Kantau, the blood-coloured mountain.

Khan Tengri is situated in the very heart of the Tien Shan, on the border triangle of Kazakhstan, China and Kyrgyzstan. Along with the **Pobeda (Victory) Peak** just south in Kyrgyzstan (less spectacular-looking, but even higher at 7,439 metres), it is the most northerly mountain higher than 7,000 metres on Earth. The range between them, which stretches over a distance of 60 kilometres along the Inylchek Glacier, is a great challenge for alpinists from all over the world. As a result, hundreds of ambitious mountaineers gather every summer in base camps at the foot of the mountains. As in all high-altitude mountain settings, the weather is unstable and unpredictable, forcing groups to wait for days or weeks before the climb can start—bad weather fronts almost every afternoon, especially in July, raise the risk factor. The climb and the descent each take six to seven days.

Above: The remote but beautiful Bayankol Valley. Above left: The pyramid summit of Khan Tengri rises towards the heavens (Christine Schwarz x2).
Left: The Khan Tengri massif is monumental in scope (Ernst Ischovits)

Purists will cringe and moan, but in the Khan Tengri 2000 Festival, 520 mountaineers from 30 countries accepted an invitation to be part of a mass ascent. Seventy-nine of them managed to reach the top—helped, however, by the fact that a helicopter service took them up to the Southern Inylchek Glacier.

In spite of such festivals and major team ascents, Khan Tengri is no playground for amateurs. The unreliable weather, deep crevasses and turbulent glacier flows, the complicated climb and not least the sheer height make conquering it still the privilege of well-trained mountaineers. However, at the foot of the range, common mortals can also honour the Lord of Heaven. If you are fit you can be guided up across the Southern Inylchek Glacier and the third mountaineer camp to the Southern Inylchek base camp at 4,000 metres, a marvellous experience that makes you feel very close to the summit.

The KanTengri Travel Agency offers various climbing routes, starting from two international base camps, up Khan Tengri, the Pobeda Peak, Marble Wall (6,400 metres) and other summits accompanied by local mountaineers. Up to 2,000 mountaineers use their services every year. If you love to be surrounded by majestic mountains but feel no need to climb them, guided trekking and mountain bike tours of one or more days are possible from the Karkara camp. Information on mountain climbing conditions can be obtained at the Kazakhstan International Mountaineering Camp Khan Tengri in Almaty, 48 Abai Avenue, tel: (7 727) 2 677 024/866.

The Zhungar Alatau Range

The **Zhungar Alatau**—often written in the Russian spelling as Dzhungarskiy Alatau—stretches over 300 kilometres from southwest to northeast along the border with China. Its highest summit, **Semyonov Tienshanskiy**, is 4,622 metres high and situated to the south of Sarkand directly on the Chinese frontier. Almost the entire area is a border district (requiring an entry permit) and therefore hardly developed and little-explored by tourists. Nevertheless, this sparsely occupied mountain region with its glaciers, forbidding summits, untamed streams, remote valleys, hot springs and clean air has huge tourism potential for mountain climbing, rafting, trekking, photo safaris and silent communication with nature at its most impressive. As with other remote areas, visitors stand a very good chance of meeting nomads and their herds who have preserved much of their traditional lifestyle.

Zharkent

The town of **Zharkent**, once called Panfilov, obtained city status back in 1882, when the borderline between Russia's conquered lands and China was determined. China's influence can be traced everywhere. Only 40 kilometres from the Chinese border post of Khorgoz, and filled with Chinese traders wheeling and dealing, it's no surprise that the bazaar is definitely worth a visit.

A part-stone, part-wooden building provides additional evidence of the Chinese influence here. With its floating roof, the Zharkent mosque looks rather like a pagoda, a cheerful combination of Chinese and Central Asian architecture. Two Chinese masters constructed the mosque without using a single nail, on the order of a rich merchant called Talibay Yuldashev. In 1911, a severe earthquake heavily damaged the building, but in 1978, after three years of restoration, it was inaugurated once more, this time as an art and architecture museum. It is located on the street named after its original sponsor, Yuldashev.

Uygurs are predominant in Zharkent and its surrounding areas. During the 1880s about 45,000 Uygurs and 5,000 Dungans entered Semirechye from western China. The voluntary resettlement was the result of a treaty between Russia and China concluded in 1881, which granted populations of the Islamic creed the right to determine their own dwelling place. In exchange, their original homeland, part of the Ili basin, was given back to China and Russia withdrew the troops that were stationed there.

Zharkent is situated on the northern edge of the Ili plain and is surrounded by a varied landscape. To the town's southeast lies the Karakum Desert, smaller than its immense namesake in Turkmenistan—what they have in common is the black sand, from which they both derive their name. To the south, the Ili feeds a swamp area, while to the north the **Toksanbay** mountain range reaches heights of more than 4,000 metres. Wonderful tours in the valleys of the rivers Usek, Burkhan, Tyshkhan and Chinzhin are possible, and provided you are fit, you can drive towards the north to **Sarybel** or the neighbouring valley of Chinzhin, climb **Mount Shakpaktastau**, almost 4,000 metres high (it takes one or two days), and trek across the glacier behind it. In the valley of Borokhudzir, northwest of Zharkent, are two sanatoriums: Zharkent Arasan and Koktal Arasan. Even if you are not having any treatments you can spend the night there; both places are modestly equipped, but serve as excellent starting points for mountain expeditions. They can be reached along a tarmac road, which splits from the main road to the settlement of Koktal, about 20 kilometres from Zharkent. It takes another 25 kilometres to reach the health resorts.

PRACTICAL INFORMATION

Hotel Asia, Zharkent, 17 Lutfullina St, tel: (+72831) 51566

Hotel Atlantik, Zharkent, 81A Pushkin St, tel: (+72831) 51229

Zharkent Arasan Sanatorium, tel: (+72831) 35363/37680

Koktal Arasan Sanatorium, tel: (+72831) 37680/33546

Kerim Aghash Sanatorium, tel: (+72831) 32838/20656

The Tien Shan's massive mountain ranges, with their jagged ridges and permanent snow cover, result in plentiful glaciers that feed the Land of Seven Rivers (Vladimir Tugalev)

Taldykorgan

Originally a nomads' winter camp, **Taldykorgan** was renamed Gavrilovka in 1868, and turned into a settlement for migrants from Russia. Situated close to the Chinese border, it was renamed Taldykorgan in 1920. Its real development came in the 1940s, as production facilities were moved from the European part of Russia to beyond the Urals. In 1944, Taldykorgan was declared a city and the region's administrative centre at the same time. Like elsewhere in Kazakhstan, with the end of the Soviet Union decline set in during the late 1980s and early 1990s. Its population decreased dramatically as many young people moved to Almaty or even directly abroad. The collapse of virtually the entire industry in the town meant there was no reason to stay in Taldykorgan—mentioning its name often brought grim, sad smiles to people's faces. Taldykorgan *Oblast* (Region) was dissolved and integrated into that of Almaty. The city seemed to have been abandoned.

But Taldykorgan, along with its 130,000 inhabitants, was saved from obscurity at the very last minute. In 2001 President Nazarbayev took people by surprise by declaring that the city was to become the administrative centre of Almaty Region. People rubbed their eyes—and

The Taldykorgan State University is once again full of students, whose talents fuel the city's economic growth (Gunter Kapelle)

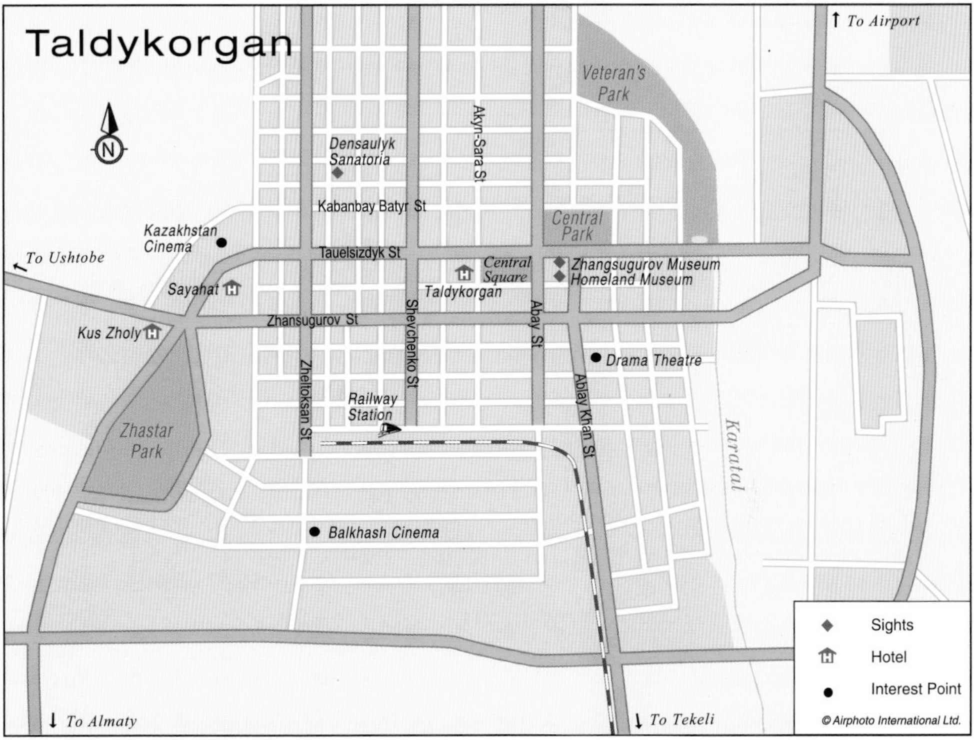

Taldykorgan
N
To Airport
Veteran's Park
Akyn-Sara St
Densaulyk Sanatoria
Kabanbay Batyr St
Kazakhstan Cinema
Central Park
To Ushtobe
Tauelsizdyk St
Central Square
Zhangsugurov Museum
Homeland Museum
Sayahat
Taldykorgan
Shevchenko St
Abay St
Zhansugurov St
Kus Zholy
Drama Theatre
Zheltoksan St
Ablay Khan St
Railway Station
Karatal
Zhastar Park
Balkhash Cinema
Sights
Hotel
Interest Point
To Almaty
To Tekeli
© Airphoto International Ltd.

УНИВЕРСИТЕТ
І.ЖАНСУГІРОВ АТЫНДАҒЫ ЖЕТІСУ МЕМЛЕКЕТТІК УНИВЕРСИТЕТІ
КАБЫЛДАУ КОМИССИЯСЫ
ПРИЕМНАЯ КОМИССИЯ

started to clear sites and build anew. New office blocks for the new administration, business accommodation, restaurants, a new hotel—the change took place with incredible speed. All the streets were torn up at the same time and remade—a cheerful chaos made the city impassable for traffic.

All of a sudden, crowds of young people populate the city once more. More than 20,000 people returned to the city in the 18 months following the decree, and Taldykorgan is once again an important centre of commerce in the region, with growth expected to continue for some time to come. The quay along the Karatal River, lit by lanterns in the evenings, has become the centrepoint for residents to meet, relax and enjoy their city's revival.

Practical Information

Accommodation options are improving constantly as the city grows, but are still relatively austere. **Hotel Taldykorgan** (128-130 Akyn Sara St, opposite the Akimat, tel: (72822) 42372) is a Soviet-style hotel undergoing renovation. Another option is **Hotel Kus Zholy** on Zhansugurov/Asanovoy St, tel: (72822) 221432, fax: (72822) 221492.

Tekeli and the Kora Valley

In spite of its off-putting factory chimneys, the relatively new mining town of **Tekeli** is actually quite a picturesque place. Situated where the rivers Tekeli, Chizhe and Kora flow together to form the Karatal, it is the entrance to the *Korinskoye ushchelye*—the 60-kilometre-long, and by and large uninhabited, **Kora Valley**.

The Kora, a wild stream fed by glaciers, forms a beautiful waterfall, the **Burkhan Bulak**, more than 90 metres high, in its upper reaches. A 47-kilometre-long hiking trail leads to the place, or you can drive or ride by jeep or mountain bike for 20 kilometres until you come to a farm with the cheerful name Ninth Bee Meadow, from where you can rent a horse cheaply and quietly trot to the waterfall. As an alternative or extension you can also make a long but very beautiful one-day trip to the **Bessonova Glacier**, which begins 15 kilometres upstream from Ninth Bee Meadow.

A particularly interesting attraction the valley offers is its relatively large population of **Tien Shan brown bears**. In spring, accompanied by a gamekeeper, you can venture into the wilderness with a good chance of observing one of the hungry bears through binoculars, recently woken from hibernation and looking for food. For fishermen, the osman, a capricious, predatory fish that usually only bites during the second half of the day, lives in the crystal-clear streams of this region.

Multi-day guided walking tours and trips on horseback from Tekeli are available with camping and full board services through the Tsentralnaya Asia tourism agency. There is a base camp near the waterfall, from where the surrounding mountains can be climbed.

The passes and glaciers in this area are no less fascinating than those in the Zailiyskiy Alatau, even though climbing up to the glaciers Tronova, Ayuksayskiy, Saposhnikova and Altynsarina requires good mountaineering expertise. And remember: you are in a border area and must be in possession of a valid entry permit.

THE KOKSU VALLEY

About 13 kilometres beyond Tekeli the world of normal vehicular traffic comes to an end. The arduous track into the mountains leads by field and meadow paths over forbidding steppe hills towards the southeast, to the **Koksu Valley**. The Koksu River is wild and tempestuous—even in summer it tosses and turns through its rocky bed. Unfortunately for nature lovers, a dam is planned to turn this potential source of energy to man's uses, and while it won't be a huge project, the consequences of the inevitable construction of access roads, etc, on the ecology are depressing. Of course the reservoir will probably become a tourist attraction in its own right, but for the present, at least, one still feels like an explorer in this undisturbed natural environment.

Not far from this site, in the mountains of **Eshkiolmes**, there are 18 short side valleys with an extraordinary collection of several hundred rock carvings from three different periods. The oldest among them, in the 2,500-year-old Scythian-Siberian animal style, are the most refined artistic works from this period in all Kazakhstan. Represented are grazing herds, eagles, leopards, deer and very realistic and detailed battles between warriors on horseback. Some of the drawings are up to one metre high.

The Koksu, meaning blue-green water, is recommended for rafting. The river, which sports some good whitewater rapids, requires full concentration even from professionals. Some tourist agencies in Almaty offer specialized trips to the area.

The river's upper reaches can only be reached by jeep; the only starting point for the neck-breaking journey is Rudichniy/Koksu, some 65 kilometres to the southeast of Taldykorgan. From here, an unpaved track leads to the **Upper Koksu Nature Park**. It follows the river to its source and even further to the Chinese border, where the Koksu's tributary, the Karaaryk (Black Tomb), has its source. It's a hard drive of several hours for the 100-kilometre route, but the reward is well worthwhile. The wild river valley scything down between the snow-covered peaks is very evocative, in some places wood-covered but mostly rough and rocky, and it is possible to trek and climb for days without meeting a living soul.

If you choose to take the southern road over the Altyn Emel back to Almaty, make sure you visit the **Chokan Valikhanov Museum** in the village of Shokan. This Kazakh nobleman and scholar spent the last months of his short life here. The lovingly maintained exhibition in the museum shows the life of this renowned Kazakh and a piece of regional history. The scholar's grave is on the edge of the village.

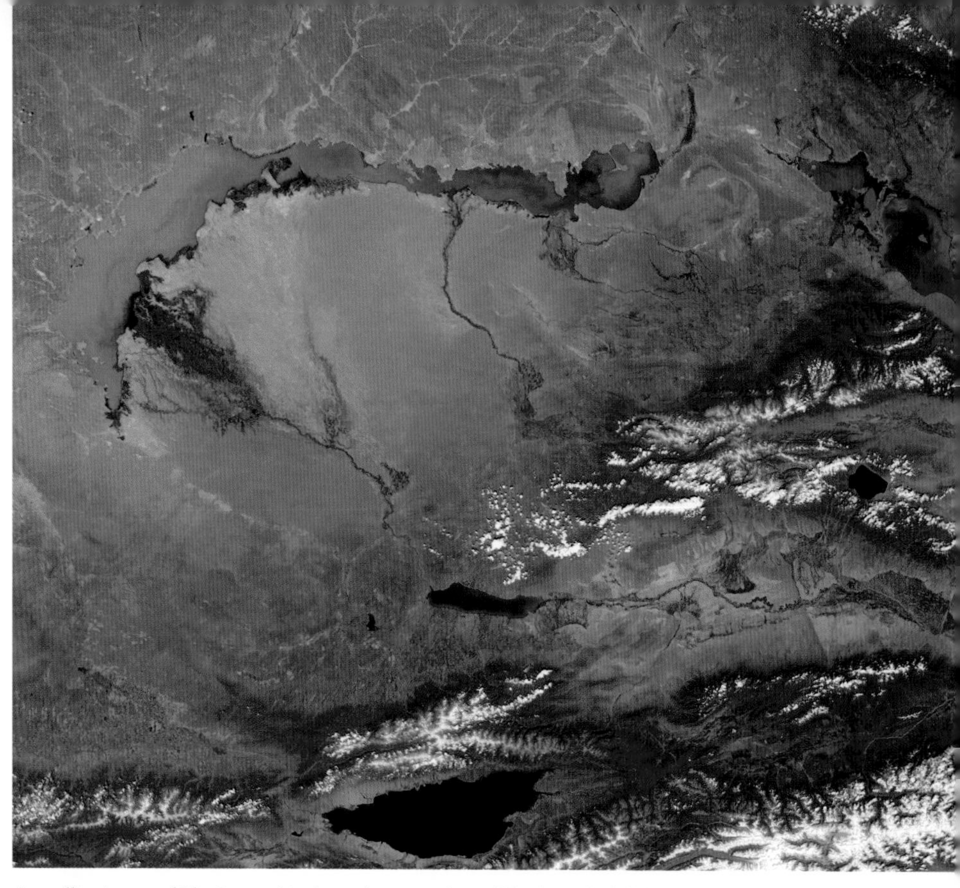

A satellite image of Zhetisu and its boundaries: Lake Balkhash and Alakol Lake to the north, the Tien Shan and Issyk Kul to the south, with the Zhungar Alatau and Ili Valley straddling Chinese territory (Image courtesy of the Modis Rapid Response Project at NASA/GSFC)

The Kapal Arasan Health Resort

In the northern foothills of the Zhungar Alatau there are numerous hot springs, the water of which is often used for medicinal treatment. The warm, slightly radioactive **Kapal Springs** in the valley of the Bien River, containing sulphur chloride and natrium, have been known for 3,000 years. Archaeological finds on the slopes of nearby **Mount Bayanzhurek**, which are among the oldest excavations in all of Semirechye, demonstrate that as early as 900 BC there were settlements here, and there is no doubt that its inhabitants also swam here. The Kapal Springs were also in use at the time of the Silk Road, a northern branch of which passed by this spot. Chokan Valikhanov mentions his visits to the then already well-equipped health resort in his journals. Kapal used to be the first and most important Russian outpost in Semirechye, at a time when Verniy was still emerging. Today, a relatively comfortable sanatorium is available not only for curative treatments, but equally for a stopover during a hiking trip. **Kapal Arasan** is situated 30 kilometres from the village of Kapal, on a side road just south of the road from Taldykorgan to Sarkand-Oskemen.

The health resort (tel: (72841) 21431, or through the office of Erkin Alaman, 15 Gogol St, Almaty, tel: (7 727) 2 300 565) has an attractive location: the main building is situated in a park with poplar and black elm trees, surrounded by steppe and with an open view south towards snow-covered mountains. A room costs from US$15 per day.

The Lepsy River and the Zhasylkol Lakes

The **Lepsy River** is yet another wild river in the Land of Seven Rivers. It draws its water from a multitude of glaciers; two of those, the Aghynykatti ("powerful current") and its tributary Kinosen are enough to maintain three beautiful lakes named **Zhasylkol 1**, **2** and **3**, which can be reached only on foot or horseback. The trip to get there is truly arduous: by bus from Taldykorgan you head in the direction of Urashal on the Alakol, then change at Kabanbay to go by car to Lepsinsk. The great German zoologist, Alfred Brehm, praised the area as one of the most wonderful steppe mountain ranges, "where milk and honey flow". From Lepsinsk you can continue by jeep in the direction of Topolevka until you meet the Aghynykatti, from where it's two or three days of walking or riding to reach the lakes.

In Lepsinsk a tourist resort has been under construction for a couple of years within the framework of an international assistance project. The aim—to provide the local population with a source of legal income through a environmentally friendly tourism project—definitely deserves support. The project is managed by a firm called Nomad in Almaty.

The milky, glacier-fed lake of Zhasylkol 1 (Dagmar Schreiber)

From Lepsinsk there are numerous very pleasant multi-day tours by jeep, but there's no denying the best way to explore, as ever, is on foot or horseback. Fit trekkers, accompanied by a guide, can go "valley-hopping" for 10-14 days along the Lepsy and its parallel streams Tentek, Aganakty, Ulken Baskan and Kishi Baskan and their tributaries to reach the village of Amanbokter. In clear weather the passes offer excellent views of the glacier-covered peaks of the Zhungar Alatau. Mount Semyon is the highest, standing out among this range of icy giants which mark the border with China and sustain the many rivers with their glaciers.

Practical Information

The **Lepsinsk Tourist Project** charges from US$10 per night in tents, yurts or in family guest rooms, and offers a variety of guided tours. Reservations can be made in Kabanbay at the office of Uygentas Agro Company, or through Dmitry of Nomad in Almaty, tel: (7 727) 2 209 510; e-mail: nomadtour@nursat.kz. You should book at least four weeks in advance to allow for the time it takes to get a permit for the border area.

The Great Plains of Zhetisu

The sand and grass deserts of Saryosek-Atyrau, Taukum and Moyinkum cover an enormous territory, stretching to the southern shore of Lake Balkhash and the three eastern lakes of Sasykkol, Alakol and Zhalanashkol. Vast and "empty" though this area may seem on maps, it is in fact far from inhospitable. The valley of the Ili River includes a rich variety of interesting landscapes, the river's delta is home to rich wildlife, the south shore of **Lake Balkhash** is a paradise for fishermen and the lakes near the Chinese border could well become an El Dorado for health resort patients.

Even in the desert, there is life. On the border that separates the Saryosek-Atyrau from the Moyinkum there are remainders of large saksaul forests, and with a good slice of luck you might catch sight of small herds of rare saiga. In olden days, when the Ili Delta ran a different course and its branches were to the east of the current mouth, caravans on one of the Silk Road's northern branches passed this way. There are four spots where the remainders of caravanserais dating from before the invasion of the Mongol hosts can still be found: **Bayauly**, **Aktam**, **Aghash-Ayak** and **Karamergen**, on the now imaginary route between the village of Bakanas in the Ili Valley and the peninsula of **Uzynaral** on the southern shore of Lake Balkhash.

The Kapshagay Reservoir

The **Kapshagay Reservoir** is like the Riviera for Almaty's residents. Only 90 kilometres from the centre of Almaty, this reservoir—into and out of which the Ili River flows—is 100 kilometres long and up to 25 kilometres wide. It can be reached by bus from the Sayakhat central bus station or with a rented car. It takes more than an hour to reach the town of

Kapshagay; pass through it, then cross the dam (payment required) for 20 kilometres in the direction of Taldykorgan. Just over two kilometres after crossing a railroad, you turn right and enter the *Zona otdykha*. Here, another payment gives you access to a water wonderland crowded with leisure-seeking city dwellers, where resort-style waterskiing, banana boating, swimming and beach volleyball is the order of the day. In most places the water is rather shallow, so you have to walk far out to swim.

Kapshagay is enjoying a building boom. A government decision in 2006 moved Almaty's casinos to Kapshagay, and a massive, multi-million dollar entertainment complex like Las Vegas is being developed. It will be called **Rose of the Winds**, featuring fountains, monorails and all the high-tech gloss you'd expect to find in a major resort; the project is scheduled to be completed in 2010. Four completely new towns with a total of more than 100,000 inhabitants are to developed between Almaty and Kapshagay, thus channelling the furious growth of Almaty. Should these plans come to fruition, the future will see a huge urban conglomeration where at present the steppe stretches away left and right of the road.

Many travel agencies offer accommodation on the lake at reasonable costs, but there are limits to their comforts, and mosquito repellent is essential.

For 500 tenge you can visit the new aqua park in Kapshagay town, but there is not much else to appeal to tourists. The original aul of Kapshagay (gorge) was a residential centre for workers who built the Kapshagay dam here in the 1960s and 70s.

THE ILI VALLEY

The **Ili**—or Ile in pure Kazakh—is the most important river in Zhetisu. Where the name originates remains uncertain. The Mongol word *ilansu* means "glittering water", while in Chinese, the river's name could also mean "eastern". One of its tributaries has its source on Kazakhstan territory, but then bends into China, where the Ili grows and then flows back into the country from the east. After absorbing many other rivers over a distance of 768 kilometres, the Ili drains into Lake Balkhash through a large delta. The caravans of the northern Silk Road often followed its course, and many stone ruins on its banks testify to ancient settlements and the intense trading activity of antiquity.

Turan tigers lived in the Ili Delta until as recently as 1939, where the reed is almost impenetrable and grows up to five metres high. Today, anglers are the most common species seen on the banks of the generally quiet river. At weekends thousands of city people head for the river because of its rich fishing—although the Amur carp, sander (or pike-perch) and giant catfish are not always the real goal of people on weekend fishing trips. (Many a man has come home with fish from the market after having spent the whole weekend with his friends living on vodka from the car boot, shashlyk from the grill, guitar music, mosquitoes and campsite romance.)

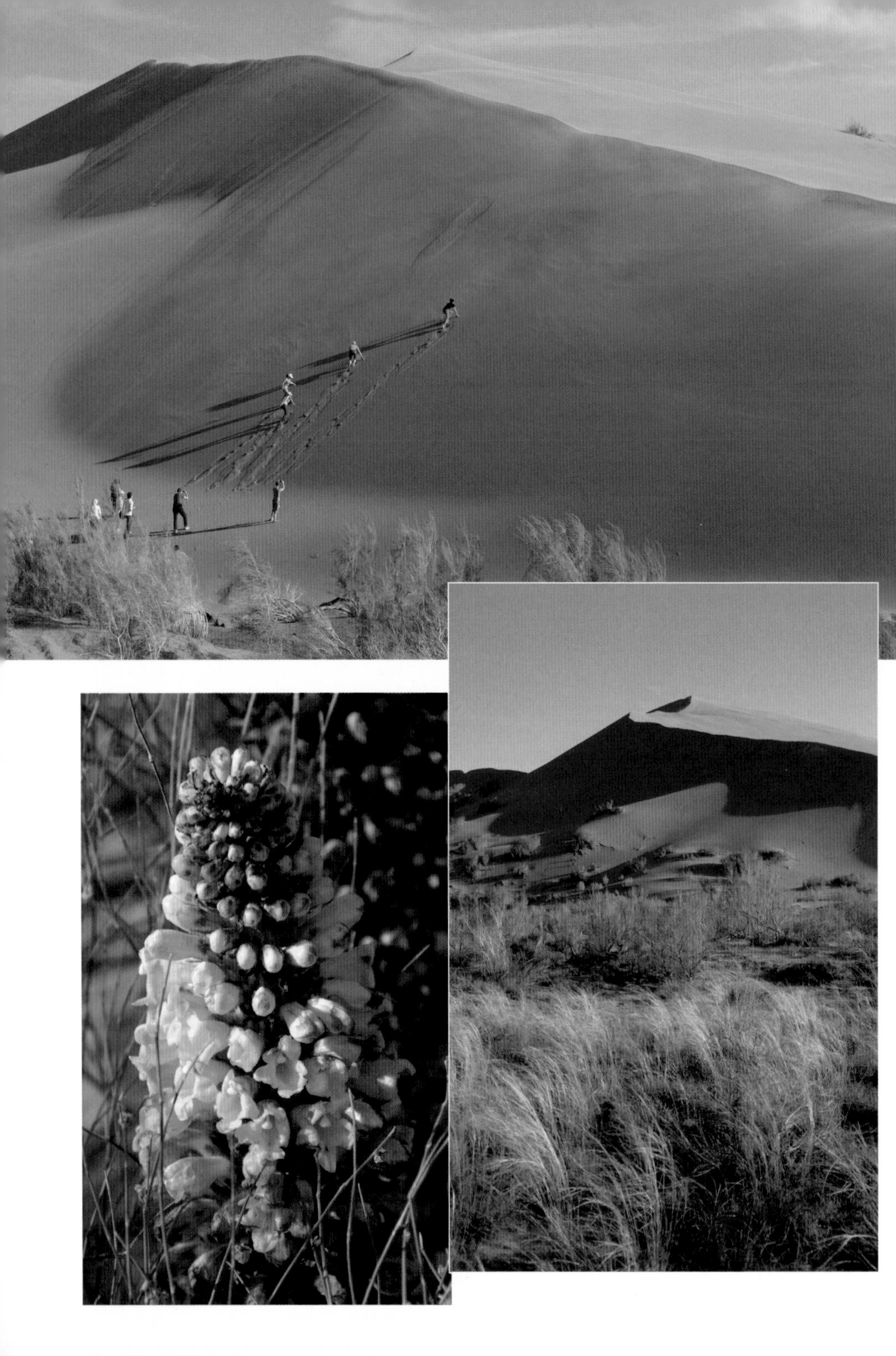

The Ili is long, and if you want a peaceful excursion away from the crowds that is easy to arrrange. Various tourist agencies offer boat trips as far as Kapshagay Reservoir, and you can continue the trip down the river beyond the dam by raft or boat. Here, the Ili winds through a picturesque landscape of steppe hills.

A particularly good day trip leads to the rocks of **Tamgaly Tas**. These rocks, the highest in the Ili Valley, are known not only for their attraction to climbers, but also for their rock carvings, the most mysterious among which are several **Buddha images**. It is assumed that the large Buddha figures and the Sanskrit inscriptions carved in the polished rock date from the 16th Century. At the time, there are said to have been Buddhist monasteries in the east of Kazakhstan, which were later dismantled by the Zhungars. The pagan inhabitants of the steppe would doubtless have added the Buddhas to their animist pantheon without any problem.

This is a wonderful place for a picnic, to explore the surrounding area, to fish or to climb. The view from the rocks, which are easy to climb, is magnificent. One can easily imagine the surrounding hills populated by large herds of horses, sheep and cattle, women in multicoloured robes and their children playing outside the yurts. There is absolute silence here during the week, but at the weekend and in summer you share this idyllic spot with anglers, picnic-lovers and shouting and singing cityfolk passing by on rafts. Local travel companies offer this tour from Almaty at reasonable prices.

Downstream, beyond the village of **Bakanas**, a dried-up river of the same name splits off to the right, to fork more than once into several branches a few kilometres further down. Many places here bear names recalling that the Ili Delta used to begin here in times past. On the edge of the easternmost dry bed (Shet Bakanas) are the remains of the **Aktam** and **Aghash-Ayak** caravanserais (10th–13th centuries AD). Some 150 kilometres to the west of Shet Bakanas are the ruins of the caravan town of **Karamergen**, on the "bank" of the dry valley Ortasu.

Those not wishing to venture so far into the desert can also visit the remains of the **Bayauly** caravanserai (10th–11th centuries AD) on the right branch of the Ili not far from the village of Bereke. To get there you must leave the main road in Bakakbakty and drive through Birlik, which has the only normal bridge crossing the right branch of the Ili.

There are no organized tours to these almost forgotten caravanserais, but if you are determined to see them, be sure to hire the services of a good local guide, take sufficient water and provisions, and a spade and wide mat to get your car out of the many sand traps to which it will inevitably succumb.

Clockwise from top: Climbing the Singing Dunes of Altyn Emel State National Natural Park is harder than you might think; feather grass bends in the breeze at the base of the dunes; a short-lived desert bloom (Jeremy Tredinnick x3)

The lower reaches of the Ili and its delta are worth exploring over a period of several days. Thousands of small and larger lakes, with swimming potential on their sandy shores (as well as on the Ili itself), a rich variety of animal life and the contrast between desert dunes, lily meadows, Togay and reed forests make this an adventurer's dream. It is wonderful country for ornithologists in particular, and each year in May, the ecological organisation Tabigat organizes raft tours on the Ili. Further information can be obtained through Mels Eleusizov (e-mail: tabigat@nursat.kz). There is no permanent tourist infrastructure as yet.

ALTYN EMEL NATIONAL PARK

On the far northeastern side of the Kapshagay Reservoir and bordering the right bank of the Ili before it flows into the reservoir, lies the **Altyn Emel State National Natural Park**, a distance of some 220 kilometres from Almaty. Among its many worthy attractions, the park boasts one that enchants tourists and draws them in a constant stream: a range of sand dunes 150 metres high, 180 metres broad and more than three kilometres long, comprised of the finest desert sand, and right in the middle of the steppe. They are called the **Singing Dunes**

Above: A huge stone-covered kurgan*, one of the 31 Beshshatyr mounds found within Altyn Emel State National Natural Park (Renato Sala and Jean-Marc Deom). Below: The semi-desert landscape of Altyn Emel bursts into colourful life in summer (Vladislav Yakushkin). Inset: Attractive wall detail at the Altyn Emel National Park headquarters (Jeremy Tredinnick)*

(*barchans*), since if you walk along their crests when the wind is blowing from a certain direction, you can hear a humming or droning sound somewhat reminiscent of an aeroplane taking off or of an organ's low bass note. Although not all tourists treat the dunes in a respectful manner (there are even snowboard contests organized on its slopes), it appears not to be eroding or suffering so far—the phenomenon that causes the dunes to remain in exactly the same spot without moving is caused by winds from different directions that meet at this spot in equal strength, replenishing the dunes with sand from the desert, and not allowing it to shift.

The dunes are situated on the right bank of the Ili, at the foot of **Mount Ulken Kalkan**. It is here that Genghis Khan is said to have broken through to the Kazakh steppe in 1219. Standing on the pass on the last mountain ridge before entering the plains, and observing the territory that he was about to conquer, he reputedly said that he felt as if he was in a golden saddle (the name Altyn Emel actually means "Golden Saddle"). Today, this 460,000-hectare territory is home to **kulan**, ***dzheyran*** (steppe, or goitred gazelle), **arkhar**, lammergeier, short-toed eagle and black stork—to name just a few of the 260 species that survive in this protected area. Some of these animals are still on the endangered list, and in theory strictly protected. The park now estimates it has a population of 2,500 kulans, 7,000 gazelles, 3,500 mountain goats and 200 argali sheep. The state pays locals to guard the park, but the sad truth is that some hunting still continues, and the dzheyran and arkhar are still at risk.

A guide is essential—you can arrange one at the park's administrative office in the entry town of Basshy—he will help you to find the park's various sights and the location of the animals, though you may not get closer than a hundred metres or more before the herds and family groups take off in a cloud of dust. The Singing Dunes are not far from Mynbulak Pond, a pretty little oasis inhabited by the hospitable family of a park ranger. The climb up the dunes is best managed from the northern side. It's a tough climb, best undertaken with bare feet, but the view of the steppe, the colourful mountains, the Ili plain and the dunes themselves is fantastic. You can hear the sand sing when the ground is dry and the wind blows from the west—late afternoon or sunset is the best time to see the dunes in all their golden glory.

At the western edge of the national park, at the foot of the mountains, are several groups of grave mounds, including what are possibly the most important kurgans in the Land of Seven Rivers. The 31 mounds of **Beshshatyr** ("Five Tents") were erected by the Sak between the 6th and 3rd centuries BC in honour of their rulers, captains and warriors, buried beneath the mounds. The Beshshatyr kurgans are only one group of more than 1,000 such burial mounds in the Zhetisu region. Nowhere else in Eurasia are there such large numbers of Sak burial sites.

Of the Beshshatyr kurgans, 21 are covered with stones, while the other 10 are covered with pebbles and earth. The largest kurgans, dedicated to rulers and chieftains, are between 45 and 105 metres in diameter and up to 17 metres high. The construction of each of the largest graves took 50,000 cubic metres of earth, stones and pebbles. The walls and ceilings of the four-metre-high tomb chambers consist of the trunks of Tien Shan fir trees, and this wood has survived at least 2,000 years. It is thought that under the hills there used to be catacombs and labyrinths from where a tunnel would lead to the tomb chambers. The mid-size kurgans, in which noblemen and officers were buried, are 25-38 metres in diameter and 5-6 metres high. The small mounds, graves of the brave foot soldiers, are 6-18 metres wide and 1-2 metres high. On their northwestern side, the mounds are surrounded by a semicircle of 45 man-high, upright standing stones. They are carved with images of animals, hunting scenes and figures. According to ethnologists the order in which these stones, named *miringy*, have been placed, is far from coincidental. Each Sak tribe (*ulus*) put up one stone as a token of honour to the ruler who was buried there. Each year, representatives of every ulus would gather here, and light a ritual bonfire next to the stones. Very old traces of fire on the stones tend to confirm this theory. The kurgans were excavated between 1957 and 1961. Human bones, ceramics, horse skeletons, felt and reed mats, iron daggers and bronze arrow points were found in the major tomb chambers.

The park is open to the public from April to the end of October. The park's severe continental climate—only 100 kilometres north of Almaty's relatively mild weather—can lead to intense outbreaks of cold. However, in July one must be prepared for temperatures of between 40 and 50 degrees Celsius. There is no shade; this, together with the multitude of mosquitoes near the river, is why long sleeves are recommended. In midsummer you should also wear conventional, closed shoes to climb the dunes, to avoid burning your feet.

Practical Information

The only land route from Almaty to Altyn Emel is via Basshy—all other ways in are *de facto* blocked. A permit is required, which you must get before the trip at Hotel Zhetisu in Almaty, at the branch of the national park administration. Foreigners pay about US$50, locals considerably less. The national park administration is in Basshy, where you can find rooms—there are now seven buildings catering to 8-10 people each. There are other overnight possibilities in the hunting lodges, as they are called, in the park itself (tel in Basshy: (72840) 31853, fax: 31559, e-mail: altyn-emel@nursat.kz). Spending the night in one of the cabins is relatively expensive, and you're paying more for the exclusivity of being alone with nature than for their modest comfort. The cabins are located near the shore of the Kapshagay Reservoir and also in the side valleys of Sholak, Dereges, Matay, Altyn Emel and Koyandy.

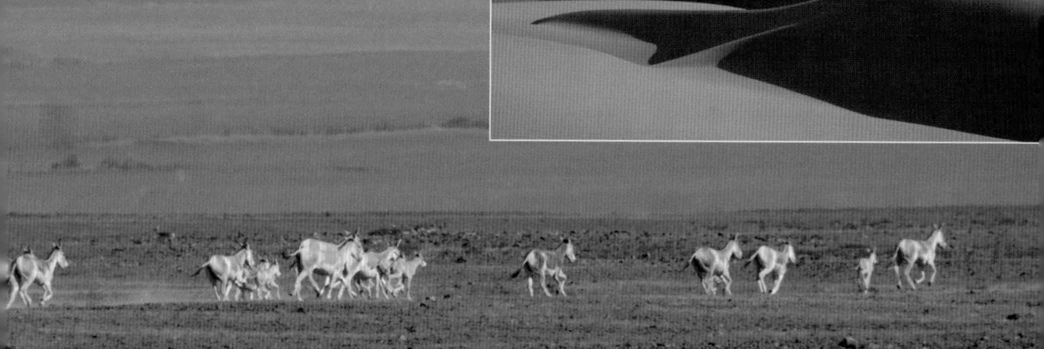

Clockwise from top left: The Ili Delta region is a labyrinth of twisting waterways, mini-lakes and marshland (Vladimir Tugalev); within the White Mountains (KanTengri Mountain Service); Altyn Emel's sand dunes turn gold in the late-afternoon sun (Vladislav Yakushkin); a herd of kulan on the move in Altyn Emel's scrub desert (Jeremy Tredinnick); a storm brews over reed beds on the shores of Lake Balkhash (Vladimir Tugalev)

AKTAU AND KATUTAU—THE WHITE AND RED MOUNTAINS

Yet another interesting natural location can be found on the eastern edge of Altyn Emel National Natural Park: **Aktau**, the White Mountains, which derive their colour from the white gypsum crystals of which they are composed. Fortunately it was decided years ago not to sell this giant gypsum resource to the construction industry. Less in vogue, but no less beautiful, are the red-violet mountains of **Katutau** (literally meaning "stiffened mountains") 10 kilometres to the west of Aktau, and particularly beautiful in the evening light.

A trip to this area is like travelling back in time to an era when the Earth was much younger. Fifteen million years ago, a vast sea covered this region; today, the bizarre, multicoloured sedimentary layers of the now uplifted mountain rocks are admired by all who visit. White and red sedimentary layers are predominant, interspersed with beautifully contrasting blue and yellow stripes. The mountains' weathered conical shapes remind the visitor of pyramids, but this area, 300 kilometres from Almaty, has not opened up for tourism in any major way, and remains untouched, without any trace of human presence, silent, prehistoric-looking, giving the impression that you have time-travelled to the dawning of the ages.

Getting to Aktau and Katutau involves the same route to Altyn Emel, passing Sarybek and Basshy then continuing on towards the southeast. The road is far from simple, so hire a guide from the national park. A 4WD is necessary.

THE ILI DELTA AND LAKE BALKHASH

Like many other places in Kazakhstan, **Lake Balkhash** has its own legend of origination. The sorcerer Balkhash had a pretty daughter called Ile who enchanted everyone on the steppe with her beauty—but most of all Karatal, a brave, good-looking *dzhigit*, or knight. His love for Ile was reciprocated. Unfortunately Karatal was poor, and Balkhash was against the liaison. To discourage the knight he imposed many difficult tests on Karatal, but he passed them all. Nonetheless, the maiden's father broke his word and refused the dzhigit his daughter. In despair, the lovers fled on their horses into the steppe. The incensed sorcerer followed them and transformed himself into a vast sea before their feet. Ile and Karatal immediately changed into two rivers that flow into the lake miles apart.

The reed-covered southern shore of the 614-kilometre-long lake belongs to the Almaty Region. Here, on the northern border of the Land of Seven Rivers, nearly all of its rivers are well preserved. The waters of the Lepsy, Aksu, Koksu, Karatal and of course the Ili, the delta of which dominates the southwestern shore's landscape, flow into it.

It is fair to say that any stay on the southern shore of Lake Balkhash requires certain sacrifices from the visitor. There are mosquitoes… lots of mosquitoes. To fully appreciate that last sentence, picture yourself standing in the middle of a forest of reeds more than head high, waving your arms around like windmills. It can be a very unpleasant experience, but nevertheless, anglers gladly suffer the inconvenience since Balkhash is a fisherman's wet dream come true. The fishing is sensational: in the waters of the relatively shallow lake—its deepest point is only 26 metres—grass or Amur carp, bream, perch and pike teem, not forgetting of course the catfish, which can grow as long as the reeds grow high. Some have been reported to be up to five metres long! It is very possible to catch a catfish that weighs between 50 and 100 kilogrammes. For either ecological considerations or for the lack of large enough pot, many angling tourists adopt the principle of "catch—photograph—release".

A trip to Lake Balkhash is also interesting for wildlife enthusiasts. There are small numbers of the rare reed cat (*felis chaus*), wild boar and wolf, as well as great white and Dalmatian pelicans (which appreciate the abundant fish resources), and numerous varieties of other water birds due to the proximity of fresh and salt water environments. Of course hunters like to visit Balkhash as well—sad as it is to think of the wildlife being further decimated by rifle-toting groups, hunting is a cultural foundation of Kazakh life, and it would be foolish to think it can be stopped entirely.

A few agencies in Almaty organize fishing, hunting and wildlife-watching trips to Balkhash; they use their own accommodation, boats and equipment. Recommended are KanTengri Mountain Service and Asia Discovery.

The Alakol Depression

The 60-kilometre-wide and 300-kilometre-long **Alakol Depression** lies in the extreme east of Kazakhstan. It is a barren, mostly flat and monotonous landscape of steppe, sparsely covered with wormwood. At first sight this is not an inviting place. A fierce wind blows all year round, in spring and autumn regularly reaching speeds of more than 100 kilometres per hour. This wind comes from the **Zhungar Gate**, a valley on the Chinese border named because it was the base for the feared and notorious Zhungar tribes, whose war hosts invaded Zhetisu for centuries. Kazakh tribes used to warn each other using fire beacons on mountaintops, whenever the enemy marched in. The remains of a city dating from the 10th-13th centuries AD near Koktuma suggest that long before the Zhungar invasions began, a branch of the Silk Road passed through this point.

Four lakes line up like a chain in the Alakol Depression. In earlier times, there were only two lakes, **Sasykkol** (Stinking Lake) and the **Koshkarkol** (Ram's Lake). Both were fed by the River Tentek, which forms a swampy delta here. These waters are wild, with reed luxuriously rampant, and surrounded by ponds, pools and puddles—in all, a bird's paradise. Dalmatian

and great white pelicans nest here, as well as little and Macqueen's bustards, gulls, cranes, herons and divers; in all, more than 200 species of bird can be observed on the lakes. A small lake of six by nine kilometres is situated directly on the Chinese border. It is called **Zhalanashkol** (Naked Lake) and strong healing powers are attributed to its mineral-rich water. Finally, there is the vast lake of **Alakol** (Multicoloured Lake), 104 kilometres long, 54 kilometres wide, and up to 54 metres deep. Actually, it can barely be called a lake, for even in clear weather the opposite shore is not visible. Only an island, **Ulken-Araltobe** (Great Island Mountain) sticks out of the water like a landmark.

The water is salty and very clear—pollution is nonexistent here since the region is extremely thinly populated and there is neither industry nor intensive agriculture within a radius of several hundred kilometres. In July and August, the water of Alakol warms up to

Landing a gigantic catfish in the Ili River can be a hands-on affair! (Vladimir Tugalev)

24–26 degrees Celsius. The particular chemical composition of Alakol's water, with a ph-value of 7.2–9.1, gives it curative powers against many persistent skin diseases. Many people suffering from psoriasis and neurodermitis make the hard journey to Alakol, enthusiastically reporting that the water helps them more than that of the Dead Sea. Healing powers are also attributed to the black shingle on the shore. Luckily, its remoteness means the lake is not yet crowded by masses of patients and tourists at health resorts along the shore; in many places the lake's banks are still pristine.

The region surrounding the lake is beautiful for all its starkness. The deserts of **Sarykum** and **Taskarkum** stretch to the southwest; the neighbouring lakes to the west, teeming with birds, are ideal for ornithologists; the foothills of the Zhungar Alatau on the way to Zhalanashkol consist of bizarre mountain formations and the canyon of the Yrgaity River; and north of the lake, beyond the **Barmakkum Desert**, looms **Tarbagatay Peak**. Fifteen kilometres northeast of the lake is the health resort of Barlyk-Arasan. For centuries, nomads have used the scattered hot springs here, and now there is also a sanatorium. Here you have actually crossed into the East Kazakhstan Oblast (Region). Alakol is a good starting point for those who want to explore the beautiful landscapes to the north; from here to the Altai, it is "only" 700 kilometres.

Left: A peaceful scene in the Ili Delta (Vladimir Tugalev)
Top left: Fishing is a hugely popular sport in the Land of Seven Rivers—and for good reason, with a number of large fighting freshwater species (O. Kormuschin)

A Funeral Feast

According to steppe custom, funeral repasts had nothing in common with obsequies. They were conducted by the so-called big toi, or assembly, at which the deceased one was thought to be present. At the same time no grieving was allowed. Instead they had games on horseback and horse races, and held wrestling and singing contests.

This time all the famous persons were invited again. The talks were focused on the coming contest of narrator-songsters: the Kipchak Kaztugan-Zhyrau with the Argyn improviser Kotan-Zhyrau, the father of Akzhol-Biy himself. Kazgutan-Zhyrau's tongue was made of flaming red calico and his teeth were sharper than a sword, whereas according to the Kazakhs he himself was less than a rook in size. Kotan-Zhyrau was over ninety but his voice was as sonorous as fifty years ago. The great hundred-year-old sage and soothsayer Asan-Kaigy, whose fame has remained through ages was to judge the contest. He was the sixth-generation descendant of the great law-giver Maikhi-Biy himself and they honoured him as a saint already during his lifetime...

...According to custom, funeral repasts had to be held in the vast expanses of the steppe, where the soul of the deceased one would be cheerful and peaceful. Besides, the coming games on horseback and horse races required much space. This is why Khan Abulkhair decided to invite his guests to the shore of Lake Akkol, west of the Ulytau Mountains. All the beks and sultans of the great Desht-and-Kipchak steppe and the settled Maverannakhr were to take part in the funeral repast.

As far as the horizon does the grass rock gently in the emerald-silvery waves of the steppe, the surface of its spicy breathing sea reaching as high as a horseman's breast. Only in the distance one can see the greyish blue outlines of the Ulytau and Kichitau Mountains, where the remains of the famed Yedighe-Batyr and Khan Tokhtamysh repose. Now and then there flare up flaming-red clusters of steppe strawberries and stone berries with necklaces of ripe blackcurrants hiding in the leaves. The sun-scorched huge peonies, trumpet-pitchers, bluebells, water lilies, roses and tulips of various tints and colours intoxicate one with their strong aroma. And in the very middle of this inimitable boundless carpet Lake Akkol stands still like a moulded silver bowl...

There is not one living soul around the lake and to all sides of it, just wild beasts scouring about and birds of passage way up in the sky. Day and night the joyful anxious voices of all kinds of game are heard, while in the very middle of the magic mirror-like surface of the lake there glides a pack of swans with their little fledglings, and from time to time the delicate flute-like sound of their calls rings out in the air...

One morning, as if by magic, three hundred big snow-white yurtas grew up on the lake's northern shore. Each one had twelve wings and inside everything was ready for receiving guests: felt mats covered with silk carpets, plenty of soft eider-down cushions and silk quilts piled up along the walls. The day before nine big caravans loaded with different provisions arrived here from Samarkand and Bukhara.

And on the most beautiful western shore, at the foot of the hill topped by the ancient idols the Horde was stationed, with the khan's headquarters and a great deal of different-sized white yurtas seeming to bathe in the blue water. Farther to the south stood the yurtas of the khan's viziers and the Genghizide sultans. Among them especially conspicuous was the huge yurta of Janybek and Kerei, as big as the khan's one. It was crowned by a white banner with a white horse-tail at its top.

All along the eastern shore there stretched a chain of black yurtas intended for numerous cooks and servants who were specially brought here from Maverannakhr, and also for hunting birds. Behind them there were twenty rows of strong, tight-stretched lassos twined from horsehair to which colts were tethered. Three thousand milk mares were driven here for all the guests to have enough koumiss. Whole herds of well-fed shiny horses and overly fattened sheep were slaughtered every day.

The feasting had been going on for a whole week now. On the very first day three hundred choice chargers started their race, or baiga, from Lake Shoindy-Kol situated at the remotest spur of the Argynaty Mountain. First prize went to the famous racer Tarlankok of Khan Abulkhair, its rider being the khan's seven-year-old grandson Muhammed-Sheibani. The moved khan promised to arrange for a special toi to celebrate the important event. After that a wrestling competition began at which Karazhan-Batyr, with arms thicker than an old camel's legs, beat all the famed palvans-wrestlers. As was the custom he was given nine presents, three times the main present being a long-legged red Arabian camel covered from head to tail in an expensive Khorasan carpet.

However, at the equestrian competitions no-one was able to pull down the Karakipchak Koblandy-Batyr. For some time, equal to the period between two milkings of a mare, the famous Argyn military leader Akzhol-Biy offered resistance to him. But in the end his horse could not stand Koblandy-Batyr's onslaught, settled on its knees and the referees recorded a defeat.

Besides the horse-races they had camel's races, women's wrestling and boys' competitions and it was only after these events that the most exciting and grand moment came: a competition of akyns, or narrator-songsters. It was fraught with many perils for the powerful and the strong, since from olden times in the steppe akyns were allowed to ridicule the weaknesses and vices of all people without taking into account their genealogy and riches, and true akyns enjoyed their right in full measure. This time the competition promised to be especially poignant because Asan-Kaigy was to judge it...

...Thousands of people were seated around the khan's Horde. Those closer sat on carpets and embroidered felt mats, those farther on plain felt cloths and those farthest settled right on the cool green grass. The old Asan-Kaigy took a long heartfelt look at the audience, looked over his dear steppe as far as the horizon and started singing:

True riches and jewels
Are kept on the bottom of the deepest seas.
True generosity and wisdom
Are kept deep down in one's soul.
The pearls watched over by the sea
Are cast ashore by hurricanes.
Wisdom is laid bare in grief,
When the heart is overburdened with wounds...

It was his famous contemplation song on the lot of his homeland, which has been preserved in the noble memory of the people for ages. Upon singing it as an introduction to the competition, Asan-Kaigy wiped his weathered sun- and age-tanned brow with a handkerchief, and turned to the akyns...

Ilyas Yesenberlin, The Charmed Sword, Part 1 of The Nomads, translated into English by the Ilyas Yesenberlin Foundation, 2000

Top: A train passes through the "Zhungar Gate" towards the Chinese border (Christine Schwarz)
Above: The Yrgaity River canyon near the northern foothills of the Zhungar Alatau (Arktur)

Practical Information

The Alakol Depression is situated in a border area, and six weeks' notice is needed to obtain an entry permit. The road from Almaty to Alakol is over 600 kilometres long; it is an interesting journey, but often torturous. Close attention is needed to deal with the treacherous road, and it takes at least 10-12 hours to get there. One should also keep in mind that there are only two "local" petrol stations—one in Beskol and the other at the border post of Dostyk, 170 kilometres farther on. Both shamelessly abuse their monopoly and charge prices according to their whim. For this reason, the trip from Almaty is perhaps better made by train, going in the direction of Urumqi in China. Get off the train in Akchi or Koktuma, from where Alakol's shore can already be seen, and continue by bus or taxi.

There is a steadily increasing number of small private guesthouses and holiday camps in Akchi and Koktuma, and the south shore of Alakol is gradually being built up as a recreation area. Before going you should try to make a booking at an Almaty travel agency. The alternative is to stay in a tent, but don't camp too close to the water, because the Alakol Depression is well known for its sudden winds, which always produce fierce waves on the lake.

Travel Agencies for Zhetisu Tours

All the travel agencies listed below are located in Almaty (city dialling code +727):

Akzhol Travel, 78/86 Zheltoksan St, tel: 2 731 041/048, 733 192, fax: 2 731 185, e-mail: motysheva@akzhol.net, website: www.akzholtravel.com

A young, friendly and reliable English-speaking team with good tours in the region and beyond, as well as assistance with hotel bookings and visas.

Asia Discovery, Office 19, 61 Abai Ave, tel/fax: 2 508 108, e-mail: asia-discovery@nursat.kz, website: www.asia-discovery.nursat.kz

Experienced, reliable and reasonably priced operator, specializing in natural science-oriented tours, as well as trekking and rafting.

Central Asia Tourism, 20½ Kazybek Bi St, tel: 2 501 070, e-mail: cat-travel@alarnet.com, website: www.centralasiatourism.com

All kinds of organized tailor-made trips for groups and individuals. CAT has branch offices throughout the country as well as in Bishkek.

Indra Tour, Office 2, Building No 4a, Abai Ave/Utegen Batyr St, Mikrorayon 8, tel: 2 254 511/741, e-mail: indratour@nursat.kz or indratour@newmail.ru, website: www.indratour.net

The company has a radio network of its own, which covers the entire mountain area. Guided walking trips; helicopter tours around the highest peaks of the Zailiyskiy Alatau

(US$75–100 per person per hour); horse riding, climbing excursions, special tours for bird-watchers.

KanTengri Mountain Service, 10 Kasteyev St, tel: 2 910 200/880, fax: 2 916 006, e-mail: kazbek@kantengri.almaty.kz, website: www.kantengri.kz

Experienced and friendly enterprise led by the Kazakh mountaineer Kazbek Valiyev who has climbed Mount Everest.

Nomad Tour, Room 220 Hotel Sedmoye Nebo, 73 Marecheka St/Mate Zalki St, tel: 2 209 510, fax: 2 760 899, mobile: Dmitriy Andreyev (director, English-speaking) 7 701 363 3339, e-mail: nomadtour@nursat.kz, website: www.nomadtour.nursat.kz

A small agency with big ideas; with the support of foreign donors, this enterprise is building up a network of ecological tourism projects. The first to be set up is in Lepsinsk at the foot of the Zhungar Alatau. Other tours on offer include the area around Burabay.

Rakhat Tour, Office 402, 65 Furmanov St/Makatayev St, tel: 2 501 625/737 495.

Fast visa and registration service, tours in the Almaty area, great multi-day tours on horseback in the Narynkol area (US$100–130 per day depending on a group's numbers).

SADMOL, Flat 16, Building 47, Samal 2, Almaty, tel: 2 588 187/630 478, fax: 2 588 199, e-mail: info@sadmol.com, website: http://sadmol.com

Tabigat Union of Environmentalists of Kazakhstan, Office 222, 115 Zheltoksan St, tel: 2 729 705, fax: 2 501 827, e-mail: tabigat@nursat.kz

Enthusiastic non-governmental organisation with friendly staff. Each year in May they organize a raft tour on the Ili. Participation costs from 30 euros per day.

Tour Asia Travel Agency, 359 Radostovtsa St, tel: 2 482 573, fax: 2 497 936, e-mail: office@tourasia.kz, website: www.tourasia.kz

Specializes in tailor-made climbing and trekking tours in the Tien Shan and the Altai. A Pamir specialist. Good English communication level.

Tsentralnaya Asia Tourism Agency, 1/F, 73a Tole Bi St, tel: 2 694 779/921 974, fax: 2 508 151, e-mail: asia@tour.online.kz

Small but well-organized agency specializing in tailor-made trips for groups of "full-blooded mountaineers" but also catering to "normal people".

Zhibek Zholy, 55 Ablai Khan Ave, tel: 2 500 400/410, fax: 2 500 416, e-mail: joly@kazmail.asdc.kz or joly@arna.kz, website: www.jibekjoly.kz

Large, experienced firm with good English skills. Tours include Silk Road trips, trekking on foot and horseback, and specialized tours for ornithologists, botanists, archaeologists, etc.

SOUTHERN KAZAKHSTAN: ALONG THE SILK ROAD

A herd of brown camels scattered on the steppe, abandoned cities, graveyards... from time to time a yurt as well... before his eyes horsemen rushed by, sometimes alone, sometimes in groups, many of them still with pointed caps as in times of old.

Chingis Aitmatov

THE SILK ROAD

Two cultures coexisted for many centuries in today's oblasts of **Zhambyl**, **South Kazakhstan** and **Kyzylorda**: the nomadic communities of the vast steppe, and the sedentary civilisation of the oases. Through this area ran an important branch of the **Silk Road**, measuring 1,700 kilometres across territory now part of present-day Kazakhstan. Trade centres and caravan stations flourished along this route, spawning the word *caravanserai*, meaning caravan palace, or caravan court. In fact, many of them did bear some resemblance to a palace, since the remains of surrounding walls have been found—and can still be seen—in the steppe and desert oases. They were usually very large, always surrounded by walls, and equipped with inns, kitchens, stables, a mosque and a storehouse for merchandise. Trade in all kinds of goods took place, from expensive cloth—such as the silk to which the route owed its name—to damask and cotton, furs and wool, precious stones, carvings, porcelain, spices, tea and fruits, arms and gunpowder, rare wild animals, noble steeds, hunting birds and hounds. The most important land trade route of all time influenced the pulse of this region for more than 1,000 years.

Southern Kazakhstan not only boasts many beautiful landscapes, but also has numerous cultural, historical and architectural treasures to offer. The sheltered, forested and well-watered **Karatau Mountains** were a dwelling place for humans as early as the Stone Age. Numerous khaganates and khanates came and went in the fertile fluvial plains of the rivers **Chu**, **Talas**, **Aksu**, **Arys** and **Syr Darya**—it goes without saying that such a naturally blessed land in the middle of desert and steppe attracted the envy of many a ruler. Unfortunately, this also led to the destruction of many cities which could otherwise have boasted today of a great Silk Road heritage. Fortunately, some of the ancient monuments have been preserved and increasing numbers are being rediscovered and restored.

The magnificent northwestern entrance to the Mausoleum of Khoja Ahmed Yasawi (Christopher Herwig)

Southern Kazakhstan is an up-and-coming region, with tourist potential that largely exceeds the existing infrastructure—something of which the regional and national governments are well aware, and beginning to remedy. An extended trip from Almaty via **Taraz** to **Otrar** and **Turkistan**, and perhaps even further on to Kyzylorda and the **Baikonur Cosmodrome**, should however also include the natural beauty of the western Tien Shan, the mountains of Karatau and classic steppe land.

A very good English language website can be found at www.southkazakhstan.com

THE FOOTHILLS OF THE TALAS ALATAU

The **Talas Alatau** marks the western end of the Tien Shan massif, and stretches to the gates of Shymkent. The tip of this relatively low mountain range, the Karatau, extends deep into the **Moyinkum Desert**. The population density in the mountain foothills is particularly high by Kazakh standards, partly due to the abundance of water from the many glacier-fed rivers, but also to the migration of Kazakh tribes from the steppe to the foothills. This policy was pursued both under the tsars and Stalin, and the dispossession and forced settlement of the nomads has put its stamp on southern Kazakhstan more than in any other part of the country. The Kazakh language and culture are predominant here, and you should take this into consideration and behave accordingly, especially in the auls.

Top left: A Kazakh woman stands in front of one of her felt rugs, made using traditional methods passed down through centuries (Jeremy Tredinnick). Left: An aerial view of the Tortkul of Tuimekent, 40km north of Taraz (Renato Sala and Jean-Marc Deom)

CHU

The fluvial plain of the **Chu River** (also known as the Shu), the upper reaches of which are in Kyrgyzstan, is notorious for its trade in hashish, which grows in particularly favourable conditions in the valley behind Aspara. Regardless of this, the town of **Chu** (Chuy) is a pleasant and quite suitable transit point if you are travelling by road. Chu is on the rail network from Almaty to the southern cities, and the train stops here for 15 minutes, enough time to explore the huge station—worthy of a city of a million-plus inhabitants—and to buy a string bag of sun-sweet sugar melons (*dyni*) on the platform. Five of them will cost as little as 50 tenge.

AKYRTAS

The town of **Akyrtas** is thought to have been the summer residence of the **Karluk khagans** during the height of their power from the 8th–10th centuries AD. Judging by the remains of its foundations, a palace certainly existed here. Another theory, however, suggests that it could have been a **Nestorian monastery**—indicated by the discovery of a stone block bearing the image of a fish, the symbol of Christianity. Whatever the case, the building was designed using very modern concepts, and excavations have revealed a most ingenious water distribution system.

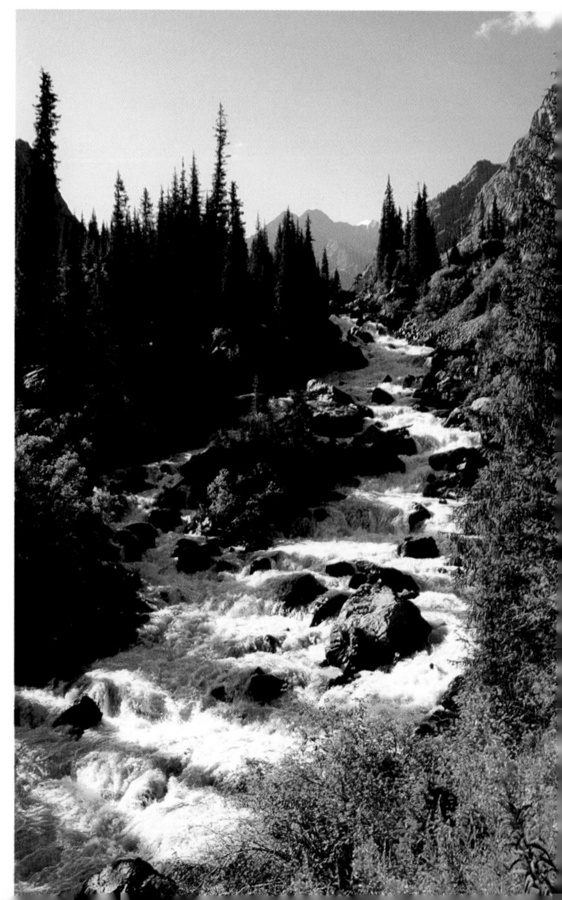

Visit it today, and you find yourself standing in front of a partly grassed, overgrown wall, with stone tubs scattered around under the open sky. It is unusual—but welcome—that none of these has yet been carried off. The best explanation for this is that it is so hard to reach the city: situated 50 kilometres from Taraz, you need the help of a local guide to find Akyrtas, off the road from Merke to Taraz near the village of **Akyrtobe**. A recommended guide is Albina Veimer (karavankz@mail.ru).

TARAZ

In 2002, **Taraz** celebrated the 2,000th year of its existence. This jubilee was slightly controversial since the city had been mentioned in writing for the first time only in the 6th Century AD. Nevertheless, with a consensus that there had been a caravan station on its location long before then, it was decided that the anniversary should take place in 2002. Regardless of the accuracy of the date, the event was greatly to the city's benefit, and much was built and restored. All houses around the central square were painted pink, giving the city the image of a big box of chocolates on the eve of the celebrations.

Together with the festivities in Taraz, to the government went to great effort to further explore and propagate the city's history. Those who are interested in obtaining a balanced and comprehensive version of the city's development can contact Rosa Golubyeva (tel: (+7262) 457 744), who has written a city guide (in Russian) containing many facts, legends and stories.

A Byzantine note dating from 568 describes this site, located on the **Talas River**, as a city bustling with traders and merchants. The city is discussed in the context of a visit by an envoy of Emperor Justinian, who was received by the Turkish khagan Dizabul, and hosted for five days with pomp and ceremony. Chinese sources dating from 630 confirm the

Above: Taraz is a green and pleasant city (Dagmar Schreiber)
Left: The Talas Alatau is blessed with an abundance of water (Vladimir Tugalev)

Ancient stone markers can be found in many locations throughout southern Kazakhstan (Gunter Kapelle)

impression of a rich merchant city with a swirling mix of nationalities. During the 8th and 9th centuries the Arabs expanded into western Turkestan (as the region was then known); in 751 they were victorious at a battle on the Talas River, which was decisive in their struggle with the Chinese for dominion over the region. But they conquered the Talas region only in 863. The name Taraz comes from Arabic and means scales—the symbol of trade.

Taraz reached its highest level of development and influence from the 10th to 12th centuries, initially as the capital of the **Karluks** and later of the **Karakhanids**, and was still a key centre on the Great Silk Road. At that time, Taraz had a land area of almost one square kilometre and included a *shakhristan* (citadel) of seven hectares. A fortress wall with watchtowers surrounded the city. Unfortunately, hardly anything from that time has been preserved, since even before Genghis Khan's army arrived, the place had been razed by the Shah of Khorezm, and afterwards it lost its significance.

A different version of the story claims that Taraz was first razed to the ground by the Mongols: **Zhu-chi (Juchi)**, Genghis Khan's eldest son, who took responsibility for the conquest, wanted to spare the city on account of its beauty, but his father replaced him with other captains who carried out his order to destroy it. Later, however, the Mongols were to acknowledge their error and founded a new city on this strategic spot, which they dubbed

Zhany (new) Taras, and which rivalled its predecessor in wealth. Until the 16th Century, when the Kazakh tribes united in their struggle against the **Zhungars**, Zhany Taras enjoyed great fame. A warlord in the service of Ablai Khan named Baba is said to have played a key role in it, for which he obtained the title Datkha. Today, his statue stands before the city hall, a place once reserved for the great leader of the Revolution, Lenin.

Following the opening of the sea route to India and the waning of the Silk Road, the city lost its glamour. The Zhungars' raids did the rest, and by the beginning of the 19th Century there was nothing left of its former glory.

The **Khan of Kokand** had the city repopulated and it is from this period that the Uzbek alleyways in the west of the city date. In 1856 the place was renamed Aulye Ata (Holy Father). Today it is thought that this is in memory of Taraz's apogee under Karakhan, who is said to have ruled in a just and wise manner until his hundredth birthday. In 1864 the Khan of Kokand lost Taraz to the Russians, and the city was destroyed once more.

In January 1936, Aulye Ata's name was changed to Mirzoyan, after the communist politician Levon Mirzoyan. He had distinguished himself in the establishment of Soviet power in the Caucasus and from 1933 until his death in 1939 he led the Kazakh Communist Party. Only 2.5 years later the city's name changed again, this time to Zhambyl after the popular folk singer. Finally, in 1997 President Nazarbayev signed a decree that returned the city to its original name.

The city's central square, formerly Lenin Square and now called **Dostyk (Friendship) Square**, is surrounded by an attractive ensemble of buildings from the early Soviet classicist period and a lovingly maintained park. East of the square, in front of the drama theatre, is a monument to the writer Baurzhan Monyshuly (1910-1982), who related his adventures in the Battle of Moscow and on other battlefields in the Great Patriotic War in numerous stories and novels. A green promenade opens up behind the row of pink-painted government and university buildings on the square.

Little is left of the old city of Taraz. The **Alye Ata mausoleum**, also known as the Karakhan mausoleum, is situated in a park not far from the stadium. Unfortunately, many of the building's original decorations were lost during its restoration, completed in 1906. New tiles have been put in place on the outside of the structure, which is flanked by minarets; only the inside of the dome and the entrance and window have retained tiles from the time of Karakhan. The mausoleum of Shamsur (Davudbek), a Mongol governor with a most gruesome reputation, is situated in the same park. The local history museum on Tole Bi Street offers a rich history of the city and its ruling classes; it is located next to the Kazakhtelecom building, and is open daily except Mondays.

PRACTICAL INFORMATION

The area dialling code for Taraz is 7262; the main post and telephone office is on Abai Avenue/Dostyk Square. There is a cash machine on Ayteke Bi Street, near a good grocery store also on Ayteke Bi Street, between Aytiyeva Street and Abai Avenue. If you can read Russian, check out www.tarazinfo.kz

TRANSPORTATION

Several trains a day depart east for Almaty and west for Shymkent, and there are several trains a week for Moscow and Siberia from the railway station on the southern edge of the city, at the end of Kolbashi Koykaylym (formerly 50 Lyet Oktyabrya). Tickets can be bought at the station or from the Sputnik travel agency on Aytiyeva Street/Tole Bi Street, opposite the Zhambyl Hotel.

The airport is situated to the west of the city, from where there are daily (except Saturday) flights to Astana. Tickets can be bought at Aerotur, 91/16 Tole Bi Street, tel: 53562/55615.

ACCOMMODATION

HOTEL GAZOVIK, 7a-1, Suleimenov St, tel: 453 681/452 042/433 991, fax: 433 233, e-mail: gazovik_hotel@nursat.kz, website: www.gazovik.kz

A new "European-style" hotel catering to both businessmen and tourists, with sauna, restaurant and conference room. Rooms from US$67.

Zhambyl Hotel, 42 Tole Bi St, tel: 452 552, fax: 451 750, e-mail: hotel-zhambyl@nursat.kz

A quiet hotel right in the middle of the city, with 75 rooms in a 1960s-style building, recently renovated, with friendly service, city tours, excursions to surrounding areas and a translator service. Rooms from US$35.

Hotel Taraz, 75a Zhambyl Ave, tel: 433 491, fax: 457 929

A large Soviet hotel not far from the town centre; 140 rooms with prices from US$20.

There is also a hotel in the railway station, on the second floor of the renovated station building, offering rooms with toilet and shower. You can pay by the hour if you are in transit waiting for a train connection.

THE AISHA BIBI MAUSOLEUM

About 15 kilometres after leaving Taraz on the road to Shymkent, you reach the village of **Aisha Bibi**, named after the mausoleum built there in honour of Aisha, the bride of Karakhan, Lord of Taraz in the 11th and 12th centuries. All Kazakhs know the tragic story of the fateful love between Karakhan and Aisha Bibi.

When the young Karakhan, ruler of the regions of western Turkestan, undertook a political mission to **Samarkand** in the year 1050, people rushed to the street in great numbers to watch him and his splendid dzhigits pass by. Karakhan noticed a young maiden of extraordinary beauty among the curious crowd. The young girl was Aisha, the daughter of the Lord of Samarkand. Karakhan was smitten, and began arranging secret meetings with her, until he was called back to his home city of Taraz to defend it against invaders from the east. Before he left, Karakhan decided to ask Aisha's father for her hand. The father, however, dismissed the young captain with insulting words. Nothing could change his opinion that Karakhan could not possibly offer his daughter a life worthy of her station.

The two lovers bade each other farewell, but not without sealing a secret bond. After waiting for a long time without any word from her beloved, Aisha decided to inform her father about the engagement and to obtain permission for the marriage. Outraged by his daughter's stubbornness, the father cursed Aisha and swore that never while he lived would he give his consent for the union. Aisha's mother, however, was concerned about her daughter's happiness and helped Aisha, dressed in men's clothes and accompanied by her old nanny, Babadzha Khatun, to flee on the best horse available.

The two women travelled for months until they saw Taraz loom on the horizon. On the bank of the River Tasaryk Aisha changed her outfit, took a long bath in the river and put on her wonderful wedding dress, which during the long months of waiting she had made herself. Then, she reached for her *saukele*, the bride's headdress. She took it out of the saddlebag and put it on her head, but at that moment a poisonous snake shot forward and bit the maiden on her cheek. The poison started to work instantly; Aisha collapsed and bade the nanny gallop forth to Karakhan and announce her arrival. But the old woman could not ride fast enough. When she returned in the company of Karakhan, his guards and a swiftly mobilised clergyman, there was hardly any life left in the girl. In despair Karakhan acknowledged that he could do nothing to save his beautiful Aisha. Therefore he ordered the clergyman to marry them on the spot, with his companions as witnesses. With mere moments left to her, Aisha signalled with a faint nod that she, Aisha Bibi—or the wedded Aisha—would be the wife of Karakhan. Then she passed away.

Karakhan swore that never in his life would he love or marry another woman—and kept his promise. He lived to 100 years old, and ruled in a wise and just manner, for which he was later dubbed Aulye Ata, or Righteous Father.

Karakhan had a splendid mausoleum built on the spot where Aisha had died. On the ruler's order, only the best construction materials were used, and the best architects engaged. Later, a second mausoleum was built as the last resting place for the nurse, Babadzha Khatun, who survived her mistress by many years, and died in honour at Karakhan's court.

Today, the mausoleums are a popular pilgrimage site for young lovers. Both buildings started to suffer the ravages of time, and for this reason they have been restored stone by stone, and now present a suitably beautiful aspect—in the way Karakhan imagined it in his designs. To get there, turn left if arriving in Aisha Bibi from Taraz, and drive for about a kilometre along a tarmac road before seeing the mausoleums, surrounded by a fenced garden.

Karatau—The Black Mountains

The mountain range of **Karatau** (Black Mountains), to the west of the city of the same name, is primarily known to palaeontologists and biologists. The former rejoice in the rich finds made here in caves and at excavations, since this area's mild climate and the shelter of its karst caves made it very attractive to primitive humans, who lived here and illustrated their world with numerous rock carvings. In the **Arpa Uzen** gorge lies the second-largest gallery of rock drawings in Kazakhstan, with 3,500 subjects. The area of **Karabastau**, where extensive evidence of settlements from the Stone and Bronze ages can be found, has been designated the **Aksu-Zhabagly Nature Reserve**. It is possible to arrange guided trips to the excavation sites from the centre of the reserve.

Biologists in turn enthuse about the wealth of wildlife in the 280-square-kilometre Karatau region, which is home to 150 endemic plants alone, as well as many rare birds. The valley of Berkara plays host to the only population of Asian paradise flycatchers north of the Himalaya.

Every valley in this mountain chain, which rises to 2,176 metres, is worth visiting. You can drive around the mountains or wander through the valleys on foot, and since there are streams everywhere, the reservation is excellent for camping. The Karatau Mountains were of strategic importance during the Silk Road era and the subsequent period of war. The ruins of watchtowers show that in times past, movement on the plains of the Syr Darya and the Moyinkum could be marked and followed from here. One such watchtower, near the settlement of **Aksun Be**, has been relatively well preserved. It is situated in the furthest northwestern foothills, and can be reached in a day's travel through Suzak.

The Aksu-Zhabagly Nature Reserve is rich in plant life, which in turn makes it a paradise for many bird species (Rolf Behlert)

The Karatau mountains do not always soar into the sky like other areas of the Tien Shan, but they are still rich in beauty and biodiversity (Yevgeni Byelousov)

The Aksu-Zhabagly Nature Reserve

Halfway between Taraz and Shymkent, and about 15 kilometres beyond the **Shakpak Pass**, is the best entry point for **Aksu-Zhabagly Nature Reserve**. The rail line passes nearby—get off at the station of Tyulkubas, and arrange to be collected or continue by taxi, following a good side road to the pretty, green district town of **Ryskulov** (formerly Vannovka) and the village of **Ak Biyk**. Close to Ak Biyk is a very beautiful cave with stalactites. In the hamlet of Zhabagly you'll find **Zhenya's and Lyuda's boarding house** (see tour agencies information on page 330), which arranges tours throughout the reservation. Around 1,400 species of flower can be found here, 27 plants are found nowhere else in the world, 238 species of bird have been recorded, and endangered mammal species such as the lynx, snow leopard, brown bear and arkhar inhabit the juniper forests of this mountain fastness.

The Steppe Lakes

Hundreds of thousands of birds migrate across the Karatau in spring and autumn each year. To the north of the mountains, where the streams flow out into the Talas, several vast lakes dot the steppe, reachable only after the snow has melted. Here, the birds make a stopover, creating a paradise for those who love the shrieks of myriad water birds, the elegant flight of terns and the romantic sight of herds of horses at water's edge. If this sounds appealing, take the opportunity to make a trip to the lakes of Taskol, Biylykol, Kyzylkol, Akkol or Darbaza, and also to the Ters Ashimbulak Reservoir to the south of the Karatau.

Aksu Canyon

To the east of Shymkent, a small but turbulent river called the **Aksu** (White Water) has carved a bizarre canyon into the landscape. The easily eroded karst rock prevailing here has been worked by nature into 600-metre-high rock walls, faults, caves and waterfalls. The upper part of the canyon is about 400-500 metres wide, but it becomes narrower and narrower as it descends from the mountains. In some places, the river completely disappears under the rocks, only to spurt out in a most impressive manner farther down. The 76-kilometre-long **Aksu Canyon** forms the western border of the Aksu-Zhabagly Nature Reserve. From Zhabagly, you can reach the deeply cut canyon by 4WD through the small village of Rayevka, beautifully situated on the high plateau, which in clear weather provides wonderful views of the highest peak of the Talas Alatau, Mount Sayram (4,454m). The faults and subterranean whirlpools can best be reached from the hamlet of Karamurt.

Another beautiful canyon lies to the east of Aksu; here, the Maskhat River has done all the work. A third canyon can be reached from Sastobe and Makhtaly; it has been shaped by the Karaungur River, flowing down from Mount Karatau.

Left: Superb wilderness in the Zhulsaly Canyon in Aksu-Zhabagly Nature Reserve (Z. Bjelousov)
Below: A botanist's dream come true—Aksu Canyon (Manuela Offenzeller)

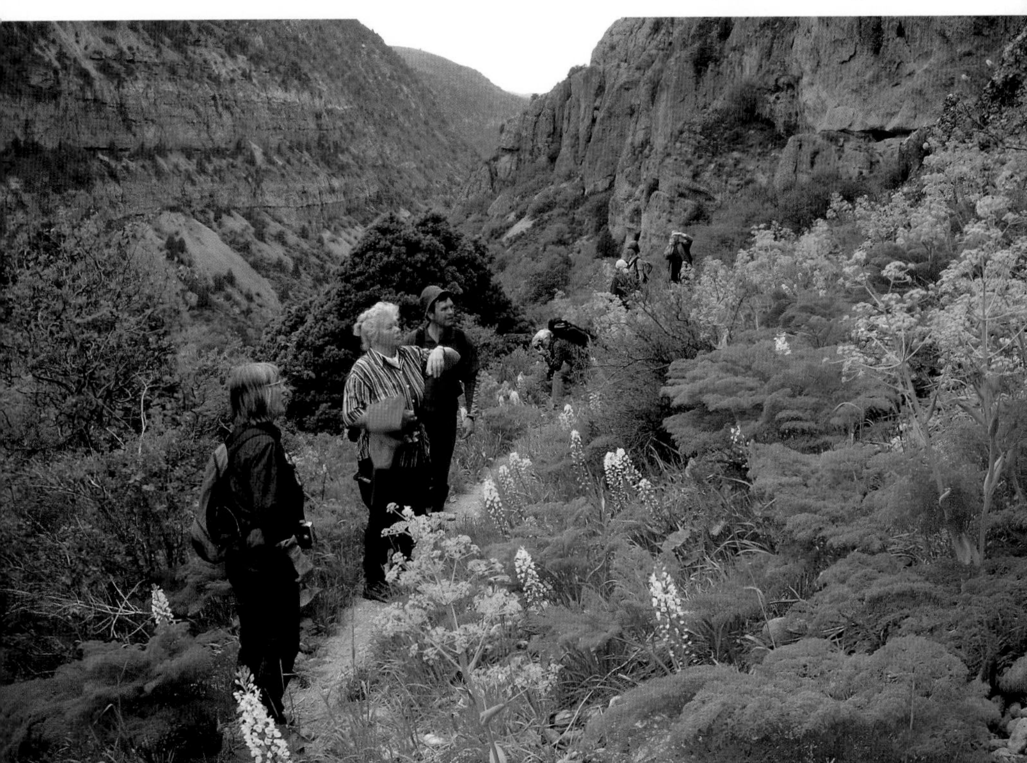

The Domalak Ana Mausoleum

In 1998, a beautiful white mausoleum was built on a hilltop near Akbastau, between Karabulak and Shayan (at the foot of the Karatau) on the site of a dilapidated medieval burial ground, said to be the resting place of a powerful fortune-teller. She predicted the death of her 12 sons, who had ridden out to avenge the theft of the family's herd of horses. Her prediction came true, and only her husband survived. The old white mare, the only horse that had not been taken, brought the stolen herd back. The **Domalak Ana Mausoleum** is the gift of a wealthy businessman named Omarov, who wanted to present his people with a memorial. "Remember your roots" is written on the tombstone inside the dome.

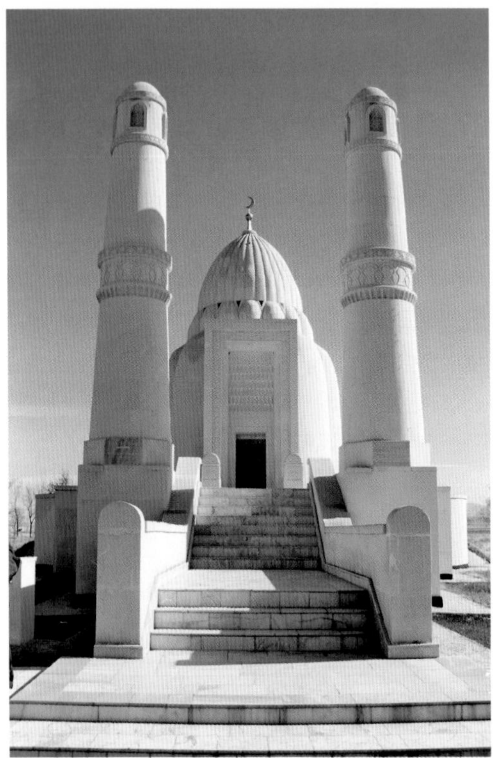

The Domalak Ana Mausoleum is a recent addition to a region where many tombs are found (Yevgeni Byelousov)

A couple of interesting places in this area are worth a detour. First is the **Ak Metshet** (White Mosque), built on top of a large cave near the auls of Kenestobe and Akmetshet. Two kilometres after Akmetshet a rough road to the right leads you to the shrine. Once back on the road, you can continue towards the mountain, to the small village of Baydibek across a mountain pass. A beautiful mausoleum has been built here in memory of the Five Wise Women (**Besh Ana**). The mausoleum of **Sangil Bibi** is hidden in a valley five kilometres after the village.

Suzak and the Moyinkum Desert

The settlement of **Suzak** on the northern slopes of Mount Karatau was once the capital of the **Kazakh Khanate** at the time of **Khan Taukel**. The sole remaining building from that period is the 16th Century mausoleum of **Kulak Ata**, while two other mausoleums, those of **Mamet Khalpe** and **Azhi Sona Ata**, as well as the **necropolis of Karabura**, date from the 18th and 19th centuries.

It's quite a journey to get there, however. The district's main town, which you must pass through to get to Suzak, is **Shayan**. Worth a visit are the mosque and Koranic school,

dating from the 19th Century, as well as the anthropological museum. Farther on, a side road leads to **Kumkent** (Desert City), the ruins of a city dating to the 10th–13th centuries. The salt lake **Kyzylkol** (Red Lake) is also worth an excursion in this region. A final stop on the road to Suzak is the village of **Sholakorgan**, where you will find the ruins of a medieval settlement, with a museum.

The landscape along this route across Mount Karatau is stark but fascinating. One should not, however, underestimate the distance—in total it is 235 kilometres from Aksu to Suzak, which is situated on the edge of the **Moyinkum Desert**. Here, a wonderful old wooden mosque still stands, and the remains of the Kazakh Khanate's old capital. Unfortunately these archaeological treasures enjoy no protection, so please treat them with respect. Adventurous travellers with sufficient water can cross a slice of desert on the road to **Zhuantobe**—a distance of 76 kilometres. In Zhuantobe you are standing on the Chu River—or you might not be: depending on the season, the river either flows through the town or has petered out entirely before it gets there. You are at a crossroads here, with a number of options. You can either turn back and return to Aksu, or continue straight to Turkistan. In the latter case, you turn right in Sholakorgan, crossing the ridge and passing through the large town of Kentau on the southwestern edge of the mountains. Or you can follow the Chu upstream through its valley. This involves one or two days' travelling through the desert on a bad but clearly visible road, passing through an aul every 50–100 kilometres. This is a Kazakhstan very few tourists see; after 400 kilometres, near Birlik, the track joins a better road, and after another 67 kilometres you find yourself in the town of Chu, half a day's travel from both Almaty and Shymkent.

SHYMKENT

Many inhabitants of **Shymkent** are of the opinion that their city has little to offer, apart from a flourishing nightlife. This is only partly true, however. The city's nightlife is indeed impressively colourful, mainly due to the multitude of street cafés and shashlyk bars that serve their clients around the clock and all through the year. They can do this because of

As you travel around the countryside you will see many of these constructions; they are simple mazars *(tombs) built from clay bricks in recent centuries—the roofs are usually the first sections to collapse (Vladimir Tugalev)*

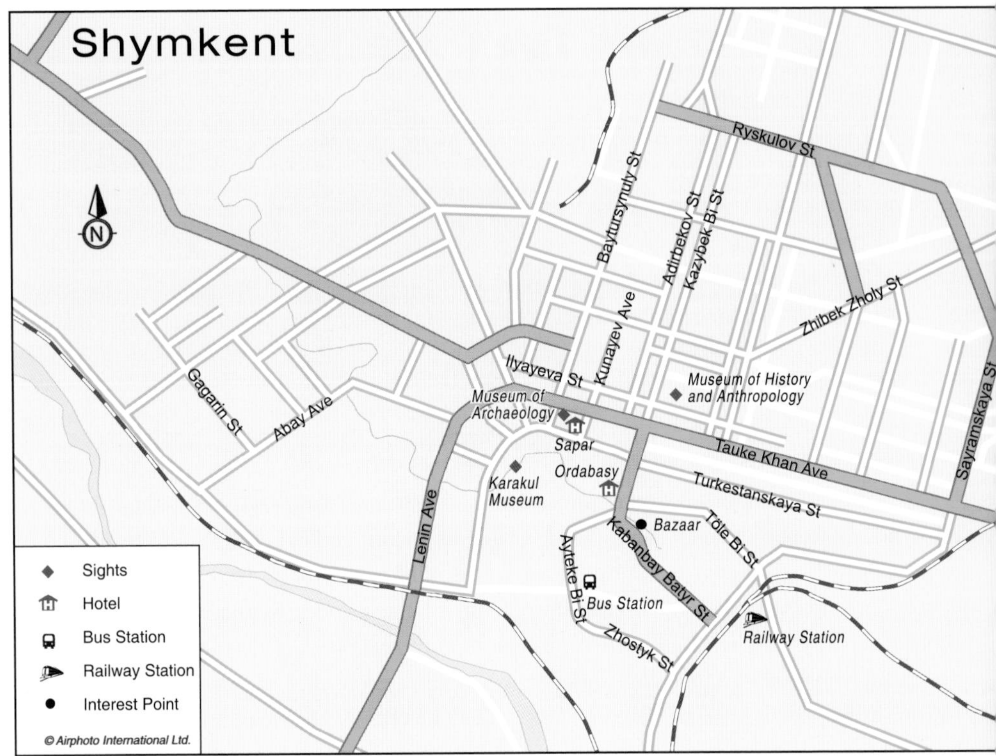

the mild climate: frost is rare in this region, even in winter. Shymkent is the most southerly large city in Kazakhstan and is situated close to the border with **Uzbekistan**. The hurly-burly on the streets has much of the Uzbek character, and many restaurants are decorated in Uzbek style, with green courtyards that make it difficult to decide which hospitable-looking establishment to choose; this is true particularly on the road that leads to Tashkent.

The name Shymkent was first mentioned in 1365, but excavations suggest that there was a major settlement on its site long before that. Russian sources from the 16th to 18th centuries identify Shymkent as Chimin or Chimin'gen. In 1915, the city was renamed Cherńyayev, in order to remind its inhabitants of the Russian general who had conquered and destroyed substantial parts of it; but in 1921 Shymkent got its historical name back. Soviet "progress" in Shymkent took shape in the form of the USSR's largest lead smelter. Its environmental consequences were devastating, with a corresponding effect on the health of the city's inhabitants. After twice going bankrupt during the 1990s, the factory is now working once again, though at half capacity and equipped with better filters. The industrial city of Shymkent also has a major oil refinery, and processing of local agricultural commodities such as sunflowers and cotton takes place here as well.

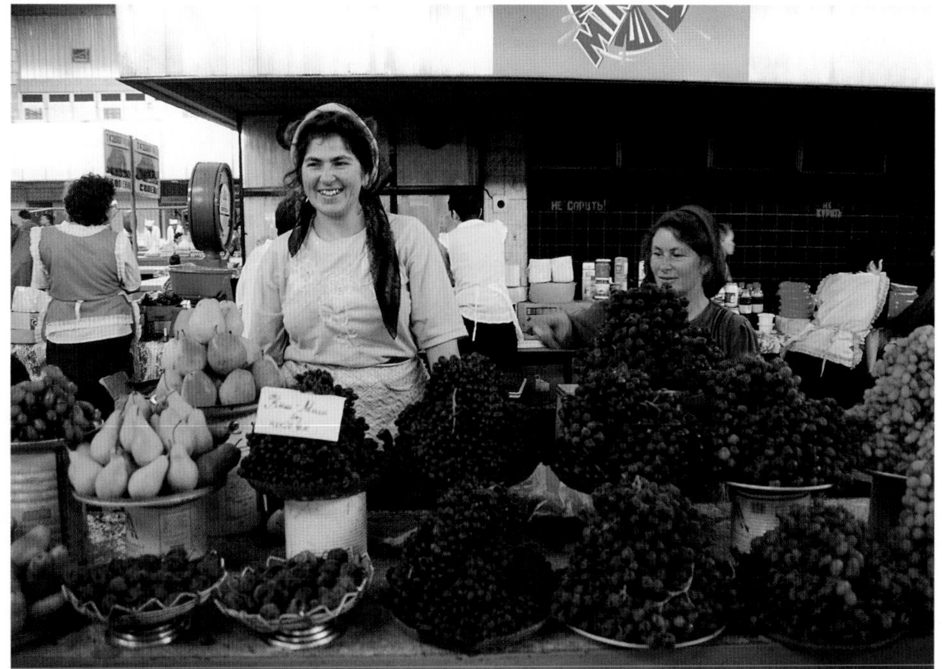

At the market in Shymkent; its southern location allows vineyards to be grown in the surrounding district, and the resulting grapes are renowned as the country's best (Gunter Kapelle)

Although there is unfortunately nothing of its old history left to see, Shymkent does have some places of interest. Worth visiting are the Museum of History and Anthropology, which includes an art gallery (23 Kazybek Bi Street), the Museum of Archaeology on Baytursinuly St, and—not recommended for animal lovers—the Karakul Museum on Lenin Square, which displays the history and processing of the legendary Karakul fur.

Practical Information

The area dialling code for Shymkent is +7252. Restaurants are all over the city—simply take your pick. You should definitely try the shashlyk roasted over saksaul wood, washed down with a cup of kumis. The bazaar on the northern side of the railway station is a typical Central Asian market.

If you decide to sample the local nightclubs, don't be surprised to see regular breaks in the dancing for pole-dancing strip shows by leggy female performers. This is a normal part of the evening's entertainment, and there is no distaste or embarrassment among the local women, who watch with as much interest as their male companions, everyone showing polite appreciation at the end of the show before resuming their own dancing once more.

TRANSPORTATION

The airport is about 20 kilometres to the north of the city, just off the road to Turkistan. There are daily flights to and from Almaty, and flights several times a week to Astana and Atyrau via Kyzylorda. The Air Astana office is at 2 Al-Farabi Avenue (tel: 549 861).

The huge railway station building is situated in the southwest of the city. There are daily trains to Almaty, Tashkent and Orenburg, several trains a week to Moscow and links to numerous other cities in the country. The bus station is situated to the northwest of the railway station on the corner of Ayteke Bi St and Zhostyk St. The easiest way to make travel arrangements is to visit Central Asia Tourism's office at 18/217 Ilayev St (tel: 211 436, e-mail cat-chimkent@alarnet.com).

ACCOMMODATION

Hotel Sapar, 17 Kunayev Boulevard, tel: 535 001, fax: 535 082, e-mail: saparhtl@mail.ru

A grand hotel in the middle of the centre, thoroughly renovated with all the features of a big city hotel. Rooms from US$87–140.

Makhambet Hotel, 68/1 Divayev St (corner of Ilayeva St), tel/fax: 535 113, e-mail: saparhtl@mail.ru

A business hotel with conference facilities. Rooms from US$120–175.

Hotel Dostyk, Adirbekov St (near Ozero bazaar), tel: 548 869, fax: 545 992, e-mail: info@hoteldostyk.kz, website: www.hoteldostyk.kz

A large but simple hotel in the city centre, near the market. Has a sauna, fitness centre and pool. Rooms US$35–60.

Kema Hotel, 93A Tauke Khan Avenue, tel: 540 736/536 568, fax: 540597

A mid-size hotel, newly renovated, situated near the market and central park and boasting a mud bath. Rooms from US$34–184.

Versailles, 114 Gagarin St, tel: 561 514

A small new hotel in the historic centre near an old park, with rooms from US$37–75.

Shymkent Hotel, 6 Republic Ave, tel: 567 195, fax: 567 194, website: www.hotelshymkent.com

A new hotel with its own nightclub and business centre. Rooms from US$37 up to luxurious US$450 suites.

SAYRAM

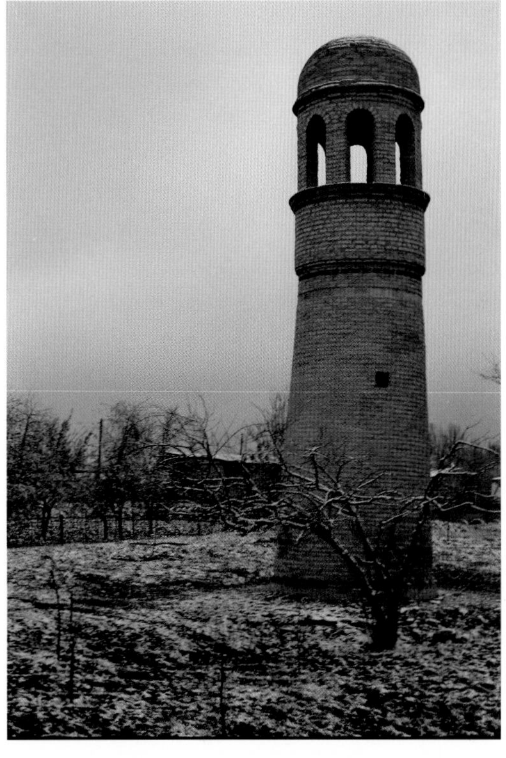

The city of Isfidzhab, mentioned for the first time in the 6th Century and later renamed **Sayram**, was once a green oasis full of gardens and farmlands and a centre of settled agriculture, manufacturing and trade. It was home to a large community of Nestorians, but in 766 AD Muslim forces swept in from the west, conquering and converting its citizens, and killing 10,000 Nestorians in the process. During the 11th Century, the scholar Mahmud of Kashgar reported on the city and was impressed by its white mansions. But following its sacking by Genghis Khan in the 13th Century, its significance declined, and, after two attacks by the Zhungars in the 17th and 18th centuries, it finally fell into decay.

A rectangular fortified area remains and has been preserved, stretching over some 500-550 metres, as well as some of the walls and the double earthworks that surrounded the city. A few important historical structures can still be visited today, thanks to partial restoration work. They include the mausoleums of **Ibrahim Ata** and **Abdel Aziz**, who was the colour-bearer of the Muslim forces who conquered the city, and whose three-domed tomb was built on the orders of Tamerlane. Sayram was the birthplace of the great prophet and Sufi teacher Khoja Ahmed Yasawi, and the tomb of his mother **Karashash** can be seen here. An architectural highlight is the 15-metre-high **Hisr Paygambar Minaret**, part of the 10th century Kyzyr mosque. There is also a **Museum of History**, which contains an old, richly illustrated Koran and stone support from the original Friday mosque. The Koran dates back 200 years, but the stone support is believed to be from that same original mosque, though it has not been carbon dated to support that theory.

Most of the historical sites lie at the edge of the town, which is 20 kilometres east of Shymkent, along the road to Lenger. Sayram has a high population density of Uzbeks, and there is relatively little Russian influence here—it has a very Central Asian feel to it, and

The architecturally simple but attractive Hisr Paygambar Minaret is over a thousand years old (Yevgeni Byelousov)

is strongly Islamic, with the Muslim call to prayers echoing out over the rooftops more noticeably than in larger cities like Shymkent. Sayram lies at the foot of **Mount Psemskiy Khrebet**, and can be used as a good base for tours in the surrounding area. The Aksu Canyon is only 30 minutes away, and three kilometres outside the town the **Martobe** group of monuments can be visited, which consists of barrows and the ruins of a 12th Century town.

Just 50 kilometres from Sayram is the idyllic campsite of Sayram Su in the **Ugamsk Canyon**. Surrounded by birch and juniper forests, and with mountain streams gushing through deeply cut rock, this is a beautiful location, and is a good starting point for walks in the delightful **Ugram Valley**, to a chain of mountain lakes and the foot of 4,454-metre-high **Mount Sayram**. Mountaineering equipment is required to climb to its summit, and those of its neighbours **Druzhba** (4,100 metres) and **Kyzyl Bash** ("Red Head", 4,200 metres). This region is still by and large virgin land, but the Shymkent administration plans to build two chairlifts—one each in the valleys of Sayram Su and Kaska Su. Developing the area into a winter sports resort is expected to be profitable.

KAZYGURT

It is said that **Mount Kazygurt** 1,775 metres high and standing alone not far from a village of the same name, was one of the landing places of Noah's Ark following the Great Flood—locals point to a hole in the ground on top of the mountain that has the shape of a boat's keel as evidence of this. Another "proof" of the legend is a large stone cross, more than 100 metres long, that lies flat on the southern slope of the mountain; it can only be seen from neighbouring mountains. The mountain is next to Km Stone 63 on the road from Shymkent to Tashkent.

THE GROUP OF ISMAIL ATA MONUMENTS AND THE VALLEY OF ROSES

Some 70 kilometres south of Shymkent is a beautiful village, again situated at the foot of a mountain. This is **Turbat**, the aul of the rose growers. In summer, this place is surrounded by blooming rose fields, grown to produce rose oil. A large town existed here from the 6th to 15th centuries, and today you can visit the **Ismail Ata protected monument** consisting of a number of mausoleums and the mosque of **Baba Ata**. While part of the walls date from ancient times, the main building has been completely rebuilt. The site is dedicated to the prophet Baba Ata, who is supposed to have worked here.

HEROES OF THE KAZAKH STEPPE

Less than an hour from Shymkent, near the town of Ordabasy, we stop for our customary lunchtime feast at a pleasant lodge located in a bend of the river. The opposite bank is cut deep to form river cliffs, but our bank is level and verdant, with trees and grassy areas where locals sit in the shade, talking excitedly as they sip bowls of kumis.

We discover that as luck would have it we have arrived on the day of this district's most important annual event: an international wrestling competition held every year for decades in honour of the town's most famous son, Kazhymukhan Munaitpas-ulu. Born in 1871, as a boy he grew uncommonly strong and brave, and even at the age of 13 could beat adult men in wrestling matches and tests of strength. Competing under the pseudonym "Yamagat Mukhanura", a Japanese name since the Kazakh nation was virtually unknown at that time, the adult Kazhymukhan Munaitpas-ulu proceeded to travel the world, beating all-comers and winning wrestling titles from Europe to Africa and America.

By 1916 he had been declared a great champion by his people, and in 1927 was awarded the title "Hero of the Kazakh steppe". His bravery and fame have inspired the Kazakhs of this district ever since, and it has become a centre for sporting achievement; there is a wrestling school boasting 70 students, but also schools of other Kazakh sporting disciplines, like boxing and the many skills associated with horse riding.

A courting couple pose on their horses before playing the traditional game of kyz kuu, *or "Catch the girl" (Jeremy Tredinnick)*

We are invited to the event, the 43rd year since its inaugural competition. We arrive at a large field to find the stands full of enthusiastic onlookers, men, women and children alike. Before the wrestling begins, we are treated to a magnificent display of horsemanship: first we watch a game of *kyz kuu*, "Catch the girl", where a young woman in gorgeous traditional clothing races on horseback away from a man, who chases after her on his own steed and, upon catching her tries to steal a kiss from her at full gallop. If he fails to catch the girl before she reaches a marked finishing point, she is entitled to chase him all the way back to the start, whipping him with her riding crop for his "clumsiness"—to the delight of the crowd.

Even greater riding skills are then demonstrated, with various riders taking up the challenge of *kumis alu*, "Pick up the coin", a traditional game and test of skill whereby a rider must, while riding at full speed, bend low over his mount's back to grab a coin off the ground. These days a handkerchief replaces the coin, but the courage and remarkable technique required prove a Kazakh rider's ability beyond doubt.

Finally comes a bout of wrestling... on horseback. Known as *auderyspak*, the rules are simple: the winner is the rider who can force his adversary down off his horse. The two compact, muscular competitors grapple, strain and tug at each other while their horses stand shoulder to shoulder, reacting to their masters' movements as they attempt to find the right leverage to force a win.

By now the crowd is whipped up to fever pitch, and as the lines of wrestlers—representing Uzbekistan, Kyrgyzstan, Russia and even Scandinavian countries, as well as national and local champions—approach the two match mats to salute the district's Akim, the stands are abuzz with speculation on

A display of horse wrestling pits two mounted contestants against each other; horse whips gripped between their teeth, they strain to unseat their opponent and win the match (Jeremy Tredinnick)

who looks strong, who is renowned for cunning and strategic nous, who has the best chance of winning his particular weight group...

The bouts are not long, but the intensity is fierce—especially between the blue-clad Kazakh wrestlers and the red-clad Uzbeks. Losers trudge off with thunder on their faces, winners with lightning smiles. We visitors have little understanding of the rules of Kazakh wrestling, which differs from the Greco-Roman style in subtle ways, and we can only guess at the importance of this event not only to the competing wrestlers and their teams, but to the entire town's inhabitants, honouring as it does the memory of their greatest son, a source of immeasurable pride that in this nation of tough, hardy men, they shine out as examples of Kazakh bravery, culture and tradition.

We must leave before the competition ends, but not, of course, before being invited into one of the yurts that surround the field, where yet another delectable feast of food is presented to us. Our host toasts us and thanks us for honouring them with a visit; we in turn make toasts of thanks for such unexpected and overwhelming hospitality. And then we are off, bellies full of hearty fare, camera's full of wonderful pictures, heads full of exciting memories... and more to come.

Having failed to catch and kiss the girl, this young horseman must now feel the sting of the girl's whip all the way back to the starting line (Jeremy Tredinnick)

THE PLAINS OF THE SYR DARYA

The Syr Darya flows across Kazakhstan territory for about two-thirds of its 3,000-kilometre course. Battles have been fought, advanced cultures developed and agriculture, manufacturing and trade practised along its banks. In ancient times the river was named the Kang, and during the early Middle Ages the Seykhun; many generations of farmers built and maintained sophisticated small-scale irrigation systems using the great river's life-giving water. Reservoirs and canals were constructed with such ingenuity that a large part of the water taken from the river flowed back into it. Evaporation was kept to a minimum, and the entire village community carried out construction and maintenance of the water works, which were crucial for survival.

The ruins of Otrar, during its heyday one of the Silk Road's great centres of commerce (Ernst Ischovits)

Soviet technocrats put an end to this era; the river was bled to death senselessly and ineffectively for the monocultures of cotton and rice. But despite the fact that the river's power is only a shadow of what it used to be, it still plays an important role in the region, with hundreds of towns and auls on its banks still surviving because of it. Initiatives to undertake cross-border water management are under way in Kazakhstan, Kyrgyzstan, Tajikistan and Uzbekistan. With luck—and commendable foresight—these initiatives, once put into practice, will have an impact on the region's future that should not be

A bird's-eye view of present-day Otrar, taken from a microlight aircraft passing to the north of the ruins (Renato Sala and Jean-Marc Deom)

underestimated. Nothing less than peace in the region is at stake here; water is life in the semi-desert and steppe areas of southern Kazakhstan, and where rivers' courses cross international borders, how they are exploited has direct consequences on the environment and human habitation further downstream.

Otrar

The ancient city of **Otrar** has had many names: Tarban, Turaband, Turar and Farab as well as Otrar. It was the birthplace of the great scholar known as Al-Farabi (meaning "from Farab"), whose face smiles out from all original Kazakhstani banknotes (now disappearing as they are withdrawn from circulation).

Otrar was among the most celebrated cities along the Silk Road during its golden era. It is thought that it was first founded as early as the 2nd Century BC, at the time of the Kang-yu confederation of states, located in the middle reaches of the Syr Darya. Also known as Kangu Tarban or Kangly in subsequent centuries, this tribe was able to retain control for a relatively long time by mingling with various Turkmen communities. Its influence only waned with the coming of Islam into Central Asia. It was during this period, from the 10th to 12th centuries, that the city, then known as Otrar, reached its zenith as a centre of trade and manufacturing. It struck its own coins, and the city's library attracted scholars from all parts of Central Asia.

In 1219, Otrar was the first city to fall victim to a horrifying campaign of revenge and conquest by **Genghis Khan** against the Central Asian oases. The governor of Otrar, **Gayir Khan**, provoked this historical tragedy. Genghis Khan, strengthened by his successful campaign against China and his entry into Semirechye, where he had met no resistance, undertook the conquest of Central Asia by diplomatic means. He equipped a large trade caravan and in the summer of 1218, the Mongol lord sent 500 pack camels loaded with precious merchandise and accompanied by 450 tradesmen to his neighbour of Khorezm.

The Mongols carried out their task in the markets of Bukhara, Samarkand and Urgench. They sold their loads, and gathered information on the region in the process. Loaded with barter goods, the camels, traders and drivers took the long road back home. They made it only to the border city of Otrar. There, accused of spying by Gayir Khan, all those who accompanied the caravan were executed—with the exception of one single driver who managed to escape and informed Genghis Khan about what had happened.

The Mongol lord immediately demanded the head of the governor from his neighbour, the Shah of Khorezm. The demand was not met, and the two envoys were reportedly put to death. In the event, this deliberate outrage was convenient for Genghis Khan, who put himself at the head of a huge punitive expedition consisting of 150,000 warriors, and by September 1219 stood at the gates of Otrar. The city was prepared for a long siege. Genghis Khan left behind 35,000 soldiers, commanded by his sons Chagatay and Ogedei, sent his son Zhu-Chi with a force to the lower reaches of the Syr Darya, and led the main army himself to Bukhara. The Pearl of the Orient fell even before Otrar did, and by March 1220 the Mongols had conquered all of **Mawernannahr**, the land between the Amu Darya and the Syr Darya.

Otrar held out for five full months, until the defence forces sent by the Shah and commanded by Karadzha Haddzhib surrendered. The hapless governor was able to hold the citadel with his followers for another month before he was forced to surrender as well. The town fell in February 1220, when the Mongol hordes burst into its alleys, murdering, ransacking and setting property on fire. The city, once so rich and beautiful, was left in utter ruin. However, Otrar did not take long to flourish once more—its conquerors soon recognized its strategic location and used it to their advantage.

Today, at the city's excavation site numerous walls remain (though in poor condition), showing the layout of large parts of the city. They clearly demonstrate that Otrar was built according to a coherent construction plan, based both on social order and hygienic principles. It must be noted that this important site, though protected by the state, is still terribly at risk; not only do the goats that roam freely around the site contribute to its continuing degradation, but tourists (mostly unwittingly) do their bit to increase the ruination as well.

The fences leave much to be desired, and many tour guides cannot prevent their groups from venturing right through the unsecured grounds. Since 2001, UNESCO, together with a Japanese-funded group, has been engaged in improving the situation. The intention to add the site to UNESCO's World Cultural Heritage list should provide the necessary means to protect it, but until then, please show restraint and proper respect for this archaeological treasure. To see vases and wall carpets found during the initial excavation of Otrar, you will have to visit the Presidential Cultural Centre in Astana.

Otrar is situated off the main roads of the modern world. In its halcyon days, it was ideally located in an oasis at the foot of a chain of hills, close to the point where the Arys flows into the Syr Darya. To get there, follow the road from Shymkent to Turkistan, turn left beyond Tortkol, cross the Tashkent-Orenburg-Moscow railway line and drive to the village of Shaulder. Here, there is a museum dedicated to the history and archaeological works of Otrar. The actual excavation site is located some 20 kilometres to the north of Shaulder, beyond Kogam aul and 1.5 kilometres off the road.

The road from Otrar to Shymkent through Arys and **Badam** provides many minor spots worth stopping to explore. As in so many parts of South Kazakhstan, every aul has something special to offer: a mosque, group of barrows or the ruins of old settlements. The road leads along the Arys River and crosses it three times. In the town of Arys the track bends left towards the east. Some 20 kilometres further down, not far from where the Badam flows into the Arys near the aul of Karaspan, are the walls of a city that stood here in the 9th and 10th centuries, as well as many barrows from various periods. The eldest among them dates from the 4th Century BC, the latest from the 10th Century AD.

Six kilometres beyond Badam is the hamlet of **Ordabasy**, part of the protected area of historic and cultural monuments of the same name. It was here, early in the 18th Century, that the Kazakhs united in their struggle against the invading Zhungars.

The Mausoleum and Mosque of Aristan Bab

The tomb-mosque of **Aristan Bab** is near Otrar, though much easier to get to, as it is close to the main road. Legend tells that this highly honoured Islamic mystic was the "discoverer" and teacher of **Khoja Ahmed Yasawi**. Aristan Bab, also known as Arslan Bab or Salmani Fars, was a follower of Mohammed's, and attended him on his deathbed, when the Prophet asked who would take his prayer chain (*amanat*) and search for his successor. Aristan Bab asked for and was granted the assignment, and went out into the world. After hundreds of years of wandering, he came to a bridge near the town of Sayram, where an 11-year-old boy, Ahmed, stopped him and demanded the prayer chain, saying: "Aksakal, give me my amanat!" Aristan Bab understood that his quest had ended, handed the amanat to the boy, and became his teacher, journeying with him to Yassi, where the boy eventually became known

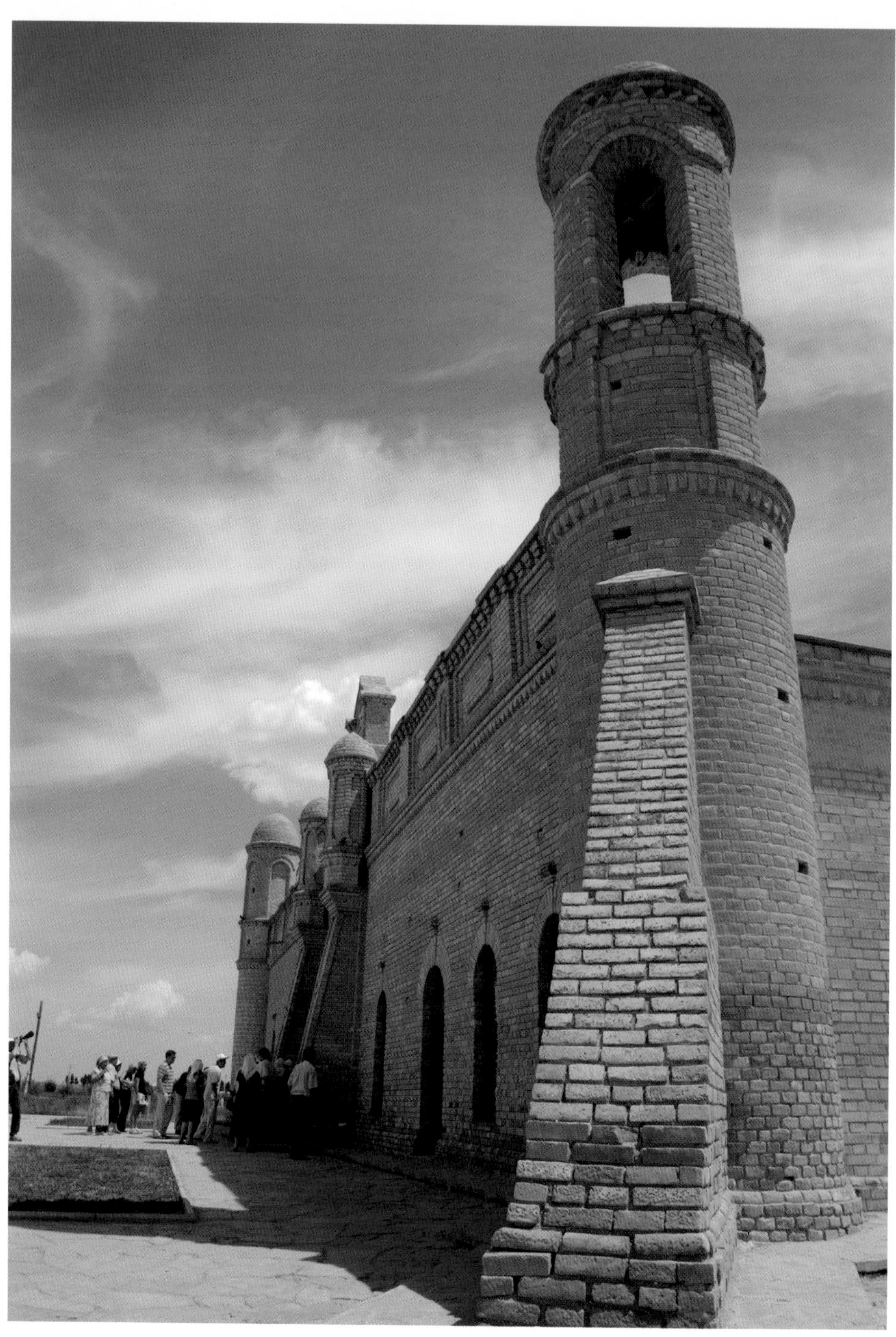

The entrance to the Mausoleum and Mosque of Aristan Bab, said to have been a disciple of Mohammed and discoverer of Khoja Ahmed Yasawi (Jeremy Tredinnick)

as Khoja Ahmed Yasawi. (Those with knowledge of Islam will observe that 500 years had passed between the death of the Prophet and the moment the amanat was handed over. But then, God moves in mysterious ways...)

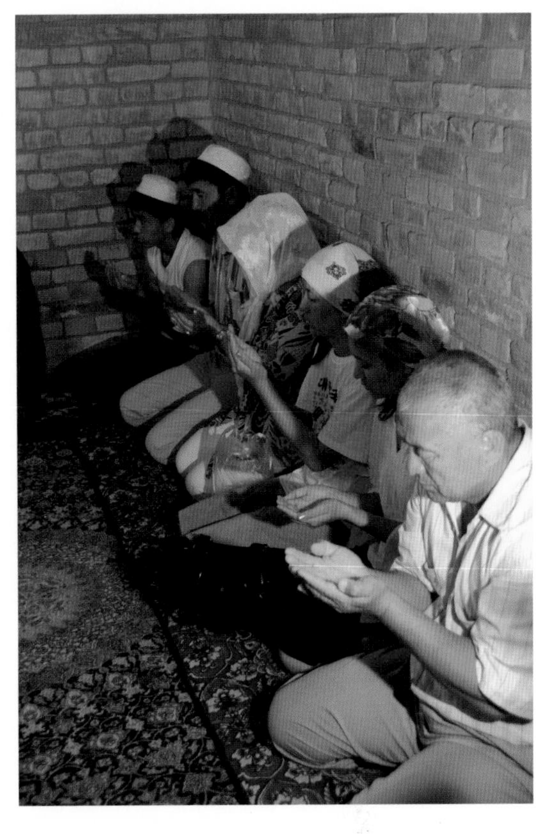

Aristan Bab died early in the 13th Century, after having taught Ahmed the basic truths of the Koran. In his honour, a mausoleum was built on top of his grave. It was destroyed several times—the building that can be seen today was completed in 1910. It has a small but attractively proportioned façade; the carpet-draped tomb in a small room to the left of the entrance is constantly full of believers praying to the great man—there can often be a long queue outside. On the right is a small but peaceful room that serves as a mosque; it is supported by ancient carved wooden pillars, and in an ante room you can admire a hand-written Koran with extraordinarily beautiful Islamic calligraphy.

Surrounding the mausoleum are hundreds of tombs, from simple graves to ornate palace-like structures, the final resting places of devout Muslims who wished to be close to Aristan Bab. A respectful stroll around these grounds can be an atmospheric and satisfying experience.

A huge and ambitious construction project is now going ahead here. Named the **Otrar Resort**, it will be a massive lifestyle complex aimed at boosting tourism. Hotels, restaurants and other facilities will be set around huge fountains in a verdant garden park, irrigated of course by channels from the Syr Darya River. The aim is to re-create something of the splendour of the Otrar of olden days, when it was a thriving and beautiful centre on the Silk Road. The project is scheduled for completion in 2010.

Pilgrims pray to Aristan Bab's tomb within the mausoleum (Jeremy Tredinnick)

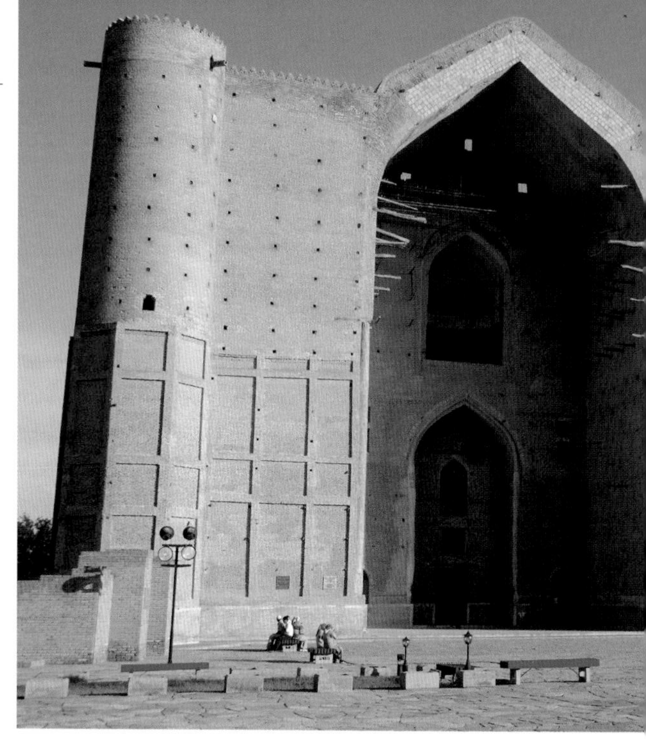

TURKISTAN

Turkistan (also sometimes spelt Turkestan) is an ancient settlement, originally known by the name of **Yassi**, the old town located on the eastern edge of present-day Turkistan. Its origin dates back to the 7th Century, when it stood in the shadow of the much larger and more significant city of Shavgar close by. It was only in the 14th Century that Yassi became the centre of the region.

From the 16th to 19th centuries the city was under the control of the Kazakh Khans. The name Turkistan, which was first mentioned in historical records in the 16th Century, has particular significance, expressing the claim that it represented the lands of the Turkic nations. This tradition remains alive to this day, and is the reason why Turkistan was chosen as the seat of the **Kazakh-Turkish University**.

The modern city of Turkistan is a typical town of the Central Asian steppe. With one monumental exception, it seems to have little to offer the tourist: a stroll around reveals the occasional traditional house with intricately carved wood gables, and the bustling and labyrinthine **Night Market** is definitely worth a visit, more to people-watch than to purchase—the mélange of ethnic nationalities going about their business is fascinating. Most shopping is done in the evening, when temperatures are more bearable, and the market serves as a social centre as well as shopping centre.

Top: The enormous southeastern portal of the Mausoleum of Khoja Ahmed Yasawi in Turkistan
Above: Early morning pilgrims rest outside the mausoleum's main door (Jeremy Tredinnick x2)

THE MAUSOLEUM OF KHOJA AHMED YASAWI

Turkistan's fame is inextricably linked to the **Mausoleum of Khoja Ahmed Yasawi**, an important pilgrimage site in the Islamic world (some claim that this mausoleum is the second most holy place in Islam after Mecca, and three pilgrimages to it equal a single pilgrimage to Mecca). The building, constructed on the orders of **Tamerlane** between 1389 and 1405 in honour of the prophet **Khoja Ahmed Yasawi** (also Hoddzha Ahmed Yassaoui), is one of the finest and most important works of architecture from the **Timurid** era. We owe this wonderful building to the generosity that came over Tamerlane after his victory over the Golden Horde and the destruction of their capital—and perhaps some noble feeling that accompanied thoughts of his imminent marriage.

Khoja Ahmed Yasawi was an Islamic prophet, poet and mystic, founder of the Sufi Tariqah order and considered by some the rightful heir of Mohammed. He was born in **Sayram** in 1094, but at the age of 11 he received the legacy of the Prophet Mohammed from the hands of Aristan Bab and followed him to learn the true teachings of the Koran. At the age of 17 he was already composing verse in Arabic, Turkic and Farsi. Ahmed refined his knowledge of Islam, oriental literature and philosophy during his studies in **Bukhara**, and following the death there of his tutor, Sheikh Youssouf al-Hamadani, he took the latter's place. After some time he returned to Yassi, surrounded himself with students and taught them the Koran in the Sufi manner of explanation and expansion that he had developed. He obtained his nickname Yassaoui (Yasawi)—from Yassi—after working for many years in the city. Ahmed's collected poetry, *Divan-i Hikmat*, (Collected Wisdom) was translated into many languages. At the age of 63, the learned teacher withdrew from secular life as a tribute to the Prophet Mohammed, who had died when 63 years old. He spent the following years meditating in an underground chamber on a hill not far from the present-day mausoleum; in time, his family joined him and then dozens of his students and followers.

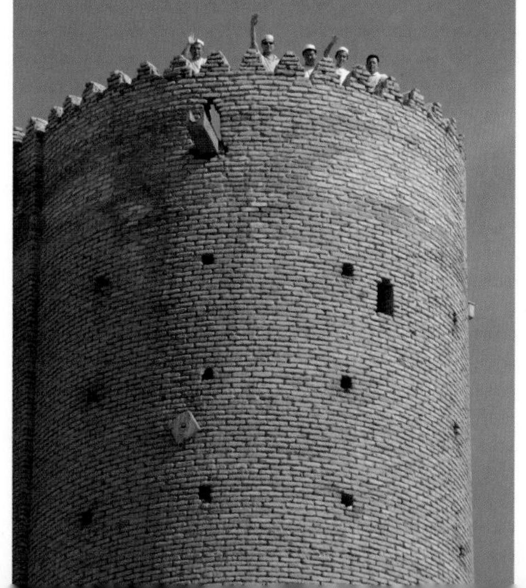

Right: Atop one of the mausoleum's minaret-towers (Jeremy Tredinnick)

Khoja Ahmed Yasawi made the commandments of Allah and teachings of Mohammed more understandable for the common people, by teaching, writing and praying in the Turkic language, Tagachay, rather than in the literary Farsi speech. His poems were learned by heart by commoners and spread far across the borders of the Kypchak Steppe. Yasawi taught unification with God through meditation, patience and asceticism—which tends to explain why he was so popular among the poor. He turned many—who had to abstain from earthly delights—into true believers. Khoja Ahmed Yasawi linked Islamic creed with elements from shamanism as well as from Greco-neoplatonic and Indian mysticism. These were spiritual missing links for a still very rationalistic Islam at the time. In contrast to many Sufis, who paid with their lives for their beliefs, Ahmed was not only honoured but also declared a saint while he was still alive. This might be due to his high spiritual status, but also reflects that religious fanaticism had much less influence in Central Asia than in the land of Islam's origin.

Khoja Ahmed Yasawi died in 1166 and was buried in great honour and splendour. A *mazar*, a domed tomb, was built on his grave. Armies of pilgrims turned up, many of them donating treasures. This led to Tokhtamysh, a Khan of the Golden Horde, attacking the city more than once in order to plunder the burial site. The mausoleum that we admire today was built on the site of the old mazar, the unbaked tiles of which were showing signs of decay at the time of Tamerlane's arrival.

It is thought that Lord Tamerlane tarried at Yassi on his way to his bride in 1389, to say a prayer. The poor condition of the mazar depressed him, and he ordered the construction of a grand mausoleum, reportedly drawing up his own detailed design for the building. The strictly proportional measures, the space plan, even the composition of the material for the sacred bronze bowl—all these are claimed to be Tamerlane's work. In the process the ruler provided an endowment in the form of land and irrigation canals (*aryks*), determined the sources of income for the mausoleum, and chose the people who were allowed to serve there.

Construction went steadily ahead, supervised by Persian master builders. The inscriptions left by mosaic artists Haddzhi Hassan and Shems abdul Wahhab from Shiraz indicate the year 1397 as the time the mosaics were put in place. Unfortunately, the construction's benefactor died in the winter of 1405, and the mausoleum was left unfinished. Even today you can see this on the main entrance, the only place not decorated with majolica mosaics. In fact this façade, with its double *ivan* (brick minarets), was only erected at the end of the 16th Century under Khan Abdullah II, though the plans made by Tamerlane were strictly followed. The façade's side walls were never completed.

The mausoleum dominates Turkistan, and can be spotted from a great distance; it is 44 metres high, and its largest dome has an outside diameter of 22 metres. It is the largest (preserved) unsupported brick dome in all of Central Asia—the mathematical rules for creating such huge unsupported vaults were only developed in the 10th and 11th centuries by scholars such as **Al-Farabi**. In 2003 the Mausoleum of Khoja Ahmed Yasawi became the first location in Kazakhstan to be listed as a **UNESCO World Cultural Heritage** site, recognizing its significance in the advancement of Islamic architecture—it was used as a template for many of **Samarkand** and **Bukhara's** future architectural masterpieces.

The mausoleum is a thing of beauty, and especially attractive in that it presents hugely differing aspects when observed from different angles: the enormous portal (*peshtak*) that looks to the southeast is massively impressive, and particularly enjoyable in the golden light of sunrise; the shining majolica domes and the lavish, intricate form of the mosaic borders on the side walls are exquisite, with the northwest façade radiating gorgeous colours as the sun dips towards the horizon. Like other great Islamic works of architectural art such as the Taj Mahal, from a distance it intrigues, from the outer complex walls it bewitches and beckons, and from close up it dazzles the eye with the beauty and scale of its detail.

Inside, in the centre of the great dome hall (*kazandyk*), stands a huge metal basin known as **the Holy Kazakh**. It is no ordinary cast bowl; it has a diameter of 2.45 metres and weighs two tonnes, but most interestingly—and significantly—it is made of an alloy consisting of seven metals: iron, zinc, lead, tin, copper, silver and gold. Water placed in the basin is believed to become imbued with trace metals that are highly beneficial to your health; the basin's capacity of 600 litres was necessary in order to give every worshipper a sip of the slightly sweet water after Friday prayers. For a long time, this sacred object was displayed in St Petersburg's Hermitage Museum, but it was finally returned to Kazakhstan and is once again proudly displayed in its historical home.

More historic treasures are hidden in the 35 rooms and chambers surrounding the kazandyk. Apart from the beautifully decorated southwestern block of the mosque and its praying niche (*mihrab*) with a view in the direction of Mecca, visitors can see the splendid sarcophagi of the Kazakh Khans Yesim, Ablai and Abulkhair as well as that of Tamerlane's great aunt Rabiga Sultan Begim. Finally, there is the main object of worship: the sarcophagus of Ahmed Yasawi in the main vault (*gurkhana*). Only Muslims can enter the gurkhana either from the dome hall or through the magnificent northwestern door. A double dome covers it, the larger one smooth and beautiful, the smaller using a multi-ribbed design, an extremely rare type of construction in Central Asia that can only be seen elsewhere in the **Bibi Khanum mosque** and the **tomb of Gur Emir** in Samarkand. The entry doors of the kazandyk and gurkhana, decorated with wonderful woodcarving by the master Safar, are also worth paying attention to.

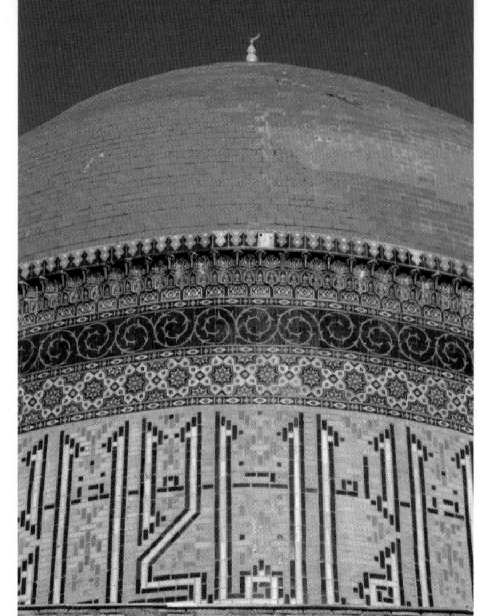

Exiting the main building on the unfinished peshtak side, it's impossible not to turn and look once again; with its two minarets it reminds one of a fortress rather than a sacred building. This is no accident; under the rule of the Khan of Kokand in the 19th Century, the entire southeastern wall between the minarets was equipped with shooting holes, and the entire building complex protected by a wall constructed of unbaked tiles, in order for the building to serve as a stronghold against Kazakhs and Russians alike.

Miraculously, the mausoleum has withstood the ravages of time, including a few earthquakes, 11 Russian artillery shell holes and even damp in the wooden rafters. Experts in architecture are of the opinion that this is due to the ingeniously simple construction of the building, which is divided into eight independent construction units. This division allowed not only structural stability, but also the possibility of harbouring different functional units within one building: kazandyk, resting-places, a mosque, a library and a *halimkhana* (dining room for pilgrims).

The buildings in the immediate vicinity of the mausoleum have mainly sacred functions. These include the Friday Mosque on the hill of Kul Tobe, a hundred metres south of the mausoleum, a domed bathhouse for ritual cleansing, a *hilwet*, or place for fasting prayers during Ramadan, an underground crypt, the mausoleum of Yesim Khan, and the small but exquisite **Rabiga Sultan Begim mausoleum** directly opposite the main southeastern peshtak. Many of these buildings, including the pentangular *shahristan* dating from the 13th-14th centuries, have only recently been restored.

As early as 1884, the Tsar's government set up a fund of 150,000 gold roubles to restore the mausoleum. This was a huge sum of money, but most of it, unfortunately, disappeared in other directions. Some improvised repairs were carried out with the remaining funds, including whitewashing over all inscriptions, but sadly many majolica tiles disappeared without trace. In 1910, the roof and parts of the walls were restored. Various minor and major repairs were then carried out during the Soviet period; unfortunately, much of historical note that had slowly built up for centuries around the main buildings was cleared and destroyed during this restoration work. Most of the real historic atmosphere that must have encapsulated the mausoleum was lost, and as a result the mausoleum stood alone in a void. During the 1990s, however, skilled Turkish workers restored the complex for a relatively small cost of US$20 million.

Today, the mausoleum is separated from the modern city by a high outer wall, along whose ramparts you can walk. There is a museum, where one can learn something about Yasawi's students and Sufism, and a large rose garden separates the holy shrine from an ensemble of small shops, where mainly devotional objects and souvenirs are for sale; most of these, inevitably, fall firmly in the category of kitsch. Northeast of the outer wall is a simple but beautifully carved statue of **Al-Farabi**, in front of a number of small buildings where traditional craftsmen and women make and ply their wares. Beautiful felt rugs, dombras and ceramics can be bought here.

The mausoleum of Khoja Ahmed Yasawi receives many thousands of tourists every year, but many more pilgrims, both from Kazakhstan and far beyond its borders. Still, a visit here feels far more peaceful and authentic than many stops on today's cultural tour circuit; you will find no beggars or T-shirt sales touts dogging your footsteps as you approach the building along one of its stone-paved paths.

Above: The interior of the Friday Mosque on Kul Tobe. Top left: Exquisite tiling on the Rabiga Sultan Begim mausoleum, which stands in front of the Yasawi mausoleum's southeastern entrance (Jeremy Tredinnick x2)

PRACTICAL INFORMATION

Turkistan's area dialling code is +72533. The town's railway station is on the main rail line between Shymkent and Kyzylorda; there is more than one train every day from Almaty and Shymkent, as well as regular trains from the direction of Moscow.

It is possible to visit Turkistan on a day trip from Shymkent, but this really does not leave enough time to explore the mausoleum properly. A much better option is to stay in one of the town's comfortable hotels, all located within easy walking distance of the shrine.

ACCOMMODATION

Hotel Turkestan, S. Kozhanov St (facing onto Yesim Khan Square), tel: 42197, fax: 41426, e-mail: too_turkestan@mail.ru or hotel_turkestan@ok.kz

New hotel in Central Asian style, five minutes' walk to mausoleum, 23 large single and double rooms, sauna, billiards, fitness room, luxury suite with its own sauna and pool. Rooms from US$40-104.

Hotel Yassy, Tauke Khan Avenue (immediately to the north of the mausoleum), tel: 40183, fax: 40185, e-mail: hotel_yessy@yahoo.com

Modernised hotel in Soviet building style, 53 rooms with 73 beds. Rooms from US$25 including breakfast.

Hotel Edem, 6 Kozhanov St, tel: 31378, fax: 31697, e-mail: edem_kz@mail.ru

Small, new hotel, noisy and cheerful, 10 minutes on foot from the mausoleum. Rooms from US$13.

SAURAN

Historians from the 9th Century reported that the city of **Sauran** had seven protective walls, a mosque and a marketplace. The discovery of underground water canals bears witness to the technological skill and craftsmanship of its inhabitants. The Mongols could not take Sauran by force of arms for many months, and only stormed the walls after they had starved the population.

Because of its strategic location not far from the Syr Darya and its significance as a trade centre on a crossroads along the Silk Road, Sauran rebounded from its sacking in the 13th Century, to become the capital of the **White Horde**. Tamerlane turned the city into a military stronghold—and again Sauran stood firm. Even the much-feared Zhungars failed to take control of the fortress.

At some stage during the 18th Century, the city fell into oblivion—in the long run, the sea route to the Indies had a more devastating impact on the Silk Road than all the hostile invasions put together. Today, the ravages of time gnaw into the remains of the circular wall that, with a diameter of just over one kilometre, sticks up out of the steppe. It is only thanks to the dry climate that the fortress, built of limestone bricks, has not disappeared altogether. Though a sign indicates that this site is protected by the state, the lack of proper road signs and the bumpy road towards its location speak a different language.

The fortress of Sauran, 45 kilometres to the northwest of Turkistan along the road to Kyzylorda, is not easy to find. Twice, signs with the word Sauran on them send the ignorant off in the wrong direction—it seems there are two villages in the area that bear the name Sauran as well. The actual site of the ancient city ruins is situated beyond those villages, some 1.5 kilometres off the road to the left (if coming from Turkistan). You must follow a dirt road that starts opposite a big copper image of an eagle. After one kilometre, you cross the Shymkent-Kyzylorda railtrack, from where the remains of renowned Sauran can already be seen.

The main road to Kyzylorda runs parallel to the railroad. Only this double line of steel bars, and the Syr Darya snaking across the plains, separate the road from the immense desert of **Kyzylkum** (Red Sands), which disappears into the south, at some stage crossing into Uzbekistan. Before you arrive in Kyzylorda you will pass vast areas of reed. Here, the extremely rare reed cat is reported to survive. The road crosses several canals that were constructed for the irrigation of rice fields. Enormous quantities of water are drawn from the Syr Darya, much of which soaks away unused since most of the canals have no concrete bottom.

KYZYLORDA

The city of **Kyzylorda** on the Syr Darya has a glorious past and, thanks to the recent discovery of the nearby Kumkol oil fields, a future as well. The present, however, is a sort of time limbo between the two, and does not necessarily invite the traveller to stay for long. Like all the newly emerging oil towns in Kazakhstan, Kyzylorda catches your attention by its extreme contradictions. On one side, there is poverty, decay, dirt and resignation; on the other, the swanky shops and homes of the oil-industry beneficiaries are impossible to miss. How should you answer the city's residents when they ask whether you like their beautiful town?

Nevertheless, tourism does exist here—the treasures of the region's history fit well with modern Kazakhstan's conscious attempt to embrace its heritage and traditions. History tells us that this was the strategic point where the caravan routes from Tashkent, Bukhara and Khiva came together, and then split to journey to western Siberia and via Torgay to Troitsk and Orenburg. There was once a large caravanserai here, on the banks of the then still powerful Syr Darya River.

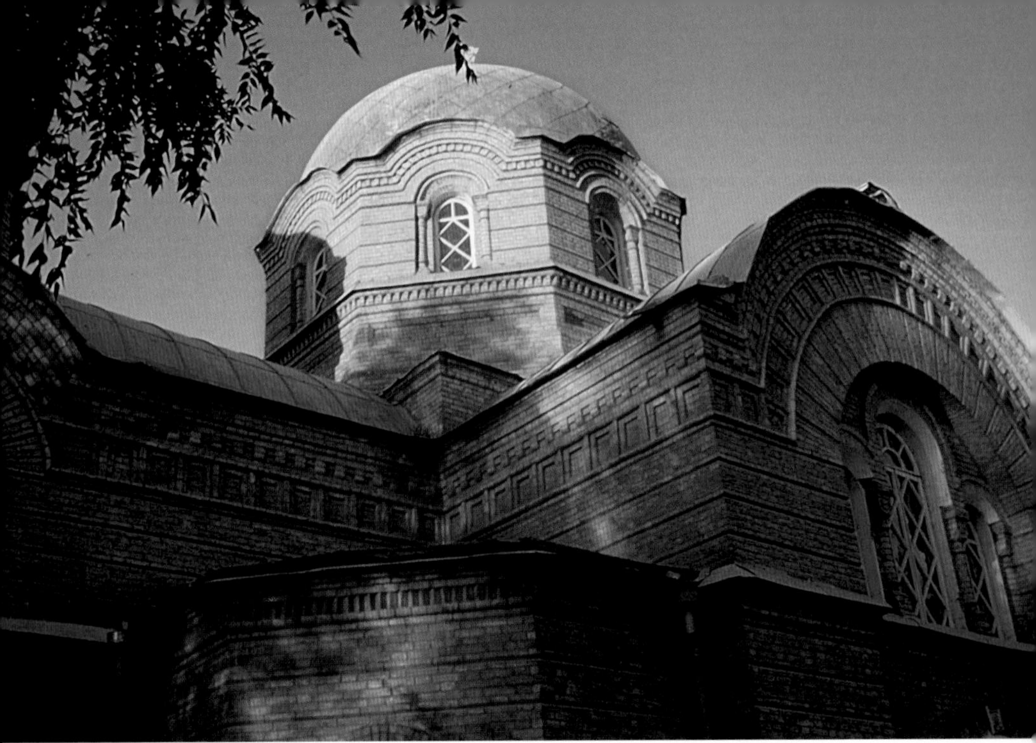

Kyzylorda's Russian Orthodox Church was built during its era as Imperial Russia's capital in the Central Asian steppe (Dagmar Schreiber)

In 1817, the fortress of **Akmechet** (White Mosque) was founded on the left bank of the Syr Darya. A year later it was decided to move the fortress to the right bank of the river, since it was more secure against the extensive floods of early summer. The Russian governorate was established in 1867, shortly after Russia's wide-ranging conquest of the Central Asian steppe, and Akmechet was renamed **Perovsk**, in honour of the Russian general Perov, who had excelled in his campaign against the Khans of Kokand and Khiva during the territory's conquest. Reminders of those days are the **Russian Orthodox church** not far from the bazaar, built in 1878 and now beautifully restored, surrounded by high trees and flowerbeds, and the numerous one-storey Russian houses in the settlement behind it. Following the October Revolution, the city was renamed Kyzylorda (Red Horde), and was the capital of Kazakhstan from 1925 until 1929.

The town has little left of its glamour as a capital these days. Not only do social contrasts show their mark, but also from an architectural point of view it has become a mix of contradictions. Kyzylorda today is a chaotic conglomeration of buildings from all periods, most of which are in a deplorable state. Next to the new mosque is the building of PetroKazakhstan, where the flags of Canada and Kazakhstan used to wave next to each other until that of China replaced the former. To the left of the Soviet classical-style theatre a block building harbours the local university, while to the right there is a so-called trade centre, which has been revamped with brown glass façades.

The **culture and leisure park** is a sad collection of fairground scrap, fallen heaps of concrete and borders overgrown with weeds. A giant bazaar throbs with life a kilometre on in the direction of the river. An Asian flair emerges here, particularly in the evenings, when women and families meet to go shopping, and thousands of feet throw up clouds of blinding dust while ear-deafening music resounds from numerous stalls. Another park has been wrested from the barren earth between the bazaar and the river, but the most pleasant place in Kyzylorda is the Syr Darya's riverbank promenade. Here, a change is in the air; bulldozers have removed shabby box-garages, and a couple of poor neighbourhoods have disappeared

Above: Kyzylorda's main train station (Ernst Ischovits)

Below: The passage of time has left its mark on the walls of Sauran, a 9th Century commercial centre along the Syr Darya trade route whose seven protective walls made it a useful military stronghold (Dagmar Schreiber)

to make room for a second bridge across the river. A stroll along the promenade, with the muddy brown river flowing silently below, is a popular activity when the weather permits. Of course the evocative monument to Korkhyt Ata, the philosopher and musician of the 9th Century, has stayed in its place.

As Kyzylorda rakes in the oil dollars it will, like so many other "nouveau-riche" towns, spend heavily on urban improvements and expansion, and it seems to have used the river as a starting point. On the eastern outskirts of town, not far from the river, new or rebuilt sport facilities help to raise living standards, and hopefully Kyzylorda will eventually return to something of its former glory.

Practical Information

The city dialling code for Kyzylorda is +7242. If you need to buy anything, virtually anything you might require can be found at the bazaar. There is also an interesting fish market not far from the railway station. The **Ethnographic Museum** is located at 20 Auezov St (tel: 276 152/274), open daily 9am–7pm.

Transportation

The Khorkhyt Ata airport is small but new. It is situated on the opposite bank 20 kilometres from town and reachable only by taxi. There are daily flights to Almaty and frequent flights to Astana and Aktau. The office of Air Astana is on 20 Zheltoksan Avenue, Office 16, tel: 270 392.

The railway station is central located, a small but nicely renovated building where you buy tickets. At least one train leaves every day for Turkistan and Shymkent, and also in the other direction, heading for Russia via Aktobe and Aralsk.

Accommodation

Hotel Samal, 53 Abai Avenue, tel: 235 617/619/622, fax: 235 623, e-mail: hotelsamal@asdc.kz

The best hotel in town, 15 rooms, 10 minutes away from the town centre. Rooms from US$96.

Zerena Hotel, 30 Begim Ata Street, tel: 275 628

New, clean and friendly, with a good fish restaurant just around the corner. Rooms from US$50.

Kyzylorda Hotel, 19 Tokmaganbetova Street, tel: 261 651/121

A large budget hotel in the town centre, with rooms from US$15.

Hotel Kair, 29 Aitbayeva St/Baytursinov St, tel: 276 797

THE KHORKHYT-ATA MONUMENT

In 1980, a huge complex of monuments was built beside the Syr Darya, 18 kilometres beyond Zhosaly. The **Khorkhyt-Ata Monument** is dedicated to Khorkhyt (or Korkut), the legendary musician, philosopher, narrator and inventor of the ***kobyz***, who is known to many Turkic nations. The architect Bek Ibrayev joined forces with physiologist S. Isatayev to construct an ingenious musical image in concrete. Comprised of four identical, eight-metre-high "half-tubes" made of reinforced concrete, each section of the monument points in a different direction, towards the four winds. The shape of this modern stele recalls the kobyz—but in more than simple form. The wind, which never fails to blow here, is caught by the concrete sections and produces a moaning tune, which can often be heard from far away. This is facilitated by the organ-like interiors of the four sections, which consist of a sound box made of 40 metal tubes. The stele is decorated with ornaments that symbolize the cosmic images of the ancient nomadic peoples.

A mausoleum is said to have been located on this spot until 1950, about which legend tells the following story: in the 9th Century, a woman in an aul along the Syr Darya bore a child, the sight of whom made all the women who had gathered in the yurt shriek and run away, since the newborn creature looked like a shapeless sack. But the mother opened the amniotic sack and a tiny baby appeared and immediately started to cry. On hearing this, the women returned to the tent and were reassured. They recommended that the mother name the child Khorkhyt, meaning terrifying. The boy grew up a clever and perceptive child, with a remarkable level of sensitivity. This characteristic remained with him, and when Khorkhyt was 20 years old, he had a bad dream, in which white-robed figures told him that he had only 20 more years to live.

Khorkhyt decided to search for immortality. He roamed the world on his female camel, Zhelmaya, and one day he met some people who were digging a grave. They answered his question by telling him that this grave was meant for Khorkhyt. He understood that he would not find immortality here. Restlessly he travelled to all points of the compass, but everywhere he met signs of death. Finally, he returned home. He sacrificed his camel Zhelmaya, built a musical instrument and covered its sound box with his beloved camel's skin. Thus was born the kobyz. Khorkhyt drew sad melodies from the instrument made from the hide of his beloved animal. This "sound from the afterlife" turned into a magic force. Death appeared but could not take Khorkhyt, who sat on the banks of the Syr Darya and played the song of life on his kobyz day and night. But eventually he fell asleep and Death appeared in the shape of a poisonous adder and took him after all. The kobyz is said to have lain there for a long time, the wind drawing soft tones from it. Ever since, music has been successfully fighting death. Where it resounds, death has no power.

Not far from the monument there is a museum and a small amphitheatre. Sitting on its stone benches, groups of travellers can see and hear prearranged performances by musicians and dancers—the melancholy sound of a kobyz at sunset makes a deep impression. For information, contact Mrs Sholpan Sultanova of the Korkhyt Ata Museum Board of Trustees (tel: 72437 22073 or 7 701 137 8886).

BAIKONUR COSMODROME

For a long time, the **Baikonur Cosmodrome** (Baykongyr in Kazakh), 250 kilometres from Kyzylorda and 50 kilometres from the garrison town of Baikonur, was inaccessible for all civilians—only technology experts and cosmonauts were brought here under conditions of the highest security. Even today, it is not possible simply to travel by train to the Tyuratam station, since the trip to Baikonur and the cosmodrome area itself requires a special access permit which can only be obtained with the help of an authorised travel agency.

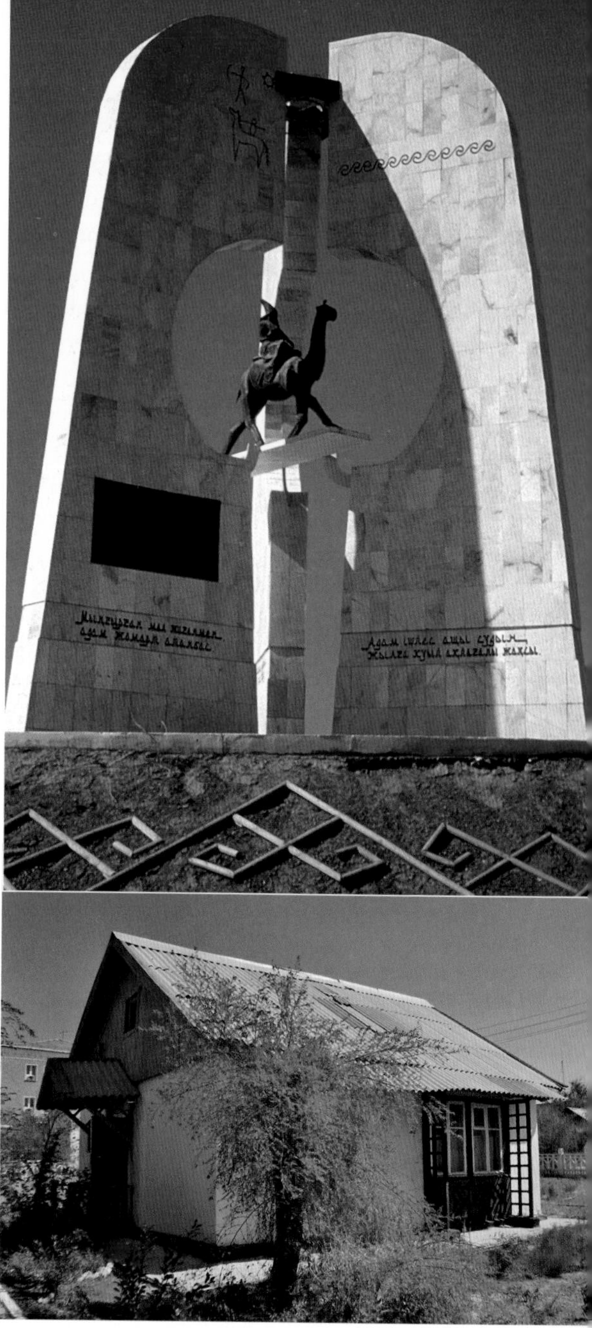

Top: The enigmatic Khorkhut-Ata Monument, dedicated to the inventor of the kobyz, *a musical instrument with a haunting quality (Dagmar Schreiber)*
Above: Yuri Gagarin's cottage in the Baikonur Cosmodrome enclave (Ernst Ischovits)

The permit includes the condition that specified locations (hotel, guided bus tours) must not be left during your visit under any circumstances. These security measures reflect the fact that Baikonur is still a **Russian enclave**, a territory leased by Russia from Kazakhstan.

The plans for the rocket-launching site were drafted in 1954. Three years later, in October 1957, the first Soviet sputnik took off—a replica of it can be seen in the Central State Museum of the Republic of Kazakhstan in Almaty. The first successful human-manned space venture, with **Yuri Gagarin** on board the *Vostok*, took off from Baikonur on 12 April 1961. In 1991, precisely 30 years after that famous flight, the first Kazakh cosmonaut, **Tokhar Aubakirov**, followed in his footsteps.

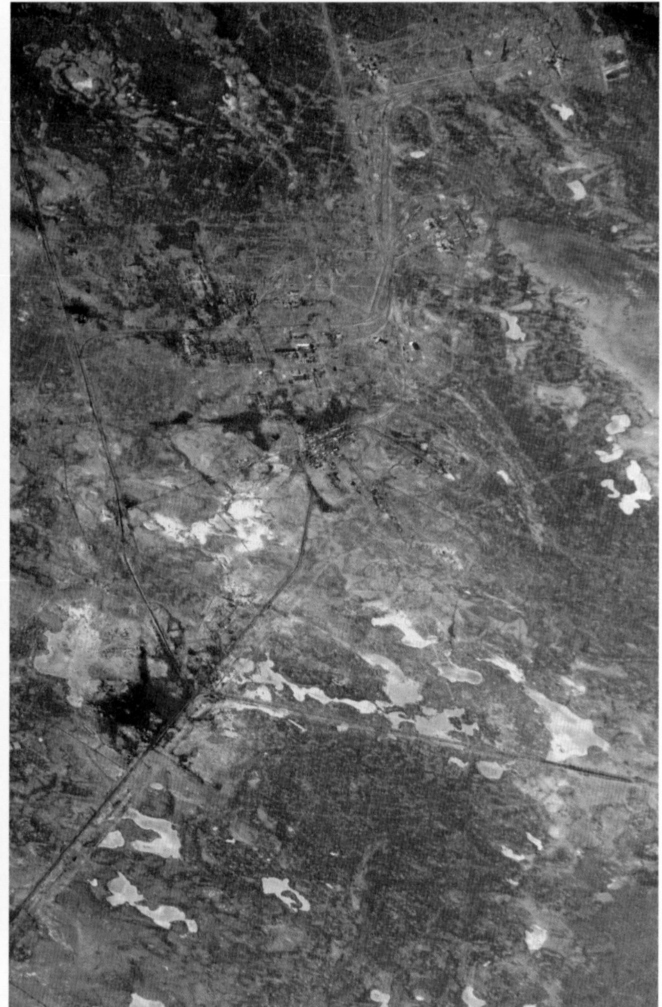

Baikonur's sprawl in the otherwsie empty steppe can be seen from this oblique-angle satellite image (Courtesy of Earth Sciences and Image Analysis Laboratory, NASA Johnson Space Center, http://eol.jsc.nasa.gov)

The collapse of the Soviet Union has changed a lot of things at Baikonur Cosmodrome. These days, tourists can witness rocket launches—from a safe distance. Such trips are expensive and completely inflexible regarding scheduling, of course. In 2001, the first space tourist, 61-year-old American Dennis Tito, went from here on a trip around the Earth, at a cost of US$20 million. Several others have followed his example, including a woman in 2007.

With a bit of luck, though, you can actually observe the launch of a space rocket from as far away as Shymkent or Turkistan—the scale of these launches makes them viewable from a distance of up to 1,000 kilometres. Overnight changes in the weather, however, create food for thought. Many inhabitants of the areas to the southeast and east of Baikonur claim that the rocket launches trigger storms over the steppe, and in addition to this, the rocket stages fall dramatically onto the steppe and hit the ground in completely random manner, often close to settlements. A path of discarded rocket parts, contaminated with rocket fuel, stretches as far as the Altai.

While it is true that the steppe is only thinly populated, nevertheless people do live there. Physicians note high levels of disease, and there are frequent protests from the population. The government of Kazakhstan has requested that Russia think about a non-contaminating fuel. At one time Russia intended to break the leasing contract, which was due to expire in 2004, and use a newly built cosmodrome on its own territory near Plesetsk. This would have been acceptable to Kazakhstan, which has the expertise to run the space-launching site on its own. The country has its own efficient research centres, which successfully develop new types of rockets and their own satellites. Marketing the world's largest cosmodrome, which stretches over 85 kilometres north-south and 125 kilometres east-west, in countries that do not have their own launching facilities, would be a source of income with high potential in the telecommunications field. But in December 2002, Russia and Kazakhstan's heads of state signed an agreement for the lease of Baikonur for another 50 years. Nevertheless, in 2006 Kazakhstan launched its own first satellite from its own facility within the cosmodrome.

For those who do visit this historical curiosity in the remote steppe, the museum of history of space travel and the modest cottage of Yuri Gagarin are very interesting. Groups can observe launch sites 1 and 2 from a relatively close position, and spend the night at the Cosmonaut Hotel, spartan, clean accommodation where in days of old cosmonauts used to sleep before the following day's launch.

Agencies offering excursions to Baikonur include Central Asia Tourism, Turan Asia, Silk Road Adventures and Sayakhat (see the end of this chapter). Bookings need to be made three months in advance.

Baikonur Cosmodrome: Space Age in the Steppe

By *Michael Steen*

The first thing that strikes a visitor to the Baikonur Cosmodrome is just how remote it is. A final piece of Russia-controlled land lost in the vast Kazakh steppe—the Russian Federation pays Kazakhstan US$115 million a year in rent to maintain jurisdiction over the site—driving to the space rocket launch site involves hour after hour of bumping along a potholed Soviet-era road through vast expanses of flat and featureless landscape or, the quicker option, flying over it in a Tupolev charter plane likely to originate in Moscow. There's a good reason for this isolation: during the 1950s, the Soviet planners who built Baikonur had not even started thinking about space. Rather, they were looking for a place to set up a secret military base that could construct, test and launch nuclear-tipped intercontinental ballistic missiles.

That also explains why Baikonur Cosmodrome was for many years not actually marked on any maps as Baikonur. The missile range and later cosmodrome was built at a railway junction named Tyuratam alongside the Syr Darya River. But once the Space Race got under way, the Soviet press referred to the Soviet Union's launch site as "Baikonur", the name of a mining town a few hundred kilometres to the north. It is thought this was done in an attempt to confuse the United States as to the site's true location. The fake name stuck, and in the mid-1990s the town that serves the cosmodrome was renamed from Leninsk to Baikonur.

A whiff of Soviet-era secrecy still hangs over Baikonur today—and this, indeed, is part of its appeal to many would-be visitors. The last nuclear missiles were shipped away in 1983 and Baikonur is now gradually moving towards entirely civilian control. But uniformed officers are still everywhere and, together with the neat rows of old Soviet apartment blocks, many of them no longer inhabited, they lend the place the feel of a provincial garrison town. Russian roubles are the main currency, although the Kazakh tenge is also accepted. A Russian mobile phone network was the first to provide mobile connections and the police and security staff patrolling the roads of the cosmodrome are Russian. To keep out the curious and the unauthorised, military checkpoints guard the entrances to both town and the sprawling but

Clockwise from right: Tight security measures follow a space rocket's progress across the steppe; the massive rocket moves slowly along a rail track towards the launching pad; the launch is an exciting moment for all; a thumbs-up from a cosmonaut undergoing final checks prior to the launch (Michael Steen x4)

high-security cosmodrome—a great expanse of steppe dotted with launch pads, giant rocket assembly halls, rocket fuel factories, radar arrays... the remains of decades of industry devoted to rocket science.

Small piles of rusting metal are scattered among the pale reddish mud and green scrubland of the cosmodrome. It's not that the Soviet space programme was particularly haphazard; it's just that there was no obvious need to keep the vast territory tidy. Baikonur has become increasingly profitable in recent times as a site for launching communications and other commercial satellites. Ironically, some of them are launched using "Dnepr" rockets, which are decommissioned nuclear missiles. Weapons that were once aimed at Western cities now put satellites in orbit to beam TV signals to those same cities. But there are also large swathes of the cosmodrome where time has stood still, leaving nothing but long-abandoned Soviet-era projects and empty missile silos.

One notable example is the decaying shell of a Soviet Energiya-Buran space shuttle—a craft very similar in appearance to its US counterpart, but one that only flew once in an unmanned test flight. The gantries of the enormous launch pad, built to accommodate the Buran, creak in the fierce wind. This is a harsh, semi-desert environment with freezing winters and sweltering summers, so even the enormous rocket assembly halls that are still in use have a battered appearance. To the casual eye, much of Baikonur looks derelict, as if the Space Age had come and gone.

But the casual onlooker would be mistaken. In order to get its cosmonauts into orbit, Russia still deploys Soyuz rockets, first used in 1966 and based on the design of the R-7 intercontinental ballistic missile. Russian space officials are proud of the heritage, simplicity and reliability of this technology, although they also like to point out that the craft has been updated continually (the Soyuz capsules that returned to Earth started to be kitted out with satellite telephones and GPS positioning devices after a capsule veered off course when landing in 2003. Once on the ground, the craft had not been able to radio mission control).

Yet for all its simplicity, Soyuz has surpassed the US Space Shuttle in safety and played a crucial role in keeping the International Space Station going. Following the Space Shuttle *Columbia* disaster in 2003, the only way for NASA astronauts to get to the space station for several years was by hitching a ride on Soyuz. These days NASA officials and former astronauts mingle with Russian space officials at Soyuz launches, often marvelling at just how close they are allowed to get to the craft during the "rolling out", when a train slowly pulls Soyuz from its assembly hall to Launch Pad No. 2, also known as the Gagarin Start.

Baikonur's manned launches blast off from the same launch pad that sent Yuri Gagarin into orbit as the first man in space in 1961. Under the gantries that hold the rocket in place, a Soviet-era mural proclaims: "Here, by the genius of Soviet man, the audacious storm of the cosmos began in 1957." It is more than the usual empty rhetoric: Baikonur is the place from which the first Sputnik satellite was launched in 1957. Aside from Gagarin, Valentina Tereshkova, the first woman in space, and Alexei Leonov, the first person to complete a spacewalk, both launched from Baikonur. And many years later, Baikonur would also be the site from which the first space tourists blasted off.

Today, Kazakhstan operates its own National Space Agency—called Kazkosmos—within Baikonur. In June 2006 it launched *KazSat-1*, its first communications satellite, designed to provide telcomm services for

Kazakhstan, Kyrgyzstan, Uzbekistan, Turkmenistan and even part of Russia. Plans were put into place to follow *KazSat-1* with *KazSat-2* and *KazSat-3*, as well as a number of scientific satellites designed to predict earthquakes. The plans also include developing a capacity to provide commercial satellite launch services to other countries. Kazakhstan has also had two cosmonauts training at the Russian space training centre for a number of years, and they are now ready to head to space in the near future. Previously, during the Soviet era, two Kazakh cosmonauts, Tokhtar Aubakirov and Talgat Musabaev, flew to space under the Soviet space programme. Musabaev is now the Chairman of Kazkosmos.

The Kazakhstan government has made the building of a major new launch site, named "Baiterek", a priority in its own space programme—President Nazarbayev is keen to develop the country's space industry, and a national space programme is being drafted reaching to the year 2020. Baiterek, jointly developed with Russia, will have the capability to launch the more environmentally friendly Angara launch vehicles—an alternative to the Soyuz booster, and capable of carrying 26 metric tons of payload to low-Earth orbits.

Watching a launch is exhilarating. Even from the safe distance of the viewing platform one kilometre away from the launch pad, the noise is overwhelming. A deep roar like the sound of an enormous gas cooker reverberates through one's body as the craft takes off and streaks up into the sky. There is something awe-inspiring about seeing it with your own eyes, even though the imagery is familiar from film and television.

However, getting to see a launch as a tourist is time-consuming and either expensive or difficult to arrange. Although Baikonur is officially a Russian leasehold, the government of Kazakhstan is keen to promote tourism to the site, but do not expect anything resembling the Disney-like ease with which tourists visit the Kennedy Space Center at Cape Canaveral in Florida. Since the town remains "closed", security clearance from the Russian FSB security services is required and this takes at least 45 days to obtain, once you have found a tour firm to arrange the trip. These work under the supervision of either Russia's space agency or Kazakhstan's transport ministry. For the dedicated, though, the time and trials involved in realising their dream of watching a launch at first hand, can make the whole experience even more satisfying.

For those with Space Age budgets, the company that has charged five civilian space tourists between US$20-25 million for a ride on Soyuz also offers tours of Baikonur starting in Moscow. Space Adventures (www.spaceadventures.com) advertises four-night launch tours for just under US$20,000 for a business-class ride and about US$16,000 for coach class. Several Russian travel agencies offer more modest packages also starting in Moscow and costing US$3,000–4,000, prices that Kazakhstan-based travel agencies with access authority to Baikonur (www.almata.kz, www.advantour.com, www.kazakhstan.orexca.com) will either match or beat for tailor-made tours.

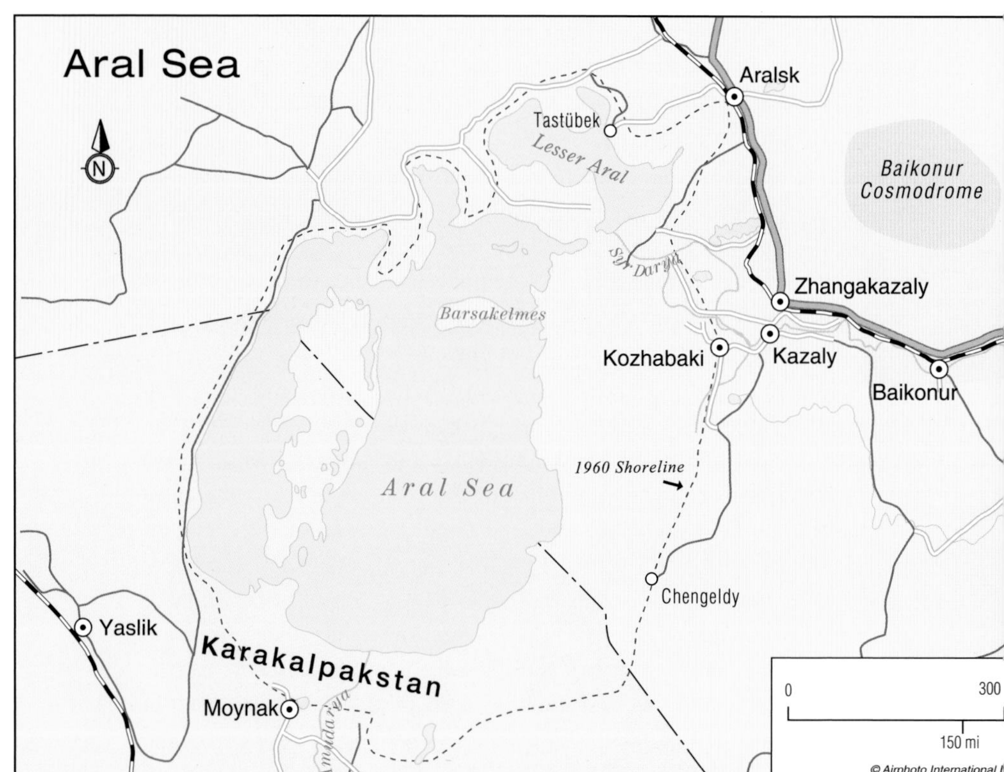

ARALSK AND THE ARAL SEA

In 1847, the Russian fortress of **Raimsk**, under the command of Colonel Yerofeyev, was built in the area inhabited by the Junior (Lesser) Horde, near the **Aral Sea**. The fortress was located 65 kilometres from the mouth of the Syr Darya. It was of strategic significance in the struggle against Kokand and Khiva to the south for control over the area east of the Syr Darya. The following year, shipping was started with the launch in Raimsk of the schooners *Nikolay* and *Konstantin*, named after Russian tsars, which navigated down the Syr Darya to the Aral Sea. Apart from the military advantage this link gave, it was highly popular among travellers as well, described as late as 1933 by the Swiss traveller Ella Maillart.

Nearby, a town for construction workers was built in 1905 right on the northeast shore of the Aral Sea, to help build the railway line connecting Orenburg and Tashkent. The town, **Aralsk**, grew rapidly and was given city status in 1938. Industry grew, most of all fish processing and a shipyard. The city did well, and the level of accommodation was high by Soviet standards. People would tell visitors the legend of the city's origin: the 40 gods, who lived under the great blue yurt (heaven), dropped a large, blue, brightly shining turquoise on the Earth during a game. The turquoise signified beauty and an abundance of

Stranded fishing vessels litter the dried-up seabed around Aralsk, once a seaside town but now many kilometres from open water (Christopher Herwig)

water and fish. The sea became famous for its fish. **Chingis Aitmatov** writes in his book *The Day Lasts More Than a Hundred Years* about the fisherman Edige, who takes the *altyn mekre*—the golden fish—from the sea for his beloved wife, Ukubala, in order to fulfil her wish for a child. The poetic description of Edige, waiting patiently for the fish, of the stormy and yet intimately known sea and the fisherman's respect for nature, is deeply moving.

Edige gave his golden fish back to the sea's wild waters, after Ukubala had admired and embraced it. Those were the days; today, nobody fetches any golden fish from the salt lake that remains. The Aral Sea is virtually dead. What is left consists of two, soon to be three, remaining partial lakes, which nonetheless are still large by most standards. The story of how it came to be this way has been told in the Geography section of Chapter One of this book, and it makes for depressing reading. The Soviet technocrats who came up with the idea of irrigating the steppe using the Aral Sea's main water sources obviously never considered the monstrous effect it would have on this once renowned and revered body of water. Global warming has also had a hand, with glaciers receding and rising average temperatures adding to the Aral Sea's woes.

Storms now carry sand and salt grains from the dry seabed right across the Central Asian steppe, onto the glaciers of the Tien Shan and even as far as the Himalaya. The Aral Sea's huge volume of water once influenced and moderated Central Asia's extreme continental climate—the sea was large enough to generate rain clouds. Now, however, the water volume is insufficient for this, and a vast region of once habitable land is falling into desertification. Though resistant plants and bushes still grow on the dry, salty seabed, the area is becoming drier, colder in winter and hotter in summer.

The 35,000 inhabitants of Aralsk hold out against the odds. Here, where once you could look out over the Aral Sea, now only sand and decay can be observed. In recent years, a kind of disaster tourism has developed. Although the town is in a state of desolation, with sand storms a daily phenomenon and one in 10 children dying before their first birthday, it still attracts many foreigners, who come here to marvel at the results of Soviet thoughtlessness and stupidity.

The only hotel worth the name on the square, a house called Aral, is at least conveniently located, though it needs renovation, like everything else. The most-frequented sightseeing spot is the **ships' graveyard**. From Aralsk, simply drive or walk for dozens of kilometres over the dry seabed. Everywhere, ghost vessels lie lopsided on their keels, scattered over the dry soil. Most of them are fishing boats, which once provided work and wealth for the region. It is certainly an emotive experience, often driving one to tears of anger over such wasteful and tragic loss.

But Aralsk's residents struggle on with great dignity. They do not give up, and even hope for the water to return one day. In 1992, inhabitants of Aralsk and many villages north of the remaining lakes grabbed spades and buckets to throw up a provisional dam with pebbles and sand in the land between the Kokaral depression and the eastern shore. The aim was to prevent the water that poured into the northern basin from spilling into the south, thus gradually raising the water level in the northern lake. Nine months after its construction the dam overflowed and breached. In 1996, a new dam was built, 14 kilometres long and up to 30 metres wide; it was strengthened in 1998. This great civil initiative in Kazakhstan gave people hope, as they held their breath and watched the water level rise and the first positive signs of improvement that resulted. Then, in 1999, a sand storm of hideous force tore the dam apart and part of the water gain was lost to the southern basin's lake, which is much larger.

However, hope has been revived once more. The World Bank has financed a 13-kilometre-long barrier dyke at the mouth of the Syr Darya. Watching the environmental disaster worsen as the water evaporated at increasing rates from the Aral Sea's surface, and understanding that it is practically impossible to save the whole remaining body of water, the decision was finally made to attempt to save and restore the northern "**Lesser Aral**". The subsequent prevention of water loss to the south has led to a significant increase in water level in the Lesser Aral. As a result the salinity is reducing, and fishing is becoming viable once again. It is hoped that the water surface will increase to about 600 square kilometres. Meanwhile, scientists are looking into ways to reduce wind erosion of sand and drifting salt. New plantation methods are now being tested on the eastern shore of the Aral Sea.

The Barsakelmes Peninsula

The **Barsakelmes Peninsula** is home to one of Kazakhstan's nine official Natural Reserves. It was established in 1939 with the aim of protecting the classic vegetation that characterizes salt-clay desert, consisting of black and white saksaul, tamarisk and 264 other typical species, as well as the corresponding fauna who inhabit this environment. Barsakelmes is also important as a breeding place for migrating birds.

Barsakelmes used to be an island in the Aral Sea with an area of 133 square kilometres. Thanks to limited access, a herd of **kulan** (wild ass), as well as **saiga** antelope and **dzheyran** (steppe gazelles) have been preserved. However, in the wake of the deterioration of climatic conditions, in particular the increase in the water's salinity, 260 kulan were moved to other protected areas during the 1980s. Yet in spite of the Aral crisis, the 50 remaining animals reproduced and multiplied in number. These days, 150 kulan continue to live here and their number increases by 20 to 25 each year.

USGS
science for a changing world

Aral Sea, Kazakhstan

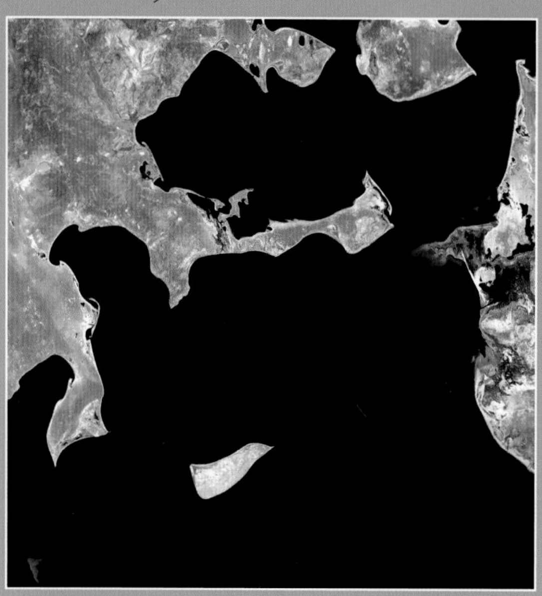

Landsat MSS
May 29, 1973

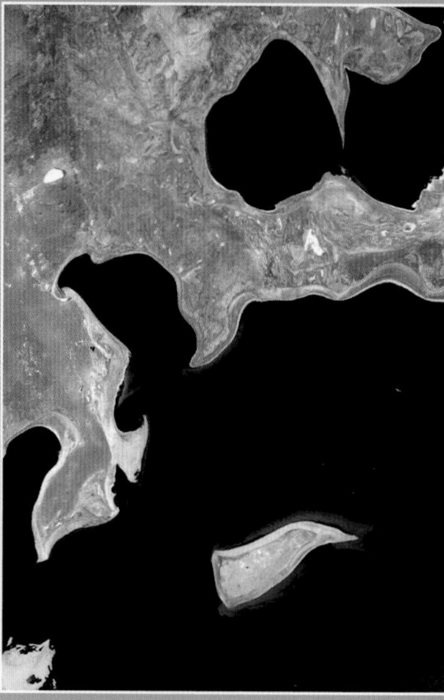

Landsat MSS
August 19, 1987

U.S. Department of the Interior
U.S. Geological Survey

In cooperation with

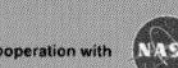

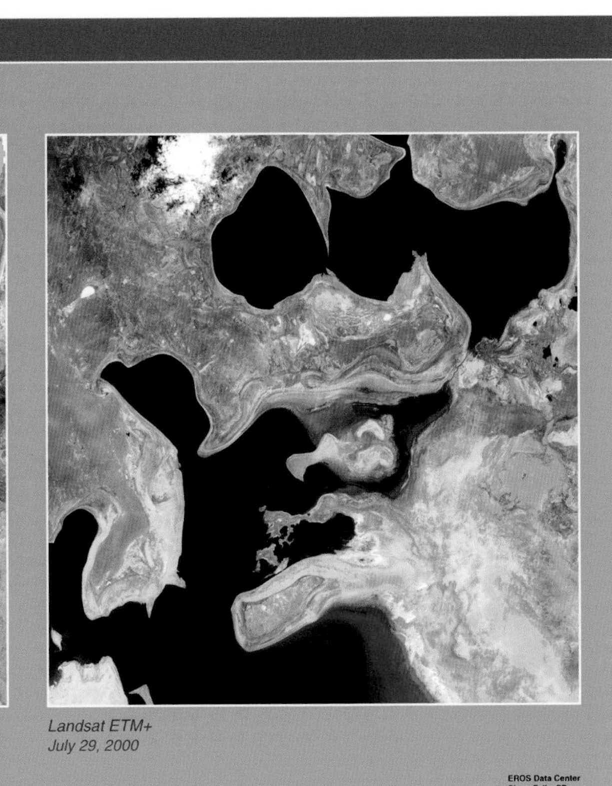

Left: Beginning in the 1960s, massive diversions of irrigation water from the rivers that feed into the Aral Sea resulted in virtually no freshwater reaching it by the 1980s. These satellite images show how it has shrunk in size, causing horrendous environmental problems. However, recent initiatives are improving the situation for the northern "Lesser Aral" (Images courtesy of the USGS Landsat science team)

Below left: As local fish populations crashed due to increased salinity, fishermen introduced flounder—which flourish in higher saline levels—into the Aral Sea in an attempt to keep the fishing industry viable (Christopher Herwig)

Because of the Aral's decreasing water level the isle has turned into a peninsula, 10 times larger than the one-time reserve. In theory, the kulan are free to roam from the area "allocated" to them, while the new link to the mainland also makes their protection more difficult. The reserve's officials want to expand the protected area by 4,000 square kilometres, in order to consolidate its status as protected land and allow unhindered resettlement of new life on the dried-up seabed. For those interested in visiting or find out more about the reserve, its director is Magzhan Tursinbayev, Street 14 of the Kazakh Militsiya, Aralsk, tel: (72433) 22231 or 7 701 663 9672, e-mail: barsakelmes@mail.kz.

For a long time, there were fears that another island, **Vozrozhdeniye**, could turn into a peninsula as well. This one-time 200-square-kilometre isle, now 10 times larger due to the receding water level, harbours a grim secret. It is here that the Soviet army had its testing grounds for biological weapons. Before the armed forces left the island, containers of anthrax, bubonic plague and probably other deadly agents were simply buried here. An inspection by American experts showed leaks in many containers. It is claimed that the viruses could easily be transmitted by insects and birds across the now shallow, narrow strait that separates the island from the mainland. Since 1991, individual cases of plague have occurred, and a mass death of saiga antelope was due to anthrax. In the meantime, American specialists have sealed the containers. Ironically, Vozrozhdeniye means "resurrection" in Russian.

SOUTHERN KAZAKHSTAN TRAVEL AGENCIES

Burkhan Shener, Turkistan, tel: (72522) 40183—a teacher and very educated guide for tours around Turkistan.

Central Asia Tourism (CAT), 18/217 Ilayeva St, Shymkent, tel: (7252) 211 436, e-mail cat-chimkent@alarnet.com.

Golden Caravan, Taraz, 111a M.Kh. Dulaty Street, tel: (7262) 459 774, fax: 346 294, e-mail: karavankz@mail.ru or karavan@tarazinfo.kz, website: www.goldkaravan.narod.ru.

Komek, 2/4 Turkestanskaya Street, Shymkent, tel: (7252) 214 305, fax: 214 307, e-mail: komek@astel.kz, website: www.komek.nets.kz.

Kuanysh, 7/15 Baytursynuly Street, Shymkent, tel/fax: (7252) 540 778 or 7 701 451 8840, e-mail: kuanysh-shm@nursat.kz.

Silk Road Adventures, 117/44 Adi Sharipov Street, Almaty, tel: (727) 2 924 042, fax: 2 926 319, e-mail: sradventure@nursat.kz, website: www.silkroadadventures.net.

Sputnik, 4/1 Gilyayeva Street, Shymkent, tel: (7252) 562 601, fax: 556 720, e-mail: sputnik-shm@nursat.kz.

Tamara Ogneva, Shymkent, (7252) 214 289 or 7 701 751 8970, e-mail: tamarahanum_o@inbox.ru.

Taraz Travel, Hotel Zhambyl, 42 Tole Bi Street, Taraz, tel: (7262) 455 989, fax: 451 750, e-mail: hotel-zhambyl@nursat.kz.

Tarazturist, 53/17 Tole Bi Street, Taraz, tel: (7262) 433 549, 433 362.

Turan-Asia Ltd, 66/8 Abai Avenue, Almaty, tel: (727) 2 337 581, 2 334 621, 2 330 371, 2 330 596, fax: 2 337 581, 2 735 874, e-mail: turanincome@belight.net or turanasia@belight.net; website: www.turanasia.kz.

Turkestan Travel, Office 103, Hotel Yassy, Tauke Khana Ave, Turkistan, tel: (23533) 40183, fax: 32533 or 7 777 229 4499, e-mail: turkestan@hotbox.ru, website: www.turkestan.land.ru.

Zhenya & Lyuda's Boarding House, Zhabagly, tel: (72538) 56696 or 7 701 717 5851, e-mail: innaksu@nursat.kz or innaksu@mail.ru, website: www.ecotour1.narod.ru.

No Wife at Home

On the outskirts of the town [Kasala—the modern-day town of Kazaly] some Kirghiz had pitched their kibitkas. These tents are the homes of the nomad tribes, and are carried by them on camels from place to place. One of these abodes was adorned inside with thick carpets of various hues, and bright coloured cushions, on which the inmates reposed. A small fire in the centre of the apartment gave out a thick white smoke, which wreathed itself round in serpent-like coils, till, gradually reaching the roof, it escaped through an aperture left for that purpose. Very pungent and trying to the eyes was this dense atmosphere—a wood, or rather sort of bramble, called saksaool, which is found in large quantities on the steppes, being used for fuel. The women in the tent appeared to have no fear of strangers, and did not cover up their faces, as is the custom amongst other Mohammedan races. They were evidently delighted at our visit, and, laying down fresh rugs on the ground, invited me to sit by their side...

...An elderly man, clad in a long brown dressing-gown thickly wadded to keep out the cold, was the proprietor of the kibitka. Pouring some water into a huge cauldron, which was suspended from a tripod over the fire, he proceeded to make the tea, whilst a young girl handed round some raisons and dried currants. The inmates were surprised when I told them that I was not a Russian, but had come from a land far away towards the setting sun.

"Anglitchanin, Englishman," said Nazar; and the party gravely repeated the word Anglitchanin. One of the men now inquired if I had brought my wife with me, and he was astonished on hearing that I was unprovided with a helpmate, the whole party being of the opinion that such an appendage was as necessary to a man's happiness as his horse or camel.

The Kirghiz have one great advantage over the other Mohammedan races. They have the opportunity of seeing the girls whom they wish to marry, and of conversing with them before the bargain is concluded with their parents—one hundred sheep being the average price given for a young woman...

..."Do you like Kasala?" I inquired of the best-looking of the girls.

"No," replied an aged female, not giving the maid I addressed time to speak; "we all prefer the steppes." And with these words she glanced contemptuously at her daughter, who, as Nazar afterwards informed me, liked the slight civilisation that Kasala was able to afford better than the beauties of nature and the trackless wastes of Tartary.

Colonel Frederick Burnaby, A Ride to Khiva: Mounted adventures in Central Asia, *1876,* The Long Riders' Guild Press (www.thelongridersguild.com)

SARY ARKA: THE GREAT STEPPE

It is summer. The trees cast their shadows, and in the meadows the flowers bloom impetuously. Busily, the summer camps are being put up, and the grass is so high in the steppe that the backs of the horses are hardly visible.

Abai Kunanbayev

THE KAZAKH MOTHERLAND

The dominant impression of Kazakhstan is of a land of endless steppe. Nowhere is this epitomised more clearly than in the **Sary Arka**, which translates as "yellow back" and is considered the heartland of the Kazakh people. This huge area, covering central and northern Kazakhstan, was home to the legendary **Kypchak** nation, a tribe of horse-masters who controlled the entire steppe from the Altai mountains to the Volga River.

The Sary Arka stretches from the **West Siberian depression** in the north to the **Balkhash-Alakol depression** in the south, and from the foothills of the **Altai** in the east to the **Torgay** valleys in the west. In some places the landscape is as flat as a pancake; in others, such as the **Kazakh hill country** (*Kazakhskiy-Melkosopochnik*), its topography is hilly, even mountainous.

Kazakhstan's new capital, **Astana**, was established right in the heart of the Sary Arka. It was considered an unusual move in 1997, but it has since proved to be a success, and the symbolism is clear: where else should people of the steppe build their capital, but in the steppe?

Left: Vast swathes of feather grass and empty sky typify Kazakhstan's Central Steppe (Dagmar Schreiber)

Far left: Wrapped up against the cold wind, three Astana residents go for a stroll beneath the city's landmark Baiterek tower (Christopher Herwig)

ASTANA

The location of Kazakhstan's capital began as nothing more than a ford across the **Esil River** (also Yesil, or Ishim in Russian), close to which a settlement called **Akmola** emerged, not far from a trading route that originated on the main branch of the Silk Road. Akmola was used as a staging post by travellers, and trade in cattle and merchandise from China and the towns of the Central Asian steppe flourished. Scholars differ on whether the name refers to the nearby white barrows or graves (*ak mola*) or the "white abundance" (*ak mol*) of sheep's wool, cotton and mare's milk. Fresh excavations on nearby Lake Buzuk suggest that there used to be a settlement called Ak Zhol (White Track), situated on a side branch of the Silk Road at the time of the Desht-y-Kypchak from the 10th to 12th centuries AD. In 1830, the Russians established a fortress here and named it **Akmolinsk**.

The stronghold at first served as a shelter for the Kazakhs against attacks from warlike neighbours such as the Kalmyks, Bashkirs and Cossacks, but later on its role changed to that of an outpost in Russia's campaign to colonize the nomadic steppe peoples. In 1838, it was captured and razed by **Kenesary Kasimov**, the leader of the largest Kazakh revolt against Russian colonialism. But Russia's ambitions could not be held back; Akmolinsk was rebuilt, the settlement grew in size and importance and in 1862 it obtained city status. Mining became its predominant industry and it also became an important railway junction.

The city retained its name of Akmolinsk until 1961, by which time it had gone through a period of being used as a place of exile. Many **Volga Germans** were deported here and turned large areas into productive land, and during World War II almost 70,000 Ukrainians, Belarusians and Russians were evacuated from the battle zones to the Akmolinsk region. Whoever arrived, however, was received with great hospitality according to Kazakh tradition, and most of them stayed on after the war.

The opening-up of the lands surrounding Akmolinsk was carried out on a grand scale as part of the **"Virgin Lands"** scheme. Tens of thousands of young people came here from Alma-Ata, Moscow and many areas of Russia and Ukraine, some voluntarily, others "delegated". They built dozens of settlements and made the land productive, with numberless square kilometres of new land put under the plough. The city in the centre of the area was renamed "Virgin Lands Town" or **Tselinograd** in Russian.

In 1992, following Kazakhstan's declaration of independence, the city was given back its old name Akmola. However, in 1998 the government suddenly—and surprisingly—announced that Kazakhstan's capital status was to be shifted from Almaty to Akmola, and the city was to be renamed **Astana**—meaning "capital"—with immediate effect. (Apparently, the name Akmola was not to the liking of the city planners because its literal meaning of

White Tomb, or perhaps deadly winter, had negative connotations for the President's risky and hugely ambitious project.)

There are a number of reasons why charming, green Almaty, with its tremendous mountain scenery and its mild climate, had to surrender its position as the capital in favour of an incongruous town in the steppe—somewhere to which unwanted people were once banished, somewhere extremely hot in summer and gruesomely cold in winter.

As a result of the more recent history of Kazakh settlement and in particular Russia's colonization of the nomadic steppe peoples, Kazakhs and Kyrgyz had been gradually pushed towards the south, while the north was increasingly inhabited by Russians, Ukrainians and, later, Germans (Almaty being an exception). This division triggered many economic, social and political challenges. In the middle of the 1990s, almost 80 percent of the money that circulated in Kazakhstan was located in Almaty and its surrounding areas. The shifting of the capital city farther north was intended to narrow this gap and improve the prospects for the northern provinces. Moving the capital should also bring about a better-balanced ethnic mix, a cooling of separatist tendencies among the Russian population groups in the north of Kazakhstan, more single-minded economic development in so far undeveloped parts of the country, and a halt to the exodus of human resources in the region.

Other arguments have been put forward for the shift from Almaty to Akmola/Astana, from the fact that Almaty is earthquake-prone, to increasing environmental problems in that city in recent years, in particular air pollution. Putting greater distance between the staunchly secular Kazakhstan government and its much more religious—if not militant—Central Asian contemporaries to the south could also have been a factor.

A revamp of the ageing generation of long-established civil servants was promised in setting up the new capital, and a new cadre of young, ambitious state employees were recruited in order to fill the government's ranks in the new capital. Moving the capital in 1998 was of course a tough ordeal for state officials who had to relocate there immediately. There were insufficient offices for the numerous newcomers, and appropriate residences were scarce, with little worth classifying as luxurious. Flats from the 1960s, 70s and 80s dominated the city, and it was obvious that the cityscape had to change fundamentally—and fast.

It has certainly done that: since 1998, building in the new capital has been taking place on a massive scale and at warp speed. The provincial airport of Akmola became the Astana International Airport, to which Air Astana, Lufthansa and KLM now fly. The **Presidential Cultural Centre**, with its blue dome in the shape of a yurt, was completed in 2000; a new national university was opened, the Eurasian Gumilyov University, named after the

Left: The view from Baiterek's golden sphere towards the Presidential Palace. Right: Sculptures and construction cranes share the skyline as Astana continues to grow (Jeremy Tredinnick x2)

spiritual father of the notion of a united Eurasia; and many modern architectural gems have followed. The mix in building styles gives an impression of a capital where Western and Eastern cultures meet. Turkish and domestic construction firms have built—and continue to build—colourful skyscrapers of many different designs on the bank of the Esil River, creating a skyline worthy of a new metropolis.

Astana is neatly split down the middle by the Esil—but it wasn't always this way. The old town of Akmola was situated almost entirely on the river's right bank, with only the city's central park and a few roads on the left bank acting as a buffer for the open steppe to the south. This area, however, was designated as the site for a brand-new city that would rival the ultra-modern metropolises of Dubai and Hong Kong—and so it has turned out to be. In fact, one could say that the fantastic city development plan drawn up by Japanese architect Kisho Kurokawa has in fact been overtaken by the reality and successes of the achievements so far.

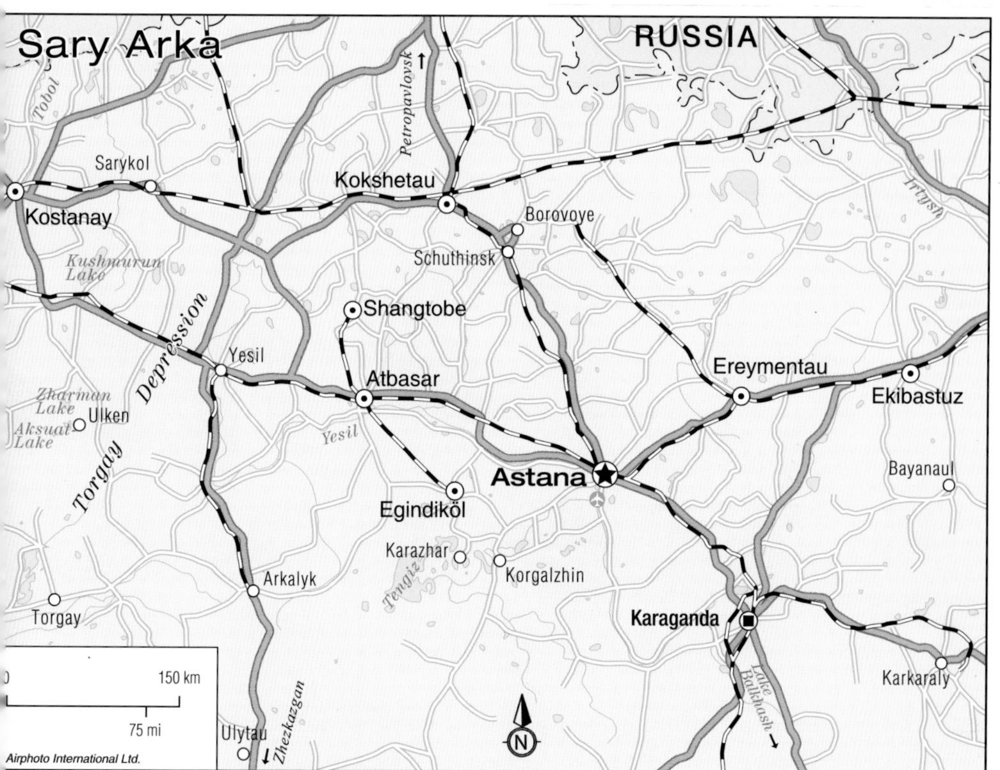

The new **Presidential Palace**, the **Baiterek** observation tower—a landmark for the city and the country—Kazakhstan's largest mosque, the modernistic **KazMunaiGaz building**, many more government and business complexes with glass and steel façades, gigantic residential complexes in imperial styles, an oceanarium, a national library and archives, a special zone for diplomats… there is no end in sight to the building boom on the Esil's southern bank. In 2006, Sir Norman Foster's architect firm completed an inspirational glass pyramid named the **Palace of Peace and Concord** (and the only major new landmark building on the right bank) that has garnered praise around the world; it was created to be the definitive meeting place for the leading representatives of world religions. Such was its success that Foster's company has been commissioned again, this time to build an even bigger construction, a colossal 150-metre-high, tent-shaped cone named **Khan Shatyr**, which will provide 10,000 of the capital's residents and visitors with a massive recreation centre protected from the elements by a transparent plastic compound that absorbs the sun and regulates the temperature inside, allowing people to sip coffee and even sunbathe by an artificial lake while it is well below freezing outside (during the cold steppe winter).

Meanwhile, flowers, shrubs and trees planted on spacious green axes throughout the city attempt to reduce the effects of the extreme weather caused by Astana's continental climate. With Astana, Kazakhstan is presenting a completely new, ultra-modern face to the world, one that shows its ambitions both within the region and on the global stage, and also its economic and financial power. Economists say that the President has allocated over US$10 billion for the construction of his new city—and that's without taking foreign investment into account.

Above: Astana is growing so fast that maps and other images are out of date almost as soon as they are created (NASA Landsat image courtesy of USGS and the Global Land Cover Facility, www.landcover.org). Right: The apex of the Palace of Peace and Concord (Jeremy Tredinnick). Previous pages: Rock outcrops in the Central Steppe rise like islands of stone in a sea of grass (Vladislav Yakushkin)

The original plan was for the President's dream of a true capital to have come true by the year 2030, when the metropolis should have a population of over a million. Already, however, the growth in population puts these expectations in the shade, with the 500,000th resident born in 2002 (that milestone was originally forecast for 2007). Wander down the river promenade and you'll be part of a vibrant scene as people go walking, skateboarding and jogging by; across the river, the aqua park, recently completed, is full of life. Everywhere, businesses, cafés, restaurants and hotels are emerging. A lively nightlife is developing, perhaps not yet as exciting as Almaty's, but time may change that. Against the odds, the new metropolis is being accepted, and all those embassies, banks and enterprises who refused to move from Almaty to the steppe—well, they will have to reconsider.

Sights

If you want to get some idea of what Akmola, Tselinograd or Akmolinsk was like, you should do it now. Many old houses on the right bank of the river are still standing, mostly in the area between the railway station and Moscow Street. There is little hope, however, that many of them will survive the coming years, since systematic neglect has left them in such a state that razing them seems to be the only practical solution. Curiously, and in contradiction to the norm, this city's most interesting sights all date from very recent times.

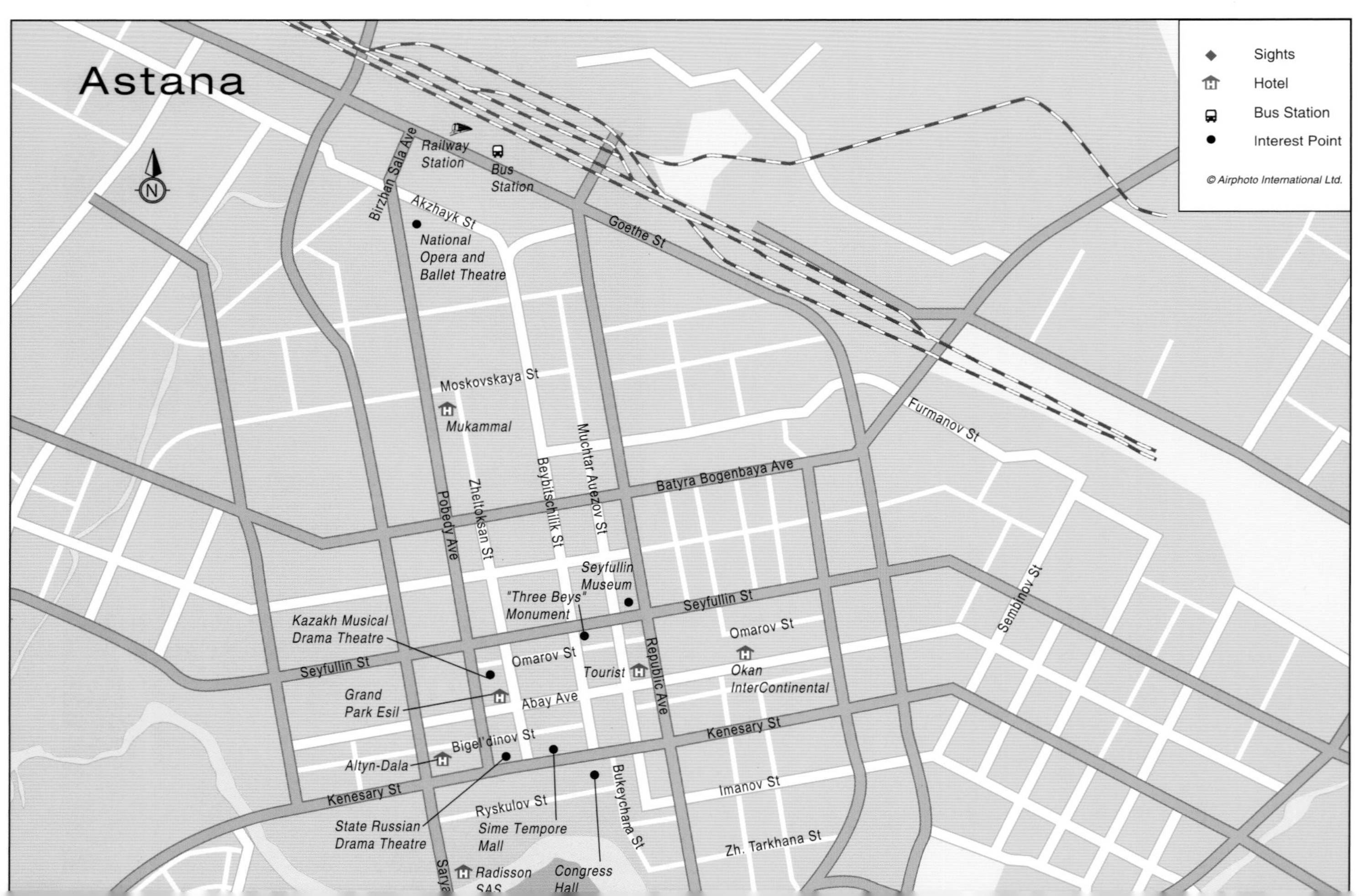
Astana
N
Sights
Hotel
Bus Station
Interest Point
© Airphoto International Ltd.
Railway Station
Bus Station
Birzhan Sala Ave
Akzhayk St
National Opera and Ballet Theatre
Goethe St
Moskovskaya St
Mukammal
Furmanov St
Batyra Bogenbaya Ave
Pobedy Ave
Zheltoksan St
Beybitschilik St
Muchtar Auezov St
Seyfullin Museum
"Three Beys" Monument
Seyfullin St
Sembinov St
Omarov St
Okan InterContinental
Kazakh Musical Drama Theatre
Tourist
Republic Ave
Grand Park Esil
Abay Ave
Bigel'dinov St
Kenesary St
Altyn-Dala
Imanov St
Ryskulov St
Sime Tempore Mall
Bukeychana St
State Russian Drama Theatre
Zh. Tarkhana St
Radisson SAS
Congress Hall

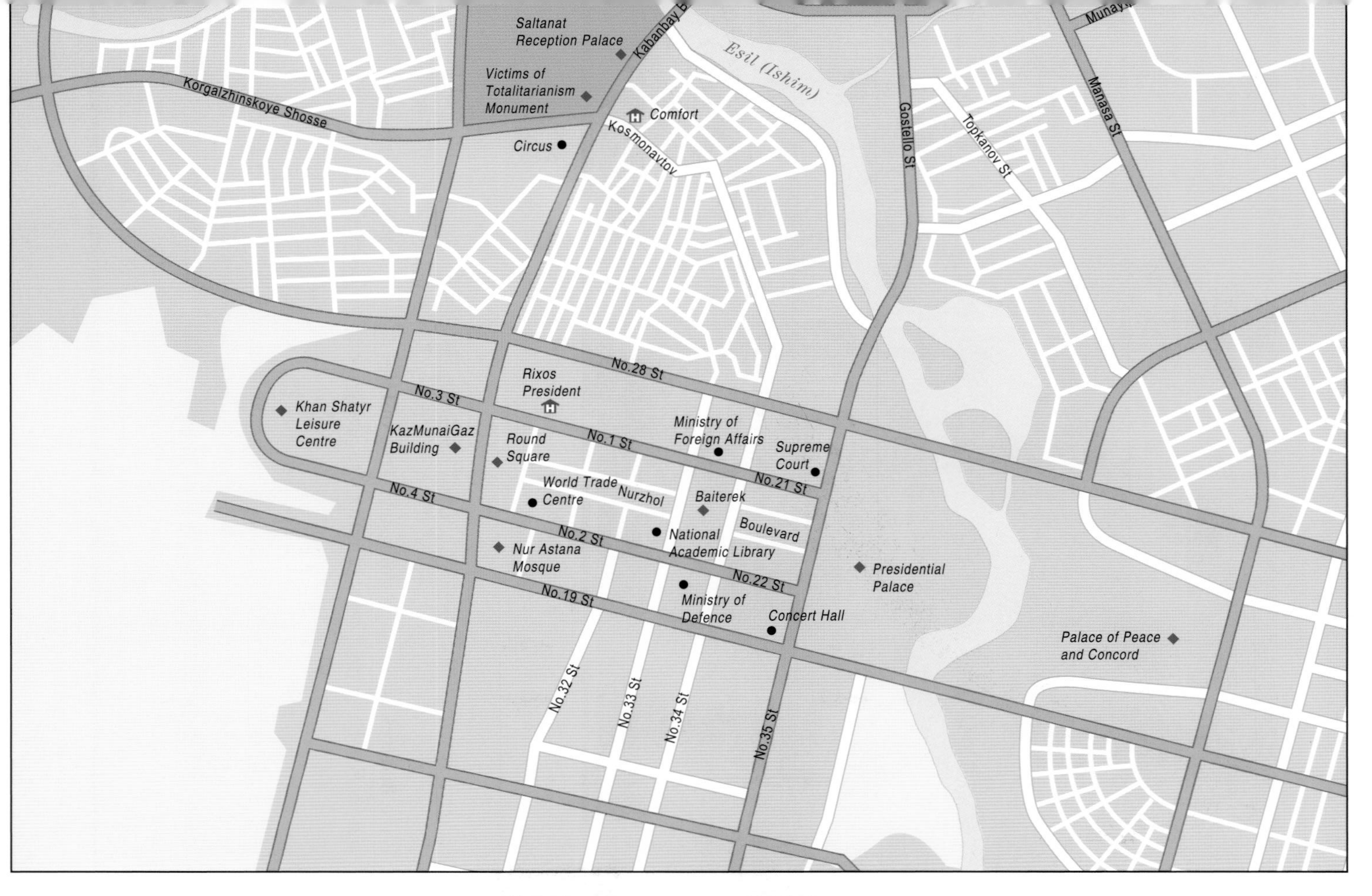

Saltanat Reception Palace
Victims of Totalitarianism Monument
Korgalzhinskoye Shosse
Circus
Comfort
Kosmonavtov
Esil (Ishim)
Gostello St
Topkanov St
Manasa St
No.28 St
Rixos President
No.3 St
Khan Shatyr Leisure Centre
KazMunaiGaz Building
Round Square
No.1 St
Ministry of Foreign Affairs
Supreme Court
No.21 St
World Trade Centre
Nurzhol
Baiterek
Boulevard
No.4 St
National Academic Library
No.2 St
Nur Astana Mosque
No.22 St
Presidential Palace
No.19 St
Ministry of Defence
Concert Hall
Palace of Peace and Concord
No.32 St
No.33 St
No.34 St
No.35 St

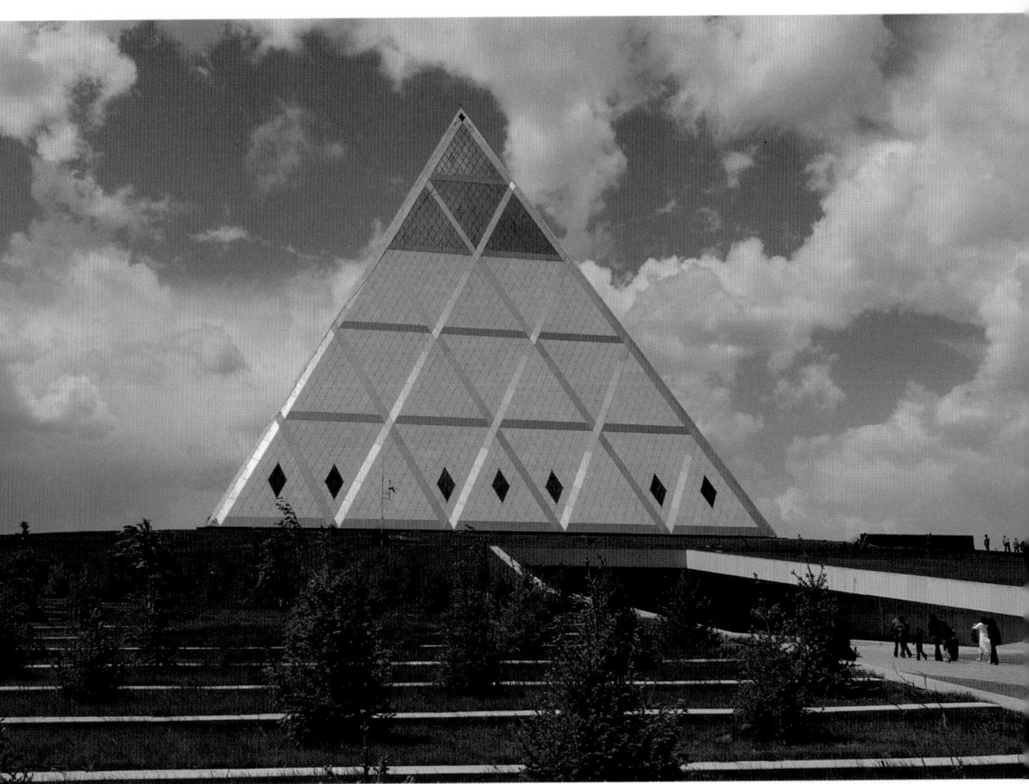

Above: The Palace of Peace and Concord, built by Norman Foster's firm in 2006. Right: Baiterek and the office blocks and other architectural marvels that surround it catch the golden light of the setting sun (Jeremy Tredinnick x2)

As you drive from the airport towards the city, the first thing that stands out from a distance is a very tall structure on the right, crowned by a golden, glittering globe. This is the **Baiterek** observation tower, the "**Tree of Life**". It was President Nazarbayev's idea, and he also has a clear view of it from his living room, for his new residence is located in full sight of the 97-metre-high structure. According to legend, the magic bird **Samruk** would lay a golden egg on the top of every tree that was out of reach to humans. All the secrets of human desire and passion were hidden inside the egg, as well as the answers to all their dreams for the future. With the building of Baiterek the egg is no longer out of reach, since two elevators whisk visitors up to the golden, gleaming globe set within the opening concrete "branches" of the white-trunked tower. From this vantage point, looking out through the gold-tinted glass, you may not grasp the secret of life's passions and desires and the key to their satisfaction—but at least you can admire how the President's vision of the future is rapidly taking shape.

Baiterek occupies the centre of a huge quadrangle, the showpiece of Astana's recent development. Occupying the eastern end of this long rectangle is the marbled splendour of the **Presidential Palace**, while facing it, albeit from a considerable distance, is the glass-fronted façade of the **KazMunaiGaz building** in the west. Between the country's political focal point on one side and the headquarters of the country's most powerful business corporation on the other, two rows of impressive buildings—housing top government and business offices—make up the remaining sides of this elongated rectangle. It makes a powerful statement of economic wealth—no doubt the intention—but it also happens to be a pleasant place to walk, since the quadrangle's inner space has been made into an attractive park, with flowerbeds and modern bronze statues of stylized traditional figures. Walk down towards the KazMunaiGaz façade and on your left you'll see the country's largest place of worship, the **Nur Astana Mosque**, whose 40-metre height symbolizes the age of Mohammed when he first had revelations from God, and whose gleaming, 63-metre-high minarets symbolize the Prophet's age when he departed from the world of man.

A wide road leads north from here towards the river and the right bank of the city. To the left stands a monument to the memory of the victims of totalitarianism, situated on an artificial hill, and dedicated to the many millions who between the 1920s and 50s lost their homes and/or lives under the Stalinist repression—many of them right here in the heart of the Kazakh steppe. Included in this sad category are the victims of forced collectivisation, dissidents shot by people's commissars, intellectuals sent to Stalin's camps, Germans, Tatars, Caucasians and other nations deported to the Kazakh territory.

Closer to the river is another grand dome supported by pillars. This is the **Saltanat Reception Palace**, where state and other official receptions and banquets are held. Nearby is the **Atameken Ethnic Memorial Park** (6 Kabanbay Batyr Street), which features a 1.7-hectare model of Kazakhstan, highlighting many architectural and other interesting sites around the country. It is open from 11am to 11pm. The large **Central Park** occupies the wedge of land created by a 90-degree bend in the Esil River; it is very popular with the city's residents, offering peace, shade and some shelter from the dustiness of the streets—

the constant construction and perennial winds of the steppe often combine to make walking around town an unpleasant experience. Within the park are cafés, a **Fantasy World** with carnival rides, ponds and many nooks and crannies where people relax on benches or picnic under the trees.

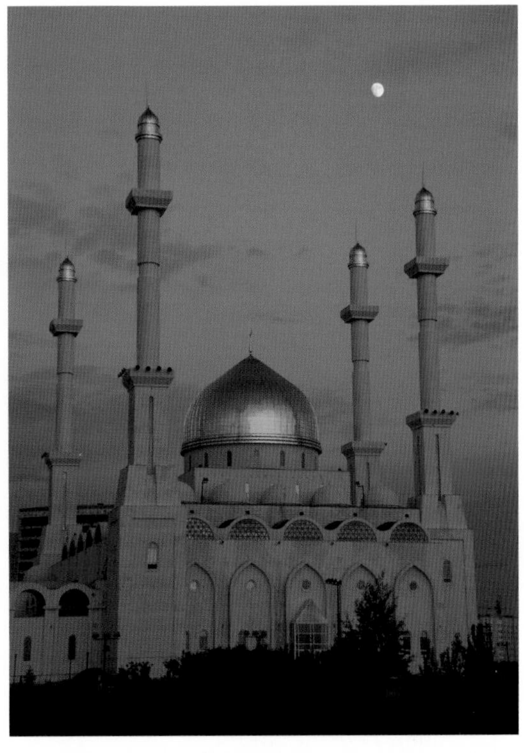

Cross the bridge over the Esil River and the large building facing you is the **Presidential Cultural Centre** on Republic Avenue, a large, white building shaped like a giant yurt with a blue dome, which houses a large library, a concert hall and a museum of Kazakh history. The museum in particular is well worth a visit, since it offers a very good overview of the origins and development of the Kazakh state. It features, among other things, a fascinating collection of gold dating from the Sak period, as well as many finds from excavations in Otrar, an original piece of the façade of the Mausoleum of Khoja Ahmed Yasawi in Turkistan, as well as that of the Aisha Bibi mausoleum near Taraz. There are works of art from modern-day Kazakhstan on the top floor.

In a building next to the Presidential Cultural Centre more than 3,000 paintings, sculptures and works of applied art are displayed in the **Museum of Modern Art**. Here too there are regular exhibitions of work by contemporary artists. The interesting **Saken Seyfullin Museum**, dedicated to the statesman, poet, writer and philosopher (1894–1938), is located farther north at 80 Auezov Street, just off Seyfullin Street.

The monument to the three renowned Kazakh jurists **Tole Bi**, **Ayteke Bi** and **Kazybek Bi** stands in front of the beautiful white building of the **High Court of Justice** on Beybichilik Street/Omarov Street. "The strength of a nation lies in its unity", reads the monument's pedestal in Kazakh, Russian and English. Also impressive is the monument to the **Pioneers of the Virgin Lands** (*Pamyatnik tselinnikam*) at 15 Munaytpasov Street.

Above: The Nur Astana Mosque bathes in the final rays of the setting sun as the moon rises over the steppe (Jeremy Tredinnick). Above left: An artist's drawing of Khan Shatyr, a colossal tent-shaped recreation complex scheduled for completion in 2008 (Courtesy of khanshatyr.com)

PRACTICAL INFORMATION

The dialling code for Astana is +7172. The main post office is at Mukhtar Auezov St/ Bigeldinov St, open Mon-Friday, 8am–7pm.

All credit cards are accepted by the cash machines at the entrances of Hotel Tourist and Hotel Okan Intercontinental. Good exchange rates can be obtained on Republic Square between Ivanov and Kenesary St.

Tuskiiz. Beginning of the 20th c. central Kazakhstan. Wool, cloth, velvet, felting, appliqué work, ending. 620 x 210 cm
Needlewoman Barlybayeva
CSM PR KPD 4611

TRANSPORTATION

Astana International Airport is located 25 kilometres to the south of the city (Infoline: 174 400/333 743). Several air links connect it with Almaty every day, and there are regular flights to most important urban centres throughout the country. Domestic flights are usually handled in the left terminal. Air Astana has daily international flights (except Saturdays) to Moscow, as well as non-stop flights to Frankfurt (four times a week) and Hanover (once a week), and twice-weekly flights to Istanbul. Lufthansa also connects Astana with Frankfurt.

Airline booking offices:

Air Astana, 9 Republic Ave, tel: 210 764—also in the Okan InterContinental Astana and Tourist Hotel.

Aerotur, 86/1 Abai Ave, 62 Beybichilik St, tel: 327 312—all Kazakh airlines plus Aeroflot and Pulkovo, open daily.

Central Asia Tourism, 30/4 Republic Ave, tel: 327 844/333 982, fax: 324 538, e-mail: cat-astana@alarnet.com—all domestic and international flights including connecting flights around the globe. Flight-hotel and flight-holiday packages available.

Aviaservicetour, 169 Kenesary St, Apt 3, tel: 215 455/216 550.

Premier, 52 Pobediy Ave, tel: 239 848/239 824.

East-West Travel Agency, Imanova St/Republic Ave, branch office at the airport, tel: 391 838/394 988.

The railway station is in the north of the city: go to the end of Pobedy Ave and into Birzhan Sala Avenue, where you'll find the ticket office (Information tel: 142 100/770 707/380

Above: Traditional rug and blanket making incorporates a number of different techniques and materials (Courtesy of the Central State Museum, Almaty)

6455
o. Berkutshi. Beginning of XX c. Pavlodar oblast. Black and white, matt photographic paper.

707/383 333). Other rail ticket desks are located at 44 Pobedy Ave, in the Okan InterContinental Astana, and in the Evrazia shopping centre (Ablai Khan Ave). Rail lines go in all directions from Astana—rail travel is the most popular way to cover the huge distances involved in most journeys, and thus the rail network is very good.

The Saparzhay Bus Station is on the right side of the square in front of the railway station (Information tel: 770 990/381 135, open 6am–12 midnight). Both suburban and long-distance buses leave from here: there are services to Siberia and the Urals, Almaty, Karaganda, Pavlodar, Oskemen (Ust-Kamenogorsk), Petropavl, Semipalatinsk and Kokshetau, among others.

Taxi fares in Astana are higher than those in Almaty. Drivers tend to try and get whatever they can from their customers, but there are fixed fares for certain distances within the city: short trips around town cost locals 500 tenge, but foreigners should expect to be charged 800 tenge. A fare from the airport to the city centre should not cost more than 2,500 tenge. There are plans for meter-taxis to be introduced in the near future.

Accommodation

There is huge interest in hotel properties in Astana, with luxury brands such as Four Seasons and Shangri-La all planning new establishments in the coming years. Currently there are two five-star luxury properties, one on each side of the river, and a burgeoning list of low- and mid-range business and tourist hotels. Following is a sample from across the range:

6435
Photo. Manufacturing of alasha – carpet. Eastern – Kazakhstan oblast.

Top and above: Two black-and-white photos document Kazakh life on the northern steppe in the early 20th Century (Courtesy of the Central State Museum, Almaty)

Rixos President Hotel Astana, No 1 Street, Administrative Centre, tel: 245 050, fax: 242 760, e-mail: astana@rixos.com, website: www.rixos.com—located next to the new embassy residential complex, and just a few minutes' walk from the Baiterek tower, this is the newest and most opulent hotel in the city (it opened in 2005), with 168 rooms, basement spa and pool, golden conference rooms and a superb lobby area where many important business deals are sealed. Rooms from US$259.

Okan InterContinental Astana, 113 Abai Ave, tel: 391 000, fax: 391 010, e-mail: astana@interconti.com, website: www.interconti.com—a 228-room, five-star international hotel near the "old" city centre, offering all the luxuries you'd expect from an InterContinental property. Deluxe rooms from US$299.

Grand Park Esil, 8 Beybichilik St, tel: 591 901/327 343, fax: 328 818, e-mail: reservations@grandparkesil.kz, website: www.grandparkesil.kz—a large, renovated four-star hotel opposite the old presidential palace. Rooms from US$155.

Mukammal Hotel, 53/1 Pobedy Ave, tel: 382 939, fax: 302 912, e-mail: info@mukammal.kz, website: www.mukammal.kz—located at the corner of Pobedy/Moscow St, a new glass-fronted business hotel. Rooms from US$83.

Comfort Hotel, 60 Kosmonavtov St, tel: 221 021, fax: 221 030, e-mail: info@comforthotel.com, website: www.comforthotel.kz—an established four-star hotel on the left bank of the Esil River close to Central Park, a quiet environment only 10 minutes away from "either" city centre. Rooms from US$37.

Radisson SAS Hotel, Sary Arka 4, tel: 990 000, fax: 992 222, e-mail: info.astana@radissonsas.com, website: www.radisson.com—located next to the bridge leading to the new city, this 181-room hotel is part of a large complex built on a two-level podium with four towers. Rooms from US$160.

Akku Hotel, 22 Rysulkova St, tel/faz: 324 199, fax: 324 199—rooms from US$110 including breakfast.

Egorkino, 93 Auezova St, tel/fax: 323 554—a small hotel decorated in an idiosyncratic but wonderful Russian style, with a friendly pub next door. Rooms from US$90.

9670
Er – tokym.- woman's saddle with harness. XIX c- beginning of XX c. East Kazakhstan. Wood, leather, metal, corals, beads.

Altyn-Dala, 19a Pionyerskaya St, tel: 327 749, fax: 320 978—centrally located near the finance ministry, a good-value two-wing hotel with new interiors. Rooms from US$60 including breakfast.

Tourist Hotel, 23 Republic Ave/Abai Ave, tel: 330 204/5/6/7, fax: 330 201/330 414, e-mail: akmtourist@mail.online.kz—a mid-range 273-room hotel dating to the 1970s. Rooms have been renovated and equipped with all necessities, and from the upper floors there is a beautiful view over the city. Rooms from US$57 including breakfast.

FOOD AND DRINK

In a city that's changing so fast it's impossible to keep up with all the epicurean delights on offer. Russian and Kazakh food, not surprisingly, are of a high quality here, but as the population becomes more cosmopolitan there are plenty of new cuisines to try—for a price. The following stalwart dining establishments get good reviews:

Restaurant Farkhiy, 3 Alikhana Bokeykhan St, tel: 321 899, fax: 320 406—next to the children's and youth palace not far from the bank of the Esil, built in the style of a yurt with a beautiful interior, good atmosphere, soft music and a wonderful summer garden, not forgetting the very good Kazakh cuisine at modest prices.

Pyetshikiy Lavotskiy, 130 Auezov St, mobile tel: (8) 701 533 5200—a rustic and tastefully decorated Russian restaurant with excellent cuisine and very attractive prices.

Egorkino, 93 Auezov St, tel: 323 878—bar-restaurant in the hotel of the same name, furnished in the style of a Russian village, with excellent Russian fare.

Agora, 113 Abai Ave, tel: 391 000—this café at the Okan InterContinental offers good shashlyk, pizza and fast food at astonishingly low prices considering the setting.

Isida, 119 Pobedy Ave, tel: 148 242—a large restaurant with international cuisine and live music.

Rancho Druzyeiy, 1 Gulmilyov St, tel: 376 094—a haven for those craving good old American food.

Venezia, Sime Tempore Mall, 9 Beybichilik St, tel: 153 906—the best Italian fare in Astana.

Left: Saddles and harnesses are often works of art in themselves, such is the importance of the horse in Kazakh culture (Courtesy of the Central State Museum, Almaty)

KAZAKHSTAN'S BUSINESS BONANZA

By *Anthony Robinson*

Central Asia's most dynamic economy first showed up on the financial world's radar screen when an obscure copper mining company called Kazakhmys (*mys* is the Kazakh word for copper) sold some of its shares on the London Stock Exchange in 2005. The timing was perfect. Soaring demand for energy and raw materials from China and India was forcing commodity prices to record levels. The chance to own a stake in 20 copper mines scattered across the Kazakh steppe but much closer to China than any other big producer proved irresistible—especially as gold, silver, zinc and other minerals were valuable by-products.

Within a year, Kazakhmys, restructured as a Western-style corporation registered in London, and with senior Western executives in key positions but still under the control of its powerful Kazakh majority shareholders, more than doubled in value to over US$10 billion. Then it bought its first oil field in Kazakhstan—and suddenly what 15 years ago was a collection of run-down mines supplying the Soviet war machine began to be seen as Kazakhstan's first home-grown, world-class resource company.

The rise of Kazakhmys is the most potent symbol of Kazakhstan's astonishing climb from obscurity to player in global markets in 15 short years. The pace is likely to accelerate over the next decade as oil output more than doubles to an expected 150 million tonnes a year—3.5 million barrels a day—by 2015, when big offshore oil wells in the Caspian Sea come on stream, and Almaty gets into its stride as a financial hub for Central Asia and beyond. By then Kazakhstan will also probably be the world's largest producer and exporter of uranium.

Other Kazakh companies took advantage of the powerful slipstream generated by the Kazakhmys IPO. As its share price soared, a raft of smaller Kazakh mining companies, together with the state oil and gas company, KazMunaiGaz, and two of Kazakhstan's three largest banks, piled in to London to take advantage of the euphoria. They raised over US$5 billion. Many more such deals are in the pipeline as Kazakh companies and banks gear up to finance strong economic growth ahead and foreign investors seek access to the new Caspian success story.

These are heady times for an economy that has enjoyed "Asian tiger" style growth of around 10 percent a year since the year 2000 and has the resources and ambition to continue indefinitely. Growth at this rate doubles the size of an economy every eight years—and the energy released is palpable not only in the big cities of Almaty and the capital Astana, but also in the new ports and rapidly growing oil towns of western Kazakhstan, which were sleepy backwaters in Soviet times. Cranes dominate the horizon and welding torches flash from high-rise buildings as armies of labourers, including immigrants from neighbouring central Asian states and Turkey, work around the clock to build luxury apartments, supermarkets, sports, health and educational facilities and gear up for massive, long-term infrastructure investments.

It is fair to say that the six-fold rise in oil prices since the US$11 per barrel lows of 1998 sparked off the recovery. But a series of financial, legal and tax reforms since the currency reform that ditched the Russian rouble and launched the tenge as the national currency in 1993, created the necessary framework to attract investment and underpin growth. Rising oil revenues have kept government revenues buoyant, with windfall oil money flowing into a specially created National Fund. Designed on similar lines to the Norwegian Oil Fund, over US$18 billion had flowed into the fund by April 2007 and been invested abroad to curb overheating at home and provide a reserve for future generations.

In future, more of the oil money will be used to fund ambitious domestic infrastructure projects. But the governor of the National Bank of Kazakhstan, Anvar Saidenov, has admitted that keeping inflation in check with so much ebullience around is a worry. Another concern is the growing skills shortage—which the government is seeking to address by obliging foreign investors to spend heavily on transferring skills to Kazakh citizens and attracting expatriates where necessary.

Over the next decade more than US$30 billion will be poured into the infrastructure needed to give the world's ninth largest country—with only 15.4 million people—the all-weather roads, railways and ports required to sustain future growth and capitalise on Kazakhstan's transit potential as a 3,000-kilometre "land bridge" between China and Europe. The Chinese government wanted to build a standard—European and Chinese gauge—railway through southern Kazakhstan so Chinese exports could run straight through to European and Middle Eastern markets.

Kazakhstan and China recently agreed to build new lines that could also join up with the existing north-south routes coming up from Uzbekistan and Turkmenistan. Once built, the new lines will link China with Europe through Kazakhstan, and provide an alternative to the traditional northern route through Russia, but shortening journeys within Kazakhstan will also make the whole rail network more efficient.

China is the big new factor in the Kazakh economy. In Soviet times the border was closed and foreign relations were the monopoly of Moscow. Now an energy- and resource-hungry China is particularly keen to invest in neighbouring Kazakhstan, which not only produces virtually every mineral Chinese factories need, but is close enough to deliver oil and gas by pipeline—even if the main oil fields are 3,000 kilometres away in the west of Kazakhstan. Chinese companies are also discussing new coalmines in northeastern Kazakhstan and new power plants and grid connections to deliver electricity to China.

But President Nazarbayev, who sees the US and the European Union as "strategic partners", is a consummate balancer between his two powerful neighbours, and trade and investment links with Russia are also developing fast, especially in areas like uranium mining, aerospace and nuclear engineering. The president wants to develop such high-tech sectors as part of a strategy of diversification through the creation of a "smart" economy alongside the traditional oil and minerals money-spinners.

Russia's strategic aim is to ensure that as much Central Asian oil and gas as possible flows through Russian pipelines, ports and railways. While sensitive to Moscow's desires, Kazakhstan is also developing its own alternative oil and gas export routes east to China and south to European markets through the Caucasus and the Black Sea.

With growth in the basic energy and resource sectors now assured, the government's focus has shifted to developing the "non-oil" economy. The government offers tax and other incentives to companies prepared to develop so-called "clusters" of related industries and suppliers and develop "special economic zones"—including new processing and assembly plants on the road and rail crossover points with China. The idea is to add value to Kazakh exports, and not just export raw materials and hydrocarbons in their raw, unprocessed state.

Over 80 percent of the economy is now privately owned, including the bulk of the oil industry where multinational oil companies have invested billions of dollars a year over the last decade and committed to as much as US$100 billion over the life of their long-term production sharing agreements (PSAs). Under these PSAs the hugely complex wells and processing equipment needed to treat the hot, sour Caspian oil will revert to the Kazakh state after 40 years—and in the meantime the government receives a rising stream of oil and gas tax revenues.

The national oil and gas corporation, KazMunaiGaz, will play an increasingly important role in developing future offshore fields under the Caspian Sea. Against a background of growing economic nationalism around the world, Kazakhstan appears to appreciate more than most the essential role played by the international oil companies, but a new tax system introduced three years ago raises the government share of revenues in new projects.

Meanwhile, President Nazarbayev is keen to turn Kazakhs into a nation of small shareholders, and called on his fellow citizens to take the US$10 billion he estimated that people were hoarding under their mattresses and invest in Kazakh companies. Impressed by the way Kazakhmys and others improved their governance in order to raise money from foreign investors, the president has also created two new state holding companies, Samruk and Kazyna, to bring Western-style management methods and transparency to the big state-owned monopolies, including the railways and KazMunaiGaz. Samruk, whose board of directors is chaired by Sir Richard Evans, former head of BAE, the UK-based Aerospace company, will also coordinate investment projects.

The president, who has been in power since 1986, engineered the seamless transition from Soviet state into a sovereign republic in December 1991, and has set a target for joining the world's 50 most productive economies by 2030. The intention is to make sure that the country's oil and mineral wealth is not just dissipated, but used to create a diversified, sustainable economy.

Diversification is a reality. Banking and increasingly sophisticated financial services have already become the fastest-growing sector of the economy—alongside the booming construction industry, which grew at four times the overall 10.6 percent growth rate in 2006—helping to push the gross national product (GDP) up to a record US$76 billion and creating many new jobs.

While the construction sector helped to soak up unemployment and start redressing the great shortage of housing, the banking sector opened up new credit lines for mortgages and consumer goods which boosted the housing market and retail sectors and created new perspectives for white-collar employees.

Roman Solodchenko, chief executive of Turan Alem Bank says, "the year 2006 was when Kazakhs threw off their suspicion of banks and borrowed to buy cars, take out mortgages and leverage their higher incomes." It was the year when the big six banks doubled their assets, earned record profits and borrowed billions of dollars abroad to finance their unprecedented growth.

Investors busy putting projects together inside the country say that although a construction boom, rapidly rising incomes and government encouragement for diversification are creating many new opportunities, the really big deals were sewn up in the 1990s when Kazakhstan was a faraway country, about which most people knew little—or did not like what they heard.

Western oil companies alone had the technology and deep pockets needed to develop the deep, high-pressure oil fields of the Caspian basin with its poisonous hydrogen sulphide gas and other dangerous and corrosive components. But the need for cutting-edge technology that only the oil majors could provide, and for heavy investment over a long period in huge, complex one and offshore projects, are key to explaining why the Kazakh economy has developed so well.

Negotiating complex, long-term production sharing agreements required huge effort on the government's part, but provided an invaluable learning curve for a newly independent state anxious to become part of the global economy and play by international rules. Under these pressures Kazakhstan created a tax and investment environment which, although still far from what investors want in certain areas, has helped to attract over US$45 billion in foreign investment.

Around 80 percent of this investment has been in the energy sector, but foreign investment has also been crucial in modernizing non-oil sectors of the economy. As a young man Mr Nazarbayev worked at the Temirtau steel plant. After the collapse of the Soviet Union the six-million-tonne capacity plant, like so many other Soviet era facilities, barely ticked over, surviving on barter deals and facing bankruptcy.

In 1995 Lakshmi Mittal, the London-based steel magnate, agreed to buy the plant and associated iron and coal mines, for little more than US$500 million.

After heavy investment, Temirtau now produces nearly five million tonnes of high-quality steel, mainly for export. AES, one of the biggest US-based coal and energy companies, picked up a similar bargain in northern Kazakhstan when it bought bankrupt coal mines and mothballed electricity plants near the Russian border, which it is now refurbishing as electricity demand soars.

With a fast-growing banking sector, rapidly rising incomes and local investors and pension funds looking for high-quality assets, the next stage of economic development is focused on turning Almaty into a regional financial centre similar to Singapore, Dublin and Dubai. Already way ahead of their neighbours in Central Asia, and with Kazakhstan becoming a potentially large exporter of surplus capital, Kazakh companies and banks are preparing to invest heavily in Central Asia and the Caucasus as well as Siberia and western China. Foreign companies too are increasingly viewing Kazakhstan as their springboard for regional investment.

President Nazarbayev talks about turning Kazakhstan into Central Asia's "economic locomotive." Considering how far Kazakhstan has come over the last 15 years, this is an ambitious but not an incredible goal.

Business Practicalities

Getting to Kazakhstan on business has become a lot easier thanks to streamlined visa formalities and an increase in flights to more cities. Air Astana, the national airline in which BAE has a 49 percent stake, is expanding as fast as it can train pilots and buy new planes. It also now offers its passengers "while you wait" visa applications to accompany the ticket. It is also possible to pick up a visa on arrival at Almaty airport. But be warned: in winter, when blizzards can last for days, air travel can mean long delays and surface transport is problematic with vast distances and towns and villages far apart.

International flights are multiplying—not just from European capitals but also from Dubai, Istanbul, Moscow, Thailand, Korea and Chinese cities. Most international flights head for Almaty, but oilmen aiming for Atyrau, capital of the oil-rich west of the country, can fly direct from Amsterdam—a lot more convenient than flying all the way to Almaty, close to the border with China, and then flying 3,000 kilometres back again on a domestic Air Astana flight.

Most business involving banks, lawyers and private companies is concentrated in Almaty, and is increasingly conducted along international lines, especially with the big banks and the increasing number of Kazakh companies quoted on the London Stock Exchange, AIM or other markets. But the way privatization happened in Kazakhstan means that wealth is highly concentrated in relatively few hands, and personal contacts are what count. The really big deals were done a decade ago when vast state assets were privatized and the mega-oil contracts were signed. The days when enterprising foreign entrepreneurs could buy up small, ailing oil fields, spruce them up and sell them are over. The future of oil lies offshore—and that means a lot of up-front risk and having KazMunaiGaz, the state oil company, as your partner.

Doing deals also requires dealing with the bureaucracy. And that means flying to Astana where officials are now to be found in the enormous new ministries and state institutions such as the powerful new holding companies, Samruk and Kazyna, whose aim is to make business less bureaucratic, and organized more like private business. The jury is still out.

Astana is a 90-minute flight, nearly 1,000 kilometres northwest of Almaty, but only a couple of hours drive from the mining capital, Karaganda. Big companies have satellite offices in Astana for regular government links and lobbying purposes, and that is where the embassies now are, although most keep consular and commercial offices in Almaty as well.

Although oil, gas, mining and banking is where the big money is, the government is keen to attract investors into non-oil and especially high-tech sectors and offers tax and other incentives for companies setting up in "special economic zones" and willing to help build "clusters" of related companies and suppliers. The aim is to diversify the economy, promote the development of small and medium businesses—and find niches that create jobs and can compete on world markets or fend off competition from Asia.

As for creature comforts, the international hotel chains are building hotels as fast as they can, tourism is a government growth target and the meat is great—lots of lamb and steppe-reared beef. Restaurants are springing up everywhere like mushrooms after the rain, and in summer, in leafy Almaty at least, you can sit outside under the trees in cheerful restaurants and cafés. In the cities and hotels the young in particular are happy to speak English, but Russian is almost essential and speaking a bit of Kazakh wins brownie points as national pride rises with the national income. And, as everywhere, a smile always helps.

The Central Steppe

Alzhir

It is sadly ironic that a town with a name suggesting a warm holiday resort on the Mediterranean was in fact a "detention camp for the wives of traitors to the homeland" (*Akmolinskiy lager zhyon izmennikov rodiniy*). Located near the village of Malinovka between Astana and Korgalzhin, it was here that the principle of family imprisonment was put into practice during the 1930s and 40s. Entire families disappeared: the men into prison camps from which most were never to return, the women and children into camps like **Alzhir**. It might not sound attractive as a tourism destination, but sometimes it is important to remember the past—if only to strengthen the resolve not to let it happen ever again.

Above: Migrating birds darken the sky at Korgalzhin (Lars Lachmann). Inset: A bright-eyed pratincole is alert to danger (Rolf Behlert). Right: The lakes of the Central Steppe are a magnet for bird-watchers (Dagmar Schreiber)

TENGIZ AND THE KORGALZHIN LAKES

The protected area of **Tengiz** and the **Korgalzhin lakes** lies 135 kilometres to the southwest of Astana. Almost 3,000 square kilometres in size, this vast water basin in the heart of the Kazakh steppe lies on the crossroads between two important bird migratory routes: the Afro-Eurasian and Indo-Central-Asian routes. The area is officially protected because of its unique fauna and flora, though lack of funding for the authorities makes it hard to protect even the central zone, resulting in frequent intrusions, the worst in the form of poaching.

Lake Tengiz is a steppe lake without an outlet. It takes in most of its volume from the Nura River, and the water is brackish. The lakes of Korgalzhin are fresh water, and are embedded in an immensely vast sea of reeds, home to tens of thousands of water birds. Ornithologists have counted almost 330 species of indigenous and migrant birds, almost 20 of which are threatened with extinction. Lake Tengiz hosts the northernmost and largest colony of pink flamingoes in the world, with up to 14,000 pairs making their nests out on the lake. On **Lake Sultankeldy** you can observe Dalmatian pelicans and great cormorants, demoiselle cranes, great egrets, great and little bitterns, ruffs, dozens of different types of geese and ducks, many kinds of waders, the sociable lapwing and black lark, and last but not least, numerous predatory birds such as the northern harrier, long-legged buzzard, lesser kestrel and steppe eagle, all of which populate the reserve.

In all, this is a paradise for ornithologists, but of course other animals live here too, such as the wolf and fox, marmot, ground squirrel and horse springer (a kind of jumping mouse), and even a few rare saiga antelope. The salt and feather grass steppe of this region contains more than 300 species of plant. The reserve's staff can organize either group or individual visits; the season starts in late April/early May when the tulips bloom, and ends in mid-September with the impressive autumn bird migration.

Both Korgalzhin, a rural settlement with 6,000 inhabitants where the administrative centre of the protected area is located, and Karazhar, a nearby location in the reserve proper, are accessible to individuals and small groups of up to 12 persons. You can book accommodation in one of the two modest but friendly boarding houses, including a sauna, for about US$10 per night. It is worth spending a few days here, in order to visit the very good collection of birds in the reserve's museum, and be briefed by the staff on the nature reserve's work. A wide range of interesting ornithological excursions can be organized from Korgalzhin. Karazhar has a guesthouse, a few bungalows and a yurt, equipped with communal shower facilities and a sauna. It has room for 34 people at a time, with full boarding on request. Apart from guided tours in English, boat and angling trips (outside the protected area) can also be organized. If you report directly to the reserve's administration or through the **Rodnik Society**, prices for guides and accommodation are moderate.

The Rodnik Society organizes excursions and accommodation in Korgalzhin and within the protected area; contact Lyudmila Luft, tel: (71637) 21043/21728, fax: (71637) 21043, e-mail: oorodnik@mail.ru or korgalzhin@kepter.kz; alternatively, contact Maxim Koshkin, tel: (7172) 314 486. Timur Iskakov (tel: (71637) 21064), a reservation worker who own a small boarding house on 9 Maxima Gorkovo Street, also arranges trips, but book in good time, particularly if you would like collection from the airport or railway station.

Above: The Karaganda Theatre is a grand edifice (Konstantin Kreiser)
Left: Camping near Tengiz Lake (Dagmar Schreiber)

KARAGANDA

A remarkable, spherical thorny plant named *karaghanik* grows in the central steppe region of Kazakhstan. It comes to life in stormy weather and whirls over the plain like a horde of rabid hedgehogs. **Karaganda** (Karagandy in Kazakh) owes its name to these plants.

Arrival in the town by train reveals nothing evil—the station has been newly renovated, and the view over the square in front of it, flanked by cultural and residential buildings, is impressive. The Karaganda of today is a typical steppe mining town, but it hides a tragic past: this was the place where, from 1929 until well into the 1950s, forced migrants and prison camp inmates were tasked with making one of the most forbidding environments of the vast Soviet empire fit to live in. Nowhere else in Kazakhstan was there such a concentration of prison camps as in the central steppe. The region's wealth in mineral resources was particularly effectively exploited with the help of prison labour. In 1833, an unsuspecting shepherd first discovered coal here. The owner of the plot, a Kazakh bey named Utep, sold it in 1856 to the Russian merchant Usakov, who started to mine the coal but unfortunately went bankrupt. The concession was bought by Frenchman Jean Carneau, and in 1907 it passed into the hands of a British company. The mine was nationalized after the October Revolution, but its value was not recognized and it was destroyed.

The mine was rebuilt within the framework of the Russian coal industry with the voluntary assistance of specialists from the Donbas (Ukraine's Don Basin). From 1929, the bulk of the work was done by prisoners; first came the dispossessed farmers, batches of political prisoners, the labour armies of deported Germans, and finally the German and Japanese prisoners of war. More than 800,000 inmates were put to work in a huge area called **Karlag** (*Karagandinskiy lager*). Part of the remains of this gruesome piece of history can still be seen today. The villages of Uzinka (after the Russian word *uznik*, meaning chained prisoner) and Dolinka, to the southwest of Karaganda, were originally built as prisons and inhabited by convicts.

Railways were rapidly built, also by forced labour, to transport the coal to the steel mills in the Urals. Karaganda gained importance in World War II, after the Germans occupied the Donbas, and after the war, German prisoners were engaged in the city's construction. The only part of Karaganda that qualifies as having some sort of charm, the Old City, was built during this period.

Karaganda's typical early dwelling style consisted mainly of dugouts and clay huts, which multiplied quickly since in the year of its establishment, the "city's" population grew to 70,000. Coalmining infrastructure, huge thermal electricity plants and residential areas are grouped around the mines, and Karaganda is an interesting destination for industrial romantics, for mining historians, and for those who like to explore man's exploitation of the land through machinery. The scenes of obsolete mining sites, high-tension cables and central heating pipes constructed above ground and with their cladding hanging below in strips, as well as abandoned blocks of flats, make for amazing, if macabre, photographs. What started in 1960 as a plan to revamp the industrial city and give it a human face, was grotesquely miscalculated. Greater Karaganda has lost almost half of its population—the area's administrative centre is left with hardly 400,000 inhabitants, down from 700,000 in the 1980s.

For a time, Kazakh returnees from foreign countries, the ***oralmany*** (Kazakh for "those who return home"), were settled in the abandoned residential blocks. They are the descendants of those who, during the 1930s, fled to Mongolia and China after losing their property and fearing forced resettlement. The influx of oralmany has caused some social problems, but to be fair Karaganda is actually a pleasant town now, with a large central park, tree-lined avenues and some friendly corners, such as its lovely neoclassical-style theatre, built by Japanese prisoners-of-war not far from the city centre. The **Karaganda Oblast Museum** (38 Yerubayev St) is worth a visit to understand the area's history and that of its gulags, though its displays are mostly in Russian. Close to the train station is a small but worthwhile **Fine Arts Museum** (33 Bukhar Zhirou), while an exploration of the central park will reveal an **Aqua Park** and **Ethnopark** where locals go for some fun.

PRACTICAL INFORMATION

The area dialling code for Karaganda is +7212. The **Gogol Library** on Yerubayev St stocks English, German and French books, and there are two internet cafés on the ground floor.

TRANSPORTATION

Karaganda has a relatively large airport that was extremely busy in better times. There are weekly flights to Frankfurt and Hanover, daily flights to Almaty, and several flights a week to Astana and Oskemen. The Air Astana office is at 31 Mira Ave, tel: 567 522/566 991. The CAT travel agency can be found at 55 Bukhar Zhyrau St, Office 29, tel/fax: 481 697, e-mail: karaganda@centralasiatourism.com.

Karaganda Railway Station is one of the most important rail hubs in the country. Regular southbound trains head to Almaty (six times a day), Taraz and Shymkent, and northbound to Astana (daily), Kokshetau, Kostanay and beyond. Travel time to Almaty is 18 hours, 10 hours by the Talgo express (daily). The bus station offers services to Almaty (a gruelling 20-hour trip), Astana, Pavlodar and Bayanaul, among other destinations.

ACCOMMODATION

Cosmonaut Hotel, 162a Krivoguza St, tel: 438 565, fax: 438 555, e-mail: hotelcosmonaut@nursat.kz, website: www.hotelcosmonaut.kz—a newly renovated, 46-room four-star hotel from the 1970s, conveniently located in the city centre near the park and botanic garden. Rooms from US$105.

Sozvezdie Hotel, 34 Stroiteley Ave, tel: 724 545, fax: 724 546—located in the southeastern part of the city centre near the Ethnopark, a three-star hotel with its own billiards hall. Rooms from US$50.

Dostar Alem, 28 Stroiteley Ave, tel: 400 400, fax: 740 202, e-mail: info@dostar-alem.kz, website: www.dostar-alem.kz—a new 41-room business hotel close to the Sozvezdie.

Chayka, 11 Michurina St, tel: 415 326, fax: 415 332—a small, nicely renovated hotel next to the cultural park. Rooms from US$26.

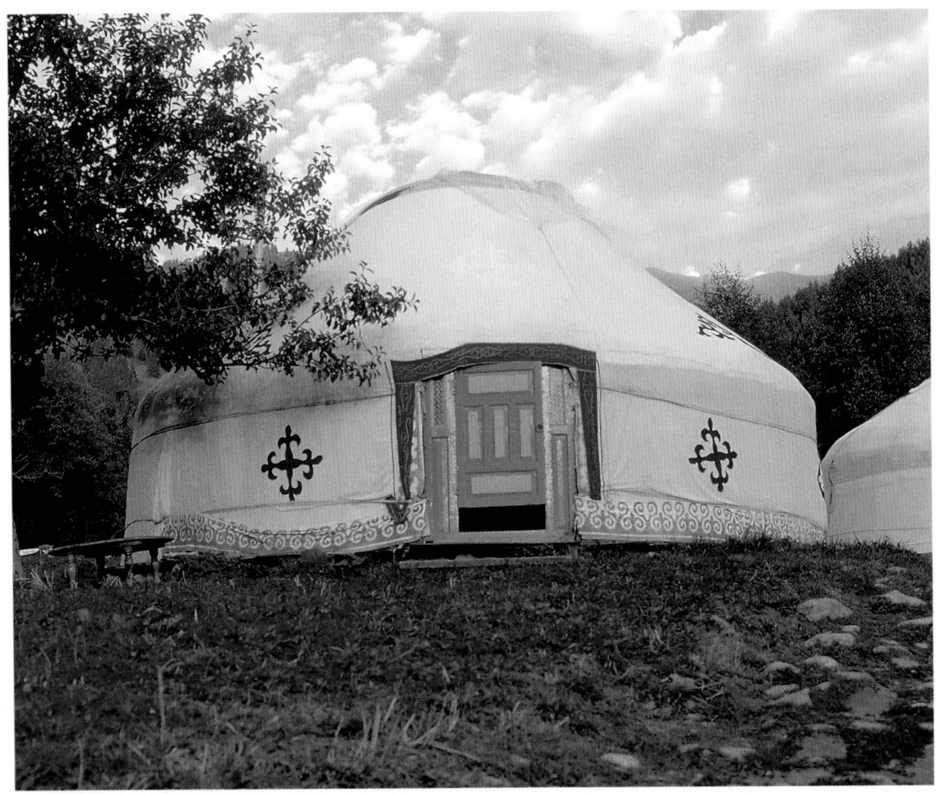

A well-made yurt will protect you from the heat of the summer and freezing temperatures in winter (O. Kormuschin)

THE HORSES OF TARTARY

Note: During the 19th century, what today is Kazakhstan's Great Steppe was known as the Kirghiz Steppe, and the peoples who lived there were generically—and mistakenly—called Kirghiz. The excerpt below was written during the author's journey across Kazakh territory; references to Kirghiz can therefore be attributed to Kazakh tribes.

The country now began to change its snowy aspect, and parti-coloured grasses of various hues dotted the steppes around. The Kirghiz had taken advantage of the more benignant weather, and hundreds of horses were here and there to be seen picking up what they could find. In fact it is extraordinary how any of these animals manage to exist through the winter months, as the nomads hardly ever feed them with corn, trusting to the slight vegetation which exists beneath the snow. Occasionally the poor beasts perish by thousands. A Tartar who is a rich man one week may find himself a beggar the next. This comes from the frequent snowstorms, when the thermometer sometimes descends to from 40 to 50 degrees below zero, Fahrenheit; but more often from some slight thaw taking place for perhaps a few hours. This is sufficient to ruin whole districts. The ground becomes covered with an impenetrable coating of ice, and the horses simply die of starvation, not being able to kick away the frozen substance, as they do the snow from the grass beneath their hoofs. No horses which I have ever seen are so hardy as these little animals, which are indigenous to the Kirghiz steppes; perhaps for the same reason that the Spartans of old excelled all other nations in physical strength, but with this difference, that nature doles out to the weakly colts the same fate which the Spartan parents apportioned to their sickly offspring.

The Kirghiz never clothe their horses even in the coldest winter. They do not even take the trouble to water them, the snow eaten by the animals supplying this want. Towards the end of the winter months, the ribs of the poor beasts almost come through their sides; but once the snow disappears and the rich vegetation which replaces it in the early spring comes up, the animals gain flesh and strength, and are capable of performing marches which many people in this country would deem impossible, a ride of a hundred miles not being at all an uncommon occurrence in Tartary. Kirghiz horses are not generally well shaped, and cannot gallop very fast, but they can traverse enormous distances without water, forage, or halting. When the natives wish to perform any very long journey, they generally employ two horses; on one they carry a little water in a skin and some corn, whilst they ride the other, changing from time to time to ease the animals.

It is said that a Kirghiz chief once galloped with a Cossack escort (with two horses per man) 200 miles in twenty-four hours. The path extended for a considerable distance over a mountainous and rocky district. The animals, however, soon recovered the effects of the journey, although they were a little lame for the first few days.

Colonel Frederick Burnaby, A Ride to Khiva: Mounted adventures in Central Asia, *1876,* The Long Riders' Guild Press (www.thelongridersguild.com)

WESTERN SARY ARKA AND THE TORGAY DEPRESSION

KOSTANAY

The mining town of **Kostanay** (Kostanai), founded in 1897 on the bank of the **Tobol River**, has predominantly Russian characteristics. The town mushroomed and obtained city rights only 14 years after its establishment. Between 1893 and 1895, it bore the name Nikolayevich in honour of the Tsar, after which it was renamed Kostanay, meaning "place for travel yurts". A handful of beautiful buildings from the time of its foundation have been preserved in the town centre, and they now house the university and some administrative offices.

Trade was the town's main activity in its early years, as its location at the ford across the Tobol made it strategically significant. Later, when the area's iron and bauxite ore reserves were opened up near **Rudniy**, the city became the centre for the region's expansive mining development. In the large mines of Sokolov-Sarbay iron ore is mined in open pits. Kaolin, titanium, zirconium, gold and brown coal are also exploited in the Kostanay area.

During the 1950s, large areas of virgin land around Kostanay were developed for wheat and other agriculture, and in 1984 an impressive-looking monument to the virgin land pioneers was erected in the regional capital. With the shift to agriculture, large food-processing enterprises were added to the city's industrial economy. Even today, the region can be described as highly cultivated, but from a tourist's point of view it is of little interest, except that Kostanay is the best starting point for a tour to the "great lakes" of the **Torgay Depression** and the **Naurzum Nature Reserve**.

PRACTICAL INFORMATION

The area dialling code for Kostanay is +7142.

TRANSPORTATION

Air Astana connects Kostanay with Hanover and Frankfurt (daily), there are daily flights to Moscow, Minsk and St Petersburg (with small Russian airlines), and there are daily flights to Astana, Karaganda and Almaty. The Air Astana office is at 95 Baytursinova St, tel: 546 875.

It is easier to reach Kostanay by train from Russia than from Almaty or Astana, since it is far closer to the Russian border than either of those cities. There are direct trains between the town and Ufa and Novosibirsk. It takes two and a half days to get from Almaty to Kostanay by train.

ACCOMMODATION

Hotel Aidana Plaza, 53 Tolstovo St, tel: 548 686, fax: 549 550—a good modern hotel close to the shopping district with rooms from US$52.

Hotel Tselinnaya, 95 Baytursinov St, tel: 543 213, fax: 545 960, e-mail: celinnay@mail.ru, website: www.hotel.kst.kz—a large, venerable, partly renovated hotel in the town centre. Rooms from US$12.

Hotel Medeo, 166A Baymagambetov St, tel: 545 945—double rooms from US$100.

Hotel Tourist, 149 Baytursinov St, tel: 544 904.

Hotel Tobol, 64 April 5th St, tel: 543 060.

The Felt Villages

Skilled craftsmen continue an ancient trade in the remote villages of **Akshyganak**, **Amantogay**, **Bestau** and **Koyandy** in the Torgay Depression. Here, felt is processed in the traditional manner. In Bestau, you can also visit the ruins of ancient mausoleums, built of unbaked clay, as well as remains of ancient settlements in the area surrounding the village. Tours are organized by the oblast's board of tourism in Kostanay, 85 Tarana St, tel: (7142) 575 330.

The Great Lakes

Five huge lakes—both freshwater and salt—occur in the Tobol River basin: **Kulykol**, **Zharsor**, **Babatkul**, **Kusmuryn** and **Tyuntyugur**. Given the most common type of trip advertised by local travel companies is for hunting, it seems the people in this area seem to think that foreign tourists are happiest when shooting wolves or flocks of water birds. Of course that may be understandable for those whose history and tradition revolves around hunting on the steppe, but for less bloodthirsty visitors there are many possibilities to stalk wildlife in a more peaceful manner.

The lakes have an immensely rich bird life, with Dalmatian pelican, whooper swan, two kinds of crane and several kinds of heron, as well as many marsh and other water birds making this region home. The largest lake, Kusmuryn, is 460 square kilometres of salty, shallow water, whose level fluctuates considerably through the seasons. The lakes can be reached from Kostanay—a tent and a few bottles of mosquito repellent are definitely recommended.

Naurzum Nature Reserve

The **Naurzum Nature Reserve** was established in 1930 and consists of wonderful forest and feather grass steppe, gnarled pines, sand dunes and reed-covered lakes. It is difficult to get there, and this has left it largely untouched and unharmed. Situated 230 kilometres to the south of Kostanay on the road to **Arkalyk**, the reserve comprises four zones: the

Following pages: The Zhezdi Reservoir provides much-needed water to the town of Zhezkazgan in the remote western steppe (Dagmar Schreiber). Inset: Typical forest and feather grass steppe in the Naurzum Nature Reserve (Konstantin Kreiser)

SAIGA SAGA

By *E.J. Milner-Gulland*

The saiga antelope is an iconic species of Kazakhstan's steppe. The Russian explorer Pishchevich, in a report to the St Petersburg court in 1884 remarked that, "in the lands of the Cossacks, there were so many saigas that in places their herds covered the whole steppe". Older people today still remember the huge migrating herds that came past their villages in the 1960s and 1970s, creating enormous clouds of dust as they went by. Nowadays, however, many children in rural areas of Kazakhstan have never seen a saiga, and even if you travel to the steppe specifically to see them, you'll be lucky to see more than a few tiny silhouettes on the brow of a hill, or tan-coloured dots in the distance as they run from the sound of your vehicle.

The saiga is the only remaining large wild herbivore of Kazakhstan's steppe and semi-desert. It is an extraordinary looking creature, the size of a goat with a pendulous nose (particularly in rutting males), huge dark eyes, and a strange flowing gait with the occasional leap into the air to look for danger. Males have translucent amber horns. They are nomadic, and undertake spectacular seasonal migrations from their wintering grounds in the clay deserts of the south to the more northerly lush steppe pastures that they graze in the summer. The population in central Kazakhstan can cover 1,000 kilometres in each direction, from the Moyinkum Desert south of the Chu River in the winter to the Karaganda region in the summer. On the way, they stop to give birth in huge aggregations—which used to number tens of thousands of animals—where the calves lie still for the first few days of their life, waiting for their mothers to return morning and evening to feed them.

These aggregations are an astonishing spectacle, visually as they fill the steppe for several kilometres in every direction, and aurally, with the honking noise of the mothers returning to look for their calves. Calves spring up from under your feet as you walk through the aggregation, invisible against the brown of earth and plant tufts until you are almost on top of them. To visit a saiga aggregation, as our colleagues at Kazakhstan's Institute of Zoology do each year to monitor the saiga's breeding success, is a true privilege, particularly as disturbing saigas during their breeding period is forbidden except for research purposes.

The saiga's story is intimately entwined with Kazakhstan's political history. By the end of the 19th century, it had been very heavily hunted for recreation, meat and particularly for its horns, which were sold to China for traditional medicines. The horns are highly prized for their fever-reducing properties, and are found in many of the same preparations as rhino horn. Like most other large game animals, its population was reduced to near extinction by the 1920s. But the advent of the Soviet Union era brought gun control, the closure of the border with China, strict game management and collectivization. The saiga is an incredibly resilient species, adapted to the harsh conditions of the steppe, with frequent mass mortalities in hard winters. This means that they are unusually rapid breeders—adult females routinely produce twins, and they start breeding in their first year of life. So unlike many other species, the saiga bounced back as soon as the hunting pressure was off, such that by the 1950s there were about a million of them and the Soviet state reopened hunting. This time it was highly regulated, state-controlled, and based on scientific advice.

Saigas remained common until the collapse of the Soviet Union. In the mid-1990s, Kazakhstan de-collectivized its agricultural sector, and overnight many rural people were left without a livelihood and with no option but to hunt saigas. At the same time, saiga management collapsed through lack of funds and the Chinese border reopened after 70 years, providing a ready market for commercial hunters. Within four years, the saiga population had halved, and it went on halving every year until around 2003.

International concern then led to the species being listed on the World Conservation Union's Red List as Critically Endangered, the highest possible category of threat of extinction. Things looked very gloomy for the saiga. However, a number of international organizations got involved, especially in supporting the anti-poaching work of the saiga management authorities. The Kazakhstan government has also started to invest heavily in saiga conservation, and is now working with international partners to designate large protected areas. These are aimed at protecting the broader ecosystem, but the saiga is one of the flagship species.

Initiatives involving local people are still patchy, and there is much to do to help rural communities themselves understand the value of conserving this species that is so emblematic of their nomadic heritage. But numbers seem to have stabilized, at least in the short term, and the saiga may yet become a conservation success story. To have twice gone to the brink of extinction in as many centuries, and to have

twice bounced back to take its rightful place in the steppe ecosystem would be an unrivalled feat. The threats on the horizon are huge—from growing demand for horns as Chinese incomes rise to infrastructural development on the steppe—but for now we can be optimistic and look forward once again to the opportunity to marvel at the saiga spectacle.

E.J. Milner-Gulland has been working on saiga ecology and conservation for 17 years, based at Imperial College London and collaborating with scientists in the countries where saigas live. The Saiga Conservation Alliance was set up by this group of collaborators in 2006, as an international network for anyone who cares about the saiga antelope. Its website can be found at www.saiga-conservation.com

Top: A wolf's tracks cross those of its saiga prey. Above left: A newborn saiga's best chance of survival is to hide and remain motionless. Above right: An adult's horns pierce the evening sky (Edda Schlager x3)

largest and a smaller one adjacent to it are located at the heart of the Torgay Depression, surrounding the freshwater lake of **Ulken Aksuat** and the saltwater lake of **Zharman**, as well as a few other smaller bodies of water. Two more zones are situated at a slightly higher level in the foothills of the **Sypsynaghash Valley** and stretch as far as Russia.

Originally, this protected area covered 3,200 square kilometres, but unfortunately it has been reduced in size by almost three-quarters. UNESCO is endeavouring to unify the Tengiz and Naurzum Nature Reserves as a protected biosphere.

ULYTAU

The region of **Ulytau** (Great Mountains) to the north of **Zhezkazgan** occupies a prominent place in the history of the Kazakh nomads. Archaeologists have found numerous remains of human settlements in this region, dating from as early as the Bronze Age. **Mount Ulytau** was a meeting place of the Kazakh khans for 400 years.

Looking at the mountain range, which gradually rises from the steppe, one can easily imagine why this particular spot was selected for important councils and actions. With an abundance of lakes, springs and rivers, the landscape is one large oasis in the steppe. Its appearance and characteristics give it a certain heavenly aura that would have appealed to the tribal leaders. Ulytau is not just the geographical centre of Kazakhstan, but was also of great importance for the ancient Kazakhs as the origin of the **Torgay River** and the **Sarysu Basin**. The steppe mountain range stretches over 350 kilometres from west to east and over 210 kilometres from north to south. Its highest peak is **Mount Akmeshit** (1,133 metres). In the second half of the 15th Century, the leaders of the three Kazakh tribal hordes and numerous subordinate tribes came together here for a great *kurultay* and sealed their unification. The inscriptions of all the tribes' coats of arms (*tanba*) on the memorial stone of **Tanbalytas** are a sign that this alliance was meant to last forever.

Among the numerous ancient tombs in the Ulytau area one is particularly significant: that of Zhu-Chi (Juchi) Khan, the eldest son of Genghis Khan. The 13th Century grave, built with baked clay tiles, has been preserved in good condition; according to age-old tradition, the sarcophagus in the inner part of the tomb is still supposed to shelter Zhu-Chi's remains.

ZHEZKAZGAN

During the 1930s only around 3,000 nomads lived in this region, in the **Kengir** aul, making it the most thinly populated area in all Kazakhstan. An aerial view reveals nothing but bare, red-brown soil. Then, out of nowhere, two vast lakes appear, along with traces of a settlement. A large town can be discerned on the bank of the snaking northern lake—this is **Zhezkazgan**, situated in the middle of the steppe, but nevertheless provided with a plentiful supply of water from the huge **Kengir and Zhezdi reservoirs**, which stand in sharp contrast to the bare, dry steppe scenery. The reservoirs were built in the 1930s to supply the industry, population and embryonic agriculture of the region.

The most central and also the remotest town in Kazakhstan is hardly ever visited by tourists. It is as though every effort has been made to make the place as forbidding to visitors as possible. Only one flight and one train every couple of days links Zhezkazgan to other parts of the country, and the railroad ends here. Bus trips from the "nearby" cities of **Karaganda** to the northeast and **Kyzylorda** to the southwest are a nightmare, if only because of the poor state of the roads. Also places of interest are scarce in Zhezkazgan. The surrounding land is far from idyllic, and the continental climate is at its most extreme.

Indeed, it is probable that no one would have settled this region if it weren't for its rich mineral resources. Not for nothing were convicts sent to work down the mines here—in fact Kazakhstan's largest prison camp was located here. It was designed for 70,000 people, but due to the difficult supply lines it never functioned at full capacity. Copper and coal reserves have, however, resulted in increased interest from mining conglomerates, and even foreign companies are being attracted to the promise of oil prospects. A railway linking Kyzylorda to Zhezkazgan has long been planned, and should this project materialize, hardy tourists will no doubt start to arrive in greater numbers.

THE NORTH

North of Astana, on entering the southern Siberian Lowlands, the steppe changes its visage, becoming a rich landscape of water, hills and forest, a glorious and versatile region that is one of Kazakhstan's most photographed areas. The area between Astana and Kokshetau is known as the "Kazakh Switzerland", and though its hills can hardly compete with the Alps in grandeur, the picturesque scenery of rocky peaks, forested slopes and jewel-like lakes rightly attracts tens of thousands of holiday-makers from Kazakhstan and Russia throughout the summer months.

KOKSHETAU

The name **Kokshetau** means Blue Mountain—although there are no peaks, blue rivers or sea close to this northern town. Like all Kazakh names, however, it originates from the reality of its surroundings, and in this instance those are some distance away: in clear weather, the blue-tinged skyline of a ridge of hills can be discerned on the horizon. Kokshetau is located on the edge of the northern foothills of the low mountain range of the same name. It is a region rich in forests and lakes, and its highest peak, Mount Kokshetau in the **Burabay-Kokshetau National Park**, reaches to 947 metres (the Kazakh name Burabay has officially replaced the Russian **Borovoye**, though you will hear and see both names used). The town was once the administrative centre of Kokshetau Oblast until the territorial reshuffle of 1997, when the North Kazakhstan Region was created with its administrative centre in Astana. In doing this the new capital gained a beautiful hinterland—and a weekend leisure spot where its resident's could escape the city and relax in natural splendour.

You can still see reminders of Kokshetau's role as a centre of provincial administration. The broad streets with pot-holed pavements are flanked by magnificent Soviet-style buildings, a relief to the eye after the desolate uniformity of multistorey residential blocks. The many abandoned industrial complexes in the city and on its outskirts contribute little to making the place look more cheerful—Kokshetau has suffered more than many other towns in the north since the exodus to their homeland of a large number of ethnic Russians after Kazakhstan's independence—the town is estimated to have lost one-fifth of its population.

Unfortunately, Kokshetau is used only as a stopping-off point for tourists on the way to Burabay and Astana, and has little tourism potential of its own.

BURABAY (BOROVOYE)—THE "KAZAKH SWITZERLAND"

Borovoye, now renamed **Burabay**, lies over 200 kilometres to the northeast of Astana and almost 100 kilometres to the south of Kokshetau—which by Kazakh standards makes it very accessible. It's a name that is treasured by all Kazakhs, referring not only to the famous lake that lies in the middle of the mountains, but to the whole **Burabay-Kokshetau National Park**. Only 630 square kilometres in size, it is one of the smaller nature reserves in Kazakhstan. Burabay is dominated by its large, clear, spring-fed lakes, and the deciduous ash and birch forests that surround them (the Russian name Borovoye signifies a landscape covered by *Bor*, or "little forest"). The park owes its clean, fresh air to these woodland trees—which in turn has granted it a reputation as a health resort, together with its mild climate and soothing scenery. Small guesthouses, hotels and children's holiday camps are scattered everywhere, but in spite of this there is plenty of pristine landscape still remaining, and even during the high season between June and September there are plenty of places to find peace and solitude.

September is considered the best month to visit Burabay: the birch trees are turning a fantastic golden-yellow, the swarms of mosquitoes have disappeared, the water in the lakes is still warm enough for swimming and there is space in the guesthouses. Moderate temperatures invite long walks and climbs up the bizarre-looking rock formations. One of these, in the shape of a camel lying down, gave the area its Kazakh name: Burabay, meaning "rich in camels".

There is, of course, a legend connected with the Burabay rock: once upon a time there lived a beautiful white camel that would change its shape whenever an enemy approached, fly onto the mountain and warn the people with loud bellows. In this way, it protected the local population from danger. One day, however, the camel was on its way to the waterside to drink when it met the hunter Kasym Khan, who considered the fine animal merely as game and shot an arrow at it. The wounded beast began to bellow and sank to its knee, while still trying to reach the watering place, but the merciless hunter kept shooting arrows at it and mortally wounded it. The camel never reached the waterside, died on the spot and turned into a stone hill, from that day forward known as *bura*, or camel. These days, hunting is strictly forbidden, and 223 different species of bird and 54 different species of mammal inhabit the national park.

The legend of the region's formation tells how God granted the Kazakhs this wonderful landscape after they had complained about the scanty steppes, which had been allotted to them during the world's creation. Roaming through the forests and climbing up to vantage points to take in the view, it's easy to imagine the Kazakhs of old, believers in the spirits of nature, coming together on this holy spot and wondering how these formations had come into existence with their shapes of camels and fortresses, witches and sleeping knights. It is only natural that each peculiar rock formation should be given its own magical tale of origin, such as the following:

In an aul there once lived a batyr who knew no fear. When the **Zhungars** invaded the area one day, the batyr called upon his peers to march against the enemy with him, but none heeded his call, since feuds between the various tribes forbade them to act as one. Therefore, the young warrior took his horse, put on his helmet and battle gear and marched towards the battlefield on his own. He lost his eyesight in the fight, was severely injured but never once backed away. Inevitably, he could not hold out against the overwhelming enemy host on his own, and when finally his mighty body collapsed, the batyr sank into an eternal sleep. There he lies to this very day, in the forest of Borovoye, his face towards the sky. From a great distance one can discern his profile while looking at the hill called **Zheke Batyr**—the Sleeping Knight.

If you want to spend some time in Burabay during the summer, make sure you make your reservation well in advance, since all accommodation is usually fully booked weeks or months ahead of time. In comparison to other areas in Kazakhstan, Burabay is well developed; not only are there parking areas and campsites, but the walking trails have even been signposted. The most popular destination, **Lake Borovoye**, can be circumnavigated at a leisurely pace in a single day. Circular in shape, it boasts many bizarrely shaped—and named—rocks, from Zhumbaktas ("Unresolved riddle", but also called the Sphynx) to its nearby counterpart Okzhetpes ("Unreachable for arrows"), as well as the Three Sisters and the Bastion. A climb up the rocks between Lake Borovoye and **Bolshoye Chebachye** is rewarded by a wonderful view over the two lakes.

Climbing the highest peak in the area, Mount Kokshetau, is not an easy venture. It is very rocky and, relatively low as it is, the difference in altitude should not be taken lightly. But the view from the summit is breathtaking, and apart from the lakes already mentioned, you can also look out over the **Maloye Chebachye** salt lake, the picturesque lake of **Shchuchinsk** and a multitude of smaller steppe lakes. The view also includes the Camel and the Sleeping Knight. Hikers in good condition can walk around the lakes of Bolshoye and Maloye Chebachye in a single day. It takes half a day to walk to the beautiful forest lake of **Katarkol** and its eponymous village. The multitude of children's holiday camps, however, does not make this walk a quiet one during the summer. Lake Borovoye is the most popular for swimming, with a lovely pebble beach under age-old pine trees. To be alone, try escaping to Lake Bolshoye Chebachye. The water is crystal-clear, and there are hidden bays that can only be reached from the rocks above. The view towards the east differs greatly from that of Lake Borovoye. From here, you are looking out over flat, unforested plain. This is steppe in its most classic form. The eastern shore of Lake Shchuchinsk and almost the entire shore of Lake Zhukey on the southeastern border of the park are also good for swimming. The latter is situated to the east of the forest-covered **Mount Berkut**, which is easy to climb. Its opposite shore, however, is completely unforested. A little-known secret is the small lake of **Karasu** (Karashye in Russian), located two kilometres to the northeast of Lake Shchuchinsk. The president has a remote, idyllic holiday home here—proving he definitely knows where his country is at its most beautiful.

However, the government has recently chosen Lake Borovoye to be the site of one of three major tourist developments, to be built as part of a five-year tourism plan. The **Borovoye Lake Resort** will commence construction in 2008, offering modern, high-tech hotel and leisure facilities in a huge project based around the lake. The idea of buzzing jet-skis and all the other trappings of the modern resort model so popular around the world today will no doubt have its supporters, but gone will be the possibility of tranquillity in that particular natural Eden and, worryingly, questions about the results of any environmental impact assessments remain unanswered, raising the question of how a large increase in infrastructure and volume of people, with the consequent rise in air, noise and water pollution levels, will ultimately affect the environment of "Little Switzerland".

Preceding pages: Lake Borovoye is one of Kazakhstan's most picturesque—and popular—tourist destinations; its clear water is surrounded by thick forest and fascinating rock formations (Christopher Herwig)

PRACTICAL INFORMATION

The area dialling code for Burabay/Borovoye is +71630. There is a range of accommodation available in villages around the region, but demand is huge and reservations are essential, unless you want to camp around the lakes—a good option if the weather is fine.

TRANSPORTATION

An early morning train leaves from Astana for Shchuchinsk, the nearest station to the lake area, and there are trains from Kokshetau too. From the station you can catch a minibus or taxi to Burabay village. You could see the main sights in a day trip, returning by train in the evening, but this would be doing the park an injustice.

ACCOMMODATION

Luxury accommodation does not, so far, exist in Burabay-Kokshetau National Park. This will change when the new resort complex opens, but for now mod-cons are the exception not the rule, and prices are accordingly low.

Saturn Pensionat, Borovoye, tel: 71899, fax: 71851—a new European-style building on the lakeshore; 11 rooms for 26 guests, good cuisine, sauna, excursions, boats, angling equipment and skis for rent. Double rooms from US$74 with breakfast.

Hotel Nursat, Borovoye, Kenesary St (opposite the museum of natural science), tel: 71301/72401, fax: 71504—a new hotel with rooms and suites for 35 guests, restaurant, sauna, swimming pool. Prices from US$20–75 with breakfast.

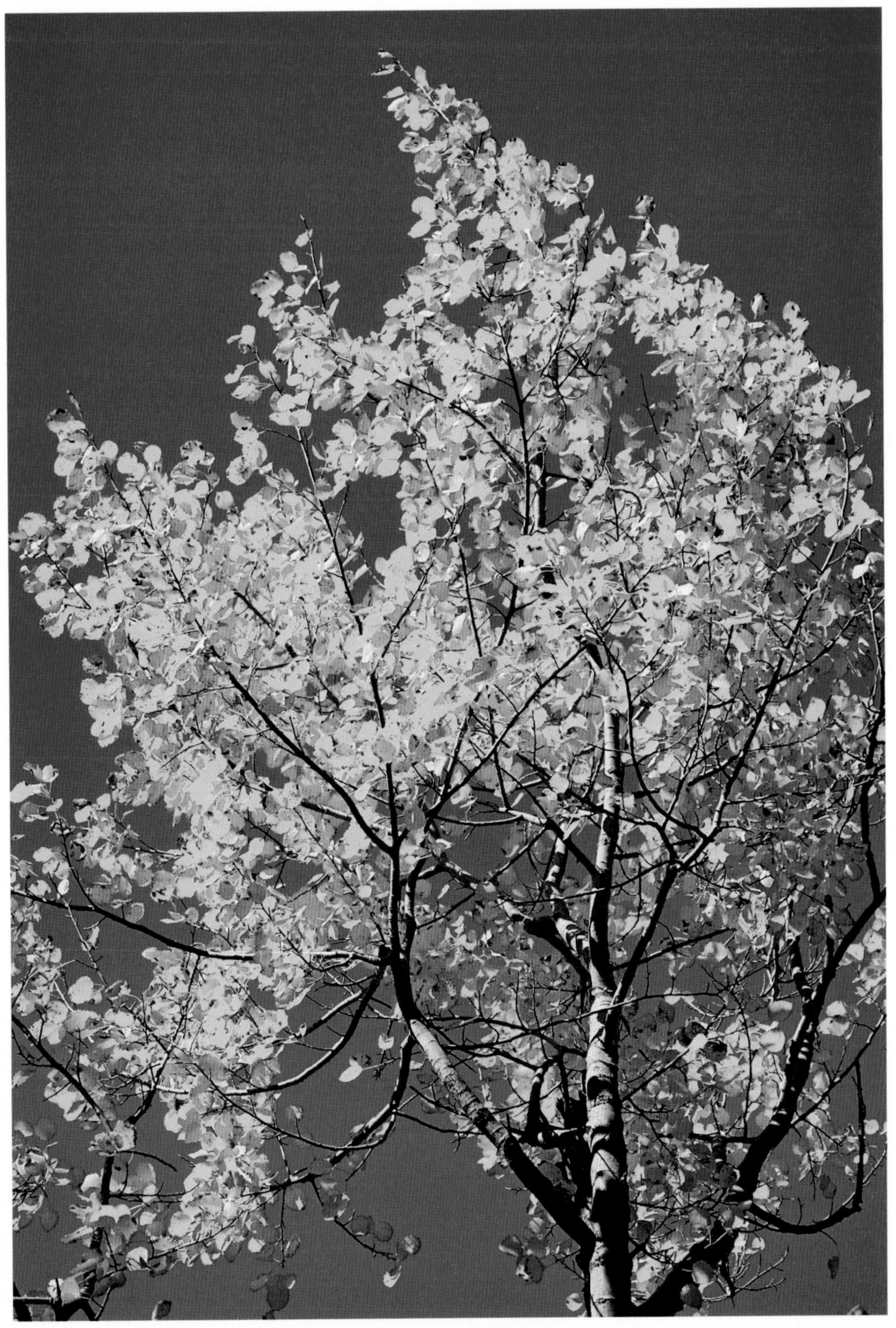

Above: The golden colours of autumn turn Kazakhstan's lowland forests into visual feasts (Vladimir Tugalev). Left: The Sphinx, or Riddle Rock, on Lake Borovoye (Dagmar Schreiber)

Hotel May Balyk, tel: 74003, fax: 74621, reservations possible through Astana (7172 216615) or Almaty (7272 632484)—a quiet stone-built hotel located between lakes Bolshoye Chebachye and Telekol, with room for 65 people in the main building and bungalows; good Russian cuisine, many sports facilities, mud-bath treatment on request. Rooms from US$15 with breakfast, full board available.

Sanatorium Zelyoniy Bor, tel: (71636) 90294, fax: 45098—a renovated Soviet sanatorium on Lake Shchuchinsk, nine kilometres from the town of the same name on the opposite bank of the lake. Health treatments on request, room for 262 people divided between two stone buildings and two bungalows, wonderful views, beach, wide variety of sports facilities, including horse riding. Rooms from US$16.

Akmolaturist Travel Agency Guesthouse, Borovoye, 50 Kenesary St, tel: 71511, reservations through Akmolaturist, 23 Republic Ave, Astana, tel: (7172) 330 101, fax: 330 201/330 414, e-mail: akmtourist@rambler.ru—a very clean inn with modest prices right on the crossroads entering the town from Shchuchinsk; it is self-service, with a kitchen available.

The Eastern Sary Arka

Between the foothills of the **Altai** and the northern shore of **Lake Balkhash** is a landscape where the Sary Arka pays full tribute to its name. The topography consists of yellow, sometimes reddish ridges, in some places strongly fissured. It gradually rises from the **Ertis Plain** to the highest level of the Kazakh steppe, the **Aksorang** on the **Kyzyltas Plateau**, and from there gradually declines to Lake Balkhash, or **Ak Tengiz** (White Lake) as the Kazakhs used to call it.

The land in the middle reaches of the **Shagan River** is a typical steppe zone, with low hills that are the perfect home for large herds of horses. This typically Kazakh grassland has a rich but haunting history. Here the national poet **Abai** lived and worked, along with the poet and philosopher **Shakarim** and the writer and playwright **Auezov**. Here also, two cultures met with great results, one the ancient nomad tradition, the other the European heritage borne by the young Russian intellectuals who were exiled here. Medicinal herbs used to be gathered in the **Karaul Mountains**, and the milk of the local mares was considered particularly healthy.

Until 1948, that is, when everything changed. The Soviet decision to use this region as an atomic test zone, and the subsequent disasters that turned it into a death zone, deprived it of promise, and almost destroyed its future. The Kazakhs living here have been through a heartbreaking ordeal. However, most of them have stayed put, and some of them continue to fight the prejudice and preconception that this part of Sary Arka is uninhabitable and unfit for tourism. The state has taken much care of late to make this region, so important to all Kazakhs, fit to live in once more.

BORLI AND THE AUEZOV MONUMENTS

From the East Kazakhstan Region town of **Semey** (Semipalatinsk) it is a long drive south through the steppe to the heights of the **Kashikbay Pass**, from where the view stretches endlessly towards a distant horizon (when the weather is clear). The water that flows from a well at the foot of the "mountain" here is said to make your wishes come true.

After one hour's driving from Semey you arrive at **Borli**, an aul where, at the winter residence of Auez, a cattle owner, the great writer **Mukhtar Auezov** was born. His home, converted into a museum after the author's death, has been restored with the help of state funds, and a splendid mausoleum for his parents has been built nearby.

In the museum there is much to learn about the close territorial and spiritual family ties between the Auezovs and the Abais. Both writers received their inspiration from their homeland, as the museum shows, for example with the carefully fitted-out model of the double yurt in which Auezov's first play, the 1917 drama of *Enlik and Kebek*, was performed. The tragic love story of Enlik and Kebek is also a story about the hostility between Kazakh tribes that weakened the nation and ultimately led to its historic defeat.

Enlik and Kebek belonged to two different tribes, the Tobykhty and the Naiman, which were engaged in a feud. The explicit ban by the tribal elders did not prevent the two from falling deeply in love with one another, but since it was impossible to live among their fellow tribespeople, the young couple fled to **Mount Chingistau** and went into hiding in a nearby cave. Here, Kebek bore a son. Enlik fed his small family on meat from the animals he hunted, but while out on a hunting sortie he was spotted, and their hideout was discovered. Once more the two lovers had to flee, riding on horseback with their baby in a cradle. In the rush, however, the cradle slid from the horse. The parents stopped to save the child, and were overtaken and caught. Their subsequent punishment was horrifying: Enlik and Kebek were sentenced to be drawn and quartered, and their baby son was thrown off the highest peak of Chingistau into a ravine. Some say that at sunset one can still hear him crying.

There is a monument to the memory of Enlik and Kebek at Km Stone 117 on the right-hand side of the road from Semey to **Karaul** and **Ayakoz**. Hundreds of ribbons have been wound around its lower part, and it has become something of a pilgrimage site.

Zhidebay and the Abai and Shakarim Monuments

Two white towers point skywards from the steppe on the edge of the aul of **Zhidebay**, 180 kilometres to the south of Semey. They are visible from up to 20 kilometres away, but coming nearer, the entire complex of monuments, including the double mausoleum for the national poet **Abai Kunanbayev** and the philosopher **Shakarim Kudayberdiyev** come into view. Both men's fate is closely linked to Zhidebay: Abai spent the winter months here during his childhood, while his younger relative Shakarim was brought up by his father's family.

Zhidebay was the winter residence of Abai's father, a wealthy Kazakh who had been authorized to act as administrator with the title of sultan over a large area between **Karkalinsk** and Semey. It was a very lively home; the family was closely intertwined and Abai liked to invite his Russian friends from Semey. After his eldest son Ospan had married, the Kunanbayev patriarch gave him the estate and moved with the rest of the family to the **Akshoky Valley**, 50 kilometres away. After Ospan's death, Abai took over the estate and went to live there with his three wives, Dilda, Aygerim and Erkezhan. His marriage with

Dilda had been arranged without his agreement and in spite of the fact that he was in love with another girl. Aygerim was his great love in later times and this marriage had been his dearest wish. As for Erkezhan, she had been Ospan's wife and, in line with steppe tradition, came under her late husband's brother's care. Mukhtar Auezov gives a wonderfully gripping and colourful description of Abai's life in conflict-ridden 19th Century Kazakhstan in his renowned book *Abai's Way* (also known as *The Path of Abai*).

Today, the house of the Kunanbayevs is a museum in which numerous objects of the family's daily life are displayed. The books in particular show many interesting aspects of the lifestyle of a wealthy Kazakh family during the second half of the 19th Century.

The mausoleum stands nearly a kilometre off the road. Even on days when it is supposed to be closed, there is always someone in the aul ready to open it and invite visitors on a guided tour. An ideal guide is Gizat Kuzembayev, a highly respected aksakal who is the head of the Abai Museum. At the age of 21, he took part in the storming of Berlin—he will proudly show visitors a copy of the book *Limits of Courage* by a Belarusian writer, which features a description of how he, Gizat, saved the life of his commander in Belarus at the age of 19.

In 1995, the double mausoleum, designed by architect **Bek Ibrayev**, was opened in the presence of President Nazarbayev and 20,000 other guests. It is 180 metres long and 60 metres wide. It is crowned by two elegant, tower-like mausoleums: the biggest is 37 metres high and nine metres in diameter, and dedicated to Abai; the smaller one, 35 metres high, is in honour of Shakarim, who perished in Stalin's purges in 1931.

Above: The ribbon-festooned monument to Enlik and Kebek. Left: Idiosyncratic architecture at the Abai and Shakarim double monument complex (Dagmar Schreiber x2)

The mausoleums stand on a structure shaped like a pyramid and composed of three stone plates on top of one another. The dark one on the bottom symbolises the ancient history of the Kazakhs, the pink middle stone stands for the life and times of Abai and Shakarim, and the white sandstone plate on top represents the present. An extraordinary library has been built inside the mausoleum's foundation. It receives daylight from above and forms a ring around an amphitheatre embedded in the foundation. Each year a recital competition is held here, for schoolchildren from the eighth to eleventh school years. The record was set by a schoolgirl who recited—by heart—400 poems and songs by Abai.

This unusual architectural complex is completed by a futuristic mosque, designed with moving simplicity and consisting of four round spaces, each crowned by a conical tower with the obligatory *mihrab* as their sole decoration.

The Centre of Eurasia

Also in Zhidebay, close to the home of the Kunanbayevs, there is a simple stone monument consisting of a circular block with a small pyramid on top. According to geographers, this is the **centre of Eurasia**. The location is supposed to have an extraordinary level of positive radiation. Some historians claim that this concentration of energy explains why the region has produced so many geniuses. Whether you believe this or not, it can do no harm to stand here for a while and let a bit of energy flow through you.

Bayanaul Nature Reserve

Draw an imaginary line between Astana and Semey, and at the halfway point, 180 kilometres southwest of Pavlodar, you will find the **Bayanaul Nature Reserve**. Kazakhs call it "Nature's Museum"; it has charming lakes, mountains, pinewoods with strangely formed trees, bizarre rock formations, steppe—there is a bit of everything here, an idyllic coexistence in an area of only 450 square kilometres. The beautiful **Bayan**, a well-known figure in Kazakh folklore, was said to have set up her aul here. Many people, most of them young men, travelled from far and wide to see Bayan. Today, they come to admire the landscape rather than a woman's beauty, but nature puts on a wonderful show, and seems almost animated here. This is the reason why, according to general opinion, Bayanaul has produced so many famous Kazakhs, such as the academic **Satpayev** and the poet **Toraygyrov**. In 3–5 days you can visit everything worth seeing: the holy cave of **Konyr Auliye**, the **Kempirtas (Witch) Rock**, **Mount Akbet**—the area's highest peak, the **Soap Lake** and the **Satpayev Museum**.

Bayanaul is a popular leisure resort during the summer months, with its guesthouses and holiday camps filled with families enjoying Mother Nature's bounty. But off-season it is also worth visiting, and then it is an ideal place to relax. Bayanaul can be reached in four hours by bus from Pavlodar and in two hours from Ekibastuz. **Guesthouse Bayanaul** and the **Chayka Health Resort**, which belong to the Pavlodartourist travel agency (1 Toraigyrov St, Pavlodar, tel: (7182) 327101, fax: 317101, e-mail: pturist@pavlodar.kz) can be booked for as little as US$10 per night with full board. They are located on the bank of Lake Zhasybay, 15 kilometres from the village of Bayanaul, and have boats for rent.

THE KARKARALY MOUNTAINS

Very few foreign tourists make it as far as the **Karkaraly Mountains**. They are far off the main roads, and there are no regular organized excursions there except for a few summer packages for Kazakhs in the few sanatoriums that still function. Though remote and with rather decrepit facilities, this is a wild and beautiful area, and in the 1960s and 70s the woods of Karkaraly were the site for many Pioneer (youth movement) camps and trade union homes.

Karkaraly is located around 200 kilometres to the southeast of Karaganda, three to four hours by car through the steppe along the trunk road to Ayakoz. The monotonous landscape is broken by the soaring eagles, buzzards, harriers and falcons that make this seemingly empty land their home. Along the way, a side road leads to the large salt lake of **Karasor**, known for the healing qualities of its water. The end of the journey is in sight when, 30–40 kilometres away the mountains, blue and full of promise, start glimmering on the horizon. As you draw nearer, you discover that they are covered with dense forest—a great contrast to the bare steppe hills that surround them. The highest peak gives the whole mountain chain its name: Karkaraly, rises to 1,400 metres high, and is so named because it looks like a *karkara*, a headdress for women. The legend goes that a young woman who fled in front of the groom she renounced threw her headdress off from her galloping horse. Immediately, the headdress transformed itself into a mountain chain, hiding the girl from the eyes of her pursuer, hotly intent on marriage, and allowing her to escape.

The 700-square-kilometre zone can be explored in a couple of days; the mountain slopes harbour bizarre-looking rock formations and an abundance of mushrooms and blackberries—as well as an even greater amount of mosquitoes. If these prove too ferocious for camping, try booking into the sanatorium located behind the building that houses the nature protection post, a small anthropological museum and a zoo, five kilometres before **Karkaralinsk**. It's slightly shabby accommodation, but the wonderful landscape and clean mountain air make up for the lack of creature comforts.

Following pages: Naiza mountain in the Bayanaul Nature Reserve (Vladislav Yakushkin)

North of Lake Balkhash

The immense mountainous steppe to the north of **Lake Balkhash** is among Kazakhstan's least developed areas. Here stands the highest peak of the Sary Arka, the 1,565-metre-high **Aksorang (White Prominence)**. From the air, you look out over a seemingly barren, empty landscape. A few red mountain folds rise from the desert, traces of mineral deposit workings can be seen, and a single road leads straight through the desolation.

Still, there is life here. A railway leads along the northern shore of Lake Balkhash, linking **Moyinty** with **Aktogay** and thereby with the main rail links Almaty-Astana and Almaty-Semey. The town of **Balkhash** on the lake's north shore is the **copper centre of Kazakhstan**, built in 1937 with the opening of the first mine. Here, 80,000 people make a living from copper—and the lake. In spite of the pollution caused by the town's industry, Lake Balkhash is still a rich fishing ground. This is obvious if you are travelling by train from Almaty to Astana; at the lakeside stations both old and young push forward on the platforms to offer catfish, pike-perch (sander) and carp to travellers. The smell of smoked fish fills the air, and along with the fish hawkers, beer sellers do good business as well—to travel by train well provisioned with fish and beer is a quintessential experience both in Russia and Kazakhstan. The quality of the fishing is a popular draw for anglers; there are plenty of spots sufficiently far from town where the huge fringing reed beds clean up the water.

Many spots are also suitable for swimming. The north shore of Lake Balkhash is less rocky than its southern shore, and in some places beaches provide a pleasant seaside atmosphere. The nicest is situated 60 kilometres to the south of **Sayak**, on the salty part of the lake. The settlement of **Priozyorsk** is on the peninsula in the bay of **Saryshagan**, 12 kilometres from the Priozyorsk railway station. This used to be a closed area, allegedly meant only for Soviet cosmonauts to relax after lengthy space trips. The legendary Kenesary is also supposed to have stayed here, not to relax, however, but during his flight from his pursuers. Deposits of agate and amethyst occur in the steppe mountains, and with a bit of luck, you might spot—from a distance—a few of the approximately 1,000 saiga antelope that survive here. In late summer, having brought up their young, the saiga form herds and roam over the steppe. In winter, wolves form packs and are so numerous in this region that it is permitted to hunt them. The winter season is also interesting for anglers in search of a great atmosphere (vodka included) while fishing through holes in the ice for catfish and sander, or pike-perch.

Above: A small stone pyramid marks the Centre of Eurasia (Dagmar Schreiber)

Sary Arka Travel Agencies

Akmolatourist, Astana, 23 Republic Ave, 2/F of Hotel Tourist, tel: (+7172) 330 204/330 209, fax: 330 201/330 414, e-mail: akmtourist@rambler.ru or akmtourist@cmgp.online.kz—excursions around town and to Burabay, Tengiz natural reserve and the lakes of Korgalzhin.

Sayat, Astana, Kabanbay Batyr Ave, tel: (+7172) 240 687, fax: 243 159, e-mail: sayat777@mail.ru—official invitation partner for "care-free" entries (visa at Astana airport), flight and hotel bookings, excursions in Astana and surroundings, angling and hunting tours.

Aruzhan, Astana, 18 Zheltoksan St, tel: (+7172) 328 518/327 275, fax: 328 027, e-mail: aruzhan@kepter.kz, website: www.aruzhan.kz.

Tsentr Dyelovich Initsiativ, Astana, 26 Beybichilik St, tel: (+7172) 324 080/316 474, mob: (8) 701 511 0369, e-mail: kazantsev@mail.kz—complete service for businesspeople as well as excursions in the area, including falcon hunting and shooting.

Tsentr Regionalnych Problem, Priozyorsk, 5 Fruze St, tel: (+71039) 42577/44877, fax: 42338, website: www.uozera.narod.ru—hotel accommodation, jeep-safari tours to places of geological, historic and zoological interest, (ice) angling, wolf, water bird and hare hunting.

Gloria Tour, Karaganda, 2 Lenina St., tel:/fax: (+7212) 425 682, e-mail: gloriatur@mail.ru—tailor-made individual tours in the region.

Intour, Karaganda, 54 Yerubayeva St, office 62, tel: (+7212) 478 730/478 923, e-mail: intur@host.kz—trips to Burabay, Karkaraly, Bayanaul and Balkash.

Kviai Tour, Karaganda, 66 Bukhar Zhyrau Ave, tel: (+7212) 425 229/484 559, fax: 425 208, e-mail: kvizitour@nursat.kz—eagle, falcon and tazy hunting in the Aksu Ayulu steppe; for more peaceful tourists show performances and wildlife-watching excursions.

Shara, Semey/Semipalatinsk, 4 Shugayeva St, tel: (+7222) 626 991/624 771, fax: 623 317, e-mail: shara@relcom.kz—excursions to the home museums and memorials of Abai, Auezov and Shakarim, trips to Mount Chingiztau, accommodation and visa service.

Semeyturist, Semey/Semipalatinsk, 9 Zhambyla St, tel: (+7222) 424 113, fax: 424 229—health resorts on the northern bank of Lake Alakol.

Leader, Shchuchinsk, Ablai Khan St, tel: (+71636) 45013, fax: 45525, e-mail: rema@lta.kz, website: www.lta.ru—hotel and sanatorium accommodation in Burabay.

Arlan Centre for Natural Protection, Karaganda, mikrorayon Vostok-5, building 34, apt. 60, tel: (+7212) 232 006, e-mail: acbkarlan@nursat.kz or arlan70@mail.ru—this organization aims to protect wildlife species and develop eco-friendly tourism in cooperation with the UNDP. Exploration tours for small groups only.

THE ALTAI MOUNTAINS AND IRTYSH PLAIN: A BREATH OF SIBERIA

Sun-bathed, blue-haloed summits, peaks, jagged ridges, conical hills, slopes and valleys; it was mountainscape of such splendour that the soul cheered at the sight of it.

Alfred Brehm

GATE TO THE EAST

In the early 18th Century, having consolidated all of Siberia under the Russian crown, **Tsar Peter I** was interested most in expanding his sphere of influence towards the east, and China in particular. Between Russia and China lay the Kazakh steppe. The steppe lands bordering **southern Siberia** and the **Altai Mountains** were the most easily reached, so Peter prepared a large expedition. In the early summer of 1715, **Colonel Buchholtz** led 3,000 men from the Siberian fortress of **Tobolsk** towards the Altai. They followed the course of the **Irtysh River** (**Ertis** or **Yertis** in Kazakh), and in 1716 built the fortresses of **Omsk** and **Yamyshevsk**. These served as bases for a new expedition, which set out in 1717 to drive further upstream on the Irtysh. Under the command of **I. Stupkin** the fortresses of **Zhelezinsk** and **Semipalatinsk** were founded. Between 1719 and 1720, led by Ivan Likharyov, the mission extended further with the foundation of the fortresses **Ust-Kamenogorsk** and **Koryakovsk**. With them, the Irtysh defence line was completed, and it was to play a crucial role in Russia's defence against the brutal Zhungars and other would-be invaders. It also played an important strategic role in the gradual colonization of the Kazakh tribes. Tsar Peter acknowledged that this was the key to the "Gate of the East".

THE ALTAI

Of all Kazakhstan's many regions, no other is so steeped in legend as the **Altai**. It is the original homeland of the Turkic nations, and contains impressive rock carvings and mysterious tombstones dating back millennia. The legendary peaks of **Shambhala** and **Byelovodye**, and the double peak of **Mount Byelukha** (considered the "navel of the Earth") are still the home of shamanism, giving the Altai a mystical reputation. Geologists, archaeologists, ethnologists, botanists and zoologists have all come here from around the world, drawn by this ancient mountain region's many treasures. The great German explorer **Alexander von Humboldt** travelled through the area in 1829, sponsored by **Tsar Nicolas I** to explore and report on what he discovered; the result was Von Humboldt's masterpiece, *A Sketch of the Physical Description of the Universe.*

Left: Classic Altai scenery in the Berel Valley (Jeremy Tredinnick)

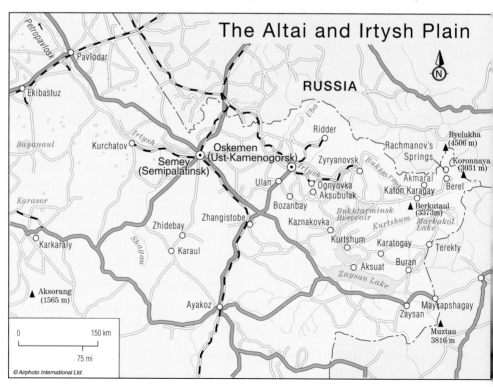

Only a small part of this large mountain range in the heart of Asia is situated in Kazakhstan. The major part of the Altai, with its continuation into the **Sazhany Mountains**, is in Russian territory, while another large section stretches into China and further into Mongolia. The mountains are incredibly rich in natural splendour, home to rare plants and animals, historical landmarks and other places of geological and anthropological interest. Not without justification is this region called the Altai, meaning "Golden Mountain" in Mongolian. Scientists called the Altai a "concise continent", a term that reflects the extraordinary variety of landscapes found within its relatively limited area: there is desert and steppe, low mountain chains covered from 600–2,000 metres altitude with taiga forest (accounting for 47 percent of the region), more than 300 high mountain peaks covered with glaciers (on Kazakhstani territory alone), and approximately 2,000 lakes and 1,200 rivers. Twenty-seven species of reptile, 36 fish species and 333 types of bird call Kazakhstan's Altai home. The **World Wide Fund for Nature (WWF)** has included the entire Altai in its list of 200 areas in the world with exceptionally important value in terms of biodiversity. Kazakhstan has acknowledged this by putting large areas of its share of the Altai under protection. Visitors to the Altai should be aware that they are guests in a by and large untouched realm and should behave accordingly.

It would be easy to spend several weeks or months in the rolling steppe, foothills, valleys and high mountains of the Altai, without losing interest or enthusiasm in the many and varied experiences it offers. Everything from inexpensive two-day excursions to lengthy Altai tours by car, bicycle, boat, on horseback or hiking are possible. The city of **Oskemen (Ust-Kamenogorsk)** is the most convenient starting and finishing point for trips. Since many of the finest areas are situated in the border area with China, the obligatory permits are required, though arrangements can be made through any authorised agency without too much trouble.

The climate in the Altai is uncharacteristic for Kazakhstan. Winters are long and harsh, with snow often more than two metres deep, while summers are relatively cool, especially in the mountainous areas. Rain is also more abundant, both in summer and winter.

Oskemen (Ust-Kamenogorsk)

In 1720, **Ivan Likharyov**, envoy of Tsar Peter I, approached the Altai at the head of a Russian expedition and designated the spot where the Ulba flows into the Irtysh as the location to build a fortress. The stronghold was named **Ust-Kamenogorsk** and formed the eastern flank of a complete fortification line along the bank of the Irtysh that was created to protect the land from the Zhungar hordes and to serve as a base for the conquest of Central Asia. In 1757, the **Zhungar Khanate** was defeated, after which Ust-Kamenogorsk's significance as a military stronghold diminished. Instead, the town gradually developed into a trade centre and an outpost for the opening up of the Altai. Because of its forbidding climate and remote location, Ust-Kamenogorsk also served the tsars as a place to exile political undesirables. Many "**Decembrists**", participants in the revolt of December 1825, as well as adherents to a movement called Nationhood, ended up here. To a large extent it is thanks to

Above left: The grandiose entrance to Oskemen's Palace of Culture, built during the city's golden era of mining prosperity. Above right: Beautiful ceiling art inside the building (Jeremy Tredinnick x2)

these young, well-educated Russian democrats that the area lost its backward status and evolved in terms of education and enlightenment. In 1869 the town, which had swiftly grown in size, was granted city status. It gradually gained importance as an industrial centre thanks to its favourable location at the foot of the Altai Mountains and on the bank of a navigable river. A port was constructed, as well as a rail link to the iron ore mines of **Ridder** (**Leninogorsk** in Soviet times). The silver needed to mint coins in Russia came from the Altai Mountains, and settlement by Russian farmers on the left bank of the Irtysh increased the importance of agriculture. Factories were built in Ust-Kamenogorsk to process agricultural commodities.

The struggle between Bolsheviks and White Guards between 1918 and 1919 saw fighting in the city, but subsequently the rail link with the Turksib line was built and more and more light industry developed. During the Great Patriotic War, a large number of heavy industries were moved to Ust-Kamenogorsk, and many of them remained in place after the war ended. Hydraulic power plants were built, and in **Rudniy** (ore) Altai the foundations were laid for the development of one of the largest polymetallic mining complexes in the entire Soviet Union. Tens of thousands of skilled metallurgy workers found jobs in eastern Kazakhstan.

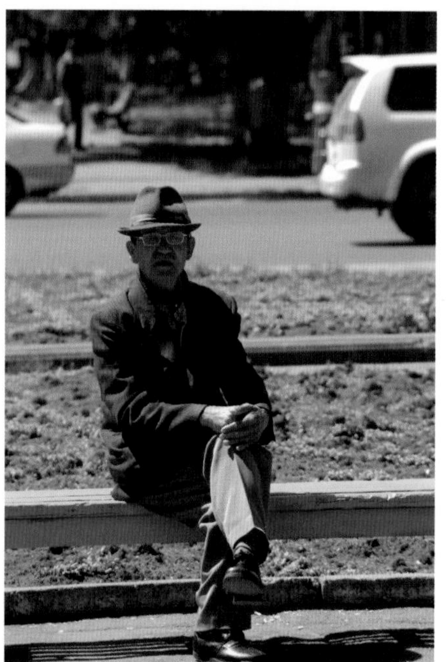

However, the shock of the break-up of the USSR, the disruption of trade relations with Russia and the opening up of global markets dealt a huge blow to the region. Many enterprises were forced to stop production and suddenly Ust-Kamenogorsk was faced with an army of unemployed. Many skilled workers emigrated to neighbouring Russia and most of the ethnic Germans who lived in the region returned to their homeland. Today, the worst has been overcome, and recovery has started. Zinc, lead, tantalum, beryllium and mercury are always in demand, and both domestic and foreign investors

Above: The towering War Memorial at the Strelka. Left: A rest in the park (Jeremy Tredinnick x2)

are gradually bringing present-day enterprises up to world standards. Skoda, the car manufacturer, has built a production centre in the city. A positive side effect of the industrial crisis in the 1990s has been the improvement in the environmental situation. The region is now in a better position to advertise and develop its ecotourism potential. **Oskemen**, the new Kazakh name for Ust-Kamenogorsk, has started to concentrate on bringing tourists to the Altai's mountain regions, but has also undertaken efforts to polish the image of the city itself. In recent years much has been built and renovated, and business centres and hotels now compare favourably with other regional capitals.

The city today, while officially called Oskemen, is still referred to as Ust-Kamenogorsk by virtually all its residents. Its location surrounded by green hills, and its broad tree-lined

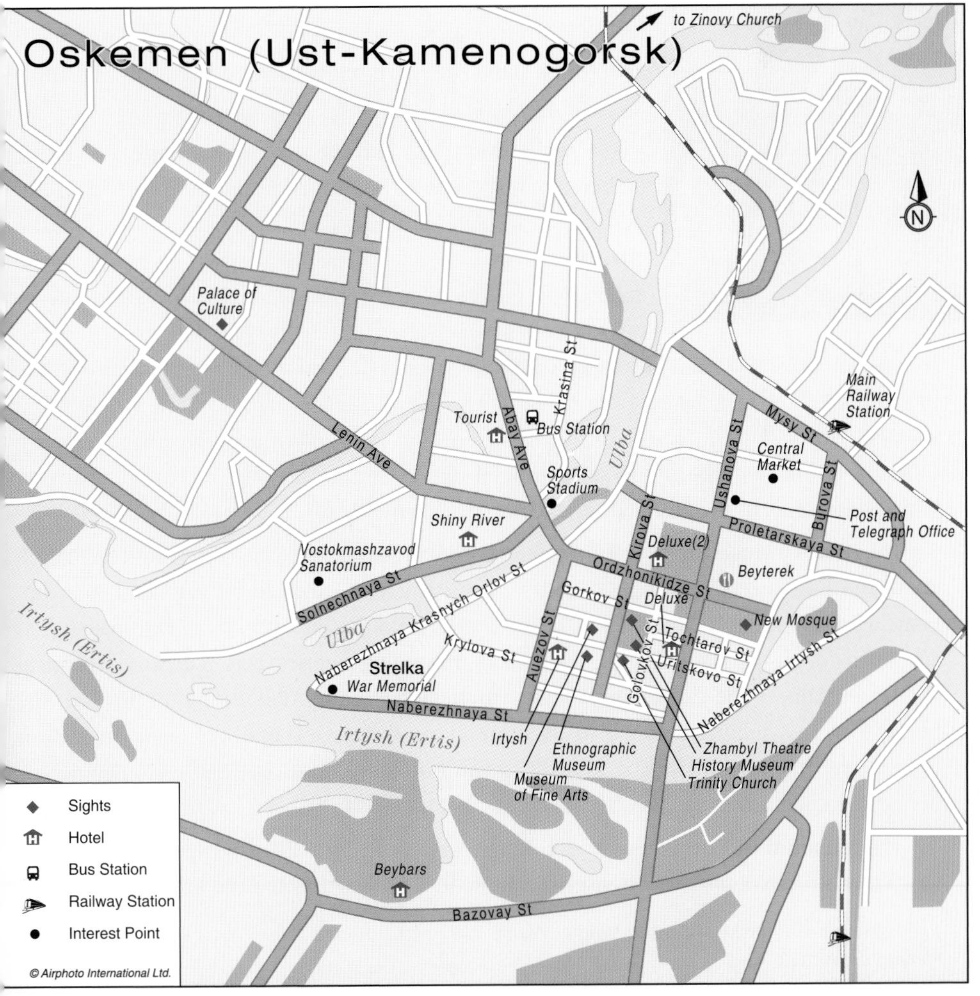

streets, parks and squares make it a pleasant place to explore. All that remains of its original history as a fortress is a small section of old town surrounding the **Trinity Church**—which was used as a storage facility for cars during the Soviet era—and the small but interesting **Kirov Park**, which contains antique farming machinery and a re-creation of an old Russian pioneers' village. The city authorities have recognised the value of keeping this area instead of modernizing it, and are renovating the neighbourhood, house by house, and laying out public gardens with fountains, as well as a small pedestrian zone. Attractive wooden houses are used as shops and businesses, and intricate iron balconies and gates add to the flair. The old town is situated between Mira (now Golovkov), Gorkov, Kirov and Uriskovo streets.

A walk down the **riverbank promenade** on either Naberezhnaya Krasnykh Orlov beside the Ulba River, or Naberezhnaya Irtysh along the Irtysh, brings you to the ***Strelka*** (Arrow), the confluence of the two rivers where the fortress once stood. The river is splendid to look at whatever season of the year you visit, flowing fast and smooth in the summer months, hidden under thick ice from November till April or surfacing again in May from under a turbulent maelstrom of ice floes. The meadows on the southern side are a popular barbecue picnic site for residents at the weekends and in good weather. At the tip of the land a huge dark-stone **War Memorial** pierces the sky, flanked by curving walls on which the names of the city's fallen soldiers are inscribed.

The **History Museum** (40 Uritskovo Street) is small but packed with interesting information about the East Kazakhstan region and well worth a visit (arrange for a guided tour, but bear in mind that only Russian will be spoken). A natural history section features stuffed specimens of all the wildlife of the Altai and surrounding steppe; there is an archaeological display explaining the explosion of human population in the Altai during the Bronze Age because of the mineral-rich soil of the region, as well as examples of Scythian kurgan excavations and stone figures; and finally a third section houses fascinating contemporary items, including Soviet memorabilia and old photographs of the city's early days.

The **Museum of Fine Arts** on 56 Tokhtarov Street and the **Ethnography Museum**, 29 Golovkov Street are also worth visiting. The latter is housed in the old school building of

Right: Oskemen's downtown Central Mosque. Above: The Central Mosque's iman poses for a picture (Jeremy Tredinnick x2)

Ust-Kamenogorsk, one of the few remaining two-storey houses that were a common sight in the city towards the end of the 19th Century. The **Zhambyl Theatre**, 77 Tokhtarov Street, a former "people's pavilion" and more than 100 years old, is also among the better-preserved buildings from those days (its original construction cost was 7,500 roubles).

To the north of the city centre a beautiful new church has been built with donations from wealthy local entrepreneurs. The **Zinovy Church** was consecrated in 2004; its walls are covered with both old and new works of religious art, but the highlight is a 100-year-old painting on wood panels of the baby Jesus held by Simon and flanked by Anna, Mary and Joseph. When a local brought it to the church only the faces could be seen dimly, but since then, amazing colour and detail has emerged, so that the robes and feet of the characters can be clearly seen—it has been hailed as a miracle, and draws many devotees. A new **Central Mosque** has also been built in the city centre, between the main square in front of the Akimat and the river.

The present-day printing house was once the home of a 19th Century gold miner named Menovchikov. The Altai branch of the Institute for Geological Science (21 Karl Liebknecht Street) is in the former villa of Menovchikov's competitor Valitov. Each year, those two gentlemen were responsible for supplying 700 kilogrammes of gold to the Russian Crown.

Practical Information

The area dialling code for Oskemen is 7232. The main Post Office is at 67 Ushanov St, open Monday-Friday 9am-6pm, Sat-Sun closed.

Transportation

From Oskemen (Ust-Kamenogorsk) there are daily flights to and from both Almaty and Astana, and several flights a week to other urban centres such as Karaganda and Pavlodar. There are daily flights to Moscow, and several flights a week to Germany (Hanover and Frankfurt). For flight information, call 428 484. The Air Astana office is at 70 Ushanov St, (tel: 243 233), and Central Asia Tourism can be found at 4/48 Auezov St (tel: 252 850, e-mail: cat-oskemen@alarnet.com).

The Zaschita railway station is located on the northwestern edge of the city—tram number 3 goes there from downtown. Trains arrive from and depart for Almaty, Semey and Russia here. Trains to Almaty go via Russian territory to Semey, then head south; if you do not have a Russian visa, or want to save a night's travel, catch a taxi or minibus south to Zhangistobe and connect with the train there—the town is two hours south of Oskemen. Trains to Ridder and Zyryanovsk also depart from Zaschita, but you can also leave from the smaller railway station in the city centre on Burov St.

Left: The Zinovy Church lies in the city's northern suburbs, and is a recent addition to its attractions (Jeremy Tredinnick)

The bus station is on the corner of Abai Ave and Krassina St. Buses and minibuses leave for all townships in the province, daily to Semey (3.5 hours, and much easier than getting the train), and almost hourly to Ridder. Long-distance buses go to Pavlodar and Astana, and to the main cities in Russia across the border.

ACCOMMODATION

Shiny River Hotel, 8/1 Solnechnaya Street, tel: 272 525/636, fax: 271 418, e-mail: reservation@shinyriverhotel.kz, website: www.shinyriverhotel.kz—Oskemen's top hotel, newly built with 72 rooms, an ornate marble lobby and business centre with high-speed internet. Located across the Ulba Bridge close to both the commercial district and downtown. Rooms from US$89.

Hotel Deluxe, 28a Uritskovo St, tel: 240 993, and 62 Kirov St, tel: 248 802, e-mail: deluxe-ukg@mail.ru—the Deluxe runs two properties, both centrally located on the edge of the old town district, with good, well-priced rooms from US$65.

Hotel Beybars, 8 Bazovay St, tel: 265 309, fax: 218 865—a 15-room retreat slightly out of town in a forest on the Irtysh, including a swimming pool. Rooms from US$90.

Hotel Irtysh, 22 Auezov St, tel: 252 933, fax: 250 985—a typical Soviet-style hotel in the city centre, with 77 rooms from US$20.

THE SIBINSK LAKES

Sixty kilometres south of Oskemen five large lakes lie hidden in the folds of a granite mountain range, arranged like five fingers. The landscape is dominated by steppe hills, dry valleys and Kazakh villages, and presents a rather stern beauty. The mountains are composed of mattress granite, as it is known, the layers of which look like piles of mattresses—or rather, to make an even more striking comparison, like semolina pudding, overboiled several times, and rapidly stiffened. These mountains, with their solid, easily scaled bare rock, invite you to climb them; reach a good vantage point, and you'll have a breathtaking view over the **Sibinsk Lakes** (*Sibinskiye ozyora*). There is no visible inflow of water—they get their water from underground springs. The lakes are ideal for swimming, and the flat southern shores are ideal for camping. However, take care while climbing the rocky slopes, which quickly get slippery if it starts to rain, turning the descent into a nightmare. In recent years the lakeside has been partially developed.

To get to the lakes, follow the road towards **Zhangistobe** and Almaty. From time to time, curious collections of stone line the side of the road—these are **Zhungar tombstones**. This area was long a bone of contention between the Zhungars and the Kazakh tribes, but the Kazakhs eventually won through. The ruins of the Buddhist monastery of **Ablayinskit**

Right: Clambering on the rocks near the Sibinsk Lakes—but watch out for the rain (Hermann Schulz)

still recall memories of the Zhungars' savagery. This monastery in the **Sibinka Valley** was famous for its learned monks and their precious Tibetan paper scrolls. Today, the structure has fallen victim to the ravages of time, to the extent that it can now hardly be recognized as such. Approximately 40 kilometres from Oskemen, a road leads off to the left in the direction of Targyn. The lakes are located on the left side of the road, up in the range of the clearly visible rocky mountains. A narrow gravel road leads up to them. From the Sibinsk Lakes, it's possible to continue to the **Bukhtarminsk Reservoir** and **Zaysan Lake**.

Karmen Kuus

East of the Sibinsk Lakes is the village of **Asubulak**. To the south lies an area that is a paradise for stone and mineral lovers; on the banks of the Asubulak River, which originates as a spring on the mountain pass of the same name, A trail leads upstream through meadows to a picturesque site where large deposits of precious stones are easily accessible. Kazakhs call this place **Karmen Kuus (Snow Camp)**. Granite and porphyritic rock, formed 280 million years ago, triggered the eruption of a new mass of granite some 250 million years ago. This mass is seamed with mineral veins; experts have identified more than 100 different materials including feldspar, rose quartz, rock crystal, aquamarine, tourmaline, apatite, garnet and other precious stones, especially in the southern part of the 400-hectare site, where the soil has been broken up by tectonic movements and big lumps are scattered all over the place. Collectors can forage to their heart's content here—so far, no one has

The Bukhtarminsk vehicular ferry cuts travel time around the reservoir (Vladimir Tugalev)

thought of forbidding people from taking samples. Some minerals contain traces of tin, tantalum and niobium; this area was mined as early as the Bronze Age—bronze arrowheads and fishhooks have been found nearby. The discovery of bones belonging to mammoth, woolly rhinoceros and giant deer also shows that this region was populated by the largest ancient mammals 30,000 ago, when the climate was milder and vegetation more abundant. Of course what for some is a sensational geological and mineral open-air museum, is for others simply a beautiful river valley—there are two springs surrounded by trees and picturesque groups of junipers and crooked pine trees on the slopes.

Bukhtarminsk Reservoir

It does not really look like one, but **Bukhtarminsk Reservoir** (*Bukhtarminskoye vodokhranilishchye*) is not only the largest reservoir in Kazakhstan but among the largest of its kind in the world. Only a small slice of land was lost when the Irtysh was diverted to this water basin, 340 kilometres long, 25 kilometres wide and up to 68 metres deep. A valley with rocky subsoil was filled up, resulting in a clean, natural-looking lake.

Around 120 kilometres from Oskemen, the lake has become a weekend resort for city residents, who come to relax, make use of the beaches and clean water, and watch the pretty sunsets. Popular places include the bays of Ayuda and Altai, the more remote location where the **Bukhtarma River** flows into the reservoir, and most of all **Blue Bay** (*Goluboy zaliv*). This is on the northern shore of the lake not far from the road to Zyryanovsk, just beyond the hamlet of Bukhtarma, where there is the obligatory sanatorium as well as small cottages for rent. Booking through a travel agency is recommended, since Blue Bay is in great demand during the holiday season, although off-season there is often nobody there at all. Temperatures are good for swimming until early September. Buses from Oskemen to Blue Bay cost 500 tenge and take two hours, but a more enjoyable way to get there is to take to the river on a *raketa*—a reconstructed Soviet hydrofoil, which in summer shuttles between Oskemen and the reservoir. They shoot upstream to the lock at Serebryanka, where the dam is bypassed. A one-and-a-half hour trip on the raketa costs 700 tenge.

A water-borne experience can be had by crossing on one of the boats that ferry people and vehicles from shore to shore, reducing travel time between Oskemen and the far northeast reaches of the region. In most places the western shore is flat and bare, and to the south of the **Kurshum ferry** there are even desert dunes. The eastern shore is lined with hills, and on the northernmost bays the forests reach down to the shore, offering a wonderful contrast with the clear, blue water in autumn. One can drive around the entire lake, and the road often remains close to the water along the east shore, before heading into hills filled with groves of silver birch. In spring and summer the road is lined with bright-yellow flowers, the rolling green hills punctuated with ploughed fields of black earth, showing how rich the soil is in iron and other minerals. Villages in the Altai foothills are filled with modest but well-built houses, with steep-sided roofs (to shed the heavy falls of snow that shroud the land in winter) and bright-blue window shutters—a common theme throughout Kazakhstan, but particularly attractive here, surrounded by such a vivid display of nature's colours. The road eventually crosses the hilly heights, revealing a sweeping panorama of the broad **Narym River Valley** and the line of 3,000-4,500 metre Altai peaks that hide **Markakol Lake** and the Chinese border beyond.

A popular tour route taking in Bukhtarminsk Reservoir and the region to its south goes via the town of **Kaznakovka**, either from the lakes of Sibinsk or from Asubulak, then crosses the reservoir by ferry to the east shore and heads down through **Kurshum** to **Aksuat** on Zaysan Lake.

ZAYSAN LAKE AND KIYN-KERISH

The area around **Zaysan Lake** was once famous for the herds of wild Bactrian camels and Przewalski's horses that grazed on its shores. Until around 100 years ago, tiger, kulan, saiga and dzheyran could also be found here, with herds counted in the thousands; biologists came from all around the world to observe this Earthly paradise.

Zaysan Lake is a very large water basin on the southern outskirts of the Altai, and a rich fishing ground. It is approximately 100 kilometres long, up to 31 kilometres wide but only eight metres deep, fed by the **Black Irtysh**, which comes from China and widens here to create an area of more than 1,800 square kilometres. Since ancient times, people have moved through the natural gateway through the mountains created by the river: caravans, conquerors, nomads and entire nations searching for new places to settle. The northernmost branch of the **Silk Road** once ran along the foot of the mountain chains of **Saur** and **Manyrak**, beyond Zaysan. Here, on the south bank of the lake, is the only driveable road that leads from the Chinese border near **Maykapshagay (Fat Gorge)** via Semey to Pavlodar.

The lake's shores consist of exotic desert landscapes. To the south lie the wild mountain spurs of Manyrak and the mighty snow-covered Saur, with its 3,816-metre peak **Muztau (Ice Mountain)**. Behind it stretches the **Tarbagatay** mountain range, much of which has probably never been properly explored by humans. Here Arkhar sheep and snow leopards still find refuge. On the north shore, there are places where you could imagine yourself to be on the planet Mars. Red and yellow clay hills dominate the areas bordering the **Bay of Shakelmes** and in the territory of **Kiyn-Kerish (Flaming Rocks)**. Melting water has eroded the rock into bizarre-looking and wonderfully carved formations. With a bit of imagination it's possible to imagine an entire city spread over 300 hectares: towers, castles and yurts, all glowing in various hues. Extreme heat and a lack of water characterize this rough, fantasy landscape.

Kiyn-Kerish is only accessible by jeep, either by turning right on the road from Kurshum to **Buran** where the branch road to **Karatogay** begins, and driving across the lifeless desert in the direction of Amana, or trying to make it along the lake's shore. Whichever way you choose, a knowledgeable guide is essential.

Camping on Zaysan Lake is an experience. From time to time at night, in the absence of human-made noise, one hears a wind-borne sound over the lake and between the mountains that is reminiscent of the humming of telegraph lines. It is to this Aeolian tune that the lake owes its Mongolian nickname of **Khut-khutu Nor (Lake of the Ringing Chimes)**.

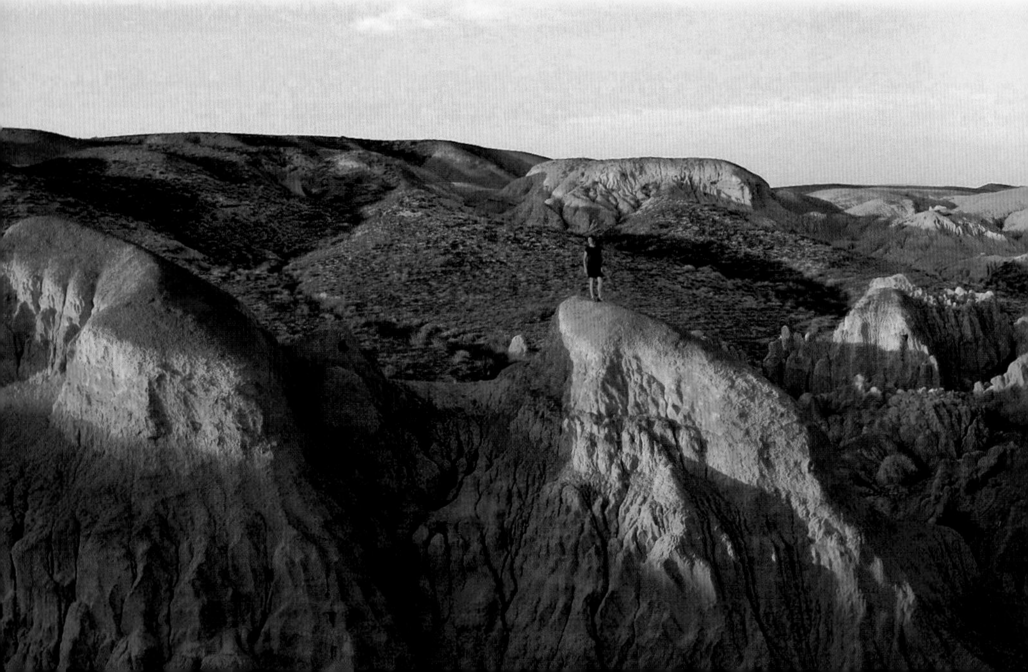

THE ROAD TO MARKAKOL

A road runs from the northern shore of Zaysan Lake in the direction of the central Altai. On his travels in the region, Alfred Brehm described the scenery along this route thus:

> In front of us, the lower ranges of the Altai towered over one another, with the high peaks glowing, some covered by snow, looking down on us below. Light and shadow, brightness and darkness, masses of fallen rock and rolling spring-green meadows, changed irregularly from one to the other. Sun-bathed, blue-haloed summits, peaks, jagged ridges, conical hills, slopes and valleys; it was mountainscape of such splendour that the soul cheered at the sight of it. It overlooked the valley of the Irtysh, half of which is occupied by Lake Zaysan, and through which led one of the three ancient routes of nations' migration in Central Asia. On the other side of it, now almost behind us, Mount Saur rose in all its glory with its still snow-covered peak, almost as high as its peers of the Altai. From here, the eye could discern the shapes of the mountain chains from Mount Saur deep into China, and from wild Mount Manrak far towards the west.

Brehm must have been on the road to **Markakol Lake**; his passionately described views perfectly fit those of the **Marble Pass**, which winds up beyond **Terekty** and the border post of **Moyildy** in steep, serpentine curves. Once at a height of 1,399 metres the view opens up dramatically, stretching out north and south over the mountains, as well as over

Otherworldly scenery near the Bay of Shakelmes on Zaysan Lake (Hermann Schulz)

the **Akkum (White Sand) Desert** in China. Continuing on to Markakol takes a long time, since the one-time bitumen and crushed stone track is now potholed and extremely rough. Indeed, it is open for only part of the year, and even travel agencies in Oskemen cannot predict if a trip will be possible. For those who are lucky, arriving at their destination instantly makes the considerable effort inconsequential.

MARKAKOL LAKE

From Oskemen it is a distance of some 500 kilometres—and a demanding journey of 12–16 hours—to reach **Markakol Lake**. The variety and beauty of the landscape along the way, however, goes some way to offsetting the difficulty and arduous nature of the trip. The first view of the "real Altai" is revealed beyond the Marble Pass, when the track winds down into the green valley of **Akzhaylyau (White Summer Pasture)**, before ascending to the **Tikkabak Pass** and down again to finally reach the "Pearl of the Altai", as Markakol Lake is known. This high mountain lake is the most picturesque of its kind in Kazakhstan. The lake and its surroundings of splendid mountain taiga forest were officially declared a 75,000-hectare natural reserve in 1976; especially in late September, this gorgeous place looks like something from a fairy tale, with its larch trees glowing yellow in the crisp mountain air, and the clear streams and springs bubbling down to the lake, whose water shines sometimes yellowish, sometimes green, but most often turquoise and royal-blue—though under some conditions it even takes on the colour of anthracite.

Markakol Lake is considered one of Kazakhstan's most beautiful locations, named the "Pearl of the Altai" and part of a state nature reserve due to its immense biodiversity (Hermann Schulz)

Markakol Lake is 38 kilometres long, up to 19 kilometres wide and up to 30 metres deep. Situated at 1,485 metres, it is enclosed in the chain of valleys between the mountain ridges of **Kurshumskiy** and **Azutau** to the north and south respectively. The lake's northern shore offers a wonderful view of the **Sarymsakty (Garlic) Ridge**, with its snow-covered peaks of **Burkitaul (Eagle's Eyrie**, 3,373 metres) and **Aksubas (Head of White Water**, 3,308 metres).

More than 100 streams flow into Markakol Lake, but only a single river, the **Kalzhyr**, flows out, south towards the Black Irtysh. The lake is renowned for its crystalline water and its abundance of *uskutsh*, a local subspecies of the Siberian *lenok* trout. Some uskutsh can reach eight kilogrammes in weight, and are a big draw for anglers.

In 1976, a state nature reserve was founded on Markakol Lake in order to protect the 700 species of vegetation, 254 bird species and rare mammals such as the snow leopard, *manul* (Pallas's cat), red wolf, *maral* (Siberian red deer), brown bear, sable and striped and flying squirrels. In all, 714 square kilometres are under the strictest protection here—in theory; as in almost all other cases, however, the area lacks the necessary funds to pay for wildlife rangers and monitoring systems, and is thus vulnerable to poachers, especially from across the Chinese border, which is very close. The lake and its environs are still largely undeveloped, mainly because the area was closed to both foreign and domestic tourists until relatively recently.

A house with limited accommodation has been renovated by the Oskemen-based tour agency Altai-Expeditions in **Urunshkaya**, a village of 500 souls on the eastern point of the

Horses graze peacefully on the shore of Markakol Lake near the village of Urunshkaya (Vladimir Tugalev)

lake. It includes a Russian sauna, situated on a murmuring brook in the middle of a birch forest which also offers idyllic conditions for camping. From Urunshkaya you can set off for tours on foot or horseback along the lakeshore and into the mountains. In midsummer, the water temperature reaches a refreshing 16–18°C. From here, you can make a trip by boat to the bee pastures of **Zhukov** and **Samoylovo**, the honey from which is claimed as the best in the world. Life is simple for the inhabitants of Urunshkaya and the small settlements surrounding it, based on raising livestock, harvesting berries and honey, fishing and growing potatoes and other vegetables in their gardens. Careful development of low-impact tourism would benefit the region without doubt, but if ever the much-bandied term "ecotourism" were a necessary requirement to non-harmful development, it would be in this beautiful spot.

Shortcut to the Northeast

It is a day's journey from Markakol to the **Narym Valley** and thence to the most northeastern peak in Kazakhstan's Altai territory: the renowned double summit of **Byelukha**. However, those who want to drive in any sort of comfort must go back to the Bukhtarminsk Reservoir, follow its shore and finally turn east up the Narym Valley, an interesting route in itself, but all the same a detour of some 500 kilometres taking much longer than a day. The "shortcut"

is known as the **Austrian Road**, named after the Austrian prisoners of war who built it in 1915. Its condition seems not to have been upgraded since that time, and it is only due to its solid construction that one can still drive on it. Good maps show the track as no more than a dotted line—meaning the lowest level of quality. People with weak nerves are advised not to attempt this road.

North from Markakol the track bends up through a dry riverbed to the picturesque valley of the **Sorvyonok River (Little Havoc Maker)** and from there to the **Altaiskiy Pass** (1,967 metres). A steep and treacherous track down from the pass leads into the **Karakaba River Valley**; this wild river flows into China where it ends up in the Black Irtysh. The roaring stream is crossed over the **Kabinskiy Most** bridge—it is best to close one's eyes while doing so, as the bridge's steel structure is heavily affected by water, ice and the substantial rocks carried along by the river, and you can see the foaming water through the many holes.

The road continues through a picturesque gorge, but three more bridges have to be crossed. If the weather is clear, you can see the Altai's highest peak (in fact the highest in all Siberia), **Mount Byelukha** (4,506 metres), in all its glory from the **Burkhat Pass** (2,141 metres). The view stretches more than 100 kilometres from here on clear days.

Above: The school house in Urunshkaya. Left: A rest stop at the Marble Pass on the way from Zaysan Lake to Markakol Lake (Hermann Schulz x2)

A serpentine gravel track now winds down to the **Bukhtarma River Valley**, with a difference in altitude of 1,000 metres—the view should take your mind off the faint feeling in your stomach and the pressure-popping in your ears. Once in the valley you are back on tarmac road. From here, you can either turn west and head back towards Bukhtarminsk Reservoir, or turn right and head towards **Rachmanov's Springs** in the northeast.

KATON-KARAGAY NATIONAL PARK

In the summer of 2001, a huge 1,300-square-kilometre area in the Altai was declared a national park. It includes almost the entire territory between the borders with Russia and China, the villages of Soldatovo and Medvyedka and the northern slopes of the Sarymsaktiy and Tarbagatay. Though **Katon-Karagay National Park** does not have the strictest protective status, it has improved the situation by imposing more severe penalties on poachers and hunters of the endangered species that inhabit this region. This measure became necessary because of the increasing impact of steadily growing tourism, and because of the increasing exploitation of natural resources by the local population during the 1990s. It's important to note that most of the families in this area's villages are extremely poor; many move out and head for the cities, and the villages begin to stagnate, while those who remain take what they need for their daily survival from the forest. When traders, mainly Chinese, began to come in increasing numbers illegally to buy maral antlers, brown bear bile, and the musk scent glands of certain rare species, the temptation to poach animals was strong, as a single animal could garner a poacher the equivalent of a month's income.

Inevitably the wildlife populations of threatened species declined, but as penalties became more severe, poaching has become less appealing. Other measures have also been employed to combat the problem; the most significant is the successful "farming" of domestic marals for the medicinal extract **pantocrine** that is found in abundance in their newly formed antlers (see Special Topic "The Miracle of Maral Medicine" on page 418).

Top: Farm hands at Katon-Karagay Maral Farm. Above: The maral, or Siberian red deer, is a large and powerful animal whose antlers are highly valued for their medicinal properties (Jeremy Tredinnick x2) Left: A test for your vehicle on the Austrian Road (Hermann Schulz)

Above: A mountainous setting for the rural village of Akmaral. Inset: meadows filled with bright-orange trollius and myriad other flowers are a feature of the Altai in spring and summer (Jeremy Tredinnick x2)

The region's main town, also called **Katon-Karagay**, is situated on the Narym Valley floor. Small and neat, it has a tiny museum dedicated to the famous Kazakh novelist **Oral Khan Bokeh**, who was born here and lived in a tiny house that houses the museum, displaying paraphernalia from Bokeh's life, including gifts presented to him from admirers during his travels. There is talk of an airport being built in the valley near to Katon-Karagay; this would of course result in development and economic progress for the local population, but responsible tourism growth is a must; local officials seem to understand this, and hope to develop tourism models that preserve the ecology and culture while allowing more visitors into the region, improving living standards for local people without causing irrevocable damage to their land.

AKMARAL

North of Katon-Karagay town, some five kilometres up a rough track from the road leading to the **Berel Valley**, you come to the picturesque village of **Akmaral**, location of a large maral breeding and farming operation. The **Katon-Karagay Maral Farm** (www.katon.kz) started with 50 marals in 1990, but now keeps 2,500 of the deer, which run free in huge fenced areas of the reserve. A fully grown maral's antlers can weigh up to 20 kilogrammes; valuable pantocrine is extracted from the freshly sprouted antlers (*pant*), which are sawn from the animals' heads while still covered with velvet (the deer is said to feel no pain and suffers no ill effects from the antlers' premature detachment). Pantocrine is famous in

A Bactrian camel peers suspiciously at the camera while one of his mates peeks shyly over his shoulder (Jeremy Tredinnick)

Oriental medicine for its alleged strengthening and rejuvenating powers—documents referring to its wondrous effects have been found in the tomb of a Chinese emperor dating to 170 BC. Huge maral farms exist on the Russian side of the border, as well as in China (New Zealand even farms deer for their antler products), but Kazakhstan's pantocrine is considered the highest quality, perhaps because the animals are left to roam and graze at will through pristine meadows and pinewoods, and their winter diet is supplemented with wheat.

The farm also houses a sanatorium of basic wooden chalets, in which rooms containing bathtubs are used for health treatments involving the pantocrine product. Hot-spring water is piped direct into the tubs, and mixed with varying amounts of medicinal pantocrine liquid depending on your physical fitness—a 10-minute soak is all that's required at any one time. Despite its very basic facilities, the sanatorium is famous among Russians and Kazakhs, who come for treatments, either to aid an existing illness or simply for the healthy benefits. The farm's director, Nurlan Toktarov, has big ambitions for the operation; a programme of upgrading and improvement is under way, and the family-run business will open two new sanatoriums soon, one a more luxurious establishment catering to only 32 people at a time, the other a larger facility in the main valley.

THE VALLEY OF KINGS

In 1998, the permafrost soil in the upper reaches of the **Bukhtarma River** revealed a long-hidden secret that caused a sensation among historians and ethnologists. At a height of 1,200 metres, near the village of **Berel**, the fully preserved body of a **Scythian prince** was discovered in one of 36 kurgans (funeral barrows) scattered over the daisy-strewn meadows of the valley floor. Another body accompanied it, first thought to have been his wife, but now considered his mother, and the remains of 13 horses with richly adorned bridles were laid around the humans. Dating to the 3rd–4th centuries BC, archaeologists from the Institute of Archaeology of the Kazakh Academy of Sciences and the National

continued on page 423

The Miracle of Maral Medicine

Late in the afternoon the weather turns, the lowering sky replaced by cotton wool clouds punctuating the deep blue of the mountain sky and mirroring the snowy frosting of the high mountain ridges. Our van turns off the main valley road and bumps and grinds over a puddle patchwork track into rolling hills simply bursting with green life. High fences follow the contours of the land endlessly as we journey through a mixture of open fields and thick forest; above us an eagle soars, watching for a chance to swoop down on one of the many marmots who scurry to safety by the side of the road as we pass.

At last we reach a village of well-worn but homely wooden houses, cross a ramshackle log bridge, and pull up outside a long, single-storey building. Gratefully stretching my legs—road travel in the Altai is a lesson in durability for vehicles and passengers alike—I am introduced to Nurlan Toktarov, founder and director of the Katon-Karagay Maral Farm, where we will overnight. The director's handshake is strong and testing, his eyes clear and penetrating, his face open and inscrutable at the same time; he is the highly respected patriarch of this community, and we will dine with him that evening.

Before supper, however, I'm shown round the farm's health sanatorium complex by Aldiyar, Nurlan's youngest son. An offshoot of the farm's main industry—the production of pantocrine-based products derived from the antlers of the *maral* (a type of large Eurasian red deer)—the rustic sanatorium buildings contain "treatment" rooms with bathtubs that are filled with steaming water piped directly from nearby hot springs, with an addition of

a silty red-brown "soup" taken from the cauldrons in which the deer antlers are boiled during pantocrine extraction. Short baths in this solution are said to provide huge health benefits, even miraculous solutions to long-lasting ailments. The explanation of the full treatment process is somewhat lost in translation for me—something happens after the bath, but I'm not sure what—and I am told I will be given a treatment later; having had many late, enjoyable but exhausting nights recently, I figure I could do with a pick-me-up. But first... food.

Our repast, as ever in Kazakhstan, is a feast of nature's bounty: the table groans under the weight of dishes of meat, fresh vegetables, aromatic bread, dried fruit, honey... and the inevitable bottles of vodka and cognac. Between mouthfuls we trade toasts of welcoming, thanks, gratitude and good fortune, and I learn of the farm's history. Nurlan worked for the government once, but made his fortune as the owner of a business manufacturing high-tech agricultural parts. An Altai Kazakh, he returned to his homeland after the collapse of the Soviet Union and independence, to find it suffering cruelly: the price of maral deer antlers, an important source of local revenue, had plummeted from US$1,000 to US$200 per kilo; the marals were disappearing from the forests; work was scarce, and the locals, unable to make a sustainable living, were leaving in droves.

Nurlan made a decision: he began buying land, which was cheap at the time, brought in 50 marals and began a deer farming operation. His persistence and dedication paid off; today, the farm is a family business employing 42 people who live on and work the land, and its extensive forests are home to 2,500 marals, from whose new antlers the amazing chemical extract pantocrine is drawn.

Left: Allowed to roam freely through field and forest, these maral grow strong and healthy
Above: In the stockade, prior to the removal of its antlers (Jeremy Tredinnick x2)

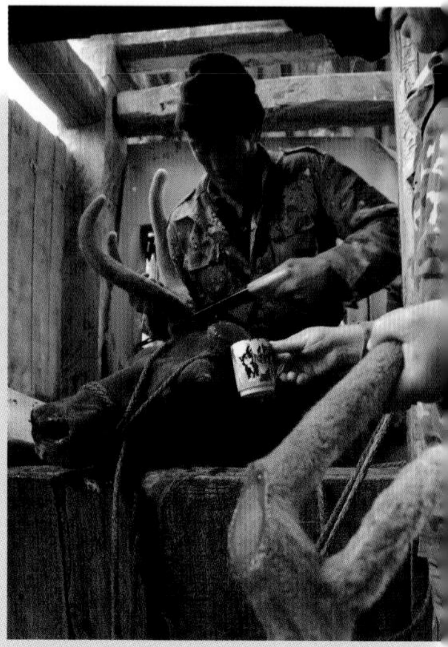

Maral keeping first began in this part of the Altai in the 17th Century, but the medical benefits of deer antler extract have been praised for thousands of years by various Asian cultures. Only relatively recently, however, have modern scientists understood its chemical properties. Pantocrine (*Cornu cervi parvum*) has a nutritional profile including collagen, amino acids, essential fatty acids, important phospholipids, minerals, trace minerals and other functional proteins, all vital components for human metabolism. It promotes protein synthesis, building lean muscle and tissue, has shown to increase work capacity and appetite, and improve sleep. It also has an anti-catabolic action that reduces wasting and debilitation, and increases production of red and white blood cells, thereby accelerating healing and recovery. In other words... pretty good stuff.

The Katon-Karagay Maral Farm has come to national attention because of a particular pantocrine product it produces. This "elixir" ("Vostochnyi") is a concoction of pantocrine, local berries, nuts and different plants, developed by the farm in association with the Kazakhstan Academy of Sciences. After an international competition, it was selected to accompany a manned space flight in 2001 as an energy booster for the Russian, American and Kazakh cosmonauts, who all gave it the thumbs-up on their return. Nurlan's aim now is to make it one of Kazakhstan's top-five products; that's a tall order, but Nurlan himself travels to Hong Kong, South Korea and Singapore selling direct to shops (a smart business move to cut out the middleman), and I wouldn't bet against someone with as much quiet authority, energy and drive as the director.

We end the evening meal well past midnight, toasting each other with tumblers of elixir-vodka mix. I'm ready for my bed, head swimming with all the alcohol I've imbibed, sleep deprivation making matters worse. It's then that I'm told a member of staff will now take me for my treatment! Looking bleary-eyed towards the door, I see a vision—a beautiful young Kazakh woman stands patiently waiting... and she's dressed in a nurse's uniform.

Above: One antler off and the other under the saw, a cup is placed to catch any dripping blood before a sandy poultice is placed onto the antler stumps. Right: Nurlan inspects an antler (Jeremy Tredinnick x2)

As my new friends say their goodnights and head off to their beds, I follow the nurse towards the sanatorium, mesmerised by her sashaying, voluptuous figure, trying to imagine myself in a more surreal situation, but hardly able to walk straight. Entering the building I'm greeted by another nurse, a no-nonsense matron who sits me down and takes my blood pressure: it's 120 over 80, which is good; with this knowledge they prescribe the amount of pantocrine mixture I will have in my bath—too high a concentration can be dangerous to your system, I have been told—and my gorgeous attendant leads me into my bathroom. With sign language—my translator has retired for the night and my Russian is as nonexistent as the nurse's English—she instructs me to strip, lie in the already prepared bath for 10 minutes, gently scooping water over myself, and when I hear her knock on the door to get out, dry and dress myself, and meet her outside.

So here I am, in the remote northeast corner of Kazakhstan, at two in the morning, having a bath in the secretions from maral antlers, much the worse for vodka, with a lovely young female nurse waiting just outside my door. The mind boggles—well, I'm not too sure what my brain is doing, but although the water is slightly greasy and has an odour reminiscent of a pine-tar solution I used to use for itchy skin, I find I'm incredibly relaxed and comfortable. My bizarre reverie is disturbed by a gentle knocking, and I obediently struggle out of the bath and back into my clothes.

Outside, my blood pressure is taken once again—it's now down to 90 over 70, whatever that means—and then I'm off again, being led towards my chalet bedroom by my raven-haired beauty. She ushers me inside, motions for me to get undressed again, sit on the bed and wait, for she will return, then disappears. Suddenly my mind goes into overdrive. The strictest decorum has been followed at all times, I have no reason to think what I'm thinking, but in my brain-addled state a number of outrageous scenarios pop into my mind—forgive me, I am only human, and she is very attractive.

I strip to my boxers, sit on the bed—surely this can't be happening—and wait for whatever is coming. Another quiet knock, the door opens and in she comes—she really is heavenly—holding something, I'm not sure what. Smiling, she gently pushes me onto my back, then over onto my side, pulls my boxers down… and very professionally slides a syringe into my rectum, swiftly administering 15ml of pure elixir into my colon—the final part of the treatment. She signals me to lie on my side for 20 minutes, then leaves.

I pass out.

I'm up at dawn, and despite once again having had far less sleep than necessary, I feel fine. No, I feel great. Who would have guessed it?

Before moving on to my next Altai adventure, Nurlan and Aldiyar take me to see a few marals being assessed. In a stockade much like a cattle ranch, each huge animal is driven in turn into a confined padded area, where a tough farmhand sits on its back and holds it still to keep it from hurting itself—or any of us. Nurlan inspects the massive velvet-covered antlers, feeling the tips, and deciding whether they are ready to be removed. One animal is released with his antlers intact, but the other two are deemed ready for harvesting. It takes only a dozen seconds or so for the farmhand to saw through each antler—there is a brief oozing of blood, caught in mugs by the onlookers, before the stumps are packed with a sandy poultice to protect them from infection, and the wild-eyed animal is freed.

I ask Aldiyar if the deer feels any pain. "No, it is like cutting your nails," he replies, "there is no pain." The maral is afraid of course, so the processing is done as fast as possible to minimize its discomfort, but the animals seem to calm down as soon as they are freed, and are soon grazing happily again, perhaps even happy to be free of 20 kilos of horn on their heads. The antlers, meanwhile, have been inspected, weighed, tagged and sent off to the boiling sheds, where they will begin a process of boiling, heat-drying and wind-drying that can last for a month.

The end result, packaged neatly in small bottles blazoned with a proud prancing maral on the label, will be sold around the world at high prices. My last taste on this trip, however, is straight from the source, as a cracked mug filled with a bloody mixture of maral essence and… you guessed it …vodka, is pressed into my hand. And why not, I think. Bottoms up!

Research Centre of France found many objects alongside the bodies, from which they learned much about the Scythian way of life. They included wooden tables with carvings, gold jewellery, felt and woollen rugs, and household tools. The excavators suspected that the ancient Scythians used a special technology for building the kurgans, which allowed the bodies of the deceased to freeze swiftly, thus preserving them in amazing condition. (One horse, upon exhumation, was so well preserved that red meat was still present on the corpse.) In summer, the soil defrosts only down to 2–4 metres at this altitude; the kurgans were constructed in such a way that their chambers are in a permanently frozen state.

Locally dubbed the Valley of Kings, the kurgans are spread out but in clusters. There is no infrastructure here at all, in fact no buildings can be seen nearby—only the stone mounds surrounded by green grass and forested mountain slopes. It is an idyllic spot; true, there is little to actually see at the kurgan sites—Kurgan No 11, where the prince was found, is simply a mud- and water-filled crater surrounded by stones—but the location and an atmosphere of antiquity make it a worthwhile stop. Not all of the kurgans have been excavated, so who knows what else may be waiting to be discovered under the frozen valley soil?

Rachmanov's Springs

From Berel it's a long, hard drive up into a landscape of high peaks and deep valleys, the road clinging to the mountainside at times high above the rushing river far below. A 4WD is almost essential, though vans can make the trip if the track is dry enough. Around 30 kilometres to the northeast, the road ends at **Rachmanov's Springs** (Rahman Kaynary), a small mountain village community situated near picturesque **Rachmanov Lake**, and boasting a health resort (www.altaytravel.com) that has counted a number of luminaries as its guests over the years. In 1995 President Nazarbayev visited the lake resort; when the locals asked for a better-quality road to be built up to their home, the president refused, saying that it was vital to "preserve the natural beauty" of the region. This was a massive disappointment for the local community, but it is likely that the fragile ecology of this area would be ruined if hordes of tourists were allowed to rush in.

The lake and village got their name from an 18th Century hunter named Rachmanov, who discovered the nine hot springs that feed into the dark, mysterious lake in this remote corner of Kazakhstan. Rachmanov lived to the ripe old age of 102, and the springs soon became famous for their medicinal qualities.

Following pages: Trekking in the picturesque Berel Valley (Hermann Schulz)

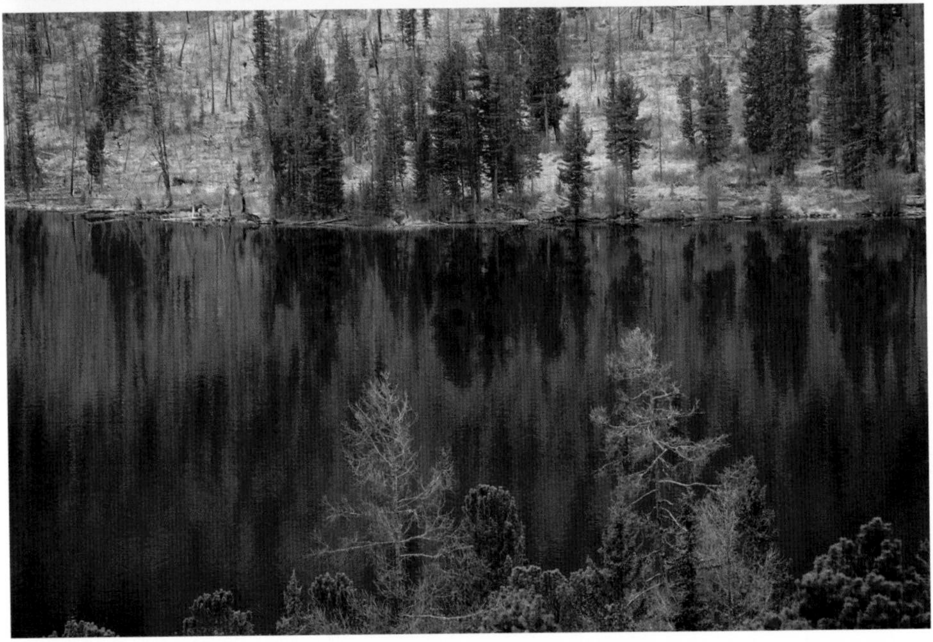

Top: Kurgans in the Valley of Kings. Above: Rachmanov Lake in mysterious mood. Right: A view of the valley floor from the jeep track up to Rachmanov's Springs (Jeremy Tredinnick x3)

The health resort is now privately owned—the government sold it to a wealthy car dealer in Oskemen—and work is forging ahead on a number of new chalets, all kitted out with kitchens, modern bathrooms and satellite TVs. The plan is to attract high-end tourists who will be flown in by helicopter (an exhilarating flight of a few hours instead of the 12 hours or more by van or 4WD), but there will be a limit of 120 guests at a time. (This of course does not count the numerous other tourists who make the long trip up by road and either camp or rent rooms at homestays in the village.) The main hot spring building is built around the largest spring pool. Complete with relaxation area, changing rooms and a tiled pool area with reclining loungers, the pool itself is gravel-bottomed, thigh deep and a soothing 40°C. Bathing is nude, and men and women bathe separately. Medical staff are on hand for specific treatments, and other spring pools in the close vicinity are now undergoing the same building treatment.

Many people—mostly Russians and Kazakhs—come here to cure numerous diseases by soaking in the springs, but there is much more to this place than that: the clear lakes and beautiful cedar forests are an example of alpine environment *par excellence*—the main lake (there is another to the south) can be toured in speedboats driven by ex-army rangers, and the hiking possibilities are endless. The forested mountains hem the lake in tightly, waterfalls like the Veronica's Hair Fall cut through the granite like fine white tendrils from the perennially snow-dusted ridges, and there is even a location known as the Valley of Bears: Siberian brown bears are common here, growing to two metres in length and potentially very dangerous animals—hence the need for rangers and experienced guides.

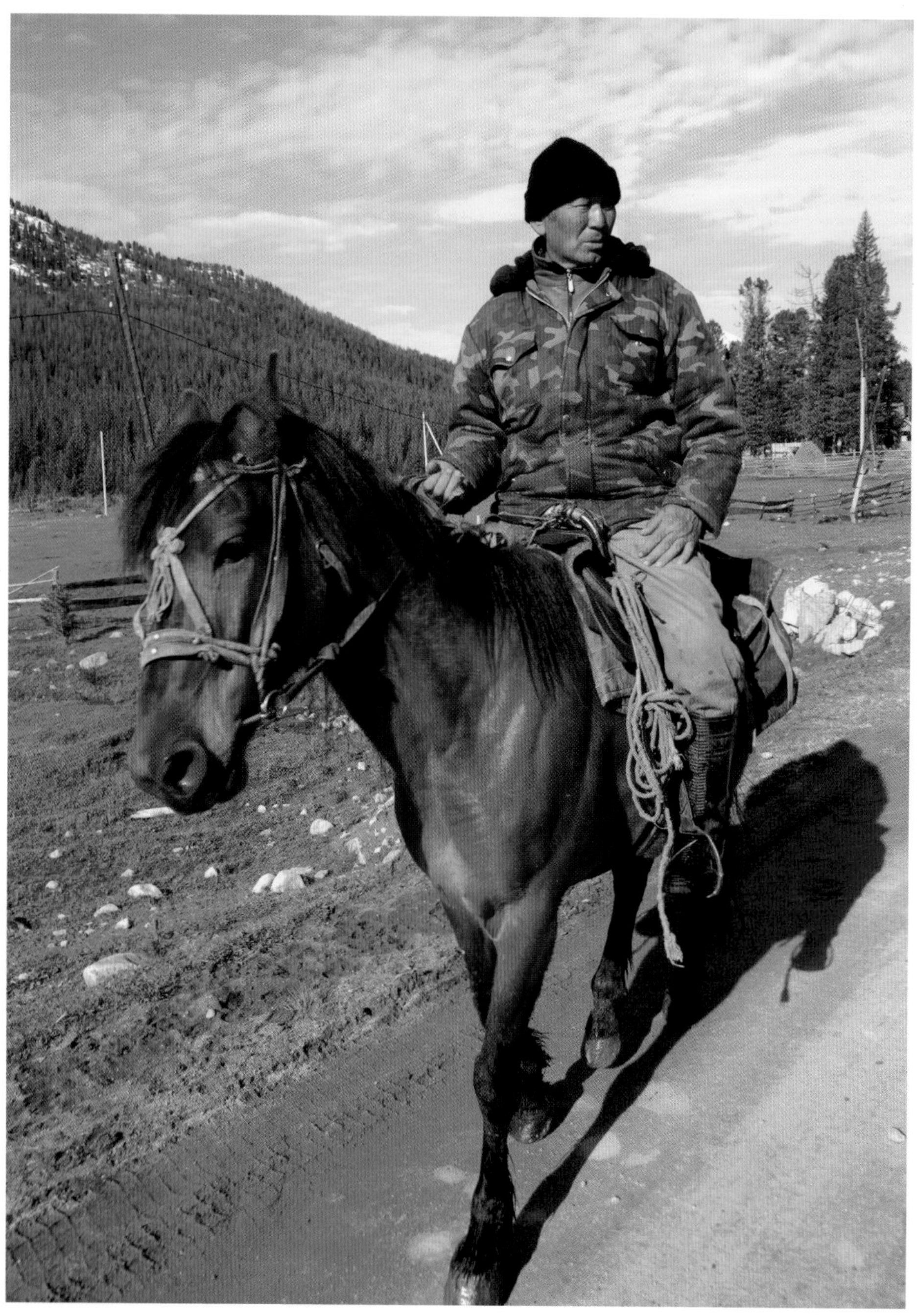

A Kazakh horseman at Rachmanov's Springs (Jeremy Tredinnick)

Top: The best two methods of transport in the Altai mountains—horse or 4WD. Above: A newly built chalet at the Rachmanov's Springs resort (Jeremy Tredinnick x2)

Another popular reason for coming to Rachmanov's Springs is to either simply get a look at, trek to the base of, or even climb, the Altai's highest and most revered peak: Byelukha.

MOUNT BYELUKHA

Gaze at the inspirational twin peaks of **Mount Byelukha (White One)** and you will understand why it is revered by the Siberian shaman culture as a holy mountain. Buddhists also honour it as the spiritual centre of the Earth, or Shambhala. For the adherents of the ancient Turkic Tengri cult, rough-looking, sky-piercing **Khan Tengri** was the dwelling place of the chief (male) god, Tengri, but Byelukha's twin peaks look like the upward-pointing breasts of a goddess, lying on her back. The water of the mountain brooks and streams that spring from the mountain's glaciers foams white—like an ancestral mother's milk. **Byelovodye (White Water)** is the name of this land of shamans.

At 4,506 metres high, Byelukha is the highest peak in all of Siberia. It is the main landmark of the central Altai, or the **Katun** mountain range. Its summit was "officially" conquered in 1914 by the Russian mountaineers Boris and Mikhail Tronov. Climbing to the summit, or both summits (the lower of the peaks is 4,440 metres high, and a glacier separates the two), is not a simple venture: the difference in altitude between the base camp on the Russian side and the summit is in the order of 3,000 metres, there are treacherous glaciers to be

The twin peaks of Mt Byelukha are the highest in the Altai (Vladislav Yakushkin)

braved, and the weather is extremely unpredictable; many an experienced mountain climber has failed on Byelukha.

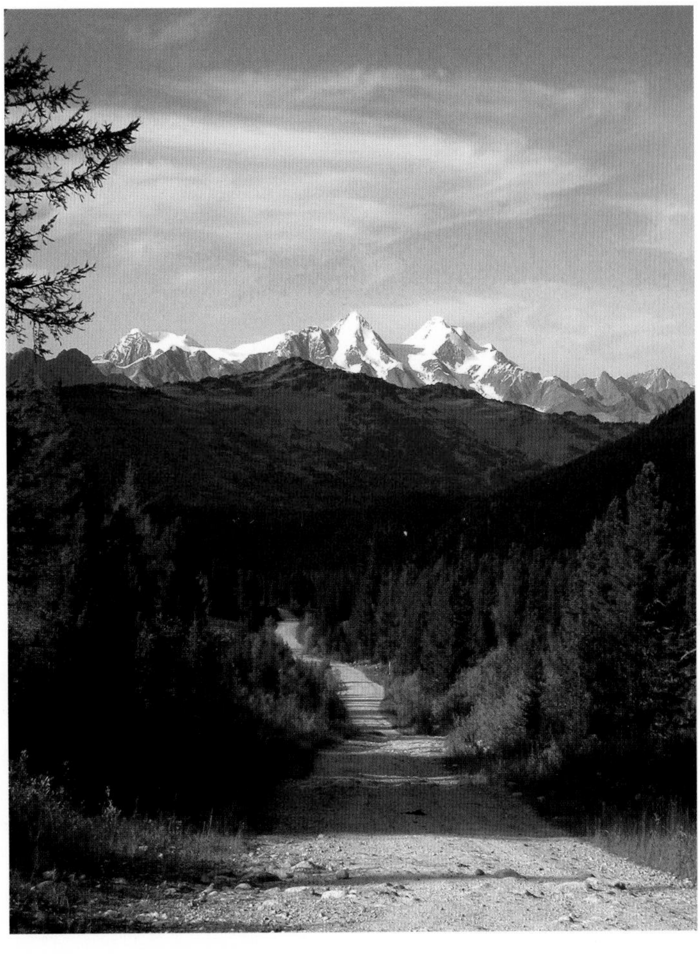

But the majority of travellers will not be aiming so high; for most, simply getting close enough to gaze upon it and experience its pristine environment is more than enough. You can actually get a distant but good view of the mountain on the track some four kilometres before Rachmanov's Springs, at **Radostniy (Cheerful) Pass**—weather permitting of course. Better, though, is to immerse yourself in this beautiful landscape on a two-day trek from the Springs to the tongue of the **Berelskiy Glacier** at the foot of the mountain, crossing two passes on the way, or from the **Greater Yazyovoye Lake** over a distance of some 40 kilometres through beautiful landscape. In this alpine wonderland you will pass the **Black and White Berel rivers**, whose cascades and many tributaries invite a bracing swim. Buddhists believe that there is a spiritual bridge at Mount Byelukha that leads to **Chomolangma (Mount Everest)**. Some trekkers are almost prepared to believe them, since the crystalline light and some natural source of energy seems to permeate this timeless region—and those who visit it.

Above: On a clear day Byelukha can be seen from the jeep track to Rachmanov's Springs (Andrey Yurchenkov). Following pages: At the old miner's camp in Kokkol (Hermann Schulz)

KOKKOL MINE AND CASCADE

The **Bolshoy Kokkol River (Great Green Water)** is a tributary of the White Berel. In 1936, the geologist A. Nikonov discovered fragments of quartz and **wolframite** in its upper reaches, at a height of 3,000 metres. A later expedition confirmed that the quartz veins that breached the surface here bore abundant concentrations of wolframite and **molybdenum**—enough to justify a mining operation. In 1938, the operation was launched and the mine and a settlement for workers were built. A second settlement was built for the miners' families, with a school, a bakery, a sauna and stables further down, in a forest some eight kilometres away from the mining site. Quartz was mined here in large quantities until 1954; it was processed into concentrate *in situ*, and carried down the valley to the village of Berel by horse.

A ghost town is all that is left now, below an impressive, thundering waterfall. Wandering about, you will find many tools still lying around, and work reports and accounts from the days when the village was very much alive have been found in the buildings. The larch-wood bridge across the White Berel, four kilometres below the lower settlement, has so far withstood all floods, and the stone track to the upper settlement has remained in good

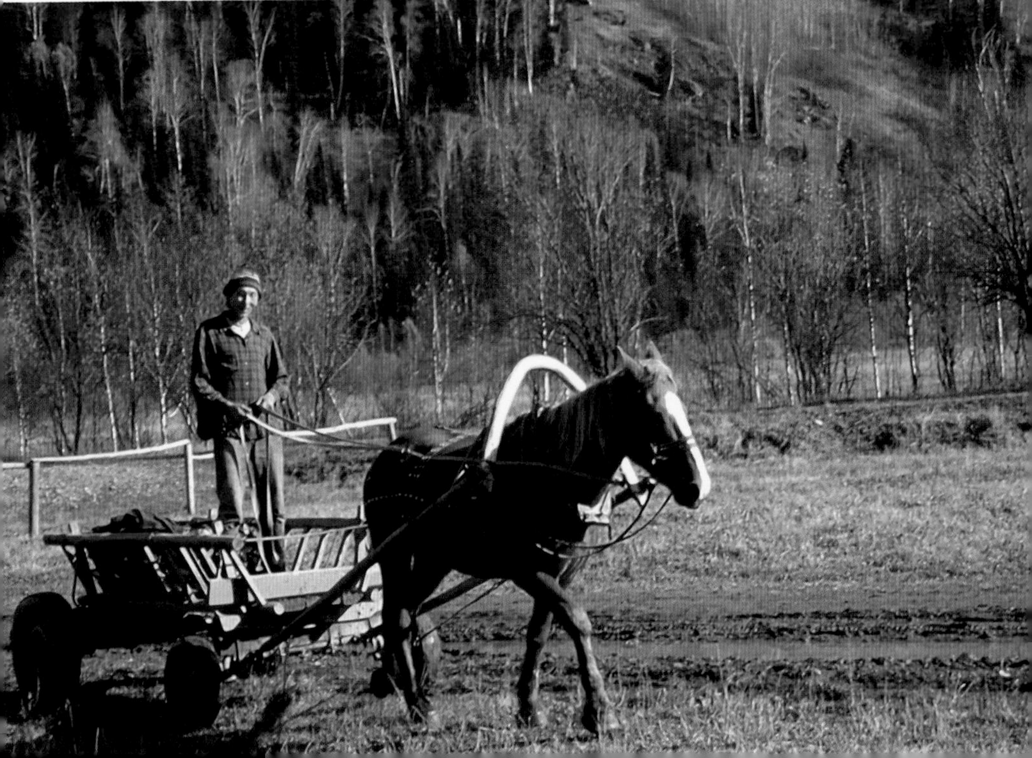

condition. Two houses have been preserved in the lower settlement, which are used by tourists who come to camp here. **Kokkol** is a suitable base camp for tours on foot to the base of Byelukha, the cascade and the upper camp. It takes about two days to walk from here to Rachmanov's Springs.

BURKITAUL

Mount Burkitaul is the highest mountain of the Sarymsakty chain. It is 3,373 metres high, and situated 18 kilometres to the southwest of Katon-Karagay town. It is popular among mountaineers for its wonderful pyramid shape and its three glaciers. The greenish-black volcanic rocks make a striking contrast against the white snow and the bluish glacier tongues on the northern slope. At the foot of the mountain there are extensive birch woods, famous for their abundance of mushrooms and berries, but farther up the landscape changes into dark coniferous taiga forest consisting of larch, cedar and spruce. Arkhar and ibex dwell on the pastures above the treeline. Mount Burkitaul can best be reached from the village of **Topkayin** on the road from Oskemen to Katon-Karagay. From here, it is 16 kilometres to the summit; unusually for Kazakhstan, on the mountain slopes there is a hut that can accommodate fairly large groups of climbers.

MAYMYR

The charming village of **Maymyr** is located on the road from Oskemen to Katon-Karagay. Five kilometres beyond the village, a side road leads to **Soldatovo**, and down a track near here, where the Maymyr stream foams out of its narrow mountain gorge, there is a small resort with a wooden house, flower gardens, a few yurts, horses and dogs, a wagon and a Russian sauna. This leisure oasis belongs to an enterprising local named Alexei Mekhnin and his family. Accommodation here is reasonably priced, and it makes an excellent base for delightful hikes and horse rides in the broad steppe valley of the Narym River and its wild, forest-covered side valleys. You can book rooms through easttour@ukg.kz or nva_nov@mail.ru, or through Altai-Expeditions (see end of chapter).

ZYRYANOVSK

The town of **Zyryanovsk** came into being at the start of the 19th Century with the discovery of valuable deposits of lead and silver. It quickly grew into an important mining centre, and during Soviet times was known for its polymetallic mining and processing complex and its lead smelters. More than 50,000 inhabitants made a decent living from this industrial sector, while agriculture, mainly wheat and sunflowers, as well as beekeeping and horse and cattle breeding, added to the prosperity of the region. Today, the town has a run-down feel, and it's easy to see the lack of funding that came with the decrease in mining activity.

Left: For Altai farmers the traditional methods are still often the best (Dagmar Schreiber)

However, in true Kazakh fashion, the district has refused to give up and is now developing its huge tourism potential, from beach and ski resorts to tours of the surrounding **Rudniy Altai** mountains.

Situated not far from the eastern end of **Bukhtarminsk Reservoir,** Zyryanovsk is a good starting point for tours in the largely untouched **Khamir Valley** up to the mountain ridge of **Kholzun** (*Khrebet Kholzun*). A road leads up to **Stolbukha**, crosses the Bukhtarma near Lesnaya Pristan and then continues to **Putintsovo**, a popular ski resort in winter. A basic road also leads from Stolbukha to the neighbouring **Chernovaya Valley**.

Another interesting tour goes to **Turgusun**, where the river of the same name flows into the Bukhtarma. From here, you can drive to **Kutikha**, a village of **Old Believers**—Christians who refused to comply with the Orthodox Church and prefer to live peacefully with their own beliefs. From here, you can continue west towards the mountains where there is a protected botanic area called **Nizheturgusunk**. To the north rises a snow-covered mountain ridge, the highest peak of which, **Vysheivanovskiy Byelok**, reaches 2,775 metres in height. Four mountain chains come together in this range, named **Chorniy Uzel (Black Knot)**. This is the highest point and also the most important source of water in the western Altai. The rivers Uba, Malaya Ulba, Gromotukha and Turgusun all originate here.

Just seven kilometres southwest of Zyryanovsk lies the **Oryol Ski Resort**, on the slopes of **Oryol (Eagle) Mountain**. There is a hotel catering to 30 people, three four-person cottages, a sauna bath-house and café-bar, while two ski lifts covering 2.2 kilometres allow skiers and snowboarders to schuss down runs with a 400-metre vertical drop. The ski season runs from December until mid-April, and skis, snowboards and snow vehicles are for rent. A leisure resort on Bukhtarminsk Reservoir also allows for summer holidaying with waterskiing, swimming and relaxing on the beach and rocky shore of the reservoir lake.

Above: Altai honey is superb, a product of the wealth of flowering plant life in the region (Vladimir Tugalev). Right: A traditional house in Ridder (Dagmar Schreiber)

Ridder

The road to the valleys of the White and the Black Uba rivers to the east and north respectively, and to the mountain range of **Ivanovskiy Khrebet** beyond, leads through the town of **Ridder**, sitting in the picturesque Uba Valley in the western Altai. Called **Leninogorsk** during the Soviet era, Ridder reverted to its historical name in 2002, named after the German geologist who, in the middle of the 18th Century, discovered rich polymetallic deposits here. The town was established in 1786, and it swiftly developed into a centre of mining and processing. A railway was constructed and the population grew to 70,000. Today, however, Ridder finds itself in a deplorable condition. Many enterprises that provided economic stability went under along with the Soviet Union, and those that remain in business can only do so with reduced numbers of staff. Part of the lead and zinc industrial processing on the northern and southern outskirts of the town are still operating, but there is not much else. As with Zyryanovsk, however, tourism development is giving some of the inhabitants a future once more.

West Altai Nature Reserve

The territory stretching beyond Ridder to the Russian border is now the **West Altai Nature Reserve**, established in 1991 and totalling 56,000 hectares of rich taiga and tundra, with 564 plant species, 120 species of bird and 30 mammals recorded in its range. It includes the mountain ranges of **Ivanovskiy**, **Lineyskiy** and **Koksinskiy Khrebet**, as well as the

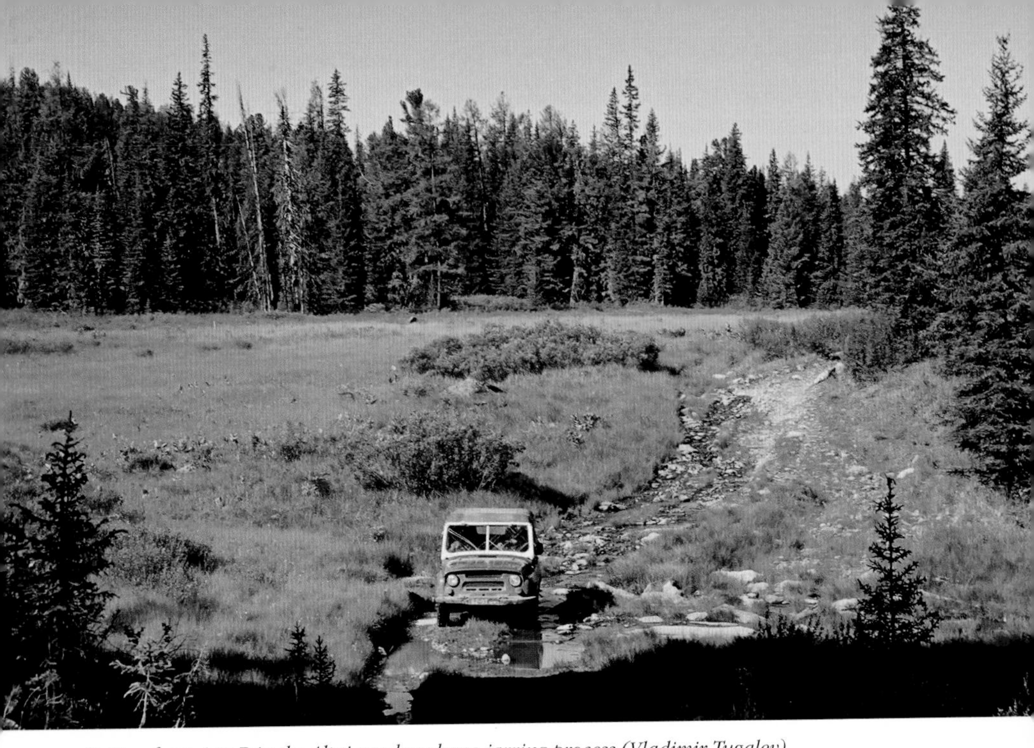

Getting from A to B in the Altai can be a bone-jarring process (Vladimir Tugalev)

Khrebet Kholsun, and consists of coniferous taiga forest and mountain tundra. Thick, overgrown woods grow in this area, known for the highest rainfall in the Asian part of the Commonwealth of Independent States, with up to 3,800 millimetres of rain in some years. As a result, there is an unusual abundance of berries, mushrooms and medicinal herbs as well as a great variety of wonderful trees, from Siberian cedar and spruce to fir, larch, aspen and birch.

Bears and wolves inhabit the reserve in large numbers, and the inhabitants of remote farms can relate numerous stories about encounters with them. Worth a visit are the lakes **Shcherbakova**, **Kedrovoye** and **Byeloubinskiye Ozyora**, as well as the **Maloulbinskoye Vodokhranilishche** with its wooden dam and primitive electrical installations built in 1926. Massive granite pillars up to 30 metres high have formed in the most astonishing shapes where the Ivanovskiy and Lineyskiy mountain ranges clash together.

Only 4WDs can make it along the road through the heavily forested Uba River valley. On the White Uba (*Byelaya Uba*), some 40 kilometres to the north of Ridder, there is a small, pretty leisure resort bearing the same name, and comprising a dozen log cabins built in the Russian style, with a fantastic sauna and a tiny but beautiful church. Byelaya Uba is an ideal starting point for hikes and rides into the side valleys and up Ivanovskiy Khrebet.

Right: Semey's old mosque has Russian elements to its construction (Dagmar Schreiber)

You can spend time here in any season: in spring, when water levels are high, the Uba is fit for rafting, and in winter the snow-covered valley is good for cross-country skiing.

Some of the remote side valleys are inhabited. Most of the recluses here, living without electricity and other modern comforts, are beekeepers and shepherds. There are also some individuals who have turned their back on civilisation, and seek only to be close to nature, surviving on a few animals and the land's bounty. Among their ancestors are the Old Believers, who moved from Russia into the Siberian forests and the Altai's all but inaccessible valleys to escape persecution. Convicts who escaped from Siberia's labour camps and serfs on the run also found refuge in the Altai, but the settlers are friendly towards visitors. If you would like to visit them, keep in mind that a pack of tea, coffee or cigarettes is a luxury here, and such gifts would be hugely appreciated.

THE IRTYSH PLAIN

The **Irtysh River** (although officially now the Ertis, the Russian name is still used everywhere) pours out of the foothills of the Altai, through Oskemen, and flows steadily towards the plain through pasture woods consisting of broad-crowned pine. A man-made dam near Shulbinsk disrupts its peaceful progress, made principally to control the flow of water.

The northern branch of the Silk Road once ran along the Irtysh, from Mongolian territory through today's China to the Bukhtarma Valley. Gold and silver from the Altai was transported along this route, and continued through the centuries right up until 1991. Hundreds of thousands of hooves marched along it each year, belonging to the massive

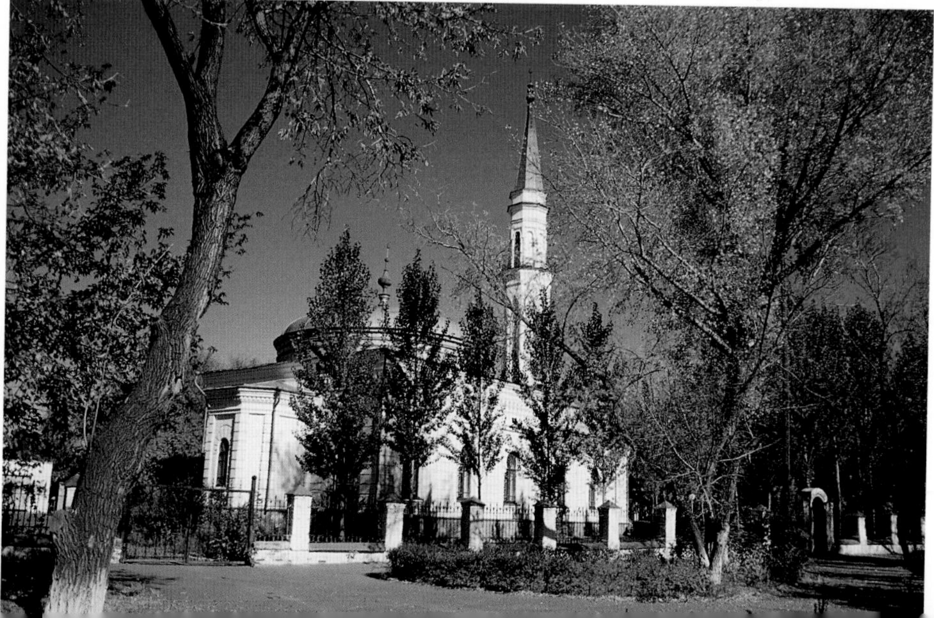

herds of sheep, each up to 2,000 strong, that were driven from Mongolia to Semipalatinsk (as it still was then), to end up in the Soviet Union's largest slaughtering and meat processing complex, which provided the army with meat. Each week such a herd, bleating and throwing up clouds of dust, and accompanied by shepherds on horseback and dogs, moved through the Altai and along the Irtysh in this way. Along the route, at 20-kilometre intervals, were sheep pens and log cabins for the shepherds. There are even plans to restart this trade and have the old sheep drive revived.

Following the Irtysh downstream from Oskemen, the next large city is historic Semipalatinsk/Semey.

SEMEY (SEMIPALATINSK)

On hearing the name **Semipalatinsk**, most people think of atom bomb experiments on test sites in the Kazakh steppe. As a result, few would think of choosing this place as a travel destination. This, however, does a great injustice to the city, now known by its Kazakh name of **Semey**. Not only did the tests stop in 1991, but radiation has dropped to significantly below internationally recognized maximum levels of tolerance in both the city and its surroundings. There is much to see here as well—residents of Semey proudly refer to their city as the spiritual capital of Kazakhstan. In doing so, they can draw on a rich history.

In 1616, word reached Russia about a city by the name of **Dorzhinkit**. It was said to be located on the right bank of the Irtysh, at the site of an ancient Lamaist monastery of Zhungar origin. This city, located in the fertile Irtysh Plain, had flourished thanks to the trade routes that crossed the river through a nearby ford.

The name Semipalatinsk dates back to the year 1718, when Tsar Peter I ordered Dorzhinkit to be turned into a fortress, including seven grand buildings that formed the city's centre. However, the name was only officially given in 1760 to a second fortress that was built on the spot where the present-day city is situated; apparently the first fortress, a rectangular wooden structure named **Fort Yamyshevsk**, was severely damaged on several occasions by the untamed Irtysh's spring floods, so it was decided to choose a better location at a higher level. In 1776, the fortress was again moved, this time a distance of 18 kilometres, and named Semipalatinsk. It swiftly developed into an important trade centre, and by the middle of the 19th Century, annual revenues from exchange of goods from Russia, China and Central Asia amounted to a million gold roubles. There was no end to the influx of caravans, and Semipalatinsk grew rich. Since that time, the city's coat of arms has featured a camel, symbolizing the caravans that once crossed the Irtysh here, bringing success and wealth to the city.

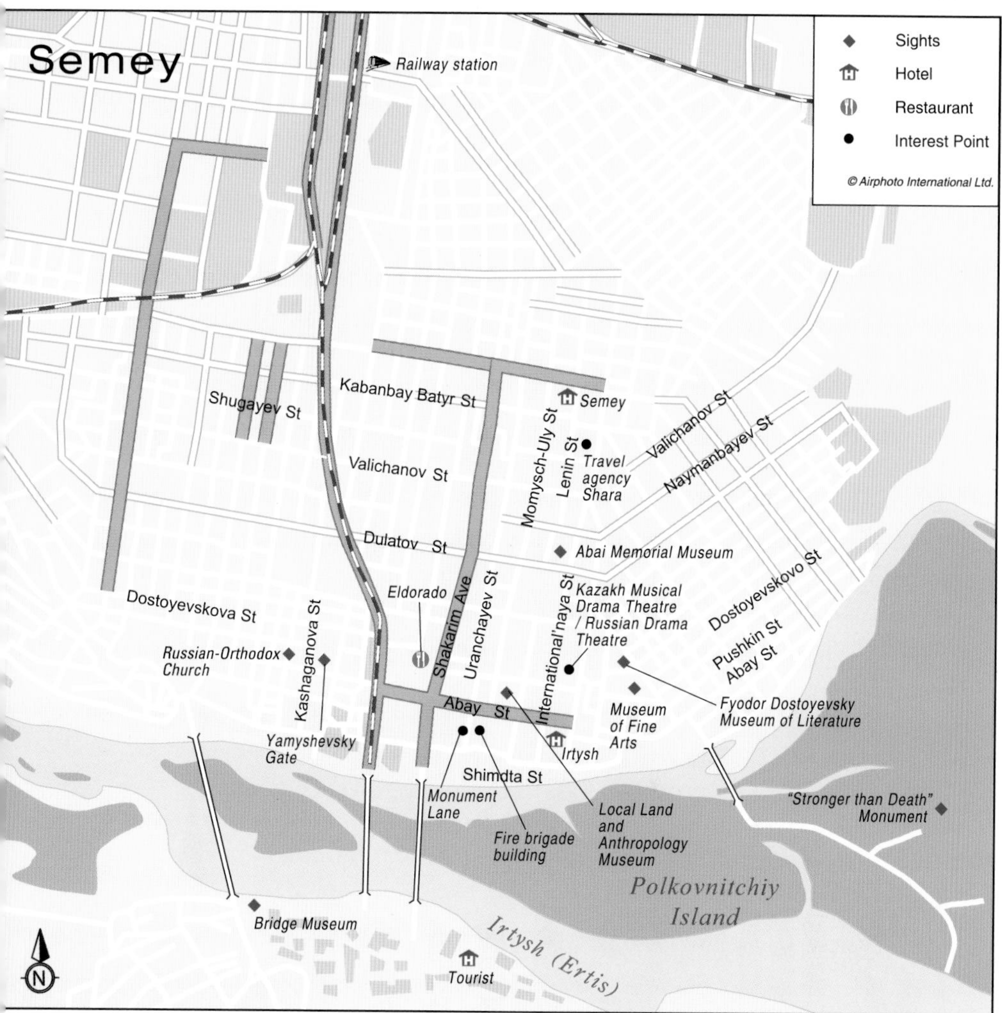

Contrary to expectation, the Kazakh name for the city, Semey, is not derived from the Russian. It comes from an ancient Turkic word meaning holy or spiritual site. The Kazakh tribes of old appear to have given this name to the site, a prophetic decision since many of Kazakhstan's outstanding luminaries, in whom the nation takes great pride, originate from Semey, including the great poet **Abai Kunanbayev**, the writer and founder of Kazakh theatre **Mukhtar Auezov**, the poet and philosopher **Shakarim**, the founding fathers of the nationalist party **Alash Orda** and a number of important musicians, singers and other creative artists.

The people of Kazakhstan have the 19th Century Russian tsars to thank for this, because they used Semipalatinsk as a place of exile. The young, democracy-minded aristocrats who, from 1825 onwards, began to strive for reforms in the tsarist autocracy usually ended up here. But their exile did not stop these well-educated, energetic noblemen from proclaiming their ideas. Libraries, museums and schools were opened. Scientific societies and cultural circles were established. In all, though unwittingly, the tsars had done the area an immense favour. Intellectual life in the garrison town increased by leaps and bounds thanks to the presence of great people such as **Fyodor Dostoyevsky**, **Yevgeny Mikhaelis**, the four **Byeloslyudov brothers** and many others. The establishment of the city library dates back to that time, as well as that of the Society for Geographical and Statistical Science.

Young Kazakhs such as Abai Kunanbayev, eager to learn, were welcomed into the company of Russian democrats, and an extensive mutual enrichment was the result. The development of the minds and personalities of people like Abai and Shakarim was a natural result of this concentration of brilliant and critical minds at a time when all over Russia social contradictions were crystallizing. Considering this, it is no surprise that the founders of the nationalist party **Alash Orda**, which in 1917 stepped forward to claim independence, should come from Semipalatinsk. The fact that all the inheritors of Abai's legacy, including

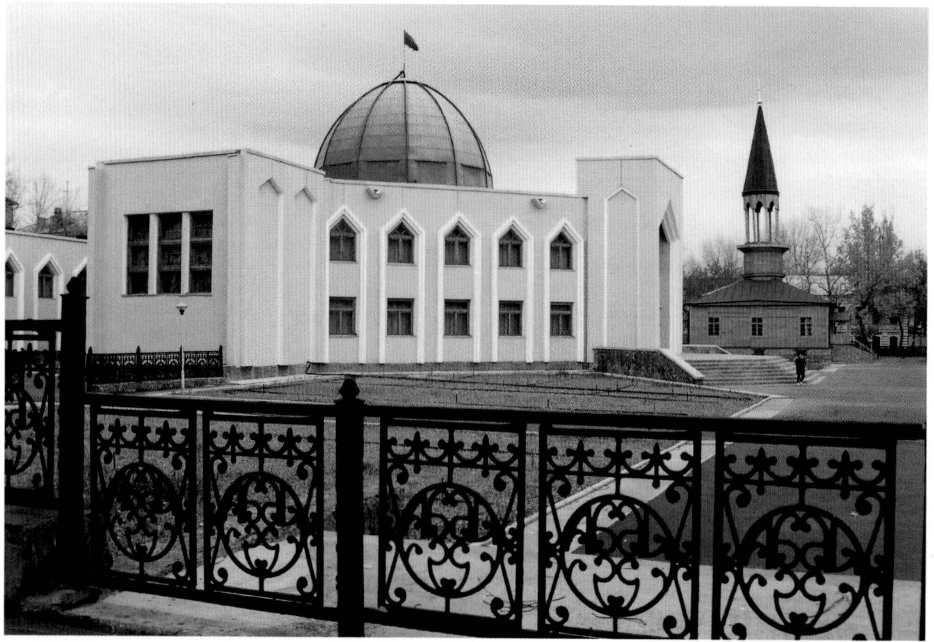

The highly recommended Abay Memorial Museum (Agency Semey)

the leadership of Alash Orda, the philosopher Shakarim and with them the bulk of the Kazakh intellectual class, were to be caught and murdered in the 1930s by the **People's Commissariat for Internal Affairs (NKVD)**, was an immeasurable loss both for Russia and the Kazakhstan to come.

It is a gruesome historical irony that a city with such a glorious past and reputation should be nominated as the location for a testing ground for atomic weapons. As a result, the entire area of Semipalatinsk was forbidden territory for years. Half a million people lived here, but were not allowed to receive any visitors from the outside world. They lived well enough, to the extent that social services and living standards were exceptionally good, but the effect on the social psyche was horrific. Plenty of information about the "inside story" of life in Semipalatinsk during those years can now be found at the **Anatomic Museum**, located in the imposing building of the Military Medical Academy (1 Lenin Street, tel: 627 905).

From the 1990s on, the city authorities and citizens made an effort to improve its image. Many buildings have been newly built or restored; educational and cultural excursions are organized for both schoolchildren and adults from all over Kazakhstan; and changing the official name to Semey is an attempt to make people forget the bitter taste the name Semipalatinsk has left behind.

Fortunately, the city and its surrounding area still bear many traces of their history in the form of museums and monuments, which have been or are being restored, and are definitely worth exploring. The **Local History Museum** (a kind of museum called *Muzey krayevedyeniya*—"local lore, history and economy museum" in Russian) is a good start for a cultural tour around Semey. Situated on Abai Street/Lenin Street, it was established as the **Gogol Library**, with an appropriate exhibition, by exiled democrats led by Yevgeny Mikhaelis. It is hard to overestimate the huge merit of this initiative, which for the first time held a mirror in front of the region through which it could see its own history. The oldest exhibits include a collection of 60 household tools from the Kazakh daily life of old, donated to the museum by Abai.

The **Abay Memorial Museum** is a must for every visitor to Semey. The generously furnished building on Dulatov Street/Internatsionalnaya Street, next to the Koran school in which Abai used to study, houses a lovingly—and didactically—clever collection of exhibits that provide information about the sources of Abai's creative force, his life and work, his experience, as well as the work of his students, and the way his heritage has lived on through the course of time. Abai's manuscripts, the household tools mentioned earlier and other testimonies to his life and times are impressive, but of particular interest are the many artistic works depicting the topics and tales in Abai's literature. Wonderful goblins by

Shamyl Koshanov and expressive graphics by **Yevgeny Sidorkin** offer foreign visitors a true reflection of Abai's broad creative imagination. These works can rightfully be included in the most important works of art in Kazakhstan today. The hall of yurts provides a very realistic idea of the Kazakh nomad's way of life. The fully furnished yurt is a masterpiece of craft which makes the visitor share the feeling as described by Abai in his poem "Spring": the utmost joy that fills the hearts of shepherds and their families when, after a long winter, they can finally put up their yurts in the broad, green steppe again.

The historical tour around the city continues with a visit to the **Fyodor Dostoyevsky Memorial Museum of Literature** at 118 Dostoyevskovo Street. The great Russian author spent the second stage of his exile here in Semipalatinsk, from 1854 till 1859, having already spent five years in the southern Siberian city of Omsk. His work *Notes from the House of the Dead* is dedicated to that first period of his exile. Along with more than 100 other members of the St Petersburg literary circle, Dostoyevsky was arrested and convicted after an informant of the Tsar's secret police had reported on their discussions about Russian serfdom. The sentence for the writer, already well known in Russia, was changed to exile literally seconds before he was to be executed.

Above: A statue of Dostoyevsky and Chokan Valikhanov sits next to the former's museum. Above right: The powerful and emotive "Stronger than Death" monument (Dagmar Schreiber x2)

Once in Semipalatinsk, Dostoyevsky received the support of Governor Spiridonov and Baron Wrangel. The latter arranged for the author to get back his officer's rank and his civil rights. This made life in exile a lot more comfortable for Dostoyevsky, and he lived in relative peace here. It was in the city that he met his first great love, married her and went to live in a two-storey wooden house in the Tartar neighbourhood. This house, with a large building attached to it, is now the museum. A guided tour reveals much of the man behind the famous author. A metal statue of Fyodor Dostoyevsky and the young Kazakh scholar and travel explorer, Chokan Valikhanov, stands next to the museum, documenting the many friendly encounters in the city between these two men of genius.

It may come as a surprise to know that Semey is also the home of one of Kazakhstan's largest museums of fine art. Its home is the splendid mansion at 108 Pushkin Street, adorned with pillars, which once belonged to a rich merchant family. The **Museum of Fine Arts** was opened in 1985, after the Muscovite art collector Nevsorov donated 500 works of art from Russia and Europe. Its 3,000 other works also include Kazakh paintings and sculptures. Temporary exhibitions are displayed on the ground floor, and the museum is open every day from 10am–5:30pm. Since guided tours are very detailed, you should allow at least two hours for a visit.

In addition, Semey has a miniature puppet museum with 800 puppets representing historic personalities, a printing museum and one of Kazakhstan's oldest fire brigade buildings. Other places of interest include the **Yamyshevskiy Gate** on Abay Street, built in 1776, the **Russian Orthodox church** on Abay Street/Kashaganova Street, and two mosques, one of which has a double minaret. You should also take time to visit the "**Stronger than Death" monument** on Polkonovich Island, dedicated to the victims of the atomic tests. The artistic reference to the 40 years of human suffering and endurance is stark, but it goes straight to the heart.

The latest landmark is the new bridge over the Irtysh, which is already quite broad here. Built in 2001, its span of 750 metres makes it one of the longest of its kind. It was built by Japanese, Turkish and local firms, and looks particularly impressive at night. There is a museum on the left bank providing an overview of the technical details of this engineering gem.

A final attraction is a collection of sculptures representing historical characters in a park on Schmitdta Street/Urankhayeva Street, not far from the pontoon bridge over the Irtysh (also worth seeing). All sorts of bizarre pieces have found a home here, especially the grotesque busts of Lenin which are touching in a peculiar way—Kazakhstan takes its history lightly. To round off a very heavy day's touring or two, take a steamboat ride on the Irtysh—a pleasant end to an exploration of one of Kazakhstan's most underrated but fascinating cities.

Practical Information

The area dialling code for Semey is +7222. There is a general tourist information point at 4 Utepbayev St (tel: 425 059). The main post office opens daily, and can be found at 48 Uritskovo St. Good exchange rates can be had at the Rakhat department store on Internatsionalnaya St. There is an internet café at 18 Shakarim Ave, though such places open and close at lightning speed these days, so ask a local.

Transportation

The airport is 18 kilometres to the southeast of the city. Air Astana has five flights a week to Astana, and a weekly flight to Frankfurt, Germany. Other airlines connect the city to Almaty and, in the summer season, to other cities as well. Flight information and ticket reservations: tel: 447 377. The railway station is located at the end of Shakarim Ave (Information, reservation and ticket sales: tel: 983 232), and the bus station is at 158 Valikhanov St (information tel: 626 925, reservations: 626 917).

Accommodation

Hotel Semey, 26 Kabanbay Batyr St, tel: 663 604/5, fax: 663 606, e-mail: hotsemey@relcom.kz, website: www.satline.info/hotel-semey—a clean, centrally located Soviet-style hotel, with prices in line with quality. Rooms from US$5–60.

Hotel Irtysh, 97 Abay St—no telephone at time of writing due to renovation, but still open. All rooms have a view over the Irtysh River, but facilities are basic. Rooms from US$10–40.

Tourist Hotel, 9 Zhambyl St, tel: 666 413, fax: 623 850—a small, centrally located renovated hotel in an old Russian merchant's mansion. Rooms from US$13.

Prophylaktorium Stroitel, tel: 624 771—on the edge of the city in a small pinewood on the banks of the Irtysh is this modest but picturesque inn; bookings through travel agency Shara.

Kurchatov and the Polygon

The **Polygon** was the name used to describe the atomic test site in the steppe to the south and west of Semey. A large part of this territory, 15,000 square kilometres in all, is still out of bounds for all visitors. Guided tours, however, are possible in some areas, and the museum at **Kurchatov** is open to the public.

Most trips lead first to the **Atomic Lake**, a vast water-filled hollow that was formed by a nuclear explosion in 1965. The experiment is said to have been an attempt to learn whether a canal could be dug using this kind of explosion, with the intention of diverting certain Siberian rivers to the Aral Sea, which was drying up. The result was sadly one horror scenario only adding to another.

You can also visit a few former rocket silos and the town of Kurchatov, named after the atomic scientist who was in charge of the atomic engineering team, and where staff used to be lodged. The town was also dubbed **Konyechnaya**—the Russian word for end station.

Between 1949 and 1989, not less than 470 atomic and hydrogen bombs were exploded here in the steppe—an average of one explosion per month. Inhabitants of Semey, 150 kilometres down the road, still relate how they could tell exactly when an explosion occurred—mostly on Sunday mornings—because the earth would tremble. They therefore took to drinking endless amounts of vodka on Saturday evenings, since vodka was considered the best available remedy against the effects of radiation.

Once the Irtysh leaves all this behind, it is as though the river takes a deep breath. Its valley broadens to a width of 20 kilometres, and the river meanders in broad snaking

Left: The Fyodor Dostoyevsky Memorial Museum of Literature is located in the house where he lived (Agency Semey)

curves, forming sandbanks and branches, lagoons, islands and shallows. It flows quietly, but a fresh trial is not far off. The **Irtysh-Karaganda Canal** draws up to 75 cubic metres of water per second from the river at **Yermak (Aksu)** for the farms and factories of Karaganda, a distance of 458 kilometres to the southwest. It took from 1962 till 1974 to complete this mammoth project, the merits of which are doubtful at best. The canal reaches a depth of seven metres and is between 20 and 40 metres wide. Since the water must virtually flow uphill, there are 22 pumping stations to force it in the right direction.

What is left of the Irtysh continues to the northwest and after 30 kilometres reaches **Pavlodar**.

PAVLODAR

The year 1720 saw the construction of **Fort Koryakovsk** as part of the Irtysh defence line. It seems that clever officials gained city rights for this rather insignificant outpost, despite the fact that the low population failed to justify it, by giving it the name **Pavlodar**, or "gift to Paul"), the forename of Tsar Peter 1's son. The scheme succeeded, but only for a while,

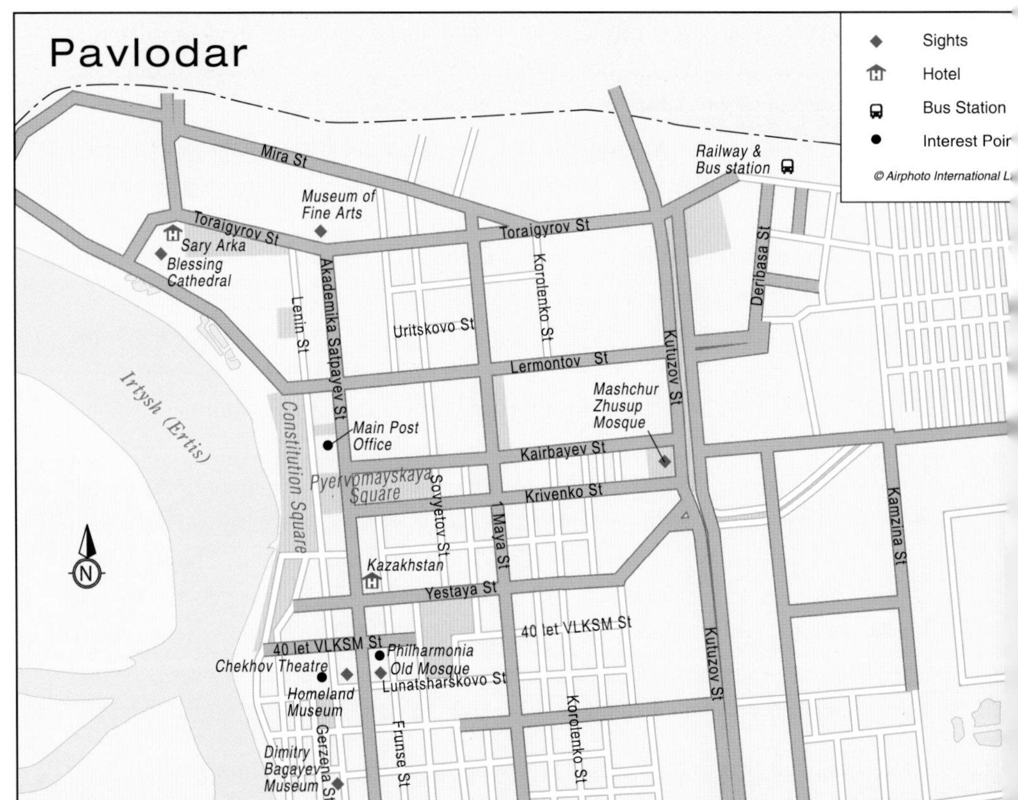

Superb wood carving in Imperial styles is a legacy of Kazakhstan's Russian past (Gunter Kapelle)

for in 1838 the town's status fell back to that of a Cossack settlement and was given back its original name of Koryakovskiy. That lasted until 1861, when the name Pavlodar was restored along with its city status and the tax privileges connected with it, the number of city dwellers finally justifying it. Today, Pavlodar has more than 300,000 inhabitants; mechanical engineering, coal mining, oil and aluminium processing facilities have largely contributed to the city's growth. Pavlodar and its satellite city, **Ekibastuz**, are the heart of an eponymous territorial production complex, a typical economic unity as created in the Soviet Union in regions abundant with resources and infrastructure.

A towering, newly constructed mosque does not hide the fact that Pavlodar is first and foremost a Russian city, with broad, long, perfectly straight avenues flanked with apartment blocks built in Soviet times, the appropriate cultural institutions and much greenery. The small wooden cottages dating from pre-revolutionary times are now threatened by the construction of new, fenced-in villas and shopping centres belonging to the post-Soviet wealthy classes.

The Irtysh flows along the city's western edge, providing it with a lavish green riverbank promenade. The river flows broad and calm here, and a large, clean beach attracts numerous swimmers during the summer months. Terraces from here lead up to **Constitution Square** (*Ploshchad Konstitutsiy*), where the administrative buildings are located, including the

Akimat. The city of Pavlodar has no real centre, and public life strolls along Toraigyrova, Akademika Satpayev and Lermontov streets. This makes the city "compact", according to its inhabitants. Pavlodar is also called the "city of shortcuts", although this is a relative qualification in Kazakhstan. Two tramlines run along Toraigyrov, Kutuzov, Pyervomayskaya and Lomova streets, and there is a good bus network.

Pavlodar has a number of impressive places of worship. The domes of the large **Russian Orthodox Cathedral of the Benediction** (*Blagoveshchenskiy sobor*), completed in 1999 and modelled on a Moscow Kremlin church, shine on the bank of the Irtysh, next to the hotel Sary Arka where Toraigyrov Street begins. It was inaugurated on the historic spot on the steep bank of the Irtysh, clearly visible to the ships that pass up and down the river, where until 100 years ago Pavlodar's largest church stood.

The **Mashchur Zhusup Mosque** (107 Kairbayeva Street/Kutuzova Street) was only inaugurated at the start of the new millennium. It was named after the poet **Mashchur Zhusup Kopeyuly**, who lived here from 1858 to 1931. This hugely impressive mosque looks as though it could welcome all Muslims of northern Kazakhstan at once; its massive structure contains ritual, cultural and social facilities under a single roof. A less forbidding and more charming old mosque can be found on the corner of Lunacharskovo and Frunze streets. A walking tour through the city from here leads down Lenin Street; on the corner of Lunacharskovo Street at house number 147, is the **Museum of Local History**. Palaeontological treasures, found in excavations on the banks of the Irtysh not far from the city, are displayed here: bones of antelope, giraffe, rhinoceros, sabre-tooth tiger and other species, all of whom wandered this region 12–14 million years ago. Across the street, the garden of the **Chekhov Theatre** gives an opportunity for peaceful reflection, sitting on a bench and breathing in the contemplative atmosphere, which differs strikingly from most theatre forecourts. Walk a short way south and turn right, and you're in the old riverside neighbourhood, where you can still get some idea of how romantic this place must once have been. The riverbank promenade starts here, running north with relaxing views over the broad Irtysh.

A small wooden house at 200 Lenin Street houses a small museum dedicated to the committed local historian and photographer **Dimitry Bagayev** and has some of his work on display. At the entrance to a large residential block (44/1 Toraigyrov Street) there is a **Museum of Fine Arts**, which shows exhibitions of modern work by artists from the Pavlodar region in large, brightly lit rooms. In front of the museum is a monument to the young poet, teacher and patriot **Sultanakhmut Toraigyrov**. His highest goal in life was to grant all children of Kazakhstan a superior education. He was also an ardent believer in Soviet power, but he died at the age of 27 in 1920—too early to experience the warping of that power.

PRACTICAL INFORMATION

The area dialling code for Pavlodar is +7182. The main post office is located at 50 Akademika Satpayev St, open Mon–Fri: 8am–7pm, Sat-Sun: 9am-6pm.

TRANSPORTATION

There are daily flights to/from Almaty, and three times a week to/from Astana. International flights go three times a week to Moscow and once a week each to Hanover and Frankfurt. Air Astana's office is at 34 Satpayev St, Office 43 (tel: 320 091).

The railway station is a large, new building on Toraigyrov St, at the end of Deribasa St. The bus station is on the square in front of the railway station.

ACCOMMODATION

Hotel Irtysh, 79 Ak. Beturov Street, tel: 320 209, fax: 326 862,—a gleaming new four-star hotel boasting 85 rooms, six suites and even a presidential suite. A business centre and swimming pool completes the package.

Hotel Kazakhstan, 71 Akademika Satpayev St, tel: 320 520/320 508, fax: 320 533—a friendly, renovated hotel with 23 large rooms and suites for one to four persons. Rooms from US$27-70 with breakfast.

Druzhba Hotel, 21/1 Kutuzov St, tel: 545 222, fax: 546 141—a good, modern hotel with business centre with all necessities.

Sary Arka (also called Hotel "Sunkar"), 1 Toraigyrov St, tel: 560 040/561 986/327 101, e-mail: pturist@pavlodar.kz, website: www.pavlodarturist.kz—a huge hotel with 300 beds on the bank of the Irtysh with a view over the Victory cathedral. Fairly basic, not yet renovated.

PETROPAVLOVSK

The city of **Petropavlovsk** is not situated on the banks of the Irtysh but some distance away on a broad river plain; the Irtysh continues on its way, crossing into Russia and eventually flowing into the **Ob River**. Petropavlovsk is on the right bank of the Esil, which is a tributary of the Irtysh. It is the northernmost city in Kazakhstan, only 60 kilometres from the border with Russia and part of a Russian network of roads and railroads. **Omsk** and **Chelyabinsk** are virtually next door.

Petropavlovsk's history dates back to a time when a Kazakh settlement called **Kyzylzhar (Red Bank)** was situated here. It was used by Tsar Peter I to build a fortification along the Irtysh defence line, but did not play any major role. It obtained city rights in 1807, and today up to 200,000 people live here, most of them ethnic Russians.

In summer, Petropavlovsk has a particularly friendly atmosphere, with numerous hospitable cafés and restaurants. Many young people stroll along its well-tended avenues and parks. The newly built Russian Orthodox church is worth a visit—but also recommended is a tour into the surrounding taiga, especially for those who love to gather berries and mushrooms.

Practical Information

There are four flights a week to Astana, with a connection to Almaty, and Air Astana also flies between Petropavlovsk and Frankfurt twice a week. There are daily train connections to Astana, as well as Omsk and Chelyabinsk across the border. Accommodation can be found at the **Hotel Skifiy** (118 Parkovaya St, tel/fax: 7152 468 807/461 065, e-mail: skif@ae.kz), a mid-range hotel in typical Soviet style, in a central but quiet location, with rooms from US$10–100.

Travel Agencies for the Altai and Irtysh Plain

Ak Nyet, 38/1 Kalinina St, Pavlodar, tel: (7182) 474 938, fax: 474 921, e-mail: ak_niet@nursat.kz—excursions through the Irtysh Valley, city tours around Pavlodar, steam boat trips on the Irtysh, trips to Bayanaul, the gold miners' town of Maykain, and the world's largest open coal pits in Ekibastuz.

Altai-Expeditions, 46 Gorkov St, Oskemen (Ust-Kamenogorsk), tel/fax: (7232) 245 709, e-mail: altai-expeditions@dvn.kz or nomad_altai@mail.ru, website: www.ukg.kz/altai-es—well-conceived walking and jeep tours through the Altai and its foothills (Zaysan, Bukhtarminsk), with its own accommodation on Markakol Lake. Fishing tours, geological and ethnographical excursions, rafting, ski holidays, horseback and mountain bike tours, assistance in bookings to climb Mount Byelukha. Tailor-made tours possible, and visa and border area entry permits arranged.

Ecosystem, 19 Karla Liebknechta St, Oskemen (Ust-Kamenogorsk), tel: (7232) 257 447, mob: (8) 333 294 1387, e-mail: undp_ukg@ukg.kz, website: http://altai-es.ukg.kz—offers the

Above: A game of chess in the park in Petropavlovsk (Gunter Kapelle)

same services as Altai-Expeditions, as the two companies are run by brothers. The owner Yevgeny Yurchenkov and his son, Mikhail, speak good English.

Globus, 9 Lenin St, Semey, Office 301, tel: (7222) 623 455—health resorts and sanatoriums, visa arrangements and ticket reservations.

Intourist, 27 Gorkov St, Oskemen, tel: (7232) 264 747, fax: 264 251, e-mail: intourist@ukg.kz—camping tours in the West Altai Nature Reserve.

Izumrudniy Altai, 160 Proletarskaya St, Oskemen, tel: (7232) 242 329, fax: 243 026, e-mail: chilikin@ukg.kz—trekking, rafting, fishing, horseback and mountain bike tours, historic, ethnographic, geological and wildlife excursions. The company has its own health resort at Bukhtarminsk Reservoir on Ayuda Bay, with neat wooden houses and sauna at economical prices.

Pavlodartourist, 2/F Hotel Sary Arka, 1 Toraigyrov St, Pavlodar, tel: (7182) 561 986/564 111/327 101, e-mail: pturist@nursat.kz, website: www.pavlodartourist.kz—owns the Chayka health resort in Bayanaul; also offers city tours.

Rachmanov's Springs Tourist Company, 11 Tikhaya St, Oskemen, tel/fax: (7232) 552 100, e-mail: rahmani@reliz.kz, website: www.altaytravel.com—reservations for accommodation and tours based around the Rachmanov's Springs and Mount Byelukha area.

Sajakhat-East Ltd, 106-41 Krilov Street, Oskemen (Ust-Kamenogorsk), tel/fax: (7232) 258 849, e-mail: svostok@vpnet.kz—linked to the East Kazakhstan Regional Akimat, offers extensive tailor-made trips into the Altai and Semey regions.

Shara, 4 Shugayev St, Semey, tel: (7222) 624 771/626 991, fax: 623 317, e-mail: shara@relcom.kz—well-guided tours around town, excursions to the Abai, Auezov and Shakarim monuments in the steppe to the south of Semey, trips to Mount Chingiztau, excursions to the atomic testing grounds and the "secret city" of Kurchatov, accommodation and visa arrangements.

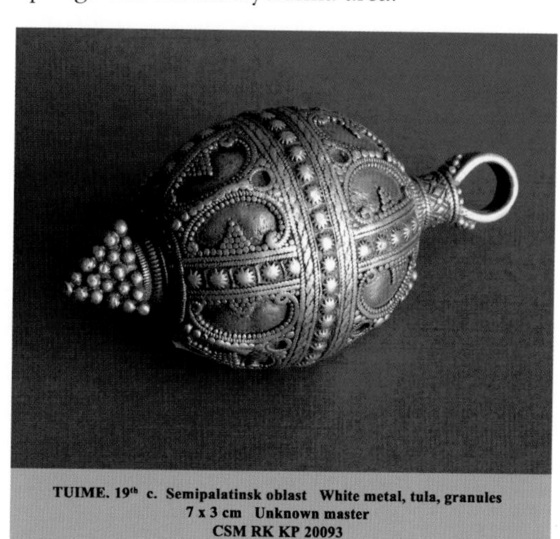

TUIME. 19th c. Semipalatinsk oblast White metal, tula, granules 7 x 3 cm Unknown master CSM RK KP 20093

Above: Superb craftsmanship in metalworking was a natural consequence of eastern Kazakhstan's immense mineral wealth (Courtesy of the Central State Museum, Almaty)

The Western Regions: Kazakhstan on Sea

God gave Kazakhstan its many natural riches so we would have strength to handle the many difficulties to come our way.

Aksakal, from the introduction to Wayne Eastep's *The Soul of Kazakhstan*

Beside the Caspian Sea

The **Caspian Sea** is a long, long way from the centres of power in Almaty and Astana—on the flight between Central Europe and Almaty you will be halfway to your destination by the time you cross it. A piece of Kazakhstan about half the size of Scotland lies to the west of the **Ural River**, and is thereby actually accounted part of Europe. The **Atyrau**, **West Kazakhstan** and **Aktobe Regions (Oblasts)**, consisting of the **Ural Basin** and the **Turan Lowland** in the north, and the **Mangystau Region** that stretches from the **Mangyshlak Peninsula** to the **Ustyurt Plateau** in the south, are two areas of the country which now have great prospects thanks mainly to the discovery of vast reserves of oil and natural gas. So far, however, the majority of this enigmatic region has been preserved in its original state. It is a fascinating part of the country that few tourists know about or visit.

The Mangyshlak Peninsula

When Russian envoys arrived here in the first half of the 18th Century, they found a fully functioning nomadic community, whose way of living amazed members of the Russian Academy of Sciences. The daily life of the tribes living on the shores of the Caspian Sea differed from that of the indigenous communities to the north and east. Fishing and seal hunting were practised here, and some agriculture had been adopted from nearby Turkmen tribes. But something else fascinated explorers, for, apart from the roaming auls of the **Kazakh Lesser (Junior) Horde**, there were many traces of half-sedentary life on the vast territory of the **Mangyshlak Peninsula**, including an extraordinary abundance of necropolises. Mangyshlak has more than half of Kazakhstan's ancient architectural history. Most etymologists track its name back to the Turkic words *myng kyshlak*, meaning "thousand settlements"; the half-buried traces of settlements in the desert sand point to times when water supplies on the peninsula must have been considerably better than the present day.

Following pages: Monumental natural towers shoot skywards from the barren plain of the Ustyurt Plateau (Vladislav Yakushkin)

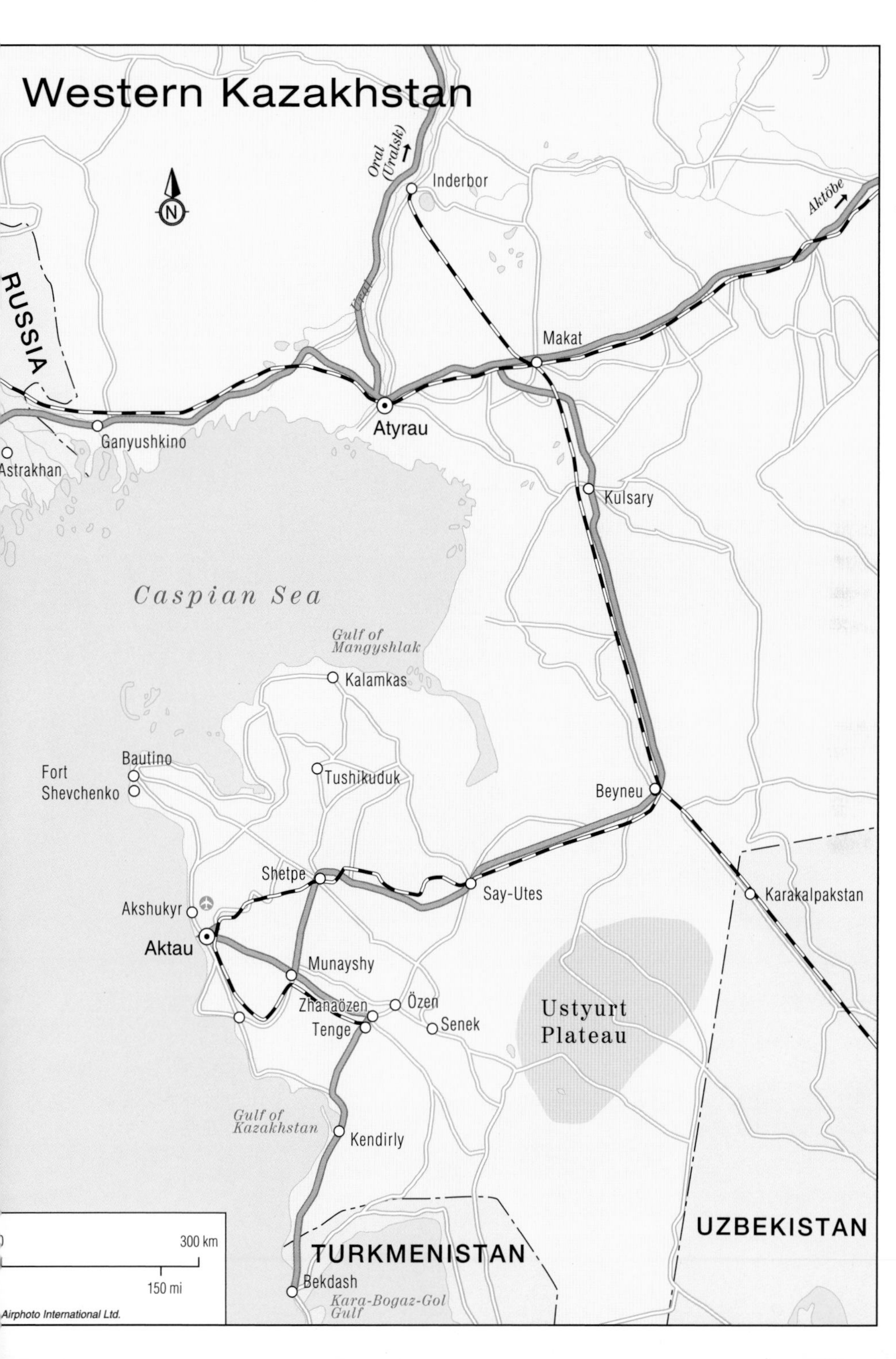
Western Kazakhstan
Oral (Uralsk)
Inderbor
Aktöbe
RUSSIA
Ural
Makat
Atyrau
Ganyushkino
Astrakhan
Kulsary
Caspian Sea
Gulf of Mangyshlak
Kalamkas
Bautino
Fort Shevchenko
Tushikuduk
Beyneu
Shetpe
Say-Utes
Karakalpakstan
Akshukyr
Aktau
Munayshy
Zhanaözen
Özen
Tenge
Senek
Ustyurt Plateau
Gulf of Kazakhstan
Kendirly
UZBEKISTAN
300 km
150 mi
TURKMENISTAN
Bekdash
Kara-Bogaz-Gol Gulf
Airphoto International Ltd.

19th c. Western Kazakhstan. White metal, carnelian. d- 6,5cm; width-5,8cm Unknown maste
CSM RK KP 3809, 3810

Its strategic location on the shore of the Caspian turned the Mangyshlak Peninsula into a transit corridor for trade caravans. The locations of old caravanserai sites are idyllic in this region because they occur next to watering holes, which form surprisingly green islands in the barren landscape. For caravan travellers, of course, survival depended on these regularly spaced out oases, and the owners of the sites knew how to exploit that. People paid in cash and precious merchandise at each caravanserai, which turned them into prosperous enclaves in the midst of the peninsula's desert.

Other locations on the peninsula and its hinterland today contain important sites of pilgrimage for modern visitors. Most of them are mausoleums, as well as a number of underground meditation chambers (retreats), used by famous Sufi figures of the past,

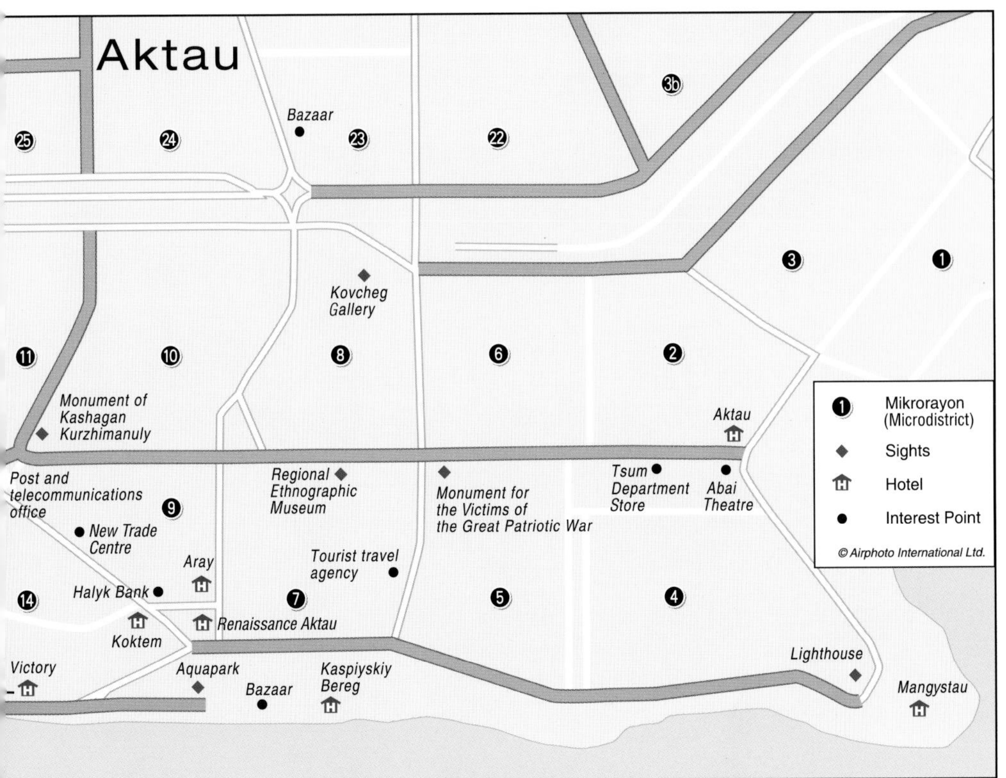

generally described as mosques because of their sacred nature and the rock-hewn rooms in which pilgrims pray, though strictly speaking this is an inaccuracy. Whatever you wish to call them, however, they are treasures of Islamic spiritual art. There are also extraordinary landscapes unlike anything you will see elsewhere in the country; add all these attractions together and you can easily fill two weeks of fascinating exploration.

Aktau is the usual starting point for tours in the region, but midsummer is not the time to go—the heat can be unbearable; spring and autumn are much better options.

Aktau

Aktau (White Mountain) is the name of the young city situated on the shining chalk cliffs, and also the name of Kazakhstan's only deep-sea port directly to its south. Formerly called **Shevchenko**, Aktau has a spacious feel about it; like all Kazakh cities, it is surrounded by multi-storey residential blocks scattered around the surrounding area, but its location on the shore gives Aktau a skyline, while the numerous sunny days give the city a holiday-like image. The city "fits in" to its environs—most of the buildings have been constructed with mussel chalk from the coastal region or with large yellowish clay bricks.

Left: The Monument for the Victims of the Great Patriotic War in Aktau (Dagmar Schreiber). Above left: Ring and bracelet combinations from the 19th Century (Courtesy of the Central State Museum, Almaty)

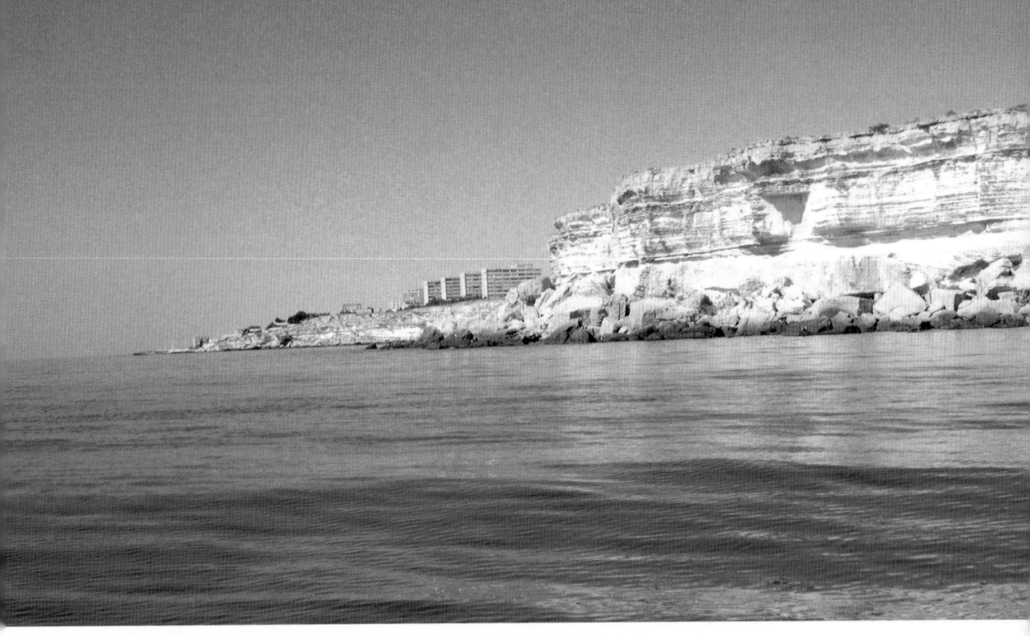

Cliffs and construction on Aktau's Caspian coastline (Valeri Balikhanov)

Aktau's first stone was only laid as recently as 1958, soon after oil reserves were found underground on the Mangyshlak Peninsula. It was decided to build a large residential complex here to house staff, and a port to ship the area's future source of wealth. In 1965, the Mangyshlak Peninsula produced its first oil; however, with the construction of the new town came major difficulties in providing water. The problem was solved with a fast-breeder reactor, which generates power for a desalination plant, but it is sometimes closed because of technical defects.

Newcomers to Aktau are often left completely confused when looking at the city map. There are no street names—only numbers that indicate blocks called *Mikrorayons* (Microdistricts) which are situated next to one another without any recognisable order, stretching both along the coast and inland. The explanation for this administrative muddle is simply a matter of chronological construction.

Mikrorayon 1, directly on Aktau Bay, was the first residential complex to be completed. It is distinguished by two- to four-storey houses in a 1950s style, with much greenery in its midst. Mikrorayons 2 and 3 were built in the 1960s and stretch to the north and the northwest. They are also characterized by their modest height and shady courtyards. The 1970s witnessed the construction of mikrorayons 4 to 9 on the steep shore to the north of the earlier residential areas. They consist of large nine- or 10-storey blocks with plenty of space for playgrounds, schools, stores and administrative services between them. These neighbourhoods form Aktau's present-day centre and dominate the city's overall character.

Left: Despite its oil associations, the Caspian's shore is still clean and very attractive near Aktau (Dagmar Schreiber)

Intensive construction is going on here, directly on the coast and the strips inland—Aktau is developing fast into an oil metropolis with a fastidious polish. Mikrorayons 11 to 15 are situated to the north, all of them relatively close to the sea; to the west of the route from Aktau that heads southeast towards the town of **Zhanaozen** there are the more newly constructed neighbourhoods numbered from 20 onwards and, apart from the bus station in Mikrorayon 28 and the bazaar in Mikrorayon 23, there is little reason for tourists to go there.

The city can be explored in a single day. It's best to start in the morning on the large square in front of the **Akimat** and the **Abai Theatre**, walk uphill north from here, turn southwest at the **Akyn Kashagan Kurzhimanuly Monument**, wander down to the seashore and stroll along it in the late afternoon and evening sun, south and then east until the circle is closed. This walk—of about 10 kilometres—takes you past some interesting sights that belie many people's perception of Aktau simply as a dormitory town.

The **Tsum Department Store** directly behind the Abai Theatre is a Soviet-style building; even if you don't buy anything, it's interesting to look at what's on offer and people-watch. Behind the department store, the **Laguna** is a modern leisure centre including a casino and restaurant among other establishments. Walking through the pedestrian zones between residential blocks you'll see many buildings decorated to advertise the powerful oil, gas and transportation companies that dominate the city.

A large, circular monument stands between Mikrorayons 7 and 9. The five massive concrete panels are positioned around an eternal flame, which burns here to commemorate the **Victims of the Great Patriotic War**. Each panel is decorated with a relief and represents a year from 1941 to 1945. In the same fashion as the eternal flame in Almaty's Panfilov Park, brides and grooms come to lay flowers and observe a minute's silence in memory of the many soldiers from Kazakhstan and other Soviet republics who lost their lives in World War II.

Above and opposite: Huge pictures of Kazakh heroes Tole Bi and Ablai Khan decorate the walls of residential buildings in downtown Aktau (Dagmar Schreiber x2)

Across the intersection and farther north, hidden behind a new shopping centre and located in the side wing of a bank, the **Regional Ethnographic Museum** houses an impressive collection of excavated items from antiquity, as well as Kazakh household tools from the 18th, 19th and 20th centuries; the region's geology, flora and fauna are also displayed in great detail. The museum used to occupy the entire building but it is now difficult to find its entrance: it is not through the iron gate with its name on top, but through another gateway on the left of the building, and then to the left through a modest-looking doorway—the sign that indicates the museum is hardly visible.

Past the museum in the direction of the unfortunately heavily neglected botanic garden, and on the opposite side of the street you pass a gallery of **national heroes** displayed on the sides of residential buildings: **Ayteke Bi**, **Kazybek Bi**, **Tole Bi**, **Ablai Khan** and now, also, **Nursultan Nazarbayev** all gaze down on passers-by.

Down by the sea is the **Aquapark**, beside which now stands the new Hotel Renaissance, looking like an ocean liner stranded on the shoreline. Unfortunately the sand beach is rather dirty, but people still swim here. Along the shore there are many opportunities to relax and have a snack in numerous small seafront cafés; further south you come to the monument of **Taras Shevchenko** in a small, nicely laid-out park with steps and ramps down onto the beach. Here the attractive, water-stained chalk rocks and houses above make a nice picture. A small tower on the roof of one of the multi-storey buildings is actually the **Lighthouse**, put there simply to save money. It is possible to climb up to it, admire the top of the small but posh Hotel Mangistau, then turn east and end up at your original starting point in the Akimat square.

Seven kilometres to the south of the city lies the oldest excavation site in Kazakhstan, the Neolithic settlement called **Koskuduk**, situated close to the sea. To visit it, try contacting Andrei Astayev (tel: +7292 436 309), the passionate historian, geographer and ethnologist who is in charge of the excavations.

Aktau has been chosen as one of three locations in Kazakhstan to undergo substantial development as tourism centres of the future (the other two are on the **Kapshagay Reservoir** near Almaty, and **Borovoye Lake** north of Astana). Aktau will represent the country's massive—and highly significant—natural energy resources; it will be known as the **"City of Energy"** and will take an estimated 7–12 years to complete, at a cost of at least US$15 billion. What exactly this massive development will entail is not clear yet, but it is obvious that the concept of a "Kazakhstan on Sea" destination offering sun, sand and water sports to both local and international tourists is appealing to the powers that be in Astana.

Practical Information

The area dialling code for Aktau is +7292. Addresses in Aktau are indicated by two or three numbers: the first indicates the mikrorayon, the second the building and the third the apartment. The post office and telecommunications building are both in Mikrorayon 14; the post office is open Mon-Fri: 8am–7pm, Sat/Sun: 9am–6pm; the telecom office is open daily: 8am–8pm. There is also a branch office of Kazkommertsbank here. Cash machines at the Halyk Bank (9/6), in the *oblast* Akimat (Mkr 4), in Hotel Renaissance (Mkr 9) and in the business centre (8/39) accept all credit cards.

Transportation

The freshly renovated airport is some 25 kilometres to the northwest of town. There are daily flights to Almaty, Astana, Atyrau and Aktobe, a daily flight to London (Gatwick) via Oral (Uralsk), several flights a week to Kyzylorda and once a week to Shymkent. Regular flights go to Moscow, Kaliningrad (Russia) and Baku (Azerbaijan). Information

tel: 421 324, fax: 421 322. For air ticket reservation try **Transavia** (Mikrorayon 8/9a, all airlines, open daily), **Central Asia Tourism** (western wing of the Aktau Hotel, tel: 517 504/515 185, fax: 514 719, e-mail: cat-aktau@alarnet.com) or **Air Astana** (Mikrorayon 8/39a, tel: 511 565).

The **Mangyshlak Railway Station** is located outside town—only a freight line runs into Aktau proper. The **bus station** is situated on the crossroads where Mikrorayons 26, 27 and 28 meet.

ACCOMMODATION

Renaissance Aktau Hotel, Mikrorayon 9 (right on the Esplanade), tel: 300 600, fax: 300 601, email: rhi.scobr.gm@renaissancehotels.com, website: www.renaissancehotels.com/SCOBR—part of the Marriott Group, this new hotel has all the attributes of an international luxury hotel. Rooms from US$150.

Mangystau, Mikrorayon 4 (opposite building 7), tel: 513 029, fax: 431 151—a white, single-storey hotel on the cape of the town peninsula; very elegant with a fantastic view over the sea, and high security as state officials often stay here. Rooms from US$60.

Koktem, Mikrorayon 14, building 10, near the Aquapark, tel: 434 479/433 487, fax: 434 487, e-mail: koktem_aktau@mail.online.kz—a small, neat hotel in the city centre, with a view over the sea. Rooms from US$78.

Hotel Zelyonaya, Mikrorayon 3, building 154, tel: 517 304, fax: 511 752—a small renovated hotel with large apartments, friendly and clean, 10 minutes' walk from the city centre. Rooms from US$88.

Hotel Viktory, Mikrorayon 15, building 4, tel: 439 516, fax: 439 501—located on the seafront, with large, well-renovated apartments and glass balconies, 15 minutes' walk from the city centre. Friendly and clean, all apartments with a view over the sea and soundproof windows. Rooms from US$50.

Hotel Aktau, Mikrorayon 2, tel: 510 298/514 707, 514 201, fax: 512 401, e-mail: laura1@pochta.ru,—a large, Soviet-style hotel built in 1972, with views over the sea. Rooms from US$35.

Stigl, 18 km south of town, tel: 300 138/139/140—a new leisure resort right on the beach, with 55 luxurious rooms, three good restaurants, sauna, and water and other sports. Rooms from US$200.

Above and below left: Images of Ayteke Bi and Kazybek Bi are also on display (Dagmar Schreiber x2)

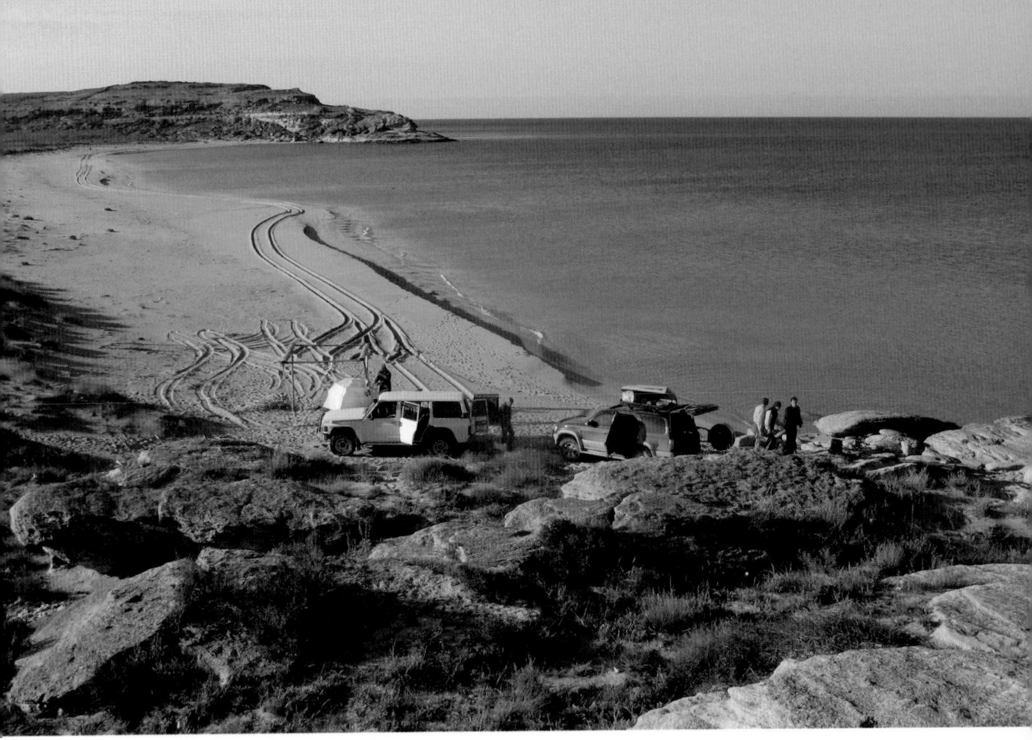

Beautiful, deserted sand beaches can be found both north and south of Aktau (Dagmar Schreiber)

Karagiye Depression

Forty kilometres from Aktau is the 10-kilometre-wide, 40-kilometre-long **Karagiye Depression**, whose lowest point is 132 metres below sea level. It lies in the triangle of wilderness between the roads to Zhanaozen and **Kuryk** (on the south coast) and the shortcut that links them. The most impressive spot in the depression is on its eastern slope, where the terrain rises abruptly to 200 metres. An observation platform halfway from Aktau to Munayshy on the southeastern road towards Zhanaozen gives a magnificent view over the area in clear weather.

Lake Karakol

The long lake of **Karakol (Black Lake)**, surrounded by a thick belt of reeds, is on the western side of the Karagiye Depression. It can be reached by driving 20 kilometres from Aktau along the road to Kuryk, and turning right towards the health resort (*zona otdykha*). The lake is on the left of the road—don't confuse it with the large basin (for water purification) to the north. The water in Karakol is extraordinarily clean and rich in fish. This attracts pelican, flamingo and other water birds, even in winter, since Karakol is a resting-place for a number of species of migrating birds on their journey from the north of Kazakhstan and Siberia.

Mangyshlak's Beaches

The waters of the Caspian Sea on its east coast are still a clear, transparent turquoise, as yet unspoilt by the constantly increasing oil drilling at multiple locations in the region. North and south of Aktau there are several beautiful beaches with fine sand and small bays between mussel-chalk rocks, where you can find yourself completely alone outside the high season of late May to early September. The most beautiful beaches can be found by turning west onto one of the tracks off the road from Aktau to Fort Shevchenko.

Eighteen kilometres south of Aktau is the sophisticated beach resort of Stigl (see Akatu Accommodation section), offering every imaginable water sport and other resort facilities. There is, however, an entry fee. The north shore of the **Kazakh Gulf** (*Kazakhskiy zaliv*), south of Kuryk on the way to the Turkmenistan border, also has several beautiful, wild beaches, but they are only accessible by 4WD.

Since 2002 there has been a small, modern holiday resort called **Kendirly** in a calm, deepwater side bay of the Kazakh Gulf, about 2.5 hours' travel from Aktau. For US$80 (and up) per person it's possible to have a typical beach holiday here—it's particularly popular as a holiday destination in winter due to its balmy climate, warmer than virtually everywhere else in Kazakhstan. Kendirly is currently administered by KazMunaiGaz, and a stay can be booked through Hotel Aruna in Zhangaozen (tel: 72934 63388, email: recepshen@tnsplus.kz) or through Caspian Tour in Aktau. There is a master plan to develop Kendirly into a huge leisure complex for schoolchildren over the next few years.

The Mangyshlak Peninsula is dissected by countless narrow and winding canyons (Dagmar Schreiber)

FORT SHEVCHENKO AND BAUTINO

Fort Shevchenko is just over 100 kilometres to the north of Aktau, on the western cape of the Mangyshlak Peninsula. It is named after the Ukrainian national hero, poet, painter and democratic thinker **Taras Shevchenko**, who lived in exile here from 1850 to 1857, after having been convicted by a military court. The fort was built in 1846 and was called **Novopetrovsk**, in honour of Tsar Peter I. In 1847 it was renamed **Fort Alexandrovich**, which it remained until 1939, when it was given its present name.

Today, only a heap of ruins on the coastal mountain, a chapel at its foot and the **Shevchenko Museum** remind one of the town's glorious past. The museum is housed in the dwelling of the former fortress commander, and is definitely worth a visit to see the collection of Shevchenko paintings that depict the daily life of Kazakhs in 19th Century Mangyshlak. The small ethnographic museum should also be visited. It displays a well-composed and well-maintained collection of artefacts and household tools from Kazakh auls in the surrounding area, with detailed explanations by Russian scholars. The mussel-chalk quarry on the edge of the town contributes to the burial site culture of the region, providing the desirable white stone for the tombs and mausoleums.

The boomtown of **Bautino** is not far from Fort Shevchenko, on the far point of the **Tyub Karagan Peninsular**. It was originally a fishing village, then later an officer's housing area. Oil company AGIP is building this well-situated settlement into a logistics base for its petroleum business, and it is currently dominated by three business hotels. The local population is to be resettled in Fort Shevchenko, to clear the way for the land's exclusive use as an oil terminal.

For those interested in staying here, there is no shortage of space at either **Hotel Chagala Bautino** (Nadyrbayev St, tel: 72983 24634, email: reservation.bautino@chagalgroup.kz—96 rooms, high season from US$150 per night) or hotels **Dostyk** and **Tengiz** on the west shore of the peninsula (tel: 7292 203 153, fax: 72938 24946, email: info@tupkaragan-group.kz—40 rooms, high season from US$100).

The Shevchenko Museum is fronted by a bust of the famous poet-painter (W. Balikhanov)

TAMSHALY AND THE NORTH COAST CANYONS

The whole north coast of the Mangyshlak Peninsula is fissured with canyons, both small and large. They are accessible in 4WD vehicles on the route from Fort Shevchenko to **Kalamkas** around the **Mangystau Gulf**. About 30 kilometres east of Fort Shevchenko a bad track leads to the **Meretsay** and **Tamshaly canyons**, the latter an idyllic spot with a small oasis and lake overgrown with reeds, fed constantly by spring water from a semicircular rock hollow. The giant rockfall at **Zhyghilan**, about 15 kilometres farther east towards the sea, provides not only the bizarre view of strangely eroded rocks, but a treat for palaeontologists as well: 15–20 million years ago, primitive animals such as three-toed horses and large predatory cats left deep footprints in soft deposits that became large stone slabs. At the edge of the neighbouring side canyon of Borly/Sultan Epe lies the **Sultan Epe Shrine**. The eastern end of this canyon landscape is formed by the deep, white chalk canyon of **Kapamsay** and the wide canyon of **Shakpaktasay**, in the porous walls of which the retreat/underground mosque called **Shakpak-ata** has been cut. Numerous necropolises, mostly well signposted, can be seen scattered left and right of the road on the way to Kalamkas, but the canyons themselves are not indicated, so it is best to be accompanied by a knowledgeable driver.

Tamshaly Canyon is steeped in legend: once upon a time, there was a rich aul ruled by an *aksakal* (wise man). After his death, the village went into decline; droughts hammered the land, the cattle began to perish, and it soon became clear a decision was needed. The wise man had appointed his wife as the aul's new chief, and she came to the conclusion that it was pointless to wait passively for rain to come, that it was better to pack up and leave the place where everyone had lived all their lives, and go in search of a new location for their village with water, even to settle by the seashore. Thus all was packed up, and the aul set off. The villagers travelled for a long time, looking in vain for water. More cattle died, and finally the people reached the limits of their endurance. They were camping on the edge of a high, barren plain. The aksakal's wife stood up and told the villagers that they had to dig for water, but the exhausted tribesmen did not react, so she herself started digging with her bare hands. Nothing happened and what little strength she had faded, but the moment she collapsed, dying, drops of water suddenly sprang from the rocks, as though they were weeping. From all sides, the water flowed down and formed a small lake, from which a small brook made its way towards the sea. The people drank, the cattle quenched their thirst, and the aul survived. Thus the Tamshaly Canyon was formed.

Climb up from the reed lake and you'll get a view over the high, bare flatland from whence the aul is said to have come. Follow the valley, through which the brook runs on rare rainy days, and you reach the village of Kanga and from there, the sea.

THE MANGYSHLAK NECROPOLISES

The Mangyshlak Peninsula is famous throughout Kazakhstan for its numerous "cities of the dead". The oldest of these date back to the Iron Age, but the majority of the tombs are from the 17th–18th centuries onwards. Kazakh nomadic tribes, especially the Nogai and the Adai, migrated to the peninsula around this time. Although they left no trace of their daily life, due to their nomadic lifestyle, they did leave many surviving monuments to their dead. Analysis of these mausoleums is a science in itself. The tombs—their fences, gravestones and memorial slabs of varying shape—tell the stories about the origins of the dead, their trade and their favourite occupations.

The grave of a poor Kazakh is usually adorned with a simple flat or upright tombstone. Most often his/her name and tribal symbol are carved in them, and occasionally objects that were characteristic of the person, such as a sabre or a horsewhip. These gravestones are known as "small forms". Better-off Kazakhs were buried under 3–5 tombstones of a particular shape put together as a pyramid. The images they bear can consist of treasure boxes, saddles, helmets or stylised animals. The graves of wealthy Kazakhs were often surrounded by an ornamented wall with a small viewing window.

In days of old, mausoleums were reserved for saints only. The status of sainthood could be obtained during one's life through great wisdom and/or benevolence that contributed to the wellbeing of the community. Today, successful entrepreneurs and high officials are also rewarded with a mausoleum when they die. These "modern saints" are honoured with a splendid dome, often lavishly adorned on the outside. Inside the mausoleum there is always an impressive coffin and often a mat on which people who visit the tomb can sit and pray.

Where a Kazakh's ancestors are buried is his home. He will always tend to return to the place where his forefathers were buried, to communicate with the deceased in whatever way he feels is right. This is why one can often see benches around the fences of richer people's tombs.

There are hundreds of burial sites in the semi-desert landscape of the Mangyshlak Peninsula. The view of bright domes and white walls rising on the horizon like a mirage across the flat, barren land is truly unforgettable. One of the largest groups of necropolises is located to the north of Aktau, next to the village of **Akshukyr** near the airport. This site, named after a saint called **Koshkar-ata** who is buried here, includes many large new mausoleums in opulent shapes, including a rare one with its foundation in the form of a triangle. But don't overlook the ancient, weathered gravestones scattered between the impressive new constructions. Near the entrance is a particularly interesting old tomb bearing a statue of a ram. Islamic law traditionally bans the use of images of living creatures, but here it has been violated in a most beautiful way. Sheep used to be, and still are, popular ornaments on tombstones, but are usually represented in a stylized manner, with little more than the animal's trunk recognizable and known as *khoy-tas* (sheep's stone); the statue here is entirely different, and is called a *khoshkar-tas* (ram's stone).

Large numbers of these grave sites can be found along the roads, but also in the middle of the steppe where there are no roads whatsoever. Although superficially monotonous places, each site comes with its own interesting background and tale – if you have a guide who knows and can relate them (see Special Topic "Mangyshlak's 'Cities of the Dead'" on page 472).

Above: Images of argali wild sheep carved into a tomb wall. Left and above left: The graves of Mangyshlak's necropolises range from simple stone piles to elaborate mausoleum constructions (Dagmar Schreiber x3)

MANGYSHLAK'S "CITIES OF THE DEAD"

By *Renato Sala and Jean-Marc Deom*

In spite of its very dry climate and consequently poor habitat, the mountainous Mangyshlak Peninsula has long been crossed by migratory tribes. This is reflected in the number of cemeteries strewn across the barren landscape. These necropolises (locally called *beit*, "cities of the dead") were located several kilometres from human settlements and, when hosting the tombs of local saints with an accompanying mosque, became important places of pilgrimage (see the Special Topic "Mangyshlak's Sacred Caves" on page 480). The graves have a special architecture, peculiar to this region, of sculpted blocks and fences, with stone stelae (*kulpytas*) next to the tombs, and petroglyph figures engraved on some sections.

This burial tradition is widespread in what was once the territory of the Lesser Kazakh Zhuz (a tribal confederation), which included the northeastern pre-Caspian region, the Ustyurt Plateau and northwestern pre-Aral (today pertaining to the provinces of Mangystau, Atyrau and Aktobe). However, the richest architectural and artistic variety and inventiveness is found on the Mangyshlak Peninsula, a fact partly explained by the local availability of a soft limestone bedrock most suitable for carving. Although most of the cemeteries consist of monuments dating to the last three centuries, many tombs and stelae are much older, attributed to earlier periods from the Iron Age to the Medieval period.

HISTORY

In western Kazakhstan, the history of fenced graves with kulpytas developed through three phases. The prototypes of this burial architecture can be found in Massagetian and Sarmatian cemeteries dating to the Early Iron Age (400 BC–100 AD) and located on the western border of the Ustyurt Plateau. They include dozens of sanctuaries (Baite, Dykyltas, Koskuduk, Karamunke, Meretsai, etc) consisting of round stone enclosures up to 10 metres in diameter, anthropomorphic statues (more than 100 have been discovered), large monolithic altars known as "sacrificial tables" and petroglyph engravings. The anthropomorphic statues show a standing man of mixed Europoid and Mongoloid traits (slanted eyes, straight nose, thin moustache), the right arm lowered along the body flank and the left one placed on the waist, wearing a military costume with weapons typical of the Scythian-Sarmatian culture. They are interpreted as sculptures of deceased tribal ancestors and heroes from whom protection was invoked through animal sacrifices. Petroglyph representations of animals, chariots, mounted warriors and clan seals (*tamga*) are engraved on some of the statues and on the encircling stones (mainly in the Baite cemetery), which are very similar to petroglyphs and tamga executed during the subsequent medieval and modern periods on the tombs of the region.

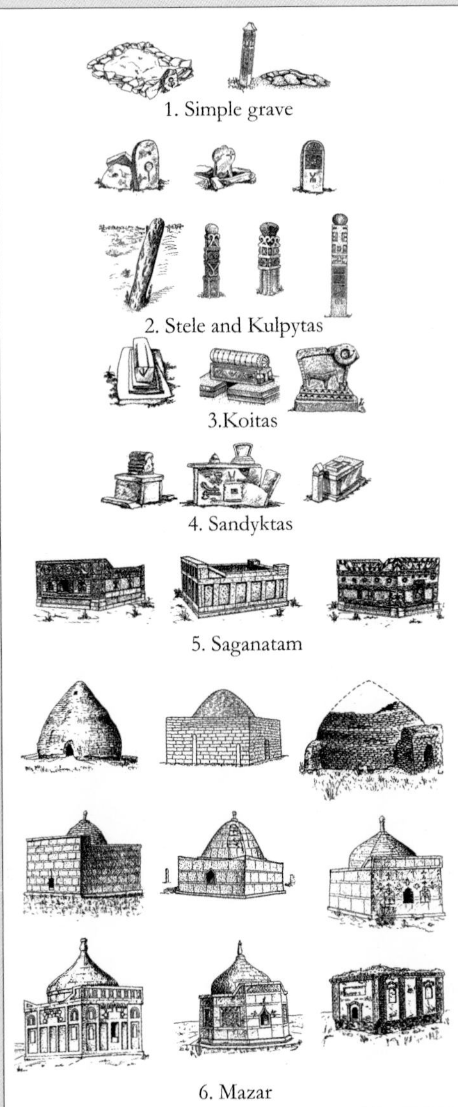

The next important phase of burial architecture was during the Middle Ages. Related to the Oguz and Kypchak cultures (1000–1200 AD), the tombs are dispersed across a very large territory comprising the Emba River, the Syr Darya Delta, the Ustyurt Plateau and the Mangyshlak Peninsula. They consist of small and shallow stone *kurgans* (burial mounds) using a very simple stone slab of which the upper part is rounded or sometimes crown-shaped, its surfaces engraved with geometric bas-reliefs and tamga.

Above: Burial architecture elements found on the Mangyshlak Peninsula (Renato Sala and Jean-Marc Deom)

The last phase of burial architecture concerns only the Mangyshlak Peninsula and consists of the cemeteries and tombs belonging to the proud and warlike Adai tribe, part of the Lesser Kazakh Zhuz of northwestern Kazakhstan, who inhabited the peninsula from the 18th century. The richest and most beautiful necropolises built in Mangyshlak are, from west to east, those of Shakpak-ata, Ushkan, Kenty-baba, Karagashty-aulie, Sultan-Epe, Koshkar-ata, Karaman-ata, Kamysbai, Masat-ata, and Seisen-ata (see map on page 482).

Structure and Design

The graves of the Mangyshlak necropolises comprise three architectural elements: the tomb, varying from a simple stone pile (see illustration on page 473) to a monumental ram-shaped statue (*koitas*); the enclosure, varying from a simple circle of stones to an elaborated box-shaped fence or a large vaulted mausoleum; and sculptural monuments around the tomb in the form of stelae (kulpytas). As a whole, the graves can be classified into five categories, from the most simple to the most elaborate:

The necropolis site at Masat-ata (Renato Sala and Jean-Marc Deom)

• simple graves consisting of a stone pile, sometimes with a stone enclosure and a standing stone (kurgan).

• graves superimposed on a pyramidal platform made of 3–5 steps with, on top, a stone sculpture in the shape of a sheep, varying from a simple sub-rectangular or cylindrical form to an elaborate sculpture of a ram (koitas, *koshkar-tas*).

• graves in the shape of a sarcophagus or a casket made of stone slabs (*sandyk-tas*). The sandyktas were often cenotaphs built for warriors whose body couldn't be found.

• graves encircled by a box-shaped and roofless enclosure with sculptured stone walls (*saganatam*).

• graves covered by a stone or mud brick cupola-shaped mausoleum (*mazar*). Some of these mausoleums are sophisticated miniaturized replicas of mosques with decorations on the exterior and interior walls.

The standing stelae are the most characteristic element of the Mangyshlak necropolises, their shape and ornamental design often being extremely elaborate. Kulpytas were generally carved in limestone or sandstone with two basic morphological styles, as flat stone slabs

Top: The Shakpak-ata necropolis, with its underground mosque in the background. Above: A kulpytas, *or stele at Beket-ata, clearly showing a battleaxe carving at its base (Renato Sala and Jean-Marc Deom x2)*

or as a sub-rectangular sculptured column. The stelae of the first type are older, found in medieval tombs. Those of the second type belong to the ethnographic period (Adai culture), and are more complex and composed of three parts: the top part is often shaped as a sphere, a cone or an octahedron; the middle section is covered by intricate decorations with geometrical, vegetal and sheep-horn shaped patterns (*koshkar-mys*), the same still found on the felt carpets of modern Kazakhs; and the lower part frames uniform geometric designs or Arabic inscriptions.

Bas-relief engravings and petroglyphs are found on stelae and on the sides of differing burial structures (koitas and pyramidal platforms, sandyktas, saganatam and mazar). The bas-reliefs consisted of five categories of subjects:

1) horses, horsemen and saddles;

2) military banners and flags, weapons such as battle-axes, swords, daggers, rifles, bows and quivers with arrows, leather belts with hanging accessories, etc;

3) dwellings and domestic utensils such as embroidered textiles, hat-stands, kettles and bowls;

4) female ornaments and objects such as jewellery, headdresses, combs and shoes;

5) tools of craftsmanship such as hammers, files, pincers, chisels, etc.

Petroglyphs were executed using a scratching technique in a linear style, which was favoured due to the softness of the chalk and limestone material, and they showed a predilection for elongated forms and elegant shapes. Their subject matter included figures of horses, horsemen, arkhar (bighorn sheep), military equipment and weapons, tamga, handprints and Arabic inscriptions. They mostly date to the 18th–19th centuries.

Both ancient and contemporary petroglyphs are also found on the walls of the underground mosque of Shakpak-ata and on chalk rock faces of small canyons of the Western Karatau mountains, with a main concentration in the area of the Kurmambet necropolis. Their representations include horses and horsemen, scenes of battles with bows and rifles, arkhar, weapons and handprints.

The Gulf of Mangyshlak

Approaching the Mangyshlak Peninsula by air from the east, a hallucinatory sight appears below, a long, sabre-shaped depression filled with water of a deep-pink hue. This is the former Komsomolets Gulf, now the **Gulf of Mangyshlak**, which borders the peninsula to the east. The water's pink colour is due to both an abundance of plankton in the shallow gulf water, and the huge flocks of **flamingos** that are drawn here to feed.

Caspian seals can be spotted in the shallow coastal waters of the Caspian Sea during the cold season. It is here that the animals spend the winter, bear young in spring, and subsequently leave to spend the summer in deeper waters. However, since the Caspian's water temperature is rising, and the ice layer each winter consequently becomes thinner, the seals find it hard to locate safe places to bring up their young. It is generally assumed that this, along with pollution of certain reed areas due to the oil industry, has caused the seal population's current decline.

The Gulf of Mangyshlak stretches more than 200 kilometres inland, and it could extend even farther in the future. If the Caspian Sea rises again, large areas of coastal strip will be turned into marshland. The eastern shore of the Gulf is safer, since it is high and steep. This is an ideal place for those who are fond of real solitude, but it is very hard to reach. A track that links the railway stations of **Say-Utes** and **Ustyurt** runs along the cliff for 15 to 20 kilometres, but from there you have to go by jeep or on foot. This trip could be combined with a visit to the necropolis of **Seysan-ata**, some 45 kilometres to the north of Say-Utes and just over two kilometres from the coastal cliff. It contains hundreds of tombstones dating from the 14th to 20th centuries, as well as a few remarkable mausoleums from the 19th Century.

The "Underground Mosques"

The sandstone and chalk landscape of the Mangyshlak Peninsula hides many natural caves that have served through the centuries as shelters, hideouts and religious retreats. These retreats are usually described as "underground mosques", but were actually places of meditation for Sufi masters, who withdrew from the world to fast and make direct spiritual contact with God. Wherever meditation was systematically practised, and where there were also evidently schools, there is today a lively traffic in pilgrims.

People come, often by difficult routes, to pray to the saints for fulfilment of their wishes, healing of illness or remedy to disputes; anything from childlessness to loneliness or poverty can be cause to visit the venerated, ancient masters of Sufism. All the major locations have "hospitable houses", as they are called, where you can stay the night in simple comfort on a sleeping mat, and be treated to bread and tea round the clock. At their discretion guests leave a small gift, such as food and drink or money.

The oldest cave complex is located at **Shakpak-ata**, in the north of Mangyshlak near the wide bay of **Sarytash** on the **Tyub Karagan peninsula**. It was hewn out of the rocks around the 10th Century (see Special Topic "Mangyshlak's Sacred Caves" on page 480), and is reached from the hamlet of **Tauchik**, but a 4WD and guide are recommended for the rough 35-kilometre route. The route from Fort Shevchenko covers 60 kilometres along a gravel track that leads along the cliffs to the winter camp of Sarytash. Shakpak-ata has three entrances, the main one on a ledge, a secret entrance located in a side valley, and a third one up on the plateau, where the location of the central hall is marked by a rectangular dome. The rock wall next to the main entrance looks like Swiss cheese with its burial niches and small holes that offered shelter to pilgrims.

Not far from Shakpak-ata is the complex of **Sultan-Epe**, patron saint of fishermen and sailors, hidden in the canyon that bears the same name. The caves, as with most of the peninsula's main pilgrimage sites, are located near a necropolis which features four tomb stones crowned by very realistic ram statues. These *koshkar-tas* are surrounded by much more straightforward tombstones, some of which bear only the tribal sign of the deceased.

The most renowned religious location on the Mangyshlak Peninsula is that of **Beket-ata** in Oglandy, of whom many legends are told. After studying in Khiva and returning to his home territory, Betek-ata became a master of clairvoyance, healing, physics, mathematics and astronomy. These skills, combined with an immense physical strength, earned him high esteem among the simple people, as a result of which Sufism became widespread in the

Top: One of thousands of bizarre stone balls, in varying states of erosion, found in the Karatau region (Dagmar Schreiber). Above: A religious guard reads the Koran at the Sultan-Epe complex (Edda Schlager)

area. Like Mohammed, Beket-ata died at the age of 63, and was buried in the underground mosque at Oglandy, one of the four mosques he is said to have built in the region (see page 485).

Every day, busloads of pilgrims come to the Beket-ata cave complex. On Islamic holidays the sanctuary and its surrounding areas have to cope with a vast number of visitors. The retreat was redecorated for Beket-ata's 250th birthday; roads were built, outdoor facilities such as toilets put up, and a guesthouse for travellers. Beket-ata is located 150 kilometres east of Aktau on a tarmac road, passing Zhanaozen and Tenge towards Ozen and Senek. The road's condition worsens as you drive east and, from Senek on, becomes very rough. Sixty kilometres before you reach Beket-ata is another famous site, the **Shopan-ata** complex. According to legend, Shopan was a pupil of Khoja Ahmed Yasawi. In the centre of the necropolis is a circular mosque, without any decoration on the outside, hewn out of the flat sandstone rocks. Believers think that before visiting Beket-ata, one must stop at **Masat-ata** and Shopan-ata. Ignore this rule and a pilgrim will not be able to find Beket-ata, and even if he does manage to locate it, his visit will be in vain.

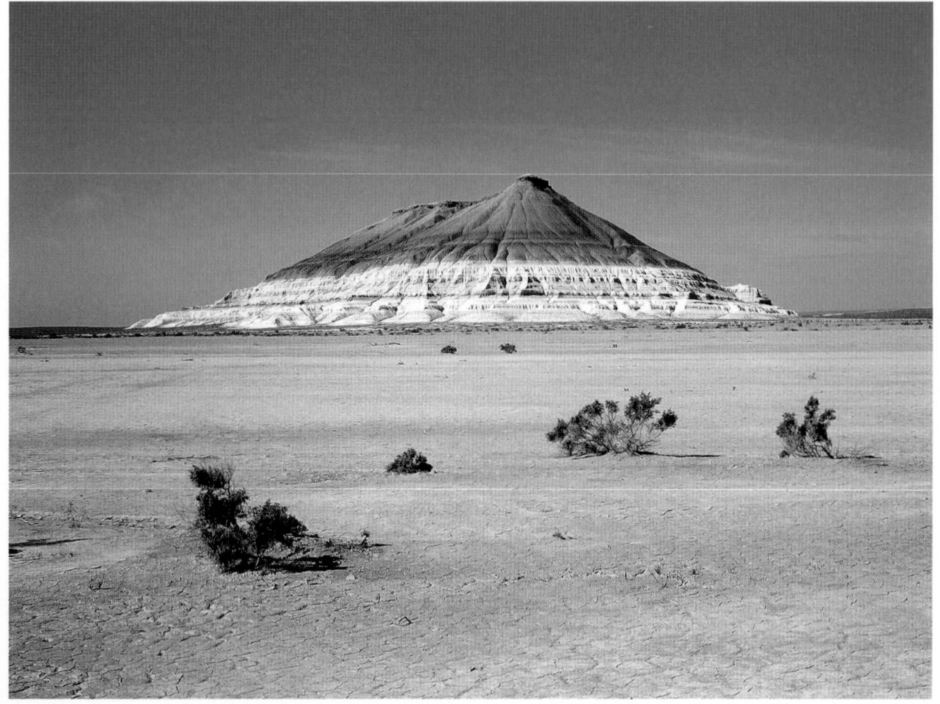

Mt Bokhty on the Ustyurt Plateau (Vladislav Yakushkin)

continued on page 488

MANGYSHLAK'S SACRED CAVES

By *Renato Sala and Jean-Marc Deom*

The arid Mangyshlak Peninsula is a mountainous extension of the Ustyurt Plateau stretching into the northeastern part of the Caspian Sea. With its high concentration of cemeteries, mosques and places of pilgrimage it is considered a holy and sacred land within Kazakhstan. Here you will find hundreds of necropolises in addition to "underground mosques", which are always coupled with the tomb of a saint, and huge cemeteries. The extraordinary location of these sites is not strange when you consider the unique features and exceptional natural beauty of the landscape, as well as the fact that for centuries this region provided winter camps for pastoralists en route to and from the Urals and the Caspian coast.

The Ustyurt Plateau and the Mangystau chain to its west (the latter being the backbone of the Mangyshlak Peninsula) constitute a huge, raised flatland of sedimentary limestone situated between the Aral and Caspian seas and bordered by huge precipices. Until the Quaternary Era, the whole area was submerged beneath a large sea, but tectonic events raised the plateau above the water to an altitude of 556 metres above sea level, at the same time dropping other areas to 132 metres below sea level. The steep cliffs of the lifted areas show layer upon layer of multicoloured clays and marl (a clay/limestone mixture containing shell fragments). In many places at the foot of the cliffs, the natural resurgence of water and artificially dug wells have created small green oases that contrast with the white chalky hills surrounding them, creating a beautiful and dramatic landscape. In addition, many natural caves have been created in the highly friable karst and carbonate rocks, and since ancient times they have provided ready-made shelters that could be artificially enlarged into underground architectural complexes.

There are around 15–20 underground mosques on the peninsula (there is no complete inventory), all connected with the graves of local Sufi saints (362 saints are buried in the region, almost one for every day of the year), with cemeteries generally dating from the 9th to 19th centuries AD. They represent important destinations of pilgrimage across the peninsula, the most visited being, from west to east: Shakpak-ata, Sultan-Epe, Karaman-ata, Shopan-ata, Beket-ata (Oglandy) and Beket-ata (Beineu) (see map on page 482).

Some of these mosques have been dated to the period of the earliest tombs (9th–10th centuries AD) and are attributed to different peoples, listed in chronological succession: Khazar, Oguz, Kypchak, the Golden Horde, the Nogai Horde and Kazakh. The group that was most active in building funerary complexes was the Adai tribe, belonging to the Baiuly large tribe of the Lesser Kazakh Zhuz (tribal confederation), which inhabited the Mangyshlak Peninsula in the 18th century and controlled the territories of northwestern Kazakhstan. The Adai were well known among the Kazakhs as an endogamic and warring tribe who led many battles against the Turkmens, Chorezmians of Khiva, Zhungars and Russians. This is well reflected in the frequent representations of weapons and epic scenes engraved on the gravestones of the cemeteries and on the walls of some underground mosques, particularly those of Shakpak-ata.

Some of the saints buried inside these mosques are recorded through local legend as contemporary with the mosque's construction, but most of them are reported as living during the last three centuries and buried in pre-existing structures. They were all said to be spiritual masters, high politicians and/or military leaders. In Mangyshlak, as in South Kazakhstan, the lineage of the saints is connected to the Sufi master Khoja Ahmed Yasawi, who lived in Turkestan between 1103 and 1166 AD. First among them was Shopan-ata, a direct disciple of Yasawi who passed on the initiation to the other saints of the region.

The architectural plan of the caves consists of several rooms, three to seven in number. The mosque is always located inside the cave and the grave of the local saint is sometimes built outside near the entrance. When both mosque and grave are inside, the mosque consists of a simple prayer room and the most important room is the burial chamber itself.

SHOPAN-ATA

This underground mosque is located 60km northeast of the village of Novyi-Uzen, on the northeastern edge of the Mangystau chain. It is situated at the foot of a promontory (Mount Shopan-ata) dividing the sandy desert of Bostankum to the west from a saline depression to the east. The cave is found at the bottom of a low limestone cliff, the top of which has been carved into a crater in order to collect water for ablutions. It is surrounded by a cemetery dating from the 10th to 19th centuries AD, from the Oguz to the Adai period, the latter constituting 70 percent of the funerary complex.

Shopan-ata is one of the oldest in the Mangystau Region (10th–12th centuries AD) and hosts the grave of the saint Shopan-ata, who lived in the 12th century.

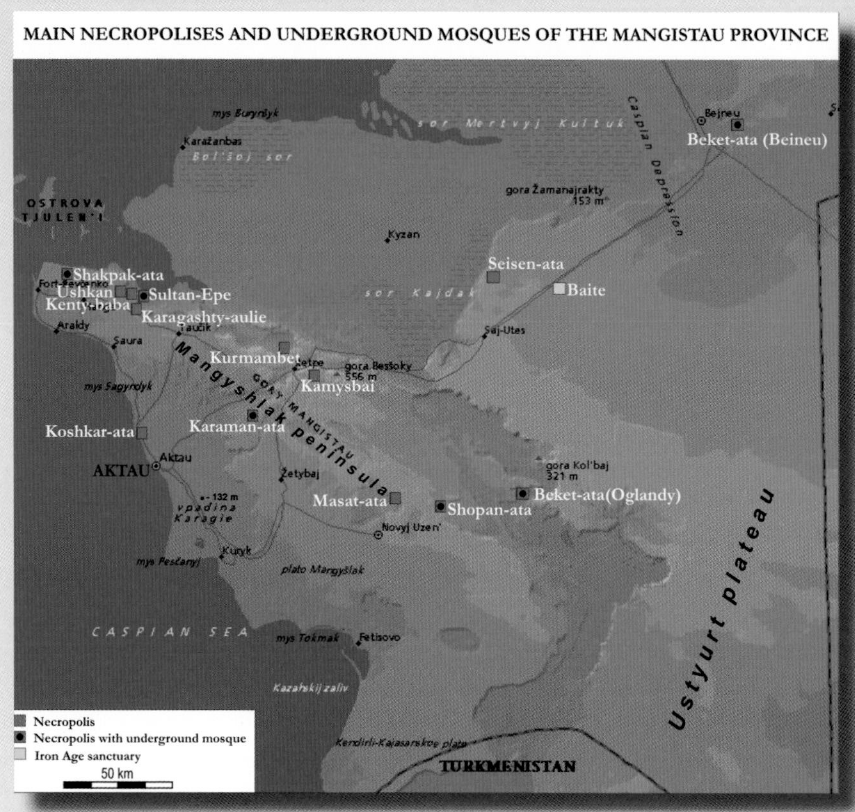

The entrance opens onto the side of a rock face and the cave consists of four rectangular rooms connected to each other by corridors: an entrance hall, a prayer room (the mosque) and two funeral chambers containing the tomb of Shopan-ata and that of his daughter. Two other doors situated to the left of the mosque's entrance give access to pilgrim dormitories.

Shopan in Kazakh and chaban in Russian mean "shepherd": Shopan-ata is in fact the patron saint of shepherds. Legend says that he was a dervish, a disciple of Ahmed Yasawi. One day, Master Yasawi summoned his disciples to a yurt, told them to shoot an arrow through the round hole of the *shangyrak* (roof opening), and go and spread Sufism as shepherds in the place where their arrows landed. Shopan-ata's arrow reached the Mangyshlak Peninsula on the site of the actual mosque,

Above: A map of locations of necropolises and cave complexes on the Mangyshlak Peninsula (Courtesy of Renato Sala and Jean-Marc Deom)

Top: The main room within the Shakpak-ata cave complex. Above: The entrance to Beket-ata (Edda Schlager x2)

in the land of a rich *bai* (landlord) named Bayan, to whom the saint subsequently proposed his service as a shepherd. Bayan agreed, saying that at the end of the year he would pay Shopan-ata by the number of white sheep born during the season. That year all the newborn sheep were white, but Bayan postponed his payment, saying that he would pay the following year according to the number of newborn black sheep. The following year, all the newborn sheep were black, and finally Bayan understood that he was facing an extraordinary man, offering Shopan-ata all his belongings.

The legend continues, saying that Shopan-ata had two grandsons, Shakpak-ata and Karaman-ata, who are buried and revered in other underground mosques in the Mangyshlak region. It is also said that he was a hero in battle, dying on the battlefield, and that his powers were such that a visit to his tomb and the invocation of his name have magical healing properties. In 1764 his tomb was visited by the young Beket-ata (subsequently buried and revered as a saint 50km east of Shopan-ata), who was inspired to go to Khiva to study Islam.

Shakpak-ata

Located 90km north of Aktau, on the cliffs of the northwestern tip of the Mangyshlak Peninsula, this mosque is cut into the vertical slopes of limestone bedrock bordering a valley with a seasonal stream. Shakpak-ata dates to the 9th–10th centuries AD, making it the oldest in Mangyshlak, and overlooks a huge necropolis. The entrance consists of a portal flanked on both sides by artificial grottoes, each occupied by a burial place, including the later grave of Shakpak-ata. The inside of the cave has a complex cross-like shape, with a series of lateral niches and a central vaulted room which, supported by four columns and having a hole in the roof, clearly imitates a yurt. The plan of Shakpak-ata is unique in Mangyshlak, and shows similarities with some early Persian mosques and with the mausoleum-mosque of Shir-Kabir in Dehistan (Turkmenistan), also dated to the same time. Another unique aspect of this underground mosque is that large portions of its walls are covered with petroglyphs and graffiti. The oldest images, attributed to the Oguz people, represent handprints, and the later drawings, attributed to the Adai tradition, represent horses and scenes of battle executed with a very high aesthetic value.

Legend tells that Shakpak-ata was the grandson of Shopan-ata. He was an ascetic dervish who took refuge in the cave with his disciples at a time when enemies were assaulting the region, and spent the last years of his life as a hermit, never leaving the cave. It is also said that the ancient Sufi masters gave asylum to sick people in their underground shelters in order to heal them, and that even today a night spent in these caves in the company of benevolent spirits will cure most diseases.

Beket-ata (Oglandy)

This underground mosque is located at Oglandy, 55km east of Shopan-ata, between the northwestern tip of the Mangystau mountains and the western edge of the Ustyurt Plateau. It is built into the slopes of a limestone and chalk cliff hanging 100 metres above a depression, together with a cemetery with tombs dating from the 10th to 19th centuries.

The date of the first building of the underground complex has not yet been determined. Access to the cave is by a staircase along the cliff, and the underground architectural plan consists of seven rooms. The mosque, vaulted with concave walls, is also built with architectural features similar to the shape of a yurt. The huge tomb of the saint is located outside to the right of the entrance. The pilgrims' dormitories are situated on the top of the hill and, nearby, there is a small museum displaying artefacts related to the Sufi master, including his brother's fur hat and a whip. The site has been recently restored and the brick wall supporting the platform of the entrance has been rebuilt in its original shape. The mullah of the mosque claims to be a descendant of Beket-ata.

Legend has it that Beket-ata was born in 1750 in Kulsary (on the lower course of the river Emba, 170km east of Atyrau) into a family of brave warriors. His great-grandfather was Eset-batyr, a well-known hero (*batyr*) of western Kazakhstan. At the age of 14, Beket-ata went to worship at the tomb of Shopan-ata and, on the third night of his stay, received a visit from the saint who told him to go to Khiva and study Islam. At the age of 40 he returned to Mangystau, where he first taught children to write, then started to heal people and act as a judge in conflicts. His preaching of good morals spread among the Adai people but at the same time, like his great-grandfather, he acted as a military strategist in the wars against the Kalmyks (Zhungars). He died at the age of 63, but the legend goes that his body remained alive in the tomb for 100 years longer, and his hair and beard were regularly cut by his disciples.

There are four mosques dedicated to Beket-ata in western Kazakhstan: the mosque of Ak-Mechet in Kulsary, the mosque Baishatyr on the Ustyurt Plateau, the underground mosque Beket-ata in Oglandy and the underground mosque Beket-ata in Beineu. Local people say that the four mosques correspond to the four seasonal camps of the Adai shepherds.

The Ustyurt Plateau provides awe-inspiring views that demonstrate the stark beauty of the natural world (Dagmar Schreiber). Inset: A study in the powers of erosion (Vladislav Yakushkin)

SHETPE, KARATAU AND SHERKHALA

The area around the village of **Shetpe** is the most varied landscape on the Mangyshlak Peninsula. About 100 kilometres northeast of Aktau in the direction of **Beyneu**—the easiest way to get there is by train, since the road takes a detour via Munayshy—are the **Karatau (Black Mountains)**, the highest peaks of which rise more than 500 metres, a considerable height in the middle of this flatland. This mountain range is known for its unusual geological deposits and bizarre forms of erosion—Kazakhstan's geologists would like to see it turned into a protected area.

One of the most spectacular natural monuments is **Mount Sherkhala (Tiger Town)**, a wonderful pinnacle of rock that from one side looks like a white yurt, but from the other reminds one of a sleeping tiger. Its aspect at sunset is particularly impressive, when it appears to be floating over the grey plain.

Just a few kilometres from Sherkhala lies the ruined caravan city of **Kyzylkhala (Red City)**, thought to have played an important role during the height of the Silk Road's golden era. The excavation site is closed at the moment to prevent looting, while Kazakh archaeologists wait for state funding. An hour away by 4WD is perhaps the most beautiful location on Mangyshlak: the **Akmystau Mountains**, also called the **Valley of Castles**, after a painting by **Taras Shevchenko**. Dramatically eroded mountains half surround and lie scattered on a broad plain, looking for all the world like the pinnacles and towers of a fairytale city.

Northwest and southeast of **Shair** village are extraordinary collections of huge stones—full globes, half globes and other geometrical shapes with diameters of up to three metres; they look like nothing so much as abandoned toys for giants. Scientists speculate that they are concretions from the seabed, the centres of which consist of fossilized maritime microorganisms, which over the course of millions of years formed concentric layers of mineral rock.

Above: Bizarrely eroded sandstone formations on the Aktolagay Plateau (Dagmar Schreiber)

THE USTYURT PLATEAU

The **Ustyurt Reserve** was established in 1984 as a state nature reserve occupying more than 2,200 square kilometres and including the western edge of the Ustyurt Plateau with its monumentally eroded rock cathedrals. The plateau in its entirety—some 200,000 square kilometres of semi-desert—stretches far into territory belonging to **Turkmenistan** and **Uzbekistan**, from the so-called "Western Chink" between the **Gulf of Mangyshlak** and the **Karynzharyk Desert** to the "Eastern Chink" on the west bank of the **Aral Sea**. It is fair to call this area the best-protected nature reserve in Kazakhstan, since its topography and the absence of any infrastructure condemn visitors to travel by helicopter, or hundreds of kilometres by jeep or on foot—something, fortunately, only very few visitors can afford or endure.

The Ustyurt Plateau's chalk escarpments, known as "chinks", are hugely impressive and starkly beautiful. The giant terraces stretch hundreds of kilometres to the north and south, in the east reaching heights of up to 219 metres on the border with the Aral Sea, while those to the west rise up to 341 metres high. Here in particular, the cliffs have been shaped by fault ruptures, water, wind and sand erosion into a rich and varied landscape. Numerous rock caverns in the central, eastern and southern areas, some very large, have offered shelter to man and animal alike for thousands of years. In spring, large expanses of the plain at the foot of the cliffs lie under water, and the contrast with the bald, oddly coloured mountains is otherworldy. The most prominent features of this section of the plateau edge are **Mount Bokhty**, about 40 kilometres east of **Senek**, and the **Bozzhira Massif**, about 30 kilometres farther on. The most difficult to reach is a mountain formation called the **Three Brothers** (*Tri Brata*), 40 kilometres north of the Kazakh-Turkmen border.

The plateau proper consists of a flat, waterless highland plain, covered with sand in some places and with gypsum crystal in others. A type of black saksaul grows only in this region, in the form of proper trees rather than bushes. Relatively large groups of the unique Ustyurt moufflon (a rare type of wild sheep) live in the reserve, as well as a small population of the lynx-like caracal, which is threatened with extinction, Indian porcupine, saiga antelope and some 20,000 dzheyran—half Kazakhstan's total population of the pretty gazelle. Many reptiles and rodents are endemic here, and at night the long-eared desert (Brandt's) hedgehog snuffles through the dark. Apart from the Houbara bustard, the large birds that live here are mainly raptors: the rare Turkmen owl (a subspecies of the Eurasian eagle owl), the saker falcon, short-toed and golden eagles and scavengers such as the Egyptian vulture. Every seven to nine years there is a time of glut for these birds when the *zhut* (a severe blizzard) leaves thousands of hoofed animals dead. This phenomenon, most feared by the nomads, takes place when, after winter rains, temperatures suddenly drop sharply and the desert freezes. Unable to find food, the animals swiftly die.

The Ustyurt Plateau is most easily visited from Aktau via Zhanaozen and Senek. The tarmac road ends here, and further travel is on sand and clay tracks to the foot of the fissured limestone escarpment of the Western Chink. There are only a few places to ascend to the plateau by jeep or on foot. A guide is absolutely essential, someone who knows all the ins and outs of the area, as the network of tracks is unclear and intact, water-bearing wells are extremely rare. Any planned itinerary to this region should include not less than five litres of water per person per day. Expedition supplies can be bought in Zhanaozen, where the **Hotel Aruana** (tel: 72934 63388, fax: 63342, email: recepshen@tnsplus.kz) is found, the last good place to enjoy comfortable accommodation before travelling to the hard-won but rewarding pleasures of the Ustyurt Plateau.

The Turan Lowland

An immensely vast, uniform desert landscape stretches from the Russian border down to **Atyrau**, featuring sand dunes and scant vegetation, if any at all. The unpaved roads are flanked by humble settlements about every 50 kilometres, and in between them the occasional shelters of a winter camp. This area, part of the **Turan Lowland** (also called the **Turan Depression**) includes the **Menteke**, **Buzanay**, **Kosdaulet** and **Batpayskagyr** deserts—all in all not a very inviting tourist destination. Almost the entire region lies below

Above: A camel seems unimpressed by its surroundings in Akmystau, the Valley of Castles. Right: A lone soul is dwarfed by monumental rock on the Ustyurt Plateau (Dagmar Schreiber x2)

sea level, and the soil is saline. The highest "mountain", **Mount Kaday**, rises 14 metres above sea level, and to the north the region borders the **Ryn Desert**. Only camels seem to prosper in this desolate area with its ungenerous soil, although sheep somehow also survive. In Soviet times, this was a closed area for testing mid-range missiles.

However, the assumption that there is only flat and forlorn steppe in the **Atyrau**, **West Kazakhstan** and **Aktobe Regions** (Oblasts) is somewhat misleading. The easternmost branch of the **Volga Delta**, the **Kigach**, flows through Kazakhstan territory, emptying into the Caspian Sea to the south of **Ganyushkino**. The small strip of land alongside it is more densely populated than all the rest of rural Atyrau Region, since its marshland is fertile. The landscape forms an interesting mix between flat steppe, desert, river and reed lake.

To the east, the Turan Lowland is bordered by the **Aktolagay Plateau**. This remote place is accessed down 80 kilometres of rough road south from the village of **Says**, which lies 250 kilometres along the road from Atyrau to **Aktobe**. Eventually a bizarrely shaped rock wall, reminiscent of a jagged sandcastle, looms ahead. The heavily cleft plateau, with its fossil-rich chalk mountains, is crowned by a chess queen—a white mountain, the original peak of which has eroded into a round skull.

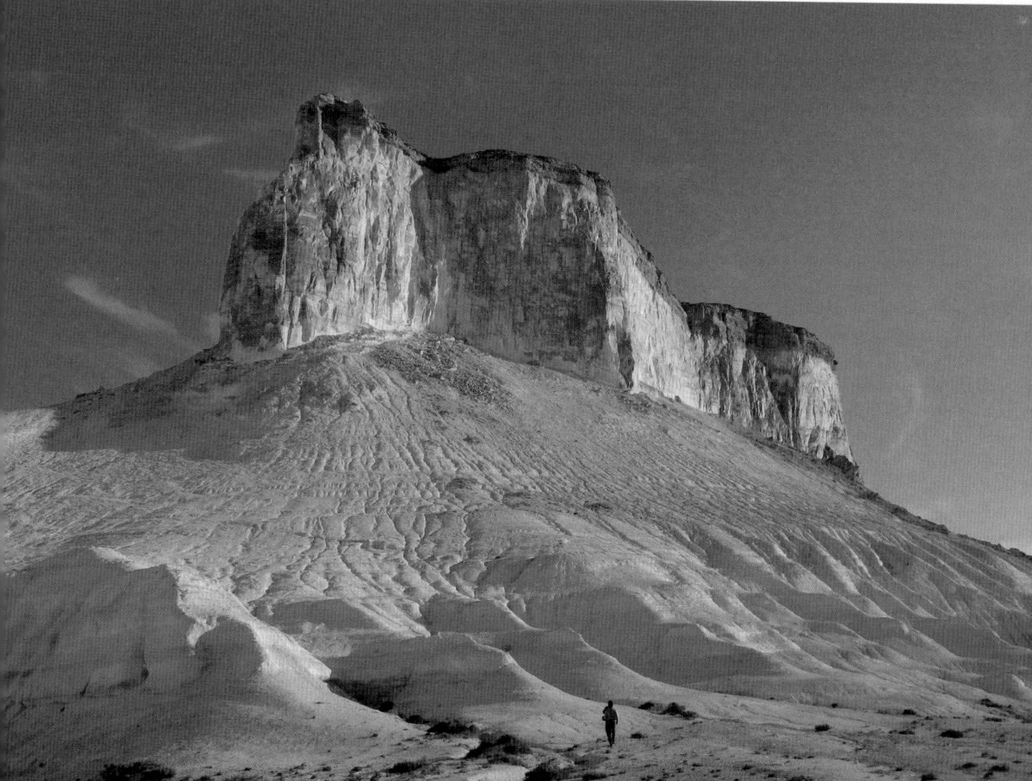

Oral (Uralsk)

Uralsk—or **Oral** as it has now been officially renamed—lies on the left bank of the middle reaches of the **Ural River** (Oral or Zhayik in Kazakh). Far from Kazakhstan's other urban centres, it is actually closer to Warsaw, Poland's capital, than Almaty. It has done much to change its image in recent years. The remnants of the original Russian town, which dates back to 1775, have been renovated with considerable care; the streets and avenues in the city centre now present a grand and attractive sight to visitors. Worth visiting are the attractive **Russian Orthodox Cathedral**, the **Pugachyov Museum** and the riverside park. Oral has 210,000 inhabitants, most of whom are employed in various industries associated with the burgeoning oilfields to the southeast. The bridges across the river make Oral an important crossroads on the border between Europe and Asia.

Practical Information

The area dialling code for Oral is +7112.

Transportation

The airport is 15 kilometres to the south of the town. There are daily flights to and from Almaty, Astana, Atyrau, Aktau, Moscow and London (Gatwick). The Air Astana office is at 188 Dostyk Ave, tel: 515 151. There are daily rail connections with Almaty (via Aktobe, Kyzylorda and Shymkent) and Moscow.

Accommodation

Hotel Chagala, 67/1 Temira Manasa St, tel: 509 855, fax: 510 459, e-mail: chagala.uralsk@nursat.kz—a modern hotel in the centre not far from the market. Rooms from US$80.

Pushkin Hotel, 148b Dostyk Ave, tel: 513 560, fax: 513 566, e-mail: rencopushkin@mail.ru, website: www.pushkinhotel.com—a four-star hotel in classic style in the city centre.

Sayakhat Hotel, 38 Temira Masina St, tel: 510 330, fax: 500 951—a large, centrally located renovated hotel. Rooms from US$20.

The Ural (Zhayik) River

The **Zhayik River**, better known as the **Ural River** in books and on international maps, flows free and wide through the Kazakh steppe between **Oral** and **Atyrau**. The water is far from clean due to the many concentrations of industry along its course, both in Russia to the north and around Oral. The river, 2,428 kilometres long, flows across Kazakhstan's territory for more than 1,000 kilometres. It flows sluggishly through its broad basin, forming side branches, islands, swampy lagoons and lakes. These steppe lands belong to the most ancient sedentary areas of the Kazakhs—but were also popular among the Russians. This was the original meeting point of the two cultures, but the Russian decree of 1756, which banned the rights of Kazakhs to let their herds graze on the right bank of the Ural, immediately led to clashes over land control.

Two roads lead from Oral to Atyrau, both of which keep close to the river. The road on the west bank is relatively well frequented, while the one on the opposite bank is in a worse state and therefore quieter. Both are just over 500 kilometres long, which makes for a day's tough travel. Bumpy side roads from both main roads lead to villages on the river's banks. You should think carefully about which road to take, for ferries across the river are scarce along the whole stretch. Between December and March a change of mind can be corrected, however, because the river freezes over and can be driven on. To see (and hear) the ice drift as it breaks up in late March and early April is quite spectacular.

ATYRAU

Kazakhstan's westernmost large city has two remarkable features. First, it straddles two continents: given the historic decision to count the Ural as the line that separates Europe from Asia in this region, the city districts located on the western bank of the Ural River are geographically in Europe, while crossing the bridge brings you into Asia.

Secondly, and far more significantly, **Atyrau**—formerly **Guriyev**—is well on its way to become Kazakhstan's oil metropolis, a boomtown where construction is under way everywhere you turn. Foreign oil companies erect their office buildings one next to the other in the city, and construct ghetto-like dormitory buildings for their staff, surrounded by walls and ugly fences. The town's authorities have a hard time trying to impose constraint on the uncontrolled construction work and develop some sort of sophisticated city planning. On paper a master plan does exist, the first stage of which basically consists of tearing down the old town of Guriyev. Following that, both banks of the Ural will be turned into a modern metropolis with green parks between the skyscrapers. By then, the town's current 250,000 inhabitants will have a mass of new neighbours, and department stores and leisure centres will be added to the cityscape.

But much needs to be done before this vision is realized. In its present state, Atyrau is a large, somewhat chaotic settlement without a proper city centre. Merciless mosquitoes discourage those who usually like to explore towns on foot—defying them requires powerful repellent cream—while in order to enjoy the area's most popular sport, angling, mosquito nets as well as protective creams are essential.

Guriyev was the first Russian town built on Kazakh territory. After having conquered the khanates of **Kazan** and **Astrakhan** under **Tsar Ivan IV (the Terrible)** in the middle of the 16th Century, the Russians found themselves in the immediate neighbourhood of the Kazakh tribes. In order to consolidate their position on the western bank of the Ural, a fortified post, constructed of tree trunks, was built and named **Ustik Yaitsk**. There had been a fishing settlement named Uyshik there previously, but the Russians developed the fishing industry further, and farmers, brought in from the Don Basin, settled down on the riverbank. Regiments of soldiers were also stationed there to provide security; this was much to the dislike of the indigenous Kazakh inhabitants, who tried to destroy the fortification more than once—only to attract a stronger Russian presence each time.

In 1645, having obtained property rights for the entire coastal area between the mouths of the Ural and the **Emba**, the **Guriyev family**, one of Russia's wealthy trade clans, received the order to fortify the town in order to be able to resist further attacks from Kalmyks and Cossacks alike. Between 1647 and 1662, a better-equipped fortress was built, this time with stone walls and eight watchtowers equipped with 17 guns. Relations with the neighbours out in the steppe improved, after the latter appeared to have decided to live with the situation. In 1734, the town was awarded city rights and was named after its founder Guriyev. Once more, the spark of revolt flared in the lower reaches

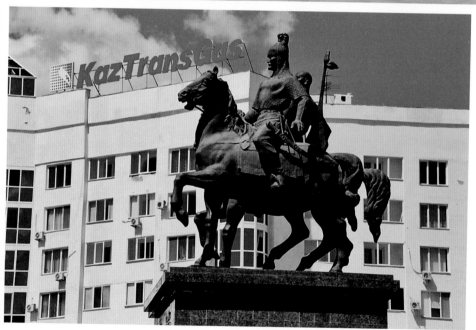

Clockwise from top left: Although modernizing fast, remnants of the old Atyrau still remain (Gunter Kapelle); ice fishing on the Ural, or Zhayik, River (Ernst Ischovits); a more modern look to the city; the river's bounty for sale in the fish market (Edda Schlager x2)

of the Ural River after the Russian crown imposed tougher regulations on settlement, thereby depriving the Kazakh nomads of their grazing rights. For 14 years, a peasant army led by **Srym Datov** held out against the Russian troops until he surrendered in 1797, after discovering treachery being plotted within his own Kazakh ranks.

Popular anger once more exploded in 1836 in an uprising led by the poet **Makhambet Utemisuly** and his comrade-in-arms **Issatay Taymanov**. As before, grazing rights were at stake in the area between the Volga and the Ural. For two years, the area controlled by the Junior Horde was ravaged by insurgency, only to end with the defeat and the death of Taymanov. Utemisuly was murdered in 1846.

But before the end of the century people discovered that in this particular area neither sturgeon nor grazing lands were the real wealth. The first oil deposits were discovered as early as 1890, and in the beginning of the 20th Century their exploitation took off. It was only after World War II, however, that systematic exploration and development operations started. Today, petroleum and fish are the main sources of income for the city. It has become a crossroads for transportation routes such as pipelines and railways between East and West, and shipping lines from Atyrau's seaport to Baku, Iran, Turkmenistan and along the Volga, the Volga-Don Canal and down the Don to the Black Sea, and on into Europe.

In 1992, Guriyev was renamed Atyrau by presidential decree. At this time the city began to transform itself. American presence is strong and will increase, since USAID and the local authorities have signed an agreement for the implementation of the overall development of Atyrau.

The city is relatively compact, and it does not take too long to walk from one end to the other (if you decide to brave the mosquitoes). A good starting and orientation point is the pedestrian bridge, built in 2002, between **Pobedy (Victory) Park** and the residential zone for the oil workers. This suspension bridge between Europe and Asia has a span of 405 metres. Across the bridge, you can walk along the riverbank through the city towards the north, passing the river's horseshoe bend until you come to the road bridge. This is the city centre, divided into two by the river and stretching no more than two to four blocks away from the riverbank. Here and there, a few parks testify to attempts to conquer the saline soil and produce some greenery.

Two museums are located on the crossroads between Momysh Uly Street and Azattyk Avenue, the **Local History Museum** (1 Momysh Uly Street) and the **Museum of Applied Arts** (11 Azattyk Avenue). Both are well worth a visit, like all regional museums of their kind in Kazakhstan. The **Museum of Regional Traditions** highlights the life and work of Makhambet Utemisuly (Utemisov), who lived in the area of Guriyev in the first half of the 19th Century and whose aphoristic and expressive poetry greatly contributed to the education of the common people. Also interesting is the exhibition about **Sarayshik**, the city of the **Golden (Nogai) Horde** that was first destroyed by Tamerlane in 1395 and later again by the Cossacks in 1580. Remains of the walls of Sarayshik have been found recently during construction work on the Ural. Atyrau's own Golden Man can also be seen here. It is an accurate replica of the golden mantle of a Samartian warrior and dignitary. This treasure and many other revealing objects were only excavated in the year 2000 near the village of **Araltobe**.

A mosque is located on Satpayev Street, just over a kilometre to the west of the road bridge. A second one, the **Kuspan-Molla Mosque**, is to the northwest on the street of the same name. The freshly restored **Uspenskiy Cathedral** adds cheer to the remains of the old town on Isataya Avenue, some way northwest of the city centre.

The cattle market of **Tuma**, on the western edge of town, is recommended to those who like "authentic" impressions of day-to-day life. The fishing port **Atyraubalyk** and the river port to its south, with the oil terminals in the background are also rather colourful. The best way to see them is from the western riverbank, since direct access to the sites is impossible.

Practical Information

The area dialling code for Atyrau is +7122. The Post Office is located at 52 Smagulov St, open Mon–Fri: 8am–7pm, Sat-Sun: 9am–6pm.

Transportation

Atyrau has an international airport (www.atyrauairport.com), located to the west of the city. There are daily domestic flights to Almaty and Astana, several times a week to Aktau, Shymkent and other urban centres in Kazakhstan, and international flights to Amsterdam, Istanbul and Russia.

Air Astana's office is at 3 Abai Ave (tel: 255 345); Central Asia Tourism's branch office can be found at 25 Azattyk Ave (tel: 354 075/6, fax: 354 077, e-mail: cat-atyrau@alarnet.com).

Atyrau is located on the Astrakhan-Orsk-Chelyabinsk rail line, with branch lines to Aktau and Almaty further down the line. The passenger railway station with ticket sales desk is on the northern edge of the city, at the end of Baymukhanov St. The bus station is located in the west of the city, to the south of the road to the airport (Kurmangazy St).

Accommodation

Renaissance Atyrau Hotel, 15B Satpayev St, tel: 909 600, fax: 906 606, email: Karina.Galustyants@marriott.com, website: www.renaissance-hotels.com/GUWBR—a Marriott Group hotel, with all the attributes of an international luxury hotel. Rooms from US$180.

Hotel Atyrau, 6 Satpayev St, tel: 921 100, fax: 271 827, e-mail: reservation@hotel-atyrau.kz, website: www.hotelatyrau.kz—a beautiful hotel in the business district, not far from the river on the main road. Rooms from US$150.

Hotel Kaspiy, 15 Satpayev St, tel: 213 307, fax: 212 511—a small, 20-room establishment with restaurant, sauna, swimming pool and fitness centre. Rooms from US$70.

Chagala, 1 Smagulov St, tel: 996 096, fax: 996 095, e-mail: atyrau@chagala-group.kz, website: www.chagalagroup.com—a good quality hotel right on the Ural River. Rooms from US$80.

Krasniy Drakon, 1 Karymsakov St, tel: 259 042—a good hotel off Azattyk Ave, in front of the Shalkyma department store. Rooms from US$120.

River Palace, 55 Ayteke Bi St, tel: 255 239—large, new and expensive, located on the riverside. Rooms from US$160.

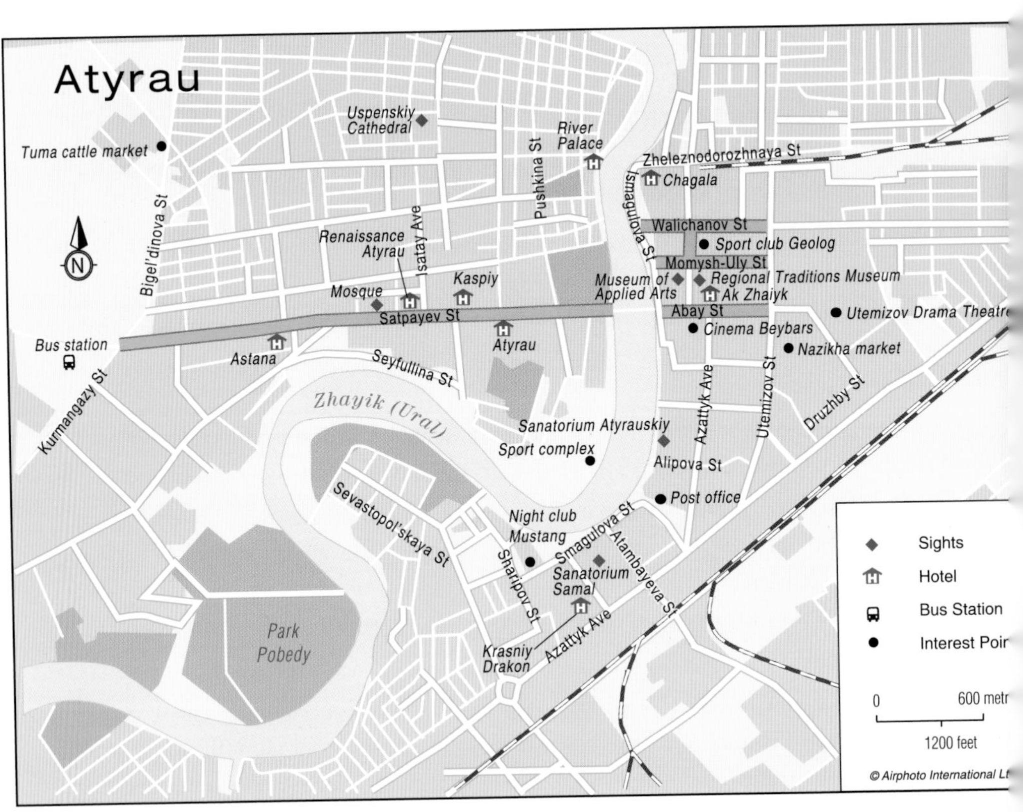

A Caviar Caveat

Caviar may be an expensive luxury at champagne parties, but it is just ordinary food in some villages on the Caspian shore. The Caspian littoral states produce 90 percent of the world's "real" caviar. This, however, could soon be a thing of the past. The larger Caspian sturgeon such as the osetra, the beluga (the largest—and the only predatory—sturgeon) and the sevruga are being mercilessly overfished. Rising prices tell the story: in the summer of 2002, prices in Kazakhstan doubled over those of the previous summer, averaging 25,000 tenge (US$160 at the time) per kilogramme. True, this is still a trifle compared to the US$1,800–2,500 one has to pay for a kilogramme of genuine caviar in some Western countries. But the fishermen see little of those huge profits, which mainly go to Russian

Top: Home to the world's best "real" caviar, prices in Atyrau are shockingly cheap to foreigners. Above: Fishing for sturgeon in the Ural Delta (Edda Schlager x2)

middlemen. An entire "mafia" participates and enriches itself in the international caviar trade. Protection schemes are no match for criminal organizations—the illegal trade in caviar is 10 times that of the legal commerce.

For a long time attempts have been made to regenerate the fish population. On the Iranian side, millions of fingerlings are raised in ponds and released into the Caspian annually. However, it takes a sturgeon 20 years to mature, and as they reach a considerable size some time before that, it still pays to catch them earlier than that. Poverty in the villages along the coast and the rivers Volga and Ural—where the fish come to spawn—inevitably drives people to fishing, exacerbating the problem.

It is actually possible to harvest caviar without killing the fish. Shortly before the eggs are laid, one can "milk" them from the female. This even produces the finest and tastiest caviar of them all, according to experts. Those who want to sample of the very best caviar should observe the following:

- Red caviar comes from salmon
- Sturgeon caviar is black or grey
- Its true taste is only preserved if it is kept in glass, as tins distort the flavour
- Caviar has only been produced in a genuine and legal manner if the glass's lid bears a GOST certificate and the serial number of the producer as well as the dates of production and expiry
- Grease on the glass indicates bad preservation or the addition of improper agents
- The lid should not bulge outwards
- The best way to take caviar is with a shot of ice-cold vodka—this accentuates the delicate taste, rather than distorting it as champagne does.

A healthy catch of huge sturgeon—but will it last? (Photographer unknown)

The Ural Delta

The Ural River flows into the Caspian Sea to the south of Atyrau as a large delta, and is a protected nature reserve. The **Ural Delta** contains hundreds of islands of varying size, plentiful reed forests, and is home to water birds and sturgeon which come here to spawn. Nowhere in the world, not even in the **Volga Delta** not far to the west, can such a dense population of sturgeon be found. From mid-March until mid-June in particular, when the sturgeon come to the surface to spawn, a good angler can catch beluga sturgeon up to three metres long and weighing in at more than 300 kilogrammes.

These fish must be released immediately, however—the sturgeon has been placed under strict protection, especially in its spawning area. Its population in the Caspian Sea is heavily overfished, so efforts are being made to allow them to reproduce here.

Aktobe

The city of **Aktobe** is located in the southern foothills of the **Ural Mountains**, which peter out into the **Turan Lowland**. Most of the vast territory of the **Aktobe Region** (Oblast) consists of scarcely populated steppe across which numerous salt lagoons are scattered, but the landscape to the northeast of Aktobe, in the rising Urals, is more picturesque, especially in June when the wind makes waves of the long blades of feather grass on the rolling steppe. Here you find the green valleys of the **Zachsi Kargaly** and **Zhaman Kargaly** rivers, where a nice reservoir looks inviting to those who seek to relax or fish.

Aktobe was first built along the northern defence line that in 1869 formed the frontier between Siberia and the Kazakh khanates. Today it has a population of 200,000, and is a centre of iron metallurgy, chrome smelting and a petrochemical industry. It is not a particularly attractive town for tourists, although it does have the usual pleasant parks, two reservoirs where locals seek R&R during fine weather, a local museum, mosques and Orthodox churches.

German civilians, who were deported east on the orders of Stalin after the German invasion of the Soviet Union, were put to work repairing the nickel mines to the northeast of the town. Many of them died of starvation, cold and exhaustion. A graveyard with a high cross and a memorial stone not far from the village of **Badamsha** recalls those innocents who had to pay for the megalomania of their political leader.

Practical Information

The area dialling code for Aktobe is +7132. The city has its own website—www.aktobeinfo.kz —but tellingly, it is only in Russian.

Transportation

There are daily flights to Astana, Almaty and Aktau, four flights a week to Atyrau and a weekly flight to Kostanay. Several flights a week go to Moscow, and there are connections with Cologne and Bonn in the summer. The Air Astana office is at 67a Abulkhair Khan Ave (tel: 548 501); Central Asia Tourism's office is at 84 Abulkhair Khan Ave, office 36 (tel: 523 841/514 227, e-mail: cat-aktobe@alarnet.com).

Accommodation

Hotel Best Eastern Albion, 13 Ayteke Bi St, tel: 241 603, fax: 210 018, e-mail: albion@akparat.kz or albion_hotel@rambler.ru—a small but good hotel in the city centre. Rooms from US$150.

KazTransWay, 11 Lomonosov St, tel: 210 693, fax: 518 387—a small hotel in the historical centre. Rooms from US$50.

Hotel Aktobe, 44 Abulkhair Khan Ave, tel: 562 829/562 915, fax: 567 772, e-mail: hotel@aktobe.kz or hotel-aktobe@rambler.ru—a large three-star, Soviet-style hotel in the city centre. Rooms from US$15.

Travel Agents in Western Kazakhstan

Turist, Mikrorayon 9, building 4/110, Aktau, tel: (7292) 430 000/511 929, fax: 338 602/310 171, e-mail: pbatalov@nursat.kz, website: www.tourist-aktau.com—ISO certified, a well-run and enthusiastic firm dedicated to proving to both domestic and foreign tourists that Mangyshlak is not a monotonous piece of barren semi-desert. Trips include beach tours, swimming excursions to Mangyshlak's beaches and Kendirly, multi-day tours to historical sites such as Fort Shevchenko, the "underground mosques" and necropolises, Mount Karatau, the Valley of Castles, Tamshaly, Mount Sherkhala, the Neolithic excavations of Koskuduk.

Caspian tour, Mikrorayon 14 (in the Wedding Palace), Aktau, tel: (7292) 426 654, fax: 426 661, email: menzhan@rambler.ru—this firm is headed by Ginayat Menzhan, for many years a leading member of the regional tourism administration; 4WD and helicopter tours to all the sites on the peninsula, Kendirly beach resort bookings, hotel bookings, interpreter service and many other possibilities.

Andrey Astafyev, Aktau, email: aasta@mail.ru—an archaeologist, historian, ethnologist and passionate guide for the entire Mangyshlak Peninsula; also organizes drivers and jeeps.

Panorama, 163 Furmanov St, Oral (Uralsk), tel: (7112) 505 632, fax: 240 675, mob: +7 777 558 9407, e-mail: contacts@panoramatour.kz, website: www.panoramatour.kz—excursions to Shalkar salt lake (75km southeast of Oral), health treatment holidays, fishing tours, assistance on all issues concerning tourism. The company owns an idyllic campsite named Mechta (Dream) between Lake Tyoploye and the Ural River about 20 kilometres north of town.

Atyrau Club of Hunters and Anglers, 38 Balgimbayev St, Atyrau, tel: (7122) 271 435, fax: 271 434—fishing trips for sturgeon and other species. The organization runs a hotel-boat in the Ural Delta.

Sputnik, 58/1-3 Abulkhair Khan Ave, Aktobe (ask for Zhalgas Balgozhin), tel: +7 701 351 0656, e-mail: sputnik-akt@mail.ru—all the usual tourism services, coordinated with agencies throughout the country.

Tourism Section of the Department for Enterprise and Industry, 40 Abulkhair Khan Ave, Aktobe, tel: (7132) 564 608, fax: 595 221, e-mail: aktobe_obltour@mail.ru—the enthusiastic section chief herself prepares interesting tours and knows a great deal about her region.

Above left: Atyrau's Uspenskiy Cathedral (Gunter Kapelle)
Below: This ship has been cleverly converted into a restaurant in Aktau (Dagmar Schreiber)

A–Z TRAVELLER'S TIPS

ACCOMMODATION

The quality of accommodation in Kazakhstan covers the full gamut from five-star hotels to the most basic rural hostels and cabins (sometimes complete with rickety, wind-blown toilet sheds in the yard, surrounding a simple hole in the ground). Prices vary accordingly. In the more remote areas, rustic inns with all the charm of boy scouts' camps prevail.

In Atyrau and Astana, in particular, seasonal shortages occur in standard hotel accommodation, causing problems for those who try to check in without a reservation. An alternative option is to try the sanatoriums, which also rent rooms to the healthy—this is best done through a local travel agency. Some agencies will also arrange rooms in private homes, which is also quite a convenient option.

For those who can read Russian and are staying in-country longer term, periodicals such as *Karavan* and *Iz ruki v ruku* publish both real-estate agencies' offers and classifieds. The Scot Holland Real Estate website (www.realestate.kz) has a number of links to real-estate agencies (most of them in Russian, some also in English) which can be consulted for residential and business accommodation. The best known in Almaty (+727) are:

- Asia Realty, 107 Abay Ave/Bayzakov St, tel: 2 430 961, tel/fax: 2 430 941/430 971
- Capital Real Estate, 62 Ayteke Bi St, tel: 2 505 015, fax: 2 505 025, e-mail crec@kaznet.kz
- Almaty Real Estate, 115 Ablai Khan St, Office 13, tel: 2 501 645, e-mail: realty@nursat.kz

AIRLINES AND AIR TRAVEL

Kazakhstan has an extensive air network consisting of 54 airports. Twelve are recognised as international airports, the most important being Almaty, Astana and Atyrau, as well as the oil and mining cities that are linked mainly to Russia and Germany.

The national carrier is Air Astana (www.airastana.com), which operates international schedules to Moscow, Amsterdam, Hanover, Frankfurt, London, Istanbul, Antalya, Dubai, Delhi, Bangkok, Seoul and Beijing.

Other airlines that fly a variety of routes into Kazakhstan are:

Air Arabia
Asiana Airlines
China Southern Airlines
Iran Air
KLM Royal Dutch Airlines
Air Company SCAT
British Airways
Georgian National Airlines
Kam Air
Krasnoyarsk Airlines

Lufthansa German Airlines	Pulkovo Aviation Enterprise
Sayakhat Air Company	Transaero
Travel Servis	Turkish Airlines
Ukrainian-Mediterranean Air	Uzbekistan Airways

Air Astana has a comprehensive domestic network, and some other airlines also fly domestic routes within the country. A list of airline offices in Almaty can be found at www.kazakhstaninvestment.com, or contact Central Asia Tourism (www.centralasiatourism.com), which is a general sales agent for many of the listed airlines.

Alcohol

Strong alcoholic drink is an "imported" culture from Russia, and it is almost as much appreciated here as in Russia proper. Since alcohol is particularly cheap, it's easy for one's health to suffer. Wherever you go you will have drink pressed on you by your hosts, and they will be insistent; good excuses are needed to refrain from drinking—such as "My doctor has forbidden me to drink", or "I *never* drink".

Sadly, a new drinking culture is developing in the cities with the rise of a middle class with spending power, and young business people are most at risk of alcoholic excess. Even Kazakhs who cherish their traditions are unlikely to escape the problem.

These days there are a number of good locally made beers on the market such as Amstel, Tien Shan, Derbes and Karagandinskoye. Kazakh wines from the areas of Yesik and Turgen are drinkable. Domestic vodka must always have a tax label on the cap. Buy it only in good shops—the brands offered in kiosks are often of doubtful origin.

Banks and Bureaux de Change

All banks open from Monday to Friday 9am–6pm, with obligatory lunch breaks 1pm–2pm. Some banks in Almaty and a few other cities also open on Saturday mornings, with a few branches (eg in shopping centres) open on Sundays as well. Leading local banks are KazKommertsbank, Bank Turan Alem, Halyk Bank, CenterCredit, Caspian Bank and ATF. Their cash machines accept a variety of credit and bank cards. Foreign banks operating in Kazakhstan include ABN AMRO, HSBC and Citibank. The service charges of foreign banks are high, though.

Most of the better hotels, restaurants, supermarkets, shops and travel agencies accept payment with Visa, MasterCard, American Express, Carte Bleue and others. Be careful not to take more cash out of the country than allowed or than you brought in and showed on your entry declaration form. It is best to keep all receipts for money drawn from ATMs ready for the customs check on departure.

Bureaux de change have extended opening hours. The best rates are offered in Almaty—they are significantly worse in provincial towns. Always count your cash at the desk to avoid "misunderstandings". Most shops accept cash payment only in tenge, though in northern parts of the country Russian roubles are in wide circulation as well. Exchange rates can be obtained through the National Bank's website www.nationalbank.kz—English pages are available.

Border Areas

Kazakhstan has a long border with China. Its frontier provinces include some of the most marvellous untrodden regions of wilderness, such as the Bayankol Valley, Mount Khan Tengri, part of the Zhungar Alatau, Lake Alakol and part of the Altai. Travel to any of these areas requires permits and thus the assistance of a local travel agent. There is no question of buying the necessary documents by yourself, or going without them and trying to "persuade" border zone officials to let you through. Arrangements through agencies such as Central Asia Tourism, Turan Asia or KanTengri in Almaty, or Altai-Expeditions in Oskemen, cost on average US$15–25 per head depending on the size of a group. Licences must be applied for at least six weeks in advance to ensure all formalities have been finished and approved before you arrive. Agencies also offer guides, which is more than worth it for the sake of security.

Bribes

Whatever you have been told, try to do without them. The "gift" may well be gladly accepted and often bluntly demanded by officials, but at the end of the day pride, honour and reputation are arguments that often weigh more heavily than swift gain. Being courteous, friendly and patient almost always does the trick.

Camping

Two *very* basic toilets and a tap is the best you can hope for at most campsites throughout Kazakhstan, with only a handful of exceptions. Free camping is allowed almost everywhere and there is no lack of beautiful, convenient sites. National parks charge between 300 and 500 tenge. Camping next to a nomad camp requires permission from an

elder; the answer will never be no, but be prepared for an invitation to a sumptuous meal and expect to be the centre of attention.

Canoeing and Rafting

The rivers Ili, Sharyn, Koksu, Karatal and others in the Almaty Region and Uba, Bukhtarma and others in the Altai are ideal for canoeing and rafting. Silk Road, MTA and Morgana Travel in Almaty, and Altai-Expeditions in Oskemen offer organized excursions of one or more days.

Car Travel and Hire

Travelling to Kazakhstan by car is only for real adventurers or those who travel in convoys—cars can easily be reduced to scrap by the often incredibly rough road conditions. Companies like Hertz and Avis are building up rental car networks these days in the big cities of Almaty, Astana, Aktau and Atyrau, which also sometimes have small car rental firms. An international driving licence is required to drive in Kazakhstan. More convenient than a self-drive rental car, and possible almost everywhere, is the option to rent a car with a driver. Costs are in the order of US$100 per day (depending on the route), plus fuel.

Chemists and Healthcare

An international health insurance policy is required by law for foreigners travelling in Kazakhstan (see Insurance section). Local doctors can be relied on for general diagnosis; technical equipment in surgeries, clinics and hospitals is poor compared to Western standards, however, especially in the provinces—serious diseases or complicated operations always require treatment back home. The nationwide telephone number for medical urgencies is 03. Major hotels have their own emergency systems.

The Kazakh word for a chemist or pharmacy is *derikhana* (*apteka* in Russian). They are found on most street corners and in every shopping centre in cities and towns, even in larger rural villages. All general necessities can be obtained, even without a doctor's prescription. This liberal attitude requires care by those who have allergies, eg to certain antibiotics.

Above and left: Kazakhstan boasts countless superb locations for camping in environments ranging from mountain fastnesses to rolling steppe to semi-desert (Karlheinz van der Meer, left; Alex Binder, above)

In Almaty (+727), medical assistance can be sought from the following addresses:

- Central Chemists, 51 Furmanov St/Gogol St, tel: 2 710 271
- Doctor Narymbetov Clinic, 115 Abay Ave, tel: 2 503 164
- Doctor-U, 42-44 Abay Ave, tel: 2 924 333
- Medical Centre/Interdent, 15 Gogol St, tel: 2 306 690
- Interteach, 83 Ayteke Bi St, tel: 2 588 100
- Dental clinic Daris-TTE, 8 Tulebayev St, tel: 2 794 151
- Denta Lux, 140 Zheltoksan St, tel: 2 624 618
- Private clinic of Dr Dieter Seitzer, Mikrorayon Miras, building 54, tel: 2 961 200/210, fax 2 961 201

International SOS in Almaty works around the clock and takes care of repatriations, 11 Luganskogo St, tel: 2 581 911/2 913 030 or (+7) 701 744 1111, e-mail: askthedoc@international-sos.com, website: www.internationalsos.com

Crime

Low standards of living among large parts of the population have led to the rise of petty crime, especially in big cities and leisure resorts such as Burabay. Theft of cars and other belongings, pick-pocketing and mugging are the most common forms of street crime. However, though caution is advised, crime rates are no worse than those in Western Europe—not to mention many parts of the Americas.

Currency & Credit Cards

Kazakhstan's national currency, the tenge, was introduced in 1993, following independence. Originally pegged to the Russian rouble, the rate was floated in the middle of the 1990s, and the tenge made fully convertible. In 1999, following dramatic depreciation, the tenge was pegged to the US dollar at 140 per greenback. Over the turn of the millennium, exchange rates witnessed an initial slump, following by a significant appreciation during 2005 and into 2006. Since this development followed a similar one in the Russian Federation, these days the Russian rouble is the most reliable benchmark for the exchange rate of the tenge. "Official" exchange rates based on the Almaty currency exchange are published daily by the National Bank: www.nationalbank.kz (page in English available).

Officially, payment in the national currency is obligatory, although euros, US dollars, sterling and (especially in the north) Russian roubles are accepted in all major hotels, supermarkets, travel agencies and clubs. All currencies can be exchanged without formalities (as opposed to Russia) Credit cards such as Visa, American Express, Carte Bleue and MasterCard are also accepted—there are usually labels on the door. Bank cards are accepted by major foreign and some local banks, include EC and Maestro.

Coins are of one, two (almost disappeared), five, 10, 20, 50 and 100 tenge. Banknotes are of 200, 500, 1,000, 2,000, 5,000 and 10,000 tenge. New banknotes in the same denominations were issued in November 2006; old ones are valid for normal circulation for a fixed period, after which they can still be exchanged at commercial banks. It is best to always carry some change and small banknotes while shopping, since change for a 5,000 or 10,000 banknote can be a problem.

Prices are usually—and by law—expressed in tenge, with the exception of some upmarket shops with expensive imported goods. Here, goods are priced in "YE" (*uslovniye yedinitsi*)—appropriate units or simply US dollars, but to be paid in tenge according to the current exchange rate. Almost all banks in Almaty and other major cities have Western Union for swift transfers to and from the rest of the world. Here, legal formalities are obligatory and the receipt should be retained.

CYCLING

Kazakhstan offers some fantastic opportunities for mountain bikers (forget ordinary bikes—they will not last). However, constant attention to safety is essential on the road, with traffic hazards a real threat, especially in towns—drivers pay little or no attention to cyclists, so the onus is on you to be vigilant and safety-conscious. Fortunately, some roads are so bad that even jeeps cannot move at more than 30 kilometres per hour. There are delightful routes for mountain bikers in the valleys of the Zailiyskiy Alatau, Bayankol and the Altai. Agencies like Turan Asia, Asia-Discovery, KanTengri Mountain Service (all in Almaty) and Altai-Expeditions/Ecosystem in Oskemen offer guided tours for groups and help with individual excursion planning.

DINING

Kazakhs have certain table manners that differ from those in the Western world. At the dinner table, Kazakhs tend to smack their lips noisily in order to demonstrate their appreciation of the food. In the same way, tea is slurped rather than sipped. Any guest who imitates these habits will be heartily applauded for it. It is impolite to stop your host or hostess from serving food. If you empty your plate it will be filled again, so once you have had enough leave a small amount on your plate—this is a polite way of saying it was delicious, but it was enough.

The precedence for seating is a very sensitive issue. The eldest or otherwise most important person usually sits at the head of the table. His (occasionally her) role is also that of *tamada*—a Georgian word that means toastmaster. He makes the crucial toasts himself (opening, closing, in honour of the guests, etc), and he can introduce other people to make a toast—no refusal accepted. If you wish to make a toast on your own initiative you should ask his permission—it won't be refused.

Eating starts together and ends together. Religious Kazakhs end their dinner with a solemn Omin—or Amen, cupping there hands in front of them, then wiping their face with both hands. It is highly appreciated if guests follow suit.

Disabled Travellers

In cities, most pavement steps have a wheelchair ramp, which is mainly the result of a high number of wheelchair users in the wake of World War II. Buildings, except for recently built ones, are less easily accessible, as is public transport. The greatest comfort for the disabled is the attitude of local people. When asked, or even immediately on seeing someone struggling, young and old will never hesitate to lend a hand.

Driving

On the roads of Kazakhstan survival of the fittest is rule number one, sometimes at the expense of pedestrians. It's important to understand certain local road habits. For instance, the wish to overtake is usually expressed by using the horn rather than the indicator, but the horn can also express simple anger or joy. Abrupt moves by the car in front of you can occur at any time, either because of holes in the road, or simply because many people have little idea how to drive—few bother to pass a test since they can simply buy a driving licence anyway...

Driving in Kazakhstan is on the right-hand side of the road—at least in theory. Traffic signs are in the European style, but are not always up to standard. The official national speed limit is 90 kilometres per hour except for some modern, multi-lane highways. Residential areas impose a maximum speed of 50 kilometres per hour. It is wise to observe those limits in order to circumvent holes, cows, sheep and other pitfalls, including the draconian penalties imposed by the omnipresent traffic police.

Except for city centres, which have modernized systems, traffic lights tend to be on the far side of the crossroads, so you must remain on the lookout for them at all times. Except for a few main routes in Almaty, there

Above: A table replete with delicious dishes is a common sight
Left: A roadside warning about the dangers of bad driving
(Jeremy Tredinnick x2)

are virtually no "green waves" in Kazakhstan; turning right or left means being on the lookout for pedestrians—not giving them priority is a serious offence.

Safety belts are obligatory, even though local drivers limit themselves to thrusting them loosely over their shoulder. Traffic police, however, tend to be less liberal in their interpretation of the law. Whether the payment remains "unofficial" or by the book, payment there shall be. Traffic police (GAI is their Russian acronym) bearing a "*pozhaluysta*" ("please") badge can stop any car for a "routine" check. Whenever this occurs, you should step out, documents in hand. An old habit still used by those who know they have committed an offence, is to place a 1,000 tenge bill discreetly within the documents.

Parking is recommended only at guarded parking lots. Parking at random for the night, especially in courtyards, can easily be at the expense of a mirror, a windscreen wiper, a lamp or even the car itself.

Available petrol includes European standard (in theory) A95 (lead-free), A93, A92 (similar to the old leaded "Super"), A76 and A73 (formerly "Normal"). In cities, prices are in the order of half European prices, in rural areas a bit higher. Since not all grades of petrol are always available, and because outside the cities petrol stations are often very far apart, it is advisable to bring a few jerrycans along to fill with spare fuel wherever you can.

EARTHQUAKES

The southern provinces of Kazakhstan to the north of the Tien Shan are within a large earthquake-prone strip that reaches from western China to the Caucasus, caused by the movement of the Indian subcontinent plate in the direction of Eurasia. The plate edges northwards at a speed of five centimetres per year (on average) and leads to frequent minor tremors and occasional major ones. Southern Kazakhstan, western China, Tajikistan, Uzbekistan, Afghanistan, Iran and Pakistan are particularly exposed. Special steel construction devices have been used in Almaty and other southern cities to secure buildings from subterranean activity. Almaty's highest building, Hotel Kazakhstan, boasts that it can resist even the heaviest earthquake.

From time to time there are also tremors in the Altai mountains.

Catch of the day on a fishing trip to Lake Balkhash (KanTengri Mountain Service)

ELECTRICITY

Reliable electrical power cannot be guaranteed anywhere, although it is much improved from the 1990s, when the theft of a large amount of cable—which was sold on the black market—together with worn-out equipment led to frequent disruptions. Plugs are two pin round, EU standard. Visitors from Britain and the US, especially, should bring adaptors along since even in Almaty they are hard to find. Kazakhstan's network is 220 Volt with a frequency of 50 Herz.

EMBASSIES AND DIPLOMATIC MISSIONS

A full list of Kazakhstan's consulates and diplomatic missions abroad can be found at the website of the Ministry of Foreign Affairs of the Republic of Kazakhstan: **www.mfa.kz**

A full list of foreign embassies and consulates within Kazakhstan can be found at the Almaty Expat Site's website: (**http://expat.nursat.kz/?3611**) and also at **www.kazakhstaninvestment.com/foreign-embassies.html**

ENTRY BY TRAIN

As early as 1930, the "Turksib", as the east-west line across Central Asia was called, was connected through the Altai with the Trans-Siberian railway. Sixty years later, the Druzhba station on the border with China was opened, and with it the link to the Chinese city of Urumqi. The train ride from Urumqi to Almaty takes around 40 hours; the border crossing is at Dostyk, where the train stops, sometimes for several hours, then on past the southern shore of Alakol Lake to Aktogay and south to Almaty. You cannot get a visa at the border going in either direction, so make sure your documents are valid before buying your ticket.

There are rail connections from Europe via Moscow to Almaty and Astana. Seats need to be booked well in advance. Stopovers are possible in around 50 cities, towns and other stops. The trip to Astana takes four days and to Almaty five. From Russia you can enter via Samara and Orenburg, through Aktobe and down past the Aral Sea to Kyzylorda and Shymkent; from Novosibirsk through Semey and Aktogay to Taldykorgan and Almaty; from Kurgan to Petropavlovsk and on to Astana; or from Astrakhan in the far west through to Atyrau.

EQUIPMENT AND LUGGAGE

Tents, foam mattresses, boats, skis and other leisure and sports equipment can be hired on the spot. On the grounds of hygiene, comfort, practicality and safety it is better to bring your own sleeping bag, climbing boots, fishing rods and climbing equipment.

The risk of lost luggage is no higher than anywhere else. Important documents, cameras and laptops belong in your hand luggage. Baggage insurance is recommended.

On domestic flights in particular, staff do not handle suitcases, bags and (in particular) rucksacks with much care. For a fee, luggage can be wrapped in polythene for protection at the airport before checking in.

Fishing

Fishing is a popular hobby among Kazakhstanis, partly for the opportunity it provides for fresh air and to picnic socially around a small campfire. The fact that rivers such as the Ural, Ili and the Black Irtysh, and lakes such as Balkhash, Alakol and Zaysan, as well as the Caspian Sea, are rich in fish and can provide a good source of income, has led to the growth in fishing trips and related tourism for foreign tourists. Many tour operators in all the major cities now offer a variety of excellent fishing trips, especially to catch monster fishes such as the catfish, sturgeon and battling pike-perch.

Gift-Giving

It's a good idea to have a few small gifts to hand—the Kazakhs have a long-standing tradition of hospitality, you will very probably be invited to someone's house on more than one occasion, and the giving of gifts is a marvellous ice-breaker. Since there is hardly anything practical that cannot be bought at local markets, it is hard to find a surprise gift once in the country. Therefore, think ahead and bring food or drink specialities, or souvenirs and coffee-table books, from your own country—these will always be highly appreciated. "Real" coffee, which in most of Kazakhstan remains hard to get at affordable prices, is a welcome gift. Men tend to appreciate diaries, organizers and pens; women adore international brands of cosmetics. If all else fails, there's always a nice bouquet of flowers for the hostess, a bottle of cognac or French wine for the host and sweets for the children.

Health Resorts

Kazakhstan is full of salt lakes, hot springs, medicinal mud sources and mountain valleys with clean air. This offers plenty of opportunities to improve one's health. Not all sanatoriums are up to Western patients' expectations in terms of comfort, and communicating with doctors is often difficult... but prices are all the more attractive for it. Most sanatoriums charge from US$120 to US$550 for a 20-day stay plus treatment costs. Health cures can be booked through Akmolatourist in Astana, 33 Republic Ave, tel: (+7172) 330 025, fax: 330 201, email: akmtourist@cmgp.online.kz, website: www.tourist.astanainfo.kz

HELLO AND GOODBYE

A typical Kazakh handshake between men takes place with both hands. A tight hug and a kiss on the cheek, especially between men who have not seen or will not see each other for some time, is also something you should expect if you have made friends. Women, however, are barely acknowledged, maybe with a nod.

Expressions of tenderness between women in public can often be even more passionate. Elderly and country people in particular, are reluctant to show any physical cordiality between men and women in public, but this is becoming much more relaxed among the younger generation. Many Westernized young people in the cities ignore those traditions—except for the handshake and the hug. Aggression in public against foreigners is extremely rare and if it occurs it is mainly due to drunkenness.

HITCHHIKING

This is one of the rare things that in principle is a lot easier in Kazakhstan than in Europe or the US. Drivers will ask for modest compensation, though, according to a longstanding, easy-going tradition that has continued since Soviet times. Unfortunately, this tradition is no longer risk-free. The best way for foreigners to get around is to socialize around town, and ask people whether they have a friend or a relative with a car who would not mind taking them to the next destination at a friendly price. He will usually earn some extra money by picking up passengers along the road and on the way back (for a little extra money he will refrain from doing so while you are in the car). If you want to try spontaneous hitchhiking it's best not to do it after dark, and never alone. Generally speaking, provincial coach lines (from two tenge per kilometre) or *marshrutkas* (minibuses) are just as cheap, a lot safer and offer better opportunities to socialize on the way.

HORSE RIDING

This is the national sport of Kazakhstan in its many and varied forms. Almost every Kazakh can ride and remain in the saddle for many hours. The country's horse breeds are well adapted to the demanding climatic and geographic conditions. They are sturdy, tough, enduring, good-natured, and suited to the mountains and steppe. Trekking on horseback is a wonderful way to see the country and gain an insight into one of Kazakhstan's most important and binding cultural foundations. However, you will need stamina, some

Above: A friendly smile from a dried-fruit seller—open hospitality can be expected everywhere you travel in the country (Gunter Kapelle)

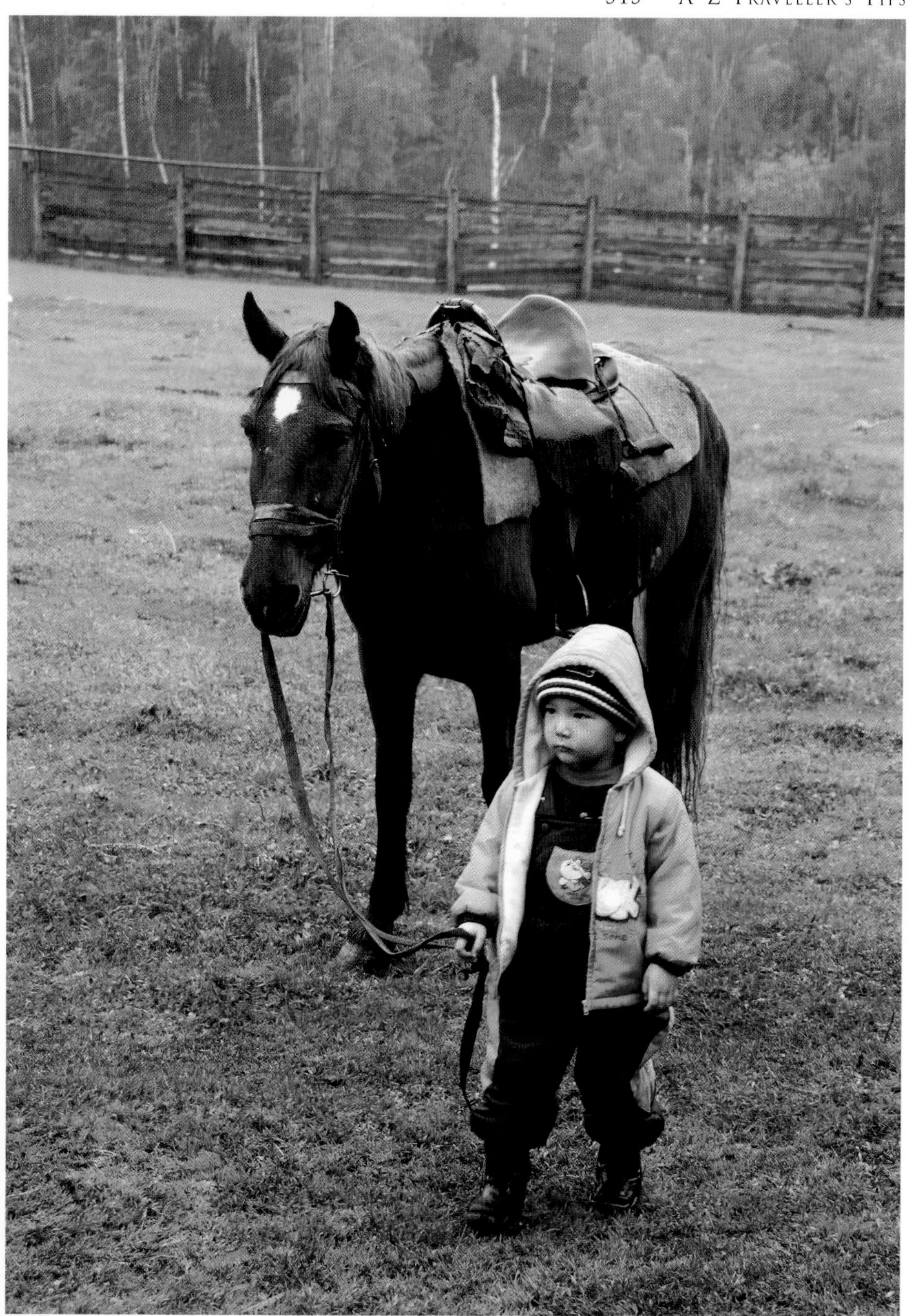

In the Altai Mountains, Kazakh children can literally ride before they can walk (Jeremy Tredinnick)

experience and to be in reasonable physical condition; you should also bring strong footwear with plain soles, trousers without inside seams, appropriate headwear and be able to adapt to local habits with bridle and saddle.

Hunting

A passion for hunting has brought several breeds of animal to the very brink of extinction in Kazakhstan. The hunting of eagle, snow leopard, kulan, saiga antelope, dzheyran, Tien Shan brown bear, red wolf and Turkestan lynx is now completely banned. Annual quotas have been imposed on hunting other animals, but they are largely ignored by poachers. Thus, only a few arkhar (argali wild sheep) may be shot each year at a cost of US$16,000 each; ibex, maral and Siberian wolf are a bit cheaper. Hunting is seasonal, restricted to a few species and numbers as well as to certain limited areas. Waterfowl, black cock, partridge and quail can be hunted at certain times and places. Some tour agencies specialize in making arrangements for foreign hunters: try Asia Discovery, Olympia Reisen (Almaty), Tsentr delovikh initiativ (Astana) or Kvizi-Tour (Karaganda).

It is also possible to arrange hunting with golden eagles, though this is expensive. For information, contact Andrey Kovalenko in the village of Nura, east of Almaty, tel.(+727) 2 420 675, e-mail: akoval@nursat.kz

Hygiene

Tap water must always be boiled and/or purified. Water pipes are porous, so sewage water tends to leak into them, and storage facilities are badly cleaned. Everything packed and properly labelled can be trusted. Fresh fruit and vegetables should be carefully washed, since fertilizers in the country can still include manure. Hands must be washed before eating.

Insurance

Basic health insurance for all visitors, and car insurance if you will be driving, are obligatory in Kazakhstan. It is highly recommended to arrange a full travel insurance policy covering your entire trip and including global health care, travel accident and personal liability, baggage and personal belongings, and repatriation insurance.

Internet

Wherever there is Internet, it is used enthusiastically and creatively, and the advantages of this fast and borderless form of communication are being increasingly recognized even in the countryside. All cities now have plenty of Internet cafés charging very reasonable fees, and Internet corners can also be found in department stores, hotels, public libraries (free of charge) and travel agencies. (See Useful Websites.)

LANGUAGE

Russian is the *lingua franca* in Kazakhstan. Although Kazakh is the official language, few Kazakhstanis—including ethnic Kazakhs themselves—speak it fluently. This may change, as the government has declared that all Kazakhstanis must learn Kazakh and English to a high level of competence within the next few years. But for now, Russian is what you need to get around. If your Russian is nonexistent, you will need the help of a translator for all but the most basic sightseeing. English is spoken in the cities by only a small percentage of people, mostly within the tourist service industry or by students, but confidence is not very high among the majority of the populace. If you are looking for help, a good trick is to find and frequent a local university café, where you are likely to meet students who will be happy to practise and improve their English by assisting you.

MAPS

Maps are in short supply in Kazakhstan. Some bookstores have maps except for the ones people really need. The bookstore on 17 Abay Ave in Almaty has the best offer, with maps of most regions on a scale of 1:1,000,000. There are no proper road maps and those that exist have a scale of 1:350,000 and, given the country's sheer size, are therefore not very helpful. Outside Kazakhstan, Moskva bookstore on Tverskaya Street in central Moscow, Stanford's in Long Acre, London and a number of specialized travel shops in cities in Europe are the best bets. Despite the difficulty, up-to-date maps are a real plus in Kazakhstan, so bring what you can. Many street and place names have changed in recent years. Ask three people for directions and each will offer a different answer.

MEDIA

The leading local television stations are NTK and Khabar, with all programmes in Russian and Kazakh. Caspionet is a local station with programmes in English as well, but is only available on cable. A number of service companies offer cable packages, which often include BBC World, CNN, Fox, TV-5 and sports and adventure channels in English, as well as Spanish and Italian stations. Online news on Kazakhstan can be obtained through the state news agency, Kazinform (www.inform.kz) and the independent agency Kazakhstan Today (www.gazeta.kz).

A number of glossy magazines appear, mostly covering leisure and show business, in Almaty, plus some more serious ones, the most important being *Exclusive*, which covers business and economics. Weekly papers include the community-style *Almaty Herald* and the more analytical *Kazakhstan Monitor*. Caspian Publishing House publishes a monthly periodical, *Caspian Digest*, a free circulation paper which can be obtained through subscription and is available at a number of hotels, restaurants, bars and other meeting

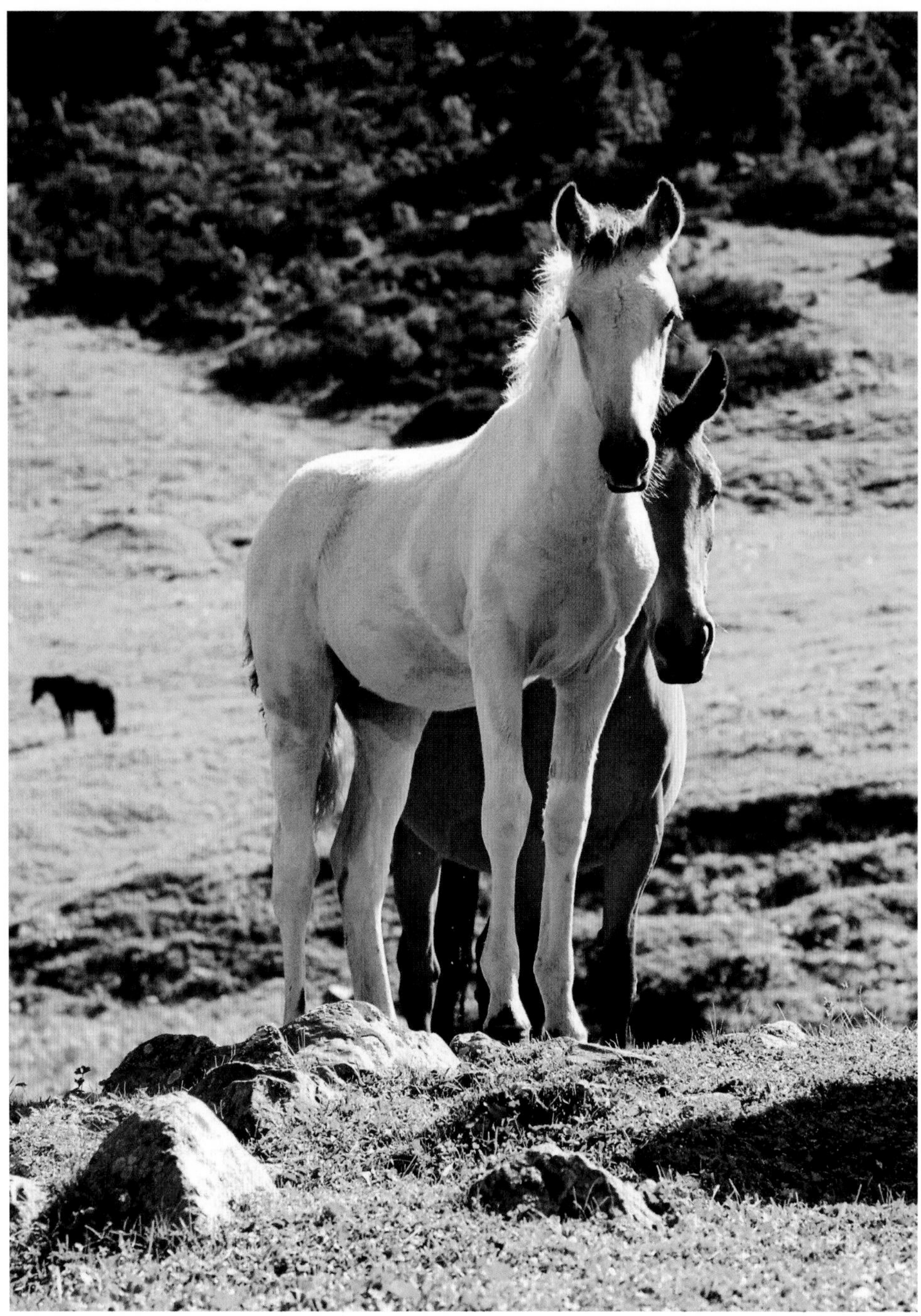

The significance of the horse within Kazakh history cannot be overstated (Vladimir Tugalev)

Top left and right: The saker falcon is coveted by falconers the world over (Jeremy Tredinnick x2)
Above: An eagle screams with impatience on a berkutshe's *arm, as it waits for its chance to hunt (O. Kormuschin)*

points, and which contains analytical background articles on geographic, ecological and economic issues. For those who read Russian, leading newspapers in Kazakhstan include *Kazakhstanskaya Pravda, Panorama, Novoye Pokoleniye* (general interest) and *Dyelovo Nedyelnikiy* (business and economics). Leading Russian papers such as *Kommersant* and *Izvestia* can be bought in major cities.

MOUNTAINEERING

The Tien Shan in the southeast of Kazakhstan and the Altai in the northeast offer plenty of opportunities for mountain climbers. Trips and expeditions of all degrees of difficulty are available—the northernmost 7,000m-plus peaks in the world, Khan Tengri and Pobeda, are true challenges for very experienced mountaineers only. Dozens of fascinating mountaineering excursions can be undertaken, even in the immediate surroundings of Almaty. The best thing to do is to bring your own gear—some agencies even insist on that for safety and liability reasons. Good trips at fair prices are offered by KanTengri Mountain Service, Indra Tours and Tour Asia (Almaty) and Altai-Expeditions/Ecosystem (Oskemen).

OPENING TIMES

Almost all shops are open daily, many till late in the evening. In big cities and increasingly in the country as well, shopping can be done between 8am and 10pm. Smaller shops and "kiosks" are open around the clock. At night, the door is closed for security, but a knock on the small window opening will do the trick.

PHOTOGRAPHY, FILM AND VIDEO

For the most part people are happy to have their pictures taken almost anywhere, to the extent that they tend to push themselves in front of your camera. It is illegal to photograph or video people wearing state uniforms (although few of them care), as well as facilities of state security such as radio stations, military installations, border posts and checkpoints. As a rule, taking photos or video of infrastructure at airports or railway stations is also banned. Penalties for violations of these regulations can be pretty severe, and even include expulsion from the country. To stay on the safe side, it is wise to ask a uniformed official *"Mozhna fotografi?"* before raising your camera. People who live in visibly poor circumstances should be asked for permission too.

Police

The nationwide telephone number for police service is 02. Despite their reputation, the Kazakh police are overall friendly and helpful. If you behave in a cooperative manner you are more likely to find a correct attitude, willingness to help, and to receive swift assistance. In most cases, displaying respect for state officials takes one much further than pulling out one's wallet.

Post and Telecommunications

Post offices are mainly open daily from 9am–7pm, in smaller towns only on weekdays. Major hotels have post desks as well. A letter within Kazakhstan takes three to five days to reach its destination. Deliveries to and from Europe take between one and two weeks. Courier services such as DHL, Fedex, EMS and UPS work faster but even they take three to five days to get a letter or a parcel delivered abroad. Smaller communities are not served by them, and the receiver must go to their nearest office in town to pick up his mail.

Public Holidays

Offices and factories are closed on public holidays and often also on the preceding day—called *pryedpradznikiy* (preparation days). Almost all shops remain open. The following public holidays are observed:

1–2 January	New Year
8 March	International Women's Day
22 March	Nauryz Bayram, the coming of spring and the ancient Zoroastrian New Year
1 May	Day of Unity
9 May	Defenders' Day
30 August	Constitution Day
25 October	Day of the Republic
16–7 December	Zheltoksan, or Independence Day

Schools in Kazakhstan close for the months of June, July and August. Universities have shorter holidays, and, besides, nearly all of them hold summer courses. Only private educational institutes of various levels have longish winter holidays. Care should be taken in trying to arrange important business meetings in summer, since most business people simply cannot be reached during the hot season.

Punctuality

Clocks tick at a different rhythm in Kazakhstan, particularly in the countryside. Things get done, but exactly when they get done is not considered of great importance. However, discipline is steadily improving in the cities as global business connections begin to exert influence on the working population. Public transport, including buses, trains and planes, usually departs on time (depending on the weather).

Radioactivity

Levels of radiation in all accessible areas of Kazakhstan are within the strict standards included in European legislation. This is also true for the city of Semey (Semipalatinsk) near which atom bombs were tested during the Soviet era. Present-day travellers, suspicious enough to carry along a Geiger counter, can confirm that there is no danger involved in visiting this region.

Registration

Immigration police registration forms are handed out on the plane and are also available at the airport. Once it has been stamped by the immigration service, the form should stay in your passport at all times. Citizens of the European Union, USA and some other countries, including Australia, Canada, Republic of Korea, Malaysia, New Zealand and Singapore, who enter the country at an international airport are automatically registered for three months. They only need to go to the Department of Migration Police (best known by its old name—OVIR) for additional registration after three months.

Those not travelling on a single-entry tourist visa or a diplomatic pass must report to the OVIR within three working days after entry in order to fulfil the formality of registration. A number of travel agencies offer this service to visitors for a small fee. NB: when leaving one's passport at the agency you should obtain a stamped photocopy of the main page and the page with the visa on it for temporary use. For information visit the Ministry of Foreign Affairs website at **www.mfa.kz**

Top: A rural postbox in the countryside (Dagmar Schreiber). Above: The interior of a yurt is filled with interesting items, many of which can be bought as souvenirs in shops and markets (Vladimir Tugalev)

Romance

The age of consent in Kazakhstan is 16 for men and women alike. In contrast to most Asian and even Western countries, women in Kazakhstan often tend to take the initiative. Be wary, though, lords of creation—most of them are not out for just a short-lived fling but are looking for something much more serious. When they succeed, they tend to be very loyal, but also very possessive. One more thing to be aware of: in cities, exuberant and provocative dress codes among women do not automatically mean that an approach is being solicited.

Homosexual men and women in Kazakhstan have the same legal rights and restrictions as their heterosexual peers. In most parts of the country and in most layers of society, however, the law is far ahead of social acceptance—even though traditional lore amply illustrates that the lords of the steppe used to be quite fond of swinging both ways. Two centuries of Russian Victorianism, however, have left their stamp on Kazakhstan. These days, only the young elite are as frank and tolerant towards various sexual orientations as the younger crowd in Western Europe—and even their gay members do not often display their affections in public. Overall, mum remains the word except in clubs, city centres and some upmarket leisure resorts.

Due to deteriorating socioeconomic conditions during the 1990s, prostitution has unfortunately blossomed. It takes place in parks, clubs of dubious reputation or simply on the street. It is strongly recommended to resist such temptations, both for health and security reasons. Prostitution, widespread as it may be, remains illegal in all circumstances and police can create serious trouble for those caught in the act.

Top and above right: Wonderful carpets, felt blankets and wall hangings are just some of the excellent mementoes worth looking out for during a Kazakhstan trip (Jeremy Tredinnick x2)

The risk of STDs remains a major threat in amorous relations in Kazakhstan, as it does in Russia and most other former Soviet republics. The necessity of using condoms and other protective measures to prevent exposure to HIV/AIDS and other diseases is unfortunately but frequently not taken seriously enough. Visitors looking for a physical relationship are strongly urged to insist on the necessary precautions.

Security

According to most foreign embassies in Kazakhstan, the risk of acts of terror in Kazakhstan is no more than the global average. Unlike some other Central Asian countries, religious fanaticism is virtually absent. Though some crimes have been committed since independence that were thought to have political motives, there have been no signs of political violence in any organized form.

Crime has been steadily on the rise over the turn of the millennium, in particular in big cities. Foreigners do not run any particular risk in Almaty, and it is sufficient to take the same precautions the local population does: do not carry large amounts of money or valuables, avoid "unofficial" taxis after dark, and make sure you carry a local mobile telephone with the emergency number of your embassy in it. Foreigners who are in for a longer stay are strongly advised to register with their embassy.

Police harassment in cities, Almaty in particular, has dwindled. However, police retain the right to check the legal documents of anyone, including foreigners, on any occasion. Whether these documents are in order or not, extortion attempts still do occasionally occur and can amount to several hundreds of dollars, which is one more reason to limit the amount of cash in one's wallet. Moreover, false policemen are still a presence, especially in the countryside, though in smaller numbers than they used to. Any policeman who does not wear a visible ID badge should be considered suspicious.

Souvenirs

Anything made of felt (rugs, slippers, puppets, miniature camels and yurts) is very popular indeed, as are leather articles including horsewhips (*kamchiy*) and saddle bottles. Jewellery includes finely wrought white silver medallions with semiprecious stones set in them. Musical instruments are also sold at most souvenir stands. Items of national dress consist of decorated long mantles and waistcoats, caps and hats. Woven rugs are also in vogue. It's possible to buy really beautiful paintings and other works of art in galleries and at auctions. In this case, however, export requires certain formalities. Travel agencies and major hotels, and also some of the museums, galleries and art shops, can be of service here.

Kazakh brandies (called "konyak") and vodkas in the upmarket sector are good, and you are free to take them out of the country within certain quantity limits. Also worth taking home are honey, herbs and spices. Caution should be observed in the case of caviar—not so much in exiting Kazakhstan, but in bringing it in to your home country. Usually only labelled pots, with a stamp and serial number, can be brought in, and then only in limited quantities for one's own consumption. Allowable quantities are updated every half-year by the UN protection watchdog CITES.

Swimming

Rivers in Kazakhstan cascade out of the mountains with wild and untamed power; even when they seem to be quiet and easy flowing they often have strong, volatile currents. It's best to swim in water where other people can be seen swimming, and even then take great care: everywhere, there are gravestones or crosses—silent reminders of drunken merrymakers who overreached themselves while swimming.

Most running water is relatively clean—the clouding of water flowing from mountain slopes is natural. The large lakes of Zaysan and Alakol are also clean. The latter is salty and can be recommended for people with skin problems. The same is true for the numerous salt lakes in the steppe, which can serve as a substitute for a trip to the Dead Sea. However, Lake Balkhash is unfit for swimming in the vicinity of the town of the same name.

Swimming in the Caspian Sea is recommended on the Mangyshlak Peninsula, where the water remains remarkably warm into October. The Kapshagay Reservoir is a popular swimming resort and the least dangerous. In most places it is shallow and warm; while swimming, though, it is wise to wear sandals since injuries can be caused by sharp stones and broken bottles, an unfortunately increasing problem caused by partying fishermen.

Taboos

It is not done, certainly not in the countryside, to greet a woman with a handshake. On entering a mosque, women should have their hair, their shoulders and their legs, including their knees, covered. Sneezing and snorting, especially at the dinner table, is considered unhygienic, but sniffing and spitting in public on the street seems to be perfectly acceptable.

Conversations, especially in business meetings, should start with a long and polite introduction. Getting to the point at once is considered discourteous.

In the countryside, toilet facilities can be very basic—although the surrounding scenery is excellent compensation (Dagmar Schreiber)

Taxis

There is hardly any distinction in price between regular taxis and ordinary drivers who pick up people for a bit of extra cash. Taxi meters, if there are any, tend to remain unused. You should agree a price before you step into the car. Major hotels have their own taxis, which can be ordered at the reception.

Telephone

Local telephone calls can be made from call boxes by using a *zheton*, a disc that can be bought at the post office, numerous shops and most newsstands. Prices are minimal. For a call to a different zone in Kazakhstan you need to dial 8, then the other zone's code followed by the number. For calls abroad dial 8, wait for another dialling tone and then 10, followed by the country code (without the preceding 0), city/area code and number. Kazakhstan is in the same country zone (+7) as Russia and Belarus, while other former USSR member states have separate codes. Phone cards for long-distance calls can be obtained in hotels (expensive), at Kazakhtelecom desks, in some kiosks and in larger supermarkets. Calls between 3am and 6am are substantially discounted.

The two leading mobile companies are K-Cell and K-Mobile. Mobile phones are for sale everywhere, but stalls and even shops have a habit of disappearing, so buy at your own risk. Better is to bring your own mobile—local SIM cards can be installed in your own phone. K-Cell has (+8 or +7) 701 as a pre-dialling code, Beeline/K-Mobile (+8 or +7) 705 or 777. There is also Dalacom with (+8 or +7) 700. A locally bought SIM card is much more cost-efficient than paying the high in-room phone rates charged by hotels.

Fishing, canoeing and camping combine on many of Kazakhstan's rivers (Vladimir Tugalev)

Time Zones

Kazakhstan now has two (it used to be three) time zones. The eastern and central parts of the country are on Greenwich Mean Time (GMT) plus six hours and include Almaty, Oskemen (Ust-Kamenogorsk), Pavlodar, Semey (Semipalatinsk), Astana, Taraz, Shymkent and Kyzylorda as far as Baikonur. The western part is on GMT plus five hours and includes Aktau, Aktobe, Atyrau and Oral (Uralsk). Now that Kazakhstan has abolished summer and winter time, the difference becomes five and four hours respectively in summer.

Tipping

In Soviet times, tipping was taboo, even considered an insult, especially if coming from a foreigner. In reality, though, on a communal level bartenders, in particular, were often favoured with a "present", especially by groups of people. For today's young waiters a tip (*chay*—"tea") is as much appreciated as it is in the West. A service commission of 10 percent is often included in the bill, but whether it reaches the staff in all cases is uncertain; better to leave a separate cash tip on the table if you want to show your appreciation for good service.

Toasting

Dinners, cocktails or any other occasion to raise glasses (and there are many) are seized upon and enjoyed with singular purpose. Drinking without at least saying in Russian "*na zdarovye*"—"to your health"—is considered highly impolite. The more extended and the more eloquent a toast, the louder the applause will be. Glasses are filled during the toast speech, and are expected to be emptied in a single gulp.

Any official or semi-formal banquet is conducted by a *tamada* or toastmaster (see also Dining), who makes the key toasts; he (only rarely she) is the only one who can do so without anyone else's permission; he appoints people to make a toast and gives permission to do so on request. Guests are never ignored in this process, and their obvious task is to thank the head of the family for hosting them, which is bound to be responded to by the latter expressing his appreciation for the guests doing honour to his table. This series of exchanges usually takes up the first round of toasts. There follows a range of toasts to each of those present in order of importance. Later in the proceedings, toasts can be made to happiness, prosperity, brotherhood, the respective nations of host and guests, to all the people present, to all the people absent, to the women in the world, to the young generations, to the old generations... In Kazakhstan the last-but-one toast is always in honour of the hostess, with thanks for her generosity and hospitality. This is followed by the last "official" toast which is nicknamed *pasachok* (Russian)—literally "walking stick cup". Those still thirsty can comfort themselves with the very last toast, or *stremyenaya* (Russian)—"mounting cup" which in times of old used to be made when the guests were already on horseback.

Toilets

Kazakhstan contains a concise encyclopaedia of toilets, ranging from holes in the ground surrounded (or not) by a shaky fence, to the finest state-of-the-art facilities. The low-tech variants can be seen in rural areas and provincial towns, sometimes as part of guesthouses. Their high-tech counterparts are found in larger cities in modern hotels and restaurants (although not in all of them, and keeping them clean is often low on the agenda). In Almaty, well-maintained public pay toilets have recently been built in several parks. But it is always wise for travellers to carry sufficient amounts of toilet paper and disinfection towels wherever they go. The Russian indications M for men and *Zhenshchiny* for women (sometimes in Kazakh) are in widespread use, though in plenty of cases the choice is left to the user. Since many of the more basic facilities are rather indiscreetly visible, Westerners have to overcome a certain amount of embarrassment

Travel Agencies

Following is a short list of some of the most experienced and reputable international travel companies offering tours either to Kazakhstan alone or including the country as part of extended Silk Road tours:

Mir Corporation, 85 South Washington St, Suite 210, Seattle WA 98104, USA, tel: (206) 624 7289 or (800) 424 7289, e-mail: info@mircorp.com, website: www.mircorp.com

Abercrombie and Kent, 1520 Kensington Road, Suite 212, Oak Brook, Chicago, Il 60523 2156, USA, tel: (630) 954 2944 or (800)554 7016, website: www.abercrombiekent.com

Sundowners Travel, Suite 15, Lonsdale Court, 600 Lonsdale Street, Melbourne 3000, Australia, tel: (61 3) 9672 5300, fax: (61 3) 9672 5311; UK Office: Suite 207B, The Business Village, 3–9 Broomhill Road, London SW18 4JQ, UK, tel: (44 0) 20 8877 7666, fax: (44 0) 20 8877 9002, website: www.sundownerstravel.com

Silk Road and Beyond, 371 Kensington High Street, London W14 8QZ, UK, tel: (44 0) 20 7371 3131, e-mail: sales@silkroadandbeyond.co.uk, website: www.silkroadandbeyond.co.uk

Silk Road Tours, 300–1497 Marine Drive, West Vancouver, BC, V7T 1B8, Canada, tel: (604) 925 3831, fax: (604) 925 6269, e-mail: Canada@silkroadtours.com, website: www.silkroadtours.com

Explore, 1 Frederick St, Aldershot, Hants GU11 1LQ, UK, tel: (01252) 319 448, e-mail: info@explore.co.uk, website: www.explore.co.uk

GW Travel Ltd, Denzell House, Denzell Gardens, Dunham Road, Altrincham WA14 4QF, UK, tel: (44) (0)161 928 9410, fax: (44) (0)161 941 6101, e-mail: mail@gwtravel.co.uk, website: www.gwtravel.co.uk

Steppes Travel, 51 Castle Street, Cirencester, GL7 1QD UK, tel: 01285 651010, fax: 01285 885888, e-mail: east@steppestravel.co.uk, website: steppestravel.co.uk

Within Kazakhstan, the following are all accredited members of the NGO Kazakhstan Tourist Association (KTA):

Almaty

ACS Agency, Gallery Journey office, Samal-2, 63, office A, 050059 Almaty, tel: (+7 727) 2629037 (adm), 2622858 (tickets), 264 4949 (tourism), fax: 2642845, e-mail: office@acs-almaty.com. Branch offices:

4 Imanova St, 010000 Astana, tel: (+7 717) 2216541, fax: 2324780; e-mail: astana@acs-almaty.com

Hotel Aktau, Mikrorayon-2, 130000 Aktau, tel: (+7 729) 2509112, fax: 2503201;

Mikrorayon-11, office 6, tel: (+7 729) 242 8012/013, fax: 243 9951, e-mail: aktau@acs-almaty.com

Acvilon Travel, Samal-2 Tower, 97 Zholdasbekova St, Almaty, tel: (+7 727) 2584207, fax: 258 4210, e-mail: info@acvilontravel.com, website: www.acvilontravel.kz

Akzhol Travel, 78/86 Zheltoksan St, 050004 Almaty, tel/fax: (+7 727) 2731185, tel: 2731041/2731408/2733192, e-mail: info@akzholtravel.com, akzhol1@akzhol.net, akzhol4@akzhol.net, website: www.akzholtravel.com

Following pages: A rural idyll on Markakol Lake (Vladimir Tugalev)

Central Asia Tourism (BCD Travel), 20½ Kazybek Bi St, 050100 Almaty, tel: (+7 727) 2501070, fax: 2501707, e-mail: catfvk@BCDTRAVEL.com

Almaty Airport office: Hotel Ak Sunkar, room 114, tel: (+7 727) 2572230, fax: 2573264, e-mail: cat-airport@BCDTRAVEL.com
Branch offices:

Astana: (+7 7172) 333125, fax: 323357; cat-astana@BCDTRAVEL.com

Aksai: (+7 71133) 93166/93171, fax: 30590; cat-aksai@BCDTRAVEL.com

Aktobe: (+7 7132) 523640/523841, fax: 514227; cat-aktobe@BCDTRAVEL.com

Atyrau/1: (+7 7122) 354075/320428, fax: 354077, cat-atyrau@BCDTRAVEL.com

Atyrau/2: (+7 7122) 320428, fax: 320430; cat-atyray@BCDTRAVEL.com

Karaganda: (+7 7212) 412826, fax: 423606; cat-karaganda@BCDTRAVEL.com

Aktau: (+7 7292) 525576, fax: 525576; cat-aktau@BCDTRAVEL.com

Shymkent: (+7 7252) 548633, fax: 561739; cat-chymkent@BCDTRAVEL.com

Ust-Kamenogorsk: tel/fax: (+7 7232) 252850; cat-oskemen@BCDTRAVEL.com

124 Chuy Ave, 720040 Bishkek, Kyrgyzstan, tel: (+996 312) 663664, fax: 600420; e-mail: cat@cat.kg

1 A.Donish St, 734013 Dushanbe, Tajikistan, tel: (+992 1372) 252543, fax: 218155; e-mail: JAM@cat-dushanbe.tg

CGTT Voyages, 17 Kairbekov St, 050002 Almaty, tel: (+7 727) 2782299/2979425, fax: 2782378, e-mail: cgttala@mailbox.kz, website: www.cgtt-voyages.fr

Complete Service, 110 Tole Bi St, office 79, Almaty, tel: (+7 727) 2922698/2923587/2928918/2925599, fax: 2784522, e-mail: complete@ysa.kz, completeservice@ysa.kz, website: www.completeservice.kz

Diamond Tour LLP, 7a Satpayev St, 050052 Almaty, tel: (+7 727) 2633325, fax: 2633290, e-mail: dtour@diamond.kz

Branch offices:

67 Beibitshilik St, 010000 Astana, tel: (+7 7172) 397360/397039, fax: 396990; e-mail: raushan@diamond.kz

9 Momysh-Uly St, office 39, 160018 Shymkent, tel: (+7 7252) 338701, fax: 561681; e-mail: dtour_uko@diamond.kz

Daphne Travel International, 20a Kazybek Bi St, 480100 Almaty, tel: (+7 727) 2917171/2722570/2960606; fax: 2722892, e-mail: daphne@daphne.kz, daphne@daphnetravel.kz, website: www. Daphne.kz

Ecotourism Kazakhstan, 71 Zheltoksan St, 050000 Almaty, tel/fax: (+7 727) 2798146/2780289, e-mail: ecotourism.kz@mail.kz, website: www.ecotourism.kz

Ellas Tourist Company, 13-18 Valikhanov St, 050016 Almaty, tel/fax: (+7 727) 2711841/2737012; e-mail: ellas_e@nursat.kz

61 Kirov St, Oskemen (Ust-Kamenogorsk), tel: (+7 7232) 579070, (+7 777) 2292476; e-mail: ellas@ukg.kz

Global Air—American Express, 7 Chaikovskovo St, 050004 Almaty, tel: (+7 727) 2332297/2332298/2332272, fax: 2335736.

Branch offices:

Almaty: (+7 727) 2583939/2584444; almaty@globalair-kz.com
Atyrau: (+7 7122) 586159; atyrau@globalair-kz.com
Aktau: (+7 7292) 426767; aktau@globalair-kz.com
Aktobe: (+7 7132) 549066; aktobe@globalair-kz.com
Astana: (+7 7172) 592554; astana@globalair-kz.com
Aksai: (+7 7113) 332149; aksai@globalair-kz.com
Shymkent: (+7 7252) 569190; shymkent@globalair.com

Gulnar Tour, 120-124 Raimbek Ave, Almaty, tel/fax: (+7 727) 2734215; 2734468/2739604/2730362/2739432/2737899, e-mail: almaty@gulnartour.kz

Branch offices:

107a Abai Ave, office 18, Almaty, tel/fax: (+7 727) 2427270/2426908;

118/13 Gogol St, office 20, Almaty, tel/fax: (+7 727) 2331347/2331465;

5 Internationalnaya St, Astana, tel: (+7 7172) 213248/211043/217554, fax: 213324, e-mail: astana@gulnartour.kz

61 Lenin Ave, Karaganda, tel/fax: (+7 7212) 435138/409070/409097, e-mail: karaganda@gulnartour.kz

KanTengri Expeditions, 10 Kastayev St, 050010 Almaty, tel: (+7 727) 2910200/2910880, fax: 2912010, e-mail: kazbek@kantengri.almaty.kz, website: www.kantengri.kz

Muay Travel, 45 Valikhanov St, 050002 Almaty, tel: (+7 727) 2737983/2738259/2912986, fax: 2738259, e-mail: muaytravel@muaygroup.kz

Nuka Travel, 72 Kazybek Bi St, Almaty, tel: (+7 727) 2676650/651/652/653, fax: 2724287, e-mail: info@nuka.kz

Robinzon, 49 Kunayev St, 050004, Almaty, tel/fax: (+7 727) 2506380/2735406/2735514/2733544, e-mail: robinzontour@mail.ru, tourism@robinzon.kz, website: www.robinzontour.nm.ru

For most locals, train travel is the most popular form of getting around the country—and a great way for travellers to experience this land's variety of people and terrain (Hermann Schulz)

Silk Road Kazakhstan, 30 Tole Bi St, office 30, Almaty, tel: (+7 727) 2938093/2914498, fax: 2839343, e-mail: srkplus@mail.ru, website: www.srkplus.com

Sky Eagle, 81 Aiteke Bi St, office 91, 050000 Almaty, tel: (+7 727) 2791854/2780822/2795960, fax: 2780821, e-mail: bella@sky-eagle.kz, info@sky-eagle.kz, website: www.sky-eagle.kz

Sputnik, 48 Baytursinov St, 500012 Almaty, tel: (+7 727) 2929895/2930516/2929967, fax: 2930516, e-mail: sputnik_2006@mail.ru, general@sputnik-kz.com, tours@sputnik-kz.com, website: www.sputnik-kz.com

SunTours Kazakhstan, 37/21 Ablai Khan St, Almaty, tel/fax: (+7 727) 2798242/235/271, e-mail: suntour@belight.net

Tour Agency Silk Road of Kazakhstan, Altyn Zaman Complex, 9b Satpayev St, 050010 Almaty, tel: (+7 727) 2558238/235/245, fax: 2558252, e-mail: info@srk.kz, sns@srk.kz, avia@srk.kz, website: www.silkroad.kz

Branch offices:

36 Abai St, office 2, 010000 Astana, tel: (+7 7172) 333321/333322/320178/320089, fax: 333322; e-mail: east_tour@mail.kz

17a Satpayev St, 060011 Atyrau, tel: (+7 7122) 203921/203923, fax: 203922; e-mail: msb@mail.kz

Mikrorayon 6, 39/1, 130000 Aktau, tel: (+7 7292) 530036/530037, e-mail: miraaktau@ok.kz

Tour Asia, 359 Radostovtsa St, 050060 Almaty, tel/fax: (+7 727) 2482573/2497936; e-mail: office@tourasia.kz, website: www.tourasia.kz

Travel Club, 42-44 Abai Ave, Almaty, tel: (+7 727) 2585117, e-mail: info@travelclub.kz

Branch office: 24 Beibitshilik Ave, Astana, tel: (+7172) 591570, e-mail: astana@travelclub.kz

Yassawi, 48a Kurmangazy St, 050000 Almaty, tel: (+7 727) 2617177/2616805/2610527/2610479/2614479, fax: 2729627, e-mail: yassawi@yassawi.kz, east@yassawi.kz, west@yassawi.kz, website: www.yassawi.kz

ASTANA

Agency Premier, 20 Pobedy Ave, 010000 Astana, tel/fax: (+7 7172) 580818/239824/239825/239848

Avangard Travel, 50/1 Molodezhny Mikrorayon office 2, 010000 Astana, tel: (+7 7172) 580156/580157/580167, fax: 580169, e-mail: travel@atr.kz, avangard_travel_@mail.ru, website: www.atr.kz

Sayat Tourist Agency, 23 Kabanbay Batyr St (Chubary Microdistrict), Astana, tel: (+7 7172) 555544, e-mail: sayat777@mail.ru

AKTAU

Tourist, Mikrorayon 9, house 4, off.110, 466200 Aktau, tel: (+7 7292) 430000, fax: 310171, e-mail: pbalatov@nursat.kz, website: www.tourist-aktau.com

TRAVEL ESSENTIALS

One should always carry the following items:

- passport—police checks can take place anywhere and at any time
- some cash—not too much and in small notes and coins; keep your hand on your wallet in a crowd
- tissues or toilet paper—in the countryside, even if there is a toilet or privy, there is rarely any paper
- diarrhoea tablets—a universal problem in developing countries, it tends to occur abruptly
- earplugs—Kazakhs are a merry nation and celebrations can cause sleepless nights

- pocket knife—in smaller inns and restaurants knives are put away in order to avoid bloodshed should disputes get out of hand, which can happen
- sandals or any kind of strong slippers—a necessity on trains and in older hotels
- a torch—power disruptions are the rule rather than exception in the countryside, and can even occur in major cities
- a sleeping bag—temperatures can drop severely and unexpectedly due to the country's volatile climate
- something to read—for the long waits and endless journeys

Travel Within the Country

For quick, smooth travel between the country's main cities air travel is the way to go—Air Astana has a very good domestic route network and a number of smaller airlines such as Skat, Sagakhat and Atyrau Aue Zholy also operate useful routes. Some expect that these smaller airlines will be incorporated into Air Astana in due course. From 2008 only modern aircraft will be in use and the old Soviet ones discarded.

Time and flexibility is needed to travel along Kazakhstan's 13,400-kilometre railway network. It is relatively good value for money (depending on your choice of class), but, for example, the 1,200 kilometres from Almaty to Astana take more than 18 hours on a "normal" fast train. Nevertheless, time requirements aside, the rail network serves most major centres of this huge country; however, there are a number of direct links missing, resulting in huge detours. Thus, there is no direct line from Almaty to Aktau—it is necessary to change somewhere up the line to Orenburg, travel across to Atyrau and then south to Aktau. The route is even more complicated from Almaty to Oskemen: from Semey you switch to another train to Barnaul in the Russian Federation, change again and travel back through Russian territory into Kazakhstan to Oskemen. This requires a double entry visa for Russia and a multiple one for Kazakhstan, and timetables for connections are confusing. There is a simple way to avoid this huge inconvenience—by getting off the train before Semey and using a taxi or bus to cover the relatively short distance to Oskemen from the rail line. Indeed, bus lines and, for shorter distances, marshrutkas or even taxis are often a convenient substitute where rail links fail. Buses cost from two tenge per kilometre.

An important and very useful development has come with the completion of the rail link between Almaty and Astana v.v. for the Talgo Express, the Spanish compromise between the conventional express train and the TGV. It leaves Almaty at 6:30pm and arrives sometime between 8am and 10am the following morning. The train is fully air-conditioned, has a bar and restaurant and cabins with two, four or six couchettes. Prices start from around 8,400 tenge and up. Tickets can be bought at Almaty Station-2, from where the train leaves, and at most travel agencies. Reservations should be made days ahead, especially for the weekends, since the trains are fully booked throughout the year.

Regular bus services are maintained between cities and towns throughout Kazakhstan. Modern coaches operate between the major urban centres; for smaller destinations, the good old Ikarus remains staunchly in place. Some of the remote townships are only served once a week, with even smaller and older types of vehicles. Those who want to travel by bus at short notice can try to buy a ticket from the driver on departure, provided there are any seats left.

Journeys by car are best done in a sturdy 4WD vehicle. A car with a driver is recommended for those with little driving experience in Kazahkstan. Once the roads peter out altogether, the value of the horse becomes apparent.

Useful Websites

Governmental Websites

http://en.government.kz—website of the Government of the Republic of Kazakhstan

www.kazakhstanembassy.org.uk—website of the Embassy of the Republic of Kazakhstan in the United Kingdom of Great Britain and Northern Ireland

www.kazakhembus.com—website of the Embassy of Kazakhstan to the US and Canada

www.kazakhstan-tourist.com—Ministry of Tourism and Sport

www.bksoc.org.uk—websiteof the British-Kazakh Society

http://aboutkazakhstan.com—comprehensive country information

Regional Websites

http://astana.kz/eng—the official website of Astana City

http://expat.nursat.kz—the Almaty Expat Site

www.southkazakhstan.com—official website of South Kazakhstan Region

www.infokz.com—Almaty City Business Directory Online

General Info

www.airastana.com—the national airline Air Astana

www.steppemagazine.com—high-quality glossy periodical covering all of Central Asia

www.inform.kz—Kazinform, an online national information centre

www.gazeta.kz—Kazakhstan Today, an "information and analytical portal"

http://kazakhstan.orexca.com—general information about the country, including hotels, tours, maps, etc

http://en.wikipedia.org/wiki/Kazakhstan—general rundown on the country

A paraglider gets an eagle's view of the Khan Tengri massif and its massive glaciers (Vladimir Tugalev)

http://www.lonelyplanet.com/worldguide/destinations/asia/Kazakhstan—info and up-to-date travel information forums

https://www.cia.gov/library/publications/the-world-factbook/geos/kz.html—CIA Factbook

http://wikitravel.org—the online worldwide travel guide

www.kazakinfo.com—includes forums on current topics

www.almadf.kz—Almaty and vicinity online photo album

www.exkz.org—online community for expatriates in Kazakhstan

Environment and Energy

www.ecotourism.kz—Ecotourism Information Resource Centre

www.iccs.org.uk/SaigaAlliance.htm—Saiga Conservation Alliance

www.fauna-flora.org—Fauna & Flora International

www.unesco.kz—UNESCO's Kazakhstan website

www.lgakz.org—Laboratory of Geoarchaeology, Almaty

http://www.eia.doe.gov/emeu/cabs/Kazakhstan/Background.html—US Energy Information Administration

Helicopters are used frequently in the high mountain regions for mountaineering expeditions, heliskiing and other sports (Vladimir Tugalev)

Medical and Travel Advice

www.fco.gov.uk—Foreign & Commonwealth Office

www.dh.gov.uk/en/policyandguidance/healthadvicefortravellers—UK's Department of Health

www.fitfortravel.nhs.uk—travel health information

www.travax.nhs.uk—UK National Health Service

www.fit-for-travel.de/en/default.aspwww.cdc.gov/travel

www.who.org—World Health Organisation

http://travel.state.gov—US Department of State

Vaccinations

The World Health Organisation currently has no special recommendations for Kazakhstan. However, if you plan to travel to remote or little-developed areas, it is wise to be properly vaccinated. Usually advised are vaccinations against diphtheria, tetanus and hepatitis A; others to be considered are typhoid fever, tuberculosis, hepatitis B, rabies and tick-borne encephalitis. A yellow fever certificate is required if coming from a yellow fever risk area.

Visas

In virtually all Western countries, travel agencies include visa provision in their travel arrangements. Only specialized agents, though, know the correct formalities—ordinary agencies often make mistakes, to the customer's disadvantage.

Kazakhstan distinguishes between tourist, "private", transit and business visas. A one-month single-entry tourist visa no longer requires an invitation. For most other visas, a letter of invitation is required. In the case of a business visa, the invitation must come from the business partner in Kazakhstan. Local travel agencies are allowed to act as such.

Services at Kazakh embassies and consulates throughout the world have improved significantly since the turn of the century. Tourist, transit and private visas take one to four working days. Tourist visas and sometimes the more complicated ones can often be applied for in the morning and picked up by the end of the same day. For those travelling unexpectedly, these three categories can be obtained at Almaty airport on arrival. (**NB:** if the flight has a stopover on Kazakh territory before landing in Almaty, passport and customs checks take place at the stopover, which has no such facility.)

Costs vary from about US$50 for a simple tourist or transit visa to several hundred dollars for long-term private or business ones. Officials working for humanitarian organizations, cultural exchange programmes and foreign investors in Kazakhstan can hope for (though not rely on) a visa free of charge.

Those who apply for a visa with a letter of invitation should make sure that the document contains the following items:

- name, surname
- gender
- date and place of birth
- nationality
- passport number, place and date of issue, and expiry date
- job description
- employer's details
- home address
- place of application
- kind of visa requested
- purpose of visit
- means of transport
- dates and places of entry and departure
- visit duration
- address in Kazakhstan

For details and updates on visas and other entry conditions, consult the Ministry of Foreign Affairs website at **www.mfa.kz**

WEATHER

Located in the centre of Eurasia, and one of the farthest countries in the world from any ocean, Kazakhstan features a classic continental climate: extreme cold in winter, extreme heat in summer, and a mainly dry atmosphere throughout the year. Different geographic conditions, though, bring variety in regional weather conditions. Thus, while in July you'll never freeze in the steppe, high up in the mountains the danger is all too real even in midsummer; and while the desert of the western regions is bone dry, it can be pouring with rain in the Altai. The trick is to research the area you are going to visit, and prepare for the conditions. Detailed weather conditions and forecasts can be obtained from www.wunderground.com as well as through local websites (see Useful Websites).

WEIGHTS AND MEASURES

Kazakhstan uses the standard metric system.

WINTER SPORT

The skiing and skating season runs from November till April, and for alpine skiing up amidst the glaciers from October till May. Skis and snowboards can be hired in the skiing resorts to the south of Almaty. The well-maintained pistes are serviced by cable chairs, and winter sport hotels and chalets line the road up from the lower valley. Although popular with locals, the ski runs are rarely crowded and you won't have to suffer the long queues for the chairlifts that typify many comparable ski havens around the world. The Tien Shan gets huge amounts of snowfall regularly during winter, and the quality of the powder snow is said to be excellent. For the more daring, heliskiing is also possible in the high montane zone, with huge descents from peaks as well as glacier skiing—at a price and at one's own risk, of course. Expansion of resorts is planned in the mountains close to Almaty, as this is seen as a big growth market. The Altai also offers possibilities for those passionate for powder snow. Several good ski resorts can be reached from Oskemen and Zyryanovsk, some of which are equipped with ski tows. Prices are moderate and day passes extremely affordable. The possibilities for cross-country skiing in Kazakhstan's snow-rich mountain ranges and hill steppe are virtually endless.

WOMEN TRAVELLING ALONE

As a modern, secular state, Kazakhstan poses no specific risks or dangers for women travelling on their own. Excessive use of make-up is usually frowned upon, as is smoking or drinking in public without male company, especially in the rather conservative south of the country. Also, well-meant questions about the wellbeing of one's husband and (preferably numerous) children should be replied to in a "positive" way—whether they exist or not! Indecent proposals from men should be declined politely but firmly. In emergencies, loud requests for help from nearby people almost always works.

The happy face of Kazakhstan's future (Bengels)

GLOSSARY

Akim: regional governor, local political and administrative leader

Akimat: regional government, government building

Aksakal: "white beard", respected elderly man

Akyn: bard, improvising poet

Arkhar (Argali): very large wild sheep with huge curving horns

Aryk: artifical irrigation channels

Aul: village or communal district

Aytis: contest in singing and declamation, most significant performance of folk poetry

Bars (Russian): snow leopard

Batyr: knight, hero, warlord

Bayga: straightforward horse race over a set distance

Berkut: golden eagle

Berkutshe: trainer of hunting birds

Betashar: wedding custom in which the bride's face is uncovered

Bey: tribal aristocrat

Bi: tribal judge, wise man

Buran: long-lasting northeasterly wind that blows across Central Asia—causes ferocious sandstorms in summer and blinding blizzards in winter

Caravanserai: traditional trailside building with accommodation for the night, protected courtyard for beasts and merchandise, and shops/stalls for restocking supplies

Chachana: teapot

Dastarkhan: literally "tablecloth", a dining place where feasts are served and eaten

Desht-y-Kypchak: tribe that dominated the steppe through the 11th-15th centuries

Dzheyran: steppe (Persian) or goitred gazelle

Dzhigit: mounted warrior, well-spoken youngster

Ephedra: bush that grows in the steppe and in the desert

Haus: sturgeon

Hilvet: place of prayer during the Ramadan (month of fasting)

Irbis (Mongol): snow leopard

Ivan (also ***livan***): a high, vaulted portal opening onto a courtyard

Kaganat: state structure of the early Turkish tribes, led by a Kagan

Kalpak: traditional Kazakh felt hat

Kamsol: vest for women down to the hip

Karagach: steppe elm tree

Kazakhdyk: sacred room in which a kettle with holy water is kept

Kerege: wooden concertina framework forming the wall of a yurt

Kimeshek: cylinder-shaped turban wrapped in a cloth, traditionally worn by married Kazakh women

Kiyiz üy: felt house, or yurt

Kokpar: also known as buzkashi, a team sport of horsemen battling to win a goat carcass and fling it across the opponents' goal line

Kulak: large-scale farmer

Kurultay: gathering of Kazakh tribes

Kyul: ancient Kazakh musical instrument

Kobyz: Kazakh fiddle with two or more strings

Kulan: rare Asiatic wild ass

Kumis: fermented mare's milk

Kurgan: Scythian or Turkic burial mound

Kystau: Nomads' winter camp

Kyz-kuu: "catch the girl", horseback game where a young man tries to catch a girl and kiss her at full gallop

Majilis: Lower House, House of Representatives within the Kazakh political structure

Maral: Siberian red deer

Mayolika: coloured ceramic tile

Mazar: Kazakh graveyard or mausoleum

Melkosopochnik: the Kazakh Uplands

Mihrab: niche for praying in a mosque

Mikrorayon: microdistrict, section of a city

Nawruz: the Kazakh New Year

Oblast: region, province

Oralmany: Kazakh emigrants who have returned to their homeland

Ordy: tribal clan

Pechak: portal in mosque or Koran school, mostly decorated

Rayon: district

Saiga: Central Asian antelope threatened with extinction

Saksaul: desert bush or tree (haloxylon) with needles adapted to dry and extreme climates—used for shashlyk barbecue sticks

Saukele: traditional tall bridal hat

Shakhristan: artisan and trade area in a city, often adjacent to the mosque

Shambala: Buddhist realm of eternal happiness, supposed to be located in the Altai

Shangyrak: oval roof opening of a yurt

Shapan: long, decorated mantle

Shubat: camel's milk

Tamada: toastmaster at a dinner table

Tazy: type of borzoi hunting dog used by Kazakhs

Tugai: section of riverine land lined with trees, rich in biodiversity

Tyubeteyka: traditional round cap

Ulus: tribe

Zapovedniki: protected nature reserve

Zhaylau: Nomadic encampment

Zhuzy: horde, tribal confederation

Zhyrau: singer, interpreter of Kazakh lore

Zistankhe: large, candle-shaped steppe and semi-desert plant

LANGUAGE

Although Kazakh is the official state language, Russian is commonly spoken by the majority of the population (except in heavily ethnic Kazakh regions such as parts of South Kazakhstan and the mountains of the Altai). It is fair to say that if you speak Russian you will get on fine anywhere you go in the country; however, using a few Kazakh words will earn a handsome return in surprised exclamations, laughter and warm smiles—and probably result in an invitation to dinner! Two pronunciation tips—in Kazakh the stress almost always goes on the last vowel in a word, while in Russian the unstressed letter 'o' is pronounced as 'a'.

The list below will give you a very basic but valuable start to communication in the country:

English	**Kazakh Transliteration**	**Russian (**Transliteration**)**
Hello (formal)	Salemetsiz be	Здравствуйте (Zdrastvuyte)
Hi (informal)	Salem	Привет (Privet)
How are you?	Kaliñiz kalay?	Как дела? (Kak dela?)
I'm fine	Kalim jaksy	Х орошо (Kharasho)
What's your name?	Sizdiñ atiñiz kalay?	Как тебя зовут? (Kak tebya zavut?)
My name is…	Menym atym...	Меня зовут... (Menya zavut...)
Good morning	Kayirli tañ	Доброе утро (Dobroe utra)
Good afternoon	Kayirli kün	Добрый день (Dobryi den')
Good evening	Kayirli kes	Добрый вечер (Dobryi vecher)
Goodnight	Kayirli tün	Спокойной ночи (Spakoinoi nochi)
Goodbye	Saw boliñiz	До свидания (Do svidaniia)
Cheers!	Densawli iñiz ü in!	Будем здоровы! (Budem zdarovy!)
I don't understand	Men tüsinbeimin	Я не понимаю (Ya ne panimayu)
How much is this?	Bul kansa turady?	Сколько это стоит? (Skol'ko eta stoit?)

Excuse me/Sorry	Kesiriñiz	Простите! (Prastite)
Thank you	Rakhmet	Спасибо (Spasiba)
Where is…?	…kaida?	Где…? (Gde…?)
Where's the toilet?	Azhetkhana kaida?	Где туалет? (Gde tualet?)
How do you say… in Kazakh/Russian?…	...Kazaksa kalay aytiladi?	Как сказать... по-русски? (Kak skazat'... pa-russki?)
Help!	Kömektesiñiz!	Помогите! (Pamagite!)
Stop!	Tokta!	Стой! (Stoi!)
Hotel	Konaq uy/meymankhana	Гостиница (Gastinitsa)
Train station	Temir jol vakzal	Вокзал (Vakzal)
Expensive	Kimbat	Дорогой (Daragoi)
Good	Jaqsy	Х орошо (Kharasho)
Monday	Duysenbi	Понедельник (Panidelnik)
Tuesday	Seysenbi	Вторник (Ftornik)
Wednesday	Sarsenbi	Среда (Sreda)
Thursday	Beysenbi	Четверг (Chitverg)
Friday	Zhuma	Пятница (Pyatnitsa)
Saturday	Senbi	Суббота (Subota)
Sunday	Zheksenbi	Воскресенье (Vaskrisenye)
1	Bir	Один (Adin)
2	Yeki	Два (Dva)
3	Ush	Три (Tri)
4	Tort	Четыре (Chityri)
5	Bes	Пять (Pyat)
6	Alty	Шесть (Shest)
7	Zheti	Семь (Sem)
8	Siyegz	Восемь (Vosim)
9	Toghyz	Девять (Devit)
10	On	Десять (Desit)
100	Zhuz	Сто (Sto)
1,000	Myng	Тысяча (Tysyacha)

Geographical spellings in Kazakhstan are often confusing and ambiguous. Even road signs and maps can display a confusing variety of options ranging from subtle differences (for example Karaganda can also be spelt Karagandy or Karaghandy) to completely new wording (Shevchenko is now Aktau). The Russian Cyrillic—and Russian street and town names—that were prevalent prior to independence has now been officially changed to Kazakh Cyrillic—with in many cases brand-new street and town names. However, many Russian names and spellings are still much in use, and it will take time for the transformation to be fully completed.

Within these pages, in most instances the new Kazakh spelling is used, with the old Russian spelling added in brackets afterwards (occasionally, where virtually constant local common usage dictates, a traditionally Russian name is still used, ie the Irtysh River, and Karaganda). However, given the overwhelming use of Russian in the cities, names of streets and places of interest on city maps are spelt according to transcription from the Russian language, not Kazakh.

New Spelling (Kazakh)	Old Spelling (Russian)	New Spelling (Kazakh)	Old Spelling (Russian)
CITIES		**RIVERS**	
Almaty	*Alma-Ata*	*Ile*	*Ili*
Aral	*Aralsk*	*Ertis, Yertis*	*Irtysh*
Aktau, Aqtau	*Shevchenko*	*Esil, Yesil*	*Ishim*
Aktobe	*Aktyubinsk*	*Oral, Zhayik*	*Ural*
Atyrau	*Guriyev*	*Sharyn*	*Charyn*
Karaghandy, Karagandy	*Karaganda, Karagandy*	*Shelek*	*Chilik*
Kostanay	*Kostanai*	*Shu*	*Chu, Chuy*
Oral	*Uralsk*	*Torgay*	*Turgai, Torgai*
Oskemen	*Ust-Kamenogorsk*		
Shymkent	*Chimkent*		
Semey	*Semipalatinsk*		
Taraz	*Dzhambul, Zhambyl*		
Turkistan, Türkistan	*Turkestan*		

Recommended Reading

Abazov, Rafis, *Culture and Customs of the Central Asian Republics* (Greenwood Press, 2006)

Adshead, S.A.M., *Central Asia in World History* (London, 1993)

Aitmatov, Chingiz, *The Day Lasts More Than a Hundred Years* (Indiana University Press, 1988)

Akiner, Shirin, *Formation of Kazakh Identity: From Tribe to Nation-State* (Royal Institute for Foreign Affairs, London, 1995)

Barthold, V.V., *Four Studies on the History of Central Asia* (translated from Russian by Vladimir and Tatiana Minorsky) Leiden, 1956–1963

Barthold, V.V., *Turkestan Down to the Mongol Invasion* (translated from Russian) South Asia Books, London, 1968

Bissell, Tom, *Chasing the Sea: Lost among the Ghosts of Empire in Central Asia* (Pantheon, 2003)

Boulnois, Luce, *Silk Road: Monks, Warriors & Merchants on the Silk Road* (Odyssey Books & Guides, 2004)

Brezhnev, Leonid, *Virgin Lands: Two Years in Kazakhstan*, 1954–5 (Pergamon Press, Great Britain, 1979)

Burnaby, Frederick, *A Ride to Khiva: Travels and Adventures in Central Asia* (The Long Riders' Guild Press, 2001)

Dawson, Christopher, *The Mongol Mission: Narratives and Letters of the Franciscan Missionaries in Mongolia and China in the Thirteenth and Fourteenth Centuries* (London and New York, 1955)

Demko, G.J., *The Russian Colonisation of Kazakhstan 1896-1916* (Indiana University, Bloomington, 1969)

Dulles, Foster Rhea, *Eastward Ho!—The First English Adventurers to the Orient* (John Lane The Bodley Head, London, 1969)

Eastep, Wayne (photographer) **and Kunanbay, Alma** (essays), *The Soul of Kazakhstan* (Eastern Press, 2001)

Elias, N. (editor), *A History of the Moghuls of Central Asia being the Tarikh-i-Rashidi of Mirza Muhammad Haidar, Dughlat* (Curzon, London 1898)

Frye, R.N. and Bernard Lewis (editors), *The Heritage of Central Asia: From Antiquity to the Turkish Expansion* (Princeton: Markus Wiener, 1996)

Furgus, Michael (editor), *Kazakhstan: Coming of Age* (Stacey International Publishers, 2004)

Galiyev, Anwar, *Traditional Institutions in Modern Kazakhstan* (Slavic Research Centre, Almaty, 1998)

Ginatullin, Marat G., *Zhetisu: Nature And Lore. A Lexicon* (Caspian Publishing House, Almaty, 2006)

Hopkirk, Peter, *Foreign Devils on the Silk Road* (University of Massachusetts Press, USA, 1994)

Hopkirk, Peter, *The Great Game: The Struggle for Empire in Central Asia* (Kodansha Globe, 1997)

Keenan, Brigid, *Diplomatic Baggage: The Adventures of a Trailing Spouse* (John Murray Publishers, 2005)

Kelaart, Lucy and Coish, Summer, *A Hedonist's Guide to… Almaty and Astana* (Hg2, 2007)

Kleveman, Lutz, *The New Great Game: Blood and Oil in Central Asia* (Grove Press, 2004)

Knobloch, Edgar, *Monuments of Central Asia* (I.B. Taurus, London, 2001)

Kozybayev, M.K. (editor) **and Romanov, Yuri** (compiler), *History of Kazakhstan—Essays*, Gylym, Almaty, 1998 (English translation available)

MacLeod, Calum, and Mayhew, Bradley, *Uzbekistan: The Golden Road to Samarkand* (Odyssey Books & Guides, 2004)

Mayhew, Bradley, Bloom, Greg, Noble, John and Starnes, Dean, *Central Asia* (Lonely Planet Publications, 2007)

McGovern, William Montgomery, *The Early Empires of Central Asia; a study of the Scythians and the Huns and the part they played in world history, with special reference to the Chinese sources* (Chapel Hill: University of North Carolina Press, 1939)

Olcott, Martha Brill, *Kazakhstan: Unfulfilled Promise* (Carnegie Endowment for International Peace, 2002)

Olcott, Martha Brill, *Central Asia's Second Chance* (Carnegie Endowment for International Peace, 2005)

Paksoy, H.B. (editor), *Central Asia Reader, The Rediscovery of History* (M.E. Sharpe, New York/London, 1994)

Pierce, Richard A., *Russia in Central Asia 1867–1917—A Study in Colonial Rule* (University of California Press, San Francisco, USA, 1960)

Privratsky, Bruce, *Muslim Turkistan: Kazak Religion and Collective Memory* (Curzon Press, London, 2001)

Robbins, Christopher, *In Search of Kazakhstan: The Land That Disappeared* (Profile Books Ltd, 2007)

Robertson, Robert and Gaggiotti, Hugo (editors/main authors), *Business Leadership In Central Asia* (Caspian Publishing House, Almaty, 2006)

Rosten, Keith, *Once in Kazakhstan: The Snow Leopard Emerges* (iUniverse Inc, 2005)

Schatz, Edward, *Modern Clan Politics: The Power of "Blood" in Kazakhstan and Beyond* (University of Washington Press, USA, 2004)

Schayakhmetov, Mukhamet, *The Silent Steppe: The Story of a Kazakh Nomad under Stalin* (Stacy International, 2006)

Silk Road Map (Illustrated): Featuring the Ancient Network of Routes from China to Europe (Odyssey Maps, 2007)

Stewart, Rowan, *Kyrgyz Republic* (Odyssey Books & Guides, 2008)

Tay, Alan, *Welcome to Kazakhstan (Welcome to My Country)* (Gareth Stevens Publishing, 2005)

Thubron, Colin, *The Lost Heart of Asia* (Perennial, 1995)

Torday, Laszlo, *Mounted Archers: The Beginning of Central Asian History* (Seattle: University of Washington Press, USA, 1998)

van der Leeuw, Charles, *Kazakhstan: A Quest For Statehood* (Caspian Publishing House, Almaty, 2006)

Wendelken, Rebecca Woodward, *"Red Metal on the Steppes: The Spassky Copper Mines, Ltd., 1904–1919"* (Ph.D dissertation, Emory University, Florida, USA, 2000)

Whitfield, Susan, *Life Along the Silk Road* (University of California Press, USA, 2001)

Wood, Frances, *The Silk Road: Two Thousand Years in the Heart of Asia* (University of California Press, USA, 2003)

Yesenberlin, Ilyas, *The Nomads* (The Ilyas Yesenberlin Foundation, Almaty, 2000)

Zhunusova, Zhanylzhan, *Democratic Traditions in Kazakh Nomadic Society* (Osaka University, 2000)

INDEX

steppe SUMMER 2007
WWW.STEPPEMAGAZINE.COM
steppe two · SUMMER 2007 · UK £10 · US $18
steppe
A CENTRAL ASIAN PANORAMA
КАССА